PONTIFICAL INSTITUTE OF MEDIAEVAL STUDIES

STUDIES AND TEXTS

6

PRINTED BY UNIVERSA WETTEREN (BELGIUM)

THE WILL
IN MEDIEVAL ENGLAND

From the Conversion of the
Anglo-Saxons
to the End of the Thirteenth Century

MICHAEL M. SHEEHAN, C. S. B.
Pontifical Institute of Mediaeval Studies

TORONTO
PONTIFICAL INSTITUTE OF MEDIAEVAL STUDIES
1963

To my Father and Mother

PREFACE

TESTATORS of the thirteenth century were sometimes pleased to begin their wills with a statement of their debts. The practice seems an attractive one — certainly it is a pleasure to devote the first page of this volume to the acknowledgement of my obligations to those whose assistance and encouragement have made it possible.

The need for a modern study of the early history of the English will was suggested by M. le professeur Joüon des Longrais in the course of a seminar investigating English institutions at the Ecole pratique des Hautes Etudes, Paris, in 1953. My thanks must be extended first of all to him, not only for this suggestion and for the initial orientation in the subject made under his direction, but also for his assistance still, though necessarily less frequently, available to me after my return to Toronto. During the later stages of my investigations I was fortunate to enjoy the direction of Most Reverend George B. Flahiff, C. S. B., archbishop of Winnipeg, then professor of history at the Pontifical Institute of Mediaeval Studies; his patience and competence were a constant inspiration. I am especially indebted to Rev. J. Ambrose Raftis, C. S. B., editor of this series, not only for his help in preparing this work for the press, but also for his invaluable suggestions and generous assistance at all stages of this study. Finally, may I thank Professor Stephan Kuttner for the loan of microfilm from the Institute of Research and Study in Medieval Canon Law, Professor Bertie Wilkinson and Rev. Laurence K. Shook, C. S. B. for precious comments on portions of this book, and Basilian confreres, especially Rev. Robert W. Crooker and Rev. Arthur F. Waligore, who aided me in preparing the manuscript for the press.

My debt extends to the owners and custodians of the wills and other documents used in the present study. Their generosity in putting this material at my disposition is much appreciated. It is not possible here to acknowledge this assistance in detail; it will be a pleasure to do so later when many of these documents are published. For the moment I must be content to express my obligation to the British Museum, the Public Record Office, the Dean and Chapter of Canterbury and the Lincolnshire Archives Committee. I also wish to thank the librarians and staffs of the Bibliothèque Nationale, the libraries of Harvard University (here there is a special obligation to Robert H. Haynes) and the University of Toronto Library.   Last of all, may I thank Rev. John F. Stapleton, C.S.B., librarian of this Institute.

There is one final obligation.   It is to that long and honourable line of editors of texts, extending from Dugdale and Rymer, through the great editors of the nineteenth century, to those responsible for the latest volumes of the different groups and societies that still carry on the essential work of publishing public and private records.

M. M. S.

Pontifical Institute of Mediaeval Studies
Toronto, November, 1962.

TABLE OF CONTENTS

LIST OF ABBREVIATIONS

B.   W. de G. Birch, ed. *Cartularium Saxonicum,* 3 vols. (London, 1885-93).

B.C.   Mary Bateson, ed. *Borough Customs,* 2 vols., Selden Society, XVIII, XXI (1904-6).

B.M. Facs.   E. A. Bond, ed. *Facsimiles of Ancient Charters in the British Museum,* 4 vols. (London, 1873-8).

BN   Bibliothèque Nationale, Paris.

Br. Mus.   British Museum, London.

C.A.   Irene J. Churchill, *Canterbury Administration,* 2 vols. (London, 1933).

C.C.   A. S. Napier and W. H. Stevenson, eds. *The Crawford Collection of Early Charters and Documents,* Anecdota Oxoniensia, Med. and Mod., VII (Oxford, 1894).

C.C.R.   *Calendar of Close Rolls.*

C.Ch.R.   *Calendar of Charter Rolls.*

C.P.R.   *Calendar of Patent Rolls.*

C.R.R.   *Curia Regis Rolls.*

DdB   *Domesday Book.*

DDC   *Dictionnaire de droit canonique.*

EHD   *English Historical Documents.*

EHR   *English Historical Review.*

EYC   *Early Yorkshire Charters,* Vols. I-III, ed. W. Farrer (Edinburgh, 1914-6), Vols. IV-X, ed. C. T. Clay, Yorkshire Archaeological Society, Record Series, extra series (1935-55).

Gesetze   F. Liebermann, ed. *Die Gesetze der Angelsachsen,* 3 vols. (Halle, 1903-16).

H.   Florence E. Harmer, ed. *Select English Documents of the Ninth and Tenth Centuries* (Cambridge, 1914).

Haddan and Stubbs   A. W. Haddan and W. Stubbs, eds. *Councils and Ecclesiastical Documents of Great Britain and Ireland,* 3 vols. (Oxford, 1869-78).

H. *Writs*   Florence E. Harmer, ed. *Anglo-Saxon Writs* (Manchester, 1952).

JL.   P. Jaffé, *Regesta pontificum romanorum ab condita Ecclesia ad annum post Christum natum MCXCVIII,* 2nd ed. by S. Loewenfeld *et al.* under the direction of W. Wattenbach, 2 vols. (Leipzig, 1885-8).

K.   J. M. Kemble, ed. *Codex Diplomaticus Ævi Saxonici* 6 vols., English Historical Society (London, 1839-48).

Mansi   J. D. Mansi, ed. *Sacrorum conciliorum nova et amplissima collectio*, 31 vols. (Florence and Venice, 1759-98).

MGH   *Monumenta Germaniae historica*

O.S. Facs.   W. B. Sanders, ed. *Facsimiles of Anglo-Saxon Manuscripts*, 3 vols., Ordnance Survey (Southampton, 1874-84).

P. and M.   F. Pollock and F. W. Maitland, *The History of English Law*, 2nd ed., 2 vols. (Cambridge, 1911).

PL   J. P. Migne, ed. *Patrologiæ cursus completus. Series Latina.*

Potthast   A. Potthast, *Regesta pontificum romanorum inde ab anno Christum natum MCXCVIII ad annum MCCCIV*, 2 vols. (Berlin, 1874-5).

PRO   Public Record Office, London.

R.   Agnes J. Robertson, ed. *Anglo-Saxon Charters* (Cambridge, 1939).

Regesta   *Regesta regum Anglo-Normannorum*, Vol. I, ed. H. W. C. Davis; Vol. II, eds. C. Johnson and H. A. Cronne (Oxford, 1913-56).

Rot. Lit. Cl.   *Rotuli litterarum clausarum in turri Londinensi asservati*, ed. T. D. Hardy, 2 vols., Record Commission (1833-44).

Rot. Lit. Pat.   *Rotuli litterarum patentium in turri Londinensi asservati*, ed. T. D. Hardy, Record Commission (1835).

RS   Rolls Series

Sharpe   R. R. Sharpe, ed. *Calendar of Wills Proved and Enrolled in the London Court of Husting*, 2 vols. (London, 1889-90).

T.   Testament

Thorpe   B. Thorpe, ed. *Diplomatarum Anglicum Ævi Saxonici* (London, 1865).

W.   Dorothy Whitelock, ed. *Anglo-Saxon Wills* (Cambridge, 1930).

Wilkins   D. Wilkins, *Concilia Magnae Britanniae et Hiberniae, 446-1718*, 4 vols. (London, 1737).

Y.B.   Year Book.

ZRG Germ. Abt.   *Zeitschrift der Savigny-Stiftung für Rechtsgeschichte (Germanistische Abteilung).*

ZRG Kan. Abt.   *Zeitschrift der Savigny-Stiftung für Rechtsgeschichte (Kanonistische Abteilung).*

INTRODUCTION

R ECENT studies of English law and institutions have devoted
considerable attention to the analysis of the last will during the
later Middle Ages. Thousands of written wills have survived from
that period, and many have been published or calendared. Year Books,
episcopal registers, and the *acta* of ecclesiastical courts supply information
on the execution of wills and the procedure of enforcement. This
material has provided the basis for a successful analysis of the will and
of its place in the society of the fourteenth and fifteenth centuries.

These studies have been hampered by the fact that there is no
monograph on the early history of the will which incorporates the
results of recent investigations. It is true that certain aspects of the
matter have been studied in detail. Thus, due to the efforts of Miss
Dorothy Whitelock and other scholars, good editions of the Anglo-Saxon
wills are now available. Furthermore, the late Professor H. D. Hazeltine
provided a careful analysis of these documents from a theoretical point
of view in his introduction to Miss Whitelock's volume; there, he related
the Anglo-Saxon will to the forms of donation in use among Germanic
peoples on the Continent, and gave it its proper place in the general
history of law. But very little recent work has been done on the
history of the bequest of property during the period following the
Norman Conquest. This is a serious lack, for the hundred years prior
to the reign of Edward I saw the English will take on the qualities that
have remained essential to it ever since. Our knowledge of this
important development remains inadequate. Certain elements of the
problem have been studied in detail, but the general understanding of
the distribution of property at death, during this period, remains much
as Pollock and Maitland left it more than sixty years ago.

In the meantime, the efforts of learned societies and individual
scholars have prepared the way for a more detailed examination of the
will. Most of the public records of the reigns of Richard I and John
—an era that is crucial for the development of the will—are now
available in print. Furthermore, the publications of local historical
societies and of the Historical Manuscripts Commission have made
scores of thirteenth-century wills available, or have indicated where they
are to be found. The organization and procedure of the courts of the
Church are being investigated. Finally, much valuable progress has
been made in the study of canon law; collections of decretals and the

glosses of decretists and decretalists have been published or described so that it is now possible to relate certain important events in the history of English law to a movement of theoretical analysis and practical elaboration that was carried on throughout the whole of the western Church. Each of these areas of investigation provides valuable material for the study of the English will.

The aim of the present study is to investigate the rather complex historical evolution that produced the last will of English law. It follows the development of this institution from the time when the Anglo-Saxons first came under the influence of Christian missionaries until the second decade of the reign of Edward I. Interest is not limited to a consideration of the theory of the will, nor even to a description of the procedures of execution and administration. These matters are studied, of course; but an effort is made to interpret the development of this institution in terms of the desires and needs of society, to show the motives that caused it to appear, and its effects on the law of succession and on the accumulation of family fortunes. Although the distribution of the property of the intestate was influenced by testamentary procedures and is a topic of considerable interest, it has been treated here only inasmuch as it has a direct bearing on the will. Occasionally references are made to the Continent, especially Normandy, to Ireland and Wales, and to documents of the fourteenth century. Here the author may seem to stray beyond the limits in space and time set to this investigation. It will be seen, however, that the matter in question sheds some light on English practice during the period under consideration.

In setting the temporal limits of this study the reasoning was as follows. It was decided to begin with three short chapters dealing with the bequest of property in the Anglo-Saxon period. As was indicated in an earlier paragraph, important contributions towards the understanding of the will during those years have already been made by Miss Whitelock and Professor Hazeltine. My great debt to them will be immediately evident to those who read the early chapters of this work; most of Professor Hazeltine's conclusions on the theory of the will have been accepted, and are presented below without further discussion. Miss Whitelock's edition of texts and her consideration of the social implications of the will, in the second volume of the *Pelican History of England,* have been drawn on again and again. But it was decided to include this material for three reasons. First, to add further support to Professor Hazeltine's contention that the Anglo-Saxon will was an oral act. Second, because it soon became evident that Professor Hazeltine was correct when he surmised that the date, 1066, was not an important one in the history of the law and practice of wills. The Conquest did not fundamentally alter the number of persons to whom a testamentary right was extended, nor the property which they were allowed to bequeath. The profound change in the theory of the will came a century later, and it is best understood if seen in relation to events in England in Saxon as well as in Norman times. The third reason is related to the preceding and is the most important: the motive of the English will must be related to a general pattern of development characteristic of all the nations of Europe as they fell under the influence of the Christian religion. This development was long and very complex, and is best seen as a continuous process extending from the time of the Anglo-Saxon conversion to the last years of the thirteenth century.

In many ways the history of the will in England is a supreme example of the part played by Christianity in the growth of western civilization; it illustrates how the injection of a religious notion into a society was able to enrich and develop several secular institutions, while at the same time involving religious leaders in secular affairs until their activity was out of all proportion to the original purpose of their intervention. The process began with the Christian desire to give alms, a form of charity providing a constant motive for the right of bequest. This notion was confronted by the forms of property holding and distribution accepted among the Anglo-Saxons, yet it was powerful enough to lead to the creation of legal instruments that made the bequest in alms possible. At this stage the impact of Christianity was in the moral order only. The new religion provided the ideal of the bequest in alms and the notion that bishops should concern themselves with its fulfilment, but there was no ecclesiastical institution to enforce the bequests of a will or to determine its nature and formalities. The legal structure into which Christianity had been introduced provided these elements. However, as the years passed the Church tended to go beyond teaching the faith and the principles of the moral life; she began to provide institutions to support and even to enforce her teaching. This tendency became especially evident during the period following the Gregorian reform when a vast structure of law and institutions administered by the Church was extended over Europe. As part of this process the church courts of England not only imposed a new notion of the will, but also supervised it and saw to its enforcement; eventually these courts found themselves charged with heavy legal and financial duties that had little relation to the protection of the bequest in alms that had been the original reason for their interference. This important

English development did not occur at the time of the Norman
Conquest; it began more than a century later.

Most of the implications of the testamentary jurisdiction of the courts
Christian were evident by the second decade of the reign of Edward,
the date selected as the terminus of this investigation. By that time
the theory of the canonical will was accepted and the basic procedures
for examination and enforcement were established. Furthermore, the
common law had admitted the representation of the testator by the
executor and had refused to allow a testamentary capacity in the
married woman and the villein. Though many problems yet remained
to be solved, it can be said that the theoretical and practical bases of
the will in English common law had been established by the time of the
Second Statute of Westminster (1285).

CHAPTER I

THE BEGINNINGS OF DISTRIBUTION OF PROPERTY
AT DEATH AMONG THE ANGLO-SAXONS

THE era that saw the conquest of Britain by Germanic peoples is a time of unique obscurity. The historian's knowledge of the arrival and settlement of the invaders is clouded by a host of questions to which answers are not easily found. Political organization and social institutions can be described only in the most general terms.

One of the many unknowns is the custom regulating inheritance. It is necessary to go back to Tacitus to find a description of this custom among the Germans.[1] He tells us that the tribes of his day did not use the testament and that the succession to property was controlled by strict family rules. This meagre information would have served only as a basis for further question even in Tacitus' time; the extent to which it can be applied to the tribes of the fifth century is still more problematical.[2] However, it seems certain that among the Anglo-Saxons recently settled in Britain the family succeeded to the possessions of a deceased householder.[3] The manner of succession was regulated by custom, but the details of that custom remain largely unknown: the time and the rate at which co-ownership was abandoned, whether there was preference of the eldest son, the details of provisions for daughters, whether the dying owner made suggestions as to the disposition of some of his wealth, are all problems to which adequate answers are not possible.[4]

---

1 "Heredes tamen successoresque sui cuique liberi, et nullum testamentum; si liberi non sunt, proximus gradus in possessione fratres, patrui, auunculi" (*Germania*, ch. 20).

2 See R. H. Hodgkin, *History of the Anglo-Saxons*, 2nd ed. (Oxford, 1939), I, 32.

3 See F. M. Stenton, *Anglo-Saxon England*, 2nd ed., Oxford History of England, Vol. II (Oxford, 1947), 277, 312-314.

4 Benedict Biscop spoke of parents' preference for their eldest child, during his last illness: Bede, *Historia Abbatum*, ed. C. Plummer, *Venerabilis Bedae Opera Historica* (Oxford, 1896), I, 375-376. When he was about to join battle with Grendel, Beowulf asked that, in the event of his death, his precious corslet, *Welandes geweorc*, should be given to his lord and uncle, Hygelac. The corslet was a family possession since it had belonged to Hraedel, father of Hygelac and grandfather of Beowulf. This is, in all likelihood, the payment of the heriot, which may have been due to Hygelac on two counts: he was Beowulf's lord and

In the era immediately following the introduction of Christianity there are indications that the customary rules of succession by the family were giving way to conceptions of property and inheritance that tended to increase an owner's power over his wealth. He began to determine those who would enjoy his property, or part of it, after his death. The early development of this right to distribute property at death and the manner and extent of its use among the Anglo-Saxons are the object of analysis in the first part of this study. The present chapter is intended to show the first steps productive of this important change. It occurred when Christian teaching on the giving of alms began to influence the older German custom of inheritance.

I. GERMANIC PRACTICE

At least one break in the solid front of family succession among the Germans is known to have occurred before they penetrated the Roman Empire. It was indicated by Tacitus: certain equipment — arms, jewellery, clothing — which had been especially associated with the dead man, was burned or buried with his body.[5] During recent years, historians have come to realize that, whatever the purpose of this practice,[6] it contains one of the sources of the notion of individual property[7] and of the idea that the needs and desires of a property owner should be satisfied even when he is dead and no longer able to enforce his commands in any physical way.

The burial of personal possessions with the ashes of the invaders of Britain was very common: much of our reconstruction of that story is based on the information that these burials yield.[8] Recent investigations have shown considerable variation in burial customs among different

---

probably the head of the family as well. Beowulf exercised a freedom of choice, however, in that he designated the piece of equipment that was to be given (*Beowulf*, lines 452-455). See W. S. Holdsworth, *A History of English Law*, 3rd ed. (London, 1923-52), II, 90, 92-93, and below, pp. 81-82.

[5] "...sua cuique arma, quorundam igni et equus adicitur" (*Germania*, ch. 27). See Jan de Vries, *Altgermanische Religionsgeschichte*, 2 vols. (Berlin, 1956-7), I, 187-197.

[6] Various suggestions as to the purpose of this endowment among the Germans have been assembled by Hodgkin, *History*, I, 27-28, nn. 19-22.

[7] E. F. Bruck, *Totenteil und Seelgerät im griechischen Recht* (Munich, 1926), and "Kirchliche-sociales Erbrecht in Byzanz," *Studi in onore di Salvatore Riccobono* (Palermo, 1933), III, 377-423. On the primitive notion of the dead as subject of rights and duties, see H. Brunner, "Das rechtliche Fortleben des Toten bei den Germanen," *Deutsche Monatsschrift für das gesamte Leben der Gegenwart*, XII, (1907), 18-32.

[8] See R. G. Collingwood and J. N. L. Myers, *Roman Britain and the English Settlements*, 2nd ed., Oxford History of England, Vol. I (Oxford, 1937), 448-450.

groups. In some areas inhumation was replacing cremation, and grave endowment was in decline during the sixth century.[9] When Christian missionaries began to make notable progress in the conversion of the Anglo-Saxons, different notions of the after-life became current. As a result, there occurred a general change in burial technique and the abandonment of the physical endowment of the dead.[10]

The adopting of a new conception of life after death and of the burial practices which were derived from it did not involve the loss of the initial tendency in the direction of personal property; the religion which required the change was already possessed of doctrines and practices which would further such development. But it should be noted that an initial penetration of the ancient Anglo-Saxons' customs of possession and inheritance had already been made by pagan burial practice. Thus the Anglo-Saxon mind was not unprepared for the Christian teaching that some of the property of the deceased should be used for his future good. At the same time one should not exaggerate the importance of this Germanic experience in the distribution of property at death. Twelfth-century documents often refer to a portion of an estate, frequently a third, over which the owner had full right of devise. Brunner, whose studies are fundamental in many of these matters, considered that this "share of the soul" (Seelteil) was a direct development from Germanic burial custom. The practice was adopted by the Church and was used for a somewhat different purpose: goods formerly provided for the equipment of the dead in the after-life were employed as alms for the remission of sin.[11] This interpretation dominated the field for many years. However, the studies of the late Alfred Schultze, and especially those of Professor Eberhard Bruck, have shown that the development was more complex and was due mainly to the influence of Christian teaching as outlined in the writings of the Fathers.[12] The

9 Hodgkin, *History*, II, 83-85.

10 E. T. Leeds, *Early Anglo-Saxon Art and Archaeology* (Oxford, 1936), p. 96, shows that the rapidity with which Christian beliefs changed pagan burial customs has been exaggerated.

11 Brunner's position was stated in "Der Totenteil in germanischen Rechten," *ZRG Germ. Abt.*, XIX (1898), 107-139, and in "Das rechtliche Fortleben des Toten ...". The chief authors who have accepted this interpretation have been listed by Schultze in his article "Der Einfluss der Kirche auf die Entwicklung des germanischen Erbrechts," *ZRG Germ. Abt.*, XXXV (1914), 89, n. 3, and more recently by Professor Bruck in *Kirchenväter und soziales Erbrecht* (Berlin, 1956), p. vi, n. 3.

12 Brunner's thesis was criticized by Siegfried Rietschel in the article "Der Totenteil in germanischen Rechten," *ZRG Germ. Abt.*, XXXII (1911), 297-312, and the basis of the alternate thesis was provided by Mario Falco the same year in *Le Disposizioni 'pro Animo'*

early Christian writers lived in the Roman Empire where there was remarkable freedom of distribution of property at death.   They sought to provide reasonable rules whereby their co-religionists might decide the portion of their wealth to bequeath in alms.   The recommended amount varied in the writings of different Fathers,[13] but the idea of the share of the soul, a fraction of an individual's possessions, spread rapidly during the fourth and fifth centuries.   Now the share of the soul, usually a third or a quarter of an estate, did not by any means equal the total wealth that could be freely distributed at death within the Empire.   But when this teaching reached the newly converted Anglo-Saxons it made contact with customs of inheritance that were much less advanced.   Thus it was not a question of teaching the new converts to devote a portion of their free estate to the good of the soul.   A preliminary step had to be taken first: it was necessary to plant in them the desire to free a portion of their property from family claims so that it might be distributed in alms after their death.   The fact that the new converts were accustomed to grave endowment made this step much easier,[14] but the idea of a precise portion of an estate being used for the soul was rooted in the Fathers rather than in the Germanic past.

St. Augustine arrived in England in 597.   By that time the invaders on the Continent had already begun to employ procedures for transferring property after death to persons not entitled to it by customary rules of succession.   In the areas bordering the Mediterranean, where

Fondamenti dottrinali e forme giuridiche (Turin, 1911).   Schultze suggested the Christian influence in the article cited in the previous note.   Later, in *Augustin und der Seelteil des germanischen Erbrechts* (Leipzig, 1928), he related the doctrine to the teaching of St. Augustine. Professor Bruck had already begun to move away from the position of Brunner in *Die Schenkung auf der Todesfall im griechischen und römischen Recht*, Teil I, Studien zur Erlauterung des bürglischen Rechts, 31 Heft (Breslau, 1909), pp. 141-145.   In *Totenteil und Seelgerät im griechischen Recht* (Munich, 1926), he developed his thesis at considerable length.   Quite recently, in *Kirchenväter*, pp. 1-119, he has shown the influence of the Fathers, especially those of the Eastern Church.   For details of the dispute regarding the Germanic and Patristic sources of the share of the soul, see *ibid.*, pp. i-viii.

13 Bruck, *Kirchenväter*, pp. 1-119, and below, pp. 12-16.

14 This was true in the Empire as well, for the cult of the dead among the pagans provided a fertile ground for the Christian teaching regarding the value of alms for the good of the soul of the deceased.   Some Graeco-Roman customs, the anniversary feast for example, were continued for centuries and often proved embarrassing to Church leaders. On the cult of the dead, see Bruck, *Totenteil*, pp. 227 ff., and "The Growth of Foundations in Roman Law and Civilization," *Seminar*, VI (1948), 1-19.   For the Christian practices of burial before the Germanic penetration of the Empire, see J. Quasten, "Vetus Superstitio," *Harvard Theol. Rev.*, XXXIII (1940), 250 ff.   These practices were not without influence among the Anglo-Saxons: see below, pp. 12-16.

the tribes experienced a very marked influence from the institutions of the conquered peoples, the Roman testament was used for this purpose.[15] A similar influence is not entirely inconceivable in that part of the Empire which fell to the Anglo-Saxons: the testament of Roman law can be presumed to have been known and employed by some levels of society in Roman Britain. It seems, however, to have disappeared with the social and economic orders which created it and which it helped to maintain. Later, the testament was known by at least those members of the Anglo-Saxon clergy of the first generation who were continental by birth or experience. These men supplied the chief motive for the distribution of property at death. Yet even after the conversion of England the testament was not used.[16] The word *testamentum* occurs from time to time. Except in a few cases, such as the distribution of property by St. Wilfrid,[17] and some scriptural commentaries,[18] where it is used in the strict legal sense, the word simply implies a written document.[19] It was to maintain this meaning in England and on the Continent for many centuries.

Several national codes were assembled on the Continent about the year 500. They show that the invaders were employing certain expedients which produced, at least in part, the effect of the Roman testament. Of chief interest are the *thinx* of the Lombards, and the *affatomie* of the Franks. From a legal point of view, these institutions did not interfere with the general customs of succession, for, in the beginning, they were acts of adoption.[20] At first their use was limited

---

[15] In the Mediterranean provinces of the Empire, the situation was quite different from that in the northwest. Population and institutional survival were much greater. The testament continued to be used for centuries in these areas, though not without changes produced by Germanic custom and ecclesiastical needs; see H. Auffroy, *Evolution du testament en France des origines au XIIIe siècle* (Paris, 1899), pp. 231-363, and R. J. R. Goffin, *The Testamentary Executor in England and Elsewhere* (London, 1911), where the findings of French, German and Italian scholars are presented, pp. 13-15.

[16] P. and M., II, 317.

[17] See below, pp. 32-33.

[18] As in the Commentary on *Heb.* ix, 15-17 by Alcuin (PL 100, 1073-4) and by Sedulius Scottus (PL 103, 264).

[19] See P. and M., II, 317, n. 2; Auffroy, *Testament*, pp. 220-225. Examples of this usage may be found in B. 25, 149, 165. In the last example cited, the sentence of interest—"Haec autem testamenti..." may be a later addition; see J. Armitage Robinson, *St Oswald and the Church of Worcester* (British Academy, Supplemental Papers V, London, 1919), p. 11.

[20] See A. Heusler, *Institutionen des deutschen Privatrechts*, 2 vols. (Leipzig, 1885-6), II, 621-625; Goffin, *op. cit.*, pp. 16-18; Auffroy, *Testament*, pp. 146-166; J. Brissaud, *A History of French Private Law*, The Continental Legal History Series, III (Boston, 1912), pp. 624-625,

to those who had no kin; later they were employed by those without children.[21]   In its earliest form, the *affatomie* required an intermediary who received conveyance from the donor and later conveyed the property to the beneficiary of the act.[22]   By the time it appeared in the Salic law, it was already concerned with the transfer of property, rather than with the adoption of an heir.   In the Ripuarian law further change is evident: the forms of the *affatomie* have assumed greater simplicity and the intermediary has disappeared.[23]   Though no evidence of an Anglo-Saxon equivalent of these institutions has come down to us, the rather close relationship that obtained between the laws of the different tribes makes it reasonable to suppose that a similar instrument existed to be used in special cases, such as that of a family which faced extinction.[24] By the time the *post obit* distribution of property appeared among the Anglo-Saxons, these institutions were already in decline on the Continent. Their place was taken by a group of acts which openly contradicted the principle that property passed to the heirs after the owner's death, and which were usually concerned with no more than a part of an estate. These transactions assumed two basic forms.   The first was an act at the end of life, known as the *verba novissima*.   The second called the *post obit* gift, was made during the life of the donor, but its material consequences were delayed until his death.   Both forms of donation are to be found in use among the Anglo-Saxons.

685-689; and R. Huebner, *A History of Germanic Private Law*, The Continental Legal History Series, IV (Boston, 1918), sect. 110, especially the bibliographical study, p. 740, n. 1.

[21] Brissaud, *op. cit.*, sect's 450, 488; Heubner, *op. cit.*, p. 741; Auffroy, *Testament*, pp. 149-150.

[22] Heusler was of the opinion that the second act was performed only after the death of the donor (*op. cit.*, II, 622).   This theory was criticized by Auffroy (pp. 150-159), whose position is generally accepted; cf. E. Chenon, *Histoire générale du droit français public et privé des origines à 1815*, vol. I (Paris, 1928), p. 459.   These institutions were probably in use before the invasions began; see Auffroy, p. 146.

[23] *Lex Salica*, XLVI, ed. J. R. Behrend, 2nd ed. (Weimar, 1897), p. 95; *Lex Ribuaria*, XLVIII, ed. R. Sohm, *MGH*, LL. V, 236-237.   The disappearance of the intermediary is but one of the changes whereby the *affatomie*, in form and effect, approached the *post obit* gift which was coming into use at this time; see Auffroy, *Testament*, pp. 147-150, 204-209, and below, pp. 24-27.

[24] Huebner, *op. cit.*, p. 661; Holdsworth, *History*, II, 95.   There is a vague reference to adoption in a grant of 956 by King Eadwig to Ælric, "adoptivo parenti meo" (B. 949, 950), but there is no indication that the adoption was concerned with the transfer of property; cf. *Essays in Anglo-Saxon Law* (Boston, 1905), p. 126.   Vinogradoff used the word *affatomia* in a wider sense, meaning a form of donation that was not restricted to donations taking effect after death, and considered it to be related to certain modes of procedure used in Anglo-Saxon England; see "Transfer of Land in Old English Law," *Collected Papers*, 2 vols. (Oxford, 1928), I, 150, n. 2.

II. CHRISTIAN PRACTICE

The giving of alms during life and at death was one of the penitential practices recommended to the early Christians.   It was well established on the Continent by the time of St. Augustine's appearance before Æthelberht of Kent. The connection between the state of perfection and the generous gift of alms had been clearly stated in the New Testament itself.   The Fathers of the Church developed this notion considerably, and at certain times their teaching went very far in its demands.   As a general rule, they recommended that alms be given during the lifetime of the donor: the sacrifice was greater and freedom from the attraction of wealth was more firmly established. Gifts made during life had the additional advantage that they were certain of accomplishment.   The giving of alms was urged, not only for the good of the donor, but also to supply the needs of other men.   The offerings of the faithful were used to support the many social and liturgical obligations which the Church had assumed.   A profound concern for the fate of the orphan and the widow, the sick and the starving, is to be seen in most of the writings of the Fathers which urge the donation of alms.   In spite of the manifest preference for alms given during life, the bequest for pious causes was also recommended.[25]   The Church was not content to urge that these legacies be given; she even interested herself in their accomplishment. Councils of the fifth century excommunicated those who failed to distribute bequests in alms according to the wishes of the dead.[26]   The bishop became concerned with the supervision of the delivery of these legacies, and in time the laws of Justinian confirmed certain rights to him in this regard.[27]

The gift of alms at death took on special importance in the late fifth century when, in certain areas at least, it became attached to the sacramental preparation for death.   In southern Gaul, due to the fact that penance was ordinarily administered but once, and because the penitential state was difficult in itself and in its social and legal consequences, public penance was almost completely neglected.   The

---

[25] Patristic texts dealing with the giving of a last alms by testament are conveniently assembled by M. Falco, *op. cit., passim;* Auffroy, *Testament,* pp. 121-127; E. Lesne, *Histoire de la propriété ecclésiastique en France,* 6 vols. (Lille, Paris, 1910-43), I, 162-172; and especially by Bruck, *Kirchenväter* pp. 1-119.

[26] E.g., II Concilium Vasense (442), c. 4 (Mansi, VI, 453); Concilium Agathense (506), c. 4, ed. G. Morin, *Sancti Caesarii episcopi Arelatensis Opera Omnia,* 2 vols. (Maretioli, 1937-42), II, 38; cf. Lesne, *La propriété,* I, 5, n. 4.

[27] *Codex Justinianus,* I, 3, 45.

sermons of St. Caesarius of Arles indicate that penance *in extremis* was the common practice of his day.[28] Under these circumstances the interval between confession of sinfulness and reconciliation, an interval during which penance was usually performed, had to be omitted. The only penitential practice that remained possible for the dying Christian was the giving of alms. This last donation was accomplished by gift *inter vivos* or by testament. The latter form of donation became so common in some areas of the Church that the making of a testament was associated with the last confession. This point of view received an extreme statement in a sermon of St. Caesarius of Arles, where the giving of alms on the death-bed seems to be as important as the priestly absolution.[29] In those parts of the Continent where the Roman testament survived it often contained nothing more than a group of legacies in alms. In some cases it became known as an *eleemosyna*.[30]

This teaching was probably known to the Christian population of Roman Britain. But in this as in so many other things the Christianity of the older population, whether in the conquered areas or on the frontier between the two groups, seemed incapable of influencing the conquering Anglo-Saxons. A profound Christian influence entered the lives of the invaders only with the arrival of the missions from Rome and from Iona.[31]

III.   DEATH-BED ALMS AMONG EARLY ANGLO-SAXON CHRISTIANS

In the theological literature of Anglo-Saxon England, there is scarcely any reflection of the insistence on the necessity of bequests in alms as found in St. Caesarius. The importance of a charitable gift, as a penitential discipline, and the value of the death-bed confession are

---

[28] "Cum enim omnes homines paenitentiam velint in finem vitae suae accipere" (Sermo LX, ed. Morin, I, 255); cf. C. Vogel, *La Discipline pénitentielle en Gaule des origines à la fin du VIIᵉ siècle* (Paris, 1952), pp. 47-54, 116-127, 164-166.

[29] "Tertius modus paenitentiae aliquibus esse videtur, si aliquis semper male vivens, in exitu vitae se reservet ad paenitentiam, et ea spe peccet, ut per ipsam subitaneam paenitentiam et cuncta aestimet peccata dimitti, et tamen, postquam eam acceperit, et illud quod male rapuit nec in simplo reddat, nec inimicis suis toto corde indulgeat, nec in corde suo deliberet, ut si evaserit, quamdiu vivit, cum grandi conpunctione et humilitate paenitentiam agat, nec portionem sibi et Christo pro redemptione peccatorum de substantia sua cum filiis suis faciat. Sic accepta paenitentia, si sine istis remediis, quae supra memoravimus, exierit de hac vita, quid de eo futurum sit, licet nos dicere dubii simus ..." (Sermo LX, ed. Morin, I, 253-254).

[30] A. Perraud, *Étude sur le testament en Bretagne* (Rennes, 1921), p. 33, n. 1.

[31] Stenton, *Anglo-Saxon England*, p. 102; P. and M., I, xxviii-xxx; M. Deanesly, *The Pre-Conquest Church in England*, An Ecclesiatical History of England, I (London, 1961), p. 62.

emphasized, but the two notions are not connected.[32] Thus the *Penitential of Theodore* states that a priest has a serious obligation to give absolution to the dying.[33] This teaching appeared earlier in the *Penitential of Finnian,* and was to re-appear, often in Theodore's words, in many penitentials of the British Isles and the Continent.[34] Almsgiving is one of the most frequently recommended penitential practices of this literature. Yet, with one possible exception,[35] the giving of alms is not connected in any way with the death-bed confession, until it appears about the year 1000 in the so-called *Canons of Ælfric.*[36]

[32] Many examples are assembled by J. T. McNeill and Helena M. Gamer in *Medieval Handbooks of Penance,* Records of Civilization: Sources and Studies, XXIX (New York, 1938), p. 457, *s. v.* "Alms"; cf. T. P. Oakley, *English Penitential Discipline and Anglo-Saxon Law in their Joint Influence* (New York, 1923), p. 134.

[33] Bk. I, viii, 5; ed. P. W. Finsterwalder, *Die Canones Theodori Cantuariensis und ihre Ueberlieferungsformen,* Untersuchungen zu den Bussbüchern des 7., 8. und 9. Jahrhunderts, I (Weimar, 1929), p. 300. A critical summary of the problems posed by the Penitential of Theodore and of the reaction of various scholars to the conclusions of Finsterwalder is available in McNeill and Gamer, *op. cit.,* pp. 179-182.

[34] *Paenitentiale Vinniai,* 34, ed. F. W. H. Wasserschleben, *Die Bussordnungen der abendländischen Kirche* (Halle, 1851), pp. 115-116.

[35] The *Penitential of Cummean (ca.* 650) mentions that the penance of the sick may be a donation in alms (VIII, 28, trans. McNeill and Gamer, *op. cit.,* p. 111). On the date of this collection, see *ibid.,* pp. 98-99, 181, nn. 23, 24, and Finsterwalder, *op. cit.,* p. 201, where it is suggested that the compiler of the *Penitential of Theodore* knew this text or a slightly different version of it.

[36] Letter I, to Wulfsige, bishop of Sherborne (ca. 998), ed. B. Fehr, "Die Hirtenbriefe Ælfrics in altenglischer und lateinischer Fassung", *Bibliothek der angelsächsischen Prosa,* IX (Hamburg, 1914), 21. The text is also in B. Thorpe, *Ancient laws of England,* Publications of the Record Commissioners, 28 (London, 1840), p. 444. A text connecting the gift of alms with the final confession of the dying, erroneously ascribed to Theodore, was frequently cited in the eleventh and twelfth centuries; it is even found in the *Decretum Gratiani* (C. 26, q. 7, c. 1) and in the *Sententiae* of Peter Lombard (IV, d. 20, 4). Friedberg remarked in his edition of the *Decretum* (Vol. I, 1041-2), that the text was not to be found in the version of Theodore that was at his disposition. The earliest ascription to Theodore that a rather extended search has been able to locate, is that of Burchard of Worms, *Decretum,* XVIII, 14 (PL 140, 941); see P. Fournier, "Etudes critiques sur le Décret de Burchard de Worms", *Nouvelle revue historique de droit français et étranger,* XXXIV (1910), 304-308, 326-330. The text appears with the same ascription in modern editions of the *De Sacramentis* of Petrus Comestor (ed. R. Martin in an appendix to H. Weisweiler, *Maître Simon et son groupe De Sacramentis,* Spicilegium Sacrum Lovaniense, Etudes et Documents, fasc. 17 [Louvain, 1937], p. 83) and of the Penitential of Bartholomew of Exeter (ed. A. Morey, *Bartholomew of Exeter, Bishop and Canonist* [Cambridge, 1937], p. 207). It is to be found, without the ascription to Theodore, among the canons of the council of Mainz of 847 (*MGH,* LL. Cap. II, p. 182, c. 26); cf. Auffroy, *Testament,* p. 351, n. 1.

The case of Drythelm of Northumbria as reported by Bede is another manifestation of the same point of view.[37]   Drythelm died one evening, but came to life the following morning and, after prayer in a nearby church, divided his possessions among his children, his wife and himself. A short time later, he gave his own portion to the poor and entered the monastery of Melrose on Tweed.   This account, witness to a division in thirds as it seems to be, has long been of much interest to historians. Bede himself seems to intend that it serve merely as an introduction to what follows.   His main purpose in including the narrative of this event is that he might re-tell the vision seen by Drythelm during the time of his apparent death.   The dead man saw the next world and the places of the blessed and the damned; between the two, in a deep valley of insufferable cold and heat, were the souls of those who had delayed confession until death, but who had been given time for the reception of the sacrament at that hour.   Drythelm's guide informed him that those souls would be saved at the time of final judgment, and would come to bliss even sooner through the prayers, alms and masses of the living.   Here we have a very clear assertion of the value of penance *in articulo mortis,* but once again there is no mention of the giving of alms by the dying.

Yet there is literary evidence that the death-bed alms was frequently practised, and Bede provides some of it.   In his account of the life of the Irish ascetic, St Fursa, he tells of a vision in which the saint, in the company of three angels, visited the next world.   As he passed through the fires of hell, one of the damned was hurled forth by the devils and struck Fursa, burning his shoulder and jaw.   One of the angels promptly threw the sufferer back into the flames, but the devil remarked that Fursa should have been willing to share the man's suffering, since he had shared his wealth after his death.[38]   From the answers of Fursa and the angel, it appears that the saint had accepted the cloak of a man who had died in his sins.   The gift had been received, not out of avarice, but that the man's soul might be saved.   Bede ends the story with the remark that the angel told Fursa many things of great value regarding the souls of those who came to repentance at the hour of death.   The *Life of St. Fursa* which Bede recommended to his reader has survived.[39]   The directions of the angel, of which Bede approved,

37 Bede, *Historia Ecclesiastica,* Bk. V, ch. 12, ed. Plummer, I, 303-310; see B. Colgrave, "Bede's Miracle Stories," in *Bede His Life, Times and Writings,* ed. A. H. Thompson (Oxford, 1935), ch. 7.

38 Bk. III, ch. 19, ed. Plummer, I, 163-168.

39 Plummer shows, *ibid.,* II, 169, that Bede used the latin life of St. Fursa that is printed in *Acta Sanctorum,* 3rd ed., January, vol. II, 401-405.

are to be found there: penance may be received even at the hour of death and with it, the giving of alms is fitting. However, if penance is not received, then a gift from the dying man may not be accepted. The priest who attends the dying sinner is to urge him to repent. If he seeks forgiveness, his alms may be distributed to the poor. The priest himself should not share in this gift, but he is to dispense it to the needy by the tomb of the donor.[40]

This account makes it clear that there had been considerable abuse of the charitable gift: men of evil life had sought to obtain forgiveness by alms, when in health or when death approached, while continuing their evil ways. Worse still, priests had been fostering this state of affairs for reasons that, to say the least, were selfish. The abuse is criticized by both the author of the *Life of St. Fursa* and by Bede in a manner that presumes that the death-bed alms was a common occurrence, at least in Ireland and in the Northumbrian church at the end of the seventh century. It is quite probable that the same was true of East Anglia, where St. Fursa paused for a time, and, at the invitation of King Sigeberht, established a monastery in an old fortress of which Burgh castle in Suffolk is perhaps the site. Even in Bede's day, his memory was still fresh in this region.[41]

In Mercia, Wessex and the kingdoms of the south and east, there is less evidence of the giving of death-bed alms in the first century after the conversion. Such a donation is mentioned, however, in a letter of St. Boniface. His manner of discussing it indicates that he saw nothing unusual in the practice.[42] Later, during the second half of the eighth century, information about the distribution of property at death is more common; most of it comes from the southern part of England. In the earlier period, however, there is no indication that the practice had become general there. Legislation dealing with the giving of alms at death shows a development of remarkable precocity in the Celtic church,[43] so that it seems likely that this form of donation received more emphasis and made a more rapid impression among the part of the Anglo-Saxon population that was converted by missionaries from the north.

Thus, although the penitential literature fails to connect the giving of alms with the death-bed confession, it can be concluded that the bequest

---

40 *Ibid.*, p. 404; cf. Bede's commentary on *Luke* xi (PL 92, 483-485).

41 Stenton, *Anglo-Saxon England*, pp. 116-117.

42 Epist. 10, *S. Bonifatii et Lulli Epistolae,* ed. M. Tangl. *MGH*, Epistolae Selectae, I, 7-15. This letter is discussed below, pp. 35-36.

43 See below, pp. 80-81.

for pious purposes was used soon after the conversion and, in some areas at least, was sufficiently ancient by the first quarter of the eighth century to have arrived at the stage of abuse.

IV. Motives for the free Disposition of Property at Death

Among the Anglo-Saxons, as among all the Germanic peoples during the Middle Ages, the primary motive for the disposal of property at death was religious.[44] These last gifts in alms eventually became so general that they ceased to be entirely voluntary. In spite of continued opposition by Church councils, they often took the form of a tax, levied by law on the property of the deceased, in favour of the church of burial.[45]

Religion provided a motive for the *post-obit* distribution of property in another way as well. The giving of alms was not of its nature in any way connected with death. It has already been seen that the penitential writings urged the donation for pious causes without relating it to the final confession. Anglo-Saxon homiletic literature manifests an unmistakable preference for alms-giving during the lifetime of the donor.[46] But such an outright gift involved the immediate loss of property. If made on a large scale, it demanded a considerable sacrifice of the donor, one that at times must have been difficult, if not impossible.[47] Hence many preferred to give the property during life, but retain its use until death. Even in this case the profound religious motivation of the gift is quite clear. The phrase *"for mine soule"* is like the reponse of a litany, repeated again and again in the documents that speak of these gifts. This manner of expression occurs so frequently

---

[44] See A. Schultze, *Die langobardische Treuhand und ihre Umbildung zur Testaments Voll-streckung*, Untersuchungen zur deutschen Staats- und Rechtsgeschichte, 49 (Breslau, 1895), p. 14; "Der Einfluss . . ." pp. 81-98; L. Palumbo, *Testamento Romano e Testamento Longobardo* (Lanciano, 1892), p. 323 (cited by Goffin, *op. cit.*, p. 15); Auffroy, *Testament*, pp. 182 ff; H. Würdinger, "Einwirkungen des Christentums auf das angelsächsische Recht," *ZRG Germ. Abt.*, LV (1935), 129-130. The earliest landbooks were concerned with gifts to the Church, a fact that was made abundantly clear by the phrasing of the proem and by the grant itself.

[45] An offering to the church of burial became obligatory by a law of Athelstan (925-936); see below, pp. 79-80.

[46] E.g., *Blickling Homilies*, ed. R. Morris, Early English Text Soc. (London, 1880), pp. 51-53, 101, 195; alms given in life were less likely to be recovered by the donor's family.

[47] In the seventh and eighth centuries such gifts were made almost exclusively by the king. In the tenth century, however, large grants were made to monasteries during the lifetime of the nobility: thus Æthelwine at Ramsey and Brihtnoth at Ely preferred to endow their foundations by immediate transfer of possession; cf. J. A. Raftis, *The Estates of Ramsey Abbey*, Studies and Texts, 3 (Toronto, 1957), pp. 6-9, and E. Millar, *The Abbey and Bishopric of Ely*, Cambridge Studies in Medieval Life and Thought, N. S. 1 (Cambridge, 1951), pp. 16-25.

that the historian is led to ask whether it had become common form, with the resulting danger that the religious motive was really less important than it might appear to be. However, the elaborate arrangements made to ensure the delivery of alms and the offering of masses and prayers for the deceased indicate that these statements correspond with the actual sentiments of the donor. The religious motive, then, led men to seek and to perfect means for the *post obit* disposition of property. These bequests were part of the immediate preparation for death, or were made long before as one of the means of fulfilling the ordinary obligations of the Christian.

Affection,[48] the acquittal of special responsibilities,[49] the desire to obtain protection for oneself and one's heirs,[50] also found expression as motives for *post obit* gifts. Family disagreement over the division of property could be prevented by its arrangement beforehand by the owner.[51] Disapproval could be manifested and punishment inflicted by defeating an anticipated succession.[52] Motives of this sort were probably more frequent and important than surviving evidence of them would indicate. Documents witnessing to such donations had considerably less likelihood of survival than those concerned with alms. The account of the will of the Herefordshire widow, who disinherited her son in favour of a kinswoman, may reflect a fairly common occurrence.[53] In this case, there is no mention of a bequest in alms. However, the woman in question had not yet come to the end of her life; she may well have seen fit to arrange for an offering for her soul before she died.

The notion that man continued to live and to have needs after death was the most important force in Germanic society, impelling towards the assertion of the rights of the individual against the rights of the family. This motive was important, not only because it was an imperious one, but because it was to be found among men in all circumstances and on

---

[48] An early example is to be seen in Bede's gift to the priests of his monastery; see below, p. 34.

[49] Wulfric Spott provided by his will for his "poor daughter"; her disability is not indicated, but her father sought to protect her as well as her holdings (W. XVII, p. 46, line 27, p. 48, line 3).

[50] This motive is evident in H. II (835), R. VI (*ca.* 845).

[51] Asser tells us that King Æthelwulf distributed his property before his death to prevent discord among his sons; see *Asser's Life of King Alfred,* ed. W. H. Stevenson (Oxford, 1904), p. 14. The wills of Æthelwulf, Æthelred and Alfred were the basis of the settlement of the dispute between Æthelred's children and Alfred (H. XI, pp. 16-17).

[52] E.g., R. LXVIII, p. 70.

[53] *Ibid.*; see below, p. 50.

2

all levels of society. The old rules of succession yielded before it. Individuals were allowed to provide for themselves in the next life, and legal forms were invented to make it possible to do so. This religious purpose remained of prime importance all through the Middle Ages. It was not the only motive however: once the initial steps had been taken, other reasons for the distribution of property appeared as well. Affection, justice, even enmity, led men to arrange that certain persons should enjoy their wealth and that others should not.

Chapter II

THE ANGLO-SAXON WILLS,
THEIR LEGAL NATURE AND EFFECT

H ISTORICAL documents of the first centuries after the conversion of
England supply sufficient information to permit the conclusion
that the Anglo-Saxons made considerable use of the donation of property
after death. The purpose of this chapter is to study the same sources to
learn something of various legal acts whereby these donations were
effected. This is a much more difficult task, for there are few descriptions
of these transactions. Even where such information does occur, the
vagueness of the legal thought of the time makes it very hard to penetrate
beyond the external forms of acts to an understanding of the theory that
lay behind them. Another difficulty, a modern one, is the question of
terminology. Before beginning a description and analysis of the
donation of property after death, it is necessary to establish the meaning
of the terms that will be used to describe it.

The connotations of the words "testament" and "will" vary in different
times and in different places. Inasmuch as they possess a precise
meaning today, "testament" and "will" are misleading when applied to
legal transactions in Anglo-Saxon England, because the modern meaning
involves the notion of a document. For some at least, this document is
an instrument that is actually capable of effecting the legal transfer of
property. But the legal act whereby the Anglo-Saxons attained such an
end was an oral act; the drawing up of a document does not seem to have
been essential to it.[1] The use of the word "testament" can be, and is,
avoided. But the term "will," employed as it has been by English legal
historians and by the editors of Anglo-Saxon documents, is so generally
accepted that its use is imperative. Nevertheless, distinctions are
necessary: when "will" is used within the part of this study dealing with
the Anglo-Saxons it is intended to imply one of a variety of oral legal
acts. To speak, then, of making a will is to describe an oral transaction
in which gifts were made which were usually completed only after the
death of the donor.

---

[1] See below, pp. 47-54, and W., p. vii.

Within the general class of legal acts known as wills three types are distinguished. The first of these was a will made *in extremis*—made, as is to be seen, under whatever conditions the situation allowed. It is called the "gift by *verba novissima*" or the "death-bed gift." The two remaining kinds of wills were made during life. The principal may actually have been in danger of death, or at least prompted to his act by illness, but the act was not made *in extremis*; there was still the likelihood of continued life. One of these acts is known as the "*post obit* gift"; it was usually concerned with a single donee to whom one property, or a group of allied properties, was given. The other was also an act made during life; in many ways it is but a development and complication of the *post obit* gift, but it can be profitably distinguished from it. By this transaction many gifts were made to a varied and, sometimes, large group of donees. It is called the "*cwide*". On first consideration there is much to be said against employing this last term. Among the Anglo-Saxons, *cwide* could be used of an act transferring property both *inter vivos* and after death.[2] It was applied to the gift of a single property or of many.[3] Originally the word had an oral connotation, but even this virtue soon disappeared when the meaning was extended to include the document that was evidence for the oral act.[4] Nevertheless historians of law have tended to use "*cwide*" to signify those multiple donations which are distinguished from the *post obit* gift. Recent studies have emphasized the earlier oral sense[5] and so the term, understood in this way, has been adopted here.[6]

As has already been implied, a document descriptive of the oral act or will was frequently made.[7] A few of these have survived in their original form; a somewhat larger group is preserved, in varying degrees of completeness, in cartularies and other collections. Throughout this book italics are used to distinguish these documents from the oral acts of which they are witness: they are called "written *wills*" or simply "*wills*". Subsidiary terms, referring to persons and things with which the wills

---

[2] W., pp. xii-xiii; cf. J. Bosworth and T. N. Toller, *An Anglo-Saxon Dictionary* (Oxford, 1898, *Supplement*, 1921), *s.v.*, *cwide*, *cwyde*. *Cwide* was also used of a decree: see W., p. xv, n. 5.

[3] Cf. W., p. 92, line 7 and p. 26, lines 11-12.

[4] On the naming of a document after the oral act of which it is evidence, see W., p. xiii, n. 1.

[5] As in P. and M., II, 319-320; Goffin, *The Testamentary Executor*, p. 35; Holdsworth, *History*, II, 95.

[6] Cf. W., pp. xii-xiii and T. F. T. Plucknett, *A Concise History of the Common Law*, 5th ed. (London, 1956), pp. 732-735.

[7] See below, pp. 52-54.

were concerned — "testator," "legatee," "bequest," "legacy" — are used with the special meanings required by the legal nature of the acts to which they refer.

I. DOCUMENTARY EVIDENCE FOR THE DISTRIBUTION OF PROPERTY AT DEATH

Our knowledge of these acts is supplied, first, by several descriptions of the proceedings during which division of property, to take effect *post obitum,* was made;[8] second, by the record of a few cases of litigation dealing with such division;[9] third, by a number of documents, in style and structure rather like the landbook, which in a variety of ways gave property after death to a donee;[10] finally, by a somewhat larger group of texts in Old English that are commonly known as the Anglo-Saxon *wills.*

The *wills* are of special importance. Their study has been much advanced by Miss Dorothy Whitelock's excellent edition of thirty-nine of them; twenty more are to be found in the editions of Miss Harmer, Napier and Stevenson and Miss Robertson.[11] Of these documents, fifteen are concerned with only one estate[12] and, in some cases at least, were written on the landbook of the property in question.[13]   Miss Whitelock

---

8 Several examples were cited in chapter one; in addition see: B. 313; R. LXXVIII; *Liber Eliensis,* ed. D. J. Stewart, Anglia Christiana Society (London, 1848), Bk. II, ch. 11, pp. 124-126; *Chronicon Monasterii de Abingdon,* ed. J. Stevenson, 2 vols., RS, 2 (1858) I, 459; Thorpe, p. 453; *DdB,* I, 177a.

9 B. 156, 256, 378, 445; H. XV, XXIII; R. XLI. CV; K. 805; Thorpe, p. 385; *Chronicon Abbatiæ Rameseiensis,* ed. W. D. Macray, RS, 83 (1886), pp. 168-171.

10 B. 192, 283, 303, 380, 1006; H. IV, V, VI (?); R. LXXXVI. See below, pp. 56-57.

11 Dorothy Whitelock, *Anglo-Saxon Wills* (Cambridge, 1930). This edition includes the confirmation of a will by King Ethelred (XVI, 2), and two *wills* of the same person (XXXVII, XXXVIII). The remaining *wills* are in Miss F. E. Harmer, *Select English Historical Documents of the ninth and tenth Centuries* (Cambridge, 1914): Nos. II, VII, VIII, X, XI, XX, XXI ; A. S. Napier and W. H. Stevenson, *The Crawford Collection of Early Charters and Documents,* Anecdotia Oxoniensia, Med. and Mod., No. 7 (Oxford, 1894): Nos. 9, 10; Miss. A. J. Robertson, *Anglo-Saxon Charters* (Cambridge, 1939): Nos. III, VI, IX, XVII, XXVII, XXIX (?), XXXII, LXII, XCII, CI, CXVI and an undated fragment from what is probably a post-conquest will (Appendix II, VIII, p. 252); B. 1162 is the sanction clause of what was probably an Old English *will,* the date of which (1032-1038) has been suggested by C. Hart in *The Early Charters of Essex: The Saxon Period,* Department of English Local History, Occasional Paper No. 10 (Leicester, 1957), p. 23, no. 45.

12 W. V, VI, VII, XXII, XXX, XXXV, XXXVI; H. VII; R. IX, XVII, XXVII, XXXII, LXII, XCII, CXVI.

13 That the text of the donation is added to the original charter is stated in B. 192; cf. W. VII; R. IX, X and p. 277.

has called them "bequests" as distinguished from the *wills* which include several legacies.[14]   In addition, there are entries in cartularies and monastic histories which preserve latin translations of the complete or partial text of Old English *wills*.[15]   Yet in all these forms, less than a hundred documents of this sort are all that survive from the last three hundred years of the Anglo-Saxon kingdom.   There is good reason to maintain, however, that many others have disappeared.[16]   Mention of disposition of property after death is made in scores of places, and of many of these legal acts a written witness was made.[17]   The very distribu-

---

[14] The word "bequest" (*quide*) is also used of grants completed *inter vivos*, as in R. XIII; see above, n. 4

[15] A document of the last quarter of the seventh century is described by Birch (B. 29) as the testament of Abbot Hean.   Stenton has shown that it is spurious: *The Early History of the Abbey of Abingdon* (Oxford, 1913), p. 10.   B. 330 is also called a testament.   It is rather the charter of a gift *inter vivos*, though it is clear from B. 445 that the donor of B. 330, Earl Oswulf, did make a distribution of his property after death and that it was described in a *will*; see H. I, and comment thereon, p. 69.   Selections from what is alleged to be the *will* of Edward the Confessor are found in a fourteenth-century hand in the *Westminster Domesday* (fol. 31b); cf. H. *Writs*, p. 540 for the text and pp. 292-294 for its criticism.   The document is spurious.   Latin versions of documents that, in many cases, were said to exist in Old English, and whose construction supports the claim, are fairly numerous.   A search that makes no claim to have been exhaustive, has produced the following: B. 402; in the *Ramsey Chronicon*: no. 31, p. 57 (B. 1059); no. 34, p. 62 (B. 1062); no. 33, pp. 59-60; no. 35, pp. 63-64 (B. 1061); no. 38, pp. 66-67; no. 63, p. 111 (K. 928); no. 107, pp. 173-174; no. 32, p. 58 (B. 1060) is probably a gift completed *inter vivos*; in the *Liber Eliensis*, Bk. II, ch. 88.   There are bequests to St. Alban's in B. 812, Thorpe, pp. 584, 586 and K. 945, 964.   In *Vita Alfredi*, ch. 26, Asser gives part of King Æthelwulf's will. It is quite possible that, as Bishop Stubbs suggested in his introduction to the edition of *Willelmi Malmesbiriensis de Gestis Regum*, 2 vols., RS, 90 (1887-9), I, xl, n. 2, Asser actually saw the written document.   Bequests of land are mentioned in K. 726 and in a charter of Wulfrun of 994: cf. W., p. 164, notes to line 7.

That the preservation of but a portion of the original in translation was intentional is clear from Asser's remarks in ch. 16 (*EHD*, I, 265) and, especially, in various selections from the *Ramsey Chronicon*.   Here, in the case of the bequest of Godric (no. 63, pp. 111-112), we are informed: "Præter hæc quoque plurima alia dona quæ aliis concessit in eodem scripto reperimus, quæ quia nos minime contingebant in figuris Anglicis neglecta remanserunt."   See, in addition, nos. 128, (p. 192), 106 (p. 173) and the introduction to no. 33 (p. 59); cf. W., p. xv, n. 2.

[16] Cf. W., pp. xl-xli; the author's observations on this, as on so many other matters concerning the wills of the Anglo-Saxon period, are deeply indebted to Miss Whitelock's edition and to Professor Hazeltine's introductory study.   Fifty years ago, H. Cabot Lodge was of a different opinion.   He considered a 'fair proportion' of the *wills* to have survived, and that their scarcity was an indication of the limited ecclesiastical influence on matters of inheritance in England: "The Anglo-Saxon Land-law," *Essays in Anglo-Saxon Law* (Boston, 1905), p. 107, n. 2.

[17] B. 192 (mention is made of a will of King Æthelberht II of Kent); B. 387; B. 402

tion of the surviving *wills* is further evidence.   As Miss Whitelock has remarked, most of them owe their preservation to the fact that they contained bequests to the Abbeys of Abingdon, Bury, Christchurch and Winchester.[18]   From the first half of the ninth century, five *wills* are extant, all from Kent.[19]   For almost a century thereafter, until the reign of Edmund, *wills* are very rare, as are documents of any kind. During these years there are three from Kent,[20] of which two are concerned with the property of the same individual, and four from Wessex.[21]   For the remainder of the Anglo-Saxon period there are only four Kentish *wills*.[22]   Between 940 and the beginning of Ethelred's reign there are three *wills* from Mercia and eight or ten from Wessex.[23] Thereafter there is a notable change in their distribution: more than a score are from the eastern counties north of the Thames, with but three from Wessex and perhaps five from Mercia.[24]   No *will* has survived from Northumbria.[25]

The distribution of these documents is, then, most uneven as to both time and place.   Yet the information they supply, supplemented by the evidence derived from other sources already mentioned, provides a basis, imperfect though it be, for the study of the will among the Anglo-Saxons.

(mention is made of the will of Archbishop Wilfrid); B. 445; H. XV; R. LXXVIII, LXXX, XCIV (spurious perhaps, cf. p. 462), App. I, p. 229 (a list of gifts of Bishop Leofric to Exeter includes the grant of chapel ornaments to take place after his death): K. 726, 819, 927, 971, 1312; Thorpe, p. 589; H. *Writs*, 2, 17, 111; *Liber Eliensis*, Bk. II, chs. 21, 26, 27, 31 (2), 35, 47, 59, 61, 64, 68, 69, 81, 83, 89; *Ramsey Chronicon*, nos. 28, 35, 68, 80, 82, 93, 107; *Abingdon Chronicon*, I, pp. 185, 429, 442, 461 (2), 476-477.

18 W., p. xli.

19 R. III, VI, IX; B. 402; H. II.

20 H. VII, VIII, X (the *will* of Ealdorman Ælfred concerned with estates in Kent and Surrey).

21 H. XI; R. XVII, XXVI, XXVII.

22 R. XXXII, LXII; CXVI; W. XI.

23 Some *wills* can be dated only within fairly wide limits, which makes greater precision impossible. The allocation of the area to which *wills* belong is also somewhat arbitrary since they are often concerned with estates in different parts of the country. They are arranged according to the area in which the chief estates with which they deal are found. Mercian *wills* are: B. 313; W. I, II.   Wessex *wills* are: H. XX, XXI; R. XXIX(?); W. IV. VI, VII, VIII, IX, and perhaps W. III and X.

24 Wessex: W. XII, XX, XXI.   Mercia: W. XIV, XV, XVII, XIX, XXIII.

25 Northumbrian estates are bequeathed in W. XVII, though the properties in question do not seem to have been the chief holdings of the testator.

II. The Nature and Legal Effects of the Acts whereby
the Anglo-Saxons disposed of Property at Death

The Anglo-Saxon, who desired to alienate at least part of his property
for the good of his soul or for other purposes, yet wished to enjoy its use
until the end of his life, sought legal means to effect his intention.
Since his purpose frequently involved at least the partial defeat of the
hopes of the surviving members of his family, the means employed had to
be capable of defending the gift against their opposition, should it
occur.[26]   These means were legal acts of considerable variety, acts that
had much of the experimental and the expedient about them.   It is to
their analysis that we must now turn.

The Post Obit Gift

The first of the transactions to be considered is that known as the
donatio post mortem or the *post obit* gift.   It is a donation with a partially
delayed effect.   By this act, the donor gave a single property or allied
properties to a donee, without himself suffering the loss of its use.   The
gift was perfected when, with the death of the donor, the object of the
gift passed completely into the power of the donee.   Legal acts of this
sort were coming into use among the invaders on the Continent well
before the arrival of St. Augustine in Kent,[27]   and it is quite likely that
under circumstances of special need the pagan Anglo-Saxons made similar
donations by this or some analogous act.   Christianity, however,
provided a more powerful and general motive for gifts of property
after death.

The legal acts thus generally described varied considerably both as
to mode of realization and legal effect.   The documents from which
information about them is derived often contain what to the modern
mind is a rather confusing statement of gift: "I give after my death", or
"We grant after the death of both of us."   Did the donor consider
himself to have conveyed any right in the object of the gift by this act
inter vivos, or was the effect of the gift entirely delayed until the death
of the donor?   There is, of course, no statement of theory on the matter
among the Anglo-Saxons, but there is evidence to show that in many
cases the donors considered themselves to have yielded some right in the
property.   At times, the landbook of the estate in question was given to

---

26 On family opposition, which should not be exaggerated, see pp. 36-37.
27 See above, pp. 8-10.

the donee.[28]   Occasionally it is stated that the donor may not alienate
or diminish the gift in any way.[29]   The formula of the gift frequently
has the same implication[30] and the conditions of the reservation imply
that some right has been conveyed.   This right was recognized in
different ways — by a token offering or by an agreement to pay rent.[31]
In a slightly different form of this last arrangement rent was paid, not
by the donor, but by the persons to whom he had reserved the use of
the property after his death.[32]   In many cases, on the other hand, there
is no indication that the donor experienced any need to recognize the
donee's right in the property.

Very frequently the donor specifically protected his own rights by
reserving the use of the property for one or several lives.   The reservation might be for the life of the donor himself; for the lives of the donor,
his wife and children; until the death of the last member of a group;[33]
or for an indefinite time.   Just at the end of the eighth century, the
priest Headda granted the family monastery, of which he was the head,
as well as other possessions to the *familia* of Worcester, on condition
that the monastery remain in the possession of his descendants so long
as they supplied a suitable cleric to rule it.   In this case, where the
post obit gift took the form of a settlement with ultimate reversion, the
interval between the gift and its completion may well have proved to
be a very long one.[34]

Some seventy years ago Andreas Heusler included an analysis of these
donations in his *Institutionen des deutschen Privatrechts*.[35]   His conclusions

---

[28] E.g., W. V: a grant to the Old Minster at Winchester by Ordnoth and his wife.
(Ordnoth reserved the right to recover his landbook should it need correction. It was then
to be returned to the donee.) W. VII: a grant to the same church by Brihtric Grim;
H. XXIII: the father of Eadgifu bequeathed land to his daughter "giving her the title
deeds."

[29] Cf. the gift of Ædnoth to Ramsey Abbey: *Ramsey Chronicon*, no. 107, pp. 173-174.

[30] E.g., W. VII: "grants the estate at Rempton ... after his death, ... on condition that
he is to have the use of the estate as long as life lasts."

[31] E.g., W. XXX: Thurstan having given Wimbish to Christchurch promised that "each
year as long as we live a pound shall be paid as sufficient proof of the reversionary right;"
cf. Miss Whitelock's translation, W., p. 79, lines 16-17.

[32] As in R. XXXII.

[33] E.g., H. II.

[34] B. 283; Birch dates the charter by the reference to Heathored, bishop of Worcester
(781-?800). J. Armitage Robinson in *St. Oswald and the Church of Worcester*, p. 8, suggests
that the bishop was already dead since the offering is for his soul. A similar reversion is
that mentioned in H. XV; here a *will* is used to support the condition of grant; recovery
proved to be very difficult.

[35] Vol. II, pp. 117-125, 621-657.

have, with some reservations as to detail, been generally accepted on the Continent.[36] He showed that the legal acts in questions were contracts completed only after the death of the donor. By these acts *inter vivos*, the donor irrevocably alienated rights in the property while maintaining its use. In the beginning such donations were concerned with a single piece of property. Delivery, especially in transactions in which clerics were concerned, was usually accomplished *"per cartam"*.[37] Within this general class of irrevocable contractual acts, certain distinctions were made on the basis of their forms and effects. One type of act effected a complete and immediate gift: by a first transaction the donor conveyed a property to the donee; then, in a second transaction, he re-acquired the use of the property for one or more lives. In a slightly different form of this first type, one that developed late in the ninth century, the donor recognized the donee's right by the payment of rent.[38] The second type of act is that to which the term *donatio post obitum* is usually applied in England. It was a simpler transaction involving a single act whereby the donee acquired ownership of the property while the donor retained possession until death. Some historians prefer to avoid stressing these distinctions, maintaining that they tended to dissappear and that from an economic point of view the results were the same.[39] In time these

[36] Heusler's treatment of the *post obit* gift was based on the monograph of G. Beseler, *Die Lehre von den Erbverträgen*, Erster Theil: *Die Vergabungen vom Todes wegen nach dem älteren deutschen Recht* (Göttingen, 1835), and his own work *Die Gewere* (Weimar, 1872). The *post obit* gift is treated in detail by R. Huebner in *Die Donationes Post Obitum und die Schenkungen mit Vorbehalt des Niessbrauchs im älteren deutschen Recht*, Untersuchungen zur deutschen Staats- und Rechtsgeschichte (XXVI, Breslau, 1888), note especially the bibliographical study pp. 3-16; and more briefly in his *History of Germanic Private Law*, pp. 744-745. Cf. Auffroy, *Testament*, pp. 194-204; Brissaud, *A History of French Private Law*, pp. 688-691; Lesne, *La propriété ecclésiastique*, I, 165-167; Goffin, R,. *The Testamentary Executor*, pp. 19-24; Chenon, *Histoire générale*, I, 454 ff.

[37] "The delivery *per cartam* having taken place in due form, it is clear that the donor has absolutely deprived himself of his property", Brissaud, *op. cit.*, p. 690, n. 6. Cf. Huebner, *History*, p. 745.

[38] Huebner distinguished two forms within this donation with the reservation of usufruct: the *precaria oblata*, where the use of the same land was given, and the *precaria remuneratoria*, where the use of a different estate was given. In the latter case, rent was usually paid; see *Die Donationes Post Obitum*, p. 116 and *History*, p. 744. Brissaud tentatively suggested that the donor's right in the land might better be considered as a limited ownership rather than a right of usufruct: *History*, p. 691 and n. 1.

[39] Brissaud, *History*, p. 690, n. 5; Goffin, *The Executor*, p. 21. Admitting that economically they were indistinguishable, Huebner insisted on the distinction: *Die Donationes*, pp. 4, 149; *History*, p. 744. Lesne, *op. cit.*, I. 166, n. 5, shows how the two forms became confused in the documents.

two types of donation took on the qualities of a simplified *affatomie* and effected the distribution of much or even all of an estate.[40]   In cases where the donor was unable to perform the formalities required for the transaction, a third party sometimes acted in his place.[41]

The extent to which this analysis is applicable to the various transactions employed by the Anglo-Saxons has until recently received little attention.[42] It is the special merit of Professor Hazeltine's introduction to the edition of the *Anglo-Saxon Wills* that it draws on the accomplishments of German and French scholars and relates primitive English practice to the general background of Germanic law, thus throwing additional light on a problem that had been largely neglected. One of the chief contributions of his essay is the suggestion that the best approach to the Anglo-Saxon wills is to consider them as contractual gifts.[43]   In the discussion among earlier writers on the Continent, it had been presumed that, in the different forms of the *post obit* gift, there was an immediate conveyance of ownership.   Interest was concentrated on the analysis of the rights acquired by the donee or retained by the donor and on a consideration of the various ways in which these rights were recognized.[44] Professor Hazeltine did not neglect these matters, but he preferred to distinguish conveyance from contract within the *post obit* gift and to emphasize its contractual aspect.[45]

Many of the *post obit* gifts were bilateral contracts. This fact is evident both in the written *wills* and in the description of the way in

---

[40] Beseler, *op. cit.*, pp. 152-196; Heusler, *Institutionen*, II, 626, 641; Huebner, *History*, pp. 744-745; Schroeder, R. *Lehrbuch der deutschen Rechtsgeschichte*, 1st ed. (Leipzig, 1889), pp. 329-330; Goffin, *op. cit.*, pp. 22-24.

[41] Brissaud, *History*, pp. 692-694 and Huebner, *History*, pp. 744-745. See below pp. 35-36.

[42] Maitland was aware of these studies and regarded them with considerable favour: "There is a great deal to show that men have thought themselves able by a single act or instrument to transfer the fee while retaining a life estate, and to make those *donationes post obitum* which have given rise to prolonged discussion in other countries. It is by no means impossible that the so-called Anglo-Saxon 'wills' were really instruments of this kind, irrevocable conveyances which were to operate at a future time" (P. and M., II, 92). Goffin summarized the conclusions but hesitated to decide the extent of their application to England: *op. cit.*, pp. 13-34, 35-36; cf. Holdsworth, *History*, II, 95.

[43] W., Introduction, pp. vii-xl. Cf. reviews of this work by T. F. T. Plucknett in *Harvard Law Review*, XLIII (1929-30), 1331-2 and R. R. Darlington in *Antiquity* IV (1930), 566-8. In his review in *ZRG Germ. Abt.*, LI (1931), 695-699, Herbert Meyer took strenuous exception to certain aspects of Hazeltine's theory of the will; this is discussed below, pp. 52-54.

[44] Cf. Heusler, *Institutionen*, II, 638-642; Huebner, *History*, p. 744; Auffroy, *Testament*, pp. 200 ff; Brissaud, *History*, pp. 689-691.

[45] W., pp. xx ff.

which these donations were made.   It is, of course, quite in keeping
with the primitive Germanic use of the counter-gift (*launegild*) as a
means of giving a permanence to a donation that the merely gratuitous
gift did not possess.[46]   The counter-gift is mentioned in bequests of a
single estate or a chattel and in the more complex division of property
which we have called the *cwide*.[47]   Even Bede asked prayers of those
to whom he gave presents before he died.[48]   Later *wills* reveal a wide
variety of arrangements whereby various ecclesiastics or religious institutions obliged themselves to provide burial, prayers, anniversary comme-
morations and alms for the donor.   The counter-gift was sometimes a
service or protection, and was occasionally imposed in the form of a
condition.[49]

The contractual aspect of many of these gifts is further indicated by
the fact that they frequently confirm earlier transactions which were
obviously contracts of the usual Germanic type.[50]   The very terms used
to describe the act whereby the gift was made, as well as the name given
the document that was witness to it, and the practice of making several
copies of this document so that donor, donee and possibly even a third
party might retain one, all point to the contractual character of these
acts.[51]   Further evidence is provided by the fact that the *post obit* gift
was considered to be irrevocable.[52]   The anathema clause of many of the
documents includes the statement that the donation may not be withdrawn.[53]   There are a few cases where the donor reserved a right of
revocation.   However the gift was not to be revoked at pleasure, but only
under certain conditions: for example, the birth of a child or the failure

[46] See *ibid.*, pp. xix-xx, xxv and n. 6; Brissaud, *op. cit.*, p. 704, n. 7; cf. E. Levy, *West
Roman Vulgar Law*, Memoirs of the American Philosophical Society, Vol. XXIX (Philadelphia, 1951), p. 167.

[47] In some of the *cwides*, the counter-gift was made by the chief beneficiary; cf. W.,
p. xxvi and no. V.

[48] See below, p. 34.

[49] In a *post obit* gift to Christchurch in 1032, Eadsige acquired the community's protection
in life and after death, reserving the right to revoke the gift and transfer his property
elsewhere, should they fail in their obligation to him (R. LXXXVI). In R. IX, the
property was to be delivered when the donees had completed twelve months of prayer.

[50] See W., Introduction, *passim*.

[51] The various terms are assembled by Professor Hazeltine in W., pp. xxi-xxii. On the
use of the chirograph and its purpose see *ibid.*, pp. xxiii-xxv and below, p. 59.

[52] W., p. xi and n. 2. The irrevocability of the *post obit* gift is held by authors on the
Continent; Heusler doubted it in *Gewere*, p. 472, but conceded the point in *Institutionen*,
II, 121 (cited by Brissaud, *History*, p. 690, n. 6).

[53] As in W. XI, XIII.

of a donee to fulfill his promise.[54]   It can be accepted as proved that
the *post obit* gift in Anglo-Saxon England was an irrevocable and usually
bilateral contract.

The conveyancing aspect of the *post obit* gift is considerably more
difficult to analyse.   The rights of the donor and donee are easily seen
in the first type of donation distinguished by Heusler, that in which a
complete and immediate conveyance of title and possession was followed
by a second act in which the donee recovered the use of the property or
of some other estate for a term of years.   But this form of *post obit* gift
was rarely, if ever, used in England before the Norman Conquest.[55]

It is the second type of *post obit* gift that is of interest here.   As has
been indicated above, historians on the Continent are generally agreed
that this donation included the conveyance of title to the donee.[56]
Such a right in the property was frequently conveyed in England as
well.[57]   There was much to be said for an immediate transfer of title:
the more completely the property had passed into the power of the
donee, the more likely the ultimate perfection of the donation.
However, there is evidence that this was not always done in England.
The landbook of the property, for instance, was sometimes retained by
the donor.[58]   Yet a gift of this sort was not a mere promise intended as
a provisional expression of a last will that only death could fix.   It was
rather a contractual promise that delivery of a property would be made
after the donor's death.[59]   The contract was made by a public formal act

---

[54] E.g., H. II, X; cf. Brissaud, *History*, p. 690, n. 6.

[55] Two transactions have many of the qualities of this form of donation: early in the
eleventh century, the priest Eadsige gave an estate at Appledore in Kent to Christchurch for
his soul.   Then he proceeded to buy back the property for two lives.   During the time that
it remained in the hands of the reservees, a food-rent was to be paid.   In addition Eadsige
had been given another estate for his lifetime (R. LXXXVI).   Thus the transaction bears
considerable resemblance to those double transfers of possession with the addition of a gift
to the donor for life, that are to be found in Marculf's *Formulæ* under the rubric: "Epistola,
si aliqui rem ecclesiæ ad usum habeant et eorum proprietate pro hac donant" (II, 39, ed. K.
Zeumer, *MGH*, LL. Form. V, 98-99); cf. Lesne, *La propriété*, I, 166-168.   The second case, an
agreement between Ealdorman Ælfred and Archbishop Æthelred (H. VIII), has some
qualities in common with the preceding: Ælfred bequeathed a property at Chartham
"after his day" and the bishop gave him another property for his lifetime.   There is,
however, no way of knowing whether the transaction involved the conveyance of Chartham
to the archbishop followed by its recovery by the donor.

[56] See above, p. 26 and n. 36.

[57] See examples cited above, p. 25.

[58] As in B. 378 (824).

[59] Cf. W., p. xi.

and the purpose of the formality was to impose a liability that was probably personal as well as proprietary.[60]   It is likely that the delivery of a *wedd* was intended to subject the property to certain obligations: it could not be alienated nor diminished and was required to be delivered to the donee eventually.[61]   Personal liability seems to be implied in a law of Cnut which speaks of the obligation to honour a wedded promise.[62]   Failure in this regard would constitute a *laesio fidei,* and as such could be subject to an ecclesiastical sanction.[63]   If one may be permitted to employ legal conceptions and terms which the Anglo-Saxons did not have at their disposition, it can be said that by the *post obit* gift, which included the actual conveyance of title, a *ius in re* vested in the donee; in the other case, where there was a contractual promise but no conveyance, the donee received a *ius ad rem.*[64]

At first sight it seems possible to make further distinctions within the rights of the donees by the analysis of the different payments made to them by the donors.[65]   Thus, where there had been conveyance of title, was the right of the donee who received rent more complete than that of the donee who did not receive it?   Or is it implied that there was an increase of the donee's right after the donor's death in those cases where the use of the property was reserved for several lives and the payment of rent was begun by the first reservee after the donor?   These questions have been posed by historians dealing with similar institutions on the Continent.   Answers tend to vary according to the particular theory of

[60] *Ibid.,* pp. xxvii-xxix; on the distinction between *Schuld* and *Haftung* in Germanic law see H. D. Hazeltine, *Geschichte des englischen Pfandrechts,* Untersuchungen zur deutschen Staats- und Rechtsgeschichte, 92 (Breslau, 1907), pp. 109-113 and O. Gierke, *Schuld und Haftung im älteren deutschen Recht,* Untersuchungen, etc. 100 (Breslau, 1910), pp. 182, 186, 314-317, 365.

[61] E.g., R. XXXIX, p. 82, line 27: "and on his wedd granted after his day." It is sometimes stated that the property may not be diminished or alienated; see above, n. 28. Hazeltine suggests that delivery of the property after the donor's death would constitute the redemption of the pledge; on the *wedd* or pledge see *Gesetze,* II, 237-238.

[62] *Gesetze,* I, 274 (14).

[63] Alfred, I, 8 (*Gesetze,* I, 48). English documents do not mention the pecuniary sanction that is to be found in Frankish instruments of the time; cf. Holdsworth, *History,* II, 87 and P. and M. II, 193. They frequently invoke divine punishment on those who fail in their obligations. An obscure phrase in H. XV (p. 27, lines 3 and 4) probably refers to confession of fault or performance of penance as one of the conditions in a settlement involving failure to respect the terms of a will.

[64] W., pp. xxviii, xxxviii.

[65] See the examples cited above, nn. 28-32.

seisin adopted by the scholars concerned.[66] But in England very little evidence is available and, even where it exists, we have no proof that practice was sufficiently consistent to provide a sure indication of the donee's rights. Thus such questions are not really capable of a satisfactory answer.

When analysed from the point of view of the property with which it dealt, the *post obit* gift assumes the qualities of several modern transactions; for example, the settlement,[67] the mutual gift between spouses,[68] the reversion[69] and the release[70] are to be found among these acts. But all find their place within the general category of the *post obit* gift because in each case donation was made by formal contract and the gift was not completed until the death of the person or persons to whom the property was reserved.

The *post obit* gift is also found within the much more complicated legal transaction called the *cwide*. Before the *cwide* is considered, however, it is necessary to investigate another act which influenced it, the donation by *verba novissima*.

The Death-Bed Gift

Among the older Christian population on the Continent, the gift in alms, made on the death-bed by *verba novissima*, was closely associated with the testament.[71] It was, as has been seen, an act frequently connected with the religious preparation for death.[72] By means of it, the dying man, having maintained his possessions until he saw the end approaching, was able to state his will with regard to those possessions to the persons assisting him. He might even distribute some of his goods himself. Examples from the seventh and early eighth centuries in England have shown that disposition by *verba novissima* occurred very soon after the conversion of the country, and repeated references give abundant proof of its continued use to the time of the Conquest and

---

[66] The dispute between Beseler and Heusler is summarized by Auffroy, *Testament,* pp. 200-201.

[67] E.g., H. II.

[68] E.g., R. III. Sometimes two parties made agreements whereby the survivor was to receive property that had belonged to the deceased: e.g., W. XIX, XXXI, XXXIV.

[69] R. XXVII.

[70] W. XXXIX.

[71] On the gift by *verba novissima* see Heusler, *Institutionen,* II, 642-645; P. and M., II, 316; Auffroy, *Testament,* pp. 350, 406, 653; Schultze, "Der Einfluss," pp. 102-106, especially the bibliographical note p. 104, n. 1; Brissaud, *History,* p. 691; Holdsworth, *History,* II, 95.

[72] See above, pp. 12-16.

beyond. Occasionally a phrase such as *cum moreretur dimisit* occurs
with such regularity in a cartulary that one has reason to suspect that
the compiler had concluded that the proper way to refer to a monastic
acquisition was by describing it as a death-bed gift.[73] The phrase would
not then be an accurate description of the manner in which the gift was
made. There is danger too that the words may refer to the completion
of the gift by delivery of possession after the death of the donor, rather
than to the actual gift itself which may have occurred much earlier.
However, there is often supplementary evidence to show that donations
so described were actually made at the end of the donor's life.[74] Gifts
of part or, occasionally, of the whole of an estate were made in alms and
for other purposes by this act. Sometimes the death-bed gift was the
occasion for making final arrangements that had been neglected or
intentionally delayed in earlier more formal acts.[75] As would be
expected at a time when penitents were examining their consciences with
more than ordinary care, this act was also used for the rectification of
some injustice.[76] The reinforcement and completion of earlier grants
and agreements also found a place there.

An excellent example of the use of the death-bed gift to supplement
earlier transactions is found in the account of St. Wilfrid's distribution
of his estate.[77] Wilfrid was journeying to his monastery at Hexham
when he was struck down by a serious illness. His followers prayed
that he might be granted a longer life to "dispose of his monasteries
and divide his possessions." Wilfrid was restored to health and
proceeded to distribute his lands and other property. In the eyes of his
biographer this was a very important act. At Ripon, he caused his
treasures to be laid out before eight witnesses and then divided his
wealth. The best portion was to be sent to Rome by messengers, since
Wilfrid was unable to deliver it himself as he would have preferred.
Of the other three portions, one was to be distributed to the poor for
Wilfrid's soul, another to the abbots of Hexham and Ripon that they
might purchase royal favour, the third to the companions of Wilfrid's
exile. He then arranged for the appointment of an abbot and set out

---

[73] As in the *Liber Eliensis*, Bk. II, chs. 21, 26, 31, 35, 47.

[74] E.g., *ibid.*, Bk. II, chs. 59, 61; *Ramsey Chronicon*, nos. 67, 79, 80.

[75] E.g., R. XXVI: "I shall verbally bequeath Æscmere to such of my young kinsmen as
obey me best."

[76] E.g., Thorpe, p. 453.

[77] *Vita Wilfridi I. episcopi Eboracensis auctore Stephano*, chs. 61-65, ed. W. Levison, *MGH*,
SS. Merov., VI, 257-261. The Latin text is edited with translation by B. Colgrave, *The Life
of Bishop Wilfrid by Eddius Stephanus* (Cambridge, 1927).

for the court of Ceolred, king of Mercia. On the way, he visited several of the communities subject to him, repeating at each the will which he had made[78] and distributing lands and money "as though ... he were sharing his inheritance among his heirs before his death." But Wilfrid did not live to complete this distribution. His final illness came upon him at the monastery of Oundle. There, in his *verba novissima*, he rehearsed the gifts of land already made, indicated his will with regard to the distribution of other lands not mentioned earlier, and ordered that the monastery of Hexham be given to the priest Acca.[79]

The extent of Wilfrid's wealth and the account of his generous distribution were not likely to be minimized by his admiring biographer. Eddi's errors are many and manifest and his work has been the object of severe criticism.[80] None the less, the account of Wilfrid's death is the part of the *Life* that is least likely to contain error. Eddi himself was present and, what is perhaps equally important, wrote the biography at the command of Bishop Acca and Abbot Tatberht who were also present. The description of events that touched their lives and offices so closely is likely to have been written with considerable care.[81] In its main lines, the account seems acceptable: warned of approaching death, Wilfrid arranged for the distribution of most of his property—monasteries, lands and goods; he then proceeded to the actual transfer of possession. It is important to note that those who witnessed the distribution of his treasure and who were among the beneficiaries of this distribution were charged with the execution of some of its elements. Wilfrid's personal delivery of possession was interrupted by his death. In his last hours he reaffirmed donations already made and arranged for the distribution of what remained.

The death-bed gift was probably the most commonly used type of will among the Anglo-Saxons. Yet it appears in a vague and indefinite way, and it is difficult to discover its exact legal nature and effect. The laws of the period do not reflect it in England; literary rather than legal

---

[78] The phrase used by Eddi is: "Illic enim quibusdam supradicta testamenta ex ordine narravit" (ch. 64).

[79] *Ibid.*

[80] B. W. Wells, "Eddius' Life of Wilfrid," *EHR*, VI (1891), 535-550; R. L. Poole, "St. Wilfrid and the See of Ripon," *ibid.*, XXXIV (1919), 1-24. Cf. Colgrave's remarks, *op. cit.*, p. xl.

[81] Wells has already made this suggestion: "Nothing in Eddi's account of Wilfrid's last years and death seems inconsistent with his former life. Here Eddi had too many fellow witnesses to make important errors." The discussion is summarized by Eleanor Duckett in *Anglo-Saxon Saints and Scholars* (New York, 1947), p. 143, n. 65.

sources provide most of the information that we possess.   This is to be
expected: among most members of society, the death-bed gift would be
exclusively concerned with chattels, and a written record was unnecessary
since the gift was completed almost immediately.   Even when land was
donated, there was less need of a document as undying witness than was
the case with the *post obit* gift, since delivery followed quickly after the
statement of the donor's intention.[82]   The haste with which the donation
must often have been made adds to the difficulty.   It is impossible to
know what was said or done in many cases, but it seems reasonable to
conclude that the performance of the public formalities typical of
Germanic legal practice was sometimes impossible.

The first question to decide is whether the donation by *verba novissima*
differed essentially from the *post obit* gift or whether it was one form of
the latter made under special conditions.   If the attitude of the donor is
considered,   several   important   differences   become   evident.   The
connection of the death-bed gift with the last confession contributed to
a more disinterested view of material goods than would normally be
possible for the donor of a *post obit* gift.   The latter expected to live, so
he carefully provided for the indefinite delay of some of the consequences
of his donation.   But the man who bequeathed property on his death-
bed did not anticipate further need of it; his chief concern was to see
that it was received by the donee.   The characteristic of this act is that
it effects a donation as completely as possible under the circumstances.

Occasionally, especially if the property involved were not of large
quantity and conditions made it possible, the gift and actual transfer of
property took place during the donor's last hours.[83]   In his touching
description of Bede's death, Cuthbert tells us that the dying man, at
about the ninth hour of the day of his death, called the priests of his
monastery to his bed-side and there distributed to them his few
possessions—napkins, some spices, some incense.[84].   On other occasions,

---

82 Nevertheless, the preparation of a deed was no doubt desirable since it could be used
as evidence were the donee's right challenged.   An example of a death-bed gift that repeated
earlier *post obit* gifts and of which a written record was made is that of Siferth of Dunham.
It is discussed below, pp. 51-52.   Another example is described in R. XLI.

83 Cf. Heusler, *Institutionen*, II, 197-201, 644.

84 *Epistola Cutheberti de obitu Bedae*, ed. E. Van Kirk Dobbie, in *The Manuscripts of
Caedmon's Hymn and Bede's Death Song* (New York, 1937), pp. 124-125.   The insular version
contains an interesting addition: "Divites autem in hoc seculo aurum et argentum et alia
preciosa dare student; ego autem cum multa caritate et gaudio fratribus meis dabo quod
deus dederat" (lines 61-64, p. 125).   The editor considers this mention of "the charitable
propensities of his (Bede's) contemporaries" to be an interpolation (*ibid.* p. 100).

when the donee was present, a donation of land, complete with delivery of possession, could be made with the forms and symbols used for donation *inter vivos,* though under the simplified conditions that the occasion demanded.[85] The same end could probably be effected by sending a member of the family or some other third party to make the donation in the name of the dying person. It seems reasonable to conclude that some of the gifts by *verba novissima* were completed by the donor himself. But where death came suddenly, no doubt a frequent occurrence, there would be no opportunity to proceed in this way. The owner would have to be content either with the mere expression of his desire as to the future enjoyment of his property or with the agreement that a third party act in his place.

The priest assisting the dying man was most likely to be told his last desires.[86] It need hardly be said that the information he brought to the surviving members of a family, involving as it might the loss of property already possessed or anticipated, was not always well received. The first account of such a transaction shows the confessor in this embarrassing position. It occurs in a letter, written by St. Boniface in 716 to Eadburga, abbess of the monastery of St. Mildred in Thanet. At the request of the abbess, St. Boniface had investigated the vision of a monk from Wenlock in Shropshire. The vision had occurred during a period of apparent death and was similar to those described by Bede—a visit to the place of the dead during which the visionary acquired certain information that could conduce to the better life among the living.[87] Among the souls seen by the monk was one at whose death and funeral he had recently assisted. The dying man had asked him to bear witness to his last words in which he demanded that a slave, whom he and his

---

[85] The death-bed gift of Siferth of Dunham (discussed below, pp. 51-52) may have involved the complete transfer of property *inter vivos.* It is possible, however, that even here the act was but a *post obit* gift. Cf. Auffroy, *Testament,* p. 407.

[86] A Council of Nantes describes the procedure to be used by a priest when visiting those about to die. He was instructed to recite the seven penitential psalms with prayers for the sick. "Post haec omnes jubeat extra cubiculum secedere, et appropinquans lecto, quo infirmus decumbit, eum blande leniterque alloquatur, ut omnem spem suam in Deo ponat ... ut substantiam suam, dum adhuc sensus et ratio in eo vigent, disponat: ut peccata sua eleemosynis redimet ..." (Mansi, XVIII, 167). The council is usually dated 658 as in A. Perraud, *Étude sur le testament en Bretagne* (Rennes, 1921), p. 34. However, the early part of the ninth century seems the better date: cf. K. J. v. Hefele and H. Leclercq, *Histoire des conciles,* 11 vols. (Paris, 1907-52), Addenda et errata, III, ii, 1246. Similar though less detailed procedure is suggested by Ælfric in his letter to Wulfsige, cited above, p. 13, n. 36.

[87] *S. Bonifatii et Lulli Epistolae,* ed. Tangl, pp. 7-15.

brother owned in common, should be freed for the good of his soul. The surviving brother had not complied. Whatever the precise factual content of the vision might be,[88] it is clear that the monk, acting as confessor during the man's last illness, had been commissioned to bear witness to a death-bed alms and that he was doing his utmost to see that the request was fulfilled. This conclusion is corroborated by the *Dialogus Egberti,* a text indicative of practice in the region of York in the middle of the eighth century.[89]   There it is asked whether priest or deacon may witness *verba novissima* in which the dying distribute their goods. The answer is that they may, and that they should have with them one or two other witnesses lest relatives seek to prevent the execution of the will of the deceased.

Family opposition of this sort should not be over-emphasized. In all likelihood, there were strong pressures in the society of the time that tended to aid the execution of the desire of the deceased.[90]   The *Dialogus Egberti,* for instance, shows that in the region of York the Church was supporting the death-bed gift by the middle of the eighth century, and it is reasonably certain that such was the case throughout the whole country. There can be no doubt that the monk of Wenlock looked upon his action as the execution of a sacred trust: whatever the meaning of the vision, it is at least clear that he considered his penitent's donation to be valid and sought to make it effective. Families must frequently have been willing to sacrifice their own comforts for the good of deceased members. The desire to assist the dead receives an unusual expression in the account of the vision of St. Fursa described in the previous chapter. There we are told that the saint accepted the bequest of a cloak, not because he wished to possess it, but that the alms of the deceased might be completed so that his soul would be released from punishment.[91]

---

88 Boniface went to considerable pains to show the care with which he had acquired his information: he delayed writing until he had been able to interview the monk personally and he did so in the presence of witnesses (*ibid.,* p. 15).

89 Haddan and Stubbs, III, 404; cf. Oakley, *English Penitential Discipline,* p. 79.

90 Cf. Heusler, *Institutionen,* II, 644; Schultze, "Der Einfluss," pp. 102-106; Bruck *Die Schenkung auf der Todesfall,* pp. 141-145 and for England, especially, W. Würdinger, "Einwirkungen des Christentums auf das angelsächsische Recht," *ZRG Germ. Abt.,* LV, (1935), 112.

91 The devil, "repetans fallacias," suggested that Fursa should share the sufferings as well as the wealth of the deceased; but the angel replied that the saint had accepted the cloak "Non propter avaritiam, sed propter animam ejus liberandam;" see p. 14 and n. 39 above. The notion reappears centuries later in a sermon of Ælfric: *Homilies of the Anglo Saxon Church,* ed. B. Thorpe, 2 vols., Ælfric Soc. (London, 1844-6), II, 344.

None the less, there was opposition at times; it is perhaps in the investigation of the means used to surmount it that the key to the legal nature of this act is to be found. Where the donor simply declared his desire with regard to the future ownership of his property, it is almost certain that the act was without legal effect.[92] The property passed to the family by the ordinary rules of succession and its members would be only morally obliged to fulfill the wishes of the deceased by the conveyance of lands or chattels which, by the time of actual transfer, had become their own property.[93] It is evident, however, that the donor by death-bed gift usually appointed an intermediary to act in his place after his death. Conveyance of alms was made to the priest attendant, with the intention that he distribute it later for the soul of the deceased.[94] Others too, friends or members of the family, had property conveyed to them that they in turn might convey it to the donee.[95] The intermediary received a real right in the property and was expected to convey it to the person or institution indicated by the donor.[96] So far as can be seen, the dying man did not ordinarily reserve the use of his property but intended that the donee or third party should have seisin immediately.

What of the man who made donations at what he considered to be the hour of his death, yet did not die? Was the gift revocable? It has been remarked that the case would have been of such rare occurrence as to render the question unnecessary.[97] None the less, it must have occurred from time to time. Unfortunately English evidence is not sufficient to provide a satisfactory answer to the question. It seems reasonable to make certain suggestions however. In cases where the dying man merely expressed the desire that certain persons receive legacies, it can be presumed that he continued to own the property since, in the eyes of

92 It has been suggested that death-bed gifts of this sort were true *donationes mortis causa*—legacies, in the Roman sense of the term. It seems reasonable to conclude that if any notions derived from Roman law entered the Anglo-Saxon theory of the will, it was in the death-bed gift. But if the statement of the dying man were nothing more than a unilateral and revocable act it is impossible to see how it could be enforced in the ordinary process of law; cf. the opinions of D'Espinay and Esmein summarized and refuted by Auffroy, *Testament*, pp. 406, n. 2 and p. 407.

93 Coffin, *op. cit.*, p. 30.

94 Cf. P. and M., II, 318-319 and Schultze, "Der Einfluss," p. 104.

95 B. 156: the Abbess Dunne seems to have conveyed the abbey to her daughter, that she might convey it to the child Hrothwaru when she came of age; B. 192: Dunwald was taking a money legacy to Rome on behalf of the late king.

96 The rights of the third party in the legacy are discussed below, pp. 41-44.

97 P. and M., II, 319.

the law, a unilateral statement of gift was not sufficient to divest him of it. Where actual conveyance had been made either to the donee or to an intermediary, it is hard to see how the donor would be able to recover his property if the beneficiary chose to resist him. But, given the flexibility of the whole procedure as well as the relations that can be presumed to have existed between the principals of the transactions, it is very likely that the donor would be allowed the use of the property while he lived. The fact that the distribution to the poor, the payment of the mortuary, even the delivery of land, frequently took place by the grave of the deceased makes it clear that the last legal act, the completion of the gift by a third party, ordinarily did not occur until the donor had passed beyond all further need of his possessions.[98]

The disposition of property by *verba novissima* had several obvious disadvantages. In an age such as that of the Anglo-Saxons, violent and sudden death must have been an all too common occurrence. The person who delayed making arrangements about the future enjoyment of his property ran considerable risk that he would not make them at all.[99] Eventually such failure came to be considered a serious fault, even a crime, and it may be presumed that from the beginning, among the more pious at least, it was an omission that was carefully avoided.[100] Furthermore, even when there was the opportunity of uttering *verba novissima,* conditions must often have been such as to render impossible that gathering of witnesses which would best guarantee the eventual implementation of the desires of the dying man. For the wealthier members of society, whose bequests included property of considerable extent, other methods were preferred, methods that allowed the owner to enjoy his property to the end of his life, while at the same time avoiding the risk of failure due to the suddenness of death. This end was attained by the *post obit* gift, as has been seen, and also by a more complex legal act, the *cwide.*

---

[98] There are many references to transactions at the grave-side in documents of the Anglo-Saxon period: e.g., arrangements regarding leased land made on the day of the funeral of the lessee (Thorpe, pp. 378-379); payment of the wergeld by the open grave (Laws of Æthelberht, c. 22, *Gesetze*, I, 4); distribution of alms to the poor (see the account of St. Fursa, above, pp. 14-15).

[99] Alfred and his brother, King Æthelred, made arrangements for the future of their estates when they 'were all harassed with the heathen invasion" (H. XI, p. 16, lines 16-19).

[100] See above, pp. 11-12.

The Cwide

The act known as the *cwide* was much like the *post obit* gift in form and effects. None the less, the two acts are fittingly distinguished, for by the *cwide* part or even all of an individual's property was distributed among what was often a large and widely dispersed group of beneficiaries.[101] The *cwide* usually included several *post obit* gifts, some of which were made at the time while others were merely confirmed.[102] Each gift, of course, had a specific object and donee. The *cwide* also confirmed marriage settlements and contracts,[103] arranged for the payment of debts,[104] and occasionally contained what may well have been a unilateral statement of future gifts.[105] Such an act, distinguished from the primitive *post obit* gift by the multiplicity of effects, was an attempt to make in advance what would be a final and more or less universal arrangement for the enjoyment of the owner's property after his decease. In a few cases a *cwide* provided for the distribution of property acquired between the time of the act and the donor's death.[106]

There even appeared, at times, the vague notion that the legal act being performed was in some way a gift by *verba novissima*. In the *will* of King Alfred, for instance, it is stated that, having heard the explanation of the manner in which the king had acquired his estates, the West-Saxon council declared that no change should be made in dispositions that the king would bequeath on his last day. The dispositions in question were made at least a decade before the king's death.[107] Almost a century later, a document introduces itself as the "last word" (*nihsta cwide*) of Brihtric and his wife; in another of about the same time, the Ealdorman Æthelmær, scorning all time sequences, "informs his royal lord and all his friends what his will was on his last day."[108] This notion

---

[101] P. and M. II, 319-320; Holdsworth, *History*, II, 95-97. For a discussion of the similar development from the *post obit* gift on the Continent see Goffin, *op. cit.*, pp. 23-27. Professor Hazeltine does not emphasize the distinction between the *cwide* and the *post obit* gift, though he speaks of the Anglo-Saxon will as being a "bundle of post obit gifts" (W., pp. x ff.). This point is raised by Herbert Meyer in the review cited above, p. 27, n. 43.

[102] Examples of confirmation of previous *post obit* gifts are found in W. III, IV *et passim*

[103] See W. p. 135, note to line 2, and examples cited there.

[104] See below, p. 75.

[105] See below, pp. 43, 46.

[106] As in W. I, p. 2, lines 1-3.

[107] H. XI, p. 17, lines 10-12: "hit nænig mann næfre ne onwende on nane oðre wisan butan swa ic hit sylf gecweðe æt þam nyhstan dæge". The latest possible date for the transaction is 889, the year of the death of Archbishop Æthelred, whose advice is mentioned.

[108] W. XI and W. X, p. 24, lines 13-14 : « cyð on dysum gewrite his cynehlaforde and

has proved to be a tenacious one, as the continued use of the term *ultima voluntas* during the Middle Ages and "last will" in modern English amply demonstrates. The survival of the notion has been aided no doubt by the fact that such acts, then as always, were frequently made in times of special danger — illness, war, departure on a journey — so that donors knew that, whatever the legal form of the act, it might well prove to be a death-bed gift in material effect.

A *cwide* was usually made with the permission or even in the presence of the king, or at least before a group of witnesses that included persons of considerable importance in the state. It was, so far as can be seen, the preserve of the upper classes.[109]

The conclusions of Professor Hazeltine with regard to the legal effect of the *post obit* gift apply in part to the *cwide* as well. A *cwide* was often made up of a group of such bilateral acts, and occasionally took the form of a principal *post obit* gift to which certain secondary agreements were attached: the principal donee entered into contractual relationship with the donor, sometimes giving a counter-gift and, on occasion, receiving a copy of a document, witness to the transaction.[110] However, the *post obit* gift is not the basic form of all the constituents of the *cwide*. Some of the bequests, so far as can be seen from the written account of them in the *wills,* seem to have been a simple promise of future gift. The unilateral quality of these donations is especially evident in those cases in which the donee was unspecified and could not have been the principal of a contractual act.[111] It is difficult to see how such an act could be efficacious, for it fails to conform to any of the Germanic forms of donation.[112] Yet it is even more difficult to avoid the conclusion that gifts of this sort were attempted. Perhaps the constant plea for a powerful protector, found in almost every *cwide,* was intended to ensure the completion of the gifts for which the usual legal

---

eallum his freondum his cwyde wæs to his nyhstan dæge," and notes pp. 125-126. Maitland speaks of the *cwide* as a fusion of the *verba novissima* and the *post obit* gift (P. and M., II, 319-320).

109 P. and M., II, 321; Holdsworth, *History,* II, 95. H. II (*ca.* 835), is the *cwide* of a Kentish reeve, who disposed of a fairly large estate and considerable stock and money, but who was, to judge by his wergeld, a churl; cf. Miss Harmer's remarks, H., p. 78.

110 Cf. W., pp. xxiii-xxx, and e.g. in W. XIII. XIX, XX, XXX, etc.

111 It was impossible to establish a contractual relationship with the people of a county or the poor, or with a slave not yet possessed; cf. H. XXI, p. 34, lines 13 ff.; W. XIV, p. 36, lines 30-32.

112 The possibility is rejected for France by Auffroy, *Testament,* p. 107. On the other hand, it is regarded with sympathy by Heusler, *Institutionen,* II, 642-645 and Holdsworth, *History,* II, 95.

procedures did not supply.[113] Another solution probably used more often than surviving evidence would seem to indicate, was to avoid the difficulty by the use of a third party, whereby the donor provided for the delivery of part of his property after death. Thus the large sums distributed by King Eadred were entrusted to five ecclesiastics for the purpose.[114] It will be remembered that quite early in the Christian period Bishop Wilfrid arranged for the distribution of his treasure in a similar fashion.[115] The intermediary was also used for the delivery of bequests by *verba novissima,* and it is quite likely that, as on the Continent, a third party occasionally performed the formalities of a *post obit* gift where, for some reason, the donor himself was unable to do so.[116]

It has already been seen that in the earliest forms of the *affatomie* on the Continent use was made of a third party, but that, as the *affatomie* became merely an instrument for the transfer of property, the third party disappeared.[117] With the development of the *post obit* gift whereby, in the beginning at least, donations of part rather than a complete estate were made, the intermediary appeared once more. This third party has been called the *Salmann* by German historians;[118] he is usually considered to be the root from which the executor of the medieval will developed.[119]

The precise legal relation of this Salmann to the donor and to the object of the donation has been frequently discussed.[120] He acted in those cases where it was impossible for the donor to enter a direct relationship with the donee.[121] German law did not admit of represen-

---

[113] See below, pp. 43-44.

[114] H. XXI.

[115] See above, pp. 32-33. Several other examples are discussed below, n. 123.

[116] Cf. Huebner, *History,* pp. 744, 754. If the intermediary were used in the *post obit* gift in its first or contractual stage, his function would be limited to conferring the right to the property to the donee, or making the wedded promise that the property would, at the donor's death, pass to the donee (cf. above, pp. 29-30). His function in donations by *cwide* or *verba novissima* would include the actual transfer of possession.

[117] See above, p. 10.

[118] It is in Germany especially that donation by *Salmann* was employed. The medieval use of the term began long after the appearance of the institution which it signified. The earliest example is that indicated by Beseler, *Die Lehre von den Erbverträgen,* I, 263, dated 1108. For a summary of later research on the use of the word, see L. Wallach, "Der älteste chronikalische Beleg für Salmannus," *ZRG Germ. Abt.,* LIV (1934), 240.

[119] See the bibliography assembled by Goffin, *The Testamentary Executor,* p. 34.

[120] Beseler, *op. cit.,* I, 261-288; Heusler, *Institutionen,* II, 652-654; Huebner, *History,* p. 745; Brissaud, *History,* p. 542; Auffroy, *Testament,* pp. 154-159, 209-215; Goffin, *op. cit.,* pp. 24-29 and P. and M., II, 319.

[121] It was otherwise with the third party in the *affatomie,* where a direct donor-donee relationship was at least physically possible.

tation; the Salmann actually received a real right in the property of the
donor, which he in turn conveyed to the donee.   There was danger, of
course, that the Salmann would fail to make the conveyance, keeping the
property for himself.   The progress of the institution was towards the
elimination of that danger.[122]   Such, in brief, was the function of the
Salmann on the Continent.

Information regarding the use of the intermediary in England is much
less plentiful.   Where he appears, it is usually with a more limited
function.   Even in the case of the *verba novissima* he is not always
charged with the completion of all the bequests, and in the *cwide* he is
concerned almost exclusively with chattels.[123]   As on the Continent, the
donor usually conveyed to him a real right in the gift.   On occasion,
sums of money seem to have been placed in his possession so that he
might dispose of them after the donor's death.[124]   Land too probably
came into the possession of the intermediary when a *cwide* was made in
time of special danger: soldiers setting out for war and pilgrims going
"over-sea" considered the possibility that they would not return and
provided that a third party should care for their property during their
absence, restoring it to them on their return or seeing to its distribution
in the event of their death.[125]   But there are a few cases where it seems

122 Cf. Auffroy, *Testament,* pp. 209-215, Brissaud, *History,* pp. 692-694 and Goffin, *op. cit.,*
pp. 24-30.

123 W. VIII: Ælfgifu entrusted the residue of her estate to the bishop of Winchester
and the abbot of the New Minster to be distributed; W. XI: Brihtric and Ælfswith left
forty mancuses of gold to each of two relatives to be distributed for their souls; W. XVIII:
Archbishop Ælfric left the residue of his possessions to be distributed by Bishop Wulfstan
and Abbot Leofric (The text is not perfectly clear on the matter but it seems that they
were also charged with the payment of his debts and heriot: cf. lines 21-26); W. XXVI:
forty pounds were to be distributed among the servants of Bishop Ælfric, if not by his
stewards, at least according to their information. In W. XX, Æthelstan the Ætheling
directed that several sums be paid in alms or for debts by his brother Edmund, one of the
witnesses of his will.   Twelve pounds were entrusted to another witness, Bishop Ælfsige,
but it is not clear whether he was to distribute the sum or keep it himself (cf. p. 56, lines
25-26, p. 58, lines 1-2).   This will was probably made during illness and may be a death-bed
disposition of property.

124 As in H. XXI; see above, n. 114.

125 In B. 313, the owner asserted his right to make a will, entrusted his lands to friends
and then crossed the sea.   Though the fact is not stated in the account that has survived,
it is quite likely that those who held the property were charged with its conveyance in
the event of his death.   On returning, the owner recovered his property after making a
payment of some sort ("Et iterum me revertente ad patriam accepi terram meam et pretium
reddidi quasi ante pacti sumus et pacifici fuerimus ad invicem").   In W. XXXIX Bishop
Ealdred held estates on which he had a mortgage.   On their return, the testators were to
redeem them, but, if they died, the bishop was to keep the estates and distribute money for

unlikely that the intermediary acquired any right in the gift. This is especially clear in those cases where he was entrusted with the distribution of the surplus that remained after the delivery of specified legacies. Here it would be impossible for the intermediary to extend his right over the gift, since, when the *cwide* was made, the property was not yet specified, perhaps not possessed.[126]

There was the danger, of course, that the intermediary might fail to deliver the bequest. Efforts were made to eliminate this weakness in the transaction. Thus on two occasions the written *wills* indicate that the distribution of money by the persons named was to be subject to a certain scrutiny: the heirs of Thurston were to distribute the residue of his estate, but under the eye of his partner; similarly various payments were to be made by Godric, brother of Ælfric Modercope, but three other persons were appointed protectors of the *cwide*.[127] This protector, or *mund*, appears in *wills* from the beginning of the ninth century.[128] In the earlier examples, he was sometimes associated with the care of a single bequest. He was often given a gift in the *cwide* with the frankly stated purpose that he should be made more zealous thereby.[129] The fact that a powerful personage was generally known to be the beneficiary of a will would be productive of much the same effect: thus when Æthelric's treachery led to the confiscation of his property, the king informed Archbishop Sigeric of the fact, and the archbishop acted as Æthelric's advocate for the sake of the estate which he had bequeathed to Christchurch.[130] The *mund* preferred above all was the king. *Wills* frequently ask his permission and protection[131] and some indicate that

---

the deceased to the extent that the value of the estates exceeded the sum borrowed by the testators. There are several other *wills* made by persons going "over-sea," but details regarding the use of their estates during their absence are not supplied: Thorpe, p. 385; W. XXVIII, XXXIV, XXXVII.

[126] E.g., W. VIII, p. 22, lines 1-4 and W. XVIII, p. 52, lines 25-26.

[127] W. XXXI and XXVIII.

[128] Cf. W., p. 240, *s.v.*, *mund* and H. *Writs*, p. 427.

[129] In 804 Æthelric gave the estate at Westminster to his mother with reversion to the Church of Worcester, "Pro qua re ea vivente ut ibi habeat protectionem et defensionem contra Berclinga contentione" (B. 313; *EHD*, I, 471-473, no. 81). Similarly Abba gave a property to his brother that he would defend the properties of his wife, and obtained the protection of the "head of Christchurch" for himself and family by the grant of an ultimate reversion (H. II). For other examples see W. XV and XVII.

[130] W. XVI (2); cf. also the bequest to Godwin in W. XXXII, p. 84, line 26 and p. 199. Gifts made to the king, or to the lord, the value of which was often much more than that of the heriot, were intended for the same purpose.

[131] As in W. VIII, XI, XII, XIII, XIV, XV, XVII, XXI.

royal favour was obtained before the *cwide* was made.[132]   Surviving writs of the Confessor show the king acting to ensure the execution of legacies for which his support had been obtained.[133]

It becomes apparent from the above discussion that a distinction can be made between intermediaries, charged with the actual execution of one or more of the bequests of the *cwide,* and the *mund* or protector of the *cwide,* who stood somewhat aside, as it were, but was expected to enforce the completion of the donor's gift.   It would be a mistake to insist on the precision of this distinction: sometimes it is not possible to judge which function an individual was expected to perform.[134]   Yet, so far as can be seen, the *mund* did not receive any right in the legacy of which he was to oversee the delivery.   His function was often the protection of the owner and his property during the latter's life, and the protection of the owner's arrangements for that property after his death. The distinction actually appears in one *cwide,* that of Ælfric Modercope (*ca.* 1042): the brother of the testator was charged with the payment of the heriot and the delivery of a legacy to Ramsey Abbey, while Bishop Ælfric and two companions were appointed protectors of the will.[135] The development of this distinction is important: late in the twelfth century a similar distinction was to appear between the executor charged with the actual distribution of property (usually chattels) and the courts which enforced the execution of a will.

The *post obit* gift, the donation by means of an intermediary, the confirmation of previous contracts, and perhaps at times a simple promise of future gift can all be found mentioned in a single written *will.*[136] What unity was possessed by the *cwide* of which such a document gave evidence?   Did it have a legal unity based on its nature, or was it not

---

132 E.g., W. II, IX, XX. It is interesting to note that in the second and third of these *wills* the witnesses are presented as evidence for the fact that royal permission had been granted rather than as witnesses of the act in which the bequests were made: W. IX, p. 24, lines 8-12; W. XX, p. 62, lines 1-2.

133 See H. *Writs,* nos. 2, 17, 111.

134 E.g., R. XLI; it is impossible to tell in this case, whether the archbishop actually received conveyance of the estates, or whether, as seems more likely, he merely witnessed Ælfheah's will, and was expected to be its defender.

135 W. XXVIII. In her edition of this text, Miss Whitelock translated *mundes* (referring to the three men charged with the protection of the will) as "executors."   The brother who was charged with the actual delivery of a bequest and the heriot is indicated as having "to pay" a certain sum. It would, perhaps, be more suitable to restrict the use of the word "executor" to those who conveyed property to the donee; in this context *mundes* can be translated "protectors," the meaning usually given the word in other *wills.*

136 Cf. W., p. xi, n. 2.

rather a group of acts, each possessing its own qualities and purpose? The second suggestion is reinforced by an examination of the quality of irrevocability that is usually attributed to the donations made by the *cwide*.

In some cases, the possibility, even the fact, of change is mentioned. King Alfred's will provides several examples. At a meeting at Swanborough (?) shortly before he came to the throne, Alfred and his brother, King Æthelred, made an agreement whereby the survivor promised to provide for the children of the other from a portion of the deceased brother's possessions.[137] Remaining property was to pass to the survivor in accord with previous arrangements. In the prologue, Alfred mentioned that there was no indication that Æthelred had made another will, a statement that implies the possibility that he had.[138] At the end of the document, mention was made of an earlier disposition and of documents that witnessed to it. We are told that where possible these documents had been destroyed and that they were of no further validity. Thus Alfred made at least three arrangements for the disposition of his property at death, and would not have been astonished had his brother done likewise. The kings were adjusting their fortunes to a rapidly changing situation and, given their position, such adjustment was necessary. The changes, in part at least, were made by mutual consent. Alfred states that, when he made the last will, many of his former legatees were dead and that the wealth at his disposal was less than hitherto.[139]

Though the royal need for freedom in this regard was a special one, there are signs that elsewhere, too, revocability was at least considered. Four of the *wills* mention the possibility of change in the anathema clause, while another informs the king that the donor has made no other will.[140] The *post obit* gift of four estates to Bury by Æthelmær, bishop of Elmham, is especially instructive.[141] It is concluded with the remark that the donation to Bury should stand, no matter how the donor might change his will. Apparently a distinction was being made between

---

[137] H. XI, p. 16.

[138] *Ibid.*, p. 16, lines 29-30.

[139] *Ibid.*, p. 18, lines 30-35.

[140] W. II, IV, XXIX, XXXI; XIV. Professor Hazeltine remarks that it does not necessarily follow from this that alteration or revocation could be made without the consent of the donee (W., p. xi, n. 2).

[141] W. XXXV. At first sight, the document seems to describe a donation completed *inter vivos*. It was a bequest however, for Æthelmær maintained the property until his deposition in 1070; cf. W., p. 204 and R. XCVII.

an irrevocable *post obit* gift and a *cwide,* parts of which could be revoked: Æthelmær had already made a will (or he foresaw the possibility of making one) which contained binding contracts, but which also included other non-contractual elements that could be revoked. Thus different bequests within a *cwide* might have different degrees of irrevocability. Sometimes a *cwide* repeated the morning gift to the testator's wife or a contract already brought to completion by delivery, and these transactions were able to stand even against forfeiture to the king by the testator.[142] Other bequests were *post obit* gifts, irrevocable bilateral contracts completed only at the death of the donor and subject to the possibility of defeat where the testator's estate was seized by the king. Yet other bequests were donations by means of an intermediary and some, perhaps, were simple promises of future gift; it is quite possible that they were revocable at least in cases of special need.

Thus the different degrees of irrevocability possessed by the various elements of the *cwide* point, once more, to the conclusion that it was not a single legal act. The unity it possessed was external, based on the fact that all its legacies were made or rehearsed at the time. The royal promise of support for these donations as a group and the association of minor gifts with a *post obit* gift to a principal beneficiary also conduced to this external unity. But, when considered from a legal point of view — the relations set up between donor and donee, the liability of the donor and the revocability of the gift — it is clear that the *cwide* was made up of several different legal acts productive of different effects. Clumsy and imperfect though it was, it represents an attempt to make arrangements for the future enjoyment of an estate by a single transaction, even though the property with which it dealt was distributed in different ways and to different donees.

The acts which were the basic elements of the *cwide* were made in accord with the practices of Germanic law; although the donation was of delayed effect, it was an irrevocable contractual act accomplished by the performance of public formalities. Where a third party was used, he acquired a real right in the gift which he was expected to deliver to the donee. But within the *cwide* there are signs of a tentative movement beyond the methods and limits of these legal conceptions. A faint ambulatory quality appears in the bequest of an indefinite residue or of property not yet possessed, and in the notion that some elements of a *cwide* were revocable. In a few cases it is possible that the intermediary

---

142 Æthelric forfeited to the king, but his wife's morning gift was not seized. She used it to obtain the king's permission that her husband's will might stand (W. XVI).

was expected to act as a representative of the deceased, rather than as a person who had a real right in the property he delivered to the donee. These tendencies are important even though, at the time, donations of this sort could not establish obligations and rights that could ordinarily be enforced by law. The *cwide*, after all, was the preserve of the wealthy, of those who were able to obtain powerful support for their bequests.

III. EXTERNAL FORMS OF DISPOSITIONS OF PROPERTY AT DEATH

We have seen that the legal acts, whereby the Anglo-Saxons provided for the distribution of their property after death, varied considerably in nature and effect. Yet wherever information is available as to the manner in which they were made, it becomes clear that in external forms they corresponded to the general Germanic pattern of oral, formal, symbolic legal acts. Whether the disposition were effected by means of a death-bed gift with a minimum of publicity, or by one of those more impressive public acts made during life, the transaction was an oral act before witnesses. The establishing of this important fact is one of the chief contributions of Professor Hazeltine's study of the Anglo-Saxon wills.[143] There he marshalls the evidence of the written *wills*, of accounts of transactions in which wills were made, and of the practice of the courts, to prove that even when a document or written *will* has survived, the legal act that effected the author's purpose was an oral act. The written *will* was intended to be its permanent evidence.[144]

The correlative of the oral quality of the act is the fact that it was made before witnesses. They served not only as evidence for the transaction; their presence was part of its formality. In the case of gift by *verba novissima*, the number and importance of the witnesses varied considerably according to the social status of the dying person and the place and suddenness of his death. Some *verba novissima* were addressed to an individual or a very small group; here the function of the confessor would be an especially important one, as the *Dialogus Egberti* foresaw.[145] Others were made before a formidable gathering of

---

[143] W., p. ix, n. 1 and pp. x, xii, xiv-xviii, xxvi-xxxix. The oral quality of the act has been accepted by Professor Plucknett, *History*, p. 733. On the distinction between evidentiary and dispositive instruments, see W., p. viii and H. Bresslau, *Handbuch der Urkundenlehre für Deutschland und Italien*, 2nd ed. (Leipzig, 1912-31), I, 49-51, 739-740.

[144] See W., pp. xxvii, xxxi, xxxv-xxxvii. The intention of preserving the memory of an act is frequently mentioned in the documents of the time; e.g., in B. 283, the *post obit* gift by Headda, discussed above, p. 25: "litteris tradunt ne ex memoria lavetur."

[145] See above, p. 36.

personages, both ecclesiastical and lay.[146]   Between the two extremes
lay an endless number of possibilities, but it may be presumed that the
quality and number of the witnesses were as great as the situation
permitted.

Witness lists of the dispositions of property made during the lifetime
of the owner, whether the act was a simple *post obit* gift or a *cwide*,
provide interesting information on the circumstances in which such
transactions were performed.   In the late eighth and ninth centuries,
the *cwide* was usually made before a group of magnates.   Alfred's will,
and his father's too in all probability, were made, as would be expected,
before a great gathering of leaders ecclesiastical and lay.[147]   Æthelric
bequeathed his property at the Synod of Acle in 804, in the presence
of Coenwulf of Mercia, the archbishop of Canterbury, five bishops and
eight ealdormen.   Æthelric does not seem to have risen above the rank
of thegn, but his family was an important one and he disposed of a
considerable estate.[148]   Similarly, the will of Earl Oswulf was made prior
to 810 before a group that included the archbishop, abbots and friends;
and at the end of the century Earl Ælfred disposed of a considerable
property in the presence of the archbishop, two abbots, two ealdormen
and a large group, mostly ecclesiastical.[149]

Divisions by less important donors, concerned with but few estates
and a single donee, divisions that can best be classified as *post obit* gifts,
were usually made in the presence of a less imposing, though often more
directly concerned group.   Thus Abbot Headda, by a transaction in
the presence of the *familia* of the church of Worcester, gave a monastery
of which he was abbot to that church at such time as his descendants
failed to provide a suitable head for the monastery.[150]   The will of the
Reeve Abba (835), in which he made very complicated arrangements for
the future of his estate, was made under similar circumstances: reversion

---

146 The will of Ætheliva, of which a resumé is contained in the *Liber Eliensis* (Bk. II,
ch. 59), was made at the time of her death, but in the presence of the abbot of Ely,
members of her family and many others as well.   A pre-Conquest bequest by *verba novissima*,
described in *Domesday Book* (I, 177a), was made in the presence of family and friends.

147 H. XI.

148 B. 313.   His mother was abbess of Stoke and his father, Æthelmund, may be the
ealdorman of that name whose death is recorded in the *Chronicle* for the year 802; cf. *EHD*,
I, no. 81, pp. 471-472.

149 B. 445 and H. X.   The will of Ælfred, earl of Surrey, might well be expected to have
been made before the king and his council, but given the military and political situation
of those years (871-889), the failure is not surprising.   The *will* takes the form of an
address to the king.

150 B. 283.

to Christchurch took place only in the event of failure of his family, but the will was made in the presence of the community there, and the documentary account of the gift is concluded by their signatures.[151]

Religious communities were a favourite group of witnesses, even when, so far as can be seen, they were not directly concerned in the transaction. In the first quarter of the ninth century, the Ealdorman Aldberht renewed the *post obit* gift of an estate in Kent to Archbishop Wulfred, before the community of the monastery "*æt Folcanstanæ*." [152] Forty years later, an Old-English document provides another excellent example: it records a settlement between Cynethryth, widow of Æthelmod, and Eadweald, her late husband's grand-nephew. By the terms of her husband's will, Cynethryth held property which was to have passed at her death to a nephew. The nephew had died and the will apparently had failed to provide an alternate beneficiary. By this new arrangement, Eadweald and his successors were granted a right of pre-emption after Cynethryth's day, and accepted the obligation to devote the purchase price for her soul. The witnesses of the agreement, all ecclesiastics, included the archbishop.[153]

When, in the late tenth century, information about wills becomes somewhat more abundant again, certain differences in witness groups become apparent. Divisions of property of greater moment were still associated with the king in one way or another. *Wills* frequently begin with the statement that the donation was made with the king's permission, and some were made before the Witan in his presence, or before the king or queen and a small group of councillors such as that which witnessed many of the landbooks of the age.[154] Other documents took the form of an announcement to the king, so that he was likely informed of the donation even though it was not made in his presence.[155] The development that is of interest, however, is that local courts and local authorities were taking a considerable part in the making of wills,[156] both

---

[151] H. II. On the "signatures" attached to this document, see below, p. 56. Other examples are: B. 380; R. III, VI.

[152] B. 378. Their witness proved useful later.

[153] H. VII.

[154] See the references assembled above, nn. 131-132. Miss Whitelock considers the mention of royal permission to be one of the characteristic features of the Anglo-Saxon will (W. p. xli).

[155] E.g., W. XX, XXIII.

[156] Vinogradoff remarked: "Towards the close of the Anglo-Saxon history it appears as rule that any change of land ownership should be made known to the county or to the hundred" ("Transfer of Land in Old English Law," *Collected Papers*, I, 166).

in admitting the donor's right to do so, and in acting as witness to the donation. The account of a meeting of a double hundred, said to have taken place at Ely some time before the restoration of the monks, throws a little light on such proceedings. There, after some property had been conveyed to Wulfstan of Dalham, a certain Ogga of Mildenhall rose to his feet and, having obtained the silence of the court, announced the donation of a hide at Grantbridge to St. Etheldreda after his day.[157] Mention is made of this *post obit* gift only in passing, for as it happened Ogga chose to emulate the piety of Wulfstan and completed his gift immediately. But the mention of the act and place where it was made is important. About the same time, the will of Æthelwyrd, of which the community of Christchurch was beneficiary, was made in the presence of the archbishop, representatives of the communities of Christchurch and St. Augustine's, but also before a group of laymen who represented both city and county members of the lathe of Canterbury.[158]

On other occasions, when the act could not be performed before the court, the court was at least informed of it. An excellent example of this is described in some detail in the report of a transaction in Herefordshire during the reign of Cnut.[159] At a shire meeting, before bishop, earl and thegns, Edwin, son of Eanwine (?), sued his mother for certain properties. Three thegns were sent from the court to her, and before them, in a manner that is not described, she succeeded in proving her right to the estate in question. Then she summoned her kinswoman Leofflæd and made a *post obit* grant to her of the estate in question and all her other property. The thegns were asked to announce the gift to the meeting of the shire that all might be witness. There, Thurkil, husband of Leofflæd, asked that the will might stand and, this being granted, went, with the permission of the court, and had the grant recorded in a gospel book at Hereford. Even here, it will be noted, the court gave its consent, and was considered to be witness to the will.

It would appear, none the less, that some *post obit* gifts continued to be made under those almost exclusively ecclesiastical conditions which

---

157 *Liber Eliensis*, Bk. II, ch. 18: "Surrexit itaque Ogga de Mildenhale, et facto silentio ait ... "

158 R. XXXII and notes pp. 316-317. R. CXVI is a *post obit* gift of a church and homestead made *ca.* 1054 in the presence of the bishop of London, the Portreeve, and thegns from within and without. In R. LXII and XCII dated 1004 and *ca.* 1040 respectively, the ecclesiastical character of the witnessing group (which included the donees), is stressed. Important laymen were present but there is no indication that the transaction took place in a court.

159 R. LXXVIII.

were seen in examples of the ninth century. One of these grants is reported in a document of the year 980.[160] It was made by Brihtric Grim to the Old Minster at Winchester, and the witnesses included not only Archbishop Dunstan and three other bishops, but also the communities of Glastonbury and of the two minsters at Winchester. The unlikelihood that all three communities were present on the same occasion, implies that the gift was made several times. The proximity to Glastonbury of Tempton, the estate that was bequeathed, would explain the desire to have the witness of this local group, while the making of the gift in the presence of the donees was common procedure.

There is little direct information about the formalities of these acts, but that which is available suggests a use of forms and symbols in accord with the general practice of the Germanic races. The silence of the court during Ogga's announcement, the solemnity of the procedure of Æthelric and the Herefordshire wife in making their wills,[161] the importance of the group usually assembled on those occasions, all favour such an assertion. First, the donor asserted his right to dispose of his property.[162] This *notificatio* frequently included the announcement that royal permission had been obtained. Then the actual statement of gift was made, probably in formally spoken words.[163] Frequently, at least in those wills that included contractual gifts, there was a symbolic conveyance by means of the landbook or, where the donor made a contractual promise without the conveyance of ownership, by the giving of a *wedd*.[164] Donations made by *verba novissima*, acts *in extremis* as they frequently were, necessarily were made with a minimum of formality; yet it seems likely that essentially they observed the forms of other gifts.

It has been suggested, in the comment on the *post obit* gift of Brihtric Grim, that the making of a will was sometimes repeated. The account of the transactions whereby Siferth of Dunham gave two hides to the monastery of Ely provides an excellent example of such repetition.[165] Before the year 975, the donor came to Bishop Æthelwold, who was at Ely, and there, in the presence of Ethelred the future king, his mother

---

[160] W. VII.

[161] B. 313 and R. LXXVIII.

[162] B. 313, R. LXXVIII. Similar proceedings are to be found in cases of donation by *verba novissima* as in *DdB*, I, 177a, and W. XX, which was probably a death-bed disposition of property.

[163] Cf. W., pp. xiv-xvi and the examples there cited.

[164] *Ibid.*, pp. xxviii-xxix.

[165] *Liber Eliensis*, Bk. II, ch. 11, pp. 124-126. It will be recalled that St. Wilfrid's will was repeated several times: see above, pp. 32-33.

and many magnates, made the *post obit* gift, chose to be buried at Ely, and asked that those present be witness to the act. Some time later, he came to the monastery to visit the tomb of a friend. While there, he sent for the abbot, and before him and a few friends repeated the earlier agreement,[166] adding the gift of two hides in Wilberton to his daughter. Then returning home, he repeated the grant before the chief men of the locality. But even this was not the end, for when death approached he sent for Abbot Brihtnoth, and in his presence and that of some of his monks, his family and many local laymen, one of whom was the thegn of Earl Æthelwine, he repeated his donation.

On the occasion of this final repetition of the donation, a written account of the transaction was made. The chirograph, for it was in this form that the document was prepared, was read to the assembled witnesses, then divided.[167] One part was sent off to the ealdorman, with the donor's request that his will might stand. Rather than give his consent, Æthelwine sent two men back to Siferth to enquire about the terms of the will. Siferth informed them that the written document was its exact statement and, thus assured that he was correctly informed of the donor's intention, Æthelwine allowed the will to stand.

The circumstances surrounding the making of the will by Siferth are reported in unusual detail. Here, where the chirograph was drawn up while the witnesses were still present and a copy given to the donee, it might well be asked whether the preparation and delivery of the document was not an integral part of the formality of the will. The drawing up of the writing could be interpreted as a formality essential to the legal act, and the presentation to the donee as a conveyance *per cartam* of a right in the property. This interpretation of the legal import of the written *will* was maintained by Brunner and his school but, as has been seen above, Professor Hazeltine has opposed these notions, maintaining that the will was an oral act and that the written document was evidence of the act and nothing more.[168] Though his assertion has received general support, it is the part of his essay on the will that has been most strenuously opposed. Yet criticism has not weakened his fundamental position.[169] Even in the case of the will of Siferth, the

166 *Liber Eliensis,* p. 125: "...volo ut conventio mea coram vobis renovetur..."

167 On the chirograph see W., p. xxiv, n. 2, and the references cited there.

168 See above, pp. 27-28; cf. H. Brunner, *Zur Rechtsgeschichte der römischen und germanischer Urkunde,* Vol. I (Berlin, 1880), pp. 149-208, "Das angelsächsische Landbuch."

169 The criticism of H. Meyer (*ZRG Germ. Abt.,* LI (1931), 695-699) who adopted the position of Brunner, is quoted with approval by A. Campbell in "An Old English Will," *The Journal of English and Germanic Philology,* XXXVII (1938), 134, n. 5. More recently

chirograph seems to have been a purely evidentiary document whose delivery played no part in the transaction. It should not be forgotten that the right of the monastery in the property had been established before in an earlier will. The chirograph was made at the request of the abbot, a request quite in keeping with the ecclesiastical desire to have written evidence of the acts whereby property was obtained. Professor Hazeltine has suggested that the reading of the written *will* to the witnesses who had just assisted at the oral transaction, as was done in Siferth's case, was intended as a "secondary orality" which strengthened the original act of gift, although it was not essential to it.[170] This is quite possible; but given the fact that the ealdorman refused to accept the document as a statement of Siferth's distribution of property until he had received assurance of its correctness, one is led to believe that there was another motive as well for the public reading of the *will*. That motive was a very simple one: the witnesses wished to be satisfied that the written account was a correct statement of the transaction, that the undying witness was a true witness.

There are other reasons for opposing the theory of Brunner. It will be remembered that in the case of the Herefordshire wife, it was only after the *cwide* had been uttered, announced to the shire court and allowed to stand that her spokesman went to Hereford to arrange for the making of a written record. There are examples where the *wills* mention groups of witnesses whose assembly on a single occasion seems almost impossible. In such cases, the donation was repeated before different witness groups, as Siferth's was, and a document, which was really a summary of several acts, was drawn up later.[171] The *will* of Brihtric Grim, mentioned above, is best explained in that way.[172] Another, the *will* of Thurstan, made during the reign of the Confessor, mentions groups of witnesses for four different counties.[173] It seems most unlikely that this *will* is the account of a single act. It is rather a

---

Eric John maintains that the *will* was only evidentiary in *Land Tenure in Early England, Studies in Early English History*, I (Leicester, 1960), pp. 176-177.

[170] See W., p. xvii and n. 2.

[171] Siferth's *will* did not survive, so that it is impossible to know whether it included an account of the earlier donations, or whether the author of the *Liber Eliensis* drew on another source. It would have been quite in keeping with the descriptive documents of the tenth century to have included all the transactions in a single vivid account; cf. F. Stenton, *Latin Charters of the Anglo-Saxon Period* (Oxford, 1955), pp. 43-44. W. XV (2), the confirmation of Æthelric's will by King Ethelred, contains most of the elements of Siferth's transaction including the reading of the document to the witnesses.

[172] W. VII; see above, p. 51.

[173] W. XXXI.

summary of several partial distributions of property, each one before a group that was concerned in some way with the area in which the property of the gift was found, or the account of a complete distribution that was repeated in different places, before different groups.   In either case, the written account would seem to be a summary of several transactions, and was not prepared until the last legal act was complete or even later.[174]

Still another indication of the proper place that should be accorded these documents is the fact that they are sometimes only a partial report of the contents of a will.   Thus, for example, it is evident that Earl Ælfred made earlier arrangements for the enjoyment of his estate, but the written *will* merely mentions them without indicating their contents.[175] It is quite evident that some of the documents were prepared for the purposes and probably at the request of the principal donee,[176] and that if some of the other bequests appear, it is more or less by accident.   Thus the document dealing with the bequest by Ordnoth to Winchester cathedral was primarily concerned with the agreement whereby the *post obit* gift of ten hides at Candover and the place of the donor's burial were arranged.[177]   It becomes evident, however, that the transaction included the distribution of portions of Ordnoth's possessions to friends.   The amount and the persons involved were not of interest to the scribe who drew up the *will,* a document of special interest to the church of Winchester, so no mention was made of them.

All evidence leads to the conclusion that the written *wills* were intended merely as evidentiary documents, that they were made when the legally effective act was complete and occasionally much later, and that, in some cases, their information was but a partial report of the provisions of the act.   Neither the writing of the *will* nor its presentation was part of the formalities of the distribution of property at death.

IV.   The Written *Wills*[178]

A few of the oldest documents, evidence of distributions of property at death, have come down to us in Latin and they probably existed in

---

174 Cf. similar suggestions with regard to the foundation charters of monasteries, by V. H. Galbraith in "Monastic Foundation Charters of the Eleventh and Twelfth Centuries," *Cambridge Historical Journal,* IV, (1934), p. 205.

175 H. X.

176 As in the case of Siferth's gift to Ely.

177 W. V.

178 The editions of the *wills* and related documents are described above, pp. 21 ff.

that language from the beginning.[179]   Most *wills*, however, have survived
in Old English or as Latin translations from the vernacular.   The
earliest of them tend to make a distinction between the oral transaction
and the document itself: the *will* of Æthelnoth and Gænburg of the
first decade of the ninth century ends with the command that no one
should "pervert this agreement (*sprece*) in any way from what is contained
in this document (*gewrit*)." [180]   The distinction becomes less common
in the *wills* of the tenth and eleventh centuries, but occurs from time to
time until the Conquest.[181]   The earliest documents usually call themselves a 'writing' (*gewrit*).[182]   As early as the mid-ninth century however,
the word *cwide*, in itself descriptive of the spoken rather than the written
act, appears applied to the document.[183]   It does not commonly occur
with that signification in the ninth century, and in one case at least, a
gift made by Alfred to Shaftesbury, it is used to describe the deed of a
gift *inter vivos*.[184]   One of the characteristics of *wills* after they became
more common again in the mid-tenth century, is that they were called
cwide.   The word is used both of a single bequest by *post obit* gift, or of
that more complicated transaction whereby an estate was divided in
several directions by means of a group of gifts,[185] and which within this
study is called the *cwide*.   It is not used exclusively however, for the
word *gewrit* still occurs, as do others that are especially descriptive of the
transaction.[186]

The analysis of these documents from the point of view of diplomatics
is not within the compass of this investigation.   Nevertheless, even a
brief description of their internal forms provides certain facts of
interest.[187]   Although the scribes drew up the *wills* with some reference

---

179 E.g., B. 192.

180 R. III, lines 23-24.

181 The *will* of Ketel (1052-1066), begins : "Her is on þis write Keteles quide" (W. XXXIV).
Other examples: W. X, XXI, XXV; R. CXVI.

182 See Hazeltine's remarks in W., pp. xii-xiii.

183 As in R. IX, Dunn's grant in reversion to St. Andrew's Rochester: "stande simle mid
cwide seo boc..." (p. 16, line 4); the oral and documentary meanings of the word appear in
a single sentence in R. XLI: he cwæþ his cwide beforan him. & he sette ænne cwide to
Cristes cyrican..." (p. 84, lines 22-23).

184 R. XIII, p. 24, line 9.

185 Compare W. I, II, IV and W. XXII.

186 Thus in H. VII, *gedinga* (agreement), and in W. XXXIX, *feorewearde* (agreement);
W. XIII, *swutelung* (declaration); H. XI, p. 16, line 29, and XV, p. 26, line 24, and p. 27,
line 1, *erfegewrite* (written *will*).

187 Cf. J. M. Kemble, *Codex Diplomaticus Ævi Saxonici*, 6 vols. (London, 1839-1848), I, ix,
xxxi, cviii ff; J. Earle, *A Handbook of the Land-Charters and other Saxonic Documents* (Oxford,

to certain forms available to them, generally they seem to have exercised such freedom of composition that the only quality that can be ascribed to the collection as a whole is that of informality. It is possible, however, to respect the variety of the documents while arranging them in groups, not by any means mutually exclusive, but possessed of certain common qualities that seem important.

The first group, containing documents of the eighth and ninth centuries, is characterized by resemblances to the landbook. A second, by far the largest, adopts an informal narrative style. Sometimes the document may begin with the bald statement: "This is the will of X," then proceed to describe the donor's gift in the third person. At other times the donor is made to speak in the first person, so that the *will* reads like a report of his actual words. A third group takes the form of an address to the king, or to the donor's lord, in which the addressee and the donor's friends are informed of his desire.[188] Finally a few *wills* of the last decades of the Anglo-Saxon kingdom, adopt a form which reflects the writs that were coming into use at the time.[189]

The first group is the most interesting, for it shows that, in the beginning, the form of the *will* was influenced by the landbook, but that in time this influence tended to disappear. The oldest of these are in Latin. The first is that recording a grant *post obitum* by a certain Dunwald in 762.[190] The document begins with an invocation, describes the donor's office, his right in the land, and his gift; it concludes with the remark that he has caused a deed to be written, which he has "strengthened with his own hand." Four other "signatures," [191] including

1888), pp. xvi-xliii; W., pp. xxix-xxxi; H. Brunner, *Zur Rechtsgeschichte der römischen und germanischen Urkunde*, I, 149-208; J. Campbell, "An Old English Will," *passim*.

188 E.g., B. 812; H. XX; W. VIII, XVII, XXI, etc.

189 W. XXIII, XXIX; the latin version of the *will* of Leofflæd daughter of Brihtnoth, preserved in the *Liber Eliensis* (Bk. II, ch. 88), is similar in form. See Miss Whitelock's remarks, W., p. 177.

190 B. 192; *EHD*. I, no. 72, p. 460.

191 On the significance of the "signature" — cross and name — of the landbooks, see H. Brunner, *Zur Rechtsgeschichte*, I, 159 ff.; G. J. Turner and H. E. Salter, *The Register of St. Augustine's Abbey Canterbury commonly called the Black Book*, The British Academy Records of the Social and Economic History of England and Wales, II (London, 1915), p. xviii; and Galbraith, *Monastic Foundation Charters*, p. 210. In all likelihood, neither name nor cross was made by the witness *manu propria*. Turner conceded that the preparation of the landbook may have been one of the formalities of the booking of land, and that witnesses may have touched the cross beside the names. Professor Levison, on the other hand, while purposely avoiding detailed discussion of the matter, implied that some of the earlier Anglo-Saxon charters were signed by the witnesses either with signature or cross: *England and the Continent in the Eighth Century* (Oxford, 1946), p. 176.

that of the archbishop, are added. Except for the list of attestations, which is lacking, an even closer resemblance to the landbook in construction and phraseology is to be found in Abbot Headda's reversionary grant of a family monastery to Worcester. The transaction took place in the presence of the *familia* of the church there, and it is not unlikely that their signatures were to be found on the original document, which has not survived.[192] A group of Old English documents of the ninth century, documents descriptive of transactions that have strong contractual characteristics, have similar qualities, though already they differ in language. Thus the arrangement of about the middle of the century, whereby Lufu granted a food rent to be paid forever by her estates, includes a *notificatio, dispositio* and an impressive array of attestations by ecclesiastics including the archbishop.[193] Another document, which also survives in the original, or in a contemporary copy, is the same in part. Once again there is what purports to be a list of signatures, but in this case the *notificatio* and *dispositio* appear in the third person and describe rather than state the settlement.[194] Finally, there are four ninth-century *wills*, extant as originals or in contemporary copies, in

[192] B. 283; see the remarks of J. Armitage Robinson, *St. Oswald and the Church of Worcester*, p. 8. B. 303 is a document from the *Textus Roffensis*, recording a grant of land in 801 by Coenwulf of Mercia and Cuthred of Kent, to the thegn Swithun. Attached to the text in the cartulary, and quite possibly in the original, was a brief statement in Latin, containing both *dispositio* and *sanctio*, whereby Swithun gave the estate after his day to St. Andrew's Rochester.

The most enigmatic document of this type, and the only one that survives in a contemporary copy, is a grant of several properties to the *familia* of Canterbury, by Archbishop Wulfred. It has all the appearances of a gift completed *inter vivos*, but the witness list contains the subscriptions of the donor and of his successor Ceolnoth, who signs as archbishop too. There is no sign of these grants among the selections from Wulfred's will that are probably preserved within the *will* of the priest Werhard (B. 402). However the selections in question were concerned only with alms and need not contradict the possibility that the former document contains provisions for the distribution of property after death. The witness list of Wulfred's donation corresponds to that of another document of the time, the *will* of Abba (H. II), which would point to a date about the time of the donor's death (832). The document is perhaps a copy of the original *donatio post obitum*, in which one of the witnesses, the then archbishop, was given the title which he did not have when the original was made; or, as J. Armitage Robinson suggests, it may be the record of a grant made on his death-bed by Wulfred, and confirmed by Ceolnoth ("The Early Community at Christ Church," *The Journal of Theological Studies*, XXVII [1926], 238-239). The text of Wulfred's grant is edited in B. 380 and is available in facsimile (*B.M. Facs.*, II, pl. 17).

[193] H. IV: *B.M. Facs.*, II, pl. 22. The second part of this charter written around and beneath the signatures seems to be a further precision, added later perhaps.

[194] H. VII; *B.M. Facs.*, II, pl. 19.

which the chief survival of the landbook form is the list of signatures. The earliest of these, the *will* of Æthelnoth the Reeve, is of the first decade of the century.[195] It is written below the text of the royal grant to Æthelnoth on a contemporary parchment, which may well be the original landbook. Aside from the list of signatures, the landbook form has entirely disappeared from the appended *will*. The text is a bald narration in the third person of Æthelnoth's gift and its conditions. The other three *wills* are somewhat more complicated in that they deal with larger estates and provide for rather involved reversions, but aside from the fact that they are stated in the first person, the list of signatures is their sole resemblance to the landbook.[196] With the exception of a *post obit* gift from the second quarter of the tenth century, no later *will* contains a list of signatures.[197] There is frequent reference to the witnesses present when the will was made, but if their names occur, they are only mentioned, usually within the body of the text.[198]

The fact that the four last-mentioned documents still maintained the signature list has led to their inclusion in the first grouping. Aside from that fact, they are typical of the second group in one or other of its forms. Thus the *will* of Æthelnoth is one of many which state the terms of the transaction in the third person.[199] The *will* of Ælfred, on the other hand, is an example of the group which employs the first person, giving the impression that some of the actual words of the donor are preserved there.[200] Many of the *wills* exhibit the scribe's difficulty in deciding which method to use, for the text frequently passes from a purely narrative style in the third person, with the past tense, to a present statement in the first person.[201]

When the written *wills* are considered as a group it becomes evident that the influence of the landbook is most pronounced and tenacious in those that deal with *post obit* gifts of land: the irrevocable, contractual quality of the transaction is usually expressed in the document itself. On the other hand, the written *wills* which contain the multiple bequests of the *cwide* tend to abandon the landbook form: expression of the contractual quality of the act diminishes or disappears completely.

195 R. III: *O.S. Facs.*, III, pl. 8.
196 H. II: *B.M. Facs.*, II, pl. 23; R. VI: *B.M. Facs.*, II, pl. 25; H. X: *O.S. Facs.*, I, pl. 20.
197 R. XXVII (932-939).
198 E.g., W. VII, XXII, XXX, XXXI.
199 R. III, XVII, CXVI; W. V, *et passim*.
200 H. X; R. VI, XXVII; W. I, IV, VI.
201 R. IX; W. III, VIII, IX, *et passim*. On the fluctuation of tense and pronoun see W., p. xxxi and n. 1.

Thus there is much in the form of *wills* dealing with *post obit* gifts that, at first sight, seems to support those historians who have maintained that these documents were dispositive as well as evidentiary, whereas the *cwide* of the tenth and eleventh centuries does not convey this impression.

Whatever their variety and however awkward their form, the *wills* are usually a faithful presentation of the successive steps of the transaction. Even the briefest documents often begin with a *notificatio*.[202] The donation clause is reported, of course, and many of the *wills* are terminated by a sanction.[203] Early in the ninth century, there are indications that *wills* were being drawn up in duplicate and triplicate.[204] Copies were given to the principal donee, to the donor and often to some third party. After the middle of the tenth century it is frequently stated within the *will* itself that it has been prepared in the form of a chirograph and that the parts have been distributed.[205]

V. COMPLETION OF THE DISTRIBUTION OF PROPERTY AT DEATH: COMPETENCE IN DISPUTES

One of the most remarkable traits of the written *wills* is their reflection of the donor's anxiety lest his distribution fail to be completed. They show too that the testator knew that completion required delivery, and frequently contain information as to the arrangements made to accomplish it. A wife or child, recipient of an estate for life, may be directed to give a food-rent in alms to the religious house that is ultimately to receive the property.[206] Certain estates were permanently saddled with an obligation in alms and, at times, failure to acquit the obligation resulted in a reversion of the property to some religious house.[207] Frequently the heirs, wife, children or relatives, or some other inter-

---

[202] B. 192, 283; R. III; W. XXII, XXXV, XXXVIII.

[203] E.g., B. 303; W. I, II, *et passim*. This has already been demonstrated by Professor Hazeltine, both as to the parts of the oral act, and the correspondence to them of the parts of the written *will*.

[204] Three copies of the *will* of Æthelric (804) are mentioned in B. 313. It was probably drawn up in chirograph form; cf. W., p. xvi, n. 2.

[205] See above, n. 167. Some of the chirograph *wills* have been published in facsimile — W. XIII: *O.S. Facs.*, III, pl. 20; W. XIX: *B.M. Facs.*, IV, pl. 42; W. XX: *O.S. Facs.*, III, pl. 38; W. XXX: *B.M. Facs.*, IV, pl. 33.

[206] E.g., R. XXVI.

[207] As in H. II, X, XXI. According to the terms of the last of the examples, the *will* of King Eadred, an almsman was to be supported on each of twelve estates "so long as Christianity endures." Should the recipient of the property refuse his obligation, the estate was to pass to the Old Minster at Winchester.

mediary were instructed to distribute money and goods.[208]   In all cases
it was a matter of completing the original donation.   The acts required
ranged from a simple resignation of property already in the hands of
the donee, to the execution of a mere promise.[209]   These acts were
performed according to the usual Germanic forms of transfer.   Chattels
were conveyed before witnesses, the graveside apparently being a
favoured place for such distribution.   Conveyance of folkland was
made before a court with the usual publicity and observation of forms,
though in some cases it seems to have been transferred by the king's
writ.[210]   Bookland too could be conveyed by writ, though others forms
of transfer proper to it would be of more common use.[211]   But when
the conveyance did not take place, when the bequest was not completed,
the donee could seek redress in the courts.

That churchmen should have been concerned with the execution of
gifts *post obitum* was, of course, to be expected.   The religious motive
for these donations was more important than any other.   The chief
witness of the act, and the person charged with its completion, was often
a bishop or a priest.   This was especially true of gifts by *verba novissima*.
Even when the act was made while the donor was in good health, ecclesiastics were usually among those involved as witnesses or in some more
important capacity.[212]   The cemeteries themselves, which for the
Germanic peoples as well as for the citizens of the pre-Christian Empire
were places where largess was distributed for the good of the deceased,
were controlled by the Church.[213]   It would not be surprising, then, if
the clergy in England, as elsewhere, were to play a considerable part in
the legal proceedings that defended and enforced the disposition of
property after death.[214]

It is misleading to make a sharp distinction between ecclesiastical and
civil courts in either competence or membership.   All through the
Anglo-Saxon period, laity and clergy were associated in the groups that
made decisions, whether those decisions were primarily of religious or

208 Examples are to be found in H. II, X; W. III, XXVIII, XXXI.

209 The various degrees of completion required have been assembled in W., pp. xxxv-
xxxvi.

210 Holdsworth, *History*, II, p. 77; accepted by Hazeltine (W., p. xxxvi, n. 5).   In W. X
(p. 24, lines 23-24), conveyance of land is to take place at the funeral.

211 For a summary of recent opinion on the manner of transferring bookland see T. F. T.
Plucknett, "Bookland and Folkland," *Economic Hist. Rev.*, VI (1936), 64-66.

212 Cf. Kemble, *Codex*, I, cxii.

213 See above, pp. 7-8, 11-12.

214 See Dorothy Bethurum, *The Homilies of Wulfstan* (Oxford, 1957), p. 76.

temporal import, or so concerned with both spheres that an attempt to label them one way or the other would be misleading. Probably no court concerned with temporal affairs ever met during the Anglo-Saxon period after the conversion without ecclesiastical members in one capacity or another. The converse may have been true as well; laymen were present at the more important synods at least. With this proviso, and with the reservation that information is not abundant, it can be said that prior to the Danish invasions, just as the wills were made, so far as can be told, before a group which was usually ecclesiastical in character, or whose ecclesiastical membership was emphasized, so the litigation concerned with disputes rising from such wills came before courts that had a similar ecclesiastical tone.[215] In the tenth and eleventh centuries a change is noted. It has been shown that during those years wills bequeathing land were made more frequently with the permission of the king, the earl or the shire court, and often in their presence as well. Similarly the litigation of which there is evidence is much more in the hands of the king or the shire. In either case, of course, ecclesiastics were present and played an important rôle, but their function seems to have been of diminished importance. The making of wills and the competence in litigation involving wills was less the concern of the Church than in the earlier period.

The oldest case, one that is preserved in Heming's cartulary, is the dispute between Hrothwaru and her mother over a family monastery at Withington, Gloucestershire.[216] The Abbess Dunne had been granted it by Æthelred of Mercia and, when at the point of death, gave it to her grand-daughter Hrothwaru, arranging that the donee's mother should have the property and its landbook in her charge until Hrothwaru was old enough to assume the position of abbess. Eventually the latter asked for the charter and was informed by her mother, whose good faith was questionable, that it had been stolen. The matter was brought before "the holy synod of the sacerdotal council," [217] and Hrothwaru's possession of the monastery was assured, a new charter prepared, and those responsible for the disappearance of the original charter were placed under ecclesiastical censure. Furthermore, it was recalled that in the terms of Dunne's will, the property was to revert to the Church of Worcester after the death of her grand-daughter. Of the procedure in the case there is very little evidence. The mention of the reversion to

---

215 See Stenton, *Anglo-Saxon England*, p. 235.
216 B. 156 (736-737).
217 "ad sanctam sacerdotalis concilii synodum."

Worcester, though it does not seem to have been involved in the original dispute, would imply that the proof of Hrothwaru's right was based on the testimony of witnesses who recalled the original grant of Abbess Dunne.   The name given the judicial body, the fact that the sole sanction mentioned was a spiritual one, and the conclusion of the account with what purports to be the signatures of eight bishops, all point to the ecclesiastical character of proceedings.[218]

Of seven other assemblies in which decisions of this sort were made, prior to the Danish invasions, there is somewhat more satisfactory information.   The ecclesiastical character of the court is emphasized,[219] but it is evident that the courts included important lay members, the king and his councillors, in at least six of the seven cases.[220]   They were, in fact, meetings of the royal court in which the ecclesiastical membership was not only numerically important, but in which it seems to have directed proceedings.[221]   Thus the two archbishops are said to have presided at the assembly of 789, though the king was present.[222]   In the decision with regard to Æthelric's freedom to devise, and the defence of the right of the Church of Worcester against the claim of the monastery at Berkeley, the archbishop is presented as the person in charge, though again in the presence of the king.[223]   As in the dispute about the inheritance of the Abbess Dunne, the judgments of these courts were usually reinforced by an ecclesiastical sanction.[224]

It will be remembered that, towards the end of the ninth century, a law of Alfred decreed that the prevention of the alienation of bookland

---

[218] The list of witnesses is discussed by Miss Whitelock, *EHD*, I, 455, n. 6.   The decision seems to have been implemented, for the monastery was in the hands of Bishop Mildred of Worcester a generation later.

[219] B. 256 (789), "pontificale conciliabulum;" B. 313 (*ca.* 798) "synodum;" B. 313 (804), "synodus æt Aclea;" B. 445 (810), "a sancto synodo ... æt Aeclea;" B. 378 (824), "synodus;" B. 379 (824), "pontificale et sinodale conciliabulum;" B. 445 (844), the decrees of the judgment of the group are called "synodalia praecepta."

[220] The exception is the Aclea meeting of 810 (B. 445), the membership of which is not given.   It probably had the same elements as the other synods.

[221] Cf. Stenton's remarks on these assemblies "whose chief work seems to have been the decision of suits relating to property claimed by ecclesiastical persons" (*Anglo-Saxon England*, pp. 234, 235, n. 2).

[222] "praesedentibus duobus archiepiscopus" (B. 256).

[223] "... ibi Æðelheardus archiepiscopus mihi regebat atque judicaverat ..."   Later the monastery at Berkeley tried to obtain possession of one of the estates granted in Æthelric's will.   Once again the archbishop seems to have dominated proceedings: "Statuta est autem atque decreta ab archiepiscopo et ab omni sancta sinodo ..." (B. 313 and 379).

[224] B. 156, 313, 379, 445 (2).

was to be achieved by proof of restriction by the original donor or donee, in the presence of the family, with the witness of the king and bishop.[225]

All of these facts combine to point to an ecclesiastical orientation in the assemblies that judged these disputes. It is important to note, however, that in those cases where it can be discovered, the procedure was like that of contemporary civil courts.[226]

These few examples possess traits that were probably common to suits touching wills involving property bequeathed to the Church. Such suits were not numerous. The very impressiveness of the court would seem to preclude its frequent use, though the fact that five of the eight accounts are drawn from Heming's cartulary can be taken to indicate that many more would be known were the histories of other estates, ecclesiastical or lay, as fully reported.[227]

Whether litigation over bequests of interest to the laity were the object of such care on the part of ecclesiastics is difficult to know. Æthelric defended his right to bequeath before such a group, and some of his bequests were to laymen. The archbishop defended the possessions of the widow and children of Oswulf, possessions that had come to them by will. In both cases, however, there was at least an indirect ecclesiastical interest, either in an individual bequest of the will, or because the Church had a reversionary right in the property under dispute.[228] The Church or the poor were beneficiaries of almost every will that is known in the earlier period, and it seems reasonable to conclude that wills that did not make such a bequest were very rare, if they occurred at all. It has already been suggested that the making of a bequest to a powerful person

---

[225] Alfred, 41 (*Gesetze*, I, 74). Kemble considered this to be one of the laws derived from the lost code of Offa (*Codex*, I, xxxii); cf. H. Cabot Lodge, "The Anglo-Saxon Land Law," *Essays in Anglo-Saxon Law*, p. 71. Some of Offa's landbooks contain limitations such as those described in this law.

[226] B. 256: the bishop of Worcester based his action on a right to a reversion which the defendant sought to deny. The bishop advanced witnesses as proof, but his right seems to have been conceded before the oath was awarded. B. 313: Æthelric claimed to possess the right to alienate his property at death and wished to have it confirmed against the denial of his family. His charters were advanced as proof and his right was confirmed on their evidence. B. 378: the plaintiff claimed right to property by will. The right was denied by the possessor who held the landbook, so the plaintiff advanced documentary and living witnesses as evidence of his right. B. 379: the defendant had possession and the landbook of the estate. The case came to oath which was awarded to the defendant. Procedure is discussed by J. Laurence Laughlin, "The Anglo-Saxon Legal Procedure," *Essays in Anglo-Saxon Law*, pp. 236-237, 257-259.

[227] B. 156, 256, 313 (2), and 379 are from Heming's cartulary.

[228] B. 313, 445.

or community, whether intended as a means of ensuring the execution of the will or not, was in fact one of the means of doing so.

A considerable change becomes apparent at the beginning of the tenth century. Once again the properties, concerning which records of litigation have survived, were in most cases of interest to the Church. Yet disputes came before the witan and the courts of the hundred and the shire, compromise was reached before the same bodies, or a solution was found in a direct appeal to the king, an appeal that was sometimes reinforced by the purchase of his good will. The ecclesiastical aspect of the courts judging such suits is much less evident.

The first example occurs about 903. An estate at Sudbury, in Gloucestershire, had been given in the eighth century to a certain Eanbald by Bishop Mildred of Worcester, with the agreement that it was to be held by a descendant in holy orders. Otherwise, the property was to revert to the church of the donor. The agreement was reinforced by the will of the next holder, Eastmund. After his death, the family failed to honour the agreement, but for more than half a century the bishops of Worcester were unable to recover the property, until in 903 Æthelred of Mercia summoned a council at Droitwich to deal with matters "both spiritual and temporal." The dispute was not simply concerned with the execution of a bequest, yet the plaintiff's claim seems to have been based on Eastmund's will. The bishop's right was admitted and a compromise reached.[229]

A clearer indication of the character of the court concerned with such matters is supplied in the account of a dispute in which St. Dunstan was involved. A certain Ælfheah, suddenly taken ill, sent for the archbishop and *cwæþ his cwide beforan him.* Leofsunu, second husband of the deceased's daughter-in-law, seized the estate without the authority of the council (witan). At a meeting held on one of the estates in question, the archbishop, by means of an oath and with oath-helpers, proved ownership according to the terms of the will, in the presence of two bishops, the communities of London (?) and Christ-church, the sheriff and all the men of East and West Kent. The sheriff, Wulfsige the priest, is called the king's representative.[230]

229 H. XV. H. XXIII is the account of the recovery of the estate willed to Eadgifu by her father. The will did not enter the dispute however, for the suit was intended to establish whether or not the testator had acquitted his obligations to his debtor who held the bequeathed estate in mortgage.

230 R. XLI and p. 334. The dispute (1045-6) between Care, Toki's son, and Bishop Ælfwold and the community at Sherborne, came to an agreement before the shire court

A few surviving records show how royal support was obtained in disputes. When Ailwin the Black died, leaving four manors to Ramsey Abbey, a relative named Ælfric, claiming that neither royal nor family assent had been obtained for the bequest, opposed the execution of the will. Noting the power of Ælfric's friends, the abbot concluded that a direct approach to King Edward and his queen would be most effective. This approach, aided by a gift to the royal couple, produced the desired result; the will was allowed to stand.[231]

From the very sparse evidence of disputes concerning wills surviving from the tenth and eleventh centuries, no very firm conclusions can be drawn. There are indications, however, that cases involving land were decided before the witan or the hundred court, and especially before the shire court once it was established. There, clerics played an important rôle, but the assemblies in question, empowered as they were to deal with a great variety of cases, were much less ecclesiastical in character than were those mentioned in the first period.[232] Procedure was according to the regular modes. In fact there is some reason for thinking that the will of land and disputes flowing from it had found a place within the normal functioning of these courts (which may indicate that they were becoming more common). It was a very old tradition in the Church that clerics should be the defenders of wills; so we find them here. But judgment did not lie with them alone; it lay with the usual group, clerical and lay, who normally constituted the courts.

Thus, having seen how a religious motive for the distribution of property at death entered the Anglo-Saxon consciousness, and having seen how other motives quickly presented themselves, we have proceeded

---

(R. CV). In the reign of Cnut, the mother of Edwin established her right to make a will before the shire (R. LXXVIII, see discussion above, p. 50), and somewhat earlier Siferth of Dunham obtained the ealdorman's assent that his will might stand (see above, pp. 51-52). In 992 the widow of Æthelstan Mann's son tried to prevent delivery of a bequest to Ramsey Abbey, claiming that after her husband had made his will he came to an agreement with her about certain properties that had been bequeathed. The dispute was settled by compromise before a large gathering, including the archbishop, two ealdormen and many others, on the anniversary of her husband's death (*Ramsey Chronicon*, pp. 59-61). It is remarkable how frequently disputants compromised their claims or, having established their rights, were willing to leave the property for life in the hands of the defeated possessor or claimant; cf. F. Zinkheisen, "The Anglo-Saxon Courts of Law", *Political Science Quarterly*, X (1895), 136.

[231] *Ramsey Chronicon*, pp. 169-170.

[232] On the growing awareness of the distinction of the two orders during the last century before the Conquest, cf. Bethurum, *The Homilies of Wulfstan*, pp. 71-74.

to an analysis of the legal acts whereby these intentions were fulfilled. Though the end was not Germanic, the means to it definitely were. The *post obit* gift and the death-bed gift were irrevocable acts *inter vivos*. They had a pronounced contractual quality; many were actually bilateral contracts.   They were performed with the usual Germanic formalism and the use of symbols.   There was also the *cwide,* a more complex act or artificially united group of acts, which divided movable and immovable property among many donees.   The *cwide* was like a number of *post obit* gifts, but to reduce it to that is to falsify it.   It was a group of acts of varied effects.   Most possessed the properties of the *post obit* gift, but some were confirmations of earlier grants; a few, especially those to unknown donees or those bequeathing as yet unpossessed property, appear to have been simple promises.   In the latter the *cwide* showed the first signs of legal conceptions that went beyond the strict rules of Germanic law.   The *cwide* was a special act, the preserve of the powerful.   It needed external support and was to perish with the Anglo-Saxon kingdom.

The emphasis on the irrevocable and contractual character of these acts is necessary if their legal nature is to be understood.   But this emphasis can be misleading; the preoccupation of the donor was not to escape the consequences of such acts, but rather to secure their completion.   This was done by the use of a third party to deliver the legacy and by obtaining the most powerful defender of the will that could be had.

Such were the acts by which the Anglo-Saxons disposed of property at death.   The Norman Conquest did not mean the end of them.   With some changes — for the most part, changes of emphasis rather than of nature — they were to be used for more than a century after the disappearance of the Anglo-Saxon kingdom.

CHAPTER III

THE USE OF THE RIGHT TO DISPOSE OF PROPERTY
AT DEATH AMONG THE ANGLO-SAXONS

WE have investigated the beginnings of the freedom of bequest among the Anglo-Saxon conquerors of Britain, and have seen the legal transactions that were used to effect the gift of property after death. It remains to consider the Anglo-Saxon wills from the point of view of their content. We shall seek to learn the extent to which wills were used, the individuals and groups who were their beneficiaries and the different kinds of property that were bequeathed thereby. From some points of view, this part of the study will be unsatisfactory. Many conclusions will have to be based on vague literary reference or on mere surmise. Even when more definite evidence is available, it will not be in sufficient quantity to permit the desired precision in describing the persons and properties to which the right of bequest was extended. Yet an investigation of the wills from the point of view of their content will be found to yield valuable information on the family, on the wealth of the leaders of society, and on several of the social and political developments of the age.

I. Personal Limitations in the Making of Wills

Christianity provided a powerful motive for the giving of alms at death and, indirectly, for the development of the legal means to make such gifts possible. The rapidity with which the Anglo-Saxons were influenced by this religious motive depended on the rate and depth of penetration of Christian teaching among the tribes. There is sufficient information to establish a satisfactory chronology of the conversion of the different kings and of the beginnings of official Christianity in their kingdoms. But the rate at which the teaching of Christian dogma and instruction in Christian practices penetrated beyond the courts to the halls of the nobility, and eventually to the huts of the lowest classes, is not easy to estimate. Even were that known, there would still remain the problem of discovering the extent to which this instruction was able to inspire the desire to live according to Christian principles. This latter influence, one touching the manner of life of a whole society, is even harder to gauge than the rate of the spread of the faith itself; but this it was that wrought changes in the society and it is of chief importance here.

Once Christian teaching and practice had penetrated the Anglo-Saxon population generally, the religious motive, impelling to the desire to give alms during life and at death, was felt. It was at work on different levels of society, for, though wealth might have been the preserve of the few, the desire to give alms of some sort need have no such bounds. Wives, young men and women not yet established in holdings of their own, may well have been moved to seek to make such an offering. It seems unlikely, moreover, that a complete moral reform in accord with Christian ideals need have been the necessary preliminary to such desires. In fact the contrary seems to have been a universal human experience both before the Anglo Saxon arrival and since. Bede mentioned those who sought to make recompense for a life that had been evil, and continued to be evil, by the giving of alms in which there was a rather unpleasant hint of the bribing of divine justice.[1] It seems permissible to conclude, then, that Christianity provided a motive for the making of wills quite soon after its appearance, even before it had made a very profound moral penetration of society, and that the motive was not limited to the upper classes, nor to the heads of households, nor to the most exemplary Christians.

Eventually the religious motive became so powerful, in society as a whole, as to limit considerably the individual's freedom to avoid the giving of alms at death. In certain areas of Gaul, there was, in the sixth century, an opinion that doubted the salvation of the person who died without making such an offering in his testament.[2] Much later, in Europe of the twelfth and thirteenth centuries, a grave stigma was frequently attached to the failure to make a will. Perhaps the most strongly stated examples of this opinion were to be found in England.[3] Did this religious pressure attain such formidable proportions among the Anglo-Saxons? It has already been seen that, though the giving of alms in connection with the death-bed confession was practiced very soon after the conversion, the surviving penitential literature does not indicate any great urgency in this regard until the end of the period. Nevertheless, it is clear that in England, unlike the Continent, a minimum offering to the church of burial was exacted by law from the time of Athelstan and probably somewhat earlier.

1 *Epistola Bedae ad Ecgbertum Episcopum*, 17, ed. C. Plummer in *Venerablis Bedae Oper Historica*, I, 421-423.

2 See above, pp. 11-12.

3 See below, pp. 232-233.

4 I Athelstan (925-936), 4 (*Gesetze*, I, 146). Cf. Stenton, *Anglo-Saxon England*, pp. 152-15.

Furthermore, towards the end of the Anglo-Saxon period, there is evidence that, on the upper levels of society at least, the religious motive for the disposition of property after death was being reinforced by a civil one. The laws of Cnut provided that when a man failed to make a will, no matter what the cause of omission, the lord of the deceased was to take no more than the heriot that was his due, and to direct the distribution of the remainder of the estate according to customary procedure.[5] In Domesday Book, the English burghers of Hereford and the royal moneyers there, both of whom paid a heriot to the king, forfeited their property to him if they died intestate.[6] Thus at the very end of the Anglo-Saxon period, intestacy actually involved forfeiture in certain cases and, somewhat earlier at the beginning of the eleventh century, there was what seems to have been a more general movement in the same direction; the law of Cnut sought to arrest it. The basis of the claim to forfeiture is not clear. The heriot had begun to appear in written *wills* in the tenth century, and it may be that, as has been suggested, provision for its payment had become so regularly a part of the division of property that failure to provide for the lord was considered to be a crime. Or perhaps the idea had already established itself that failure to make a will implied failure to provide for the soul, and some lords, ecclesiastics perhaps, sought to use the goods of the deceased for that purpose.[7] At any rate, it is possible to conclude that among the thegn class, by the beginning of the eleventh century, there was a considerable civil pressure supplementing the religious motive to ensure the making of a will. By this time, the distribution of property at death was not necessarily a means of defeating family expectation, but in the face of growing claims of lordship was able to serve as a protection of family rights. Whereas in the seventh and eighth centuries, the will was an instrument used by the individual for his personal ends against the claims of those who would normally have succeeded to his property, in the eleventh it could be used to prevent interference by the lord and to ensure the future prosperity of

---

P. Haensel, "Die mittelalterlichen Erbschaftssteuren in England," *Deutsche Zeitschrift für Kirchenrecht*, XIX (1909), 171-195, 376-397, XX (1910), 1-50, especially XIX, 376-397 See below, pp. 79-81.

5 II Cnut, 70, 70.1 (*Gesetze*, I, 356-357). On the heriot, see below, pp. 81-82.

6 DdB, I, 179; cf. A. Ballard, *The Domesday Boroughs* (Oxford, 1904), pp. 75, 84 and P. and M., I, 313.

7 P. and M., II, 322. The family was required to provide for the soul of the intestate in the Coronation Charter of Henry I, ch. 7; see below, pp. 108-110.

the family.[8] This fact throws a momentary light on a very important social and political evolution; but of more direct interest here, is the information it yields on the use of the will.[9] In the early days of Christianity among the Anglo-Saxons, a will was an innovation, one that derogated from the normal rules controlling the succession to an estate. By the time of the reign of Cnut, and probably before it, the adjectives *cwideleas* and *intestatus,* in their privative sense, take on the deeper signification that the institution, whose lack they imply, was the normal thing. The law had to provide for the situation where a will was not made. Among the heads of the thegnly families, then, the will must have been in general use by the beginning of the second millenium.[10]

Though women held property in their own right, wives did not usually dispose of it independently during the lifetime of their husbands.[11] Mutual wills by husband and wife, with arrangements for survivorship occur.[12] However the manner in which the text of the *will* slips from the first person plural to the third person singular masculine, or from the third person plural to the direct words of the husband, indicates the prominent part the latter played in the transaction.[13] Nevertheless, such *wills* sometimes contain a paragraph in which the wife makes provision for her own property.[14] Occasionally, especially where dispositions were made by *verba novissima,* wives seem to have made wills alone, though presumably with the permission of

---

[8] Cf. C. Gross, "The Mediaeval Law of Intestacy," *Select Essays in Anglo-American Legal History,* 3 vols. (Boston, 1907-9), III, 726.

[9] Kemble was of the opinion that it was especially the king's thegns whose freedom was thus limited by the claims of lordship (*Codex,* I, cxi). However, the independence of the lesser thegns was in decline as well, as they found it necessary to commend themselves and their properties to the more powerful landowners; cf. Stenton, *Anglo-Saxon England,* pp. 48: ff., and D. Whitelock, *The Beginnings of English Society* (London, 1952), pp. 85-87.

[10] See E. Glasson, *Histoire du droit et des institutions politiques, civiles et judiciaires de l'Angle terre,* 6 vols. (Paris, 1882-3), I, 127.

[11] On the property of married women see E. Young, "The Anglo-Saxon Family-Law," *Essays in Anglo-Saxon Law,* pp. 177-180; F. G. Buckstaff, "Married Women's Property in Anglo-Saxon and Anglo-Norman Law," *Annals of the American Academy of Political and Social Sciences,* IV (1893-4), 233-264; cf. Whitelock, *op. cit.,* and Doris M. Stenton, *The English Woman in History* (London, 1957), pp. 8-28.

[12] H. II; R. III; W. V, XXXIX. Cf. Glasson, *op. cit.,* I, 128. Sir Henry Spelman, citing the *will* of Brihtric and Ælfswith (W. XI), saw in this an influence of Roman civil law and compared it with a formula of Marculf (II, 17, ed. Zeumer, p. 86); cf. "Of the Original of Testaments and Wills and of their Probate, to whom it anciently belonged" (1633) in *The English Works of Sir Henry Spelman,* 2nd ed. (London, 1727), p. 128.

[13] E.g., the *will* of Ulf and Madselin (ca. 1066-8), W. XXXIX, p. 94, lines 14-18, 2: p. 96, line 2; W. XI.

[14] H. II, W. XXXIX.

their husbands.[15] Widows freely exercised their right to make such divisions of property. Their wills often recall and confirm some of the prescriptions of the wills of their husbands and, on occasion, provide an alternative arrangement where the desire of the husband had become impossible of realization.[16]

Of the lower orders of freeman, here as in so many other things, the records yield but little information. Given the many levels of wealth and economic dependence to be found among the ceorls, as well as the change of their position in society as the tribal organization yielded more and more to a seigniorial one, it is very difficult to generalize.[17] Freemen were bound to pay church dues, and it is quite likely that many of the poorer freemen were not content that their soul-scot be limited to the minimum required by law. A Kentish reeve of the early ninth century, who seems to have been a ceorl, held bookland and a mill and disposed of them by will.[18] While their state would theoretically permit them to make a will, the actual property of which the ceorls could dispose varied from the rather considerable holdings of those, who from an economic point of view had risen to the level of the thegn, to those whose livelihood depended on the services they rendered a lord and whose personal property was of narrowly limited proportions.[19] Of those slaves who had been given their freedom, the laws of Wihtred say that the lord succeeded to their property. This regulation does not appear in kingdoms other than Kent, nor in the later laws, but references to the bequest of freedmen

[15] The death-bed will of Thurgunt, "permittente viro suo Thurkillo," is described in the *Ramsey Chronicon*, p. 175. While it would not be unreasonable to contend that the insistence on the consent of the donor's husband is really a precaution deemed necessary by the Anglo-Norman chronicler, the delivery of the property by the husband is sufficient indication of his consent.

[16] H. II, VII; R. XVII, LXXVIII; W. III, XIV, etc. In the settlement between Cynethryth and Eadweald Oshering (H. VII), the former provides for the succession to the estates of her late husband. He had made provision for them in his will, but the death of the intended legatee had made the bequest impossible. Cynethryth's arrangements seem to have been in the spirit of the earlier will, since the property was to remain in her husband's family.

[17] Cf. Stenton, *Anglo-Saxon England*, pp. 463-465; Whitelock, *The Beginnings*, pp. 98-102; and *EHD*, I, Introduction, pp. 58-59. This depression of the lower classes of freemen has been questioned by J. A. Raftis in a recent article "The Trend towards Serfdom in Mediaeval England," *Report of the Canadian Catholic Historical Association* (1955), pp. 15-25.

[18] H. II and p. 78.

[19] Compare the prosperous ceorl of the *Geþynðo*, 2 (*Gesetze*, I, 456-457), and, at the other extreme, the non-servile bee-keepers and swine-herds of the *Rectitudines Singularum Personarum*, 5, 6.3 (*Gesetze*, I, 814-815).

in the *wills* of the tenth and eleventh centuries imply that the lord still possessed some rights in them.[20]

As to the extent to which minors disposed of property at death, here too there is but little information. Presumably children of either sex, prior to their majority, though they might own property acquired by inheritance or in other ways, were entirely dependent on their fathers for its administration. Any gift in alms or for other ends, that was made by them, was made with his permission.[21] Sons who had attained their majority but were not yet heads of households would be free from paternal restrictions in the disposal of property that was their own.[22] Æthelstan the Ætheling, probably on his death-bed, made a will disposing of a fairly large estate. This was a special case, and he obtained the permission of his father.[23] Daughters before marriage would need paternal consent for such an act.

Other members of society were limited in their power of disposition of property at death by status. Their status may have been acquired or inherited. Of the clergy as a whole, it can be said that considerable freedom of bequest was exercised. Episcopal *wills* are one of the most numerous groups that have survived.[24] A distinction is sometimes made within the *will*, between the property held by the bishop as a private person, and that held in virtue of his office.[25] Priests do not seem to have been prevented by their state from divisions of property.[26] Abbots and Abbesses are frequently described as exercising a similar

20 Wihtred, 8 (*Gesetze*, I, 13); see W., p. 165 and below, p. 105.

21 Cf. Young, *loc. cit.*, pp. 162-163. In the earliest laws a boy attains his majority in his tenth year (Hlothaire and Ædric, 6; Ine, 7.2; *Gesetze*, I, 10, 92). Later it is usually at the age of twelve (II Athelstan, 1; II Cnut, 20, 21; *Gesetze*, I, 150, 322-324), and in an ordinance of the bishop and reeves of the London district there is a tendency to retard legal responsibility to the end of the fifteenth year; cf. VI Athelstan, 12, (*Gesetze*, I, 183).

22 Young, *loc. cit.*, p. 162.

23 W. XX.

24 W. I, IV, XVIII, XXVI, XXXV; *C.C.* X. A synod of the bishops of the Province of Canterbury in 816 required that one tenth of the property of a bishop be distributed to the poor in alms and all English slaves were to be freed if they had become slaves during his period of office (Haddan and Stubbs, III, 533). See below, p. 105.

25 A similar distinction is made within the fortune of the king, as in Asser, *Vita Alfredi* (ed. Stevenson, pp. 14-15), and K. 1312; cf. J. E. A. Jolliffe, *The Constitutional History of Medieval England from the English Settlement to 1485* (London, 1937), p. 127.

26 A few examples of priests' *wills* survive: B. 402; R. XXIX, LXXXVI. R. XXVIII may be a *post obit* gift; the testator of W. XXIII was probably a cleric. In B. 342, a grant of 813 by Archbishop Wulfred to the *familia* of Christchurch, the recipients are given houses which they may hold during life and bequeath at death; the beneficiaries of the future distributions were limited to those within the *familia*.

right. All cases of bequest by superiors of monasteries, however, occurred in the first centuries after the conversion, and most were concerned with provision for the future control of their houses.[27] This practice, as well as the need for it, seems to have disappeared in the last two centuries of the Anglo-Saxon period.[28] Of the lesser members of the monasteries, information is less abundant and somewhat confusing. Bede, it will be remembered, distributed a few personal effects in his last hours. Much later, a council of the early Norman period spoke of the possession of personal effects by the monks as an abuse of the Saxon Church.[29] A more serious charge is made in the Abingdon Chronicle, where it is said that monks inherited property and disposed of it, presumably by will as well as during life.[30] The investigations of Dom David Knowles show, however, that while monks sometimes administered property given to the monastery by their families for their support, its disposition lay with the monastery, not with the individual monk.[31] Abuses, whether in the possession of chattels or even of land, could exist and, on occasion, may actually have been extended to the attempting of a bequest; but of the Anglo-Saxon Benedictines of both sexes it can be said that they were excluded by their state from the disposition of property at death.

The slaves maintain their usual silence. Primitively, they could own no property, but it is clear that their situation gradually improved so that they were allowed to keep that which they had gained from labour in their free time.[32] Provision made by a law of Alfred set aside the

[27] B. 156, 283. In B. 378 mention is made of a *post obit* gift to Archbishop Wulfred by Abbess Selethryth and her brother. On the use of the will as a means of controlling the future ownership of monastic lands see below, pp. 92-94.

[28] It appears, however, that in the tenth century abbots and abbesses had been accustomed to gather money which would be offered to the king as heriot when they died. This practice was forbidden in the epilogue to the *Regularis Concordia* (ca. 970): "... iussit ut nemo abbatum uel abbatissarum sibi locellum ad hoc thesaurizaret terrenum ut solitus census, quem indigenae *Heriatua* usualiter uocitant, qui pro huius patriae potentibus post obitum regibus dari solet" (ed. Symons, p. 69).

[29] The London synod of 1075 (Wilkins, I, 363).

[30] Ed. Stevenson, I, 477.

[31] D. Knowles, *The Monastic Order in England* (Cambridge, 1940), p. 81 and nn. 2 and 3. Among the notes made by Richard James in the seventeenth century there is a summary of a deed of gift by King Eadred to the nun Eawynn (946). By it, the donee was given property at Shipland with the right to give to whom she would at death; see Marion Gibbs, *Early Charters of the Cathedral Church of St. Paul, London*, Camden Third Series, LVIII (1939), p. 6, J. 12.

[32] The *Penitential of Theodore* prohibits the taking from the slave of that which had been acquired by his labour (II, xiii, 3, ed. Finsterwalder, p. 331). The Latin version of VII

four Ember Wednesdays, that slaves might sell that which they had acquired in this way or in alms.[33]   They themselves were not required to give alms.   The *Blickling Homilies* speak of those to whom this obligation did not apply, a group that would include the slaves.[34]   Certainly the slave's attempt to make an offering of this sort would be successful only if his owner saw fit to permit it.   However, the desire to give an alms at death may well have been present, at least among penal slaves and victims of warfare, who in happier times had belonged to the classes of whom a death-bed offering was expected.[35]

II.   BENEFICIARIES OF THE WILLS

The recipients of bequests included persons on all levels of society and various religious and civil groups as well   Grants to the king, the queen and the testator's lord, often in the form of a heriot, were common.[36] Religious communities and their heads were, of course, among the chief beneficiaries.   Sometimes the completion of the donation followed immediately on the death of a donor, but very often the gift took the form of a right to a reversion.[37]   In fact, the creation of reversionary rights seems often to have been the purpose for which a will was made. A city, a county too, might receive the grant of a ship for defence, or of money for payment of tribute to the invaders.[38]   Arrangements were

Ethelred allows slaves to be free of work during the three days of national fast before the feast of St. Michael, "et operetur sibimet quod vult" (2.3, *Gesetze*, I, 260).

[33] Alfred, 43, (*Gesetze*, I, 78-79).   The translation adopted here is that of F. L. Attenborough. *The Laws of the Earliest English Kings* (Cambridge, 1922), pp. 84-87 and p. 199, n. 8 to law 43.   One version of Wulfstan's *Sermo ad Anglos* complains that slaves were not allowed to keep what they had earned in free time or had been given in charity; see *Sermo Lupi ad Anglos*, ed. Dorothy Whitelock, 2nd ed. (London, 1952), pp. 38-39, textual variants and notes to line 48.

[34] Ed. R. Morris, p. 36.

[35] Wulfstan described the state to which thegns were sometimes reduced during the Danish invasions, in his *Sermo Lupi ad Anglos*, lines 102-132 (ed. Whitelock, pp. 44-46; *EHD*, I, 857-858).

[36] E.g., to the king: W. I, II, *et passim;* to the queen: W. VIII, IX, XI; to the lord: W. XXXIV, *C.C.* IX.

[37] B. 283; H. II; W. V, VIII *et passim.*   Sometimes it is evident that it is the intention of the donor that an ecclesiastical institution succeed to the bulk of an estate only if, as one *will* expressed it, the "family dies out so utterly that there be none of them able to hold land" (H. II, p. 4, lines 17-18).

[38] Archbishop Ælfric gave ships, and King Eadred gave large sums of money to be used to pay the invaders if necessary—sad reflections on the preoccupations of the age (W. XVIII, H. XXI).   Thurketel of Palgrave bequeathed a moor to the use of a group of freemen (W. XXIV).

made for distribution to the poor in several wills.   This often took the
form of a distribution of food and money on the day of the funeral
and on its anniversaries, a practice whose roots lay deep in early Christian
and pre-Christian funeral customs.[39]   Sometimes a monastic community
replaced the poor as beneficiary, the offering taking the form of a food-
rent to provide a feast on the anniversary day.[40]   The family, of
course, benefited from the wills: as a general rule the wife was very well
provided for, though reversions usually controlled the transfer of property after her death.   Friendship was often the motive of a legacy.
Servants too were left money and other gifts in several of the surviving
wills, and one of the most common of all gifts was to slaves, in the grant
of their freedom.[41]   The legatine synod of 786 decreed that illegitimate
children should be denied a share in the inheritance.   This seems to
have been applied in succession controlled by customary rules, but in
two of the wills which, it is not unreasonable to conclude, dealt with
such children, the power of bequest was used to ensure their prosperity.[42]
Creditors were occasionally mentioned in *wills,* where instructions were
given for their repayment.[43]   Debtors too find place there occasionally,

[39] Interesting examples of these benefactions are to be found in B. 402, and especially
in H. I, where a somewhat detailed account of preparations for the distribution is given.
On the funeral meal among the Germanic peoples see de Vries, *Altgermanische Religionsgeschichte,* I, 195-197.   Similar practices existed in the Empire before the appearance of
Christianity and among the early Christians themselves; see above, p. 8, n. 14.

[40] As in R. VI, XXVI *et passim.* No doubt St. Fursa would have been quite
scandalized to see the goods of the dead used in this way: see above, pp. 14-15.

[41] See below, pp. 104-105.

[42] Canon 16 (H. and S., III, 455, and *Alcuini Epistolae,* ed. Dümmler, *MGH,* Epp. IV, no. 3,
p. 25).   The correct date is 786 (not 787); cf. Levison, *England and the Continent,* p. 16, n. 3.
In W. IV, the "kinsman" was probably illegitimate.   The son, Æthelwald, in H. X (p. 14,
lines 8-13) also seems to be illegitimate.   The editor has raised some objections to this
conclusion.   However, it is quite obvious that the child whose birth was so eagerly desired
was intended to enjoy a position superior to that of Æthelwald, for whom the complicated
arrangements described in the *will* were made.   The latter suffered some disability and
was likely illegitimate; cf. H., pp. 90-91.

[43] It is not certain whether there was active and passive transmission of debts to successors among the Anglo-Saxons; cf. Holdsworth, *History* II, p. 7.   In a few surviving examples
debts were to be collected and devoted to the payment of bequests, seemingly implying that
the testator considered the debtor's obligation to continue after his death (W. XX; C.C. X).
Instructions for the payment of debts are to be found in H. XI, p. 19, line 2; W. XVIII,
p. 52, line 22; XX, p. 60, line 22; XXVI, p. 72, line 13, and perhaps XIX, p. 56, lines 4-7.
If legal conceptions had not yet attained the notion of the transmission of obligations, it is
at least likely that a religious duty to repay a debt before death, or in the final arrangement of the testator's property, was recognized: before going off to the war in which he
died, the father of Eadgifu "not willing to go to battle leaving any man's money unpaid"
redeemed a mortgaged estate (H. XXIII).

the testator remitting their obligations as one of the charitable acts of the will.[44] From time to time, residual bequests were made to a child, a church or a friend.[45]

III. MATERIAL LIMITATIONS IN THE ANGLO-SAXON WILLS

The extent of the freedom of bequest in Anglo-Saxon society can be considered not only in terms of the person who made the will, but also in terms of the property with which the will dealt. It has been suggested that the first dispositions involved that part of the testator's estate to which the family had a less strong claim, namely those personal effects which in pagan times were intended to be of use to him after death. That, however, was but a beginning. Among the Christian Anglo-Saxons the desire to give alms, as well as other bequests, was the cause of a steady pressure tending to reduce family rights in an inheritance. The first question to be posed, then, is whether limits to the freedom of bequest, limits in a quantitative rather than a personal sense, were ever imposed among the Anglo-Saxons. It was generally true in thirteenth-century England, as in many parts of northern Europe, that a precise portion of a testator's property, usually a third, was freely bequeathed.[46] The remainder descended to his family by customary rules of inheritance. Bede tells us of a division of property in thirds by Drythelm the Northumbrian about a century after the conversion of the Anglo-Saxons began. This distribution resembled that commonly found in England five hundred years later.[47] Since the seventeenth century, historians have remarked the similarity and have asked whether the dead-man's part of the thirteenth century was but the continuation of a freely disposable third of the time of Bede. But the centuries between Bede and the Anglo-Norman kingdom are long, and to bridge them is something that those who have asked the question have hesitated

---

[44] As in W. XVIII, p. 54, lines 2-4.

[45] E.g., H. XI, p. 18, lines 27-29; W. III, p. 14, lines 22 ff: VIII, p. 22, lines 1-4; XXI, p. 64, lines 11-13.

[46] In modern writings the testator's portion is referred to as "dead man's part," *"le disponible,"* *"Freiteil,"* etc. See pp. 288-293; cf. H. S. Maine, *Ancient Law,* 3rd American ed. (New York, 1879), p. 189 and Huebner, *History,* p. 742.

[47] *Historia Ecclesiastica,* Bk. V, ch. 12; see above, pp. 14-15. The temptation to see a connection between the two cases is perhaps made a little more strong by the fact that in the Anglo-Saxon version of Bede's account, a version from the circle and time of Alfred, the phrase "tertium sibi ipse retentans," is translated "þonne þriddan, þe him gelomp" (the third which fell to him). See *The Old English Version of Bede's Ecclesiastical History,* ed. T. Miller, E. E. T. S., 2 vols. (London, 1890-8), I, 424; cf. *Essays in Anglo-Saxon Law,* p. 135.

to do.[48] The matter has been reconsidered by Professor Bruck in a recent study, which relates the case of Drythelm to one of the great cultural patterns of western Europe during the early Middle Ages. He suggests that Bede's account reflects a practice that was common in the Northumbria of his time.[49] The free use of a third of an estate for the good of the soul showed a precocious development in Ireland, a development reflected in both the Brehon Laws and Irish canonical collections.[50] Professor Bruck suggests that in this, as in so many other things, the Irish influence persisted in northern England long after the synod of Whitby.[51] A further remnant of this Irish influence may survive in a law of Ine of Wessex, whereby a third was reserved to the wife of a criminal whose estate had been confiscated.[52] This portion could possibly have been the complement of a third for the dead. But the general impression left by the laws is that, south of the Humber before the Viking invasion and in the country as a whole after it was united under the crown of Wessex, there was no attempt to limit the freedom of distribution at death to a precise portion, namely a third.[53] The impression is strengthened by the written *wills* which are still extant.

This does not mean that the Anglo-Saxon of any class considered himself free to dispose of his property without consideration of the claim of his family. The evidence, especially that of the *wills*, indicates that disposition of property was made with the intention of striking a reasonable balance between family claims and needs, and the testator's desire to distribute his possessions outside the usual lines of inheritance. The alienation of property was often made easier for survivors by the use of the reversion. In the case of a will such as that of the Abbot Headda, there was practically speaking no difference so far as property passing

---

[48] P. and M., II, 314; Holdsworth, *History*, II, 94; Brunner, "Der Totentheil", *ZRG Germ. Abt.*, XIX, (1898), 123. Various opinions are cited by Bruck, *Kirchenväter*, p. 197, n. 2 and p. 204, n. 2, to which might be added that of W. Somner, *A Treatise on Gavelkind*, 1647 (London, 1726), p. 92, cited in *Essays in Anglo-Saxon Law*, p. 135.

[49] Bruck, *op. cit.*, pp. 196-200.

[50] The development, as shown in the different strata of the *Senchas Mar* and the *Collectio Canonum Hibernensis*, is analysed by Professor Bruck *ibid.*, pp. 168-183, and its chief stages outlined pp. 183-187.

[51] The suggestion is made all the more compelling when the Northumbrian example is related to the many cases of division in thirds, which Professor Bruck has found in those areas of Europe to which Irish missionaries had penetrated; cf. the review by Jacques Michel in *Latomus*, XVI (1957), 529-532.

[52] Ine 57. It reappears in VI Athelstan, I (*Gesetze*, I, 114-115, 173).

[53] This was the conclusion of Brunner, "Der Totentheil," p. 123, and has been reaffirmed by Bruck, *op. cit.*, pp. 208-216.

to the next generation was concerned.[54]   Among the *wills* which report those more complete distributions of property, which we have called the *cwide*, it is remarkable how rarely a son is indicated.[55]   Where children are mentioned, the *cwide*, to a large extent, takes the form of a division of property among them, though the future of the estates after the lives of the children might be controlled by reversions.[56]   Two of the *wills* mention arrangements for the gift of various properties to religious houses, with the understanding that if a child were born the lands would pass to it.[57]   A third *will* is even more illuminating.   In it, Ælfred, ealdorman of Surrey, makes careful arrangements for the succession to much of his property by his wife and daughter, and for reversions to other more distant relatives.   The offering of a gift to St. Peter's, Rome, and other grants in alms are mentioned.   Finally there is a donation of bookland to an illegitimate son and provision for his further support, in the event that the king fail to allow him to succeed to the folkland held by his father.   Yet all these arrangements were to go for nought, if God granted Ælfred a son by his present wife.[58]

It is remarkable too that, in the surviving accounts of litigation concerned with the distribution of property at death, wives and children are rarely implicated.[59]   The attempt to defeat the completion of a will

[54] B. 283.   In W. II, Ælfgar disposed of a very large estate but most of it was given to his daughters Æthelflæd and Ælfflæd (cf. W. XIV and XV), and even to their children. It was only after the death of daughters and grandchildren that many of the bequests were to be completed.   From an economic point of view these legacies made no change so far as the persons, to whom the property was reserved, were concerned.   They were not free to dispose of it, however.

[55] Given the incompleteness of the transaction that is reported in the written *will*, it is temerarious to attempt to show that a given testator was childless.   Nevertheless an attempt has been made, based on failure to mention a child in the will, and on an examination of the persons for whom and of whom prayers were asked.   Testators do not seem to have had children in B. 313; R. III, IX (see p. 277, n. to line 25, where the editor suggests that mention of children may actually have been made), XXVI, XLI; H. II, VII, XX; W. V, VIII, IX, XI, XIV, XV, XX, XXVIII, XXXVIII, XXXIX.   Only daughters are indicated in H. X (a son, considered to be illegitimate, is mentioned); W. II, XVII, XIX, XXV, XXIX. Wills of priests and bishops are not included.

[56] H. XI; W. II, XXI, XXXII.

[57] H. II; R. III.

[58] H. X.   In the first part of the *will*, Ælfred spoke of his property and bookland ("mines erfes and mines boclandes").   In the grant to the son, for whom there was but a forlorn hope, he speaks of all his possessions ("alles mines erfes"); *erfe* was used to mean wealth, in goods and estates, and in this context it seems correct to consider it to mean both—"all my property."   See p. 14, lines 32-36; cf. Bosworth-Toller, *Anglo-Saxon Dictionary, Supplement*, p. 595 and Young, "The Anglo-Saxon Family-Law," *Essays*, p. 137, n. 2.

[59] Bequests were disputed by sons in *Liber Eliensis*, II, 26; K. 805; R. LIX, LXXVIII and perhaps CV.   A widow opposed a will in *Ramsey Chronicon*, ch. 33, pp. 59-61.

seems more often to have been made by relatives and others with some claim against the testator. The actual number of cases is small, too small perhaps to be the basis of a well founded judgment, yet even this evidence points to the same general conclusions. For wives and descendants adequate provision was usually made.[60] The will was used for a distribution that amounted to the dismemberment of an estate, or for a complete or nearly complete alienation from the surviving members of a family, in those cases where the family faced extinction so far as descendants of the testator were concerned. Hard and fast rules do not seem to have existed, but it is probably correct to conclude that the will that ignored the needs of wives and descendants was quite rare.[61]

Though the Anglo-Saxon testator was not usually limited to the alienation of a precise portion of his property, his freedom was restricted in another way: he was eventually constrained to make at least a minimum offering to the church of his burial. This rule appears in the first code of Athelstan among the church dues which the reeve was to enforce. It was called "*sawolsceatt*"—an alms for the soul of the deceased.[62] The practice was much older of course. One of the earliest wills of which a fairly complete report survives mentions the grant of lands to the monastery at Deerhurst, the place of the donor's burial.[63] Within the Empire, it was customary from the fourth century that Christians be allowed to choose their place of interment, and that 'some offering be made there at the time of burial.[64] The general law of the Church was opposed to the demand of such a fee, however. Instructions of popes and bishops presumed the existence of burial offerings and

---

[60] Provision for the wife was usually made in pre-marital agreements and by the "morning-gift"; cf. Young, *op. cit.*; Brissaud, *History*, pp. 754-755; and W., pp. 111, 135. 144 (cf. p. xlvii), 181, 195. As was mentioned above, these arrangements were sometimes confirmed in wills; e.g., W. XIII, XV, XXV, XXXI.

[61] Cf. Holdsworth, *History*, II, 92-94.

[62] I Athelstan, 4 (*Gesetze*, I, 146-147). Repeated in III Edgar, 5.2; V Ethelred, 12; VI Ethelred, 20; and I Cnut, 13 (*Gesetze*, I, 200-201, 240-241, 252-253, 294-295). On the *sawolsceatt*, see Bosworth-Toller, *Dictionary*, pp. 818-819, *Supplement*, p. 694; Liebermann, *Gesetze*, II, p. 647, *s.v. Seelschatz*; W. pp. 109-110; Bruck, *Kirchenväter*, pp. 204-216. On the development from a free offering to a church tax, cf. Schultze, "Der Einfluss," pp. 80-90, and Haensel, "Die mittelalterlichen Erbschaftssteuern," *Deutsche Zeitschrift für Kirchenrecht*, XIX (1909), 378-387.

[63] B. 313; see above, p. 42. Such a grant is implied in B. 256 (789). Arrangements sometimes included the agreement that clerics or monks of the place of burial would come for the body after the testator's death: e.g., W. V; *Liber Eliensis*, II, 62 describes how the monks of Ely came for Brihtnoth's body on the battlefield where he died.

[64] Cf. A. Bernard, *La Sépulture en droit canonique du décret de Gratien au Concile de Trente*, (Paris, 1933), pp. 85 ff; *Dictionnaire de droit canonique*, V (1953), 920.

permitted them, but insisted that they were not to be exacted; such procedure was considered to be simoniacal.[65]   The practice of making an offering at the time of burial appeared very soon after the conversion in England, where its acceptance was facilitated by the Germanic practice of grave endowment still generally known there.[66]   The biography of St. Fursa is a strong indication that, late in the seventh century, it was common practice to give an alms by the grave-side to the poor and to the priest who assisted at the burial.[67]   The saint himself preferred that the offering be made only to the poor.   The soul-scot was not mentioned in the laws of Ine, though other church dues found a place there.   The testimony of the *wills*, however, is adequate proof that these grants were general, long before they became obligatory in the law of Athelstan.

At first, as Lingard has stated, the burial fee was usually considered by the donor as distinct from his other alms.[68]   This is made very clear in the ninth-century *will* of Abba the Reeve.[69]   A hundred years later, in the *will* of Wynflæd, "soul-scot" is used vaguely of any gift for the soul; but *wills* of that century and the following one often continue to use the term strictly, distinguishing it from other offerings, even though they were made to the same church.[70]   Sometimes the word "soul-scot" was not used, the offering being described merely as a bequest to the place of burial.[71]   Most often however, offerings were simply made for the soul, so that it is impossible to know what part was intended as a burial fee.   In the laws of Ethelred and Cnut, where the term "soul-scot" is used in the strict sense of a burial offering, the free choice of place of interment and the ecclesiastical reaction to it can be seen: the soul-scot was to be paid to the church to which the deceased belonged, even though the body were buried elsewhere.[72]   It can be taken for granted

---

[65] Bernard, *op. cit.*, pp. 141 ff.

[66] See above, p. 6, and Stenton, *Anglo-Saxon England*, pp. 152-153.

[67] See above, pp. 14-15. Bernard, *op. cit.*, p. 165 cites Lingard as maintaining that the offering was due from the seventh century. Actually Lingard suggested that date only for the church-scot, which appears in the laws of Ine of Wessex; see J. Lingard, *History and Antiquities of the Anglo-Saxon Church*, 2 vols. (London, 1845), I, 192.

[68] Lingard, *ibid.*, stated that the soul-scot was always distinguished from other charitable bequests. This position is corrected by Stenton, *op. cit.*, pp. 152-153.

[69] H. II, p. 3, line 29, p. 4, lines 1-2: "then one thousand pence are to be given at my funeral for my resting-place, and to the community severally, five hundred pence on behalf of my soul" (p. 41).

[70] Cf. W. III (p. 10, lines 1-6), XII and XV (p. 40, lines 11-12); see also W. XVII, XVIII, XIX.

[71] As in W. XX, XXIII, XXIX.

[72] V Ethelred, 12.1; VI Ethelred, 21; I Cnut 13.1 (*Gesetze*, I, 240-241, 252-253, 294-295).

that, where this happened, there would also be a bequest to the church of burial. The offering seems frequently to have been delivered by the open grave. It was so described in the life of St. Fursa, in some of the *wills*, and in the later laws.[73] Continental practice was similar.[74]

The amount of the payment intended in the laws is unknown. In the *Collectio Canonum Hibernensis* mention is made of a cow or a sheep as a suitable offering.[75] Given the later custom in England, it is probable that there was a similar minimum soul-scot among the Anglo-Saxons. The actual donations, which can be seen in the *wills*, varied from the rings, given to Ely by Brihtnoth and his wife, to the donation of several large estates.[76] Where "soul-scot" was used to mean all the alms given for the soul, no amount seems to have been fixed. In Ireland there was rapid development of the notion that the soul's part should be a third of all the property or, at least, of the chattels. Some of the Irish laws demanded that all of this free portion be given for the soul of the deceased.[77] But except for its possible appearance in Bede, the notion that a third of the property should be devoted to alms does not appear in Anglo-Saxon England.[78] There the testator seems to have been free to give alms in excess of that amount or, having made a minimum offering to the church of his burial, to give less.

One other grant made by Anglo-Saxon testators had many of the qualities of a required offering. From the middle of the tenth century, almost every *cwide* included a payment to the lord. This was frequently called a "heriot."[79] It will be remembered that a law of Cnut restricted

---

[73] See the previous note and above, p. 15. Distribution at the funeral is mentioned in H. II.

[74] Bernard, *op. cit.*, p. 65.

[75] "*De sedatione communi.* a. *Sinodus Kartaginensis* ait: Sedatium commune, si modicum fuerit, respui non debet; si magnum, accipiendum usque ad praetium vacce; hoc sedatium aufugit regem et episcopum, cui monachus est et fratres. b. *Sinodus Hibernensis* in hoc sedatium ovem aut praetium ejus statuta demensione censuit." (Bk. II, ch. 15). A somewhat larger offering, though not necessarily for burial, is described in Bk. XVIII, De Jure Sepulturae, ch. 6: *Die irische Kanonensammlung*, ed. H. Wasserschleben, 2nd ed. (Leipzig, 1885), pp. 16-17, 57.

[76] Cf. W. XV, p. 40, lines 11-12 and *C.C.* X and W. XVIII.

[77] Cf. Bruck, *Kirchenväter*, pp. 178-183.

[78] See above, p. 14.

[79] On the heriot in general see H. Brunner, *Forschungen zur Geschichte des deutschen und französischen Rechtes* (Stuttgart, 1894), pp. 22 ff; for its use in England see H. M. Chadwick, *Studies in Anglo-Saxon Institutions* (Cambridge, 1905), pp. 375-376; *Gesetze*, II, 500-502, *s.v.* "Heergewäte;" W. p. 100, and p. 238 *s.v.* "heriot;" and the valuable suggestions of Eric Johns, *Land Tenure in Early England*, pp. 56-58. Miss Whitelock considers the payment of the heriot to be characteristic of the will in the last century of the Anglo-Saxon kingdom (W. pp. xli, 100).

the right of a lord in the property of an intestate to his legal heriot. Such an offering did not occur in the earlier written *wills*, which were concerned almost exclusively with the donation of land. It is only as more detailed descriptions of bequests, including chattels, became general, that the heriot took its place among them. This offering to the lord was intended, in part, to obtain his support for the will.[80] Frequent grants to the queen and the ætheling had the same intention.[81] According to the laws of Cnut, only men in the lay state were bound to make the payment. Yet the wills of women and of bishops often mention sizable bequests to the king, and sometimes, even in the case of a woman, the bequest is called a heriot.[82] From time to time the payment exceeded the amount indicated in Cnut's scale.[83] The motive may have been the seeking of protection; but, given the closeness of some of the testators to the royal family, affection should not be excluded. In a few wills, such as that of the East Anglian thegn, Ketel, the heriot is given to a lord other than the king.[84] Occasionally the written *wills* tell of the arrangements made for the payment of the heriot.[85]

[80] W. p. 100; R. Caillemer, "The Executor in England and on the Continent," *Select Essays in Anglo-American Legal History,* III, 750-753. Maitland suggested that the heriot may also have been intended to move the king to allow unbooked lands to be distributed by will; see *Domesday Book and Beyond* (Cambridge, 1897), pp. 298-299.

[81] As in W. VIII, IX, XI, XXIX. In W. XI, the purpose of the gift to the queen is stated: "to forespræce. þ se cwyde standan moste." (p. 26, lines 21-22).

[82] Actually, the oldest bequest of this sort to the king is found in a latin version of a woman's *will* (B. 812), dated 944-946. Other examples of such payment by women are in W. VIII, XIV, XV, XXIX, XXXII. It is only in the last of these, dated 1046, that the term "heriot" is used (cf. W. p. 198). Bishops make this offering in W. IV, XVIII, XXVI; *C.C.* X.

[83] II Cnut, 71 (*Gesetze*, I, 356-359). The existence of a scale before that time is indicated by reference to a "due heriot" in W. XVII (1002-1004), p. 46, line 8, and W. XVIII (1003-1004), p. 52, line 23. Cf. W. p. 100.

[84] W. XXXIV, cited by Miss Whitelock in W. p. 238, *s.v.* "heriot" and p. 202, n. to line 26. The *will* of Leofwine, Wulfstane's son (*C.C.*, IX), mentions the grant of an estate to Wulfstan, bishop of London, the testator's lord.

[85] W. XXIX: the children were to "succeed to the inheritance and pay the gold." The *Ramsey Chronicon* (pp. 111-112) preserves in latin translation a fragment of a document of the late 10th century, which mentions the grant of the estate of Thorington to the abbey. There was a stipulation that the abbot, brother of the donor, should pay the heriot. The document is an interesting example of the heriot-relief confusion: the translator considered the heriot to be a payment in relief by the successor, rather than an offering by the deceased owner; see W. XIII, p. 32, lines 17-18; XXXI, p. 80, lines 24-25.

IV. THE KINDS OF PROPERTY DISTRIBUTED BY THE ANGLO-SAXON WILLS

The establishment of the individual's right to choose the owner of his possessions after death was a derogation from the customary rules of family inheritance. This right was not of universal application at first, but was slowly extended over different kinds of property. As has been seen, the initial area of exercise was over that portion of an individual's goods which was most completely his own. Thus the first chattels to be bequeathed were items of personal equipment—things which the testator alone had used. Their loss did not seriously inconvenience the surviving members of his family. Other chattels, which were tools required by the family or by even larger social groups, came to be freely distributed more slowly, for their loss reduced the income of all who used them. Land was least at the disposition of the individual for it was most closely related to the needs of whole social groups; it required many hands for its tilling and many depended on it for their livelihood. Thus different kinds of property became subject to distribution by will under varied conditions and at different times. Land proved to be most resistent to the right of bequest. Yet the first detailed information regarding the property distributed in Anglo-Saxon wills is concerned with gifts of land. With their study, then, we shall begin.

The Alienation of Land by Will

If evidence of all Anglo-Saxon wills had survived and it were possible to establish statistics enumerating the various types of property bequeathed, it would be found, no doubt, that bequests of land were among the least common. The alienation of no other type of property could impose such permanent hardship on the social group, once settlement had been completed and the support of families had been associated with fixed landed estates. The notion that these holdings could be put beyond the reach of those who had come to look upon them as their own, just at the moment when a younger generation expected to assume their control, or that an estate could be broken into several holdings, had very little to recommend it to the men of that age. Yet the bequest of land was attempted, and met with some success. Our information about this development is supplied by the landbooks and the written *wills*. From their study it is possible to suggest why the alienation of land at death was introduced, and to show the extent to which it was permitted. Once again the innovation proves to be a response to a need of the Church; in this case it was to protect ecclesiastical property.

Saint Augustine and his followers were given buildings and lands for their use soon after their arrival in Kent.[86]   It may be assumed that as the first ecclesiastical communities were formed and enlarged, they were adequately endowed; protection of their property is the subject of the very first of the Anglo-Saxon laws.[87]   Charters constructed, or perhaps reconstructed, later, seek to witness to these donations, but it is not until the time of Archbishop Theodore that undisputed charter evidence of grants of land is available.[88]   It is almost a commonplace that the written document or landbook was introduced by the clergy to give greater security to their possessions.   The exact nature of the rights granted in these transactions has not, however, been the subject of such agreement.[89]   The transfer of possession of land, in some cases at least, was accomplished by the acts to which the landbooks refer.   In those cases where the land in question was already under exploitation, the gift was the donation of certain rights in the land rather than the property itself.[90]   The historian's difficulty in establishing the exact rights acquired in land by the beneficiaries of these grants is due, in part, to the vague description of them in the landbooks.   However, for the purposes of this investigation it is the quality of these rights — their duration and alienability — that is of special importance.   Here the landbooks are more helpful.   Their dispositive clauses indicate that the property was held in perpetual inheritance and, in time, show that the donee had received a power of disposal during life and even at death.

86 Bede, *Historia Ecclesiastica*, Bk. I, ch. 33, ed. Plummer, I, 70.

87 Æthelberht, I (*Gesetze*, I, 3); regarding Liebermann's dating of these laws, cf. H. *Writs*, p. 6, n. 2.

88 In a series of articles published in 1941-2, Miss Margaret Deanesly suggested that the early charters, said to be grants of Æthelberht of Kent (B. 3, 4, 5, 6), contain genuine portions, survivals of earlier documents drawn up under the influence of the Frankish members of Queen Bertha's suite.   The discussion is conveniently summarized and criticized by W. Levison, *England and the Continent*, Appendix I, "The Charters of King Ethelbert of Kent," pp. 174-233.

89 A convenient summary of this very complex discussion is in T. F. T. Plucknett, "Bookland and Folkland," Revisions in Economic History III, *Econ. Hist. Rev.*, VI (1936), 64-72.   Later consideration of the problem is in Stenton, *Anglo-Saxon England*, pp. 302-309, and T. H. Aston, "The Origins of the Manor in England," *Transactions of the Royal Historical Society*, Fifth Series, VIII (1958), 59-83.   Many fundamental questions touching the nature of book-right have been posed by Eric John in *Land Tenure in Early England*. This work was not available in time to be considered in the present study.   Though it has received rather harsh treatment by some reviewers, it makes several important contributions to the discussion.

90 Maitland emphasized the transfer of superiority involving "fiscal rights and justiciary rights" over bookland: *Domesday Book and Beyond*, pp. 231-234; cf. Aston, *art. cit.*, pp. 63-65.

Eventually it becomes evident that such rights have passed beyond ecclesiastical owners and are possessed by some members of the laity as well. The time and place of development of these statements of right are of sufficient interest to warrant careful investigation.

The oldest charter of which a contemporary text is preserved bears witness to the grant of land on the Isle of Thanet, in 679, to Abbot Brihtwold by Hlothere, king of Kent. It concludes the rather vague description of the property with a clause stating that it is to be held perpetually: *teneas possedeas tu posterique tui inperpetuum.*[91] From this time on most charters, using one formula or another, state that land given to church or monastery is to be held in perpetual inheritance. But the dispositive clauses also indicate a right of alienation; it is the explication of this power that is of special interest here. The notion appears in a charter dated 672-674, a good copy of which survives in the Chertsey cartulary. It records a grant of land in Surrey by the under-king Frithuwold. The donation clause expresses a power of alienation in general terms: "donata sunt et concessa et confirmata teneatis et possideatis. et quodcunque volueritis de eisdem terris facere tam tu quam posteri tui liberam licenciam habeatis." [92]

That the "licence to do whatever you wish" involved donation, sale and exchange, is made explicit in two charters of the last fifteen years of the century from Wessex and Kent. By the former, shortly before 688, Cædwalla, king of Wessex, grants sixty hides to three men at Farnham, Surrey, to establish a monastery. Their rights include the power of gift and exchange at will: *libertam a me habeatis licentiam donandi commutandi.*[93] The second charter is a grant of the year 694 by King Wihtred of Kent, to Abbess Æbba, of land on the Isle of Thanet. Her powers of disposition of the property are stated quite fully: "teneas possideas, dones, commutes, venundes vel quicquid exinde facere volueris liberam habeas potestatem; successoresque tui defendant inperpetuum." [94]

[91] "... you may hold it and possess it, and your successors maintain it forever" (B. 45); translated and briefly discussed in *EHD,* I, 443-444, no. 56.

[92] "... as they have been granted, conceded and confirmed by me, you are to hold and possess, and both you and your successors are to have free license to do whatever you wish with the same lands" (B. 34, *EHD,* I, 440-441, no. 54); cf. B. 67.

[93] "You are to have from me free permission to give and exchange..." (B. 72). Birch dated the charter 688, but Miss Whitelock, pointing out that Wilfrid, first of the witnesses, returned to the north the previous year, advances the date to 685-687 (*EHD,* I, 445, no. 58).

[94] "... you may hold, possess, give, exchange, sell and have free power to do what you will, and your successors may maintain it forever" (B. 86). This charter was considered spurious by Haddan and Stubbs (*Councils,* III, 242), but is probably genuine; cf. Levison,

In a final step the dispositive clause is expanded to include an explicit statement of freedom of alienation at death.   This first occurs in two charters of the last decade of the century, recording grants to Abbess Æbbe.   The first, a grant of land at Sturrey by King Oswin, probably in 690, contains the clause: "habeat possideatque proprio arbitrio, et cuicumque voluerit vivens vel moriens habeat integram facultatem condonare tantum in domino." [95]   The second charter, probably of the following year, one that in general phraseology is remarkably close to the former, states the abbess' rights in land granted by King Swæbhard: "Æbbæ abbatissæ jure æcclesiastico ac monasteriali et quibuscunque successoribus ipsa voluerit derelinquere, tantum in domino, in sempiternum possidendam perdonamus." [96]   These charters are from among the group, dealing with the estates of the church of Minster on the Isle of Thanet, transferred with the body of St. Mildred to St. Augustine's by Cnut.[97]   Long considered to be spurious, their value was reaffirmed by G. J. Turner in his introduction to The Black Book of St. Augustine.[98] However, the charters as they have come down to us have at least suffered some changes and additions,[99] so that while the clauses under

op. cit., p. 230.   The form of the dispositive clause was uncommon in England.   B. 225 and 400 are similar, though in the latter case the right of alienation at death is added.   On the Continent a similar form is found in the seventh-century Formulae Andecavensis: "... quicquid ab odierna diae ipso vernaculo facere volueritis, abendi, tenende, donande, vindende seu conmutandi, quomodo et de reliqua mancipia vestra obnoxia exinde facere volueritis, liberam abeam potestatem" (italics added): no. 9, ed. Zeumer, p. 7.   There are several examples among the deeds of Saint-Germain-des-Prés; e.g., no. IX (697), no XXIV (794): Recueil des chartes de l'Abbaye de Saint-Germain-des-Prés, ed. R. Poupardin, 2 vols. (Paris, 1909), I, 18, 38-39.

[95] "... she may have and possess under her own authority, and during life or at death has full power to give to whom she will, tantum in domino" (B. 35).   The last phrase, which has been left in latin, may imply that the new donee would have the same right as the abbess.   However it is possible that, in this text and the one cited in the following note, the words are taken from I. Cor., vii, 39 and could be translated "so long as it be in the lord."   This would restrict the power of alienation, permitting sale or donation only to other churches and would support the explanation of the introduction of freedom of bequest suggested below, pp. 91-94.   Eric John, op. cit., p. 4, n. 1 suggests that the phrase be read "tantum in domin(i)o."

[96] "... we give in eternal possession, in ecclesiastical and monastic right, to Abbess Æbbe and to whatever successors she shall wish to leave it, tantum in domino..." (B. 42).

[97] Cf. K. 1326.

[98] G. J. Turner and H. E. Salter, eds. The Register of St. Augustine's Abbey Canterbury, commonly called the Black Book, British Academy, Records of Social and Economic History, II, 2 vols.   (London, 1915-24).   The dates of the two charters in question are discussed in Vol. II, xxxiii-xxxiv.

[99] Ibid., p. xxxviii.

discussion provide a strong possibility that freedom of alienation at death was being stated thus early, it cannot be advanced with certainty. The same qualification must be applied to a Mercian charter of 692.[100] It is not for another half century that unquestionable evidence of the fact is available.

This first occurs in a group of charters of King Æthelbald of Mercia. The oldest Mercian charter to survive in a contemporary copy (736) witnesses to a grant, by this king, of land at Stour in Worcestershire to Ealdorman Cyneberht. The land was to be used to found a monastery and the donee's rights of alienation are explicit: *cuicumque voluerit vel eo vivo vel certe post obitum suum relinquendi*.[101] Another charter, probably of the same year, preserved in a much later but trustworthy copy, records the grant of land in Warwickshire. Again, it is for the foundation of a monastery and, as in the previously mentioned charter, the estate may be alienated during life or at death. In this case there is an important reservation: the grantee must be acceptable to the king and, presumably, to his council.[102] In the other kingdoms this freedom of alienation of land at death becomes explicit a little later. The grants to Abbess Æbbe excepted, the earliest case in Kent is a charter of Egbert II granting lands within the walls of Rochester to Eardwulf, bishop of the city, in 765.[103] A charter of Aldwulf, king of the South Saxons, granting land to Ealdorman Hunlabe for the construction of a monastery, is

[100] B. 77: "... et tamen se vivente vel etiam post obitum ejus cui voluerit dimittendum libenter concedendo, trado;" cf. Eric John, *Land Tenure in Early England*, pp. 74-76. In a lost charter of Wulfhere of Mercia (657-674), described by Patrick Young early in the seventeenth century, Abbot Colman received land with the right to choose his heir; see H. P. R. Finberg, *The Early Charters of the West Midlands*, Studies in Early English History, II (Leicester, 1961), p. 86, no. 195. The text of B. 60, recording the sale of land by Æthelred of Mercia to Osric, "in perpetuam, hereditatem possidendum & adhabendum, & post se in suam genelogiam qualicunque manu voluerit donandum," is probably a compilation of the ninth century; see Finberg, *op. cit.*, pp. 158-162, whose reading of the text is adopted here.

[101] "... he is to have the power, ... during his lifetime or indeed after his death, of leaving it to whom he shall wish" (B. 154; *EHD*, I, 453-454, no. 67). Cf. Stenton, *Latin Charters*, p. 34 and indications given there.

[102] B. 157; cf. Stenton, *Latin Charters*, pp. 35-36, 56. The dispositive clause reads: "et cuicumque placuerit vel se vivente vel obeunte ea condicione qua sibi traditum acceperit licenter omnino nobis concedentibus libens tradat." Similar clauses are found in B. 153, dated 723-737, which "may be genuine" (F. M. Stenton, *The Early History of the Abbey of Abingdon*, p. 23, n. 1), and B. 165, dated 716-743. Both are charters of Æthelbald of Mercia.

[103] B. 196: "... et cuicunque volueris te vivente seu moriente dare æternaliter perdono."

probably of the same year, and contains a similar phrase.[104]   The first
West Saxon example is to be found in a charter of Cynewulf in 778.[105]
Towards the end of the reign of Offa, freedom of alienation at death is
usually stated in Mercian charters.[106]   For the area north of the Humber,
there is no charter evidence.

The fact that the freedom of alienation of lands at death became
explicit in a document of 736, or even in 690, should not, of course, be
taken to mean that the right was exercised only from that date.[107]   The
charters' ability to describe legal rights developed much more slowly
than the rights themselves.   In all probability, the power they eventually
came to express was possessed and used very soon after the beginning of
the conversion.   None the less, the growing insistence on the fact that
lands and rights possessed by the Church were freely sold and exchanged
or given away, either during life or at death, is somewhat surprising.
Such holdings were apparently more fully disposable than any others
in England of that day.   General church legislation had striven for
centuries to prevent alienation of church property and had sought to
restrain the activity of bishops and abbots, the persons who were most
likely to commit such an abuse.[108]   Yet in England, perpetual inheritance with partial or full right of disposition seems, during these first
centuries, to have been what was considered to be typical of land held
by the Church.   Mr. Jolliffe has collected many interesting examples
from the earliest landbooks to show how the phrase *ius ecclesiasticum*
had come, in the eighth century, to imply possession by charter.   The
phrase not only indicated that, in the beginning, such property belonged
to a church or monastery and that an ecclesiastical sanction protected it,
but it seemed especially to describe the condition of the estate, that is,

---

104 B. 197: "... ut habeat et utatur. et post se cui placuerit imperpetum jus derelinquat."
105 B. 225; cf. Stenton, *Latin Charters*, p. 26.
106 E.g., B. 202, 203, 207, 223, 230, 247.
107 As Stenton observes, *Latin Charters*, p. 32, the earliest literary reference to charters is
in Eddi's description of the dedication of Ripon by Wilfrid 671-678. Wilfrid distributed
estates at the end of his life as has been seen, but, since his and all other Northumbrian
charters of the period are lost, it is impossible to know whether such a right was expressed
in these early documents. See above, pp. 32-33.
108 P. W. Duff, "The Charitable Foundations of Byzantium," *Cambridge Legal Essays*
(Cambridge, Mass., 1926), pp. 87-88; E. Lesne, *Histoire de la propriété ecclésiastique en France*,
I, 18, 133, chs. xxii, xxiii; T. P. McLaughlin, *Le très ancien droit monastique de l'occident*,
Archives de la France monastique, XXXVIII (Paris, 1935), pp. 241, 242, n. 1. The same
preoccupation is evident in early English councils: e.g., Privilege of Wihtred of Kent, 696-
716 (B. 91); Council of Celchyth, 816, cc. 7 and 8 (Haddan and Stubbs, III, 582); also in
many charters and *wills:* B. 214; H. XVI, XX; R. XVII. XXVI, XXVII; W. VI, XI, XVII.

possession with perpetual right and complete alienability.[109]   He might
have gone further for there are remarkably clear manifestations of this
point of view in a few charters of the third quarter of the century.   In
these documents, among the earliest to mention immunities, freedom of
alienation was specifically connected with *ius ecclesiasticum*, while the
immunities were given separate mention and connected with purchase.
An excellent example of this distinction is provided by an original text
or its contemporary copy (770), whereby Uhtred, under-king of the
Hwicci, granted land to his thegn Æthelmund.[110]   The estate is to be
held *jure æclesiastico*, with the freedom of choice of heirs.   Furthermore,
digno pretio a antedicto Æðelmundo suscepto, the land is freed from a variety
of obligations.   Such clauses do not become part of the usual phrasing
of charters, but they are of interest as a complete expression of the
tendency to consider possession with perpetual inheritance and freedom
of alienation, at death as during life, to be typical of estates held by the
Church.

The stressing of the perpetual right of the ecclesiastical donee was to
be expected.   But what purpose was served by maintaining a power
of bequest over church property?   Was it merely a blind imitation of

[109] "English Book-right," *EHR*, L (1935), 9-10. If the texts of the two charters touching
donations to Abbess Æbbe (cited above, nn. 95, 96) are accepted, then the relation of *ius
ecclesiasticum* to the notion of perpetual inheritance and alienability is to be found in the
last quarter of the seventh century: "ecclesiastico jure concedo... dono perpetuo... cuicumque
voluerit vivens vel moriens habeat integram facultatem condonare" (B. 35); "jure æcclesiastico ac monasteriali et quibuscunque successoribus ipsa voluerit derelinquere... in sempiternum possidendam" (B. 42). Cf. the interesting suggestions of Eric John, *Land Tenure in
Early England*, pp. 4-23.

[110] B. 203; *EHD*, I, 462-465, no. 74. Another charter (B. 202), somewhat briefer, and of
the year 767 seems to be concerned with the same persons and estate. In this case the
boundaries are not given, nor is the reversion to Worcester mentioned. The charter is
known only through a copy published by Hickes in the eighteenth century, and, while it is
convincing in structure and phrasing, it is impossible to know whether it represents an
earlier grant under different conditions, or whether the two documents are but different
versions of the same transaction. It is worthy of note, though, that in both charters the
choice of heir is intimately connected with *ius ecclesiasticum*, while freedom from public
obligation is connected with purchase; cf. Miss Whitelock's notes *EHD*, I, 402. A remarkable identification of the power of alienation at death with ecclesiastical right may occur
in a charter of 777, recording a grant of land by Offa to Aldred, under-king of the
Hwicci: "donabo illi ut se vivente habeat et cuicumque voluerit post se libera utens
potestate jure ecclesiastico possidendam relinquat" (B. 223). While it is true that the
words "jure ecclesiastico" are more obviously related to "possidendam," they can also be
related to "potestate" so that the phrase is translated: "... that he may have it during life
and, freely using [his] capacity by ecclesiastical right, may leave it to whomsoever he will
to possess after him." On the authenticity of this document see Robinson, *St. Oswald and
the Church of Worcester*, pp. 24-25, and Finberg, *op. cit.*, p. 94, no. 223.

model documents so that a right was implied that was never intended to
be given?   On the Continent both formulae and charters usually avoid
mentioning the right of alienation at death in the case of lands given
to the Church.   Such a right is stated in several of the formulae of the
early seventh-century Angers collection.   Here it is most clearly
expressed in a gift of land by parents to a son: "et hoc est abendi,
tenendi, seu commutandi, posteris tui, vel ubi tua decrederit volomtas,
derelinquendi." [111]   In this, as in the three other cases where these formulae occur, the land in question passes from one member of the laity
to another.[112]   The collection is, in fact, concerned almost exclusively
with transactions beween laymen.   That is not true of the *Marculfi
Formulae*.   Here the purposeful avoidance of the use of such formulae
with regard to church property is quite evident.   The dispositive clause
of a formula of grant to a layman includes such freedom,[113] whereas the
cessio ad loco sancto, which immediately follows, avoids it.[114]   The difference of attitude is best demonstrated in a deed of exchange from the
Formulae Salicae Merkelianae, a collection of the second half of the eighth
century.   The transaction in question is an exchange of land between
a layman and an abbot, and the formula states the rights enjoyed in the
property that has come into the hands of each participant.   The full
powers of alienation during life and at death by the layman are clearly
stated: "habeat, teneat atque possideat suisque heredibus, aut cui voluerit, ad possidendum derelinquat, vel quicquid exinde facere voluerit,
liberam in omnibus habeat potestatem faciendi."   The abbot's powers,
however, are much less extensive, since it was intended that the land
should serve the needs of the Church: "ad opus sanctae ecclesiae habeat,
teneat adque possideat, vel quicquid exinde in augmentum sanctae
ecclesiae facere decreverit, liberam in omnibus perfruatur arbitrium." [115]

---

111 *Formulae Andecavensis,* no. 37, ed. Zeumer, p. 16.

112 Nos. 41, 54, 55, ed. Zeumer, pp. 18, 23, 24.

113 *Marculfi Formulae* I, 14: "... habeat, teneat atque possedeat et suis posteris, Domino
adiuvante, ex nostra largitate aut cui voluerit ad possedendum relinquat, etc." (ed. Zeumer,
pp. 52-53).   Similar clauses are found in Bk. I, chs. 13, 17, 30, 33; pp. 51-52, 54, 61, 63-64.

114 Bk. I, ch. 15: "... et ipsi et successores sui habeant, teneant et possedeant, vel
quicquid exinde ad profectum ecclesiae illius, *aut* baselicae, facire voluerint, ex permisso
nostro liberam in omnibus habeant potestatem" (p. 53).   Similar clauses are found in
Bk. I, ch. 16 and Bk. II, chs. 4 and 6; pp. 53-54, 76-77, 78-79.   Two of the models in the
Formulae Marculfinae Aevi Karolini (nos. 22 and 23, pp. 122-123), are concerned with church
property, but employ the formulae that are commonly used of lay holdings.   They are
almost literal copies of Marculf I, 33 and 14, both of which were concerned with the
estates of laymen.

115 No. 20, ed. Zuemer, pp. 248-249; contrast *Marculf,* II, 23, *ibid.,* p. 91.

The continental example should have led to a limited statement of the rights of alienation vested in ecclesiastical owners. However, during the seventh and eighth centuries in England, the tendency was in the opposite direction; the formulae of the charters were enlarged until the fullest expression was given both to completeness of ownership and to the free alienation of land. This unusual development seems to represent an attempt to defend the possessions of the Church. When clerics were given land and exemption from the public obligations of land, they had to be protected from the efforts of the family of the donor to recover his gift either immediately or after the donor's death. The royal landbook was intended to place such lands permanently outside the right of the donor's kindred. The Church associated herself with this act in the charters' anathema clauses, which so closely resemble decrees of councils forbidding the recovery of donations to the Church.[116] A limited freedom of alienation was to be expected, and the dispositive clauses of charters came very quickly to express the right of sale or exchange. This would be necessary at times, as prohibitions of alienation of church property usually admitted. In fact, the land granted by one of the first of the surviving landbooks was sold by the recipient's successor, and there is evidence that transactions of this sort were fairly frequent.[117] But freedom of bequest of land was a quite different thing. It is very probable that it was introduced to meet another threat to ecclesiastical property that must have been evident almost from the beginning. This threat came from the families of church leaders.

According to the formulae of the charters, a gift was made for the soul of the donor, to God, to a saint and his church or monastery.[118] By the sixth century, churches and monasteries in some areas subject to Roman law, had attained the status of colleges and foundations. As such they were capable of legal acts including the reception of gifts and bequests.[119] This legal status would be known to the missionaries, and

[116] Priests or children who seek to recover donations made by themselves or their parents are threatened with excommunication: Council of Agde (506), c. 4, cited above, p. 11, n. 26; Council of Clichy (626-627), c. 12, printed in Mansi, X, 595, where the text is given as c. 10 of a Council of Rheims; cf. K. F. v. Hefele, H. Leclercq *et al.*, *Histoire des conciles*, 11 vols. (Paris, 1907-52), III, 260, n. 2, 264-265.

[117] B. 107, 186; *EHD*, I, 441-443, no. 55.

[118] E.g. B. 45, 200.

[119] Duff, *art. cit.*, pp. 83-89; Lesne, *op. cit.*, I, 124-131; McLaughlin, *op. cit.*, pp. 34, 46, 58, 203 ff. It should be noted that the monasteries, founded by private individuals in England, would acquire some official recognition from the landbook by which lands and exemptions were given for the monastery. In the making of the landbook both royal and ecclesiastical powers were associated.

the first foundations in Kent would, in their eyes at least, be considered in this way. But ecclesiastical property was vested in the bishops and abbots or monastic founders, and these persons, members of the highest class as they so often were, tended to obscure the community over which they presided.[120] This was especially true of many of the religious houses. As the monastic movement developed, a rich variety of foundations appeared.[121] The king might grant land directly to some ecclesiastic so that he could establish a religious house. A layman might seek land for such a purpose from the king, or he might devote his own land to it, seeking a royal charter and the privileges and exemptions usually attached to such an establishment. In the case where a layman proceeded to implement his declared intention, his own relationship to the community could be of many sorts: he might enter it as abbot, or as a simple religious; he might remain in the lay state and, having appointed a religious to direct the community, take charge of its temporal affairs; he might found a family monastery with the intention that it pass to his descendants.[122] From time to time he found himself without a community at all. In most of the smaller monasteries, and they were in the majority,[123] the abbot or founder dominated the scene. Yet, as Maitland has remarked, there was no legal theory that would make it possible to regard such a person as a corporation sole or a trustee.[124] Given these conceptions of ownership, ecclesiastical holdings must often have been considered to be the property of the bishop, abbot or founder, who controlled them. In these conditions there was considerable danger that the family of the head of an ecclesiastical body would seek to succeed to the estates which their deceased relative had controlled. It mattered little whether these possessions had been brought to the church by him or by the gift of others. In Eddi's eyes, Saint Wilfrid was the owner of many monasteries. His repeated remark that the dying abbot should make a division of his property and appoint

---

120 On the "aristocratic character" of the Church of the time, with special reference to England, see Levison, *op. cit.*, p. 27, n. 2, and Stenton, *Anglo-Saxon England*, p. 162.

121 *Ibid.*, pp. 157-162.

122 E.g., the monastery founded by Saint Willibrord's father came eventually, "legitime successione," to Alcuin; cf. Stenton, *op. cit.*, pp. 162, 163, no. 1. The monastery of Abbot Headda (B. 283), is another example; but in this case arrangements were made that if the donor's family failed to provide a suitable head for the *monasteriola*, the property was to pass to one of the greater and more stable foundations. Cf. B. 154, 236 and H. XV; also *Gesetze*, II, 539-540, *s.v.* "Kirchenherr."

123 Knowles, *The Monastic Order*, p. 22, n. 2.

124 *Domesday Book and Beyond*, p. 242.

his successors is worthy of careful consideration.[125]   Bede informs us that Cedd, bishop of London, at the time of his death in 664, gave the direction of his monastery at Lastingham to his brother Ceadda.[126] Even more important information is provided by the account of the last days of Benedict Biscop.   Here we are told that in accord with the rule of Saint Benedict and a privilege of the Pope, the new abbot is to be chosen *iuxta vitae modum et doctrinae . . . industriam,* rather than as *succesorem generis.*[127]   It is quite evident from the account that a claim to succession by Benedict's brother, a man of little merit, was anticipated. The danger extended not only to the monastery of Jarrow of which Benedict was abbot, but also to his other foundation at Wearmouth, whose abbot, Sigrid, was ill and soon to die.[128]

Whether they came from Rome or from Gaul, the first missionaries to England were familiar with the Roman testament and may be presumed to have known something of the teaching of the Fathers on its use.   They would quickly realize that there was need of some of the powers it gave a proprietor.   Historians have generally agreed that the charter was an ecclesiastical importation, but they have not given sufficient emphasis to the fact that the transaction that lies beyond the charter, in its motive and in many of its effects, was also the work of

---

[125] *Vita Wilfridi,* ch. 61, ed. Levison, p. 257: "Tunc omnis familia cum intimo cordis merore consueta arma orationum arripiens, die noctuque indesinenter canentes et deprecantes Dominum concedere ei inducias vitae, saltem ad loquendum et domus suas ad disponendas possessionesque dividendas, et ne nos quasi orbatos sine abbatibus relinqueret... Et, Deo concedente, ita factum est, ut et omnem vitam nostram in diversis locis secundum suum desiderium sub praepositis a se electis constitueret et substantiam suam intus et foris Deo et hominibus suo iudicio dispertiret, quod ante non perficerat." See above p. 91. In an act before witnesses, Wilfrid associated the priest Tatberht with himself in the rule of the monastery, with the understanding that the associated abbot should succeed: *ibid.,* chs. 62-63, ed. Levison, pp. 257-259.

[126] Bede, *Historia Ecclesiastica,* Bk. III, ch. 23, ed. Plummer, I, 176.

[127] *Historia Abbatum auctore anonymo,* ch. 16, in *Venerabilis Bedae Opera Historica,* ed. Plummer, I, 393-394.   The same events are described even more colourfully in Bede's version: *Historia Abbatum,* chs. 6, 11, ed. Plummer, I, 369, 374-376; see Levison, *England and the Continent,* pp. 24-29.   The privilege was given to Benedict for Wearmouth by Pope Agatho in 679.   It was later confirmed by Pope Sergius who probably extended it to Jarrow.   In his account of the dedication of the new church at Ripon, Eddi mentions that several abbots and abbesses made Wilfrid their heir or gave him ownership of their monasteries immediately: "Ideo namque pene omnes abbates et abbatissae coenobiorum, aut sub suo nomine secum substantias custodientes aut post obitum suum heredem illum habere optantes, voto voverunt" (ch. 21, ed. Levison, p. 216).

[128] In a private conversation Professor E. F. Bruck remarked how much the action of Wilfrid and that of Benedict Biscop resembled an adoption.   Cf. Maitland, *Domesday Book and Beyond,* pp. 242-243.

ecclesiastics.[129]   It is suggested that the reason for the introduction of this important right to control the devolution of land after the death of the owner was the desire to protect church property from the families of deceased clerics.   The right might often have been exercised in favour of a member of the family.   But even this action placed ecclesiastical office, and the control of property that went with it, in the hands of a suitable person and removed them from the power of other members of the family.[130]   When the first generation of church leaders had passed from the scene, Anglo-Saxons held most of the positions of ecclesiastical importance.   This meant that large estates were controlled by men whose families lived in England.   Given the legal system of the time, it was quite reasonable for these families to consider themselves to have some rights in the estates which seemed to be the property of their clerical relatives.   It is suggested that under these circumstances a way was found to protect church lands by the assertion of the right to bequeath them by will.   The right was not used to alienate land from the Church, but to keep it out of the control of those relatives of important churchmen who would divert it to secular uses.[131]

It is very probable that the clergy saw some advantage in fostering the possession of land with similar rights by certain lay magnates. For the laymen, who obtained land intending to use it for some religious purpose, or obtained ecclesiastical privilege for their own land with the same intention, did not always proceed immediately to found a monastery or to give the land to a foundation already in existence.[132]   Alms given during life, involving direct personal sacrifice as they did, were preferred for penitential reasons.   But, even though the grantees of bookland may have intended to carry out their foundation or endowment as soon as possible, there were often causes that militated against their doing so.   Present necessity, uncertainty as to future needs of a family, long term preparation for what was a major undertaking would frequently provide motives for the delay of transfer of property.   Though these estates were not yet in the Church's possession, those concerned with ecclesiastical needs would see many advantages in allowing them to enjoy the privileges of Church property: among other benefits, it

---

129 Cf. Jolliffe's remarks, *EHR*, L (1935), 8-10.

130 As in B. 156, 283.

131 Professor Bruck cites an example at Constantinople where abbots passed their powers on to successors by a series of wills lasting until the twelfth century. The continuance of the monastery was like that of a foundation based on a chain of trustees; cf. "The Growth of Foundations in Roman Law and Civilization," *Seminar* VI (1948), p. 18.

132 Cf. Stenton's reconstruction of the evidence concerning Abbot Haeha, *The Early History of the Abbey of Abingdon*, pp. 18-19.

permitted the gift at death, where the alms given *inter vivos* had not been forthcoming.

By the end of the eighth century, the pressures that had produced the *Eigenkirche* and *Eigenkloster* on the Continent had been felt in England and had taken their effect there.[133]   Yet in the early stages of the resistance to the movement, the freedom of alienation of property at death, which proved to be such an important apprenticeship for many Anglo-Saxons in the possibilities of private ownership,[134] was probably introduced to oppose lay encroachment and preserve as much freedom for the Church as the conditions of that very difficult time would permit.

In England of the seventh and early eighth centuries, possession of land with the right of perpetual inheritance and with freedom of alienation was virtually unknown among the laity.   The advantages of ownership in the new manner, introduced for the Church, must have been remarkable.   There were other privileges, both financial and legal, from which such estates benefited. These seem to have varied considerably and could even be added to rights already possessed in an estate.[135]   As might be expected, the laity sought to share such privileges, though at first the means adopted were considered to be reprehensible. Bede has left us an unforgettable account of the evils of such abuse.[136] However, in the reign of Offa, it becomes evident that some laymen held estates enjoying ecclesiastical privileges, and that they had been granted to them by the king without the intention that they should eventually be used to endow the Church.   An early example (779) is an original charter of this king, whereby he granted land, near the Windrush River in Gloucestershire, to his thegn Dudda.[137]   Though

[133] For a general summary of studies on the proprietary church and monastery, see Knowles, *The Monastic Order*, pp. 562-568, where the conclusions of Stutz, his school and their critics are presented and related to England.   McLaughlin, *Le très ancien droit monastique*, pp. 232-238, presents the findings of French historians somewhat more fully.   References to certain aspects of the problem may be found in Levison, *op. cit.*, pp. 27-33, 249-259. All agree that the movement was well under way in England during the first half of the eighth century.   Bede says that it began after the death of Aldfrith (704) and, in his letter to King Æthelbald, Boniface dates these encroachments from the first decade of the century: *Epistolae Bede ad Ecgbertum Episcopum*, chs. 10-13, in Bede, *Opera Hist.*, ed. Plummer, I, 414-417, II, 386; *S. Bonifatii et Lulli Epistolae*, no. 73, ed. Tangl, pp. 152-153.

[134] Wurdinger, "Einwirkungen des Christentums," *ZRG Germ. Abt.*, LV (1935), 112.

[135] B. 148 (*EHD*, I, 450-451, no. 65) is the earliest surviving document which refers to immunities.   It is clear from the text, however, that immunities were already common in ecclesiastical estates.   The charter is dated 732; cf. H. XII.

[136] See above, n. 133.

[137] B. 230; cf. Stenton, *Anglo-Saxon England*, p. 305, and Eric John, *Land Tenure in Early England*, pp. 77-79.

the document employs the usual formulae implying grant in alms, the fact that the grantee was permitted to give his land to any of his kinsmen and that they were protected from forfeiture, would seem to indicate that the grant had no ecclesiastical purpose. Such charters occurred fairly frequently, in the provinces under Mercian domination, as the eighth century drew to a close.[138]

Lay estates, held in perpetuity with hereditary right, became more and more common in the following century.[139]   In the *Rectitudines Singularum Personarum,* a document compiled in the early years of the reign of the Confessor, possession by book-right is presented as characteristic of the thegn.   This is confirmed by Cnut's law, stating that the landowner, who had acquitted his obligations, had the right of disposal during life and at death.[140]   The power to bequeath their estates was probably possessed by most lay recipients of bookland from the beginning.   No doubt, the fact that their estate was perpetual was much more precious to them than their right to alienate it.[141]   None

[138] B. 248; cf. Stenton, *op. cit.,* pp. 206, 519. This charter should be compared with the following: B. 247 (785), of which it is perhaps an expansion; B. 248 (an almost contemporary copy), which shows that the property, or part of it, had already been possessed by the grantee's father, so that the charter may deal with a grant of rights in the land rather than a gift of the property itself; B. 282 (796), which was rejected by Stevenson in his edition of Asser's *Life of Alfred,* pp. 205-206, and by Stenton in *Early History of Abingdon,* p. 27, but since accepted in its main lines by the latter, *Latin Charters,* pp. 25-27; B. 318. The formulae, derived from the grant in alms, are abandoned in B. 254 (788), a charter of King Offa. This very important document is the only one of its type to survive; see Stenton's remarks, *Latin Charters,* pp. 38-39.

[139] There was only a slight possibility that a charter granted to a layman would survive, in cases where the document and the property with which it dealt did not come into the possession of some ecclesiastical foundation. Older historians, judging on the basis of charter survivals, concluded that these grants were not common: cf. P. and M. II, 254-255; Maitland, *Domesday Book and Beyond,* pp. 257, 315-316; Holdsworth, *History,* II 70. There is one important exception: Earle, who wrote seventy years ago, considered laymen's charters to have been very common, more common, in fact, than those held by the Church (*A Handbook of Land-Charters,* p. lxxv). The recent study of the charters supplemented by a careful use of literary evidence, has shown that by the time of Alfred possession of bookland by the laity was of frequent occurrence; see Stenton's criticism of Maitland in *Early History of Abingdon,* pp. 43-44, and the developed statement of his position in *Latin Charters,* pp. 60-65.

[140] *Rectitudines,* I (*Gesetze,* I, 444; *EHD,* II, 81-83); II Cnut, 79 (*Gesetze,* I, 366-367). On the frequency of possession by book-right in the last years of the Anglo-Saxon kingdom see P. Vinogradoff, *English Society in the Eleventh Century* (Oxford, 1908), p. 255.

[141] "Every man hopes when he has built a dwelling-place on land loaned from his lord that he may rest on it for a time and hunt and hawk and fish and get a living somehow for himself from that loan... until through his lord's kindness he has earned bookland and perpetual possession" (Alfred's preface to his rendering of the *Soliloquies* of St. Augustine cited by Stenton, *Latin Charters,* p. 62).

the less, both rights were possessed. Thus, when forms of possession introduced for the Church passed to the laity, family hopes were at once increased and diminished; they were increased because the owner possessed in perpetuity and could arrange for succession by his children; but they were also diminished because it was frequently within his power to deny all family rights in his estate. He did not have to seek the permission of his children if he chose to alienate his bookland.[142]

In many of the landbooks of the ninth and tenth centuries, the clauses describing the power of alienation might seem to limit the right of bequest. In these charters, the earlier form—*cuicunque voluerit tradere... post obitum*—is often abandoned, being replaced by *cuicunque herede tibi placuerit derelinquendam,* or some similar phrase. Maitland was of the opinion that these clauses were not restrictive, the word *heres* being used in a general way, referring to any successor, rather than to a kinsman exclusively.[143] A study of the landbooks and *wills* from this point of view substantiates his position. Thus, for example, in a will of about 855, Dunn gave an estate to St. Andrew's Rochester, after the death of himself and his wife. The property had been obtained from King Æthelwulf, with the right of leaving it after his day to whatever heir (*cuicunque herede*) he wished.[144] There were restrictive forms, however: sometimes the inheritance was limited to the family, though the holder of the book was free to choose within that group; occasionally the freedom was restricted to a choice within the male line.[145]

Other estates in land were alienable by will as well. Thus land held by lease for several lives, was sometimes freely disposable at death, within the limits of time set by the lease itself.[146] It is not likely, how-

---

[142] H. Cabot Lodge, "The Anglo-Saxon Land Law," *Essays in Anglo-Saxon Law,* laid considerable emphasis on the necessity of family consent. Maitland refused to adopt this position inasmuch as it applied to bookland, refuting the argument based on B. 313 (P. and M., II, 253, n. 1).

[143] P. and M., II, 254, n. 4. Lodge, *art. cit.,* p. 71 considered the phrase to be restrictive.

[144] Compare B. 486 and R. IX; B. 449 and R. VI; B. 442 and H. VII. In the last case, a widow arranged that her husband's family have right of pre-emption in his property; the proceeds of the sale were to be devoted to alms.

[145] A law of Alfred (41) ordered that restrictions, whether made by donor or recipient, were to be acted upon; see above, p. 62. On limiations, see Earle, *A Handbook,* p. xx. Examples of limitations to the family: B. 254; in *wills:* W. XI (p. 28, line 11), XVIII (p. 52, line 29), XIX (p. 54, line 23). Examples of limitations to the male line: B. 244, 524; in *wills:* H. XI (pp. 18-19).

[146] An early example is provided by the text of a lease for two lives by Denebeorht, bishop of Worcester, to Balthun, a priest: "ut hanc etiam terram possedeat et postquam viam patrum incedat duobus post se heredibus quibus vellet relinquat;" this charter (B. 304, dated *ca.* 802) is discussed by J. A. Robinson in *St. Oswald and the Church of Worcester,*

ever, that folkland ever became sufficiently free of the claims of inheritance to be commonly bequeathed. Some seventy years ago, in an essay that has been the point of departure for all subsequent discussion of folkland, Sir Paul Vinogradoff argued that freedom of bequest was one of the qualities that distinguished tenure by book-right from other forms of possession.[147]   His basic argument remains valid for, though there have been several attempts to show that folkland was freely bequeathed at least during the last two centuries before the conquest of England by the Normans, they have not been successful.[148] It is true that occasionally such bequests occurred; but they were made with the permission of the king or the consent of the heir.[149]   There are several surviving examples which show this method of procedure in operation.[150]

During the last century of the Anglo-Saxon kingdom another limitation of the power of bequest appeared.   As the lower levels of the thegn class and free peasants tended to seek the protection of the powerful, the rising claims of lordship limited these freemen in the disposal

p. 9.   Other examples: DdB, I, 177a; R. XXXVI et passim.   In a codicil to R. XXXV the lessee indicates those who will enjoy the leased property after his death.

[147] "Folkland," EHR, VIII (1893), 1-17.   Vinogradoff developed his position in Growth of the Manor, 2nd ed. (London, 1904), p. 209 and in "The Transfer of Land in Old English Law," Collected Papers, I, 150, 157.

[148] Vinogradoff's position was criticized by G. J. Turner, "Bookland and Folkland," Essays in Honour of James Tait, ed. J. G. Edwards, V. H. Galbraith and E. F. Jacob (Manchester, 1933), p. 363; free bequest of folkland is suggested by J. E. A. Jolliffe, "English Book-Right," EHR, L (1935), 20 and in The Constitutional History of Medieval England (London, 1937), pp. 73-74.   See the summary of this discussion and the conclusions thereto in Plucknett, "Bookland and Folkland," Econ. Hist. Rev., VI (1936), 71-72; cf. Stenton, Anglo-Saxon England, p. 304 and John, Land Tenure in Early England, pp. 15-16.

[149] See Plucknett, art. cit.; P. and M., II, 254-255; W. p. xxxv, n. 1.

[150] E.g., DdB, I, 336b: Godric, son of Garewin, became a monk at Peterborough and the abbot seized a ploughland he had held in Lincoln.   The burgesses maintained, however, that the land could not pass outside the kindred and the city without the permission of the king;   cited by P. Vinogradoff, English Society in the Eleventh Century, p. 256. Ramsey Chronicon, pp. 169-170, is the account of opposition to the execution of a will bequeathing land to the abbey, based on the testator's failure to obtain royal permission or family consent.   There is probably a similar basis to the opposition by the son of Goding the monk to his father's bequest to Ely; see Liber Eliensis, BK. II, ch. 26.   In H. Writs, 2, Tole, widow of Urk, is given royal permission to bequeath land to the monastery at Abbotsbury.   K. 964, a document from the late twelfth-century register of Evesham, contains Ælfgar's testimony that Ordwicus bequeathed land to Evesham with his permission.   In its present state the document reads like a twelfth-century writ of confirmation, but the transaction which it describes is quite likely a bequest made with the lord's permission and may refer to folkland.

of their lands.[151] Many lesser thegns held their lands as a gift from their lord and, in the words of *Domesday Book,* could neither give nor sell without his permission. This limitation applied to the bequest of land as well. Many others, lesser thegns and free peasants who had estates of their own—folkland that had come to them by acquisition or inheritance—found it necessary to seek the protection of the powerful. It is also likely that, with the passage of time and the decline of family fortune. some holders of bookland were forced to seek support among the great. According to *Domesday Book* these freemen could alienate their properties without interference from their lord. Yet whatever the legal principle may have been, the complaints of men such as Wulfstan, regarding the oppression of lesser freeman,[152] lead one to conclude that these persons found the permission of the lord to be a necessary preliminary to an attempted bequest of land.[153]

The amount of land with which the wills dealt, and the size of the bequests to different individuals, varied exceedingly. The total area bequeathed by the Kentish reeve, Æthelnoth, seems to have been but three ploughlands, while the will of Wulfric Spott distributed considerably more than seventy estates spread over eleven counties.[154] Bequests of two or three acres are not unknown, while, at the other extreme, the gift of several estates to a single donee are of frequent occurrence.[155]

The Distribution of Movable Property at Death

The initial freedom of bequest among the Germanic races, as among others, was exercised over that part of a person's property which was most fully his own—personal equipment identified with the past and

---

[151] See above, p. 71 and n. 17, and Stenton, *Anglo-Saxon England,* pp. 481-483.

[152] Cf. *Sermo Lupi ad Anglos,* line 47. One version of the text has an important addition at this point: "Free men are not allowed to keep their independence, nor go where they wish, nor to deal with their own property as they wish;" see ed. Whitelock, p. 28, textual variant to line 47 and the translation in *EHD,* I, 856, n. 4.

[153] In W. XXXI, the *will* of Thurstan, a bequest of a hide at Dullingham was made to Viking, the testator's servant. In the *Inquisitio Comitatus Cantabrigiensis,* f. 90b, ed. N. E. Hamilton (London, 1876), p. 18, the recipient is presented as the "man" of Earl Harold, and could not alienate his property; cited by Miss Whitelock in W. p. 194; cf. Vinogradoff, *English Society,* pp. 473-474.

[154] See extreme examples such as R. III (cf. B. 318) and W. XVII (cf. Whitelock, *The Beginnings,* pp. 86-87).

[155] Several bequests of a few acres are to be found in the *will* of Edwin (W. XXXIII); grants of several estates to a single donee, usually a child or an ecclesiastical institution, are common: e.g., W. II, XIV, XV, XVII, etc.

future needs of the individual.[156]   Other chattels, farm stock and equipment, which in an agrarian economy were closely bound up with the productivity of the land, became fully disposable more slowly. With certain important exceptions, they tended to become suitable matter for distribution at death, as the land itself did, and it was with the land that they were usually bequeathed.

Though the total value of movable property distributed in surviving Anglo-Saxon *wills* was probably less than the value of the land with which they dealt, chattels are of special interest.   They were the most common form of bequest in a society in which the possession of land, let alone the right to alienate it, lay outside the hopes of a large part of the population.   Movable property, by its nature, did not easily lend itself to donation by *post obit* gift.   In Anglo-Saxon England there does not seem to have been a statement of the principle *donner et retiner ne vaut*,[157] but the perishable quality of many chattels imposed at least partial compliance with it.   A testator might desire and even promise to give a sum of money and a certain number of cattle, but since such forms of wealth existed to be exchanged or consumed, he could not transfer a right to the donee in any given coins or animals.   Furthermore, since many events could intervene between the making of a bequest and its execution, the total value of movable property of a perishable nature could not be determined until the time of death.   These bequests, then, took on a certain ambulatory quality that is typical of the Roman *donatio mortis causa:* the donation could not become fully effective until the time of death.[158]   On the other hand, pieces of military equipment, valuable household furnishings, jewellery, books and church ornaments were more stable forms of wealth.   They could be bequeathed with reasonable confidence that the precise thing, of which gift was made, would still exist when the time of execution arrived.

There does not seem to have been any need for an explicit reservation of the use of chattels for life, though the effect was often accomplished by attaching them to a gift of land which was so reserved.[159]   It is for this reason that the movable property, which was bequeathed with land,

---

156 See above, pp. 6-8.

157 Cf. Goffin, *The Testamentary Executor*, p. 21; Huebner, *History*, p. 745.

158 On the *donatio mortis causa* see below, p. 132.

159 This fact is made especially clear in a sentence from the bequest of an estate at Rimpton to the Old Minster at Winchester, where, the donation having been stated, the *will* continues: "on condition that he is to have the use of the estate as long as his life lasts, and afterwards it is to go to that foundation, stocked as it is with cattle and men and all things, for the comfort of his soul." (W. VII, p. 18, lines 18-21; translation, p. 19.)

leaves but little sign of its presence in the written *wills*. Specific bequest of chattels, independently of the gift of land, was very often made by *verba novissima*. It will be recalled that Bede disposed of a few possessions in this way. Other gifts of the same sort are frequently to be found among the bequests of the *cwide,* and were often made by means of an intermediary. Saint Wilfrid bequeathed a considerable fortune in gold, silver and jewellery towards the end of his life, and he entrusted several friends with its execution. It is the bequest of more precious possessions, the sort, actually, that were once part of the endowment of graves, that finds most frequent mention in literary sources and in the Anglo-Saxon *wills* themselves.

Prior to the middle of the tenth century, the written *wills* give little information on the bequest of chattels; their purpose was to serve as evidence of *post obit* distributions of land.[160] After that date, however, chattels appear more frequently and, in a few cases, written *wills* were devoted almost entirely to them.[161] Two distributions of the ninth century gave sizable and precise numbers of oxen, cattle, sheep and swine, to different donees.[162] In King Alfred's *will* stock is mentioned in passing, but large donations are indicated as money gifts, about two thousand pounds in all.[163] Where farm stock is mentioned in the *wills* of the tenth and eleventh centuries, it appears that most of it was being donated with the estate to which it belonged, or that at least a minimum complement was maintained on these properties.[164] Horses

---

[160] Cf. W. p. 100.

[161] E.g., H. XXI; *C. C.* X.

[162] The bequests of Abba the Reeve (H. II) included at least 17 cows, 14 oxen, 200 sheep and 100 swine; those of Ælfred (H. X), 2400 swine, and more if they were available,— an excellent example of the ambulatory quality of some bequests that was mentioned above, pp. 40-41.

[163] H. XI, p. 18, lines 11 ff. In one *will* of the mid-tenth century (B. 812), Æthelgiva bequeathed farm-stock in much the same manner as did Abba and Ælfred (see previous note): 20 cows, 30 oxen, 250 sheep as well as 2 horses and dogs to the king for her heriot. On the use of the term "heriot," applied to women's bequests to the king, see above, p. 82.

[164] Cf. P. and M., II, 2. Estates are usually given "with all that is on it" or "with cattle and men and all things." In some cases more details are given: Bishop Theodred arranged that stock, equivalent to that which had been on the episcopal estate at Hoxne when he received it, should remain, but that the increase be distributed for his soul (W. I, p. 4); Wynflæd held a life interest in an estate at Chinnock and gave stock and slaves to her daughter, except six oxen, four cows and four calves, which were left with the property (W. III, p. 13); Æthelflæd distributed half the stock of each of her villages, the residue remaining with the estates apparently (W. XIV, p. 37); Ælfric Modercope granted Lodden to St. Edmund's and Burgh to Ely. His sheep, he divided in two parts, "half for Loddon

appear in almost every *cwide* as part of the heriot given the king.[165]   It is quite evident that the bequest of farm-stock, as indicated by the *wills*, did not tend to strip the land of the equipment that was necessary for its cultivation.   There is evidence, rather, of considerable preoccupation with maintaining livestock at the level required for the exploitation of land.

Slaves, like animals, were included in the equipment of an estate. As will be seen, many were given their freedom as part of the charitable bequest of their owner.   However, many remained in their condition and they, too, were usually left with the land to which they belonged.[166] Occasionally slaves were moved from an estate, having been bequeathed to a donee other than the owner of the property on which they had lived.[167]

During the tenth and eleventh centuries, the usual means of making bequests of large value, separate from, and other than land, was by the gift of money.   This use had appeared even earlier among the very first reports of *post obit* distribution;[168] but the few examples of the ninth century seem to indicate that bequests were often made by the transfer of large numbers of livestock.   The sums mentioned, at least in the *wills* of the upper class, are often very large.   They indicate an important use and accumulation of precious metal and specie at the time. The sum of Alfred's distribution has already been mentioned.   King Eadred's *will* indicated bequests of considerably more than two thousand pounds and many thousand gold mancuses.[169]   He even provided the metal that two thousand of these coins might be struck for distribution. Wills of lesser persons included bequests of proportionately large sums of money.[170]

and half for Burgh"—an interesting indication of his point of view: he was providing stock for an estate given in alms (W. XXVIII).   Precise numbers of animals are mentioned in a few cases: W. XVII, XIX.

[165] The specific mention of the bequest of horses is of more frequent occurrence than that of any other kind of live stock, an indication of their special value; cf. W. p. 238, *s.v.*, "horses," and *C.C.*, X.

[166] See above, n. 164.

[167] As in the *will* of Wynflæd (W. III, p. 12, lines 26-31), where the testator had a life estate in Chinnock, but stock and men were hers.   The slaves and some of the stock were bequeathed to her grand-daughter.

[168] Wilfrid's distribution of treasure has already been mentioned.   Dunwald, donor of an estate to Christ Church (B. 192), was on his way to Rome to deliver the alms of the recently deceased King Æthelberht II (762).   Large bequests to persons or communities outside the country could scarcely have been delivered except in this way.

[169] H. XXI.

[170] E.g., *C.C.* X; W. I, III, VIII, X, XXVIII.   It has been suggested that bequests of

Of other chattels mentioned in the *wills*, there is a considerable variety, but rarely any sign of an attempt to distribute the minutia of household furnishings.[171] Here once again, to succeed to a property was, normally, to succeed to its equipment. The *wills* of men dwell with "loving precision" on war gear, horse furnishings, and the mounts themselves.[172] Ships too, sometimes fully equipped for war, are among their bequests.[173] Bishops *wills* show a special interest in relics, chalices, vestments and church equipment generally, though similar gifts were frequently made by the laity as well.[174] In the *wills* of women, somewhat more concern with detail is shown. Jewellery, tapestries, gold and silver vessels, horns, bed furnishings, gowns, were of special interest of course; but occasionally the written *wills* reflect arrangements for the distribution of more common household and personal equipment among sons, daughters and servants.[175] Tents, the use and apparent value of which are a comment both on the conditions of the time and the considerable mobility of members of the upper class, appear as bequests in several *wills*.[176]

In the time of the Confessor and long before, churches were generally owned by individuals, who could dispose of them as they wished.[177] The specific mention of the bequest of a church or a monastery is rather

---

this kind provided one of the chief sources of capital for the purchase of land during the monastic expansion of the last thirty years of the tenth century; cf. J. A. Raftis, *The Estates of Ramsey Abbey,* pp. 7-11. There are signs, however, that the money required for bequests was frequently not on hand. The testator arranged the sale of certain estates to provide it: e.g., W. XXVI, p. 72.

171 Cf. Whitelock, *The Beginnings,* p. 96. On the bequest of chattels in general see *ibid,* pp. 89-99.

172 The phrase is Miss Whitelock's, *ibid.,* p. 95. The supreme example of this sort of *will* is that of Æthelstan the Ætheling (W. XX).

173 W. XIII, XVIII; *C.C.* X.

174 Examples of such gifts by the laity are to be found in W. III, p. 10; VIII, p. 20; XX, p. 58; XXI, p. 62 *et passim.*

175 The *will* of Wynflæd (W. III, *ca.* 950) is a good example: at least thirty-two slaves are mentioned by name, and provision made for the freedom of others should there be more at the time of her death; to her daughter Æthelflæd, she left "everything which is unbequeathed, books and such small things;" further on, Æthelflæd is given "the utensils and all the things inside" (inside a homestead apparently). The *will* of Wulfwaru (W. XXI, 984-1016) contains many similar bequests.

176 W. III, XVIII, XXVIII. The last example is the tent which Ælfric Modercope took with him on his journey over-sea.

177 Cf. the study of H. Boehmer, "Das Eigenkirchentum in England," in *Texte und Forschungen zur Englischen Kulturgeschichte; Festgabe für Felix Liebermann* (Halle, 1921), pp. 319-321, cited by D. Knowles, *The Monastic Order,* pp. 593-594 and notes.

rare in the later *wills*, however.[178] . It would seem that, in most cases, churches were bequeathed with the estate to which they were attached. A phrase from a writ of the Confessor which grants a property "with church and with mill" supports this conclusion.[179] The specific mention of mills is also very rare, though it does occur.[180] In both cases, churches and mills were bequeathed with the rights that appertained to them.

It would seem that almost any right in persons or in things could be alienated at death.[181] One of the bequests most frequently mentioned in the written *wills* was the gift of rights attached to land. Their precise import is not usually indicated.[182] Perhaps the most common bequest of a right was the gift of freedom to slaves.[183] It is to be found in almost every *cwide*. In earlier *wills* a distinction was sometimes made between men enslaved for crime (*witeþeow*) and other slaves (*þeow*).[184] After Ethelred's time, the distinction disappeared.[185] A council of 816 ordered that bishops free their English slaves, and episcopal *wills* show that this prescription was obeyed.[186] Usually the slaves to be freed were indicated generally ("all the men," or "half the men"), but at least thirty-two were mentioned by name in the *will* of Wynflæd.[187] Occa-

178 Bequests of churches are made in W. I, p. 2; W. XXXVII; R. CXVI; and confirmed in W. XXIX.

179 H. *Writs*, 85, pp. 351-352; "mid circe and mid milne."

180 W. XXVI, p. 72, lines 16, 18; XXXI, p. 80, line 30; the last bequest is so worded as to imply that the testator owned several mills and apparently bequeathed them, though all but the one mentioned seem to have been included in the gift of land.

181 Cf. Jolliffe, *Constitutional History*, p. 90, n. 3.

182 "With as full rights as ever I owned it" (*so ful and so forth so ic it formist ahte*) or some similar expression was used to describe bequeathed rights in general. Some, of course, were specified: the right of ingress and egress (or the obligation to allow them) as in W. XXV, XXIX, XXXIV; fishing rights as in W. I, XVII. Cf. W. p. 242, s.v. "Swa ful."

183 Cf. *C.C.* p. 132, note to X, line 28; W. pp. 111-112, 239 s.v. "Manumission clauses."

184 Thus Bishop Theodred freed his slaves without distinction (W. I), while Archbishop Ælfric freed the penally enslaved (W. XVIII), and Bishop Ælfwold of Crediton freed both penal and purchased slaves (*C.C.* X).

185 Miss Whitelock remarks (W. p. 112) that all the later references to manumission are from East Anglia, an area in which, so far as can be concluded from the information available, the distinction was not made in *wills*.

186 Council at Celchyth, ch. 10 (Haddan and Stubbs, III, 583). See W. I, IV, XVIII, *C.C.* X. No mention of 'English' slaves is to be found in episcopal *wills*. It would appear that some bishops did not consider themselves to be bound to free the slaves on the estates that were part of their personal holdings, as distinguished from those which they held as bishop: thus at Hoxne, an episcopal estate, though only the acquisitions in farm-stock were distributed, all the men were to be freed, while at Lothingland, an estate that apparently belonged to the bishop's patrimony and which he bequeathed to his nephews, only half the men were to be freed (W. I, p. 4, lines 14-16; p. 2, lines 31-32 and p. 4, lines 1-2).

187 W. III, pp. 10-12.

sionally the testator imposed the condition of good service between the time of making the will and his death.[188] The number of slaves freed in this way gives every indication of being a large one. It shows that there was an important counter-movement to the steady recruitment of the slave class due to economic and legal difficulties. The work force, available for the farming of the estates to which slaves had belonged, was probably not largely changed, but the status, obligations and rights of the members of that force saw considerable alteration due to these manumissions by will. Occasionally the freed slave received the bequest of a homestead and equipment.[189]

Some of the *wills* contain the donation of land on which lived freedmen, geburs and others, who had a higher status than the slaves, but owed certain services to the lord of the estate. The bequest of their services is mentioned specifically in a few *wills*.[190] In other cases this donation is probably implicit in the gift of the land on which these peasants lived.

The bequest of a right of pre-emption in lands or chattels was not unknown. In a few cases, the property in question was to be sold at a price considerably less than its actual value, so that the bequest was at once a gift to the purchaser and a means of obtaining money to be given in alms, or used for some other purpose.[191]

Towards the end of the Anglo-Saxon period, the privilege of receiving the profits of jurisdiction was acquired by some private individuals. This right, too, became the object of bequest in some cases.[192] The

---

[188] As in W. XXV, p. 70, line 13; cf. W. p. 181, n. to line 13.

[189] W. XXIV, p. 68, lines 3-4; XXXIV, p. 88, lines 22-23.

[190] In W. XXXVI, Thurkil and Æthelgyth bequeath a property with its men—"half free and slaves and freedmen." In W. III, p. 12, lines 27-28, geburs dwelling on rented land are given with an estate. These bequests are donations of rights to certain payments due from members of these classes, rather than the donation of the men themselves; cf. W. pp. 112, 165, 206. Several levels of servants, owing different payments to the lord are indicated in the *Rectitudines Singularum Personarum;* see above, p. 71.

[191] A right of pre-emption of land is given in H. II, VII, and is implied in W. XIII, p. 32, lines 16 ff; pre-emption at a special price is found in H. X. In H. II, the *will* of Abba the Reeve, bequest of a sword is made to Freothomund and he "is to give four thousand for it, and of this sum, thirteen hundred pence are to be given back to him" (p. 4, lines 9-11; translation, p. 41).

[192] Wulfric Spott gave the estate at Morton to Burton Abbey, "and eall seo socna þe ðærto hereð" (W. XVII, p. 48, lines 28-29). Professor Stenton suggests that this is an example of the "sokeland" of Domesday Book, from which lords received the profits of jurisdiction even though they did not own the land itself; see *Types of Manorial Structure in the Northern Danelaw,* Oxford Studies in Social and Legal History, II (Oxford, 1910), pp. 21 ff; cited by Miss Whitelock, W. p. 158. In a writ of the Confessor it is declared that

privilege of receiving the heriot from the holders of certain lands was bequeathed on at least one occasion.[193]   Still other privileges, such as freedom from toll, were mentioned in charters and, occasionally, they were granted with the right of bequest.[194]

The rather surprising extent to which the bequest of rights was used is one of the most remarkable qualities of the later Anglo-Saxon wills. By the last years of the kingdom, the idea seems to have been accepted that it was fitting to bequeath almost any source of revenue, provided that the necessary permission was obtained.   But grants of this sort were matters of privilege; they were made by persons of wealth and, like the *cwide* in which they were included, depended on the support of the powerful.   The bequest of land was also a matter of privilege or permission.   It would be a mistake, however, to underestimate its importance in the economic and family history of the time.   There are indications that it occurred rather often and that it sometimes involved very large estates.   But the gift of chattels at the end of life was the most common form of bequest.   It was at the disposition of a large part of the Anglo-Saxon population and, after the Norman Conquest, continued to be in general use.

the abbot and monks of St. Edmund's Bury are to have sake and soke over lands bequeathed to them "as fully and completely as he had them who was their former owner" (H. *Writs*, 12, pp. 156-157).   In this second case, a bequest of juridical rights may well have been implied.   The question of the existence of private courts in Anglo-Saxon England, one that has long been discussed and on which agreement can hardly yet be said to have been reached, cannot be investigated here; an introduction to the principal opinions is available in W. p. 158, and more recently, in H. *Writs*, pp. 73 ff.   Whatever right was possessed seems to have been an object of bequest.

193 W. XVII, p. 48, lines 27-28, and p. 157.

194 A charter of Æthelbald of Mercia, found among the seventeenth-century transcriptions of Richard James, exempted one ship of the bishop of London from toll and customs, and granted the right to bequeath the privilege (*Early Charters of S. Paul's,* ed. M. Gibbs, J. 14, pp. 6-7).   In the twelfth-century Bath cartulary, there is a charter in which King Edmund granted land to his thegn Æthelere, reserving to himself the right to bequeath the thegn's services to whomsoever he would: "Et meum post obitum cuicunque meorum amicorum voluero eadem fidelitate immobilis obediensque fiat" (B. 814); cf. Jolliffe's discussion of this charter, *Constitutional History,* p. 90, n. 3.

CHAPTER IV

THE WILL IN ENGLAND FROM THE CONQUEST
TO THE END OF THE THIRTEENTH CENTURY,
ITS NATURE AND EFFECT

SEVERAL of the gifts of land mentioned in the Anglo-Saxon *wills*
were never completed, for between the making of the bequest and
the delivery of the legacy England was conquered by the Normans.
This event brought the island into a closer relationship with the
Continent and exposed it more fully to the influence of important legal
progress which was being made there. New legal notions would
eventually lead to profound changes both in the theory and practice of
distribution of property at death. But the most far-reaching of these
modifications were not to appear until the second half of the twelfth
century; for the moment there was very little change either in the
extent to which this distribution occurred, or in the legal nature of the
acts whereby it was accomplished.[1] It is the purpose of this chapter to
demonstrate the continued use of the *post obit* gift and the death-bed gift
during the first generations after the Conquest, then, having sketched
the development of the canonical doctrine of the testament, to show
how this new instrument replaced the older acts of distribution in
England. Implementation and control of the canonical will and the
forms it assumed during the thirteenth century will be considered in the
succeeding chapter. A final chapter will deal with the distribution of
property at death from the Conquest to the late thirteenth century from
the point of view of the persons who made wills and the property with
which the wills were concerned.

I. THE *Post obit* GIFT AND THE DEATH-BED GIFT IN
ANGLO-NORMAN ENGLAND

One of the results of the subjection of the country by the Normans
and their allies was a fairly rapid replacement of the upper levels of
society both clerical and lay. The very persons who employed the
cwide to distribute their property at death, persons whose closeness to the

[1] See P. and M., II, 323-325; W. pp. xxxiii-xxxix.

Anglo-Saxon king helped to ensure the implementation of their desires, constituted the group that by the time of the Domesday inquest had largely disappeared.[2]   With them perished the *cwide* and the vernacular written *will* which listed its bequests.   It would be the thirteenth century before an instrument of similar flexibility would be commonly used again.

Yet, with this important exception, the radical change of personnel did not bring about a notable modification of the will in England. Distribution of property by means of the *post obit* gift and the death-bed gift continued as before.   It was one of the claims of the new dynasty that the regime which it imposed was but a continuation of the customs of the time of Edward.[3]   In this matter the claim seems generally to have been borne out, not because of any decision to adjust Norman customs to those of the conquered, but because the two racial groups forced together by circumstances found that they were in basic agreement about the will.   Norman and Anglo-Saxon practices had developed along similar lines.

The Distribution of Property at Death in Normandy before the Conquest

The obscurity of Norman institutions in the generations before the Conquest is well known.[4]   No collections of laws, no treatises discussing legal practice have survived; it is quite unlikely that they ever existed. Cartularies and the occasional original document provide the chief source of information, and even this is comparatively restricted. Enough evidence is extant, however, to conclude that in the disposition of property at death Norman practice was generally similar to that found throughout the rest of Northern France.[5]

The *post obit* gift of land with reservation for one or several lives is of fairly frequent occurrence.   Sometimes, as among the Anglo-Saxons, the right of the donee was recognized by the payment of rent by the donor and others to whom the property was reserved.[6]   The gift of land

2 See Stenton, *Anglo-Saxon England*, pp. 614-618, 671.

3 Examples of this point of view are many.   Manifestations in official documents may be found in William's London Charter and in the Coronation Charter of Henry I, c. ? (*Gesetze*, I, 486, 522).

4 C. H. Haskins, *Norman Institutions* (Cambridge, Mass., 1925), pp. 1-5, 241-249.

5 See Auffroy, *Testament*, pp. 402-421.   On the custom in Brittany, an area from which a considerable part of the invading army was drawn, see A. Perraud, *Etude sur le testament en Bretagne*, pp. 33-45.

6 E.g., a grant (*ca.* 1060) by Godfrey the cook and his wife of an arpent of vines; they were to continue to cultivate the vineyard, but gave the monks a measure of wine each

might be part of a larger transaction involving the *post obit* gift of movables as well, and which occasionally included the immediate and complete gift of other properties.[7]   There is also evidence of the death-bed gift of land and chattels.[8]   The formal transfer of right usually took place in the presence of a considerable group, though, in the case of donation by death-bed gift, formalities were adjusted to the situation: a representative of the donor might make delivery to the beneficiary either before or after the former's death; the donee or his representative might come to the bedside of the dying to receive the gift.[9]   Whether made while death seemed remote, or during the last hours of the donor, both gifts were considered to be irrevocable donations *inter vivos*.   An initial weakening of this type of gift is already evident in the occasional appearance of the notion that the donation includes property not yet possessed, but which will be acquired before the death of the donor.[10] Donations of land seem usually to have been made with the consent of the donor's lord, and often with the consent of the family as well.[11]

The legal acts that accomplished the distribution of property at death in the areas from which the conquerors came are seen then to have been basically the same as those of the Anglo-Saxons.   Neither replacement of the defeated aristocracy nor policy of the victors was to produce an immediate change of institution, for as yet no other was known.[12]

---

year.   On the death of husband or wife, the monks received half the property, the rest passing to them on the death of the survivor;   *Cartulaire de l'Abbaye de la Sainte-Trinité du Mont*, ed. A. Deville, published as an appendix to *Cartulaire de l'Abbaye de Saint-Bertin*, ed. B. Guérard, Collection des Documents Inédits (Paris 1840), no. XIV, pp. 429-430. Another example of *ca.* 1050-75 *ibid.*, no. XIII, p. 429.

[7] *Ibid.*, no. LXXIX, p. 460 (undated); no. XLIX, p. 447 (before 1066); no. LVIII, p. 452 (1063).

[8] There are several examples mentioned in the cartulary of Sainte-Trinité de Rouen : "Gislebertus ... ad extrema veniens" grants land and rights in a mill (no. XLVIII, p. 446, *ca.* 1050); also no. LIII, p. 450 (*ca.* 1050) and no. LVII, p. 451 (*ca.* 1066).

[9] *Ibid.*, no. LXIII, p. 453-454 (*ca.* 1066); *Cartulaire de l'Abbaye de Redon*, ed. A. de Courson, Collection des Documents Inédits (Paris, 1863), no. CCCXVI, "Daniel monachus qui hoc recepit donum...," pp. 269-270 (*ca.* 1070).

[10] "Ipso die mortis nostre quicquid citra Sequanam habebimus in auro vel argento et in quacunque pecunia vel sustantia Sancti Gandregisili erit.": F. Lot, *Etudes critiques sur l'Abbaye de Saint-Wandrille* (Paris, 1913), no. 43, pp. 98-100, *ca.* 1071.

[11] The legacies of Ralph Fitz Ansere, with which the previous note deals, were confirmed by his lord, and after the latter's death by his son, who placed a charter on the altar in the presence of the donor and the monks of Saint-Wandrille.   Similarly, in the cartulary of Sainte-Trinité de Rouen, no. LVII, p. 451 and no. LXXIX, p. 460.

[12] There is sufficient evidence to conclude that similar customs existed in Brittany at the time of the Conquest.   Examples of the *post obit* gift in the cartulary of Redon:

The Distribution of Property at Death in England
during the First Century after the Conquest

The law-making prerogative of the Anglo-Saxon kings, which had been allowed to lapse during the reign of the Confessor, was resumed by his Norman successors.   In their laws and charters some information about the legal acts, whereby property was disposed at death, is to be found.   There is, in addition, a considerable mass of charter and literary material that can be used to resolve some of the questions which the laws leave unanswered.

In the Coronation Charter of Henry I it is stated that, if a king's vassal, being ill, dispose of his movable property, the gift shall stand; if he die intestate, then his wife, children, relatives or men shall make such a division for the good of his soul.¹³   The implications of this text are many, and to some of them we shall return in a later chapter.¹⁴ Two points are of interest here: first of all, the distribution of some property at death is presented as the normal thing—so usual in fact, that a system is provided to repair any omission in this regard; secondly, it is taken for granted that distribution normally occurs during the last illness.   It will be noted too that, in the case both of testamentary and intestate succession, the verb used to express the act of donation has a double form: *dabit vel dare disponet* and *dederit vel dare disposuerit*.   It is tempting to see in this construction a disjunctive use of the word *vel*, implying a distinction between a donation completed even on the death-bed of the donor by the actual conveyance of the gift, and the donation where the final step was not taken, but arrangement made that the gift be completed, perhaps by a third party.   A similar distinction seems to be implied in the second charter of King Stephen (1136).¹⁵

nos. CCXCI, CCXCVIII, CCCVIII, CCCXIII; in the *Cartulaire de l'Abbaye de Saint-Georges de Rennes,* ed. Paul de la Bigne-Villeneuve (Rennes, 1876): nos. X, XII. Examples of the death-bed gift at Redon: nos. CCXCV, CCCXX, CCCXXIX, CCCXXXVII, CCCLXXII; at Rennes: no. XLIII. Consent of the lord and the family, delivery by a third party, etc., are exemplified in these charters. See above, n. 5.

13 "Et si quis baronum vel hominum meorum infirmabitur, sicut ipse dabit vel dare disponet pecuniam suam, ita datam esse concedo. Quod si ipse, praeventus vel armis vel infirmitate, pecuniam suam non dederit vel dare disposuerit, uxor sua sive liberi aut parentes, aut legitimi homines ejus, eam pro anima ejus dividant, sicut eis melius visum fuerit": W. Stubbs, *Select Charters,* 9th ed. by H. W. C. Davis (Oxford, 1913), p. 118.

14 See below, p. 289.

15 A distinction is observed by Miss Robertson in her translation of this charter "...I grant that his personal property shall be bestowed as he himself bestows it or directs by will for its bestowal. But if he has been prevented... from bestowing his personal

At any rate, charter and literary evidence shows that death-bed gifts were made in the two manners suggested. Those same sources indicate as well that such donations were not concerned exclusively with chattels. In fact evidence of this sort usually survives precisely because gifts of land were included. Finally, this evidence shows that it was still possible to make arrangements well before death by the *post obit* gift. On examination these legal acts are found to possess the same fundamental qualities that were observed in pre-conquest England and in Normandy.

The *post-obit* gift had the advantage that it eliminated the danger of intestacy following sudden death. Is is to be found in many forms, forms which have this at least in common, that the gift was completed only after the death of the donor.[16] Most often the donation was an act involving one or several estates of varying sizes, to which the promise of sepulchre and the prayers of the donee were offered as counter-gifts.[17] Occasionally, the *post obit* gift was part of a donation which included other gifts completed by an immediate transfer of possession.[18] More rarely, it was but a secondary part of an exceedingly complex transaction performed with considerable ceremony: the so-called foundation charter of the Abbey of St. Werburgh, Chester, mentions that in addition to the estates and other property immediately conveyed to the abbey by Hugh

property or from directing its bestowal by will, etc." *The Laws of the Kings of England from Edmund to Henry I* (Cambridge, 1925), p. 281. The text is translated in *EHD*, II, 401: "If any of my barons being ill, shall give away or bequeath his movable property . . . . But if prevented . . . he shall die intestate, etc." The relevant clause of Stephen's charter is "Si quis . . . ecclesiastica persona ante mortem suam, rationabiliter sua distribuerit vel distribuenda statuerit, firmum manere concedo": Stubbs, *Select Charters*, p. 144. The translation in *EHD*, II, 403 reads: "If any ecclesiastical person shall have made reasonable disposal of his property, or intended to dispose of it before his death, I allow, etc." Since the following sentence *Si vero* etc., implies that both acts were distributions at the end of life, the translation is somewhat misleading.

[16] See P. and M., II, 323-327.

[17] An early example is found in the *Textus Roffensis*: Eadmer, London host of Gundulf, bishop of Rochester, asked for fraternity. In return, he gave half a fishery called the New Weir immediately, the other half at death. His body was to be buried at St. Andrew's and his anniversary to be celebrated there (1077-1087); ed. T. Hearne (Oxford, 1720), p. 212; translation in *EHD*, II, 954, no. 279.

[18] See the example described in the preceding note; also grants to St. Werburgh's Abbey, Chester, by Scirard and Wacelin (1093) in *The Chartulary or Register of the Abbey of St. Werburgh, Chester*, ed. J. Tait, 2 vols., Chetham Soc., New Ser., LXXIX, LXXXII (1920-3), I, 20, 50; and in *Documents Illustrative of the Social and Economic History of the Danelaw*, ed. F. M. Stenton, British Academy Records of Social and Economic History, V (London, 1920), p. 275, no. 370: Roger, son of Levenot, grants land "post obitum meum, . . . et in vita mea dedi" two other parcels of land (late twelfth century).

of Avranches and his wife, a *post-obit* gift of Weston and attached lands
was made.[19]   Yet another type, which like the preceding was performed
with considerable solemnity, was the gift of ten acres to Ramsey by
Wulfgeat,   In this case the bequest of land was part of a transaction
whereby the donor was granted an estate by the monks.[20]   Several
cartularies contain evidence of transactions involving a *post obit* gift in a
manner somewhat similar to that by Wulfgeat.   From one point of
view, the act is a grant of land by an abbey either in fee or for life.
But from another point of view it can be considered to be a *post obit*
gift of land, or more often, of chattels: land was granted in fee with the
understanding that in addition to regular services, the tenant, at death,
would be buried in the abbey and certain property would be given in
alms.[21]   In the case of a grant for life, the estate too would return to
the abbey with the body of the deceased.[22]   Yet another type of *post obit*
gift, perhaps the most common, took the form of a contract between a
layman and a religious house.   The layman promised that if he decided
to change his state he would become a religious in the monastery with
which he made the agreement.   If he remained in the lay state a share of
his chattels, or even all of them, would pass with his body to the

[19] The charter *Sanctorum prisca* is discussed by Tait in his edition of the cartulary, I,
xxxv-xliii, 13-37. In its present form it is probably a conflation of the *historia fundationis*
and a confirmation of the last years of Count Hugh (1096-1101).

[20] *Cartularium Monasterii de Rameseia*, ed. W. H. Hart and P. A. Lyons, 3 vols., RS, 79
(1884-93), II, 262. Maitland suggests (P. and M., II, 323, n. 2) that, as mention is made of
prayers for the dead before the donor made his gift on the altar, "Wulfgeat is supposed
to be making the gift 'post obitum suum'." It is more likely that the account is simply
describing the daily sequence of exercises, since prayers for the dead were regularly said
after chapter; cf. *The Monastic Constitutions of Lanfranc*, ed. D. Knowles (London, 1951),
p. xvii.

[21] Ranulf was granted land in fee, and he and his wife made a contract with the
Abbey of Ramsey whereby they received fraternity and the promise of suffrages for their
souls, and at their death the abbey was to receive "quantum possessionis ad utrumque
eorum pertinebit" (1091-1100): *Ramsey Cart.*, II, 259. Examples from the Burton cartulary
are described in P. and M., II, 324.

[22] *Ramsey Cart.*, I, 120-121: William Pecche was granted land at rental for life; he was
to have sepulchre in the abbey, "et centum solidi dentur de suo proprio ad ipsam
ecclesiam pro anima ejus, vel marca auri" (1088). There are many other examples: *ibid.*,
I, 140, 143-144, 150; W. Dugdale, *Monasticon*, ed. J. Caley, H. Ellis and B. Bandinel, 6 vols.
(London, 1846), II, 603, a donation to Thorney Abbey (1085-1112); a similar arrangement
at Rouen is found in the cartulary of Sainte-Trinité, pp. 464-465, no. LXXXIV (1075). In the
Whalley Coucher Book, a tenant bound himself and his heirs to leave a third part of their
movables in alms: *The Coucher Book of Whalley Abbey*, ed. W. A. Hulton, 4 vols., Chetham
Soc., X, XI, XVI, XX, (1847-9), I, 155.

monastery at his death.[23]   The religious house gave fraternity and the right of burial in exchange.   Aside from transactions of this sort there is very little information about the *post obit* gift of chattels.   A few charters survive that were witnesses to the donation of some article of great value, relics, jewels, etc.[24]

Whatever the form of the *post obit* gift, it was made with some public ceremonial.   Accounts of these acts frequently mention a symbolic transfer of right in the presence of witnesses by a rod or a weapon, and eventually by a charter.[25]   Sometimes the conveyance was made "by the hand" of the donor's lord or superior.[26]   Though such expressions of the lord's agreement were exceptional, gifts of land, except in certain privileged areas, were made with his permission, and that permission was usually expressed.[27]   Confirmation by the donor's family too seems to have been a normal part of proceedings.[28]   The donee's right in the

---

[23] E.g., *Abingdon Chronicon*, II, 124, 130, 168.   At the foundation of the abbey at Chester, Count Hugh ordained that all barons, burgesses, and free men should give their bodies and one third of all their substance to the monastery of his foundation.   Maitland suggested that we are dealing here with a special law of the Palatinate (P. and M., II, 325, n. 4).   The clause in question may intend permission rather than command: there is little sign that it was obeyed, only two grants of this kind, by Scirard and Wacelin, being mentioned in the cartulary; see above, p. 111, n. 18.

[24] E.g., in *EYC*, II, 429, no. 1136, we read of the *post obit* gift of a phylactery containing relics from the Holy Land to the Abbey of Bridlington (1130-39).   In a cartulary of the monastery of Sainte-Trinité de Caen (Paris, Bibliothèque Nationale, MS. *Lat.* 5660. fol. 24r) is a charter containing a *post obit* gift of chattels by Queen Matilda, the foundress. It is published in translation by Abbé de la Rue in "Memoir on the Celebrated Tapestry of Bayeux", *Archaeologia*, XVII (1814), p. 93.   Another example is described below, p. 114, n. 33.

[25] Gifts by Hugh of Avranches to St. Werburgh's of Chester and by Wulfgeat to Ramsey Abbey were made in this manner.

[26] A good example, dated 1139-1148, is to be seen in the *post obit* gift of a church to the monastery of Bec by Philip canon of Melling, made through the intervention of Archbishop Theobald: "et in manum nostram posuit eam et per nos reddidit eam ecclesie Becci;" cf. A. Saltman, *Theobald Archbishop of Canterbury* (London, 1956), pp. 399-400, no. 177.

[27] *Ibid.*, p. 261, no. 33.   An interesting variant of this type of donation is found in a document of the *Furness Coucher Book* (*ca.* 1194): Adam son of Gamel, donated land to the monastery with reservation for life.   But he had not yet obtained permission from his lord; he promised therefore to seek it: "Sciant presentes et futuri quod ego Adam filius Gamelli forestarii fidele posse meum ponam pro adquirenda gratia domini mei Michaelis Flamengi de F[urnesio] et confirmatione."   Once he or the monks had obtained permission, seisin was to be solemnly conveyed by himself or his heirs; cf. J. Brownbill, ed. *The Coucher Book of Furness*, Vol. ii, 3 vols., Chetham Society, N.S., LXXIV, LXXVI, LXXVIII (1915-9), I, 525-526.

[28] In the case cited above, n. 26, William of Melling, brother of the donor was present at the donation and his charter confirmed it: Saltman, *op. cit.*, pp. 401-402, no. 178.

8

gift was often expressed by the payment of rent by the donor, or occasionally by the immediate partial surrender of the gift or its income.[29]
In gifts involving land in the first decades after the Conquest there is
no known case where, by a double transaction, the donor surrendered
the property to the donee then received it back for life.[30]

In all these forms the donation was considered to be irrevocable.
The transaction was contractual in character, and the bilateral quality
of the agreement was usually explicit in the mention of spiritual benefits to be received by the donor.   However, in the bequest of chattels,
and occasionally in the bequest of land, that same ambulatory quality
which was seen in Normandy became steadily more common as the
decades passed: gift was made not of the possessions of the moment,
but of the property or a portion of the property that would be possessed
at the time of death.[31]   This notion is one of the forces that helped to
replace the various donations *inter vivos* like the *post obit* gift and the
death-bed gift, by the testament.   In the meantime, as the twelfth
century progressed and more rigorous requirements for the transfer
of seisin of land became general, it was found necessary to change the
act into a donation completed by transfer of possession, followed by a
re-grant to the donor for life or several lives.   In this evolved form
the *donatio post obitum* survived well into the fourteenth century.[32]   It
was especially employed for the donation of land, but as late as 1203
King John found it useful as a means whereby he was able to give
precious jewels to the shrine of St. Edmund, yet enjoy the sight of
them until his death.[33]   In this final form the *post obit* gift ceases to be

29 E.g., *Ramsey Cart.*, I, 130; *Cartulary of St. Mary Clerkenwell*, ed. W. O. Hassal, Camden
Society, 3rd series, vol. LXXI (London, 1949), p. 77, no. 117 (1160-80).

30 Maitland suggested (P. and M., II, 323), that this "would imply an analysis of the
post obit gift such as men had not yet made."

31 E.g., *Ramsey Cart.*, I, 143-144: "Pater autem ejus, et mater, cum de hoc seculo migra-
verint, corpora eorum debent ferri ad Ramesiensem ecclesiam, cum ea parte pecuniæ quæ
tunc temporis pertinebit, et ibi sepeliri" (1114-1130); also I, 150 (1133-60); Dugdale, *Monasticon*, II, 603, no. 27 (Thorney Abbey, 1085-1112); *Historia et Cartularium Monasterii Sancti
Petri Gloucestriæ*, ed. W. H. Hart, 3 vols., RS, 33 (1863-7), I, 188, no. LXXIV (before 1179)

32 E.g., Dugdale, *Monasticon*, III, 154: a gift to Bury St. Edmunds in 1240; *The Great
Chartulary of Glastonbury*, ed. A. Watkin, 3 vols., Somerset Rec. Soc., LIX, LXIII, LXIV
(1944-56), II, 341, 343-344: a gift to Glastonbury in 1340.

33 "...obtulimus ei [Sancto Edmundo] saphirum magnum et rubeum quendam inclu-
sum auro, et abbas et monachi ejusdem domus praedictos saphirum et rubeum nobis
tradiderunt tota vita nostra habendos, ita quod revertatur [sic] ad domum illam post
obitum nostrum, et nos ob venerationem dicti martyris dedimus et concessimus praedicto
abbati et conventi x marcas annuas ad Pascha..." Dugdale, *Monasticon*, III, 154-155
cf. *Rot. Lit. Pat.*, p. 37b (Dec. 1203).

primarily a means of distributing property at death and therefore passes beyond the object of this study.

The more common instrument was the death-bed gift.[34] It is to be found employed not only by the lower levels of society, where it was the usual instrument for effecting such a donation, but was much used by the powerful as well. Even where earlier *post obit* gifts had been made, it was probably a general practice to give some final alms in an act that often included the confirmation of these earlier gifts.[35] The Conqueror himself, during the last days of his illness at St. Gervase, divided his possessions both land and chattels. His rather hesitant confirmation of the earlier grant of Normandy to Robert, the letter to Lanfranc instructing him to aid William Rufus in his succession to England, a kingdom that could be considered to be an acquisition, and the gift of treasure to Henry are well known.[36] In addition, he arranged for the distribution of money and land to the poor and to churches on both sides of the Channel.[37] Even the regalia, or part of them at least, were bequeathed.[38] Members of his family, too, made final

[34] See the discussion of the Coronation Charter of Henry I above, p. 110. In the Commentary on *Hebrews*, ix, 16, ascribed to Lanfranc there is a very interesting change: writers of the seventh and later centuries had been content to say that death confirmed the testament, but the author inverts the statement, pointing out that testaments are made at the time of death—"Testamentum autem nisi a moriente non conditum" (PL 150, 396). A letter of Archbishop Theobald to Gilbert Foliot, confirming privileges of the monastery of Leominster concerning the income derived from sepulchre, speaks as though distributions made *in extremis* were usual (Saltmann, *op. cit.*, pp. 440-441, no. 217).

[35] E.g., a confirmation by Robert de Ferrières (d. 1139) of a donation of land to Tutbury Priory mentions that his mother made the donation as death approached, "sicut ipsa multis ante annis in sanitate sua Deo voverat atque promiserat" (Dugdale, *Monasticon*, III, 395).

[36] See the account of his death ascribed to a monk of Caen edited by T. D. Hardy, *Catalogue of Materials* RS, 26 (1862-71), II, 14, translated in *EHD*, II, 279, no. 6; *Orderici Vitalis Historia Ecclesiastica* ed. A. Le Prevost, 5 vols., Soc. Hist. Franc. (Paris, 1838-55), III, 229, translated in *EHD*, II, 281-282, no. 7.

[37] Record of some of these legacies has survived: 100 pounds and household furnishings to St. Andrew's, Rochester (*Textus Roffensis*, p. 32); distribution of money by William Rufus according to his father's instruction is described in the 'E' version of the *Anglo-Saxon Chronicle* for 1087, ed. B. Thorpe, 2 vols., RS, 23 (1861), I, 356; grant of the manor of Bromham to Battle Abbey was made by the same "at his father's command" (*Regesta*, I, no. 290); grant of the manor of Vains to St. Stephen's of Caen confirmed by Duke Robert (Haskins, *Norman Institutions*, App. E, no. 1, p. 285).

[38] The account of William's death by the monk of Caen mentions that crown, sword and sceptre were given to Rufus. However, in a confirmation of the English properties of St. Etienne de Caen, made by Henry II at Bayeux (1156-61), we are informed of the exchange of the manor of Briditona in Dorset, made by Henry I "pro corona ceterisque

distributions of property by death-bed gift.   Queen Matilda is known
to have granted Notham in Devonshire to St. Stephen's of Caen in this
way; in lent of 1093, during a serious illness that threatened to be fatal,
Rufus granted a church and fifteen hides in alms, in a donation that
was probably looked upon as a death-bed gift.[39]   In his account of the
preparation of Henry I for death, Archbishop Hugh of Rouen included
a description of the king's alms, and his command that his debts be
paid and money distributed to the poor.[40]

Persons of lesser importance usually left the disposition of their
property until a time of serious illness. Examples of donations of land
by them in this way are to be found from shortly after the Conquest
until the end of the twelfth century.[41] Occasionally these bequests of
land took the form of a last minute reparation of injustice and, from
time to time, the account of these restorations succeeds in conveying the
donor's frenzy lest life flicker out before its evil has been undone. As
usual, the bequest of chattels has left little trace, but all evidence
points to the use of the death-bed gift for that purpose especially.

As may have been implied by the Coronation Charter of Henry I,
the actual delivery of the land or chattels of the death-bed gift was
accomplished in two different ways.[42] By one form of gift, the donation

---

ornamentis eidem corona adjacientibus, que pater suus W. rex proavus meus moriens
Sancti Stephanus dimissit:" *Recueil des Actes de Henri II ... concernant les provinces françaises*,
ed. L. Delisle and E. Berger, 4 vols. (Paris, 1909-27), I, 262-263, no. CLII.

39 *Ibid.*, I, 267, no. CLIV; the reference is simply "regina in infirmitate qua defuncta
est," but it must refer to the wife of the Conqueror since the property was listed among
the abbey holdings in Domesday Book (I, 104a). William Rufus' donation is mentioned
in the *Gloucester Cart.*, I, 102. According to the 'E' version of the *Chronicle*, the king took
back the property on recovery (*sub anno* 1093, ed. Thorpe, I, 359), but it belonged to the
abbey in the time of Stephen; see *Gloucester Cart.* I, 224.

40 The story ends with a telling phrase: "Utinam sic fecissent qui thesauros ejus tene-
bant et tenent:" Ep. vi (1137), PL 179, 690, and William of Malmesbury, *Historia Novella*,
ed. K. R. Potter (London, 1955), pp. 13-14.

41 Many examples could be cited; the following, from various parts of the country, will
suffice to give some idea of the use of this form of gift of land after death: *ca.* 1087 Swain
gave the land of Whatley to Westminster, probably in his final illness (J. A. Robinson,
Gilbert Crispin, Abbot of Westminster, Notes and Documents relating to Westminster Abbey, 3
[Cambridge, 1911], p. 135); *ca.* 1110, *ibid.*, pp. 40-41; *ca.* 1090 Ranulf Peverel assigned an
estate to St. Paul's of London, *in obitu suo* (M. Gibbs, *Early Charters of the Cathedral Church
of St. Paul*, p. 44, no. 61); a grant to Tutbury Priory before 1139 (Dugdale, *Monasticon*, III,
395, no. xi); also *Cartularium monasterium Sancti Johannis Baptistae de Colecestria*, ed. S. A
Moore, 2 vols., Roxburghe Club (London, 1897), I, 159-160, 163, 167, 191, 312; *Abingdon
Chronicon*, II, 108-109, 170-171; *Chartulary of St. Werburgh, Chester*, I, 78-79, no. 23; Saltman
Theobald, p. 488, no. 256.

42 See above, p. 110.

was completed in the lifetime of the donor by a transfer of right and possession. The five thousand pounds received by Henry Beauclerc were said to have been received (and counted) by the young prince before his father's death. The complete conveyance of land too could be effected in this way, though here assistance was needed. In a case of restoration described in unusual detail in the Glastonbury cartulary, the donor sent his brother with his glove, whereby the gift was placed on the altar; then a monk was taken to the property itself and received seisin; finally the abbot, having come to visit the sick man, received conveyance once more.[43]

As would be expected, the completion of the donation in this way was often impossible. In that case the donor had to be content to instruct members of his family, friends, or the attending priest to make delivery of the property after his death.[44] Delivery seems usually to have taken place at the time of burial, an arrangement that was especially convenient since the church of burial was often the chief beneficiary of the death-bed distribution.[45]

When donation of land was made by death-bed gift, the transaction involved considerable preparation and formality when possible. There are many indications that permission was obtained beforehand of the heirs and even of the lord.[46] Where this had been impossible, the donee himself sometimes sought their confirmation.[47] Witnesses were

---

[43] *Grand Cartulary of Glastonbury*, I, 126-128, no. 172. A document of 1129, taking the form of a letter from Nigel de Albini to his brother William, is of considerable interest here: the former, at the point of death, informed his brother that he had already restored most of the pillage of what must have been a very busy life; but, as several estates remained in his hands, he asked that they be restored and that earlier restorations be confirmed: "ut redditiones terrarum quas ego Eboracensi et Dunelmensi feci ecclesiis . . . ut donatio mea firma sit et stabilis, vestris viribus et omnium amicorum nostrorum faciatis . . .. Et tu, Willelme, frater meus, redde Giraldo excambium suum, et Burnulfo nemus suum de Hantona:" see J. Raine, ed. *The Historians of the Church of York*, 3 vols., RS, 71 (London, 1878-94), III, 54-57; cf. *Early Charters of St Paul's*, pp. 40-41, no. 56; *Ramsey Cart.*, I, 257-258.

[44] Examples of this operation and an analysis of the powers exercised by the agent of the donor are presented in the discussion of the rise of the executor, below, pp. 152-161.

[45] E.g., *ca.* 1087, an estate bequeathed by Swain was placed on the altar before witnesses by his son and wife, the day of his burial; see above, n. 41.

[46] *Cart. Sancti Johannis Colecestria*, I, 158-163: Margaret wife of Hamo de Sancto Claro gave the manor of Stokes, part of her *maritagium*, to St. John's Abbey after obtaining the confirmation of her husband and brother. The witness lists of deeds concerned with these donations very often include the names of wives and children.

[47] To obtain the consent of the lord or the heir, the donee frequently made a money gift or surrended a share of the bequest.

present and they attached much importance to their memory of the
transaction; during the twelfth century it was looked upon as the chief
evidence of donation.   Presence at the will-making of his lord was one
of the few excuses for delay allowed the sheriff in the *Dialogus de
Scaccario*.[48]   Occasional documents show the witness' concern that his
evidence should not perish with him.[49]

The death-bed gift was an irrevocable act *inter vivos*.   By it the surrender of property by the donor was more complete than in the *post obit*
gift, since, not expecting to live, he did not reserve it for future use.
The very completeness of the act must, on occasion, have proved
awkward when death did not ensue immediately.[50]   Bilateral and contractual qualities were less marked than in the *post obit* **gift,** though
here too there is, not infrequently, mention of a counter-gift of suffrages
for the dead and place of burial.   In some cases however, especially
those in which the donee was not specified, the choice of beneficiary
being left to those who had been charged with the distribution of the
property, there was no possibility for the donor to enter such a contractual relationship.[51]   It is probable that the persons acting for the donor
were often instructed to make arrangements for the soul's need and for
burial.   Here a contractual quality would remain.   But in other cases
there is no sign that such was the intention of the donor.[52]   Under these
conditions, the gift tended to become a unilateral act.

48 Bk. II, ch. 4: "Item si idem dominus eius infirmitatis pondere pressus testamentum
coram suis condere voluerit et ad hoc cum aliis fidelibus suis ipsum evocaverit excusabitur;"
ed. A. Hughes, C. G. Crump and C. Johnson (Oxford, 1902), p. 124.

49 A document from the Bridlington cartulary published in *EYC*, II, 456 (1156-7), illustrates this matter very well: Robert de Gant gives notification that he was present when
his brother, the earl of Lincoln, on his death-bed made his will in the presence of his men.
Several properties were given to the church of Bridlington, and the donation confirmed by
charter.   The writing, reading and sealing of the document before the assembled group is
described in detail.   Finally Robert announces that he was witness of the act (he actually
sealed the document), and is prepared to defend it.   Another document of 1188-90 informs
us that John of Pinigeston was witness of the devise of a mill by Henry de WIflei and that
as he was going to Jerusalem, his brother and heir was appointed "ut hoc idem testetur in
loco meo." (*Ibid.*, III, 405).

50 See the discussion of the will of Archbishop Theobald, below, pp. 142-143.

51 E.g., London, Br. Mus., Add. Ch. 20587: notification of a grant of land to the
church of Guisho by Hugh of Rudby, executor of Stephen de Mesnil II.   Choice of donee
was left to Hugh's discretion: "Hujus igitur donationis ut optatum sortiretur effectum, me
capellanum suum et predictarum ecclesiarum personam, fidum substiterit executorem, ut
sicut unctio Spiritus me doceret, elemosinam illam dispensarem" (ed. *EYC*, III, 145-147
1189-99).   Choice of beneficiary seems to have been left to those acting for Archbishop
Theobald.

52 Such would seem to have been the case in the two examples cited in the previous note

During the last decades of the twelfth century the death-bed gift ceased to be sufficient to effect the donation of land. At the same time, new forces began to mould the act of bequest. These forces produced, as we shall see, very little perceptible change in the form of the act, but its nature and effects became quite different.

II. Development of the Canonical Theory of the Testament

Throughout Northern Europe during the twelfth and thirteenth centuries important innovations were made in the theory and practice of the legal acts disposing of property at death. As would be expected, the tempo and extent of the change varied considerably from country to country. The difference was not in the motive: the religious purpose remained very pronounced, receiving, in fact, a growing official sanction. Nor was the change most pronounced in the diminution or enlargement of the portion of property with which the act was concerned. It was the act itself, its nature, its effect and, eventually, the technique of its control and completion, that were to undergo profound modification: as a result of the juxtaposition of new knowledge and new needs, this act took on many of the qualities of the Roman testament.

The Return of Roman Law

One of the many important developments that characterize the life of Europe during the last decades of the eleventh and the whole of the twelfth centuries was the revival of the study of Roman civil law. In its wake came a considerable organization and adjustment of law, legal theory and practice. These effects were felt even in areas of customary law. The chief stages of this important process have long been known to the historian and need not delay us here.[53] What is of more immediate concern is the fact that one of the institutions that come to be better known was the testament, a legal act controlling the devolution of a testator's estate more effectively than anything that the peoples of northern Europe had been able to devise. Roman law provided a theory of the testament and its nature, prescribed its forms and the limits of the property with which it might deal, and furnished a jurisprudence for the courts which controlled and enforced it. England,

[53] A recent summary of literature on the matter is published by J. Ph. Levy, "La Pénétration du droit savant dans les coutumes angevins et bretons au moyen-âge," *Tijdschrift voor Rechtsgeschiedenis*, XXV (1957), p. 1, n. 1. Older but still useful essays in English are: P. Vinogradoff, *Roman Law in Medieval Europe*, 2nd ed. (Oxford, 1929) and H. D. Hazeltine "Roman and Canon Law in the Middle Ages," in *Cambridge Medieval History*, ed. H. M. Gwatkin *et al.*, 8 vols. (New York, 1911-36), V, ch. 21.

like the rest of Northern Europe, came to know the testament and, in part, to adopt it.

The knowledge of Roman civil law came to Northern Europe through two closely allied disciplines: directly, as object of study and analysis by itself; indirectly, through the canon law of the medieval Church. Of recent years several scholars have shown that, during the crucial period of formation of the common law in England, the interest in the direct study of Roman law in that country, was considerably greater than had been suspected.[54] It is Roman law as studied and observed in canon law that is of chief importance here however. Canon law presented a quite specialized view of the testament, a view that tended to emphasize certain secondary aspects of the civil law. It was this specialized canonical view that proved to be essential to the English development. Thus the history of the formation of the canon law of the testament is of considerable importance for the understanding of the English will.

Canon Law and the Testament

The crucial period, during which the older Anglo-Norman practices, controlling the disposition of property at death, yielded place to institutions that differed from them both in nature and effect, can be approximately located between the death of Henry I and the end of the reign of King John. Those years correspond almost exactly with the age during which the general canon law on the matter was elaborated.[55] In the early stages of the canonical development, the testament, as such, was not the object of concern. Interest was indirect, fruit of the Church's efforts to protect the property owned or administered by ecclesiastics, and to supervise the distribution of alms provided by bequests. From this interest in property, actually possessed by the Church or intended to pass under its administration, had grown a fairly complex, and not always consistent, series of canons which regulated the rights of disposition of property by clerics and religious, and pronounced ecclesiastical penalties against those who hindered the delivery of legacies for pious causes. A further interest grew from the relationship that came to exist between the giving of alms at death and the claim of the church of burial to a share of them. The free gift

---

[54] Recent material is indicated by S. Kuttner and E. Rathbone in "Anglo-Norman Canonists in the Twelfth Century," *Traditio*, VII (1949-51), p. 279, n. 4. See Vinogradoff *op. cit.*, pp. 97-118 and Hazeltine, *op. cit.*, pp. 756-762.

[55] A brief sketch of the development of the canon law of the testament is available in Auffroy, *Testament*, pp. 384-398.

was gradually institutionalized, becoming an exaction in some areas at least, and different churches, which in one way or another had some claim on the donor, sought to establish their rights to a share in his alms.   In response to these problems ecclesiastical legislators began to regulate the right of burial and its income.   But the testament as such, its legal nature, its formalities, were not of direct concern.

Canonical collections of the tenth and eleventh centuries usually reflect this point of view, devoting a few canons to the alienation of ecclesiastical property, the rights of sepulchre, and the punishment of undutiful heirs.[56]   However, a considerably more detailed treatment of the matter is to be found in the collections made in the last decade of the eleventh century by Ivo of Chartres.   In fact, two of his works, the *Collectio Tripartita* and the *Decretum*, incorporate almost all the relevant canons that Gratian was to use in his consideration of these problems.[57] Furthermore, in the last section of the *Decretum*, the book entitled *De officiis laicorum et causis eorumdem*, the author chose to go considerably further than his predecessors: drawing on Roman civil law as well as on Frankish capitularies, he assembled texts touching the sanctions that could be used to enforce the execution of legacies, and the persons, lay as well as clerical, to whom the right of *post obit* disposition of property extended.[58]   However, these canons, as those earlier ones which had

---

[56] E.g., on the alienation of Church property: *Collectio Anselmo dedicata* (ca. 882), IV, 120 (drawn from the analysis published by A. Friedberg in his edition of *Corpus Iuris Canonici*, I, xlii-xliii); Reginon of Prüm, *De Synodalibus causis* (ca. 906), I, 366, ed. F. G. Wasserschleben, *Reginonis abbatis Prumensis libri duo de synodalibus causis et disciplinis ecclesiasticis* (Leipzig, 1840), p. 169; Burchard, *Decretum* (1012-1022), I, 212, 214, 227; II, 206, 207; III 121 (PL 140, 611, 614, 660-661, 696); on sepulchre: Reginon, *De syn.*, I, 127, pp. 80-81; Burchard, *Decretum*, III, 151-162 (PL 140, 702-705); sanctions against undutiful heirs: *Coll. Anselmo dedicata*, I, 46; V, 135, X, 70; Reginon, *De syn.*, II, 389, p. 362; Burchard, *Decretum*, III, 140, 142; XV, 34 (PL 140, 701, 904).   On these collections, their date and context, see A.M. Stickler, *Historia Iuris Canonici Latini*, Vol. I, *Historia Fontium* (Turin, 1950), 146-159, and P. Fournier and G. Le Bras, *Histoire des collections canoniques en Occident*, 2 vols. (Paris, 1931-2), I, 234-267, 364-421.   A similar point of view is evident in the Penitential compiled (1150-1170) by Bartholomew of Exeter: ch. CXII deals with the goods of deceased clerics, ch. CXIII with sepulchre, and chs. CXI and CXII provide penalties against those who obstruct gifts for pious causes (ed. A. Morey, *Bartholomew of Exeter Bishop and Canonist*, pp. 275-276).

[57] The *Collectio Tripartita* is dated 1093-4, the *Decretum*, 1094; cf. Stickler, *Historia*, I, 179-184.

[58] Ivo, *Decretum*, XVI, 35, 115, 116, 233 (PL 161, 911, 927, 948), contains sanctions to be invoked against those who prevent the execution of the testament. The right to bequeath is considered in cc. 111, 188 and 302 (PL 161, 926, 941, 959). On the incorporation of texts such as these into canonical literature see Fournier-Le Bras, *Histoire des*

found place in other collections of the age, are not arranged so as to
present an organized body of doctrine on the subject, but on the
contrary are scattered here and there among texts dealing with a wide
variety of topics.   Methodical arrangement is one of the more remarkable qualities of the third and most widely known of Ivo's collections,
the *Panormia*.   Here the treatment of these topics was less developed
than in the longer works from which it was drawn.[59]   It did, however,
incorporate one of those texts from the *Institutes* of Justinian which had
been used in the *Decretum*, a text which treated of the general freedom
to dispose of property by testament, without reference to any specifically
canonical preoccupation with the matter.[60]   In this regard, then, it too
is a reflection of the growing use and study of the texts of Roman law.
This new development was to provide both a source of law and a
method of interpretation[61] and, as the use of Ivo of Chartres would
seem to promise, the canonical exposition of problems touching the
testament was to be considerably influenced by it.

   The new influence is abundantly evident less than half a century
later in the treatment of the disposition of property at death by Gratian
in the *Decretum*.[62]   The progress does not lie so much in the actual
canons that constitute the relevant parts of the collection, as in the fact
that they are related to each other, opposed, discussed and, occasionally
at least, explained.   The result is still quite incomplete, but the first
signs of a canonical consideration of the testament are at last distinguish-
able.   Once again, there is no attempt to present the regulation and
direction of the testament as an area of properly ecclesiastical interest.
Treatment comes rather as an incident in the general presentation of

---

collections canoniques, II, 72-78.   By including these texts the *Decretum* was carried beyond
the strict limits of a canonical collection, an indication of the author's concern with the
general development of law; see Fournier-Le Bras, II, 76, 357.   On Ivo's failure to arrange
these texts so as to form a compact presentation of the matter, see Auffroy, *Testament*,
pp. 387-388.

   59 On the alienation of church property: II, 50-53; on sepulchre: II, 26, 27, 29; sanctions
against undutiful heirs: II, 5, (PL 161, 1092, 1087-9, 1084).   For the date and importance
of the *Panormia*, see Stickler, *Historia*, I, 182-183.

   60 *Panormia* V, 60 (PL 161, 1223-4); the text combines two texts of the *Decretum* — XV,
185 and 188.   They are derived from *Institutes* I, 4 and II, 12 respectively.

   61 See Fournier-Le Bras, *op. cit.*, II, 357.

   62 On the originality, sources and importance of the *Decretum* see DDC, IV, 611-627 and
Stickler, *Historia*, I, 200-215.   For the date, 1140 or even earlier, see DDC, IV, 612 and
especially A. Vetulani, "Le 'Décret' de Gratien et les premiers décrétistes, d'après une nouvelle source," a summary of the author's monograph, *Dekret Gracjana* (Breslau-Cracow,
1955), pp. 156-168.

the law touching two quite distinct topics: the disposition of clerical property, and the right of sepulchre and its income. Intimately connected with the latter, of which it was ultimately the source, is the problem of the administration and enforcement of legacies for pious causes.

The canons touching sepulchre proved to be crucial. Having dealt with the property of clerics, Gratian proceeded in *Causa* 13 to discuss the income derived from tithe and sepulchre.[63] The consideration of the latter led to the question whether the individual has the right to choose his place of burial. Gratian opted for this freedom[64] and substantiated his postition by a text ascribed to Gregory the Great: *Ultima voluntas defuncti modis omnibus conservetur* (q. 2, c. 4). Then, having limited the application of the canon to the free, he proceeded to ask whether it were restricted to the liberty of choice of place of burial, or whether it extended as well to freedom of disposition of property.[65] Here at last, he found place for a momentary consideration of one aspect of the testament as such — the extent of the testator's freedom. He concluded that the *ultima voluntas*, of which Gregory wrote, could not be considered to be entirely free since Augustine taught that, where children survived, the bequest in alms should not exceed a son's share. Furthermore, even the legacy intended for pious uses was not fully controlled by the testator since, according to Pope Leo, half of it was to be given to the church of burial. Gratian returned to Augustine's position in canon 8, adding the dictum that such a portion is not a minimum but rather the maximum bequest for pious causes.[66]

Next, having asserted that the laity are free to give alms in their testaments, and having suggested some limitations regarding both the legatee and the amount of the gift, he proceeded to cite several ancient and frequently quoted canons ordering the excommunication of those

---

[63] C. 13, q. 1, *pr.*

[64] C. 13, q. 2, *dict.* §10 p. c. 3 "Ubi autem quisque tumulandus sit, legibus expressum non est, et ideo in voluntate tumulandi consistit."

[65] C. 13, q. 2, *dict.* p. c. 7 "Sed aliud est..."

[66] "Hac nimirum auctoritate mensura testatori prefigitur, non quam cogatur exsolvere, sed quam prohibetur transcendere." On the "son's share," cf. Bruck, *Kirchenväter*, pp. 84-104 and the references cited there. The text *Relatum* of Leo IX to which Gratian referred was incorporated in the *Decretals* of Gregory IX (III, 28, 2). It seems to have been included in the text of the *Decretum* available to the author of the *Summa Parisiensis;* see gloss *ad* C. 13, q. 2, *dict.* p. c. 7 (*The Summa Parisiensis on the Decretum Gratiani*, ed. T. P. McLaughlin [Toronto, 1952], pp. xiv, 167), and was apparently added at the end of the volume used by Stephen of Tournai: *Summa ad* C. 13, q. 2, *dict. ad* c. 7 (*Die Summa des Stephanus Tornacensis*, ed. J.F. v. Schulte [Giessen, 1891], p. 110).

who prevented the execution of the alms of the dead.[67]   Nothing was added to indicate procedure or the extent to which the bishop was expected to supervise such bequests.   In fact, a text of Distinction 88, which later decretists would go to some lengths to bring into relation with the canons of *Causa* 13, suggested that bishops should have very little to do with the testament: *Episcopus tuicionem testamentorum non suscipiat* (c. 5).

Finally, there is a brief discussion of the revocability of legacies and of donations made in alms at a time of grave illness.   It occurs as part of the consideration of those who in danger of death dedicate themselves to some religious institution, but on recovery wish to return to their former state.   Gratian concluded that, unless the person in question had actually made religious profession, he must be permitted to return to the world and to recover his possessions.[68]

The destiny of the *Decretum* is well known: it became the text-book of the schools and, as other text-books, was clarified, rendered more consistent, and supplemented by the glosses, *Summae*, and *Quaestiones* which were the fruit of its study.[69]

A brief sampling of the *Summae* is enough to show that in them Gratian's treatment of the testament was developed considerably.   One of the chief areas of interest within this topic was the discussion of ecclesiastical jurisdiction in matters touching the distribution of property at death.   It centered on the canon of Distinction 88 already mentioned:

---

67 Canon 9 *Qui oblationes*, and c. 11, *Clerici uel saeculares*. Examples of their use in earlier collections are cited above, p. 121.   Other cases include Ivo, *Decretum*, III, 206, 208, *Panormia*, II, 5; *Collectio Tripartita*, III, 3, 27; II, 28, 3 (PL 161, 247-248, 1083, and Friedberg, *Corpus*, I, lxvi).

68 C. 17, q. 2, c. 1.   In q. 4, c. 43 and the following dictum he considered the case of a property owner who, expecting to die childless, gives his estate to a church, retaining the usufruct.   Gratian, citing the opinion of Augustine which was similar to his own, favoured the return of the property should a child be born to the donor.

69 On the use of the *Decretum* in the schools, see S. Kuttner, "Quelques observations sur l'autorité des collections canoniques dans le droit classique de l'Eglise," *Actes du Congrès de Droit Canonique* (Paris, 1947), pp. 303-312, cited by Tierney, *op. cit.*, p. 14, n. 2.   General surveys of canonical literature between the publication of the *Decretum* and the appearance of the *Decretals* of Gregory IX are available in J. F. v. Schulte *Die Geschichte der Quellen und Literatur des canonischen Rechts*, 3 vols. (Stuttgart, 1875-80), I, 39-255; Stickler, *Historia*, I, 217-236; A. Van Hove, *Prolegomena: Commentarium Lovaniense in Codicem Iuris Canonici*, I, i, (Mechlin-Rome, 1945), pp. 423-467; S. Kuttner, *Repertorium der Kanonistik*, I, *Studi e Testi*, 71 (Vatican City, 1937), and subsequent additions and corrections published in *Traditio*, I—(1943—).   The useful suggestion that the *Decretum* invited rather than terminated discussion, is developed by C. R. Cheney, *From Becket to Langton* (Manchester, 1956), pp. 44 ff.

Episcopus tuicionem testamentorum non suscipiat. Whereas Stephen of Tournai was content to explain the technical meaning of *tuitio,* and to remark that the opening of testaments was the function of the *Magister census,* the author of the *Summa Parisiensis* noted that other canons of the *Decretum* contradicted this prohibition.[70] He concluded that bishops might defend testaments and see to their execution, so long as this function did not extend to the opening of the document and the establishment of its validity. The *Summa* of Simon of Bisignano reiterated the plea for episcopal defence, with the qualification that the testament must be just.[71] In its discussion of this same text, the anonymous *Summa Lipsiensis,* a product of the Anglo-Norman school that can be dated *ca.* 1186, repeated the statement that the opening of the testament pertained to the *Magister census.* But the author went much further, for he stated that legacies were to be sought before an ecclesiastical judge.[72] Later, in the discussion of *Causa* 13, q. 2, c. 4, he asked why the judgment of cases touching bequests pertained to

---

[70] Stephen of Tournai equates *tuitio* with *insinuatio* and *apertura testamenti: Summa ad Dist.* 88, c. 5, "*Ep. tuitionem,* i.e., insinuationem. Insinuari namque, i.e. aperiri testamenta, ante neminem licebat nisi tantum ante magistrum census" (ed. Schulte, p. 110); *Summa Parisiensis ad Dist.* 88, c. 5, "*Episcopus tuitionem.* Contrarium habuimus ubi dictum est quia episcopus debet defendere servos testamento liberatos, et in sequentibus contrarium habebimus. Determinamus ergo per legem, quia lex dicit quod quidam episcopi volebant habere potestatem ut testamenta coram eis aperirentur ibique omnimodam tuitionem eorum haberent et robur eis darent, quod lex prohibet. Et illud idem prohibet decretum in hoc loco, non quod non possint defendere testamenta et ultimas voluntates custodiri efficere, sed non debent omnimodam apertionem testamentorum eorumque valentium penes se constituere" (ed. McLaughlin, p. 69). On the *apertura testamenti* of Roman law, see the brief description in A. Berger, *Encyclopedic Dictionary of Roman Law,* American Philosophical Society (Philadelphia, 1953), p. 364, *s.v.,* "Apertura testamenti," and p. 503, *s.v.,* "Insinuatio testamenti." The function of the Magister census is described *ibid.,* p. 570. An account of the process, "Gesta de Aperiendis Testamentis" (a. 474), is printed in *Fontes Iuris Romani Antejustiniani,* III *Negotia,* ed. V. Arangio-Ruiz (Florence, 1943), no. 58.

[71] Simon de Bisignano, *Summa ad Dist.,* 88, c. 5, "*Episcopus tuitionem testamentorum non suscipiat.* Et nota quod hic non dicitur episcopum non posse defendere testamentum cum constat firmum esse et injuste improbari, sed potius interdicitur ne debeat in foro contendere et disputare ut advocatus probando illud legitime esse factum cum etiam causas proprias per se ipsos tractare non possunt excepta causa criminali, ut C. 5, q. 3, *Quia episcopus* (c. 3)." The text has been made available by Rev. T. P. McLaughlin who is currently preparing an edition of the work.

[72] *Summa Lipsiensis ad Dist.,* 88, c. 5, MS. Rouen, 743, fol. 40v, "*Episcopus usque tuitionem.* Scilicet tutelam testamentariam non suscipiat, vel tuitionem per insinuationem quod soli magistro census competebat insinuari [*lege* insinuare]... Sed queritur coram quo debunt peti legata vel fideicommissa: videtur quod sub iudice ecclesie, ut C. 16, q. 1, Admonere (c. 14)." On the *Summa Lipsiensis* see Kuttner, *Repertorium,* pp. 196-198.

bishops while other civil matters were refused them, and concluded that it was because they were allowed to make decisions in disputes involving donations to pious causes.   This second reference to the matter was concluded with the remark that the restriction of Distinction 88 applied only to the *insinuatio testamenti.*[73]

Huguccio's position, though similar, was more refined and tended to limit rather than to enlarge the area of episcopal jurisdiction over the testament.   He distinguished two quite different senses of the term *tuitio*: it could be interpreted to mean either the *apertura testamenti* or simply the defence of the testament.   With regard to the former meaning, he suggested that the usual reference to the *Magister census* was true but irrelevant.   He went on to point out that the opening of the testament before the bishop would involve him in litigation that would not be suitable to his state and must therefore be avoided.   On the other hand, if *tuitio* were interpreted to imply the defence of the testament, it was quite fitting that the bishop do so, when such matters were brought to his attention, so long as he did not become involved in the activities of the lay courts.[74]   The payment of legacies was to be enforced by the excommunication of those unwilling to execute the bequests of the deceased.[75]

This discussion makes it clear that in the minds of the decretists the bishop was expected to defend the testament.   It shows too that his primary interest was the execution of the legacy for pious uses, but that from this concern with a single aspect of the testament his interest had been extended in an imprecise manner to the institution as a whole. However, this activity was not to involve him in the secular courts.

---

[73] Fol. 80v, "Sed quid ad episcopum audire causas legatarium magis quam alias causas civiles? Et dicunt quod si qua relicta sunt ad pias causas potest de illis dictare sententiam ut C. 16, q. 1, Admonere (c. 14). Unde ibi dicitur piae. Quod autem dicitur supra, Distinctione 88, *Episcopus,* quod ad eum non pertinet tuitionem, hoc intelligendum est per insinuationem ut ibi diximus."

[74] Huguccio, *Summa ad Dist.*, 88, c. 5, MS. Paris, BN. Lat. 3892, fol. 96r. "Sed licet hoc verum sit ... haec expositio videtur esse remota ab hac littera. Potius ergo intelligo hoc capitulum in tali casu: ecce aperitur testamentum emergunt inde multae quaestiones et controversiae in quibus non debet episcopus stare. ... Et est *tuitionem,* i.e., defensionem et patrocinium, scilicet ut in causis advocatus ea defendat. Non dicit quod episcopus non debeat testamentum defendere cum causa tractatur coram eo vel aliter videt illum iniuste reprobari dummodo constet ipsum legitimum esse, sed pro eo defendendo non debet suscipere officium advocati in foro."

[75] *Ibid., ad* C. 16, q. 1, c. 14, fol. 227rb, " ... ad ecclesiam pertinet providere ut testamenta serventur et legata solvantur, praesertim quae in usus pietatis legantur. Si quis ergo non vult parere voluntati testatoris licite potest cogi ab ecclesia etiam per excommunicationem."

As for his own courts, it was clear that their jurisdiction extended to the protection and enforcement of legacies in alms, but they were not to establish the validity of the will. In addition, there is the suggestion of the *Summa Lipsiensis* and of Huguccio that episcopal authority might extend even further, in those cases at least where it was requested.

Another topic, the property with which the testament was to deal, was the object of much interesting discussion by the decretists. It will be recalled that Gratian had tempered Gregory's statement of the freedom of the last will by the imposition of two limitations which restricted the amount of the legacy and the choice of beneficiary. He did not choose to discuss the total property over which a testator had the right of alienation. His citation of Novel 123 in *Causa* 19[76] indicates his awareness of the civil law on the matter, but he seems to have chosen, with full advertence, to discuss only those rather narrow limits implied by his interpretation of the text of Augustine, and to present this property as the object of the canonist's concern. The reaction to Gratian's interpretation of Augustine was generally one of disagreement. Thus in the *Summa* of Rufinus it is stated that Augustine's purpose was not to forbid, but to dissuade a testator from giving alms in excess of a son's share; the only strict limitation was that imposed by Roman law (the *pars legitima*), as Gratian himself had implied in his citation of Novel 123.[77] A similar position was adopted in the *Summa Lipsiensis* and by Huguccio.[78] As for the amount of the *pars*

---

[76] *Nov.* 123, c. 38 is quoted in C. 19, q. 3, c. 9.

[77] Rufinus *Summa ad* C. 13, q. 2, *dict. a.* c. 9, "Due auctoritates in hoc loco inducuntur, que canonibus et legibus adverse esse videntur. Quod enim inducit Augustinum dicentem quod pater, si habet unum filium, Christum faciat alterum, i.e., non debet plus dare ecclesie quam filio relinquere, hoc est contrarium legibus, ubi dicitur quod, si quis ad monasterium vult converti, omnes res suas monasterio conferre potest, dummodo filii legitima non fraudentur, hoc est quarta vel tertia; ut infra Cs. XIX, q. III, c. Si qua mulier (9). Item quod inducit de Leone ... Sed istud Augustini non prohibitio, sed dissuasio est, scil. ut non plus conferat ecclesie quam relinquat heredi; vel ex causa intelligendum, videlicet ut non contra filium iratus hoc faciat—unde et dicit: (Cap. 8) *Si quis irascitur.* Pia vere mentis deliberatione precedente preter legitimam omnia sua potest dare ecclesie, sicut asserunt leges humane" (*Die Summa Decretorum des Magister Rufinus,* ed. H. Singer [Paderborn, 1902], p. 336).

[78] The commentary of the *Summa Lipsiensis,* MS. Rouen, 743, fol. 81r, is almost word for word the same as that of Rufinus quoted in the preceding note. The phrase "hoc est quarta vel tertia," referring to the *pars legitima,* is omitted; cf. the following note. Huguccio, *Summa ad* C. 13, q. 2, c. 8, MS. BN. *Lat.* 3892, fol. 214r: "Sed intelligo prohibetur transcendere ex calore iracundie et ex odio, vel prohibetur, i.e., dissuaditur, i.e., consilio Augustini suadetur et consulitur ei ut non transcendat eam." Cf. Bruck, *Kirchenväter,* p. 250.

legitima, it was stated to be a quarter or a third in the *Summa* of Rufinus, while Stephen of Tournai mentioned that, though it had once been a quarter, it had since become a third.[79] The latter position is found in the *Summa Lipsiensis* as well.[80] Much later, the *Glossa Ordinaria,* in a somewhat brutal fashion, will remark that Gratian was in error as his own text makes manifest, and that, excepting the *pars legitima,* the testator is free to bequeath all his property in alms.[81] Gratian's defence of the revocability of donations made while in danger of death is generally supported.

The decades that witnessed the elaboration of the *Summae* on the *Decretum* correspond with the period during which the revitalized papacy increased its activity in the ecclesiastical courts of Europe. Questions of law and procedure, of principle as well as detail, were referred to Rome; answers were forthcoming in that great stream of letters which is perhaps the most palpable indication of papal activity during the second half of the twelfth century.

Some of these letters dealt with the testament. As would be expected, the most common objects of concern were those properly ecclesiastical problems that rose from the distribution of clerics' property and the control of income derived from legacies and burials.[82] Occasionally, however, the point of view was enlarged and rulings of more general application were made. Thus two letters of Alexander III (*ca.* 1170) defended the testament made before two or three witnesses against those who would demand the more strict formalities of Roman law. The first letter was sent to judges in the city of Velletri, who had been demanding that testaments containing legacies for pious purposes should have five or seven witnesses, *secundum leges.*[83] The pope insisted that in such matters they were to proceed *secundum canones,* that is, in accord with the scriptural directive that two or three witnesses were sufficient. In the second letter, to Hubaldus, bishop of Ostia, the pope maintained that a parishioner's testament made at the end of his life before his

---

79 Rufinus' opinion is quoted above, n. 77. *Summa Stephani ad* C. 13, q. 2, *dict. ad* c. 7 "Quae [pars legitima] olim erat quarta illius partis, quam habiturus erat ab intestato. hodie per authent. tertia" (ed. Schulte, p. 219).

80 *Summa Lipsiensis, ad* C. 19, q. 3, c. 9, MS. Rouen, 743, fol. 98r, "Legitimam, id est tertiam partem illius quam habituri essent."

81 *Glossa ordinaria ad* C. 13, q. 2, c. 8 *Hac nimirum.*

82 Among the letters of Alexander III dealing with the devolution of ecclesiastical property, JL. 14046, 14116, 14347 provided texts for X, III, 26, 9; 22, 8; 26, 12 respectively. C. 15 of III Lateran became X, III, 26, 7.

83 JL. 11480 (1167-9).

pastor and two or three witnesses was valid, adding that such was the general custom of the Church.[84] In this case it will be noted that there is no indication that the papal regulation was limited to legacies intended for pious purposes.

Other letters of the same pope gave directions for the payment of the debts of the deceased. Perhaps the most interesting statement in this regard was one of several decisions in a letter addressed to Richard, archbishop of Canterbury. Here the pope approved of the practice whereby a creditor was permitted to launch an appeal to prevent the burial of a deceased debtor until the heir or other relative promised to acquit the debt.[85] Similar concern is seen in a letter in which a prelate was obliged to pay those debts of his predecessor that were contracted to supply the needs of his church.[86] Elsewhere, discussing the custom whereby a cleric who died between March and November had the right to distribute the income for the whole year, he remarked that, though the practice was hardly reasonable, it should be tolerated, especially if the cleric were burdened with debt.[87]

Yet another matter of considerable interest appears in a letter to the bishop of Le Mans.[88] Here, dealing once more with the property of

---

[84] JL. 12129 (1171-2).

[85] JL. 14312 (1171-2). I have not been able to find examples of this practice in England. It will be recalled that the clergy who attended Geoffrey of Anjou at his death refused to allow his body to be buried until they had exacted a promise from Henry II to respect his fathers division of his holdings; see William of Newburgh, *Historia Rerum Anglicarum*, in *Chronicles of the Reigns of Stephen, Henry II and Richard I*, ed. R. Howlett, 4 vols., RS, 82 (1885-90), I, 112-113. Similarly at the death of Duke Leopold of Austria, the clergy refused him the last sacraments until he had released Richard I from the unpaid portion of his ransom. His son refused to be bound by this act, but once again burial was granted only at the price of agreement. Tancredus, *ad Compilatio Ia*, II, 20, 41, MS. Vat. Lat. 1377, p. 70 went to considerable length to show that such action was opposed to the Civil law and that the decretal was merely the papal acceptance of an English custom rather than an indication of the general law of the Church: "...et hic dominus papa respondit secundum consuetudinem anglicorum, et hoc notaverunt Ricardus et Alanus." This part of Alexander's letter was included in the *Compilatio prima*, but it was omitted in the *Decretals*, though the rest of the letter, of which it was part, found a place there.

[86] JL. 14013 (1159-81); the conclusion—"Sicut filius debita patris solvere tenetur, ita praelatus sui praedecessoris pro ecclesiae necessitate contracta"—became X, III, 23, 1.

[87] JL. 13587 (1175-1180). Another letter which purports to be from Alexander III to the dean and chapter of Reims is found in the *Collectio Brugensis*, LVI, 3 (ed. E. Friedberg, *Die Canones-Sammlungen zwischen Gratian und Bernhard von Pavia* [Leipzig, 1897], p. 169). It instructs the recipients to proceed against a widow who refused to pay the debts and legacies of her late husband. She had, however, promised on oath to do so, and the violation of the oath seems to be the basis of the action.

[88] JL. 13842 (1159-1181).

9

clerics, the pope made a distinction between the donation *inter vivos* and the testament, a distinction that for Northern Europe at least was very important, for it was little understood:[89] a cleric, even when ill was permited to give alms, in moderate extent, from church property by donation *inter vivos,* while the bequest of the same property by testament was forbidden.

In an attempt to keep abreast of new legislation, whether derived from letters such as those cited above, or from the canons of councils, collections of texts were assembled in various centres throughout Europe.[90] Haphazard arrangements of varied material at first, these collections soon began to assume a more systematic structure, attaining finally to the plan that was made permanent in the *Decretals* of Gregory IX. Actually, the first of the so-called systematic collections, the *Collectio Parisiensis II,* published by Bernard of Pavia before 1180,[91] did not contain any of the decretals of Alexander III that referred to the testament and that have been assembled above. Texts dealing with this matter were drawn from councils and papal letters prior to the twelfth century.[92] Though this collection failed to incorporate the newest material on the subject, it is of considerable interest from the point of view of methodology. Canons touching the testament in any way were brought together under two titles. Of these, the first, *De peculio clericorum,* deals with the limitations of the cleric's right to alienate property, limitations that apply both to the matter of the bequest and to the recipient.[93] The second title, *De sepulturis et ultimis voluntatibus,* is of interest since the last will is mentioned in the rubric itself, though still in close relationship to the question of sepulchre.[94] In fact, three canons are given to the choice of place of burial and the division of the burial offering, while but one, the fourth, is directly concerned with the testament. It is a canon of a Council of Mainz,

---

[89] Cf. *Institutiones,* I, 7, ed. P. Kruger in *Corpus Iuris Civilis,* 3 vols. (Berlin, 1915-28), I, 15.

[90] On the general history of the Collections see Kuttner, *Repertorium,* pp. 272-385. For a convenient introduction to later literature see W. Holtzmann, "Über eine Ausgabe der päpstlichen Dekretalen des 12. Jahrhunderts," in *Nachrichten der Akademie der Wissenschaften in Göttingen,* Phil-Hist. Klasse (1945), pp. 15-36, and the remarks of S. Kuttner in "Notes on a Projected Corpus of Twelfth Century Decretal Letters," *Traditio,* VI (1948), pp. 345-351.

[91] An analysis and sketch of the contents of *Coll. Parisiensis II* is published by Friedberg, *Die Canones-Sammlungen,* pp. 21-45; see Kuttner, *Repertorium,* p. 290.

[92] C. 1 of Title LII is the exception; it is ascribed to Paschal II (1099-1118): JL. 6611.

[93] Title XLIX; limitations as to matter: cc. 10, 14; limitations as to recipient: cc. 5, 6; on the estates of intestate clerics: cc. 7, 8, 11-13 (ed. Friedberg, *Die Canones-Sammlungen,* p. 40).

[94] Title LII, *ibid.,* p. 41.

preserved in the collections of Burchard of Worms and Ivo of Chartres, empowering the bishop to force an heir to acquit himself of his obligations by preventing his enjoyment of the estate to which he has succeeded. The point of view of this collection is, then, very much the same as that which has been seen in Gratian's *Decretum* : the testament or *ultima voluntas* is of interest because it usually contains provisions regarding sepulchre and the giving of alms, and it is the bishop's duty to enforce them. Nevertheless, the fact that it found place in the rubric to the title should not be ignored, for it was to remain there until, within little more than a decade, a whole title was devoted to it.

The pertinent letters of Alexander III were, with one exception, incorporated a few years after 1180 in another collection, known as the *Appendix concilii Lateranensis.*[95] In its first redaction at least, this collection was the work of the English school. It contains two titles similar to those already mentioned in *Parisiensis II,*[96] but the treatment is more developed and includes later material. This work seems to have provided the core of the relevant parts of a very important collection published by Bernard of Pavia between 1188 and 1192, and called the *Breviarium extravagantium.*[97] In time it became known as the *Compilatio prima.* This collection is of primary importance for many reasons; it made a considerable contribution to the canon law of the testament. In it there is evidence of a conscious effort to distinguish the varied and somewhat confused points of view from which canonists had considered this matter hitherto. Five consecutive titles of Book III bear the rubrics: On Donations, On the Property of Clerics, On Testaments and Last Wills, On Intestate Succession, On Sepulchre.[98]

Of these titles, the third is of special interest. Here at last is a canonical treatment of the testament free from the usual references to sepulchre. The sources of this title are of interest: six of the fourteen canons are drawn from the letters of Alexander III; for most of the

[95] Ed. Mansi, XXII, 248-454; analyzed in Friedberg, *op. cit.*, pp. 63-84; cf. *DDC*, I, 833-841. On the provenance of the collection and its supplement, see W. Holtzmann, "Die Register Papst Alexander III in den Händer der Kanonisten," *Quellen und Forschungen aus italienischen Archiven und Bibliotheken*, 30 (1940), p. 16, n. 1, and the criticism thereof by Kuttner in "Notes," *Traditio*, VI (1948), p. 349.

[96] Tit. XXIX *De alienatione rerum ecclesiae et earumdem reparantium;* Tit. XLIII *De sepulturis et mortuorum voluntatibus.*

[97] Five texts from the earlier redaction of the *Appendix* and two others from Bk. L, which was added later, are included in the title, *De Testamentis,* of the *Compilatio prima.* This latter collection is edited by E. Friedberg, *Quinque Compilationes Antiquae* (Leipzig, 882), pp. 1-65; cf. Stickler, *Historia*, I, 225-229.

[98] Bk. III, titles XX-XXIV.

others the author reached much further back into the past, six being drawn from the letters of Gregory the Great and the remaining two from a council of Mainz of the ninth century and the third Council of the Lateran.[99]   Most of the texts, it is true, were still concerned with clerics and religious and with limitation of their freedom to alienate property at death.   Of these, however, one was the text of Alexander III making the important distinction between the testament and the *donatio inter vivos*.[100]   The last six canons of the title are applicable to the testaments of the laity as well: three deal with the testament itself, defending the validity of the nuncupative or oral will, and stipulating that, for legacies for pious purposes, two or three witnesses are sufficient.   Of the remainder, one canon treats of the bequest of property not owned by the testator, while two others instruct the bishop in the enforcement of the testament of the deceased.[101]

The contribution of Bernard of Pavia to the elaboration of the canon law of the testament did not end with his edition of the *Compilatio prima*. During the last decade of the twelfth century he published the *Summa decretalium,* a work of considerable importance from the point of view both of its originality and of its influence on later canonists.[102]   It is a methodical exposition of the ensemble of canon law cast in the form of a discussion of each of the titles of the *Compilatio prima*.   Here is to be found what is, in fact, a short-treatise on the testament.   The completeness if not the depth of its presentation becomes evident from a sketch of its contents: the distinction between the *donatio inter vivos* and the *donatio mortis causa* is made; the principal instrument by which the latter is effected being the testament, it is then discussed; a definition of the testament is given, written and nuncupative forms disinguished, formalities are discussed and a distinction made between the require ments of civil and canon law with regard to the number of witnesses discussion turns to those who are free to dispose of property by testament; the confirmation of the act by the death, physical or legal, o the testator is considered, and the various causes of revocation, including the changed intention of the testator, are outlined; the *ultima volunta* and its simplified formalities are discussed; sanctions to enforce the delivery of legacies are described; the analysis is completed by a few

99 Canons 5-10 are from the letters of Alexander III, cc. 1-3, 12-14 from Gregory I, c. 1 from the Council of Mainz, and c. 4 from III Lateran.

100 Canon 5; see above, p. 130.

101 Bk. III, tit. 22, cc. 9-14 (ed. Friedberg, p. 33).

102 *Bernardi Papiensis Summa Decretalium*, ed. E. A. T. Laspeyres (Graz, 1956), pp. 1-28. Cf. Van Hove, *Prolegomena,* pp. 447-448 and Kuttner, *Repertorium,* pp. 387-390.

lines on the testaments of former religious who have been advanced to the episcopacy.[103]

By the end of the twelfth century then, there were in existence a collection of canons and a short treatise dealing with the testament, its nature and some of the jurisprudence of its use. The next fifty years were to see a rapid elaboration of both the theoretical and practical aspects of the matter by the canonists, but already the basis for the treatment of the testament in the *Decretals* of Gregory IX and in exhaustive treatises like the *Summa* of Hostiensis were established in the two works of Bernard of Pavia. The influence of the *Compilatio prima* on the organization and structure of later collections was to prove fundamental. Of the four that appeared in the following years, and that grouped with it are known as the *Quinque Compilationes Antiquae,* three devote a title to the testament.[104] In the *Decretals,* an official collection published by Gregory IX in 1234, the treatment of donation, succession, and sepulchre follows the arrangement of the *Compilatio prima,* in five titles with the same rubrics and sequence.[105] In fact, the title *De testamentis et ultimis voluntatibus* of the *Compilatio prima* was incorporated almost completely in Gregory's collection.[106] Of the nine additional canons in the *Decretals,* five were drawn from the later *Compilationes* and four from the letters of Gregory IX himself. Several of these supplementary texts are of general interest, reflecting, as they do, the rise of the executor.[107] To them we shall return.[108]

For the moment, however, it is the accomplishment of the sixty years that followed the publication of Gratian's *Decretum* that is of special import. Ecclesiastical legislation and the studies of the canonists had arrived at a doctrine of the testament. But it was a special doctrine for a special purpose. Behind the canon law and its

---

103 *Summa decretalium,* pp. 96-99.

104 *Compilatio IIa,* Bk. III, tit. 14; *Compilatio IIIa,* Bk. III, tit. 19; *Compilatio Va,* Bk III. it. 13 (ed. Friedberg, pp. 84-85, 123, 173).

105 X, III, titles 24-28. On the *Decretals,* cf. Stickler, *Historia,* I, 237-251 and *DDC,* IV, 627-632.

106 All but one of the fourteen canons of the title, *De Testamentis,* of the *Compilatio prima* are reproduced in the *Decretals:* eleven of them find a place under their original rubric; c. 1 was not included in the *Decretals;* cc. 7 and 8 became X, III, 5, 13 and I, 9, 4.

107 X, III, 26, 13, from a letter of Innocent III (1202), maintains that the person who commits the last disposition of his property to another is not to be considered an intestate Potthast, 1796); cc. 17 and 19 are drawn from letters of Gregory IX (1227-1234), in which bishops are instructed to compel executors to carry out legacies for pious purposes Potthast, 9644, 9646).

108 See below, pp. 219 ff.

discussion, there was a competent knowledge of the testament in the strict sense of Roman law.   When the canonists spoke of legacies or the last will, they meant an act that was ambulatory and revocable, as was the Roman testament.   But they chose to leave the essential aspect of the testament, the institution of an heir, in the background.[109]   Their chief interest was in one of its secondary functions, the giving of legacies. Bernard of Pavia and others chose to define the testament in those terms.[110]   Even where the canonists insisted on the stricter meaning of the testament, their interest remained with the legacy, and with a special type of legacy — that for pious purposes.   They established special simplified formalities for making these legacies by last will or codicil, and special episcopal powers for their enforcement.   Within this limited area there was little dispute.   But the bequests found in the testaments of the twelfth century were to such a large extent a matter of alms that there was a tendency to apply these special rules to all legacies.   The discussion of the extent of the episcopal power of enforcement by the Decretists has already been sampled.   Commentators on the *Compilatio prima* and later collections, including the *Decretals,* dealt with the same problem and came to similar conclusions.[111]   The temptation to extend the use of simplified formalities was felt as well. It was remarked above that Alexander III defended legacies made before two or three witnesses against the more rigid demands of the civil law, and that there was at least the possibility that his directions

---

[109] Cf. *Inst.* 2, 20, 34; *D.* 28, 5 and 7; *Code,* 6, 24-25.

[110] "Testamentum est dispositio, qua quis disponit, quid de rebus suis post mortem suam fieri velit, et dicitur testamentum quasi testatio mentis i.e. manifestatio voluntatis" (Bernard of Pavia, *Summa decretalium,* ed. Laspeyres, p. 96); "Testamentum est voluntatis nostre iusta sententia de eo quod post mortem nostram fieri volumus ... et dicitur testamentum quasi testamento mentis ..." (Damasus, *Summa,* MS. Paris, BN. *Lat.* 15000, fol. 63r); "Testamentum est testatio mentis qua disponitur quid de rebus suis post suum decessum testator fieri velit" (Vincent of Spain, *Apparatus ad X,* III, 26, 2, MS. Paris, BN. *Lat.* 3967, fol. 134v); the *Glossa Ordinaria* to the same canon has a similar definition of the testament. In those same years, a theologian, Baldwin, archbishop of Canterbury commenting on *Hebrews,* ix, will use the description of the civil law: "Hic dicitur testamentum solemnis ordinatio testatoris in qua plerumque fit institutio hæredis" (*Liber de Sacramento Altaris,* PL 204, 665; cf. *Inst.* II, 10).

[111] Bernard of Pavia, *Casus decretalium ad Compilatio Ia,* III, 22, 12 (ed. Laspeyres, p. 340) The notion that in some imprecise way the bishop's protection may go beyond the bequest for pious purposes is expressed indirectly in the *Glossa ordinaria ad X,* III, 26, 6 (equals *Compilatio Ia,* III, 22, 11): "et hoc praecipue in his quae ad pias causas relinquuntur." Innocent IV is more explicit: "Defensio testamentum ad episcopem pertinet maxime que ad pias causas ... idem videtur etiam in non pias ..." (*In quinque libros decretalium* [Venice 1578], p. 164v).

could be applied beyond the legacy for pious causes to a legacy for any purpose. Tancred interpreted the text in this way, seeing in it a general derogation from the more strict demands of Roman law.[112] But the more common opinion adopted by Bernard of Pavia, Damasus and others, as well as by the *Glossa Ordinaria* to the *Decretals,* held that it applied only to the bequest in alms.[113] In brief, the common law of the Church developed a doctrine of the legacy for pious causes. It considered this legacy to be made by an ambulatory, revocable act. It prescribed formalities of great simplicity and ordered enforcement by the bishop. It was a special law which often might apply to only a small part of a testator's fortune. This it was that provided the basis for the general law of the English will.

English Conditions Fostering the Adoption of the Canonical Testament

By means of this long and rather technical analysis we have seen how the common law of the Church developed from an incidental concern with certain aspects of the burial of the dead and the disposition of their property to the possession of its own law and jurisprudence of the testament. The Church in England was not unaware of this progress. The studies of the late Zachary Brooke have shown that with the Normans came the knowledge of the collections which presented the original point of view.[114] Furthermore, his investigations, with the

---

112 Tancredus *ad Compilatio Ia,* III, 22, 9, Ms. Vat. *Lat.* 1377, p. 91: "*Improbamus* ... sed quia generaliter loquitur hic papa, quod hic dicitur intelligo generaliter et puto per hoc capitulum omnibus legibus derogatum quae dicunt minus sollempnem voluntatem testatoris non valere."

113 Bernard of Pavia, *Summa decretalium,* p. 97. The same position is held in his *Casus decretalium* in the discussion of III, 22, 9 and 10, *ibid.,* pp. 339-340. Here as elsewhere the *Summa* of Damasus is very dependent on that of Bernard: "Hodie vero in hiis quae relinquuntur ecclesiis duo testes sufficiunt ..." (MS. Paris, BN. *Lat.* 15000, 63v). The *Glossa Ordinaria ad* X, III, 26, 10 and 11 is of the same opinion. Innocent IV outlined various positions in his commentary on X, III, 26, 11 (*In quinque libros decretalium,* p. 165r) and in *Speculum Iuris,* II, ii, "De Instrumentorum editione" (Venice, 1576, p. 681b), Durantis held that "per ius canonicum" the two or three witnesses were sufficient for any legacy. Cf. J. D. Hannan, *The Canon Law of Wills,* Catholic University of America Canon Law Studies, 86 (Washington, 1934), pp. 274-282.

114 Z. N. Brooke, *The English Church and the Papacy* (Cambridge, 1931), pp. 82-85. Thus in the *False Decretals,* which were known in England, the usual canons regarding the legacy of church property, alms for the dead, the avoidance of secular business, the prohibition of the *tuitio testamenti,* and the excommunication of those who prevented the execution of legacies, are to be found: see P. Hinschius, ed. *Decretales Pseudo-Isidorianae* (Leipzig, 1863), p. 335, c. i; p. 330, c. iv; p. 285, c. iv; p. 304, c. xviii. The same matters appear in the collections of Ivo of Chartres which were used in England in the twelfth century; cf. Brooke, *op. cit.,* and above, p. 121.

adjustments made by later studies, demonstrate the close relationship that existed between the law and practice of English ecclesiastical courts and the common law of the Church during the twelfth century — the period when the fundamental steps were taken.[115]   The deluge of papal letters directed towards England during the decades after the Compromise of Avranches may be explained as an effort to reform a backward ecclesiastical legal structure or, as has been recently suggested, by the effort of a very competent one seeking to perfect itself.[116]   In either case, the intimate relationship of English courts to the common law of the Church is evident.

Furthermore, Anglo-Norman canonists made a not unimportant contribution to the development of legal science during the twelfth century.   They compiled several of the *Ordines iudiciarii*,[117] played a key rôle in the gathering and arranging of papal decisions in those collections that eventually found an official form in the *Decretals* of Gregory IX,[118] and, as appears from recent investigations, made important speculative contributions to legal science as well.[119]   The developing canon law was known in England; the English played their part in the process.

In the century of the great crusades and of increasing travel for purposes of pilgrimage and trade the desirability of a revocable act, such as that which the canonists knew, is obvious.   Historians of the testament on the Continent have shown the many manifestations of this

[115] This discussion and the contributions of Brooke, Professors Barraclough and Holtzman, and others, are presented by W. Holtzmann and E. W. Kemp in *Papal Decretals relating to the Diocese of Lincoln in the Twelfth Century*, Lincoln Record Society, 47 (1954), pp. ix-xvii, and Cheney, *Becket to Langton*, pp. 32-43.

[116] *Ibid.*, pp. 47-48.   There was much reference to Rome before 1172 as well: see A. L. Poole, *From Domesday Book to Magna Carta 1087-1216*, Oxford History of England, Vol. III (Oxford, 1951), p. 195.

[117] Cf. *DDC*, VI, 1132-43 and especially S. Kuttner and E. Rathbone, "Anglo-Norman Canonists in the Twelfth Century," *Traditio*, VII (1949-51), 290-292.   This article is fundamental for an appreciation of the relation of Anglo-Norman canonists to the general movement.

[118] "...more eagerly and more successfully than anywhere else:" Brooke *The English Church*, p. 98; see Cheney, *op. cit.*, pp. 46-47.

[119] "It can now be considered an established fact that the English Church throughout this period was well abreast of the developments which everywhere resulted from the growing centralization of ecclesiastical procedure, from the work of Gratian and his school, and from the ever-increasing number of authoritative responses and appellate decisions rendered by the popes in their decretal letters" (Kuttner and Rathbone, "Anglo-Norman Canonists," p. 279).   Cf. W. Ullmann, "Canonistics in England," *Studia Gratiana*, II, 519-528.

need to which the testament responded.[120]   An interesting example of the first half of the century is to be seen in the Ramsey cartulary. Siward the cleric made a *post obit* gift of land and churches to the abbey, with reservation for his lifetime and with the additional condition that, if he went on pilgrimage and returned, he would possess it as before; if he died it would remain with the abbey.[121]   In the following century, when the canonical will with the executor was established, a testator might find the solution to a similar problem by putting his executor in charge of his property during his absence with the understanding that, in the case of death, the executor would proceed to distribution in accord with the terms of the will, while, if the testator returned, he would enter once more into possession.[122]   In the interval, however, much had to be learned about the canonical will.

One of the changes that did much to lay English practice open to ecclesiastical influence, was a change in the attitude of the royal courts to the bequest of land.   In the discussion of the rules controlling succession to real estate, it will be shown that the bequest of land was never general, never easily accomplished.   Nevertheless, it was occasionally effected by means of the acts already described.   During the second half of the reign of Henry II, the king's court condemned the bequest of land.[123]   The results of this decision are many.   One that is of special import here is that land, the form of property about which the common law courts had proved and were to prove so jealous, was not usually involved in litigation over wills.   The Church already had a foothold, however vaguely defined, in the enforcing of certain bequests of chattels.   If the gift of land by will had continued, and the common law courts had exercised their usual interest in this form of property,

---

[120] Perraud, *Etude sur le testament en Bretagne*, p. 46; Chenon, *Histoire*, II, 263. On the development of the use under similar circumstances in England see Plucknett, *History*, pp. 576-577.

[121] "Et si in peregrinationem porrexerit, et redierit, habeat sicut nunc habet. Et si obierit in itinere, solutas et quietas ab omnibus heredum calumniatoribus habeat supra-criptum altare" (*Ramsey Cart.*, I, 130). The deed is dated 1114-1130. Such a form of bequest probably lay behind the transaction described in a letter of about 1180: William Than, going to the Holy Land with his lord, William Tracy one of Becket's murderers, made his wife swear that she would assign his estate and possessions to the convent at Christ Church. The letter contains the tale of her failure to do so after his death, and her subsequent attempt to correct her fault. Presumably the convent had not known of William's intention; *Literæ Cantuarienses*, ed. J. B. Sheppard, 3 vols., RS, 85 (1887-9). App. no. 13, vol. III, 359.

[122] See below, p. 146, and n. 162.

[123] See below, p. 269.

it is very doubtful that the Church's control would have expanded to the extent it did.   But the common law courts withdrew and the ecclesiastical courts gradually extended their area of activity, proceeding to state the effects of the will, the conditions for its validity, and the procedure of its implementation.[124]

To present this expanding jurisdiction of ecclesiastical law as a form of clerical aggression, or as the bullying victory of the sophisticated lawyers of one system over their simpler brothers of the other, is to show a sad lack of historical perspective.   Many of the judges and members of the royal administration who, in the time of Henry II and his sons, dispensed and actually formed the common law of England were bishops.[125] Some of them were playing a similar rôle in the organization of ecclesiastical courts and administration as well.   In those men were united knowledge of the principles and practice of common law and a considerable acquaintance with Roman law in both its civil and canonical forms.   Whatever was done by the ecclesiastical courts was done with the knowledge of the civil courts.   Whatever decisions were made as to the ability or inability of one legal system to provide for the control of the will, were made with the knowledge that the other was quite able to supply.   The crucial decision was one of division of labour between two jurisdictions made by men who were aware of the claims and the resources of each.   By the end of the reign of Henry II decisions touching the validity of wills were made by the courts of the Church.   As would be expected, the officers of those courts turned to their own law and the system that lay behind it for their theory of the will and for the formalities required for validity.

III.   THE CANONICAL WILL IN ENGLAND

The first influence of the civil law was external: immediately following the invasion and during the twelfth century there was a quite remarkable use of romanesque phraseology.[126]   One of the most common cases was to speak of making an heir — *heredem facere, heredem constituere* or *here-*

---

124 See below, pp. 164-177.
125 "Henry's greatest, his most lasting triumph in the legal field was this, that he made the prelates of the church his justices" (P. and M., I, 132).   Between 1170 and 1213, one third of the bishops combined the office of bishop with that or royal judge; see Cheney *Becket to Langton*, pp. 24 ff. and H. G. Richardson and G. O. Sayles, *Select Cases of Procedure without writ under Henry III*, Publications of the Selden Society, LX (1941), pp. lix and n. 4 cviii, cxiii.
126 P. and M., II, 328.

dem eligere.   Phrases of this sort are to be found in scores of examples in documents ranging from the very formal agreement between King Stephen and Henry (the Treaty of Westminster of 1153),[127] through borough charters, private deeds and letters, to the chronicles.[128]   An account of a lawsuit during the reign of Henry I narrates how a dying man was urged by his servants *ut testamentum faciens publice sibi haeredem substitueret.*[129]   There was even the occasional learned reference to a text of the *Code* of Justinian to justify the execution of a will.[130]

In England as in Normandy the word *testamentum*, referring to an act whereby property was distributed after the death of the testator, came into use rather slowly.   Expressions like *donum facere* and *donatio* or *donum* were commonly used, and as they were replaced the term *divisa* shared the field with *testamentum.*[131]   When it appeared, this last expression was not intended to denote a testament in the strict sense of Roman civil law; however it did refer to a dispositive act rather than to a deed or charter, witness to a donation *inter vivos*.   (It will be recalled that *testamentum*, meaning a document, was found among the Anglo-Saxons;

---

[127] "Sciatis quod ego Rex Angliæ Stephanus Henricum ducem Normanniæ post me successorem Angliæ regni, et hæredem meum jure hæreditario constitui; et sic et hære-dibus suis regnum Angliæ donavi et confirmavi" (Rymer's *Fœdera*, I, 18).   Similarly in a royal charter of 1131 Henry I describes how a property came into his hands : "sicut justum heredem suum hereditavit" (*Regesta*, II, no. 1719).

[128] *British Borough Charters*, eds. A. Ballard and J. Tait, 2 vols. (Cambridge, 1913-23), I, 73-74: "Ut unusquisque ... de quolibet alio ... heredem facere" (Burford, 1087-1107); "Et inde heredem constituere quemcunque et quandocunque voluerint" (Dunwich, 1215). An early private charter of Geoffrey de Mandeville provides a good example of a common type of phraseology: "quem mihi heredem facere disposui" (1087-97), in Robinson, *Gilbert Crispin*, p. 139, n. 15; other examples: *Ramsey Cart.*, I, 129, 252; *Abingdon Chronicon*, II, 130-131, 205-206. St. Anselm used the phrase in Ep. 126, "sibi secundum placitum haeredes eligunt," and Ep. 176, "quos vult eorum haeredes constituere:" *Opera Omnia*, ed. F. S. Schmitt, 5 vols. (Edinburgh, 1946-51), III, 268; IV, 59.   As for the chroniclers, in *Vita Sancti Oswaldi* Eadmer writes "Regni Dei fecit hæredem:" ed. J. Raine, *Historians of the Church of York*, 3 vols., RS, 71 (1879-95), II, 59; similarly in *Historia Ecclesiastica*, IV, 4, Orde-ricus Vitalis writes "quem totius terræ suæ in Anglia hæredem constituit:" ed. A. Le Prevost, II, 182.

[129] *Two Cartularies of Bath Abbey*, ed. W. Hunt, Somerset Record Society, VII (1893), 49-51.

[130] E.g., in the letters of Gilbert Foliot, Ep. 64 (1131-48), *PL* 190, 788-789: "Et quia nihil magis debetur humanitati quam quod extreme voluntatis liber sit stilus, et licitum quod ultra non redit arbitrium ..." (*Code*, I, 2, 1).

[131] *Leis Willelme*, c. 34 : "Si home mort senz devise."   In the latin version, the phrase is translated: "De sine testamento morientibus" (*Gesetze*, I, 514).   The will of Henry was called a *divisa*.   On the appearance of the term *testamentum* in France, see Auffroy, *Testament*, pp. 399, 401 and n. 1.

in this sense the word continued to be used occasionally during the century after the Conquest.[132])

Influences of this sort, however, were but external. In the second half of the twelfth century it becomes evident that Roman law was penetrating beyond the external and accidental to change the nature and effect of the very acts whereby property was being distributed at death.

The Nature and Effect of the Canonical Will [133]

The canonical will, which appears well established in England by Bracton's time, was ambulatory, that is, it did not take effect until the death of the testator. It was also unilateral and revocable. The effects of this legal act, then, were quite different from the earlier forms of donation described above. The chronology of the stages whereby it came into use in England is not easily established. The very profound theoretical difference between the canonical will and the death-bed gift, acts whose external forms could be identical, necessarily penetrated very slowly. An abstract treatment of the subject does not occur until Bracton's treatise. Glanvill remarks that heirs are bound to observe the *testamenta* of those to whom they succeed, but reveals nothing of his conception of the nature of these acts.[134] It is necessary to turn to

---

132 In the early twelfth-century translation of the *Rectitudines Singularum Personarum,* the term is used in this sense: "De Lege taini. Taini lex est ut sit dignus rectitudini testamenti sui ..." (*Gesetze,* I, 444; III, 246). The same use occurs in *Leges Henrici Primi:* "Si quis moriens debitor testamenta tradicionis uel uendicionis aliqua fecerit ..." (*ibid.,* I, 593, c. 75, 11).

133 P. and M., II, 323 ff; Holdsworth, *History,* III, 535 ff; Plucknett, *History,* 738-740. Here, as was found to be the case when treating of the Anglo-Saxons (above, pp. 19-21), it is necessary to make certain distinctions in the use of terminology. It will be noted that in the section of this chapter dealing with the common law of the Church, the expression used was "canonical testament," or simply "testament," while in the present section the term "canonical will," or "will," has been preferred. The word "testament" is purposely avoided as descriptive of the English act because of the quality of institution of an heir, which is implied in Roman civil law, and which lies behind the understanding of the word in the general law of the Church as well. Occasionally it will be necessary to employ "testament" for the simple reason that it was used in its special English connotation by Glanvill, Bracton and thousands of documents of practice. Ordinarily however, "canonical will" or "will" is used, referring to the legal act of the testator. The notion of the written document containing the act is expressed here as in earlier chapters by means of italics—"written *will,*" or simply "*will.*"

134 Bk. VII, ch. 5: Glanvill, *De Legibus et Consuetudinibus Regni Angliae,* ed. G. E. Woodbine, Yale Historical Publications, MSS. and Edited Texts XIII (New Haven, 1932), pp. 104-105. This treatise will be cited as "Glanvill," though it is not intended to imply that Ranulph de Glanvill was its author.

documents of practice, which occasionally throw light on the theory of the acts of which they are witness. Here and there certain qualities proper to the canonical will, rather than to the various forms of donations *inter vivos*, appear, and they can be used to establish an approximate chronology of the decay of one institution and its replacement by another.

The first signs of the change have already been indicated in the analysis of the *post obit* gift and the death-bed gift. A few documents mentioned the gift of chattels and even of land, which the testator did not yet possess, but which he hoped to have at the time of death.[135] In such a gift, the donee could not be said to have right in any specific property from the time of donation, though it is likely that, in the first half of the twelfth century at least, the donor considered himself to be personally obligated from the moment when the gift was made. In this case, the contractual aspect of the act is still pronounced, but an ambulatory quality is appearing as well. On the other hand, the notion of contract was weakening in those death-bed gifts where the distribution of chattels was left to the discretion of a third party acting for the donor.[136]

Another indication of novelty is to be seen in a new freedom in the choice of place of burial.[137] It will be recalled that the early treatments of the testament and sepulchre in canon law were closely linked. We have seen too that one of the chief concerns manifest in the *post obit* gift was the choice of place of burial. Usually the donor's body and property were given to the same church, and the gift of the body was considered to be as irrevocable as was the bequest of property. Thus when Ralph Basset, a special friend of the Abbey of Abingdon in which he had fraternity and the promise of sepulchre, was suddenly taken ill at Northampton and was asked where he wished to be buried, he replied that it was to be at Abingdon *sicut ante promiserat*.[138] This choice was long considered to be binding and examples of it are to be found through the thirteenth century and well beyond.[139] Where the

---

[135] See above, p. 114.

[136] See above, p. 118.

[137] On the general problem of the freedom to revoke a previous choice of sepulchre, cf. Bernard, *La Sépulture en droit canonique*, pp. 85-104.

[138] *Abingdon Chronicon*, II, 170-171 (*ca.* 1129).

[139] In the account of the death of William Marshall, the notion that he is bound to keep his early promise that his body be buried with the Templars, is placed on the lips of the dying man: *L'Histoire de Guillaume le Maréchal*, ed. P. Meyer, 3 vols., Société de l'histoire de France (Paris, 1891-1901), lines 18228-18242. On July 6, 1231, Henry III made gift of a

promiser had changed his mind and wished to choose another place of burial, there was in the early twelfth century the strong likelihood that the earlier promise would be vindicated. An example of this is to be found in the account of the dispute between Herbert de Losinga, bishop of Norwich, and the monks of Thetford over the body of Roger Bigot.[140] Thetford had been founded by Roger in the first decade of the twelfth century. Shortly afterwards, he died, but not before he had asked for burial in the church of his foundation. The family and friends of the dying man were present and apparently gave their support to his request. But the bishop, basing his plea on a promise made somewhat earlier whereby the deceased had given himself and his family to the cathedral for burial, prevented the fulfilment of this second request. By the middle of the century, however, the opinion was growing that the dying man is free to change his mind on the matter of place of burial, and that his last will in this regard must be followed. A case similar to the above occurred in 1143 when Miles, earl of Hereford, having promised his body to Gloucester Abbey, but then having founded Lanthony Priory, requested burial in the latter church. His desire was vindicated in the bishop's court in spite of the opposition of the monks of Gloucester, though certain concessions were made with regard to the burial of the earl's children. The document describing the decision ends with an agreement that asserts the principle that parishioners had the right to revoke their choice of place of burial.[141]

As late as 1161, however, Archbishop Theobald expressed a clear intention that his will should be irrevocable. In a letter to Pope Hadrian IV in the spring of 1156, he had mentioned that during a

---

manor to the master and knights of the Temple, to whom he had entrusted his body for burial, but four years later he found it prudent to issue a second charter in which he asserted his right to change his decision on the matter, though the property was to remain with the original donee (*C.Ch.R.*, I, 210-211).

140 From a fourteenth-century history of Thetford Priory printed in Dugdale, *Monasticon*, V, 153 and in *The Life, Letters and Sermons of Bishop Herbert de Losinga*, ed. E. M. Goulburn and H. Symonds, 2 vols. (London, 1878), I, 166-167, 232-234. Ordericus Vitalis describes how the nuns of St. Mary's of Lisieux claimed the body of Bishop Hugh (d. 1077), their founder, against his own express desire and the demands of the canons of his cathedral. The royal court at Rouen decided for the nuns: "In ecclesia quam condidit, locum sepulturæ sibi, memor mortis, elegit" (Bk. V, ch. 3, ed. Le Prevost, Vol. II, 309-310).

141 "...ita etiam quod si quisquam se ipsis canonicis prius reddiderit, et postea apud Sanctum Petrum sepeliri deliberaverit, absque omni contradictione a monachis suscipiatur, et liberæ sepulturæ apud eas tradatur" (*Gloucester Cart.*, I, lxxv-lxxvi). Examples of the notion that the choice of sepulchre, expressed in the *ultima voluntas* made on the death-bed, must be implemented, are to be found in the letters of Gilbert Foliot, *Ep.* 16, 45 (1143-8), PL 190, 759-760, 778-779.

recent illness that threatened to be mortal he had disposed of all his
property, except a little which was maintained for his own needs.[142]
He seems actually to have handed his goods over to the beneficiaries so
that he no longer had even their use.[143]   Nothing could be less ambulatory than this.   A second will, which has survived, was made and
redrafted between 1158 and 1161.[144]   From it, as well as from a letter
to the king in the spring of 1161, it becomes clear that he had once more
distributed all but a little of his goods and that this remainder was to
be handed over to four friends charged with the distribution of his
alms.[145]   The *will* itself is largely devoted to the confirmation of earlier
agreements made with the obedientiaries of the cathedral priory.   Of
its dispositions, there was to be no change.[146]

Yet little more than a decade after Archbishop Theobald's death, the
compiler of the first part of the *Ramsey Chronicon,* musing over some
mysterious Anglo-Saxon documents before him, remarked that they
were evidence both of outright gifts and of testaments, and that the
latter, which in the words of St. Paul are confirmed only by death, had
no effect during the life of the testator.[147]   A remark such as this is
difficult to interpret; certainly the compiler was in error when he spoke
of the Anglo-Saxon *post obit* gift as a testament.   Yet he did seem to
realize that the essential difference between the two kinds of donation
lay in the time at which they became operative.   It is very likely that
this understanding of the Pauline text reflects contemporary legal ideas.
But such notions were new and far from general acceptance, for, though
in 1182 Henry II stated specifically that his will was revocable, he stated
it so frequently that it is necessary to conclude that the revocability of
the act was not yet fully accepted.[148]   That the notion of revocability

---

[142] "...facto iam testamento rebusque omnibus usque ad victum tenuem erogatis:"
The Letters of John of Salisbury ed. W. J. Millor, H. E. Butler, revised by C. N. L. Brooke
London, 1955), no. 8, p. 14. On the date of the letter see p. 261 of this edition.

[143] See below, p. 244.

[144] *Letters of John of Salisbury,* no. 134, pp. 245-248; on the different versions of the text,
ee *ibid.,* p. 245.

[145] *Ibid.,* no. 135, pp. 249-251.

[146] "Nostra quidem uoluntas est, et quae Deo auctore numquam mutabitur:" *ibid.,*
. 245.

[147] "Testamentum quoque suum contra futuræ generationis malitiam literis commen-
abant, quatinus authentica scripta exquisitam posteris publicæ attestationis exhiberent
eritatem. Nihilominus tamen eorum aliqui ea quæ alienis deputabant propriis quoad
iverent usibus reservabant; scientes, juxta Apostolicæ sententiæ fidem, testamentum in
orte solummodo testatoris confirmari, vivente vero testatore non valere" (p. 56).

[148] After the statement of many legacies occurs the phrase "nisi eas in vita mea repetere
oluero" (Rymer's *Fœdera,* I, 47).

was spreading and had begun to threaten one of the qualities of the
post obit gift is indicated, however, little more than a decade later, in a
document witness to such a gift of books to Osney Abbey.[149]   Here the
donor saw fit to renounce the power of alienating the books in the
interval between the gift and his death.

In the first half of the thirteenth century written *wills* began to
appear in fairly large numbers. The donation clauses of the *post obit*
gift, clauses indicative of an act already effective (*dedi et confirmavi*),
were slowly replaced by the present form of the verb (*do, lego*) without
reference to the time when the act becomes operative.[150]   The statement of the right to revoke a will appears until the end of the Middle
Ages, but very rarely; ordinarily the testator seems to have seen no need
to insist.[151]   Hugh of Wells, bishop of Lincoln, made a will in 1212
and another quite different distribution in 1233.   Other examples of
revocation in whole or in part by change and addition occur during the
century.[152]   Expression of a contractual quality in the wills is very rare.
Where it does occur, it usually takes the form of an arrangement for
suffrages for the soul.[153]   Contracts of this sort were very often made

149 "Et dedi & concessi eidem ecclesie & canonicis ibidem deo servientibus omnes libros
meos de theol[ogia]; ita ut nihil liceat michi inde deinceps [facere] ad alienacionem
aliquam, nisi de [assensu eorundem] abbatis & canonicorum de Oseneya:" *Cartulary of
Oseney Abbey,* ed. H. E. Salter, 6 vols., Oxford Historical Society, LXXXIX-XCI, XCVII-VIII
CI (1929-36), III, 78, no. 1252. The deed is dated 1184-1205.

150 Donation clauses expressing an accomplished act will be found in the examples of
post obit gift cited above, pp. 111-114 The new form, in the present tense and without
reference to the time of completion is found in T. 23, T. 33, etc. However, as will be
shown below, where the form of the written *will* is analysed in some detail, the use of the
present tense did not become general until the middle of the century. On the method
of reference to thirteenth-century wills, used throughout this study, see Appendix A
below, pp. 309-312. The number after the letter "T" is intended to provide a ready
indication of the date of the will. Thus "T. 23" is a will of 1223, "T. 33" a will of 1233
etc. Where several examples are used from the same year they are cited in chronological
order as "T. 53a," "T. 53b," etc.

151 Holdsworth, *History,* III, 540, n. 3.

152 T. 12 and T. 33; Henry III obtained papal confirmation of a will in April 1244; the
Pope confirmed it—"si in eadem voluntate usque ad supremum vite exitus duxeris persis-
tendum:" *Registres d'Innocent IV,* ed. E. Berger, 4 vols., Bibliothèque des Ecoles françaises
d'Athènes et de Rome (Paris, 1884-1921), I, 111, no. 644. Henry made what is probably a
second will in 1253 (T. 53b). Two wills of Boniface, archbishop of Canterbury, are
mentioned in a letter of Gregory X in 1272: *Entries in Papal Registers relating to Great
Britain and Ireland,* ed. W. H. Bliss *et al.,* PRO, Calendars (1894—), I, 444. A previous
will was revoked in T. 68.

153 E.g., T. 30: "Ricardo Kicus vii acras terræ sub Sapwde ... ad inveniendum in Ecclesia
de Lega iiii Lampades ardentes per annum ..."

by the executors as part of the implementation of the will.[154] Occasionally there is a confirmation of an earlier agreement made by the testator or his ancestor.[155] Several of the wills were made far from home under circumstances that made contractual relationship between testator and beneficiary impossible.[156] Most contain residual clauses in which executors are instructed to distribute part of the property at their own discretion.[157] The over-all impression from the second decade of the thirteenth century is that the will, capable of effecting the transfer of bequests to many beneficiaries, and looked upon as a single unilateral act, was coming into general use.

This conclusion is confirmed by the exposition of the will in the *De Legibus et Consuetudinibus Angliæ* of Henry de Bracton.[158] Here the will (*testamentum*) is presented almost exactly at it was seen to be taking shape in the hands of the canonists. Of the essential quality of the Roman testament, the institution of an heir, there is not a word. The exposition occurs as part of the consideration of the kinds of acquisition by donation. Donation is either *inter vivos* or *mortis causa;* the latter is assimilated to the testament.[159] Bracton's speculative presentation is for the most part a selection and rearrangement of the title *De Mortis Causa Donationibus et Capionibus* of the *Digest*.[160] The donation *mortis causa* is shown to be ambulatory as to its total effect, unilateral and revocable. It can be made in two ways: either by actual delivery of the property subject to conditional return to the donor should he survive the dangers present or anticipated, or as conditional on the death of the donor. This exposition is quite awkward and unsatisfactory. Bracton failed to show that the donation *mortis causa* had been assimilated to the bequest, and that bequests were made in the *testamentum* or *ultima voluntas*.[161] In fact, the word *testamentum* does

154 See below, p. 216.

155 E.g., T. 30: "Roberto de Bosco et hæredibus suis quod pater suus ei dedit cum lia sua . . ."

156 E.g., T. 12, T. 59a, T. 67d.

157 See below, p. 218.

158 Ed. G. E. Woodbine, 4 vols., Yale Historical Publications, Manuscripts and Edited exts III (New Haven, 1915-42); all citations and quotations are from this edition.

159 "Videndum qualiter donatio dividatur. Dividitur autem sic, quod donationem alia ter vivos, alia mortis causa, sicut ex causa testamentaria, de qua inferius dicetur" (fol. 11); fol. 49.

160 Fol. 60: "Est inter alias donationes . . . hæc enim omnia instans periculum demonsant." The paragraph is constructed from *D*. XXXIX, 6, 2; *Inst*. II, 7, 1 ; *D*. XXXIX, 6, and 27. On the question of Bracton's use of Roman law cf. H. Kantorowicz, *actonian Problems* (Glasgow, 1941), pp. 58-78.

161 Azo carefully distinguished the bequest from the *donatio mortis causa*, showing as

not occur in that paragraph of the treatise which presents the qualities of the act. Then having completed the speculative treatment of the subject, Bracton abandoned the technique of paraphrase and the use of the words *donatio mortis causa,* and thereafter spoke only of the testament. Furthermore, the variant of the donation in which the property was actually conveyed, subject to conditional return, is placed, in Bracton as in the *Digest,* on an equal footing with the other form which has no effect whatever until death. Actually this form of the bequest was rarely used in England.[162] These limitations aside however, the treatise does provide strong evidence for the general acceptance of the canonical will in England.

Bracton used a text of the *Digest* to show that when the bequest is not revocable it must be considered to be a donation *inter vivos.*[163] Here he touched on a fact that must be underlined as a necessary corrective to what has gone before. Though the practical advantages and the theoretical consistency of the canonical will are evident, it would be a mistake to think that it swept all before it in the thirteenth century. There was something to be said for the *post obit* gift and the death-bed gift. From certain points of view, the fact that the will could be revoked was regrettable. This was an age when, in spite of frequent and grave moral lapses, men looked upon the preparation for death as of supreme importance. It was an age that was strongly moved by the saint's desire to die stripped of every possession, naked in a bed of ashes. Lesser men, too, sought to die unattached to things of this world. In the account of the death of William Marshal, as he bids farewell to his wife, there is even the note that for the hours or days remaining to him

---

well, the qualities they had in common (*Summa in Codicem ad lib.* 8, *tit,* 56, in *Summa Azon* [Venice, 1566], pp. 879-880). Bernard of Pavia related the *donatio mortis causa* to the testament in the initial sentence of the title of the *Summa decretalium* dealing with the testament: "Tractavimus de donationibus inter vivos et causa mortis; sed quoniam donati causa mortis solet fieri in testamentis, de testamentis dicamus ... Videamus igitur, quid s testamentum ..." (ed. Laspeyres, p. 96).

162 Under such circumstances the property given by *post obit* gift was sometimes conveyed to the donee to hold while the donor was absent on pilgrimage, etc. In the thirteenth century the property might be placed in the control of executors during the owner absence; see the *will* of Hugh de Nevill, a crusader (T. 67d): if he were taken prisoner executors were to take possession of his property and inquire whether he could be ransomed or not; another example, in this case touching the property of a pilgrim, is in *Rot. Lit. C* I, 515b.

163 "Si autem sic donetur mortis causa ut nullo casu revocetur, causa donandi magis e quam mortis causa donatio, et ideo perinde haberi debet sicut alia quævis inter viv donatio" (fol. 60; *D.* XXXIX, 6, 27).

he would live as one unmarried.[164]   Under those conditions, one would expect that many would want their offering to be effective immediately, token as it was of their turning from the things of this life to those of the life to come, and would see in revocability the very instability of purpose that they sought to avoid.   Then too, a desire, not unknown even in a later age, to express human affection by the actual conveyance of a gift to friends as they gathered around the death-bed, would help to resist the notion that the bequest was not yet effective and could be revoked.   Some continued to use the *post obit* gift: such was William of Drogheda, civilian, canonist, professor at Oxford, a man who knew and understood the revocable will if anyone did.[165]   Others made wills, but expressed their feelings on the matter by promising not to revoke them.[166]   Such promises however were effective only morally and were not enforced by the courts.[167]   Attitudes such as these were important and should not be ignored.   None the less, the general movement of English society from early in the thirteenth century was to accept the canonical will.   Written *wills,* references to will-making, the practice of the courts, canons of councils and synods, all bear witness to its increased use and the constant efforts being made to increase its effectiveness.

[164] "Bel amie, or me besereiz,

Car ja mès nul jor ne[l] ferez." (lines 18369-70, ed. Meyer, Vol. II, 300-301.) After kissing his wife goodbye, the Marshal had the mantle of the Templar placed on his shoulders. Then his wife left the chamber.

[165] The first part of his deed, which is dated 1241-2, reads like an ordinary charter of grant of property: "Nouerit uniuersitas uestra me dedisse et concessisse et hac presenti carta confirmasse deo & beate Marie et sancto Iohanni Baptiste ... domum meam cum pertinenciis quam habo aput Oxoniam ... habendam & tenendam libere et quiete, pacifice, in puram et perpetuam elemosinam sicut in carta inde confecta plenius continetur, de me & heredibus meis." The editor notes that since this is the house in which William of Drogheda died, the grant did not become fully effective until his death. After the description of certain arrangements for suffrages, the document continues: "et prefato altari lego ad opus dicte misse domum meam ap[ut] Oxoniam secundum quod in carta continetur quam tradidi dictis priori et monachis, et omnes libros meos theologie quod habeo & habiturus sum, gradale, troperium et portetorium, & calicem estimacionis duarum marcarum, et cetera vestimenta que contingunt sacerdotem ministrantem in albis, & altare:" H. E. Salter, ed. *Eynsham Cartulary,* 2 vols., Oxford Historical Society, XLIX, LI (1906-8), II, 174-175. In the same cartulary (I, 313-314), in a document of 1282-3, the donor excludes his future right to alienate or make a will.

[166] See below, Appendix B, p. 313.

[167] Cf. *Glossa Ordinaria ad Decretum,* C. 12, q. 2, c. 4; Raymundus de Pennaforte, *Summa Iuris,* ed. J. R. Serra, *Opera Omnia* (Barcelona, 1945—), I, 143-145. The position was adopted by John of Acton (d. 1350), *Constitutiones Legatinæ D. Othonis et D. Othoboni* (Oxford, 1679), p. 109; by Lyndwood in his *Provinciale seu Constitutiones Angliæ* (Oxford, 1679), p. 163; and later by the common law; see Holdsworth, *History,* III, 540.

The Rise of the Executor

The extraordinary flexibility and effectiveness of the will as it was perfected during the thirteenth century is due in large part to the development of the executor. As first presented in Glanvill, the executor seemed likely to play a minor rôle,[168] but as the control of the will came more completely under the jurisdiction of the ecclesiastical courts, his area of activity was enlarged so that he very quickly became the representative of the testator. The common law moved somewhat more slowly, maintaining several limitations to the executor's rights and obligations, but under steady pressure from the bishops and their courts came by 1285 to admit the essentials of the executor's position as representative of the deceased.[169] The later stages of these developments are known and can be briefly presented. But the process whereby this agent of the deceased managed to find a place in the will, as presented by Glanvill, is much less clear. A generation later, in Magna Carta, his function was considerably enlarged. Of this too, there is need of explanation.

The appearance of the executor at this time is not limited to England.[170] There in fact, his first assertion of importance is somewhat later than on the Continent. With a few important exceptions, it has been agreed by historians for over half a century, that the executor, though associated with the canonical testament all over Europe, was not derived from Roman law, but was rather a development from Germanic institutions.[171] According to this reading of the evidence, it was the

---

168 "Testamenti autem executores esse debent hi quos testator ad hoc elegerit et quibus curam ipsam commiserit. Si vero testator nullos ad hoc nominaverit, possunt propinqui et consanguinei ipsius defuncti ad id faciendum se ingerere. Ita quod si quem vel heredem vel alium rerum defuncti repererint detentorem, habebunt breve domini regis vicecomiti directum . . ." (VII, 6).

169 See below, pp. 225 ff.

170 For the extensive Continental literature on the subject, see above, p. 16, n. 44. Important studies on the executor in England were made at the turn of the century: Goffin, *The Testamentary Executor;* R. Caillemer, "The Executor in England and on the Continent," *Select Essays in Anglo-American Legal History,* III, 746-769; O. W. Holmes "Early English Equity," *Law Quarterly Review,* I (1885), 162-174, and "Executors in Early English Law," *Harvard Law Review,* IX (1895), 42-48, are especially important. On the general background to the development, L. Dulac, *Développement historique et théorie de l'exécution testamentaire* (Toulouse, 1899), is useful. Shorter sketches are available in P. and M., II, 335 ff. (cf. p. 335, n. 1 for bibliography), and Plucknett, *History,* pp. 737-738, this last, very brief but remarkably complete. An excellent synthetic presentation of the history of the executor, one that includes recent work, is in Holdsworth, *History,* III, 563 ff.

171 "He is nothing else than the salmann appointed to ensure the execution of a will

Salmann, considerably reshaped both in fact and theory, that was used on the Continent with the newly developing canonical testament to supply for the *institutio haeredis* which it lacked in most areas. In the beginning, the Salmann actually acquired rights in the property by public tradition, and maintained them pending delivery to the donee. Gradually the older Germanic formalism gave way. The Salmann ceased to receive delivery during the donor's life-time. He became charged with one or several bequests rather than the whole property of the deceased. Eventually his position became revocable.[172]

There are, however, important limitations to this explanation. First of all, the details of the very considerable evolution sketched above are not easily demonstrated in extant documents. Furthermore, there are signs of a form of the institution in southern France in which the third party seems to have acted as a trustee rather than in his own right.[173] Finally, there is the fact that in Byzantine and Mohammedan law, systems largely free from Germanic influence, similar institutions developed during the Middle Ages.[174] Nevertheless, it seems impossible to avoid the conclusion that the long Germanic experience in the use of a third party to act for the deceased provided the institutional source of the executor. This third party was to be quickly developed and reshaped under the pressure of the needs of the time and the determination of the church courts to use the executor as their instrument for the implementation of wills. In this evolution, notions derived from Roman law played a fundamental rôle.[175] It is not inconceivable that without the Germanic experience a similar institution would have developed. But that experience is a historical fact and in it the beginnings of the executor lie.

Of the properly Anglo-Saxon antecedents of the executor, there is much less evidence, so little in fact that some scholars have concluded

which contained nothing corresponding to the Roman instituted heir" (Goffin, *op. cit.*, p. 34); similar opinions by many other authors are assembled *ibid;* in addition, see Holmes, "Early English Equity," p. 164 and E. F. Bruck, "Zur Entwicklungsgeschichte der Testamentvollstreckung in römischen Recht," *Zeitschrift für das Privat- und öffentlich Recht in Gegenwart*, XL (1914), 545-559.

172 Cf. Holdsworth, *History*, III, 563-564 and especially, Goffin, *op. cit.*, pp. 24-34.

173 This evidence is presented by Auffroy, *Testament*, pp. 308-312, 413-420.

174 Caillemer, "The Executor in England and on the Continent," pp. 746-749; Plucknett, *History*, pp. 737-738.

175 A remarkable example of the romanesque influence is seen in the *Vita Sancti Dunstani*, written *ca.* 1090 by Osbern, preceptor of Canterbury. On the lips of the dying Æthelfleda, Dunstan's patroness, he put the words: "Illum [Deum] ergo rerum mearum hæredem acio, te vero hæreditatis tutorem constituo; ut quicquid Illum cognoveris velle, tui arbitrii it effectui mancipare." ed. W. Stubbs, in *Memorials of St. Dunstan* RS, 63 (1874), p. 87.

that the Church imported the institution, fruit of more precocious developments on the Continent, and applied it locally in England.[176] However, mention has already been made of the occasional appearance of the *mund* or protector in the Anglo-Saxon *wills,* and even more rarely of individuals whom we have called executors, and who were charged with the actual delivery of certain bequests.[177] Even beyond the evidence of the *wills,* there were signs that the attendant priest and other witnesses who received the last words of the dying were charged with a similar task of protection and delivery.[178] Whether the powers vested in them were comparable to those of the *Treuhand* or the *Salmann* on the Continent, it is not possible to say,[179] but that a third party sometimes acted for the deceased is undeniable.

For the period after the Conquest, English evidence is more satisfactory. The use of a third party occurs only rarely, if at all, in the *post obit* gifts; seemingly the publicity of the act, the permissions of lord and heir that frequently accompanied the donation, established the donee's rights sufficiently well. It was rather in cases of the death-bed gift, when strength or time was lacking to the donor that a third party was drawn into the transaction. It is very difficult to arrive at the theory that lay behind these acts. When Glanvill came to write of the death-bed gift of land, the notions of seisin then in vogue made the gift impossible ; he did not choose to write of this form of donation at an earlier day when it was effective.[180] Conclusions must be drawn rather from the evidence provided by the wording of charters. In many cases it is clear that the third party was considered to be the legal owner in the interval between the donation and the actual delivery to the donee ;[181] occasionally there is reference to the public transfer of the property to the third party.[182] There are a few examples, however,

---

[176] There is "little doubt but that this person, familiar in the continental codes of law and in the canon law was introduced into England after the Conquest" (Holdsworth, *History,* III, 565); also Goffin, *op. cit.,* p. 37.

[177] See above, pp. 43-44.

[178] *Ibid.*

[179] See above, p. 41.

[180] See below, pp. 266-273.

[181] E.g., in a document of *ca.* 1087 mentioning a gift of land to Westminster Abbey: "terram, scilicet Wateleyam, quam pater suus dedit sancto Petro pro anima sua, et de qua terra ipse Rotbertus cum sua matre fecit donacionem ... in eodem die quo sepultus est pater suus" (Robinson, *Gilbert Crispin,* p. 135, no. 8).

[182] E.g., Albreda, wife of William de Sackville was present when her husband gave five shillings of land in Colchester to St. John's Abbey "et me rogavit sicut suam conjugem ut ipsas quinque solidatas monachis constituerem et contraderem. Testes inde fuerunt ...

where he seems to have been considered to be only the agent of the donor. He had no right in the property, but simply made conveyance in the place of one who was unable to do so. This point of view is evident especially in cases of death-bed gift, where seisin was transferred to the donee even before the death of the former owner.[183] In either case, it is evident that the donation was completed by a person freely chosen by the donor, and that the third person in question entered into his office as a result of a bilateral agreement with the donor.[184]

There are many indications of a quite different development in the last quarter of the twelfth century. With the triumph of primogeniture among the nobility and its spread through the lower levels of free society (perhaps even before this was accomplished), there was a movement towards unified succession by the heir.[185] He was not the freely chosen heir of Roman law, but the heir of English law, made by God, as Glanvill said,[186] a person whose choice lay entirely outside the control of the testator no matter how objectionable he might be. It will be recalled that Glanvill had shown the death-bed gift of land to be impossible without the heir's consent. The property of which a man died seised became the property of his heir. If the latter were willing that his father's death-bed gift of land be implemented, the effects of the act so far as the donee and the family of the donor were concerned, were those of a bequest. But, in the eyes of the law, the heir made the gift of his own property and this he was not bound to do. He was obliged, however, to deliver bequests of movable property. Such was the practice described in the Assize of Northampton (1176) and Glanvill.

Ego itaque secundum voluntatem mariti mei feci quam citius potui offerens super altare Sancti Johannis totam defuncti donationem et nominatim quinque solidatas illas statutas in terra Colechestrie que michi erit commissa feci contradi monachis per Rogerum de Bruil:" *Cart. Sancti Johannis Colecestria*, I, 163 (*ca.* 1158).

183 Robert priest of Mercham bequeathed a house to Abingdon Abbey: "Et quia ille ultima infirmitate jam laborabat, et illuc ire non poterat, cuidam Uualtero de Coleshulle, cognato suo, vice sua domum eandem super magnum altare offerre præcepit:" *Abingdon Chronicon*, II, 205 (1154-89). For other examples, see above, p. 116. Occasionally it does not seem to have been clear to the executor, whether he acted in his own right or merely as agent of another: e.g., "dispono et committo et quicquid juris in rebus predictis aliquo modo et aliquo tempore habuerunt ipsi vel etiam ego ipse noscor habuisse, simul cum cartis, etc.:" (*EYC*, II, 145-147, no. 800). For early examples of this notion on the Continent, see Auffroy, *Testament*, pp. 412-415, and Perraud, *Etude sur le testament en Bretagne*, p. 37.

184 Goffin, *op. cit.*, pp. 25-31.

185 P. and M., II, 343-345.

186 Bk. VII, ch. 1.

Roman civil law had given the Church a weapon against the undutiful heir and, as we have seen, the notion that the Church could interfere in certain cases survived all through the Middle Ages.[187]   None the less, the main guarantee of fulfilment of the desires of the Roman testator was his freedom to choose as heir one who would accomplish what was desired, and to exclude the person who would not.   The institution carried the reasons for its success within itself.   The sanctions of the law were but external pressures intended to supply in those rare occasions where the institution failed to function normally.   Something of the like efficacy was needed in those lands where the choice of heir was not within the power of the individual.   Throughout northern Europe the need was filled in varying degrees by the executor.   In England, where primogeniture in the inheritance of land was an accomplished fact, and unified succession a possibility, the position of the heir promised to be especially strong.   Yet it was in England that the powers of the executor were to see their fullest development.

The first appearance of the executor in a legal treatise was not auspicious.   In the Assize of Northampton it is stated that, on the death of a freeholder, the heir is to have seisin of the land and chattels of the deceased.[188]   With the latter property he shall implement the will.   The same emphasis of the position of the heir is evident in Glanvill, but here it is said that executors ought to be named and that they should see to the execution of the will.[189]   As presented in Glanvill, the executor's position is that of a supervisor.   He did not receive the goods of the testator, much less represent him; he is reminiscent of the Anglo-Saxon *mund* rather than the Salmann.   Yet in 1215 Magna Carta will mention the distribution of a testator's chattels by the executor.   In the interval between Glanvill and the Great Charter, the executor seems to have replaced the heir as the one to whom chattels passed for distribution after their owner's death.   One wonders whether the position of the heir in Glanvill is a correct description of the practice of the time.   There are some indications that it is not.   The *will* of Henry II did not mention executors by name, but it did appoint a group of royal servants who were to distribute his property *per manum et visum*.[190]   A king's will is, of course, a special case, but there are other examples of the same

---

[187] *Novel.* I, 1; see above, pp. 120 ff.

[188] "Item si quis obierit francus-tenens, haeredes ipsius remaneant in tali saisina qualem pater suus habuit die qua fuit vivus et mortuus, de feodo suo; et catalla sua habeant unde faciant divisam defuncti" (c. 4, Stubbs, *Select Charters*, p. 179).

[189] *Glanvill*, Bk. VII, c. 6; the text is quoted above, p. 148, n. 168.

[190] See above, p. 143.

period which provide similar information. Thus in a charter of
St. Mary Clerkenwell (1180-3), we are informed that Nicholas de
Swanescans, being too ill to distribute his property himself, put executors in his place both to make his will and to implement it.[191]   Other
documents of the years around the turn of the century illustrate the
executor acting in the same way.[192]   On the other hand, some examples,
where the heir received the chattels of the deceased and distributed
legacies, are to be found in the Pipe Rolls until quite late in the reign
of King John.[193]

Glanvill probably described an ordinary situation, where the testator
was succeeded by a son or near relative.   Most of the earliest examples
where the executor, identified as such, is shown exercising the function
Glanvill reserved to the heir, are the wills of ecclesiastics.   These men
were not expected to have descendants, and their successors were often
appointed after a long delay.   Furthermore, the protection of their
property was one of the functions of the courts of the Church.   It is
very likely that, in the cases cited, the implementation of the will by the
freely chosen executor was made easier for the simple reason that the
testator had no children to act as heirs.   It will be recalled that Glanvill
considered sons and daughters to have greater right to prevent alienation than did more remote heirs,[194] and that much earlier the Germanic

---

[191] "Sciatis quod cum Nicholaus de Swanescans clericus in extremis laboraret et pro
multa et grauiter inualescente egritudine non haberet facultatem prout expediret sibi suum
condendi testamentum, ipse elegit nos ad supplendum quod pro se minus adimplere potuit
et posuit nos in loco suo ad faciendum testamentum suum et ad faciendam executionem
testamenti illius de tenementis et posessionibus suis et catallis et rebus suis.   Nos itaque
karitatis intuitu curam suscipientes quam ipse nobis inposuit vice predicti *Nicholai* concessimus et dedimus et nomine testamenti reliquimus..." (*Cartulary of St. Mary Clerkenwell*,
pp. 208-209, no. 319).   In 1184, the executors of Hawise are paid money from the estate of
her husband: "Et executoribus testamenti Hawise que fuit uxor prefati Roberti. xxij.s. et
viij.d." (*Pipe Roll*, 30 Henry II, p. 134).

[192] E.g., a deed of St. Paul's, showing the executors of Thomas the canon, selling a
house in London: "Sciant tam presentes quam futuri quod ego Radulfus de Diceto decanus
sancti Pauli Lond' et eiusdem ecclesie capitulum venditionem quam fecerunt supprior
sancte Marie de Sudwerc et R. d Storteford' magister scolarum et magister Hugo de
Lond*onia* et Hugo de Raculf' executores testamenti Thome nepotis..." (*Early Charters of
St. Paul's*, pp. 128-129, no. 167); for other examples see below, nn. 197, 200.

[193] In 1203, Robert, brother and heir of Hugh Bardolf was in charge of his late
brother's chattels; the notice includes the clause: "Vult etiam dominus R. quod testamentum ipsius Hugonis rationabile teneatur:" *Pipe Roll*, 5 John, p. 103; in 1210 Thomas son
of Ralph had his father's chattels "ad faciendum testamentum suum:" *Pipe Roll*, 12 John,
p. 35.

[194] Bk. VII, ch. 1.

peoples had seen fit to introduce a third party to act for the land owner who seemed about to die without a member of his family to succeed him.[195]   During the reign of John the ecclesiastical courts extended their jurisdiction over the will to include disputes touching the delivery of bequests.[196]   It is suggested that the growth of the power of the executor at the expense of the heir, which these courts fostered, was made easier — had its beginnings perhaps — in those cases where the testator was a cleric, one whose heir was not a descendant.   This suggestion is strengthened by the fact that, in the two earliest examples in the Close Rolls where the executors of lay testators are shown receiving goods and distributing them, the testators died childless.[197]

It is explicitly stated in Magna Carta that the distribution of a testator's bequests was to be made by his executor.[198]   The sheriffs had been seizing the chattels of deceased royal tenants, who were indebted or were thought to be indebted to the king, and had been taking more of these chattels than the debts warranted.   According to the new ruling, which first appeared among the Articles of the Barons and was reproduced in all later issues of the Charter,[199] royal officials, on receipt of instructions indicating the amount of debt, were to cause the chattels of the deceased to be viewed by a local jury, then, having taken inventory and seen to the payment of the royal debt, were to hand the remainder over to the executors for the implementation of the will.   It may be asked whether this clause involved an innovation or represented current practice.   Magna Carta was the result of clerical pressure as well as that of the laity, and it is conceivable that the bishops used it to impose a view of the executor which they favoured.   The manner in which

195 See above, pp. 9 ff.

196 See below, pp. 169-176.

197 Robert, earl of Leicester died in 1204 and left neither children nor brothers. A letter instructed the sheriffs of Leicestershire and Warwickshire not to impede his "executores testamenti" in their work (*Rot. Lit. Cl.*, 6 John, 1204, p. 13a). The following year, similar instructions were issued regarding the property of Maud, countess of Warwick, who died childless (*ibid.*, 6 John, 1205, p. 24a).

198 "Si aliquis tenens de nobis laicum feodum moriatur, et vicecomes vel ballivus noster ostendat litteras nostras patentes de summonitione nostra de debito quod defunctus nobis debuit, liceat vicecomiti vel ballivo nostro attachiare et inbreviare catalla defuncti inventa in laico feodo, ad valentiam illius debiti, per visum legalium hominum, ita tamen quod nihil inde amoveatur, donec persolvatur nobis debitum quod clarum fuerit; et residuum relinquatur executoribus ad faciendum testamentum defuncti; et si nihil nobis debeatur ab ipso, omnia catalla cedant defuncto, salvis uxori ipsius et pueris rationabilibus partibus suis" (c. 26, Stubbs, *Select Charters*, p. 296).

199 *Articles*, c. 15; *Magna Carta*, 1215, c. 26; 1216, c. 20; 1217, c. 22; 1225, c. 18; cf. W. S. McKecknie, *Magna Carta*, 2nd ed. (Glasgow, 1914), pp. 321-326.

reference is made to the executor provides what is perhaps the best answer to this question. The subject of dispute was the behaviour of the sheriffs; mention of the executor occurs only in a subsidiary clause. But it is taken for granted that he received the chattels of the deceased and distributed them. Thus, though mention in Magna Carta would greatly strengthen the executor's position, it seems that the essentials of that position had already been attained. This conclusion is supported by the evidence of the earliest *wills* of the thirteenth century,[200] by references to the activity of the executor in documents of the Exchequer and the Chancery,[201] and by the fact that early in the reign of Henry III the executor began to represent the testator.

English common law was retarded in the development of representation of any kind.[202] Thus it is not surprising that the executor's right to be the passive and active representative of the testator met long and effective resistance from the royal courts.[203] In Glanvill, the heir was responsible for his ancestor's debts and was bound even in excess of the amount received from the inheritance.[204] Presumably he could sue debtors whose obligations had been recognized before the death of the testator.[205]

Once it had been admitted that the testator's chattels should pass to the executor for distribution, the way was prepared for the latter's activity as representative of the deceased. Canon law and common law agreed

---

[200] The freely chosen executor is expected to receive and distribute the testators' chattels in T. 12, T. 16, T. 23, T. 25, etc. It was just after this time that papal letters began to take note of the executor and to instruct bishops that they enforce the correct performance of his office: see Potthast, 9644, 9646 (1227-34), which become X, III, 26, 17 and 19.

[201] The executors of Peter de Stoke are shown acquitting his debts to the king in the Memoranda Roll of 10 John, 1207-8: R. A. Brown ed. *The Memoranda Roll for the Tenth Year of King John*, Publications of the Pipe Roll Society, N.S., XXXI, 31 (1955), pp. 38-39. Executors of Gilbert Pecche were allowed seisin of his chattels having given security for the payment of his debts to the king (*Rot. Lit. Cl.*, 14 John, p. 123a); Gilbert left a minor heir and daughters: see G. E. Cokayne, *Complete Peerage*, 2nd ed., 12 vols. (London, 1910-40), vol. X, 334. In the Pipe Roll of 13 John, the "executores testamenti" of Robert of Thornham, custodian of the see of Canterbury, answer at the Exchequer for some of the debts of the deceased (p. 112). It will be noted that in these cases the executors had begun to represent the deceased in the payment of debts to the king.

[202] See Caillemer, *op. cit.*, p. 755; H. Brunner, "The Early History of the Attorney in English Law," *Illinois Law Review*, III (1908), 257-279.

[203] On the representation of the deceased by the executor, see P. and M., II, 343-348; Goffin, *op. cit.*, pp. 35-78; Caillemer, *op. cit.*, pp. 755-764; and especially Holdsworth, *History*, III, 563-583.

[204] Bk. VII, chs. 5 and 8; also *Dialogus de Scaccario*, Bk. II, 18, ed. Hughes, p. 151.

[205] Goffin, *op. cit.*, p. 39; Holdsworth, *History*, III, 573.

that all debts should be paid before the delivery of legacies was made. Given the primitive religious purpose of the will it is not surprising that the testator desired that all injustices be repaired, and that obligations of any sort be acquitted.   From the first quarter of the thirteenth century most written *wills* instruct executors to see to the payment of debts.[206]   These documents leave a distinct impression that the testators were willing to go considerably beyond their purely legal obligations.[207] Occasionally the heir was instructed to complete the payment of debts where the funds assigned to the executors for that purpose failed.[208] But the chattels, the first source to be tapped for the payment of debt, had been assigned to the executor, and it was to be expected that efforts would be made to oblige him to pay these debts.   Powerful pressures in this direction were applied almost immediately by the royal administration itself.

Reference has been made above to a few cases in the reign of John where a testator's debt to the king was collected from his executors.[209] It may be taken as axiomatic that royal servants enforced their master's rights by obtaining assets wherever they were available.   Thus it is not surprising to see them proceeding against executors, as soon as it was established that they should have control of the testator's chattels.   It appears that the procedure to be used against royal debtors, outlined in Magna Carta, was not always followed exactly.   The delay that would necessarily result, if executors were powerless to act until the sheriff was informed of the debts of the deceased, must have made the letter of the law difficult to apply.   Instead, royal servants were often instructed to obtain pledges that debts would be paid by the executors when these debts were known.   The chattels were then delivered to the executors that they might proceed to distribute legacies.   This implied that the royal administration considered the executor to be the passive representative of the deceased even for uncertain debts.   This development can be illustrated by a sampling of the Memoranda Rolls prior to 1230.   In the two rolls that survive from the reign of John, arrangements for the collection of royal debts were made with the heirs or, as in the case of ecclesiastics, with successors.[210]   A similar situation is described in the

---

206 E.g., T. 12, T. 25, T. 30, T. 33.

207 See below, p. 260; cf. the suggestion of Holdsworth that this fact explains, in part, the slow development of the passive powers of the executor (*History*, III, 584).

208 E.g., "Et si bladum prædictum ad debita sua adquietanda pertingere nequiverit, hæres suus id quod defuerit perficiet" (T. 30).

209 See above, p. 155 and n. 201.

210 There was one exception, the payment of debt to the king by the executors of

rolls of the second and third years of Henry III.[211]   But in the seventh
year of Henry's reign both heirs and executors are found to be liable
for royal debts,[212] and in the roll of the fifteenth year, sheriffs are found
to be dealing with the executors as a general rule.[213]   In this last document there is even a directive to the sheriff not to molest an heir, since
arrangements for the payment of debts had been made with executors.[214]
By that time references to the payment of royal debts by executors are
of frequent occurrence in the Close Rolls.[215]   Thus it is not surprising

Peter de Stoke in the roll of 10 John; see above, n. 201. Examples of the payment of
debts by heirs or ecclesiastical successors may be found in the roll of 1 John, ed. H. G.
Richardson, *The Memoranda Roll for the Michaelmas term of the First Year of the Reign
of King John*, Publications of the Pipe Roll Society, N.S., XXI, (1943), pp. 9, 26, 44, 64-65,
and in the roll of 10 John, ed. Brown, pp. 36-37, 41, 43, etc.

[211] References to the Memoranda Rolls of 2, 3 and 7 Henry III are drawn from typed
transcripts which are available in the Search Room of the Public Record Office. A
typical entry from *K.R. Memoranda Rolls*, 2 "Henricus Hosatus frater et heres Willelmi
Hose de Tadewic debet respondere de ix libris et iiii solidis et iiii denariis pro debito fratris
sui" (Search Room, 62/C, p. 44).

[212] E.g., "Executores testamenti Thome de Nevill' debent respondere de xii de scutagio
Pictavie de tempore quo habuit custodiam abbatie Sancti Albani" (Search Room, 62/H,
p. 17). Both the executors and the heirs of Gilbert de Tany were involved in the
payment of his debts: "Executores testamenti Giliberti de Tany debuerunt solvisse ad
festum Sancti Hylarii preteritum xx. marcas de catallis ipsius. Quilibet trium heredum
Giliberti de Tany debet pro ipso Giliberto C. libras et dimidam preter relevium suum
scilicet quilibet eorum l. marcas. Preterea executores testamenti ipsius Giliberti debent
xx. marcas" (*ibid.*, p. 17).

[213] See *The Memoranda Roll of the King's Remembrancer for Michaelmas 1230—Trinity 1231*,
ed. C. Robinson (published at Princeton as Pipe Roll Society, N.S., XI, 1933) pp. xxi, 17,
20, 39 *et passim*.

[214] "Mandatum est vicecomiti quod non distringat Robertum Musard' pro debitis Radulfi
Musard' quia ... exequtores finem fecerunt inde cum domino R." *ibid.*, p. 65. On the
other hand, where the assets in the executor's control were not sufficient to acquit the
debt to the king, payment was sought from the heir. An example of this is provided
by the first of the Exchequer Plea Rolls: "Item postea reddiderunt dicti executores.
xvij libras et iiij solidos de dicto debito et dixerunt quod nichil amplius habent de bonis
suis. et ideo recesserunt quieti et dominus Rex recuperet residuum dicti debiti de herede
dicti Ricardi de Brome" (*Select Cases in the Exchequer of Pleas*, ed. H. Jenkinson and B. E. R.
Formoy, Publications of the Selden Society, XLVIII [1931], p. 13, no. 38). The same roll
mentions a case where the sheriff delivered the chattels of the testator without taking
security for the payment of debts to the king. By the time these debts were known and
sought, all assets had been distributed. The executors suggested that the king seek his
debts from the heir: "et ideo credebant ut dicunt quod Rex capere deberet ad heredem
ipsius Ricardi de debitis suis" (*ibid.*, pp. 12-13, no. 37). Both examples are dated 1237.

[215] In 1227 the executors of William de Mandeville having undertaken to pay his debts
to the king, the sheriff is instructed to convey all his chattels to them: *Rot. Lit. Cl.*, II,
167a, 169, 180b, 189b. Similar instructions regarding the chattels of Alex. of Doreset, H.
of Nevill, and the bishop of Norwich are found in *C.C.R.*, II, 201-202, 489 and III, 384.

that a writ to the archbishop of Canterbury in 1237 should begin: "Although it is common right that the debts of persons deceased ought first to be paid by the executors . . .".[216]

Active representation was also fostered by the royal administration. The acquittal of obligations to the king depended at times on the executor's ability to collect the debts owed the testator. From the early years of the reign of Henry III the sheriffs are found to have received instructions to aid the executors in doing so.[217] Occasionally the king himself is seen admitting an obligation to the testator and paying the required sum to the executor.[218] So it came about that the collection of the king's debts led to an early practical admission of the passive and active representation of the testator by his executor.[219]

The royal courts were much slower to admit this representation. But from early in the reign of Henry III there are indications that the executor was obliged to pay debts of which the testator had been convicted during his lifetime, or which he had admitted in his will.[220] *Bracton's Note Book* preserves the report of a case of 1219 from which

[216] "Rex Archiepiscopo. Cantuariensi. Licet ius sit commune quod decedencium debita prius solui debeant ab executoribus eiusdem quadam tamen prerogatiua regie dingnitatis in hoc precellimus quod juxta regni consuetudines artare possumus per Balliuos nostros cuiuscunque dingnitatis executores ad soluenda nobis debita que a defunctis nobis debentur:" from the Memoranda Roll of 20, 21 Henry III, published in *Select Cases in the Exchequer of Pleas* pp. lv-lvii.

[217] In 1219 the sheriff of Gloucestershire is instructed to give to the executors of Walon de Cotes the sum owed to him by William de Mara (*Rot. Lit. Cl.*, I, 393b); in the L.T.R. Memoranda Roll of 7 Henry III: "et scire facias Briano de Insula et abbati de Sireburn' et aliis debitoribus ipsius Rogeri per literas tuas quod eisdem executoribus satisfaciant de debitis que ipsi Rogero debuerunt" (Search Room, 62/H, p. 72); in 1226 the sheriff of Northampton is instructed to distrain the men of Oswaldbec to pay the executors of Roger the farm owed to him while he was yet alive (*Rot. Lit. Cl.*, II, 105b). In the case mentioned above in n. 214, where the executors of Richard de Brome did not have assets sufficient for the payment of all their testator's debts, they informed the king of debts still owed the testator and of the theft of five acres of corn by the men of Earl Roger Bigod; the debtors were distrained to pay the king directly.

[218] In 1224 the king credited the executors with his debts to Roger de la Forde, late sheriff of Dorset (*Rot. Lit. Cl.*, I, 583b). Several examples of the payment of the salary of those who died in the royal service to their executors are to be found in the Gascon Rolls 1242-54: *Rôles gascons*, ed. F. Michel, Documents inédits (Paris, 1885), nos. 1243, 1672, 3114.

[219] Basing his conclusions on the Gascon Rolls, which were available in print at the end of the last century when he was preparing his studies on the executor, Caillemer illustrated these royal practices during the period 1242-54 (*op. cit.*, p. 759). Actually they were older by as much as a generation.

[220] For the details of this development cf. Goffin, *The Testamentary Executor*, pp. 37-45.

it can be inferred that mention of a debt in a will obligated the executor.[221] This conclusion is shown to be correct by the report of a dispute three years later where a writ of prohibition stayed an action in court Christian, by a creditor against executors, because the debt in question had not been admitted in the will.[222] This same source shows that in the 1230's executors were able to bring action against their testator's debtors, where the obligations had been admitted or proved before the latter's death.[223] Debts of this kind could, with but a little imagination, be looked upon as already part of the assets of the deceased, just as admitted obligations could be considered to be virtually withdrawn from his estate.[224] It is not surprising, then, that both of these actions were allowed in court Christian.

Representation of the deceased for unacknowledged debts and obligations remained, however, with the heir. The royal courts were unwilling that a debt be sought by or against an executor in court Christian, when action during the testator's life could be had only in the king's court. The heir's lot had been improved since he was no longer bound legally beyond the extent of the assets received.[225] So Bracton presents the practice of his day.[226] But the arrangement was exceedingly awkward[227] and already there was a considerable pressure to make the heir yield this area of activity too. The practices of the royal debt collectors were not without effect. The intentions of testators as manifested in their wills and the inclusion in contracts of a clause, whereby the parties and their executors were bound or named beneficiaries,[228] imply that by mid-century many desired that the

---

[221] *Bracton's Note Book,* ed. F. W. Maitland, 3 vols. (London, 1887), no. 52.

[222] *Ibid.,* no. 162. The annotator remarks: "Nota quod locum habet prohibitio si quis implacitet executores alicuius de debito defuncti quod ipse defunctus in uita sua nec in testamento cognovit nec in uita conuictus fuit;" see Bracton, *De Legibus,* fol. 407b.

[223] No. 810 (1233): executors were prevented by prohibition from suing Peter de Malo Lacu for debt because "nec idem Petrus unquam conuictus fuit in vita ipsius [i.e. the testator's] super debito illo, nec debitum illud cognitum fuit unquam in uita ipsius Galfridi, etc." Payment of debt to executors is illustrated in nos. 381 (1230), and 559 (1231).

[224] So Bracton presented them, fol. 407b; see Holdsworth, *History,* III, 573.

[225] In Bracton's time the heir's assets probably included the land inherited from the deceased; cf. Holdsworth, *History,* III, 573, 576, n. 1. For an example of an attempt to collect more than his purparty from an heir and the royal order for the adjustment of payments see *C.P.R.,* V, 4 (1258).

[226] *De Legibus,* fols. 407b, 101, 113b.

[227] "It is a roundabout scheme that would compel the heir to collect money in order that he might pay it to an executor who would divide it among the legatees" (P. and M., II, 346).

[228] E.g., in July 1251 the king acknowledged the loan of 2000 marks by Richard of

executor represent the testator as completely as possible.   Prohibitions during the last twenty years of Henry's reign show that the courts Christian sought to entertain testamentary suits touching unacknowledged debts.   Bishops and councils complained that these prohibitions and the resulting inability of the executors to collect the debts of their testators, had rendered the completion of wills impossible.[229]

There was one important group, however, that looked upon this development with misgivings.   They tried to throw part of the burden of debt back on their landed property and on the heir who received it. No doubt they feared lest the overriding claims of the Exchequer take all, or nearly all, their chattels to the neglect of bequests in alms. Beginning in 1227 is a long and rather numerous series of letters in the Patent Rolls, in which tenants-in-chief or royal servants, who were likely to be indebted to the king, obtained permission to make a will with the understanding that royal debts would be collected from the heir.[230]   Eventually it was specifically stated that executors would not be responsible for royal claims.   In one of the last examples, a letter to Roger Mortimer in 1282, the recipient was informed that as a special favour, one never granted before even to blood-relatives of the king, his executors would not be impeded, but the escheators would take themselves to the heir.[231]   Had the chancery clerk been better acquainted with the rolls of previous years, he would have known that the letter he penned was not unique.   Yet his remark does reflect an important change that occurred at about this time.   Early in the reign of Edward I the request of the bishops regarding the representative capacity of the

Cornwall, the sum to be paid to the earl or his executors *C.P.R.*, IV, 101. In "A Conveyancer of the Thirteenth Century," F. W. Maitland edited a *Forma obligacionis de pecunia mutuata* in which the debtor binds himself to pay his creditor "vel suis certis procuratoribus, vel heredibus suis vel executoribus hoc scriptum presens habentis." See *The Collected Papers of Frederick William Maitland*, ed. H. A. L. Fisher, 2 vols. (Cambridge, 1911), II, 193-194, no. 21.

229 For the efforts of the bishops and their courts see below, pp. 225 ff.

230 In 1227 the king conceded that, though Hugh Mortimer was indebted to him, he might make a will and the king would recover his debts "de heredibus suis" (*C.P.R.*, II, 169); other exs., *ibid.*, p. 201 (1228), p. 250 (1229). The attitude is especially clear in a letter concerning the will of the earl of Chester in 1232: "ita quod non remaneat occasione debitorum, que ipse comes nobis debet, quin executores testamenti ipsius comitis libere et sine impedimento executionem ipsius faciant de omnibus supradictis, quoniam de debitis que nobis debet, nos cepimus ad heredes suos et terras suas" (*ibid.*, II, pp. 472-473). In 1255 Walter Cantilupe, bishop of Worcester arranged that his executors should not be bound for his debts to the king, but that they should be paid by his successors at the rate of 25 marks a year (*ibid.*, IV, 398).

231 *C.P.R.*, (Edward I), II, 38.

executor was partially granted: actions touching debts and claims were allowed the executor, but jurisdiction remained with the temporal courts.[232] Thus the complaint of the clergy that the implementation of wills had been rendered impossible, was removed. This important decision was made quietly, perhaps in the courts themselves. It was indirectly acknowledged by the Second Statute of Westminster (1285) which gave the executors an action of account as well.[233] Henceforth the heir was obliged only where the testator had bound him by an instrument under seal; this was, in fact, of frequent occurrence.[234] But the executor had been recognized by the temporal courts as the representative of the deceased. Only after more than a century, during which the executor increased that power of representation, would Lyndwood be able to compare him to the heir of Roman law.[235] But the foundation of all later development was established by 1285.

It was the executor who made the English will the marvellously flexible and effective instrument that it was. His choice was important and, as will be seen in the following chapter, it was made with great care. The testator did all that he could to see that his man acted as he himself would act. When the choice was a failure and the executor could not be trusted to do his duty, then the Church courts intervened to enforce obedience.

The activity of the Church courts is the subject of the following chapter. For the moment it is possible to pause: the executor was accepted, at least in principle, as the representative of the deceased. With that, the proper qualities of the English will were established, and common law was committed to the principle that movable and immovable property should devolve in different ways. We have seen that the legal act whereby property was distributed at death was not fundamentally changed by the Conquest. The *post obit* gift and the deathbed gift continued to be used. Both were donations *inter vivos* with strongly marked contractual qualities. In the middle of the twelfth century, new needs and the stricter notions of seisin of the common law

---

232 See the discussion of this matter below, pp. 225-230.

233 Stat. West., II, c. 19: in cases of intestacy the ordinary was bound "eodem modo quo xecutores hujusmodi respondere tenerentur si testamentum fecessit." The action of ccount was granted in c. 23; see below, pp. 227-228.

234 See below, p. 228.

235 *Provinciale*, fol. 172, *ad Intestatus:* "Executores universales, qui loco Hæredis sunt." Dn the stages of this development, see Goffin, *op. cit.*, pp. 45-54; Caillemer, *op. cit.*, pp. 760-69 and especially Holdsworth, *History*, III, 574-585.

found weaknesses in gifts of this sort just at the time when the canonists established an understanding of the Roman testament, and of the last will — a special, simplified form of the testament.   This last will came into use in England.   During the reigns of Richard and John its popularity grew at the expense of the older acts.   By John's death the essential steps seem to have been taken.   Decisions touching the validity and enforcement of wills had passed to the courts of the Church and the delivery of bequests was entrusted to their creature, the executor. During the remainder of the thirteenth century, the implications of these decisions were worked out in detail.

CHAPTER V

THE CANONICAL WILL,
FORMALITIES, IMPLEMENTATION AND CONTROL

T HROUGHOUT most of northern Europe, during the twelfth and
thirteenth centuries, the ecclesiastical courts established a large
measure of control over the will. England was not excluded from this
development. There, in fact, it extended to lengths unknown on the
Continent. The later stages of the elaboration and statement of
ecclesiastical jurisdiction in testamentary matters have long been known
to historians and can be described with comparative ease, though many
details remain to be investigated. But the beginnings of this control
of the will are not easily discerned. Was the jurisdiction of the
courts Christian, described by Glanvill, assumed after deliberate
decision, or was it acquired by the simple performance of that which
had to be done when no other public authority seemed able to do it?
Or was it a combination of the two—an initial acquisition of certain
functions by a continuation of the protection of wills which had always
been expected of the clergy, followed by a series of decisions by royal
officials, which enabled this jurisdiction to be extended into those
areas deemed necessary for efficiency? In the fifteenth century,
Lyndwood was at a loss to provide an answer to these questions, and
though later historians have frequently returned to the problem and
are now better informed about certain aspects of the matter, their
answers still remain somewhat unsatisfactory.[1]

Perhaps part of the difficulty has been caused by a tendency to devote
too much attention to a secondary aspect of this development: the
acquisition of testamentary jurisdiction is looked upon as a result of a

1 *Provinciale*, p. 174, *gl. ad verb.* approbatis. For a discussion of this matter among later
historians, see H. Swinburne, *A Briefe Treatise of Testaments and Last Willes* (London, 1611),
pp. 17 ff.; H. Spelman, *Of the Original of Testaments and Wills, English Works*, pp. 127-132;
J. Selden, *Of the Original of Ecclesiastical Jurisdiction of Testaments, Works*, III, 1664-1675;
Wm. Prynne, *Records*, III, 140; Blackstone, *Commentaries*, III, 96-97; H. C. Coote, *The Practice
of the Ecclesiastical Courts* (London, 1847), pp. 5 ff.; Stubbs, "An Account of the Courts
which have exercised Ecclesiastical Jurisdiction in England," p. 28-29; F. Makower, *Constitutional
History and Constitution of the Church of England* (London, 1895), p. 425.

default on the part of the civil courts, with awkward results for the law of property, or it is seen as a clerical invasion of an established field of legal practice. If there was an invasion, the crucial areas were captured without serious resistance. It is the very lack of signs of struggle that is most embarrassing to the historian. In the thirteenth century there were disagreements resulting from the attempt to perfect the procedure for the implementation and enforcement of wills, and from these disagreements it is possible to show the limits of the jurisdictions concerned. But there is no indication of serious opposition to the essential steps whereby the ecclesiastical courts obtained intrinsic and extrinsic control of the will.

Given the legal situation in England in the decades following the Norman Conquest, it is not surprising that some supervision of the will was exercised by the clergy. Of the subsequent growth of common law, there was as yet no intimation. Royal law was of limited application; there were numerous private and special jurisdictions over localities. men and pleas. It was to be expected that the clergy would be concerned with certain aspects of the will, since their law demanded it of them. But from the initial desire to protect the bequest in alms, the interest of the church courts expanded until they controlled the formalities of the will, obtained jurisdiction in disputes, and established regular procedures for the control of executors and the delivery of bequests. The essential steps in this rather complex development were taken in the years between the separation of lay and ecclesiastical jurisdictions by William the Conqueror and the beginning of the reign of Edward I. It is the purpose of this chapter to investigate the will during those two centuries, showing the establishment and extent of the jurisdiction of the courts Christian, and the testamentary forms and procedure of execution of the English will as it developed under their tutelage.

I. The Acquisition of Internal and External Jurisdiction over the Will by the Ecclesiastical Courts

In the study of the will in Anglo-Saxon times, it was concluded that the enforcement of legacies did not pertain to any group that could properly be called an ecclesiastical court. On the other hand, from the few cases of disputes over legacies of which evidence has survived, it was obvious that the clergy were involved at least as defenders of the bequest in alms. In this they were performing a duty that had been theirs since the patristic age. They never relinquished the obligation during the Middle Ages, nor is there evidence of any responsible opinion that they should do so. But this was only a beginning: as the Church sought to make the defence of the bequest in alms effective, it almost inevitably became more deeply involved in the control of the will.

The crucial event in the development of the ecclesiastical courts in Anglo-Norman England was William's decision to withdraw spiritual pleas from the local courts.[2] As a result, the tribunals of the Church were free to develop and to adopt their proper law and procedure. Inevitably, they reflected the great movement of reform that was growing in the Western Church. Throughout all of Europe, efforts were being made to define fields of activity proper to the lay and spiritual authorities.[3] William's writ, reserving every plea *quae ad regimen animarum pertinet* to the courts of the Church, was the fundamental step in this direction as far as England was concerned. Bishops and archdeacons were to withdraw from the courts of the shire and the hundred. Participation of the laity in the courts and synods of the Church was discouraged.[4] The detailed implementation of this division was accomplished only gradually. While a complete separation of the courts so that they were constituted exclusively of clerics or laity was never effected (both jurisdictions were frequently exercised by individual clerics),[5] the separation of pleas was achieved as quickly as possible. But the precise area of jurisdiction included within William's definition of spiritual pleas was no less uncertain to the lawyer of his age than to the historian of our own. Many pleas touched both orders and could not easily be assigned to one jurisdiction or the other. But a division had to be made since the older arrangement whereby bishop and earl decided such cases together was no longer operative. Some decisions as to detail were impossible during the first years when law, procedure, and the courts themselves were still in primitive condition. Assignment of disputed areas of jurisdiction was made pragmatically. Sometimes decisions were taken without a clear understanding of their implications, and occasionally it was necessary to reconsider them. Much of the legal history of twelfth-century England is devoted to the experiments, disputes, and adjustments by which a frontier was established through that area of jurisdiction to which both courts laid claim.

---

2 Stubbs, *Select Charters*, pp. 99-100; for the date (shortly after 1072), see Stenton, *Anglo-Saxon England*, p. 661. On the significance of this separation of jurisdictions, see *ibid.*; also P. and M., I, 75, 89; H. Boehmer, *Kirche und Staat in England und in der Normandie im XI und XII Jahrhundert* (Leipzig, 1899), pp. 91-97; Irene J. Churchill, *Canterbury Administration*, 2 vols. (London, 1933), I, 2-4.

3 P. and M., I, 124; on the general movement throughout Europe, *ibid.*, n. 2.

4 Cheney, *Becket to Langton*, pp. 107-108.

5 Poole, *Domesday Book to Magna Carta*, pp. 201, 217-218.

The will, with the disputes it entailed, was one of the institutions of interest to both lay and ecclesiastical authorities. From one point of view it was a distribution of property at death, a secular matter. But, as a donation in alms, it came within the scope of the spiritual courts. Had it been question of awarding jurisdiction over the fully developed testamentary procedure of the second half of the thirteenth century, it would probably have been given to the lay courts. But in the first decades after the Conquest, the decision had to be made in different terms. It was question of a will that was primitive both in form and method of execution. In those circumstances, there was much to be said for allowing at least a partial control to the courts of the Church. These distributions of property were usually made by death-bed gift. Being closely connected with the reception of the last sacraments, they were looked upon as a religious act.[6] Documents of the age frequently refer to the special importance attached to the desires of a dying man.[7] Wills almost always involved a donation for pious purposes, and sometimes contained nothing else. In southern Europe, where the testament of Roman law remained known, bequests in alms were but accidental parts of a larger whole. But in England the situation was quite different. There, the bequest in alms tended to be the most evident quality of the will. This is reflected in the charter of Henry I where provision was made for the soul even in the case of intestacy.[8] It was with the making and protection of these legacies that the clergy had long been associated. In France, where a similar situation existed, the ecclesiastical courts had been extending their jurisdiction over the will since the end of the ninth century.[9]

For these reasons it was almost inevitable that, in the division of jurisdiction, the control of some aspects of the will would fall to the clergy. Yet it is not yet possible to say whether there was an explicit award of supervision, or whether the clergy simply continued to interest themselves in the execution of wills and, when there was doubt of fact or law, began to seek a decision in their own courts.[10] It is not until

---

[6] See *Lincoln Wills,* ed. Foster, II, x-xi.

[7] A phrase from the *Codex Justinianus* (I, 2, 1) was quite popular: "Et quia nihil magis debetur humanitati quam quod extremae voluntatis liber sit stilus ...;" it was used in a letter of Gilbert Foliot of 1139-48 (Ep. 64, PL 190, 788-789). A similar notion is expressed in the *will* of Archbishop Theobald: "Supremis deficientium uoluntatibus suum accomodant iura fauorem ..." (*The Letters of John of Salisbury,* ed. Millor, etc., I, 245).

[8] C. 7; Stubbs, *Select Charters,* p. 118, see above, p. 110.

[9] Brissaud, *A History of French Private Law,* p. 696; E. Chenon, *Histoire générale du droit français,* I, 458.

[10] Blackstone suggested that the Church had assumed jurisdiction by the time of

Glanvill's time that a precise statement of the testamentary jurisdiction
of these tribunals is to be found. There it is stated that though the
enforcement of legacies could be obtained by royal writ, where there
was question of the validity of a will or of the bequests made in it, the
ecclesiastical courts were to decide.[11]

At first sight, it is surprising that internal jurisdiction over the will
was exercised by the courts Christian. It has been shown above that,
though canon law of the twelfth century saw fit to prescribe certain
formalities for bequests in alms, it opposed the probate of the testament
by the bishop or his court. It is probable that in England, where there
were special conditions, a different approach was necessary. There was
no civil organization able to provide the *apertura testamenti* of Roman
civil law, nor was there any other procedure that attained the same end.
In the majority of cases, the clergy received the will from a penitent
during his last hours. Whether a man died testate or intestate very
often depended on the word of his confessor. When a written record
was made, the clergy supplied it. Where there was question of the
contents of a will, the facts could be learned from them and, sometimes,
from no one else. Thus, under the conditions of the time, an internal
jurisdiction could not be exercised without the assistance of the clergy.
Since they were expected to avoid participation in the deliberations of
secular tribunals, it is not astonishing that this jurisdiction developed
in their courts.

Glanvill's statement implies an established practice. There is no
hint that it is a recent innovation. In Becket's time, when there was
dispute over jurisdiction in pleas touching both the spiritual and the
temporal orders, wills were not mentioned.[12] Given Glanvill's evidence,
the silence cannot be taken to imply that the elaboration of the testamentary jurisdiction of the clergy had not yet begun. On the contrary,

Henry I (*Commentaries*, III, 97). Makower was content to say that the Church "drew the
decision of testamentary causes to itself" from the time of William's ordinance (*op. cit.*,
p. 425), an opinion that had been advanced, with some hesitation, by Stubbs in his
"Account of the Courts," p. 28, and in the *Constitutional History*, III, 356. Coote thought
that internal jurisdiction over the will, i.e., declaration as to validity, contents, interpretation, etc., might well have begun with the Conquest (*op. cit.*, pp. 21-22). Maitland
taught that jurisdiction was mixed and that during the reign of Henry II and afterwards
the secular courts gradually abandoned their interest in it (P. and M., II, 332-333); cf.
Selden, *op. cit.*, 1667-1670 and Holdsworth, *History*, I, 625-626.

11 Glanvill, Bk. VII, chs. 6-8.

12 Four articles of the Constitutions of Clarendon dealt with disputed areas of jurisdiction
(1, 3, 9, 15: Stubbs, *Select Charters*, pp. 164-167). Selden seems to have been the first to
remark that the right to control the will did not enter the dispute (*op. cit.*, *Works*, III. 1669).

it implies that it was already established and was unopposed. Similar evidence is provided by the silence of papal letters sent to England; problems concerning the last will are not mentioned in the voluminous correspondence during and after the conflict between Becket and Henry II. Though these decretals provided a large portion of the papal law in the collections prior to and including the *Decretals* of Gregory IX, none of the canons dealing with the testament is derived from letters sent to English addresses.[13] The implication is, once more, that the matter was not disputed and that this jurisdiction was functioning without serious problems.

An early example of a decision that required information as to the contents of a will is found in a cartulary of Bath Cathedral Priory. The account begins with a writ of Prince Henry (1118-0) ordering the bishop of Bath to seise Modbert of land bequeathed to him by Grenta, his father-in-law.[14] The bishop did not proceed immediately, but, when occasion was presented, asked a gathering of magnates to consider the matter. The prior of Bath maintained that Grenta was in possession of the land until his death and that he held it of the priory with a life interest. According to his testimony, both of these facts were admitted by Grenta in a last will in which he released the estate to the monks. The court was able to proceed to the proof of this statement immediately, since several of the witnesses of the will were present. The prior's statement was confirmed and, after the hearing of other claims, the land was awarded to the priory. The nature of this gathering is not perfectly clear. At first sight, it seems to be an ecclesiastical court, convened on the feast of Saints Peter and Paul, with two bishops presiding and with many clergy in attendance. But there were also laymen present, and the royal writ, as well as the subject of the plea, indicates that the group was probably functioning as the bishop's seigniorial or franchise court.[15] But part of the evidence turned on a statement made in a last will. Even at this early date, it is quite possible that, in other circumstances, proceedings would have been delayed while a decision on the contents of the will was sought from an ecclesiastical tribunal. But given the constitution of this court it was possible for it to function as a court Christian as well. It is important to note that

---

13 See above, pp. 128 ff.

14 *Two Cartularies of ... Bath,* ed. W. Hunt, I, 49-51; *Regesta,* II, no. 1201.

15 This is the interpretation of the case by Madox in *The History and Antiquities of the Exchequer in England* (London, 1711), pp. 74-77; M. M. Bigelow, *Placita Anglo-Normannica* (Boston, 1877), p. 117; and, most recently, by R. C. Van Caenegem, *Royal Writs in England from the Conquest to Glanvill,* Selden Society, LXXVII (1958-9), pp. 200-201.

information of this sort was sometimes needed in pleas that were not directly concerned with the enforcement of the execution of wills.[16]

It is very likely that a primitive jurisdiction of this sort was exercised almost from the time of William's separation of pleas. Any action by the clergy to enforce bequests in alms would presume the existence of a system for proving that such bequests had been made. It is not yet possible to say when it became accepted practice for lay courts, royal or otherwise, to seek this information from their spiritual counterparts. As was suggested earlier, it appears well established by the early years of the reign of Henry II. It may go back to the time of his grandfather. At any rate, an intrinsic control of the will was assumed without serious opposition.

The importance of this jurisdiction can scarcely be exaggerated. The unique control over the will exercised by the ecclesiastical courts of England is to be traced to it. Since these courts decided on the validity of wills, it was for them to establish the required formalities. Since it was their duty to establish the contents of wills and to interpret them, they provided means for assuring a clear and well authenticated declaration of the testator's intention. From the hearing of occasional pleas when the contents of wills were disputed, it was a logical step to make probate a regular part of the procedure of execution. It is very likely that the efficient exercise of this internal jurisdiction over the will by the courts Christian is one of the chief causes of the decision by the royal courts to abandon extrinsic jurisdiction to them as well.

In Glanvill's treatment of the power to enforce delivery of bequests, neither the clergy nor their courts are mentioned. He says, rather, that the writ *de faciendo stare rationabilem divisam* could be obtained for the purpose. It is difficult to believe, however, that the clergy gave up their century-old duty of defending bequests in alms. Nor is it likely that, as a result of the separation of pleas, they were expected to do so. Though Glanvill dwelt on enforcement by royal courts, he did not exclude a concomitant jurisdiction in the clergy. There is considerable evidence of their activity in this regard during the twelfth century. Thus the reference to the property of intestate clerics in the charter of

---

[16] Evidence from the last will of the deceased was advanced by both parties in the famous dispute between Mabel de Francheville and Richard de Anesty. The latter produced witnesses to show that he was the instituted heir of his uncle. Mabel based her position on the same will and on other claims. She did not produce witnesses but appealed to Rome; cf. *The Letters of John of Salisbury*, ed. Millor, etc., I, 227-237, 267-270. This case was not transferred to the courts of the Church to establish the contents of a will, but to establish Mabel's legitimacy. The will had a bearing on the case, however.

King Stephen implies that there was some supervision of the execution of clerics' wills by the Church.[17]   It is very likely that with the confusion of Stephen's reign and the failure of several organs of government, assistance for the implementation of legacies was often to be had from the Church alone.   There are specific references to the confirmation and enforcement of bequests by all levels of the hierarchy.   The pope himself confirmed the will of Walter de Ridale in the mid-twelfth century, and Innocent III stubbornly insisted that King John deliver Richard's bequests to Otto IV of Germany.[18]   When Geoffrey Plantagenet died, the bishops extracted a promise from Prince Henry that he would respect his father's bequest to his brother Geoffrey, by refusing burial until the promise was made.   A letter of Alexander III to the archbishop of Canterbury seems to imply that this practice was not unknown in England in the third quarter of the century.[19]   Before his death, Archbishop Theobald excommunicated any royal agent who interfered with the execution of his will, and, earlier in the century, the dean and chapter of York instructed pastors to warn parishioners that obstruction of legacies in alms would result in the infliction of ecclesiastical penalties.[20]   Henry II made his bishops promise to excommunicate anyone who prevented the execution of his will.[21]

---

17 The text is printed below, p. 243, n. 51.

18 Hadrian IV confirmed the will of Walter de Ridale in 1156; Alexander III confirmed the possession of Ansketil de Ridale, the legatee, in 1165 (*EYC*, II, 114-117).   Various accounts of Richard's bequests are summarized by Poole in *Domesday Book to Magna Carta*, pp. 449-450.   The letters of Innocent III are printed by F. Kempf, *Registrum Innocentii III Papae super negotio Romani Imperii* (Rome, 1949), nos. 28, 49, 69, 129, 132.   In the last letter the bishops of Ely, Durham and Worcester were ordered to compel payment, using ecclesiastical penalties if necessary.   The success of the pope's interference, or the inconvenience it caused, is indicated in a letter patent of 1202, in which the king ordered that the will of Constance, countess of Britanny, be not opposed "ne Dominus Papa, vel alius ad hoc debeat manum apponere" (*Rot. Lit. Pat.*, I, 85).   John's will, in turn, was supported by Honorius III (Bliss, *Register*, I, 45).

19 William of Newburgh, *Historia Rerum Anglicarum*, in *Chronicles of the Reigns of Stephen*, etc., ed. R. H. Howlett, 4 vols., RS. 82 (1885-90), I, 112-113; see above, p. 129.

20 The will of Archbishop Theobald is discussed above, p. 142.   The York mandate is dated 1140-54: "et nisi reddiderunt ecclesiasticam vindictam in ipsos exerciant" (*EYC*, I, 152).   A similar mandate dates from 1160-85 (*ibid.*, p. 162).

21 "Vobis etiam archiepiscopis et episcopis mando, ut per sacramentum quod mihi fecistis ... in synodis vestris sollempniter accensis candelis excommunicetis, et excommunicari faciatis omnes illos qui hanc divisam meam infringere praesumperint."   Papal support was also sought, for the text continues: "et sciatis quod dominus Papa hanc divisam meam scripto et sigillo suo confirmavit sub interminatione anathematis."   The will of Henry II is discussed above, p. 143.

In the cases cited, the sanction at the disposition of the clergy in their efforts to defend the will was a moral one. In William's writ, as in the general law of the Church, obedience to the courts Christian was enforced by means of excommunication. Even in the thirteenth century, when external jurisdiction over the will was largely in the hands of the ecclesiastical courts, no physical sanction was at their direct disposal. By that time, however, the procedure of recourse to the civil authority was perfected. William had provided for it when the separation of pleas took place, but, in the present state of the evidence from the twelfth century, it is not possible to say to what extent the Church was able to invoke secular aid to compel the delivery of legacies. Proceedings in the royal court, as described by Glanvill, had the advantage that, once a decision had been reached, it was implemented by force if necessary. But even though it cannot be shown that the Church was able to bring this ultimate sanction to bear, it is obvious that in the period between the separation of the courts and Glanvill the clergy exercised some supervision of the execution of bequests. On occasion, both secular and ecclesiastical authorities might defend a will: Archbishop Theobald excommunicated those who interfered with the completion of his will, but he sought the support of the king as well. It is implied in the account of the death of Hubert Walter that those who prevented the delivery of bequests were often royal servants and that the sanctions of the Church had to be used against them.[22] In fact, there is much evidence to show that during the twelfth century the clergy were often required to defend a will against the very persons who, according to Glanvill, could be expected to enforce it.

By 1230 a general extrinsic jurisdiction over bequests of chattels had been assumed by the ecclesiastical courts.[23] The change was completed without apparent resistance and without statement of motive. Glanvill's reference to the writ for the recovery of legacies gives the impression of a well established procedure that was in common use in his day. Yet there are few signs of it.[24] Pleas for the enforcement of bequests of

---

[22] "...ut quod extremis vocibus morituri dictitarunt, inviolabiliter observaretur, et de conniventia regis resistentes, vinculo anathematis innodavit:" Ralph de Coggeshall. *Chronicon Anglicanum*, ed. J. Stevenson, R.S., 66 (London, 1875), p. 159.

[23] Makower, *op. cit.*, pp. 426-427.

[24] The plea before the court of the bishop of Bath is one of the rare examples of the exercise of this jurisdiction; see above, pp. 168-169. Sometimes it is not possible to know where the action lay: thus in a document published in *The Cartulary of Darley Abbey*, ed. R. R. Darlington, 2 vols., Derbyshire Arch. Soc. (1945), pp. 499-500, there is record of an agreement between the abbey and Henry de Tuschet in which the former abandoned

chattels are not to be found in the *Curia Regis Rolls* of Richard and John. The *Patent Rolls* and the *Close Rolls* of John and Henry III include many royal letters to sheriffs ordering them to allow the execution of a will or to aid the executors in their task, but it can be shown in almost every case that the testator involved had been indebted to the king, or was a tenant or servant against whom the king had some claim.   The letters in question do not seem to be concerned with the recovery of legacies, but instruct royal servants to release chattels that had been seized so that execution may follow.[25]   It will be shown below that the ecclesiastical courts never entirely excluded the interference of royal courts in the execution of wills.   If the king had any claim against a testator, be it only that the deceased was indebted to a debtor of the king, then the courts acted to defend royal interests.   But with this important exception, there are few signs of the enforcement of bequests by royal courts after Glanvill.   The writ for this purpose appeared neither in the Irish register of 1227 nor in the earliest English collection which is dated not later than 1234.[26]

    At the same time, there is evidence of the growing jurisdiction of the courts of the Church.   It is to be found in the English register just mentioned, where the clause *nisi de testamento vel matrimonio* appears as a limitation of the writ of prohibition *de catallis et debitis*.[27]   This clause makes its appearance in the *Curia Regis Roll* of Michaelmas 1214.[28]

"...actionem ...adversus predictum Henricum ...pro legato patris sui." The document is dated *ca.* 1150.

[25] Selden cited several examples as possible evidence of a continued exercise of extrinsic jurisdiction by the royal courts, but admitted: "it may be, that those *Writs* in the former Chapter, and the like, were but in case of Tenants being Testators, upon whose deaths all their goods were to be seised by the Sheriff, or other such officer, and the debt (if any were) paid to the King" (*Works*, III, 1673).   In 1204, the sheriff is instructed not to impede the executors of the earl of Leicester and to restore to them any chattels removed from his estates (*Rot. Lit. Claus.*, I, 13); a similar letter was sent to the sheriff of Nottingham regarding the will of Geoffrey Fitz Peter, in 1213 (*ibid.*, I, 154).   The letter sent to Peter des Roches in 1214 is closely allied to Glanvill's writ: "Mandamus vobis quod teneri faciatis testamentum Ade de Gurdun, quod fecit de rebus suis mobilibus et omnibus aliis in Angl. secundum disposicionem testamenti, excepta terra quam de dono nostro habuit" (*ibid.*, I, 169 and 73).   But Adam was a royal servant, so that the letter was probably intended to order the release of his chattels, seized pending investigation of debts to the king.

[26] Cf. F. W. Maitland, "The History of the Register of Original Writs," *Collected Papers*, II, 139, and Holdsworth, *History*, II, 613-615.

[27] G. B. Flahiff, "The Writ of Prohibition to Court Christian in the Thirteenth Century," *Mediaeval Studies*, VI (1944), 277-279.

[28] *C.R.R.*, VII, 292-3 (Michaelmas, 16 John); cf. C. T. Flower, *Introduction to the Curia Regis Rolls, 1199-1230 A.D.*, Selden Society, LXII (1943), p. 110, and Flahiff, *loc. cit.*, p. 277, n. 79.

It is not to be found in the roll of the following year, but in 1219, when court records resume, and in subsequent years the formula occurs frequently.[29] Thus the reference to the extrinsic jurisdiction of the courts Christian became *de cursu* in the early years of Henry III. It implies a practice already well established, one that must go back to the reign of John.

It is possible that Glanvill has been misunderstood; the text of Book VII, which has been interpreted to mean that the enforcement of legacies was normally to be obtained from the royal courts, can be read in a different way. In the edition of Woodbine, it is as follows :

> Debet autem testamentum fieri coram duobus vel pluribus viris legitimis, clericis vel laicis, et talibus qui testes inde fieri possint idonei. Testamenti autem executores esse debent hi quos testator ad hoc elegerit et quibus curam ipsam commiserit. Si vero testator nullos ad hoc nominaverit, possunt propinqui et consanguinei ipsius defuncti ad id faciendum se ingerere. Ita quod si quem vel heredem vel alium rerum defuncti repererint detentorem, habebunt breve domini regis vicecomiti directum in haec verba (VII, 6).

Even in this form of the text, the subject of the verb *repererint* in the last sentence seems to refer to *propinqui* and *consanguinei* of the sentence which precedes it. In this interpretation *executores* would not be included among those who had an action to enforce the terms of a will in the royal courts. Since the words *ita quod* usually refer to that which immediately precedes them, there is much to be said for the older punctuation in which a comma or a semi-colon, rather than a period, was placed between *ingerere* and *Ita*.[30] If this punctuation were adopted, the suggested meaning would be all the more clear. Glanvill is saying that the testator normally appoints executors; but when he fails to do so his relatives and friends can proceed to execute the will, relying on the support of the royal courts if necessary. This probably implies that pleas in which executors were involved were not heard in the courts of the king; the well known reluctance of these courts to admit represen-

[29] The clause appears six times in Michaelmas, 3/4 Henry III; seven times in Easter, 4 Henry III; nine times in Trinity, 4 Henry III; eleven times in Michaelmas, 4/5 Henry III, etc.

[30] The punctuation used in the edition of Woodbine is the same as that to be found in Tottel's edition (London, 1555 [?], *STC*, 11905) fol. 49 and in G. Phillips, *Englische Reichs-und Rechtsgeschichte*, 2 vols. (Berlin, 1827-8), II, 398. But the two sentences of these editions were read as two clauses of a single sentence in the text published by M. Houard, *Traités sur les coutumes Anglo-Normandes*, 4 vols. (Paris, 1776), I, 478 and in that published with the *Regiam Majestatem* in the *Acts of the Parliament of Scotland*, Record Commissioners, 36, Vol. I (1844), 154. The two clauses were separated by a semi-colon in the translation published by John Beames in 1812 (2nd ed., Washington, 1900, p. 137).

tation supports this interpretation. We know that the powers of the
executor were increasing rapidly during the last years of the twelfth
century. Now if the tribunal for actions by or against the executor
were already the court Christian, then requests for judgment in the
royal courts would tend to disappear as the executor replaced the heir
as the representative of the deceased. This interpretation of Glanvill,
based as it is on a very literal reading of the text, is but a suggestion.
Its virtue is that it explains the fact that examples of enforcement of the
delivery of legacies by the courts of the king are so rare.

In Normandy the cognizance of pleas for the enforcement of legacies
was passing to the church courts during Richard's reign. The articles
of 1190, as reported by Ralph Diceto, show that the Church was charged
with the supervision of legacies and the distribution of the property of
the intestate whose failure to make a will was excusable.[31] This information is corroborated by the Inquest of 1205 and by the *Très ancien
coutumier,* though the latter's reference to disputes between the archbishop and the seneschal of Rouen shows that the lay courts were not
fully resigned to their loss.[32] Evidence of Norman practice cannot be
applied to England without great caution.[33] But the churches of the two
areas were in close contact and the practice of the one would be known
by the other. Furthermore, the Norman evidence shows that the church
courts which had this jurisdiction over the will, also supervised the distribution of the goods of the intestate. It seems very likely that the latter
power would be affirmed only after an extrinsic jurisdiction over the
will had been established. Now in England the first general statement
of the Church's right to supervise the distribution of the goods of the
intestate appears in Magna Carta.[34] There were to be further disputes

31 "Item, distributio eorum quæ in testamento relinquuntur auctoritate ecclesiæ fiet...
Si quis vero subitanea morte vel quolibet alio fortuito casu præoccupatus fuerit, ut de
rebus suis disponere non possit, distributio bonorum ejus ecclesiastica auctoritate fiet"
(*Ymagines Historiarum,* in *Opera Historica,* ed. Stubbs, II, 87-88).

32 *Layettes du Trésor des Chartes,* ed. Teulet, 3 vols. (Paris, 1867-75), I, 297, no. 785:
"Item diximus per sacramentum nostrum quod nulla ecclesiastica persona debet aliquem
trahere in causam pro fide vel pro sacramento quod fiat de feodo laico vel catallo hominis
laici; sed si fides data fuerit de catallo maritagii vel de legato mortui, ...de causa illa bene
possunt judicare." *Le très ancien coutumier,* I, ch. 57 (ed. Tardif, p. 47): "... Quando
eciam juratum visinetum se faciat nesciens, hoc diffinitum erit in ecclesiastica
curia, et non in laica; tamen multociens inter dominum Rothomagensem archiepiscopum et
Willelmum senescallum placitum inde audivimus."

33 Thus, according to the articles of 1190, breaches of faith were to be tried in spiritual
courts.

34 C. 27; Stubbs, *Select Charters,* p. 296.

on the matter, but the arrangement was established in principle. However, Jocelin of Brakelond describes an example of this supervision almost twenty years earlier. Hamo Blunt died and his executors, who had prevented access to him during his last hours, reported a will in which a disproportionately small sum was given in alms. Abbot Samson suspected them of collusion and refused to allow the will. He considered Hamo to have died intestate and distributed his property. This distribution included not only the portion of the goods of the deceased given in alms, but his whole fortune. Now Abbot Samson was a masterful man, capable of more strenuous action than the general law might sanction. It is not clear whether he was exercising a civil franchise or his ecclesiastical jurisdiction, but in his own eyes he was acting in the latter capacity, for he prefaced his action by the remark *Ego fui episcopus eius.*[35] It would appear, then, that the supervision of the distribution of an intestate's property by the bishop was to be found in England almost as soon as its appearance in Normandy. Thus the right or duty assigned the clergy by Magna Carta was not something entirely new. It was rather the recognition of a growing practice and of a general claim. As suggested above, this power would likely develop after the church courts had obtained a right to enforce the terms of a will. Thus another line of reasoning leads to the conclusion that there was a general withdrawal of lay jurisdiction over wills and a recognition by the end of John's reign that such pleas were normally heard in the courts of the Church. In this aspect of the will, as in so many others, the first twenty years of the thirteenth century were the time of decision. In 1230 a plea, reported in *Bracton's Note Book,* was transferred to the courts Christian because it dealt with a legacy.[36]

The motives for the withdrawal of testamentary jurisdiction from royal courts are unknown. If an attempt is made to suggest what they were, it is only that the reasonableness of the decision might become more evident. The fact that the common law prevented the bequest of land undoubtedly made the decision much easier. But, as was suggested above, one of the motives lay in the fact that the ecclesiastical courts had established an intrinsic jurisdiction over the will, whereas the courts of common law had not done so. This failure meant that any pleas for enforcement of legacies before royal justices risked delay while decisions as to the validity and contents of a will were sought in

35 *The Chronicle of Jocelin of Brakelond,* ed. Potter, pp. 91-92.
36 No. 381. Bracton considered these pleas to pertain to the spiritual courts (fol. 61), and *Fleta* explicitly denied jurisdiction to royal courts: Bk. II, ch. 57, ed. Richardson and Sayles, II, 194.

the court Christian. A second and similar motive probably lies in the rise of the executor. He was appointed by the will. Therefore the assistance of the courts of the Church would sometimes be required to establish his identity, before proceedings against him or on his behalf could begin. Thus, once again, the courts of the king were hindered from carrying testamentary pleas through to a decision without recourse to an ecclesiastical tribunal. The inconvenience could have been avoided had an internal jurisdiction been assumed by the royal courts. Instead, the normal extrinsic control of the will was abandoned to the Church. Only the final sanction, the use of force, remained to the lay power. It was to be used at the invitation of the bishop.[37]

Thus it was that, by the end of John's reign, the spiritual courts of England came to establish a unique jurisdiction over the will. In the exercise of their authority the clergy developed formalities and procedures for the making of wills and for the supervision and enforcement of their execution. As there was but little English precedent, they were able to draw on law and practice outside the country without danger of conflict with local custom.

II. FORMALITIES OF THE WILL

As the canonical will took shape in the hands of English clerics, it assumed remarkable simplicity of form. This development was to be expected, since it was the fruit of the Church's century-old attitude towards bequests. In her effort to support donations for pious causes the Church did not limit herself to the defence of wills that, from a technical point of view, fulfilled all the requirements of Roman law; she had gone further and had succeeded in reducing the formalities of this type of donation to a minimum. It has been shown above that some canonists of the twelfth century sought to apply these simplified formalities to the testament as a whole.[38] On the Continent, this question was long debated; but in England the decision was accepted, apparently without serious opposition. There the canonical will, made with a minimum of formality, was accepted irrespective of the purpose for which bequests were intended. It was also recognized in the royal courts, where a decision might depend on the validity of a will, and, for the most part, in borough and manor courts as well.

In the description of the formalities of the will in the late twelfth and the thirteenth centuries it will not be possible to draw on scientific

---

37 See p. 222.
38 See the discussion of *Decretales*, III, 26, 4, above pp. 128-130.

studies of testamentary law such as those provided for a later age by John of Acton and William Lyndwood. Nor are there series of *acta* touching the details of will-making and administration from which an exact picture of practice can be drawn. However, there are several important sources of information. There are, first of all, references to the formalities of the will in Glanvill, Bracton and *Fleta*. More complete information is found in the episcopal statutes of the thirteenth century. They provide a series of rules which, in increasing detail, describe the formalities of the will and the process of execution. This series culminates in the statutes of Bishop Peter Quivil of Exeter (1287), which include a brief but remarkably complete discussion of these matters.[39] Finally, there are the written *wills* which are to be found in increasing numbers as the period draws to a close. From these sources it is possible to draw sufficient information to provide a reasonably complete analysis of the form assumed by the will and of the requirements for its validity.

Requirements for Validity

The fundamental requisite for the success of a will was that the testator make a clear statement of the use that was to be made of his property after his death. Roman law required that the testament be made in the presence of seven witnesses and that it institute an heir. The codicil was concerned only with bequests and required five witnesses. But these stringent demands had long since failed of application to the bequest in alms. For that purpose the two or three witnesses of *Deuteronomy* were considered to be sufficient.[40] It has been suggested that the letters of Alexander III in defence of the use of two or three witnesses were part of an effort to protect a general practice of the Church against the more rigorous demands of resurgent Roman law.[41] At any rate, it is clear that this minimum requirement as to the number of witnesses was permitted in England well before his pontificate and that it was not subject to serious opposition at any time.[42]

---

[39] Canon L, *De Testamentis*, is prefaced by a paragraph in which it is stated that, although the will is treated in canon law and even more fully in civil law, most men are unable to use this material. Thus the lawmaker is moved "...quae in quotidiano sunt usu, utilia quaedam statuere..." (Wilkins, II, 155).

[40] See above, pp. 128-130; other examples are cited by Perraud, *Etude sur le testament*, p. 33.

[41] Cf. Hannan, *The Canon Law of Wills*, p. 274.

[42] There were three witnesses to the will of Gunni de Stanton (1139-1148), reported in a letter of Gilbert Foliot (Ep. 64, PL 190, 788-789), and two witnesses to the will of Ace the

The canonists tended to relate the bequest in alms, made with the simplified form, to the codicil. They usually called it *ultima voluntas* or *codicilli*. The word *testamentum* was commonly reserved to the act made with full solemnity. During the late twelfth and thirteenth centuries, either word was used in England to denote *post obit* distributions of property, though *testamentum* was much the more common.[43] Occasionally an early will, such as that of Henry II, was called *divisum*, and the French form, *devise*, was used to describe the few wills that survive in that language. During the time in question, there is scarcely any sign of the later practice which would reserve "testament" for distributions of movables and "last will" for bequests of land.[44] There is an occasional indication that "last will" was more fittingly applied to bequests made in haste on the death bed and, hence, with a minimum of formality.[45] Sometimes the act was called a last will and testament and, in a few cases, testators who were determined that their distributions of property should qualify for validity under one form or another asked that their wills be accepted as testaments or, failing that, as last wills or codicils.[46] Normally the word "codicil" was reserved to additional bequests made after a will was completed.

The presence of two witnesses was a minimum requirement. This does not mean that the making of a will before a small and intimate group was generally practised. The old notions regarding the publicity of a donation remained strong. Most testators desired many witnesses both to the fact that they had made a will and to its contents. In the fourteenth century, when witness lists were frequently included in

---

archdeacon (1194); cf. *Three Rolls of the King's court*, ed. F. W. Maitland, Publications of the Pipe Roll Society, XIV (1891), p. xxv. Two or three witnesses also sufficed for choice of place of burial; cf. *Gloucester Cart.*, I, lxxvii. For a later discussion of witness requirements, cf. *Provinciale*, p. 174, *gl. ad verb.* probatis. Glanvill demanded two or more witnesses (Bk. VII, ch. 6) and Bracton (fol. 61) and *Fleta* (Bk. II, ch. 58) were in agreement.

43 In the enrolments of the Court of Hustings for the years 1271-3 (Rolls 4 and 5), the will was usually called *ultima voluntas*. In the second of these rolls it is said that the last will was contained "in testamento dicti defuncti" or "in scripto testamentario." The more commonly used term for will, in the earlier and later rolls, was *testamentum*.

44 A rare exception is to be seen in the two Hustings rolls cited in the previous note. On this distinction in the use of terms, see R. R. Sharpe, ed. *Calendar of Wills Proved and enrolled in the Court of Husting, London, 1258-1688*, 2 vols. (London, 1889-90). I, xxxi, and *The Register of Henry Chichele*, ed. E. F. Jacob, 4 vols. (Oxford, 1937-47), II, xix-xxi.

45 E.g., Glanvill remarked that the married woman could not make a *testamentum* without the consent of her husband and that this prohibition extended even to the *ultima voluntas*. Lyndwood distinguished the two terms on the basis of the perfection of procedure, p. 173, *gl. ad verb.* voluntatem ultimam.

46 See below, p. 192.

written *wills*, the number of witnesses named was often ten to fifteen, and the lists were usually terminated with a significant *et aliis*. In some cases reminiscent of Anglo-Saxon and Anglo-Norman practice, the will was made before the chapter of the monastery or church that was the chief legatee.[47]

Yet there are occasional signs during the thirteenth century that some testators preferred that their bequests should not become public knowledge. The growth of this desire is the correlative of the right to revoke a will. It must have soon become apparent that the narrower the circle of those who knew the contents of a will, the weaker the social pressure that might prevent its revocation.[48] Many of the original *wills* of the second half of the century were folded and tied in the closed position. In a few cases it can be shown that the thong was sealed; apparently it was intended that the document remain closed until the testator's death.[49] The significance of this development and its relation to the growing importance of the written *will* is discussed below, but it is of interest here as an indication of a growing desire for secrecy.

The witnesses were expected to be of an age and intelligence required to make them capable of a legal act. Both Glanvill and Bracton spoke of them as *viri legitimi*. Neither specifically excluded women from being witnesses to wills, though the more obvious meaning of their phrase implies as much. The canonists denied this office to women. Gratian stated a general prohibition of the use of the female witness; the Decretists and the authors of several procedural treatises applied this prohibition specifically to the testament.[50] This rule does not seem to have been applied in England. Little information about witnesses as distinct from executors of wills exists for the years of interest to this study. But it is well known that women often served as executors during the thirteenth century. Furthermore, there are a few cases where witnesses who were not executors are mentioned, and women are found to be included among them.[51] As would be expected, both offices were

[47] E.g., T. 47b; the will was made "coram conventui in pleno capitulo."

[48] Cf. Auffroy, *Testament*, p. 453.

[49] See below, p. 192.

[50] *Decretum*, C. 33, q. 5, 17 *Mulier*; in the gloss on this canon in the *Summa Parisiensis*, Huguccio, and the *Glossa Ordinaria*, it is stated that a woman may be witness in all civil matters exclusive of the testament. A similar position is adopted in the *Ordo judiciarius* of the Bamberg Codex, ed. J. F. von Schulte (Vienna, 1872), p. 26, and the *Speculum iuris canonici* of Peter of Blois, ed. Reimarius (Berlin, 1837), p. 65.

[51] Women are mentioned as witnesses in T. 71b. Later examples are to be found in the *will* of Margaret of Eure, 1378, (*Wills and Inventories*, I, 35-36) and in a Yorkshire *will* of 1346 (*Testamenta Eboracensis*, I, 20).

more commonly held by men, but there is no indication that women as such were excluded from them in England.

Some local customs demanded that special witnesses be present under certain circumstances. Thus in several of the boroughs a will bequeathing land had to be made in the presence of the mayor or some other official.[52] On certain manors the attendance of the bailiff was necessary for the validity of a villein's will.[53]

In some parts of Europe the local ecclesiastical law required that a priest be in attendance when a will was made. The fittingness of the reception of the last words of a dying man by his priest was an old and well honoured tradition. But in the thirteenth century synods in many localities went further and made the priest's presence obligatory.[54] In England the rule first appeared in the Salisbury statutes of Richard Poore (1216-21).[55] Similar canons were introduced later at Canterbury, Durham and Exeter.[56] In the last of these, it is specifically stated that the priest witness should be the pastor of the deceased. This was probably the intention of earlier rulings as well.[57] Lyndwood remarked that the presence of the priest never became general law, but was required by local custom. Innovation does not seem to have been the purpose of these constitutions. Nor is it likely that they represent a reaction to a general resentment of the part played by the clergy in the making of wills. The years during which these constitutions became law saw the organization of probate by the ecclesiastical courts, and these rules probably represent an attempt to make universal a practice that was already general and of proven efficiency. No doubt it was intended

52 Cf. *B.C.*, II, 200.

53 "Preceptum est ballivus capere in manum domini omnia bona infirmorum legata ad quorum testamenta facienda non vocat' " (Wystowe, 1294): *Court Rolls of the Abbey of Ramsey and the Honor of Clare*, ed. W. O. Ault, Yale Historical Publications, Manuscripts and Edited Texts, IX (New Haven, 1928), pp. 211-212. See below, pp. 253-254.

54 Cf. Hannan, *op. cit.*, p. 276 and Auffroy, *Testament*, pp. 443-448, 598-599.

55 "Præcipimus quod laicis inhibeatur frequenter ne testamenta sua faciunt sine præsentia sacerdotibus" (*Charters and Documents ... Salisbury*, ed. Jones and Macray, p. 158). On the date and importance of this collection, see Cheney, *English Synodalia*, pp. 51-55.

56 Cf. the text of the Statutes attributed to Stephen Langton in Wilkins, I, 572n and the discussion thereof in Cheney, *op. cit.*, pp. 62-65. The Durham text is edited in Wilkins I, 583; it can be dated 1228-37. The Exeter constitutions (1287) are in Wilkins II, 155. The same notion appears in a canon attributed to St. Edmund of Canterbury *ca.* 1236 (Wilkins, I, 638); the attribution is probably false, according to Cheney *op. cit.* p. 67. The presence of the priest appears in the *Très ancien coutumier de Normandie* (ed. Tardif, p. 47).

57 The presence of the parish priest is mentioned in the canon attributed to St. Edmund; see the previous note.

that the parish priest remind the testator of his obligation to give aims, but the reason for the rule that is stated by the constitutions—that the testator's will be fulfilled—[58] was a valid one. The rule was usually obeyed. When death approached, more powerful members of society very often sent for a clerical acquaintance of corresponding importance who aided them in preparing for death, administering the last sacraments and receiving their wills.[59] Lesser persons, whose social horizon was the parish, usually asked their pastor to assist them in this way. The general impression left by the written *wills* is that the Church's effort to ensure the presence of a priest was succesful during the thirteenth century and for many years thereafter.[60] The priest was more than a witness. He seems frequently to have aided the testator in making choice of bequests and legatees, just as he aided him in the preparation for death, of which the making of a will was really a part. The priest-witness was often asked to serve as executor.

During the thirteenth century executors usually seem to have been the chief witnesses of bequests of property, In fact from about 1225 until the end of the century, one could easily conclude that there were no other witnesses. During the twelfth century and the first quarter of the thirteenth, the form of the written *will* was still much influenced by charters that had served as evidence of *post obit* gifts. Like the documents they imitated, these earlier *wills* were often terminated by a list of witnesses. This list might include the executors, but other names were mentioned as well.[61] But during the rest of the thirteenth century the executor tended to hide the witness almost completely. There are fairly frequent references to distributions of property made "in the

---

58 "...ut eorum ultimae voluntates adimpleantur." Other reasons were suggested by councils in southern France; cf. Hannan, *op. cit.*, pp. 278-279.

59 E.g., the description of the death of William Marshal, cited above, p. 146, and the account of the death of William earl of Salisbury (1226), in Matthew Paris, *Chronica Majora*, III, p. 104: "Invalescente deinde aegritudine, cum certissima suae necis indicia cognovisset, fecit episcopum civitatis ad se venire, ut ea quae Christiani sunt in confessione et viatico susciperet, et legitimum de rebus habitis conficeret testamentum."

60 Canon Foster, editor of the Lincoln Wills, concluded his discussion of this matter with the remark that the parish priest was "in most cases, the first and principal witness" (*Lincoln Wills*, II, xii).

61 Eg.., the *will* of Robert, son of Alan de Fordham, *ca.* 1200, Oxford, Bodleian, MS. Charters, Norfolk a. 6 (614); also T. 12. In the biography of William Marshal, the dying man seals his *will* in the presence of his wife and son, and asks them to seal it as well. Then he sends the documents off to the archbishop of Canterbury and two other bishops, asking them to be his executors and to seal the *will*. They do so, excommunicate those who obstruct his bequests, and return the document; see lines 18327-18350 (ed. Meyer, II, 299-300).

presence of executors."[62]   Written *wills* often mentioned their presence
and a similar phrase appeared in model *wills* of the second half of the
century.[63]   The executor was expected to bring the will for probate,
a fact which implies that he was frequently present when the will was
made, knew its contents, and knew of his own appointment.   When a
written *will* was made, it was he rather than the simple witness that was
invited to seal the document.

Yet, however much in the background, the simple witness who played
no part in the execution of the will still had a proper function.   Though
not usually mentioned in written *wills,* his presence is revealed in
accounts of probate.   Thus a text of 1231 mentioned five executors
and no other witnesses, but the probate showed that three witnesses were
examined and that only one of them was an executor.[64]   In most of the
probates of the Court of Hustings after April, 1285, the usual formula
states that the will was presented by the executors but that other persons
were examined as witnesses.[65] There was much to be said for maintaining
this distinction, for there was an obvious danger of collusion where the
same persons were witnesses of a will and agents of its execution.   This
danger is reflected in a statute of Bishop Peter Quivil of Exeter which
states that, at least for a nuncupative will, executors and witnesses must
be distinct.[66]   During the last years of the thirteenth century, the
witness who was not an executor began to appear once more in written
wills.   Formularies of model documents reflected the change as well.[67]
Yet even during the fourteenth century, it was the executor rather than
the witness who was normally mentioned in the written *wills.*

It is difficult to understand why only the executors were usually
invited to seal the written document.   The obvious and most simple
explanation is that they were the most important persons present when
the will was made.   But there may well have been a deeper reason that
represents a survival of the older technique of the *post obit* gift.   The
executor's function was an exceedingly important one.   On his action

62 As in the reference to the will of Peter des Roches, bishop of Winchester, in *C.P.R.,*
III, 166 (1236).

63 See below, p. 193 and n. 120.

64 T. 31.

65 "Dictis die et anno venerunt Thomas de Basing', Nicholas de Wynton, Robertus de
Wetheringesete, Capellanus, et Adam de Glovernia, executores testamenti Margerie filie
quondam Galfridi de Wynton ... et probare fecerunt testamentum ipsius Margerie quo ad
articulos laicum feodum tangentes per Thomam de Otteburn' et Willelmum de Leye'
testes iuratos et examinatos" (Hustings Roll 15, no. 40).

66 Wilkins, II, 156.

67 See below, n. 120. Witnesses and executors were distinguished in T. 71a, T. 78b, etc.

depended the completion of the testator's bequests. It is only reasonable to suppose that, wherever possible, his consent was obtained before he was nominated to the office in a will. Furthermore, an executor would not be appointed if it were evident that he opposed the testator's bequests. It seems reasonable to conclude that in the beginning, at least, there was some sort of agreement between the testator and his executor. In theory the testator could revoke his will and the executor was free to withdraw. But beneath the invitation that the executor seal the *will*, there may lie the notion that he was morally obliged to see to its completion. It will be recalled that the charter of *post obit* gift was sometimes sealed by those whose consent was needed to ensure the success of the gift, and who, in many cases, were expected to ensure delivery.[68]

A few of the wills, such as that of Peter of Aigueblanche, bishop of Hereford, manifested an entirely different spirit.[69] Here the witnesses came to the fore. Executors were appointed in the body of the document, but the names and seals of seven witnesses were added at the end. The attestation of the codicil was also in keeping with the requirements of Roman law. The Aigueblanche will was intended to be valid on the Continent as well as in England and, as such, was a special case. However, certain of its formalities were reflected in the wills that were more properly English. Some documents mentioned seven executors and had seven seals.[70] Lists of witnesses were sometimes prefaced by the remark that the persons in question were specially summoned to perform their function.[71] In their expositions of the formalities of the will, both Bracton and *Fleta* include this notion, which is a reflection of the *testis rogatus* of the civil law.[72]

As long as the testator clearly expressed his will in the presence of witnesses who were legally competent, the act was valid. There was no English equivalent to the institution of an heir required by Roman civil law. Eventually the executor's powers were to become so great that he was assimilated to the heir, and it was said his appointment was one of the required formalities of the will.[73] But, since the bishop had power to replace executors and to nominate them when the testator had failed

---

[68] Cf. n. 61 and the reference to the *will* of William Marshall.

[69] T. 68.

[70] E.g., T. 56.

[71] E.g., T. 98.

[72] "ad hoc specialiter congregatis" (Bracton, fol. 61, and *Fleta*, Bk. II, ch. 58); on the *testis rogatus* in Roman civil law, see Berger, *Dictionary*, p. 736.

[73] Cf. *The Register of Henry Chichele*, ed. Jacob, II, xix-xx.

to do so, the observance of this formality did not touch the validity of the will.[74]   This insistence on the appointment of the executor did not appear until well after the century that is of interest to us here.   None the less it should be noted that, in practice, the need for executors was quickly realized.   Even in the thirteenth century, the will that failed to appoint them was a rarity.

Since so much was demanded of executors, it was to be expected that the utmost care would be devoted to their selection.   *Wills* of the thirteenth century are excellent witness to the complex and ingenious arrangements made to ensure a successful choice.   In almost every case several persons were appointed to the office;[75] occasionally it was stated that, where necessary, decisions could be made by part of the group or by survivors.[76]   The appointment of new executors, should the original nominees die before their task was accomplished, was sometimes provided.[77]   Many of the *wills* of the more important members of society named a principal executor, and some were careful to state that no disposition of property might be made without his consent.[78]   In a few cases, particular executors were appointed to act in special areas of the country, or to deal with specific groups of legatees.[79]   Some of the *wills* named a second group to serve as counsellors; there are a few examples where the executors were instructed not to act without their advice.[80]

Executors were chosen from all levels of society.   Usually they were members of the testator's own class, though attempts were sometimes

[74] Holdsworth, *History*, III, 563.

[75] Simon de Montfort named his wife as sole executor; in the event of her death, her place was to be taken by their son Henry. Counsellors were appointed and they were to become executors on the death of the two first named (T. 59a).

[76] "Quod si aliquis non potuerit forte se intromittere, alii nichilominus testamentum exequantur" (T. 31); Edward I appointed eight executors but allowed four to act "en num des autrus" (T. 72b); survivors were to act in T. 33.

[77] E.g., T. 12, T. 59a.

[78] Richard Wych, bishop of Chichester, having first obtained his agreement, named the archbishop of Canterbury his principal executor and guardian of all his goods (T. 53a); consent to all decisions by the principal executor is demanded in T. 67b, T. 69.

[79] Principal executors for each ecclesiastical province were named in T. 59b, executors for England and Ireland in T. 67b. The Master of Holy Cross named his sister to distribute bequests to his poor relatives; she was not included in the list of executors (T. 59b).

[80] In T. 59a and T. 69 executors were obliged to seek advice. William de Longespee named three classes of executors: the first group, four bishops, were called *executores*; four others, including William Marshal, were to be consulted and to assist in the execution of the will; finally two men, who seem to have been his servants, were appointed 'ad dictum testamentum fideliter exequendum per consilium et auxilium predictorum virorum." The two last mentioned were probably charged with the actual distribution (T. 25).

made to have a more influential person assume this office.   Husbands and wives usually appointed their surviving partner to be an executor. Children and other members of the family were also chosen, although the notion that they were least likely to follow the testator's will had already appeared in literature of the second half of the thirteenth century.[81]   The clergy and religious were also popular choices.   As religious were limited in their legal capacity and in their ability to move about the country, the rather onerous duties of the executor's office were less suitably assumed by them.   They were forbidden this office in a canon included among the statutes of Bishop Bitton of Bath and Wells (?1252-8).   This ruling reappeared in Archbishop Boniface's provincial statutes of 1261 and was frequently repeated thereafter.[82] However, religious could obtain permission to act and often did so.[83] The Exeter statutes of 1287 urged that executors be of the diocese of the testator.[84]

[81] In *Le Manuel des pechiez* (*ca.* 1260):

> Mult ai veu, et trop souent,
> Mauueis executurs,—nomement
> A home mort sun parent (lines 5260-2);

and in *Handlyng Synne* (1303):

> Of all executours þat men fynde,
> Werst are þyn ownë kynde,
> And þy chyldryn specyaly
> Are to þy soule unkyndëly.
> Þy chyldryn alle sey þus, —
> "Whome shulde þey ȝyuë hyt but vs ?" (lines 6265-6270)

Both texts are published in *Robert of Brunne's Handlyng Synne*, ed. F. J. Furnivall, Roxburghe Club (London 1862), p. 196.

[82] In the statutes of Bath and Wells, the canon, *Quod religiosi non possunt fieri executores consiliorum* [lege *consiliarios?*] *vel administratores*, reads in part: "Et nisi vir [lege ut viris] evagandi religiosis et rebus secularibus immescendi prorsus occasio auferatur, statuimus ne in episcopatu nostro executionis honus sine nostra licencia suscipiant speciali..." (Vat. Lib., Ottob. Lat. 72, fol. 112r).   Similar canons appear in the derived collections of Archbishop Ludham of York (1259?), preserved in Br. Mus., Landsdowne MS. 397, fol. 251r, and of Bishop Gervais of Winchester (1262-5), published by Wilkins as a collection of Henry Woodlock, bishop of Winchester (II, 298); cf. the discussion of these collections in Cheney, *English Synodalia*, pp. 96-109.   The statute of Archbishop Boniface is printed in Wilkins, I, 746.   See the discussion of this matter in Lyndwood; *Provinciale*, p. 168, *gl. ad. verb.* ordinariorum, religiosus.

[83] This became the general law of the Church by a decretal of Boniface VIII: "Religiosus, exsecutor ab aliquo in sua voluntate ultima deputatus, non potest... nisi a superiore suo petita super hoc licentia et obtenta" (*Sext.*, III, 11, 2).

[84] "Curet autem testator, fideles et locupletes nostrae diocesis, et non alienae, constituere executores" (Wilkins, II, 156).

The Form of the Will

It remains to consider the manner in which the testator expressed his will. In an earlier chapter it was maintained that in Anglo-Saxon times the will was an oral act. Whether a written record were made of it or not was unimportant, so far as the legal nature of the transaction was concerned. The document was considered to be a permanent witness to the act, but the act was valid without it. Dispositions of property at death continued to be made in this way after the Conquest and, although the development of the canonical will led to the adopting of a new theory of the effects of this act, its oral form persisted for many years.[85] The essentially oral quality of most of the wills of the Middle Ages is not easy for the modern mind to grasp. The task is made difficult by our tendency to project the contemporary distinction between a nuncupative and a written will into the late twelfth and thirteenth centuries. Both forms are now considered to be manifestations of the testator's intention; both are legally effective acts. But this distinction is misleading when applied to the period under consideration. At that time, the testator usually announced his will before witnesses. This was the effective legal act. No form of words was required for its validity. In many cases the testator would be capable of little more than a few sentences or a nod of assent to suggestions made to him by those in attendance. If memory of the making of this will and of its contents remained only in the minds of the witnesses (they might commit it to writing at a later opportunity, or at least at the time of probate), then it was called a nuncupative will. But very often, especially in the second half of the thirteenth century, the testator's bequests were put into writing immediately. When the act was performed in this way it was called a written will, but it is important to realize that, in most cases, the legally effective transaction was still the oral statement of intention before witnesses.

The oral quality of the act is easily demonstrated. It is quite frequently remarked that the testator made his bequests "with his mouth."[86] The donation clauses of most of the wills of the first half

---

[85] Cf. Foster, *Lincoln Wills*, II, xvii, and F. M. Stenton, *Transcripts of Charters relating to Gilbertine Houses*, Lincoln Rec. Soc., XVIII (1922), xvii-xviii.

[86] E.g., in the *will* of Robert of Spain (1301): "Pateat ... quod ego Robertus condidi presens testamentum meum ore proprio in hunc modum" (London, Br. Mus., Harl. Ch 53 H 23); in a certificate touching the will of Harry Wheler (1478) we read that he "willed by expressed words of his mouth spoken" (London, PRO, C-146. 6615). Canon Foster printed an example from 1524 in *Lincoln Wills*, II, 14: "I utterly revoke and disanul all other willes by me herebefore made and spoken by my moth."

of the thirteenth century employed the perfect tense, implying that the act was already accomplished. The earliest accounts of the examination of witnesses also focus attention on the oral nature of the will. The examination was not intended to prove the authenticity of the document. In fact the written *will* seems almost to have been ignored and emphasis was placed on the fact that the witnesses were present when the bequests were made and heard what was said.[87] Finally, some documents made the distinction between the legal act (the oral statement of the testator) and the writing in which evidence of it was contained. Thus, for example, Gervase of Canterbury described how Henry II made a will "as though he were going to die," then added: *in scriptum quoque redigi præcepit quod testatum est.*[88] Many other instances could be given to demonstrate that the notion of the will as an oral act continued in England until well after the Middle Ages.

Nevertheless, an exclusive emphasis of the oral nature of the medieval will is somewhat misleading. There is abundant evidence that as the thirteenth century advanced the written *will* increased in importance. In many cases the chief concern was to establish the authenticity of the written *will,* and there are occasional hints that the execution of the document was considered to be the effective legal act.

One of the first indications of this change is to be found in the rather uncertain use of the word *testamentum* that seems to imply that the distinction between its two meanings—legal act and documentary evidence of the act—was becoming obscured or even forgotten. It has been shown above that the witnesses to the oral will were expected to give evidence of its contents. The written document was intended to serve the same purpose. In the second half of the thirteenth century it becomes apparent that the witnesses were being examined less about

---

[87] Thus in a document attached to T. 31, it is stated that the witnesses "viderunt, interfuerunt et audierunt." A similar description of the examination of witnesses appears in the Hustings roll in 1271: "Qui dixerunt quod presentes fuerunt et audierunt ubi dictus Walterus ... donavit, etc." (Roll 4, no. 130). The Hustings roll usually mentions the presentation of the written document as well; see the following note.

[88] *Historical Works of Gervase of Canterbury,* ed. W. Stubbs, 2 vols., RS, 73 (1879-80), I, 297-298. Other examples: "Hoc est testamentum Amalrici filii Rad' in quo extreme voluntatis sui conscribi voluit testimonium" (London, Br. Mus., Egerton MS. 3031, fol. 38, dated 1180 or earlier); a letter of King John to the guardians of the see of Chichester during vacancy—"quod permittatis quod executores testamenti domini Simonis Episcopi Cicestrensis exequantur testamentum ipsius juxta tenorem autentici scripti sui a quo sigillum suum dependet ..." (*Rot. Lit. Cl.,* I, 92a); similarly in the *will* of William de Longespee (T. 25). The distinction between the will and the *scriptum* in which it is contained appeared frequently in the Hustings roll; e.g., roll 4, nos. 130, 135, 142, etc.

the oral act than about the written *will* which lay before the court. Thus in the register of Archbishop Walter Giffard of York (1270) there is a testimonial letter in which the prelate said that he had seen a *will* and examined its seal and had questioned the witnesses *super omnibus in memoratu scriptis contentis.*[89]   A similar change can be discerned at London in the Court of Hustings.   There, the formula of probate long emphasized the examination of witnesses who were "present and heard" when the will was made.   But in the last decade of the thirteenth century the enrolment often omitted the names of the witnesses, although place was left for them on the roll.[90]   This would seem to imply that the formula of probate, with its emphasis on the oral act before witnesses, was somewhat archaic, and that the written *will*, which the scribe had at hand when preparing the enrolment, was the preferred evidence of the testator's disposition of property.   Beginning in 1273, most Hustings' probates mention the reading of the document in court and there is evidence that it was done as early as 1256.[91]   In the year 1302 a description of the examination of witnesses in the *Liber Albus* emphasized the importance of their testimony about the seal of the document.[92]   Probate seems to have become especially concerned with the proof of the authenticity of the written *will*.

The probate of the will of Master Martin of Holy Cross seemed to go one step farther, for approval was related exclusively to the examination of the written document.[93]   This case is somewhat unsatisfactory, for the statement is condensed and obscure; but the notion is clearly stated in the will of Peter of Aigueblanche, where it is said that probate was granted because, on examination, the written *will* proved to be in accord with required formalities.[94]   Now the will of Peter of Aigueblanche was a special case.   It was drawn up by a notary and the formalities of Roman civil law were observed as to witnesses and sealing. It is very likely that in the bishop's circle the function of the witnesses

[89] *The Register of Walter Giffard, Archbishop of York,* ed. W. Brown, Surtees Society, CIX (1904), pp. 164-165.

[90] E.g., roll 18, no. 64 (1287-8); roll 19, nos. 18, 42, 47; roll 25, nos. 11, 28, 41, etc.

[91] See below, p. 207 and n. 191.

[92] *Munimenta Gildhallæ Londoniensis,* ed. H. T. Riley, 3 vols., RS, 12 (1859-62), I, 403.

[93] "... nos Testamentum bonæ memoriæ quondam Domini Martini de Sancta Cruce coram nobis legitime probatum vidimus, inspeximus, non cancellatum non abolitum nec in aliqua sui parte viciatum, set integrum ..." (T. 59b).

[94] "... volumus pervenire [sic] quod nos testamentum bone memorie domini P[etri] quondam Herefordensis episcopi et codicillos quos idem fecerat examinavimus diligenter, et pronunciamus omnia predicta legitime processisse. Quare executoribus in predicto testamento damus potestatem ..." (T. 68).

was to prove the authenticity of the document and the application of the testator's seal was considered to be the legal act which constituted the will.   This would mean, of course, that the oral quality of the will had disappeared and that the essential legal act was the execution of a document.

There are several indications of this point of view during the thirteenth century.   There was, first of all, the tendency to treat the written *will* as authority for a right rather than a record of its acquisition. An example is to be seen in the *Cartulary of Darley Abbey,* where it is remarked that in place of a charter covering a bequest of rent, the *will* of the testator is held.[95]   More important is the fact that some of the written *wills* speak of bequest made *virtute istius testamenti.*[96] It would not be unreasonable to maintain that these examples are cases of the uncertain use of the word *testamentum,* indicated above, so that the reference could be to the oral act rather than to the document that was intended to be its evidence.   But there are examples where the text states that the bequests was made by the document—*per hoc scriptum legavit.*[97]   This same manner of expression appears in an Ipswich custumal of 1291, which speaks of the bequest of tenements *par testament escrit ou nuncupatyf* and in the Exeter statutes of 1287.[98]

A final example of the importance attached to the execution of the written *will* is provided by the account of the will-making of Bishop Sutton of Lincoln.   It is narrated with unusual detail in his register.[99] In May, 1291, the bishop announced to attendant clerics that he had made his will (*testamentum condidisse*) the previous day in the form contained within a document.   The document was shown to the household, read in part, then closed.   The bishop's great seal was appended and those present were asked to be witnesses.   A brief note early the

[95] "Memorandum   quod   loco   carti . . .   habemus   testamentum"; ed. Darlington, I, 84, no. A32.

[96] E.g., T. 65.

[97] T. 37; even here the argument is not completely satisfactory, for the following phrase is to be found in the same document: "ad faciendum plenarie testamentum sicut continetur in hoc scripto."   The notion is clearly stated in a document in the Reading cartulary: the executors of the will of Herbert Fitz Peter terminate their account of his benefactions to the abbey as follows: "Que omnia prefatus Herebertus predictis abbati et monachis in testamento ipsius sigillo suo signato dedit et assignavit" (Br. Mus., Harl. Ms. 1708, fol. 115r); dated 1248.

[98] B.C., II, 196-197; Bishop Quivil's canon reads—"Facto autem testamenti nuncupativo, vel in scriptis . . ." (Wilkins, II, 156).

[99] The Rolls and Register of Bishop Oliver Sutton, ed. Rosalind M. T. Hill, Vol. III, Lincoln Record Society, XLVIII (1952), lxxv-lxxvi, 103-104.

next year mentioned that the bishop made another will and that, in the
evening after vespers, he had it sealed in the presence of witnesses.[100]
In this case we do not know whether it was read or not, but two years
later he produced it, had it read aloud, and confirmed it.[101]   Changes
and additions were contained in a codicil which was drawn up and
witnessed in proper legal form.   In the case of the first will, there
seems to have been some attempt at secrecy.   The witnesses mentioned
in the register do not seem to have heard all the bequests, and it can be
presumed that they were unable to read the document since it was
closed.   To what were these witnesses to testify?   to the fact that a will
was made and to its contents, or to the fact that the document sealed
before their eyes was an authentic statement of the testator's will?   The
account stresses the fact that they were present when the document was
sealed.[102]   What then was the purpose of the formality of sealing the
document before the witnesses?   Was it to establish the authenticity of
the document? or was it the act that formally constituted the will ?

This account of the will-making of Bishop Sutton is of considerable
importance for, reported as it is, it reveals two different legal traditions
meeting in a single transaction.   From the partial and complete readings
of the document it is clear that the older notion of the oral quality of the
will was still in vogue.   On the other hand, the importance attached to
the act of sealing the document is clear, and it is hard to avoid the
conclusion that this formality was not only a means to establish an
authentic witness to the testator's intention, but constituted the will
itself.   Thus it seems necessary to conclude that, although the oral
quality of the will remained uppermost in many minds, there was
already in the thirteenth century an emphasis on the execution and
sealing of the written *will* in the presence of witnesses which shows that
these, in some circles at least, were considered to be the essential
formalities.

The Written Will

It is evident from the foregoing discussion that the precise function
of the written *will* is sometimes hard to establish.   It is clear, however
that its importance increased during the thirteenth century.   The
frequency with which these documents were made during these year

---

100 *Ibid.*, p. 182.

101 *Ibid.*, p. lxxxvi.

102 This is especially clear in the account of the sealing of the second *will*: "... idem
testamentum fecit ... consignari, advocando testimonium dicti domini [list of witnesses]
qui omnes presentes in consignatione protinus affuerunt" (*ibid.*, p. 182).

also increased; in this they reflect the growing use of the private document in various kinds of transactions. It is not the purpose of the present study to embark on a diplomatic analysis of the *wills* that survive from the time of Henry II to the end of the period of interest here. That will be the subject of another volume. It is useful, however, to point out certain external and internal qualities of these documents, since they substantiate several of the conclusions and suggestions made above.

The testator's chief concern was to provide proof of the authenticity of his will and, if he had made several, to indicate which of them was valid at the time of his death. During the thirteenth century *wills* were signed neither by the testator nor the witnesses.[103] The preferred mark of authenticity was the seal. The Exeter constitutions of 1287 urged the testator to employ the seal of another if he did not have one of his own.[104] In 1359 a wise canon of Lincoln fixed his seal to his *will*, but he arranged that the seal of the cathedral chapter be affixed as well, since his own was unknown.[105] The Exeter constitutions urged that the seals of those present be added, since a document which bore only the testator's seal could easily be forged.[106] During the period under discussion *wills* were sealed by testators and executors and only rarely by anyone else.[107] An exception to this rule is the will made according to the formalities of Roman law, where the seals of the witnesses rather than of the executors were used. Occasionally the *will* was sent to a person of importance that his seal might be added.[108] The *will* of William Longespee (T. 25) was terminated by a clause in which it was stated that the testator had fixed his seal and had invited his executors to do likewise. A clause of this sort is to be found in many

---

[103] Cf. *Lincoln Wills*, II, 14. The *will* of Walter Suffield, bishop of Norwich (T. 56) is probably endorsed by the testator's own hand. No other example of this is known for the thirteenth century. The sealing clause of the *will* of Cecilia Huse (T. 67a) reads: "In cuius rei testimonium huic testamento sigillum meum una cum signo predicti prioris et signis predictorum executorum meorum apposui." In this case the word *signo* must refer to the seals of the individuals concerned since there are no signatures on the document. A letter of Gilbert Foliot (1139-48) speaks of a *will* as though it were signed by testator and witnesses: "... in conscriptorum testium presentia ipse subscripsit" (PL 190, 788-789).

[104] Wilkins, II, 156.

[105] Cf. *Lincoln Wills*, I, 11.

[106] Wilkins, II, 156.

[107] For an early example of sealing by a witness as distinct from the executors, see above, n. 61.

[108] William Longespee, earl of Salisbury sent his *will* to the king and obtained the royal seal (T. 25). On the affixing of the seal of the archbishop, see below, p. 205.

of the *wills* of the second half of the century[109] and in model *wills* as well.[110]   Where original documents have survived, it can be seen that it was indeed the executors whose seals were appended.   Sealing by the executors, as opposed to the witnesses, seems to have continued even in *wills* of the last quarter of the century, where specific mention was made of the simple witnesses.

Another of the more interesting external features of these *wills* is that many were folded and laced in a closed position with a thong. In the rules for the preparing of a written will that are included in the Exeter constitutions of Peter Quivil the closing of a *will* before sealing is specifically mentioned.[111]   In a few cases the thong was sealed to the dorse of the folded document so that is would be possible to know if it had been opened and read before probate   As early as 1226 the *will* of Philip de Sancte Marie Ecclesia, treasurer of St. Paul's of London, was closed and sealed in the folded position.[112]

In a few cases it can be shown that several copies of the document were prepared.   An example of this practice is provided by the *will* of Henry III which was drawn up in the external form of a chirograph, although the phrasing of the document was similar to that of other *wills* of the time.[113]   Occasionally, separate documents were prepared to include bequests in different areas.   In 1293, for example, John of Sandwich had two *wills* drawn up to contain legacies of property in Kent and Essex respectively.[114]   In the fourteenth century, the practice began of executing two documents: one was called "testament" and bequeathed chattels; the other, called "last will," contained bequests of tenements.[115]   No example of this practice has been found in the thirteenth century.   A written *will* usually called itself *testamentum*. *Ultima voluntas* was used fairly often and in a few *wills* both names were united—the "last will and testament" with which we are familiar today.

Almost all the written *wills* of the time were in Latin.   A few were in French; most of the *wills* using this language can be shown to have been

---

109 E.g., T. 33, T. 53b, T. 59a, etc.

110 This is true of the model *will* of the late thirteenth century printed in *The Archaeological Journal*, XXI (1865), pp. 58-62.

111 "... ac in scriptis, si fieri potest, suum condere testamentum, quod, postquam factum fuerit, claudatur ..." (Wilkins, II, 156).

112 T. 26.

113 T. 53b; the *will* of Gilbert son of Fulc (*ca.* 1200) is another example (PRO, E-40. 11559).

114 Canterbury, Dean and Chapter Library, *Sede Vacante* Scrap Book, II, 190.   In 1341 John de Pulleney executed three documents in making his will; cf. Sharpe I, 609-610.

115 See above, p. 178, n. 44.

made under special circumstances. Thus the *will* of Prince Edward (T. 72b) was drawn up in French when he was on crusade.[116]

These documents were usually written by some cleric in attendance. A few were drawn up by notaries and, in one case, the first *will* of Bishop Richard de Gravesend of London, the testator wrote it himself.[117] Notaries usually identified themselves in the final clauses of the documents they prepared. The names of other scribes were occasionally indicated as well.[118]

The texts of those documents that served as witness to *post obit* gifts in the twelfth century assumed the forms of ordinary charters of the time.[119] But early in the thirteenth century, the structure and phraseology of *wills* took on proper characteristics, so that, as a general rule, they are easily distinguished from other documents. No precise formulae were required; the texts of these *wills* are remarkable for the variety of their phrasing. Nevertheless a common plan is usually apparent. The existance of a number of model *wills,* from the second half of the thirteenth century, shows that efforts were made to ensure that the text was reasonably well organized, and that it gave clear statement to those facts that had to be known for the successful execution of the testator's intention, namely, the legacies and those who were to receive them, the date, and the names of executors.[120]

The introductory part of the text commonly began with an invocation of the Trinity, followed by the name of the testator and the statement that he was making his will.[121] After 1225 the date was occasionally added at this point.[122] More rarely, the place and the names of the witnesses were included as well.[123] As a general rule, however, this

[116] T. 67d was also drawn up when the testator was on crusade. The *will* of Walter de Cokeseye was written in Latin, but a codicil was added in French (Worcester, Giffard Register, fol. 410). The French *will* of John de Meynaco is enrolled *in extenso* in Hustings roll 24 (no. 19, 20th November, 1294).

[117] T. 89b.

[118] Thus it is remarked within the text of the *will* of Simon de Montfort (T. 59a) that it was written by his son Henry.

[119] Cf. Holdsworth, *History,* III, 536.

[120] In addition to the model *will,* cited above in n. 110, the following have been collected: Cambridge, Univ. Lib., MS. E e, i, 1, fol. 225 (ed. F. W. Maitland, "A Conveyancer of the Thirteenth Century," *Collected Papers,* II, 195-196); Cambridge, Corpus Christi MS. 297, fol. 101v (1275-1300); Cambridge, Gonville and Caius MS, 205, p. 467 (mentions 1258 within the text); Oxford, Bodleian MS. Rawlinson, G. 5, fol. 522 (late thirteenth century).

[121] "Hoc est testamentum N" (T. 23, T. 25), or "Ego N. condo testamentum meum" (T. 28, T. 33).

[122] E.g., T. 25.

[123] E.g., T. 31.

information was part of the conclusion of the *will*. Sometimes the testator was pleased to reflect on the certainty of death and the uncertainty of the time of its coming.[124] More often he stated his condition: he was going on pilgrimage;[125] he was ill in body but sound in mind.[126]

The body of the text was devoted to a statement of the testator's bequests. His first concern was to provide for his spiritual good. He gave his soul to God and his body to the earth or, more often, the soul was given to God and the Virgin Mary and the body to the church chosen for burial. In the second half of the thirteenth century detailed arrangements for the funeral frequently occurred at this point in the *will*.[127] Next instructions were given for the payment of the mortuary and the acquittal of the debts of the deceased. Then followed the bequests in alms and to relatives and friends. The considerable variety of practice in this regard is discussed in the following chapter. The donation clauses assumed several different forms. The usual verb was *lego* or *legat*. There was also frequent use of *do et lego* and, occasionally, of *concedo* and *assigno*. The French *wills* used the form *je devis*. As was mentioned above, the verb expressing the donation was usually in the perfect tense during the first half of the thirteenth century. For the remainder of the Middle Ages the present form of the verb was preferred. When, during this later period, the verb of the donation clause was in the perfect tense and referred to the third person, the text in question was probably that of a nuncupative will.[128] The list of legacies was often completed by directions for the disposal of any residue that might remain.[129]

The final portion of the text was concerned with the execution of the will. Earlier documents, such as those of Archbishop Theobold and Henry II, were concluded with an anathema clause.[130] This rather formidable sanction fell into disuse during the thirteenth century.[131]

---

124 "Quia nichil est certius morte, nichil incertius hora mortis" (T. 71a). See Bracton, *De Legibus*, fol. 27 and *Note Book*, I, 90 and III, 192, where the phrase occurs; cf. *Digest*, 35, 1, 1.

125 E.g., T. 25, T. 53b.

126 "... languens corpore sana mente" (T. 67a etc.).

127 See below, pp. 258-259.

128 E.g., the *will* of Henry de Colebi (T. 71b).

129 The Exeter statutes of 1287 included a model clause dealing with the residue and ordered that it be incorporated in *wills* (Wilkins, II, 157); cf. P. and M., II, 339.

130 See above, pp. 142-143. Archbishop Theobald also gave an indulgence to those who aided the execution of his will.

131 One of the rare exceptions to this rule is to be found in the *will* of Bishop Richard

Executors were urged in God's name to do their duty and, occasionally, they were asked to act with the diligence that they would desire in their own executors.[132]   In some wills, they were given a legacy which was to be received if they fulfilled their obligations.   The chief concern of the concluding portion of the text was the appointment of executors. The usual verb employed was *constituo*.[133]   As was the case with the verb of the donation clause, the perfect tense was commonly used during the first half of the thirteenth century.   The testator often stated that he had fixed his seal to the document and that he had asked his executors to do likewise.   This phrase appeared in the *wills* of more important members of society during the first quarter of the thirteenth century, and by its close was to be found in *wills* dealing with quite modest fortunes.   A list of witnesses was occasionally added at this point.[134] Many of the texts were concluded with the date and, in a few cases, there is mention of the place where the will was made.[135]   Occasionally, previous wills were revoked.[136]

III.   The Implementation of the Will

In the late Middle Ages it was customary to say that the man who had made a will had not long to live.   Although the saying eventually came to embody a superstition, in the beginning it was an accurate description of a fact: most men delayed the making of their wills until death was imminent.[137]   The executor who fixed his seal to a *will* could be fairly certain that in a short time he would be embarked on the process of implementing the desires of his deceased friend.

---

of Chichester (T. 53a): "Excommunico et Anathematizo omnes illos qui testamentum meum maliciose impediunt."

[132] E.g., T. 99b.

[133] "Possuit" was used in T. 30, and "Instituit" in T. 95.

[134] E.g., T. 67a, T. 71b.

[135] Among the procedural rules included in the statutes of Cardinal Otto (1237) was the following: "In principio quoque vel fine cujuslibet scripturae auctenticae sufficientem datam inferi statuimus diei, temporis, atque loci (Wilkins, I, 655).   The place was mentioned in T. 67d, T. 72a, etc.

[136] E.g., "Et sciendum est quod testamentum meum prius conditum, per istud testamentum meum in ultima voluntate mea factum penitus adnichilat" (T. 72a).   In cases of revocation, it was necessary to establish the dates of the different acts in question; hence the importance of including the date within the text of the *will*.

[137] "Comune custume of men is to make þer testament whanne þei dien, and for to make exequies for þat day þat þei been biried" (John Wyclif, Sermon CCXXXVII, in *Select English Works of John Wyclif*, ed. T. Arnold, 3 vols. [Oxford, 1869-71], II, 212); cf. Foster, *Lincoln Wills*, II, x.

During the thirteenth century a technique was elaborated to carry this execution through from the death of the testator to the completion of all his bequests.   The process included a non-contentious probate which established both the validity of the will and its precise contents, the taking of an inventory of the assets of the deceased, the commission of administration, and the examination of accounts and the acquittal of the executors.   These procedures were elaborated with differences of tempo and sequence in the various dioceses of the country.   There is not sufficient source material to show their development in detail. However, it is possible to sketch its main lines by drawing on the episcopal statutes mentioned above, the episcopal registers, which increased in volume and detail as the century drew to a close, and the casual *acta* of testamentary administration.

Probate

It was already agreed in Glanvill's time that, when the validity or the terms of a will were in question, the decision lay with the ecclesiastical courts.[138]   During the following years this proof of the will developed from an occasional procedure, invoked in disputes, to a regular and, usually, non-contentious process through which all wills passed before execution began.   The date at which this important step was taken and the motives for the decision are not immediately evident.[139]   There was precedent for it in Roman civil law and, in fact, the *publicatio testamenti* reappeared in southern France shortly after 1100.[140]   But it was not until the middle of the thirteenth century that it was commonly mentioned in the northern area of customary law.   In those years probate was imposed by the statutes of several French councils, but did not become subject to an exclusively ecclesiastical control.[141]   By that time the non-contentious probate of the will seems to have become general procedure in England.

The necessity of probate as a prelude to any *post obit* distribution of property became clear as a result of certain developments late in the reign of King John.   Magna Carta had provided for the sequestration of the estates of royal tenants until their obligations to the king were

138 See above, p. 167.

139 Selden did not make the distinction. Thus he implied that non-contentious probate was regular procedure by Glanvill's time. He remarked, however, that he could find no example of a probate act before the reign of Henry III (*Works*, III, 1669-71). The earliest probate found during the present study is attached to T. 31.

140 Auffroy, *Testament*, pp. 519-521.

141 *Ibid.*, pp. 447-448 (The Council of Tours mentioned here should be dated 1236) and 599, n. 3.

established and acquitted.[142]   Then the goods of the deceased were to be delivered to the executors for distribution.   The necessity of providing machinery to establish the proper executors must have been evident almost immediately.   Another demand for probate was supplied by Magna Carta when it granted the supervision of the goods of the intestate to the Church.[143]   This meant that, as a preliminary to the distribution of the property of any person deceased, it had to be established whether that person had died testate or intestate.   A series of episcopal statutes from Worcester illustrate how the implication of these rules gradually became evident.   In the first statutes of Bishop William de Blois (1219) a regular process was imposed for establishing whether clergy who died in the diocese had made a will or not.[144]   Nothing was said of the estates of the laity in these statutes, which were concerned almost exclusively with matters touching the liturgy and clerical discipline.   But in a second series ten years later, the same bishop extended his interest in the will: he made provision for the regular supervision of the executors of the laity and for the distribution of property of those who died intestate.[145]   In this case there was no specific mention of probate, but it is difficult to see how it could have been avoided as the first step in the procedure imposed.   A similar concern is manifest in the third Worcester collection, that of Walter de Cantilupe (1240).[146]   Here a careful supervision of executors, including their payment, involved a knowledge of the contents of wills by the ecclesiastical authority that almost necessarily implied that probate was regularly given in the diocese of Worcester by this date.   Similar rules, with the additional precaution of the inventory (to be made before administration was given to the executors), appeared in three sets of statutes derived from those of Walter de Cantilupe.   They were published at Bath and Wells by Bishop William Bitton between 1252 and 1258, at York by Archbishop Ludham in 1259, and at Winchester by Bishop Gervais in the early years of the following decade.[147]   In the last-mentioned statutes,

---

[142] See above, pp. 154-155.

[143] See above, p. 174.

[144] "Item, si persona vel vicarius decesserit, non fiat distributio rerum suarum, antequam constiterit episcopo, vel ejus officiali ipsum testamentum condidisse" (Wilkins, I, 571). The canon continues to inform the local dean that in the interval he should sequestrate the property of the deceased.   Many letters commissioning sequestration in these circumstances are extant from the thirteenth century.

[145] Wilkins, I, 627.

[146] *Ibid.*, I, 674.

[147] Bishop Bitton's canons are found in Bibl. Vat., Ottob. Lat. 742, fol. 112r, and those of Archbishop Ludham in Br. Mus., Lansdowne MS. 397, fols. 249v-251r.   The Winchester

probate of all wills was specifically imposed as a prelude to administration. A similar rule had already appeared in a canon of the provincial Council of Lambeth in 1261, and it was to find a place among the legatine statutes of Cardinal Ottobono (1268).[148] Thus specific reference to a general non-contentious probate finally appeared in 1261. But earlier canons permit the suggestion that in some dioceses at least it was established as much as twenty years before that date. The canon of 1261 supports this deduction for it does not speak of probate as an innovation, but as a procedure to be followed *juxta morem*.

Probate *acta* of the period under discussion are not numerous. None of the act books that include them in large numbers is to be found before the fourteenth century. Our main sources of information are a number of original letters, commissions, and *notitiae* produced in the ordinary exercise of testamentary jurisdiction, and the more numerous references to probate and administration which are to be found in episcopal registers. From this evidence it is possible to describe probate procedure at least in its general lines.

According to the Lambeth statute of 1261, probate was to be given by the ordinary. John of Acton interpreted this to mean the bishop and others possessing ordinary power.[149] Bishops could and did grant probate themselves, and they quite frequently provided for it by commissions for individual instances. There are several examples of probate by the bishop's official. In the thirteenth century it is quite difficult to know whether this matter regularly fell to the official's court or whether he was acting on special commission.[150] Probate was also granted by various ministers employed by the bishop in the administration of local areas of his diocese. The few commissions of appoint-

statutes are printed in Wilkins, II, 298. See the discussion of these collections, above, p. 185, and n. 82.

148 The Lambeth constitution reads: "... et postquam coram ordinario, juxta morem probatum fuerit testamentum ..." (Wilkins, I, 754). Cardinal Ottobono's statute of 1268 is printed *ibid.*, II, 8, c. xiv.

149 P. 107, *gl. ad verb.* ordinario; cf. *Provinciale*, p. 174, *gl. ad verb.* approbatis.

150 The will of John de Brommere (T. 99c) was proved by the official of Worcester, and that of William of Arundel (T. 95) by the official of Winchester. Miss Churchill has shown that the commissary general of the archbishop of Canterbury was given the power to grant probate by his commission of appointment in 1382, and that the power was exercised earlier (*C.A.*, I, 59). The commissary general, *sede vacante*, proved wills in the thirteenth century: e.g., the will of Hugh de Panebrok (T. 93). The official gave probate at York in the fifteenth century; cf. A. H. Thompson, *The English Clergy and their Organization in the Later Middle Ages*, Ford Lectures (Oxford, 1947), pp. 192-193. But cf. Colin Morris "The Commissary of the Bishop in the Diocese of Lincoln," *Journal of Ecclesiastical History*, X (1959), p. 53.

ment of these ministers that survive from the thirteenth century are not in sufficient detail to indicate the extent of testamentary jurisdiction possessed by the appointees. Of the archdeacons it can be said that probate was one area of activity in which they seemed to vindicate their claim to ordinary jurisdiction.[151] They and their officials granted the most numerous group of probates that survive from the thirteenth century. A power similar to that of the archdeacons was exercised by those in charge of the deaneries of the archbishop of Canterbury's immediate jurisdiction, by rural deans, and by the rectors of exempt parishes.[152] Probate was also granted by cathedral chapters and certain of the great religious houses which were exempt from episcopal authority.[153] During the bishop's visitation to any of these areas or liberties, probate could be granted by the visitor.[154]

It becomes apparent, then, that the division of probate jurisdiction in England along diocesan lines was complicated by divisions within each diocese, where local officials claimed the power in the area of their jurisdiction. When the property of a testator lay within several of these areas, his executors were faced with the slow and costly process of obtaining probate from each of the officials concerned. Efforts were made to provide a regular and expeditious procedure for dealing with these cases. The solution lay in a direct appeal to the jurisdiction superior to all those involved. Since it necessarily resulted in some loss of authority by those holding subordinate offices, the solution was developed and applied only with considerable difficulty.

---

151 Recent studies by Colin Morris (see the previous note) and R. L. Storey, *Diocesan Administration in the Fifteenth Century*, Publications of the Borthwick Institute of Historical Research (York, 1959), show the rise of other officials who tended to lessen the probate jurisdiction of the archdeacons.

152 Probate was granted by the dean of Arches (T. 69) and by his commissary (T. 77). On the exempt parishes of the archbishop of Canterbury, cf. *C.A.*, I, 83 ff. In 1280, Archbishop Pecham confirmed the ancient rights of these rectors in testamentary cases: *Registrum Epistolarum Fratris Johannis Peckham*, ed. C. T. Martin, 3 vols., RS, 77 (1882-6), I, 127. The dean of Oxford gave probate in T. 71a, T. 86, etc.

153 The probate of T. 93 was granted by the commissary of the dean and chapter of St. Paul's. The Abbey of Meaux based a claim to prove wills of tenants in chapter on a privilige of Pope Alexander IV (1249-61): *Chronicon Monasterii de Melsa*, ed. E. A. Bond, 3 vols., RS, 43 (1266-8), II, 121-122; cf. Knowles, *The Monastic Order*, p. 600.

154 Compositions regulating the powers of the visiting prelate and the local authority were usually made; e.g., a composition of May 1338 between the bishop of Bath and Wells and the archdeacon of Wells arranged that during visitation the bishop was to have probate and the reception of accounts of all who wished it, as his predecessor had (Wells, *Liber Albus*, R. II, fol. 58).

On the diocesan level, when property lay within several of the minor jurisdictions, probate came to be reserved to the bishop or his official. This arrangement was presented as established procedure in a memorandum from the register of Bishop William Ayermin of Norwich (1325-36).[155] A similar arrangement was eventually adopted where property of a deceased testator lay in several dioceses. Probate and the supervision of the execution of the will passed to the prerogative jurisdiction of the archbishop.

A legatine statute of 1268 had suggested a different line of development, providing that where the deceased held "benefices" in several dioceses probate should pertain to the bishop within whose jurisdiction death occurred.[156] In his commentary on this clause John of Acton admits local custom which would allow probate in one of the dioceses in which benefices were held or in that in which death occurred, but he seems most concerned to avoid delay of probate. He adds that the accounts of the executors should be received by all the ordinaries in whose dioceses the deceased had property.[157] It was precisely over this reception of accounts that the first attempts to establish a prerogative supervision of wills met opposition. The conflict that resulted between the archbishop of Canterbury and his suffragans clouded the first years of the episcopate of John Pecham. There is much evidence in Pecham's register to show that he sometimes supervised the execution of wills in the different dioceses of his province. This activity is especially evident in the enforcement of the wills of the clergy, suggesting that the word *beneficia* in the statute of 1268 was used in the strict sense to refer to clerical property. Thus in a letter of 1280 Pecham spoke of neglect of property lying in four dioceses by the executors of William of Kilkenny, late bishop of Ely, and ordered his officers to proceed to execution.[158] But his suffragans resented and eventually opposed this activity.

Positions were clearly drawn late in 1280 during the dispute between the archbishop and Thomas de Cantilupe, bishop of Hereford, which resulted from Pecham's attempt to supervise the execution of the wills

155 *C.A.*, II, 77-78.

156 Wilkins, II, 8.

157 P. 107, *gl. ad verb.* fidem. This is the arrangement shown in practice in a letter of William Wickwane, archbishop of York (1283): Ralph of Woodborough, a cleric with goods in the archdiocese, had died in Lincolnshire, and his will was proved "coram loci ordinario, ad quem testamentorum examinatum extitit." Master Benedict of Southwell was appointed commissary to receive inventory and accounts for the goods in the archbishop's jurisdiction; *The Register of William Wickwane*, ed. W. Brown, Surtees Society, CXIV (1907), p. 83.

158 *Registrum Epistolarum*, I. 110-111.

of Henry de Hawkley and Giles de Avenbury, both members of the
chapter of Hereford. Pecham maintained that the metropolitan had
an immemorial right to receive the accounts of executors who administered a will dealing with property in several dioceses within his province.[159]
The reception of accounts remained the chief object of concern in the
rather bitter dispute that followed. In the course of the discussion,
however, metropolitan claims were stated in a wider context involving
jurisdiction over all matters concerned with the execution of these
wills; probate by the archbishop's official was included.[160]

Prerogative supervision of wills was but one of several areas of dispute
at the time; in fact there was no specific reference to it in the list of
gravamina presented to Pecham by his suffragans at the Easter synod of
1282. However it was implicit in the objection to direct appeals to the
metropolitan before local ordinaries had been allowed to deal with cases
within their jurisdiction.[161] The committee appointed by Archbishop
Pecham to study these complaints brought in recommendations that
favoured the suffragans' claims on the whole. However they admitted
that when a dispute could not be settled on the diocesan level it was to
be received by the archbishop's official. As an example of this procedure
they mentioned supervision of the will of a testator who died with
property in several dioceses of the province.[162]

It is not perfectly clear whether the report recommended prerogative
jurisdiction only in case of dispute, or whether it considered the execution of a will dealing with property in several dioceses to pose problems
that were insoluble on the diocesan level so that it necessarily passed into
the archbishop's jurisdiction. The second interpretation seems the
better, but the former is also possible. Future disputes between the
archbishop and his suffragans would be in terms of one interpretation
or the other: was the metropolitan jurisdiction to be invoked only after
neglect or by appeal from the courts of the dioceses in which the
testator's property lay? or was it to act immediately in the supervision

---

159 See the account of this dispute in Decima L. Douie, *Archbishop Pecham* (Oxford, 1952),
pp. 195-214; also Cape's introduction to *Registrum Thome de Cantilupo*, ed. R. G. Griffiths,
Canterbury and York Society (1907) and *C.A.*, I, 380-383.

160 Pecham, MS. Reg. fol. 150r (Wilkins, II, 85): "... quod cum contingat aliquem in
fata decedere, qui in pluribus dioec. beneficiatus existit, executio, et defensio, et probatio,
et omnia quae testamentum suum contingunt, ad ipsum spectare dignoscuntur."

161 *Registrum Epistolarum*, I, 328-332.

162 "... ne plures episcopi seu officiales eorum de bonis testatoris hujusmodi in suis
diœcesibus particulatim consistentibus separatim cognoscentes, contingat contrarias proferre
sententias, et unum exequi, quod alter decrevit nullatenus exequendum" (*ibid.*, I, 337-338).

of such wills to prevent the expense, delay and inconsistency that would usually result if these wills were supervised on the local level?

The commission's report was the basis of a general settlement reached at Lambeth a few weeks after Easter. It is significant that the only important area in which the agreement failed was that concerned with the supervision of wills. The meeting is described by Bishop Giffard of Worcester in a letter of 30 April to Thomas de Cantilupe. According to Giffard, Archbishop Pecham and nine of his suffragans met in the chapel at Lambeth and came to agreement on the matters in dispute. Articles were drawn up incorporating the terms of the reconciliation, though Giffard admitted that there might have been minor differences in the wording of the texts prepared.[163] The suffragans sought authenticated copies of the agreement, but these were not forthcoming. Instead, a few days later they received another document drafted in the form of an ordinance to Pecham's official. The chief discrepancy between the two documents was in the section dealing with the supervision of wills.

According to the articles of the Lambeth settlement probate was to be granted by the bishop in whose diocese death occurred. (This initial directive is a restatement of Cardinal Ottobono's constitution of 1268.) Bishops were to supervise the distribution of the portion of a testator's property that lay within their dioceses. Metropolitan jurisdiction was to be invoked only in the case of disputes that could not be solved on the local level (*ut huiusmodi perplexitas evitetur*).[164] The preoccupation with the wills of the clergy is evident once more, for the article begins "Si moriatur rector habens duo beneficia in diversis diocesibus, testamentum coram episcopo illo probetur in cuius diocese diem clausit extremum." The ruling was to be of general application, however, for the section ends with the sentence "Et hoc idem de laicis bona vel possessiones in diversis diocesibus habentibus observetur." [165]

---

163 "... articuli quidam secundum uniformem intellectum omnium, sicuti nos omnes vel maior pars nostrum quo ad substantiam in scriptis redegimus, licet modus scribendi quo ad verba forsitan per aliquod (?) mutaretur, concessi fuerant et concorditer approbati" (Reg. Godfrey Giffard, fol. 134v); there is a résumé of the letter in *The Register of Bishop Godfrey Giffard of Worcester*, ed. J. W. Willis Bund, 2 vols., Worcester Historical Soc. (1898-1902), II, 147.

164 There are two versions of the articles in Reg. Godfrey Giffard, fols. 133r-134r (*Register*, II, 146-147); quotations are from the second and longer version. The articles are also preserved in Oxford, Bodleian MS. Ashmole 1146, fol. 78r-v (cited by Miss Douie, *op. cit.*, p. 211, n. 2) and in an abbreviated form in *Registrum Ricardi de Swinfield, 1283-1317*, ed. W. W. Capes, Canterbury and York Soc. (1909), p. 32. Cf. above, no. 157.

165 Reg. Godfrey Giffard, fol. 134r.

The second document is an ordinance to Pecham's official dated 25 April; it specifically refers to the recommendations of the committee appointed to examine the *gravamina* and claims to incorporate its advice. The ordinance avoids the complexity of the Lambeth report, simply stating that the official of the court of Canterbury shall receive the accounts of executors administering the wills of those who died with property in several dioceses of the province.[166] It was intended to be provisional; within the text there is mention of further discussion at the next meeting of the bishops.[167] However Pecham's commission to his official in 1284 was expressed in similar terms.[168] Furthermore he seems to have considered the ordinance to have been a correct statement of the agreement between himself and his suffragans for in 1283, during the dispute with Bishop Sutton of Lincoln over the will of the countess of Ferrars, he stated that the metropolitan right of supervision was admitted by his bishops during a recent discussion. Presumably he was referring to the agreement of April, 1282.[169]

Bishop Giffard's letter to Thomas de Cantilupe and Bishop Sutton's disagreement with the archbishop over the will of the countess of Ferrars show that they saw the settlement of 1282 in a different light. The whole dispute was opened again in 1287, when Pecham tried to exercise his authority in supervising the wills of three wealthy clerics and met concerted opposition from several of his suffragans; it was to trouble the episcopate of Archbishop Winchelsey as well.[170] In the last stages of the quarrel the prerogative right of probate was specifically asserted.[171]

---

[166] "Inprimis igitur, volumus et ordinamus, quod officialis noster Cantuariensis ad querelas subditorum fratrum et suffraganeorum nostrorum de cetero non rescribat, præterquam in casibus specialibus, videlicet in casu negligentiæ, et in audiendis ratiociniis ab executoribus decedentium in provincia Cantuariensi habentium redditus, maneria, possessiones, et bona in diversis diœcesibus nostræ provinciæ memoratæ; nec non et in aliis casibus, qui tam de jure quam de consuetudine, nostris et prædecessorum nostrorum temporibus, eidem sunt permissi pariter et concessi" (*Registrum Epistolarum*, I, 335).

[167] *Ibid.*, p. 336. Cf. Douie, *op. cit.*, p. 212, n. 7.

[168] See *C.A.*, I, 382-383.

[169] "Memores enim sumus qualiter, cum de pace cum coepiscopis nostris tractatum habentes, in vestra præsentia turbationis remedia per viros industrios quæreremus supra debitum officii nostri, in quos fuit per vos et ceteros coepiscopos tunc præsentes consensum unanimiter ad tractandum, qui inter ceteros articulos istum dederunt nobis in scriptis, ut causæ testamentariæ defunctorum, quorum bona fuissent in diversis diœcesibus constituta, ad nostrum pertinerent indaginem pleno jure" (*Registrum Epistolarum*, II, 566).

[170] On the dispute of 1287-8 see Douie, *op. cit.*, pp. 223-225. It can be followed in *Registrum Swinfield*, pp. 33-34, 37, 41, 170 ff.

[171] See *ibid.*, pp. 33, 37, 182-183; cf. *C.A.*, I, 383.

Archbishop Pecham had tried to provide a consistent, efficient and inexpensive procedure for supervising the wills of testator's with property in several dioceses within his province.[172]   His correspondence and the ordinance of 25 April spoke of this testamentary jurisdiction as an immemorial right.   We know that when the activity of his official came under attack, Pecham had the archiepiscopal archives searched to provide precedents for the official's procedure.[173]   But the recommendations of the commission appointed to study the *gravamina* presented this testamentary supervision in a context of innovation.[174]   This commission composed of three ex-officials of Canterbury and a former official of the archdiocese of York was particularly well equipped to know the past and present extent of the archbishop's jurisdiction.[175]   The truth of its opinion is supported by the fact that non-contentious probate and the reception of accounts were themselves comparatively recent innovations.   Prerogative supervision of wills seems to have been one of several areas of metropolitan jurisdiction that were being developed in those years.   During the long dispute between Pecham and his suffragans one can see the enlargement and clarification of the conception of prerogative supervision of wills until it included the whole process of administration from the issue of probate to the acquittal of the executors. In this as in so many other beneficial reforms that he sought to bring about, Pecham's manner of proceeding was unfortunate, so that he found himself opposed by the bishop of Hereford and eventually by many of his suffragans.   For the moment he failed.   Cantilupe's successor at Hereford can be excused if it was with a complacent smile that he proved the will of the official of Canterbury and granted administration to executors who included the dean of Arches.[176]   But in the somewhat bitter discussion of his claims, Pecham came to a

---

172 Examples of wills that had to be proved in many places provide some measure of the expense and inconvenience of the system supported by Pecham's opponents: the will of Henry, Lord Grey of Codnor, dated September 9, 1308, was proved before the archdeacon of Chester (Sept. 16), was accepted as proved by Thomas, sequestrator of William, archbishop of York, at Nottingham (Sept. 19) and by the official of Rochester (Oct. 15), and was proved by the bishop of London (Oct. 15) and the bishop of Lincoln (Oct. 22): see *Hist. MSS. Comm. Report*, 64, Lord Middleton (1911), pp. 84-86.   The will of Lettice, wife of John de Lodbrok (1308), was proved before the sequestrator general of the bishop of Coventry and Lichfield (Feb. 7), the offical of the archdeacon of Leicester (Feb. 15) and the sequestrator general of the bishop of Worcester (Feb. 27): London PRO, E-40.4583.

173 *Registrum Epistolarum*, I, 172 (26 January, 1281) and above, n. 166.

174 *Registrum Epistolarum*, I, 337-338; cf. Douie, *op. cit.*, p. 210.

175 *Ibid.*

176 *Registrum Swinfield*, p. 395 (1303).

position which involved probate, supervision of execution and the
reception of accounts by the metropolitan authority. His was the
procedure that was eventually to be adopted.[177]

The procedure of probate was simple and direct. The executors
presented the written *will* to the ecclesiastical authority who by office
or by special commission was empowered to prove it.[178] The witnesses
and the document itself were examined to establish the *will's* authenticity.
If the testator had made a nuncupative will, its terms were announced
by those who were present.[179] Clarification might be sought as to the
meaning of certain phrases of the will.[180] If the statement of the
testator's intention was found to be satisfactory, and the conditions in
which the will was made corresponded with the formal requirements for
validity, the will was approved.[181] Usually the seal of the official was
added to the *will,* and often probate copies, sealed only with the seal of
the official, were made. A note, stating the name of the person granting
probate, the date and the terms of the grant, was added to the face of the
original or on the dorse. It was also included in the probate copy.

There are a few examples of wills from the time of Archbishop
Pecham which were formally proved before the death of the testator.
The written *will* was presented to the archbishop who proved it and
added his seal in confirmation of the fact.[182] In these special cases
administration was granted the executors immediately on the death of
the testator.

[177] On the later development of prerogative probate see *C.A.,* I, 383 ff. and the
introduction to Vol. II of *The Register of Henry Chichele,* ed. E. F. Jacob.

[178] Examples of the presentation of the will by the executors occur occasionally in the
thirteenth century (e.g., T. 89a). At London they were expected to present it before the
Hustings if it contained bequests of land. If they failed to do so, a legatee could obtain
the writ *ex gravi querela* to force them to act; cf. Sharpe, I, xliii.

[179] See below, Appendix B, pp. 313-315.

[180] Among the grievances brought forward by the clergy of the archdeaconry of Lincoln
in 1255 was the complaint that indistinct legacies were not devoted to pious causes as
intended by testators, but were seized by the king (*Annales Monastici,* ed. Luard, I, 361).
This income had been granted the king by the pope; an example of payment is to be seen
in the composition between royal collectors and the executors of Hervey Bede in 1256
(*C.P.R.,* IV, 514); also *ibid.,* V, 99.

[181] Several statutes make a distinction between the proof and approval of the will: e.g.,
at Lambeth in 1261—"Item, testamentis coram ordinariis locorum probatis, et approbatis..." (Wilkins, I, 754).

[182] E.g., the note of probate attached to the *will* of Anian II, bishop of St. Asaph
T. 89a) states that the executors presented the *will* already proved and sealed by
Archbishop Pecham. The ecclesiastical commissaries, "ipsam probationem approbantes,"
gave administration. Another example is described in a letter of 1283 in Pecham's
Registrum Epistolarum, II, 499.

A study has been made of the length of time usually required to obtain probate in the fifteenth century, and it shows that the matter was handled with commendable dispatch.[183]   There is not sufficient information of this sort from the period under discussion to obtain a certain conclusion.   In the rare cases where the date of probate of wills is known we are ignorant of the precise time of the testator's death. However, even if the interval between the making of the will and probate is considered, it is often found to be remarkably brief, so that it is possible to draw the tentative conclusion that the system of probate was quite efficient.[184]

The fees that were charged at this time are unknown; they were probably related to the value of the estate of the deceased.[185]   Already in the thirteenth century, the complaint against the excessive fee for probate was to be heard.[186]

The probate before the ordinary did not establish the validity of a will once for all.   Just at the moment when it can be certainly maintained that non-contentious probate had become part of the regular procedure of execution, the London Court of Hustings was to be found imposing its own examination and approval of wills as a preliminary to delivery of bequests of tenements.   In the following years a similar procedure was developed in many other boroughs.[187]

In Anglo-Saxon times it had been customary to deliver seisin of land before the local courts.[188]   Thus both the publicity of the act and its record, in the memories of those present, were assured.   The borough court continued to perform this function under the Anglo-Normans and, in time, enrolments of deeds of sale or donation began to be

---

183 See *The Register of Henry Chichele*, ed. E. F. Jacob, II, lx.

184   The dates of execution and of probate were as follows: T. 67a, April 20 and June 27 T. 67, Oct. 18 and Oct. 28; T. 86, May 8 and May 22, etc.

185 The provincial council of 1328 decreed that there should be no fee charged for th probate of wills dealing with assets of less than 100s (Wilkins, II, 553); cf. *The Register c Henry Chichele*, II, xxxiv.   In the account of the executors of Reginald Labbe (printed belov Appendix C, p. 322), a fee of 8d for probate and legal aid is indicated.   The estate of th deceased was valued at 33s 8d.

186 See the charges against the rectors of exempt parishes during the vacancy Canterbury after Archbishop Pecham's death mentioned in B. L. Woodcock, *Mediev Ecclesiastical Courts of the Diocese of Canterbury* (London, 1952), pp. 22-23.

187 Cf. *B.C.*, II, cxxxviii-ix, 194-200; Sharpe, I, xlii-xlvi.   For evidence of probate borough court other than those mentioned in *B.C.*, see E. W. W. Veale *The Great Red Bo of Bristol*, Bristol Record Society, II (1931), p. 67, n. 1, and *The Register of Henry Chiche* I, xiii, n. 5.   The earliest extant enrolment at Exeter was in 1271 (Roll I, m. 19).

188 Cf. *B.C.*, II, *cxxxviii*.

made there.   Given this background it is not surprising that these courts
sought to perform a similar function when land was transferred by will.
Nor were they content to record the delivery of a tenement by the
executors.   The Hustings showed remarkable care in its effort to find
the true intentions of those disposing of property.   Thus when a married
woman wished to sell or donate land she was examined apart from her
husband.   Similarly, when land was bequeathed, the Hustings demanded
that it be satisfied as to the testator's intention and, to obtain this,
developed is own procedure of probate.

The earliest enrolment of a will proved in borough court appeared
on the Hustings Roll of January 1259.[189]   This probate was said to be
secundum consuetudinem et usus Civitatis.   It has been suggested that a
statute in the *Liber Ordinacionum,* which ruled that there could be no
security in a devised tenement unless the will was enrolled, can be dated
as early as 1230 and indicates a procedure of probate at that date.[190]
On the other hand, there are objections to advancing enrolment and
probate of wills as normal procedure much before 1250.   Surviving rolls
begin in 1254, but the earliest will was recorded in January 1259.
Eighteen wills were enrolled that year and nine and seven were engrossed
the next two years respectively.   In the decade following 1261, no more
than three wills were enrolled.   Those years were a time of political
disturbance and records are incomplete.   Furthermore, as will be seen,
borough probate may have been partially withdrawn due to ecclesiastical pressure.   None the less, enrolments of the first twenty years after
1254 are such that it is difficult to see them as the fruit of a procedure
regularized as early as 1230.   The first certain reference to probate in
borough court is in the *Liber de Antiquis Legibus* of London.   The year
is 1256 and here, once more, probate is presented as an established
custom.[191]   But two years later an entry in the same volume records an
important decision of the justices: wills were to be proved even though

---

[189] Roll 2 (17).

[190] This statute (to be found on fol. 173) was dated *ca.* 1300 in *B.C.,* II, cxxxix; but
A. H. Thomas, in *Calendar of Mayor's Court Rolls 1298-1309* (Cambridge, 1924) I, 156, n. 1,
dated it 1230 and concluded that the "claim to probate or enrolment" of wills went back to
the early years of the century. The procedures of probate and enrolment should be
distinguished.

[191] Ed. T. Stapleton, Camden Society, XXXIV (1846), p. 24: "Hoc anno, die Lune ante
festum Sancti Andree, comparuit Willielmus de Munchanesey in Hustengo, et fecit legi
testamentum Pauline,... in quo ipsa perlegaverat omnia tenementa sua in Londoniis et
optulit ad probandum illud, sicut consuetudo Civitatis est de testamentis, aliquid tenemen-
tum, terram vel redditum tangentibus."

a claim was made against legacies contained within them.[192]   The
probate was without prejudice to future claim.   This decision involved
a precise statement of the purpose of probate—it was intended to approve
the will as a valid and clear statement of the donor's intention without
reference to the justice of his intention—and would have to be made
soon after a non-contentious probate had been established.[193]   Before
that time, some disputes touching bequests of tenements undoubtedly
hinged on the validity of the contents of a will.   In these cases the
borough court probably proceeded to establish the facts by some procedure that would be a form of probate.   Decisions of this sort may have
been given in the early years of the century or even before, just as in the
courts of the Church.   But it seems best to conclude that probate of
wills as a regular procedure in the Court of Hustings began about 1250.

The refusal by the boroughs to accept the ecclesiastical decision on
the validity of the will was resented and, in the Lambeth statutes of
1261, those laity who demanded a second probate were threatened with
excommunication.[194]   At the time of this dispute the *will* was written
on a single page.   All bequests, whether of *mobilia* or *immobilia,* were
described together, and all were included in the proof by the ecclesiastical official.   We know that the *will* was read at the Hustings and,
since bequests of tenements were not carefully separated from other
legacies, it is almost certain that in many cases the whole document was
published there.   It has already been shown that the procedure was
intended to provide proof of the will and nothing more; all decisions
touching the legitimacy of bequests remained for later consideration.
Thus, although the Hustings probate was said to be *quoad articulos laicum
feodum tangentes,* it was almost a duplication of the act already performed
in the ecclesiastical court.   Furthermore, although the earliest enrolments were a paraphrase of the clauses of the will that dealt with
burgages, they soon consisted of sections carefully copied from the *will*
itself and, occasionally, included legacies that had nothing to do with
the bequest of tenements.   In a few cases the whole will was transcribed.[195]   Under these circumstances the strenuous reaction of the

---

192 P. 41.

193 This point was made rather often; cf. *B.C.,* II, 197, n. 3.   Thus it might be maintained that the statement of 1258 was not the first.   However, the chronicler seems to
present the decision as one that was being made for the first time: "... provisum fuit in
Gildhalle inter Judicia, quando aliquis detulerit testamentum alicuius defuncti ad probandum ..."

194 Wilkins, I, 754.

195 The enrolment of the will of Nicholas Bat (Roll 2 [55], May, 1259) seems made up
of clauses transcribed directly from a written *will.*   Several enrolments contain legacies of

Lambeth Council is not surprising. The threat of excommunication may have had some effect, for only two wills were enrolled in the Hustings between the date of the council and 1269, a fact that can hardly be explained by the troubled state of the country alone.[196]   In 1268, Geoffrey of St. Dunstan, one of the guardians of the see of London during the suspension of Bishop Henry of Sandwich, sought to enforce this rule by ordering parish priests to excommunicate those of the laity who received probate.[197]   A restriction of the proof of wills by laymen may also have been intended by the legatine statute of the same year, which forbade the grant of administration to executors until they had renounced their privileged court.[198]   But the king came to the support of the citizens and the practice of the borough courts was allowed to continue.[199]   As a general rule, probate was first obtained from the ordinary and then from borough officials.   This practice was established at Oxford by 1288 and is to be found in other boroughs in the following years.[200]   Reference to the earlier ecclesiastical probate occurs occasionally in the Hustings enrolments.[201]   Several original *wills* bear notes of probate by the two jurisdictions.   Here too the prior decision by the ecclesiastical authority is evident, for, in all the examples that it has been possible to consult, the borough probate bears the later date.[202]

In London, the will was presented to the Hustings Court for probate by the executors.[203]   Two witnesses were examined as to the circum-

movables and include information about the sealing of the *will*, etc.; e.g., Roll 14 (44); Sharpe I, 63. The full text of the will of John de Meynaco was enrolled: Roll 24 (19); Sharpe, I, 116-117. Similarly, at Exeter, the enrolment of the will of Amery de Ponte contains bequests of movables: Roll 14 (18-19 Edward I) m. 14d.   Cf. C. Gross, "The Mediaeval Law of Intestacy," *Select Essays in Anglo-American Legal History*, III, 7.

196 Cf. Sharpe, I, 8-10.

197. *Liber de Antiquis Legibus*, ed. Stapleton, p. 106.

198 Wilkins, II, 8. The text may refer to the renunciation of privileged ecclesiastical jurisdiction. See the discussion of the different officials who gave probate in each diocese, above, pp. 198-199.

199 *Liber de Antiquis Legibus*, p.106.

200 Cf. *B.C.*, II, 195-196. Sharpe (I, xliii) questioned the truth of this statement for London.

201 The enrolment of the will of Henry de Coventre includes the note: "Istud testamentum probatum est sufficienter coram Offic' Arch' Lond', die sancti Vincencii, etc." (Roll 14 [44]; cf. Sharpe, I, 62-63).

202 E.g., T. 78a received ecclesiastical probate April 23 and Hustings probate, May 6; T. 82b received ecclesiastical probate July 17 and Hustings probate, Nov. 29; T. 71a was proved before the dean of Oxford on June 18 and before the mayor and bailiffs on Nov. 10, 1273.

203 If the executors refused to act, legatees could obtain the writ *ex gravi querela*; see n. 178, above.

stances when the will was made and about the written *will* itself.   It was then read.   Objection to its contents could be made then or later, but if the will were judged to be valid it was declared proved;[204] the relevant clauses were enrolled in the Hustings roll and the written *will* was endorsed with a note indicating the date and the place of probate. Other boroughs varied the process somewhat, but the basic procedure of probate was usually similar to that of London.[205]   At Ipswich a will bequeathing tenements was to be proved within forty days of the death of the testator.   The more common time limit was a year and a day, but there are examples to show that probate in borough court was sometimes delayed for years.[206]   There are a few cases where the testator presented his will to the Hustings for probate before his death.[207]

Copies of wills and extracts from them are to be found on the rolls of manorial courts; eighteenth-century treatises, dealing with procedure in these courts, speak of manorial probate as a power commonly exercised.[208]   It was suggested by Pollock and Maitland that this jurisdiction is to be traced to the rights of probate held by monastic and other ecclesiastical bodies in virtue of their peculiar jurisdiction.[209] This suggestion has usually been accepted, and in many cases it can be shown that jurisdiction of this sort was ecclesiastical rather than manorial in origin.[210]   However, in an unfinished essay, published only after her death, Elizabeth Levett pointed out that there is strong evidence that in

204 See the description of probate in a letter of the Mayor and Aldermen of London to their counterparts at Oxford, dated July 1325: "In London a will is proved by two witnesses sworn and examined, and if, after proclamation made, anyone challenge the will, then the will and the challenge are enrolled, and execution is granted;" in *Calendar of Plea and Memoranda Rolls of the City of London*, ed. A. H. Thomas, Vol. I (Cambridge, 1926), p. 9.

205 Veale, *op. cit.*, p. 67, n. 1; *B.C.*, II, 196-200.

206 *B.C.*, II, 197, n. 1; cf. the reference to practice at Norwich in *The Register of Henry Chichele*, II, xiii, n. 5.   Cases reported in the Plea and Memoranda Rolls of London in the fourteenth century, sometimes show long delays; e.g., vol. I, 82.

207 See the memorandum prefixed to the enrolment of the will of William Kelwedon in Sharpe, I, 74.

208 E.g., T. Gurdon, *History of the High Court of Parliament and the History of the Court Baron and the Court Leet* (London, 1731), pt. ii, p. 608.

209 P. and M., II, 341-342.   This position was adopted by N. J. Hone, *The Manor and Manorial Records* (London, 1906), p. 22.   More recently, in *Some Documents of Barnoldswick Manor Court of Probate*, Yorks. Arch. Soc. Rec. Ser., CXVIII (1951), p. 53, G. E. Kirk says that this was "usually" the case.

210 Thus in "Norwich Cathedral Priory in the Fourteenth Century" *Bulletin of the John Rylands Library*, XX (1930), pp. 98-99, C. R. Cheney shows that the probate by the "dean of the manors" was an exercise of the prior's peculiar jurisdiction.

some cases at least manorial courts exercised a probate of wills.[211]   Miss
Levett's essay included the texts of wills inscribed on the St. Albans
court rolls.   She was able to show that while the wills of freemen which
were included had been proved before the archdeacon, who exercised
the abbey's peculiar juridiction, the wills of villeins were proved
"before the cellarer in the halimote." [212]

The examples cited were from the middle of the fourteenth century.
It will be shown below[213] that villeins of some manors were allowed to
make wills in the presence of manorial officials more than a century
earlier.   It would seem that in these cases there would have to be proof
that the will had been made in the special conditions for validity
required by local custom.   No doubt that proof was most easily obtained
in manorial court.   In time, the procedure of probate probably assumed
some of the characteristics of the parallel process in ecclesiastical or
borough courts, including enrolment of the will itself.   Some historians
have suggested that the proof of wills by manorial officials goes back
to Anglo-Saxon times.[214]   It is probably true that in that age and in the
period following the Conquest, the lowest members of society made
their wills, when they made them at all, with permission and under
conditions imposed by the lord of the manor.   No doubt there was
some supervision to see that those conditions were observed.   If the
word probate is used to apply to this supervision, it would refer to a
practice that was indeed very old.   But if taken in the proper sense of a
procedure to establish whether a deceased person had made a will,
whether due formality had been observed, and the contents of the will,
then probate can hardly be said to have existed until the early years
of the thirteenth century, when the making of wills by villeins had
become accepted custom on some manors.[215]

The Inventory

The procedure of probate established whether a will had been made
and whether it was valid.   It also published the contents of the will.
If the deceased had made no effort to bequeath his property, or if, for
one reason or another, the will was invalid, the deceased was declared

[211] *Studies in Manorial History,* ed. Helen M. Cam, M. Coate and L. S. Sutherland (Oxford 1938), pp. 208-234.

[212] *Ibid.,* pp. 208-209, and p. 209, n. 1.

[213] Pp. 253-254.

[214] Selden (*Works,* III, 1667) suggested this; also Stubbs, *Constitutional History,* III, 356, and Makower, *op. cit.,* p. 425, n. 109.

[215] Cf. Miss Levett, *op. cit.,* p. 209, where it is suggested that this control of the will by the manor court existed in the early years of the thirteenth century.

intestate and the proper procedure for the distribution of his goods was begun.[216] But if the will was approved, the executors began to implement it.

At the time of probate, an initial decision by and about the executors was made. Those named to the office did not have to accept. Sometimes the unwilling nominee suggested another to act in his place; in other cases he simply withdrew.[217] If the ordinary found an executor to be unsuitable, he refused to allow him to act.[218] It was not always necessary to replace these executors because testators, anticipating incapacity or unwillingness in those named to the office, often appointed more than were needed to administer the will. If the executor accepted the office, he was expected to carry it through to completion. As will be seen below, he could be removed for failing in his task. Anyone who acted as executor, though not named to the office, was liable for the debts of the deceased.[219]

By 1261 it becomes evident that the executors' first duty was to prepare a list of the goods of the testator. In that year the taking of an inventory was generally imposed throughout the southern province by the Lambeth Council. This investigation of the assets of the deceased and the preparation of a written account was already a very old practice. Provision for it in certain cases is to be found among the laws of Justinian.[220] What is more important for our purposes here is the fact that from the fourth century canons of councils had provided for the listing of the goods of deceased clerics, especially bishops.[221] The repetition of these canons and the occasional mention of the taking of an

216 On the development of ecclesiastical supervision of the intestate's property and on the procedures used, see Holdsworth, *History*, III, ch. 5.

217 An example of the substitution of a new executor at the suggestion of the executor withdrawing from the office is provided by the register of Bishop Godfrey Giffard of Worcester in 1281: "Memorand' quod ... Domina Alda Relicta Domini Willielmi Corbet et Executrix testamenti defuncti ipsius substituit loco sui Eadmund' de Neubury clericum per litteras suas ..." (fol. 114). A decade earlier, Archbishop Walter Giffard of York wrote the executors of Walter de Cantilupe and informed them that he did not intend to assist them in their task: "Nec in hoc negotio procuratorem ordinare volumus ut tanquam executor aliqualiter habeamus" (*The Register of Walter Giffard*, ed. W. Brown, p. 178).

218 Replacement of executors by the ordinary could lead to difficulty in borough court. According to some local custom, probate was to be given in the presence of the executors named in the will; cf. the Oxford example of 1288 cited in *B.C.*, II, 196, n. 1.

219 Cf. *Y.B.*, 20-21 Edward I, ed. ed. A.V. Horwood, pp. 374-376. On the "executor de son tort" see Holdsworth, *History*, III, 571-572.

220 *Codex*, 5, 37, 24, and *Digest* 26, 7, 5-7; 27, 3, 1; 42, 5, 15. Cf. Berger, *Dictionary*, p. 373, s.v. *Beneficium inventarii*.

221 Hannan, *The Canon Law of Wills*, pp. 172-173.

inventory show that the practice was never entirely lost during the early Middle Ages. In a rather idealized picture of the Anglo-Saxon church, Ordericus Vitalis presented the taking of an inventory as part of the ordinary procedure following the death of abbots and members of the clergy. He also presented a similar practice as one of the facets of the good government that obtained under the Conqueror.[222] Provision for an inventory of bishops' property appeared in the *Decretum* and was glossed by the Decretists.[223]

Early examples of this practice are rare in England. However in the account of Abbot Samson's administration of the estate of Hamo Blunt, the listing of the goods of the deceased was mentioned without comment.[224] Magna Carta had imposed the taking of an inventory as the first step in the administration of the estate of royal tenants.[225] It seems reasonable to conclude that it was frequently done during the first half of the thirteenth century, especially in those cases where the validity of a will or the manner of its execution was called into question. The first official mention of the inventory is in the statutes of William of Bitton, bishop of Bath and Wells (1252-8).[226] There it is stated that immediately after the testator's death the executors are to arrange that a written account of all movable property be made before witnesses. The inventory was to be prepared within fifteen days if possible. The same canon appeared in the statutes of Archbishop Ludham of York in 1259.[227] The Lambeth Council of 1261 imposed the inventory through-

---

[222] *Historia Ecclesiastica*, Bk. VIII, ch. 8, and Bk. IV, ch. 9 (ed. Le Prevost III, 313; II, 200).

[223] C. 12, q. 2, c. 45. In the *Summa Parisiensis* the inventory is defined as "charta continens summam eorum quæ inveniuntur in possessione defuncti" (ed. McLaughlin, p. 161); Rufinus likened it to the inventory of Roman civil law; *gl. ad* Caritatem (ed. Singer, p. 328). There is a treatment of the inventory in the *Summa casuum* of Raymond de Pennaforte (ed. 1503, pp. 196-197) and in Durantis' *Speculum iuris*, Bk. II, pt. ii, De Instrumentorum editione (ed. 1576, pp. 729-730).

[224] *Chronica Jocelini de Brakelonda*, ed. Butler, pp. 91-92. When Ralph, abbot of Battle Abbey, died (1124), two men were sent by Roger of Salisbury to make an inventory of the abbey and its appurtenances: *The Chronicle of Battle Abbey*, trans. M. A. Lower (London, 1851), p. 66.

[225] C. 26, Stubbs, *Select Charters*, p. 296.

[226] "*Quod fiat inventarium in testamentis et executores debitam habeant sustentacionem de bonis defuncti. Ut testamenta circum quaque procedant rite precipimus quod exsecutores testamenti statim post mortem defuncti bona ipsius mobilia ubicumque fuerint reperta fideliter sub fide dignorum testimonio conscribi procurent...*" fol. 112r; see above, p. 185, n. 82.

[227] Fol. 251r; see above, n. 82. A canon of similar import but with different wording is included in the statutes of John Gervais, bishop of Winchester (1262-5), edited by Wilkins, II, 298.

out the southern province, and from that date reference to it occurs in most synodal statutes.[228]

The Lambeth Council ruled that administration of the testator's goods was not to be given the executors until the inventory had been presented to the ordinary. A legatine statute of 1268 repeated the rule, adding punishment of executors who disobeyed.[229] In some areas at least, this requirement was an innovation.[230] It must soon have become evident that certain arrangements for the custody of an estate had to be made immediately, and that even the preparation of an inventory involved a certain degree of administration.[231] In the following century, allowance was made for this in statutes like that of Archbishop Stratford, which permitted executors to arrange and pay for the funeral and perform other acts that could not be delayed.[232] The Exeter statutes of 1287 described all stages of execution with unusual detail, but did not specifically demand the completion of an inventory before the award of administration.[233] The completion of the inventory within fifteen days was suggested, but the statutes imply the possibility of its delay until after the probate and the award of administration. This procedure was often adopted in practice, as an examination of probate *acta* makes abundantly clear. Executors, having sworn to take an inventory and give an account of their activity when demanded by the ordinary, were granted administration of the goods of the deceased.[234]

---

228 Wilkins, I, 754. The Exeter statutes of 1287 (*ibid.*, II, 156) required that the debts and obligations of the deceased be included. Several of the extant *wills* have an inventory attached; e.g., T. 26, T. 78b, T. 83. They usually include a summary of debts and obligations.

229 Wilkins, II, 8.

230 This is clear from a letter in the register of Bishop Bronescombe of Exeter (1264): in a particular case, he ordered his official to grant administration only after inventory had been taken, then added that henceforth this should be the general practice. He also referred to the council, presumably that of 1261: "Hanc autem formam in testamentis aliorum auctoritate Concilii volumus et mandamus observari:" *Episcopal Registers of the Diocese of Exeter*, ed. F. C. Hingston-Randolph, Vol. I, *The Registers of Walter Bronescombe and Peter Quivil* (London, 1889), p. 283.

231 In 1280, Archbishop Pecham allowed executors to deal with the perishable goods of the late bishop of Winchester, pending a final grant of administration (*Registrum epistolarum*, I, 118-119).

232 Wilkins II, 705. John of Acton allowed administration for these matters (p. 107, *gl. ad verb.* inventarium), as did Lyndwood (*Provinciale*, p. 176, *gl. ad verb.* prius).

233 Wilkins, II, 156.

234 E.g., the note of probate attached to T. 71a: "... & iurat[is] de fideli inuentario faciendo & computo reddendo commissa fuit administracio executoribus nominatis in testamento ..."

The Administration of the Will

Having received the grant of administration, the executor proceeded to implement the will.[235] In carrying out his duties, he acted as a continuation of the person of the deceased, completing the business arrangements described by the will and exercising throughout a remarkable power of decision.

It was the executor who made the English will the flexible and effective instrument it was.[236] The testator's desire, as revealed in surviving documents, and the obvious intention of the ecclesiastical courts, was to make the executor's powers as much as possible like those of the person for whom he acted. In the last stages of the dispute touching representation, royal advisers even suggested that there was an effort to exceed these powers. As the thirteenth century advanced, the executor tended more and more to become a projection after death of the legal personality of the deceased. First of all, it can be concluded from Magna Carta and from documents dealing with individual cases that he received all the movable property, not merely that which was included among the bequests of the will.[237] In the administration of this property he was given remarkable discretion. Sometimes all decisions as to beneficiaries were left to him;[238] at others, the testator was content to sketch his intention in the broadest terms, leaving details to his determination.[239] The executor might even be ordered to

[235] See below, Appendix C, p. 316.

[236] Holdsworth, *History*, III, 574-585.

[237] It will be noted that, though c. 26 of Magna Carta (quoted above, p. 154) distinguished the part of the chattels freely disposable by will from the parts reserved to the wife and children, it states without reservation that once royal debts were paid the chattels were to be given to the executor. Bracton's description is similar: "et residuum catallorum executoribus relinquatur" (fol. 60b). Residual clauses found in *wills* from the beginning of the thirteenth century, imply that such was the practice. References to the control of property in other documents support this conclusion; e.g., in 1228 the king informed the executors of Robert de Ros that William, son of the deceased, had arranged to pay his father's debts, and instructed them to give him the part of his father's goods that pertained to him (*C. Cl. R.*, I, 124).

[238] In 1234 Robert son of Walter was given permission to make a will or assign others to make it (*C.P.R.*, III, 43). Innocent III defended this type of will in a letter that was included in the *Decretals* (III, 26, 13). The *Glossa Ordinaria* to this canon held that it was not a true testament, because it did not institute an heir. Actually the papal decree carefully avoided the word *testamentum*, using, *extrema voluntas* instead. Archidiaconus maintained that to give such powers to another was to make him heir: *Lectura super decreto ad* C. 12, q. 2, c. 46 (Lyons, 1516, fol. 198ra).

[239] E.g., the *will* of King John (T. 16); also T. 59a. Certain bequests, to minor servants, etc., were often left to the discretion of the executors.

rearrange the terms of the will if it were considered necessary to do so.[240]   Occasional remarks indicate that the executor of a royal servant was sometimes called upon to complete some of the duties of the deceased.   He is to be found holding a castle after the death of the castellan, collecting royal moneys, rendering an account at the Exchequer, performing various tasks pertaining to the office of sheriff.[241] In many wills the residue of the chattels was left to be distributed for the soul of the deceased as the executor saw fit.[242]   By means of this instrument the testator was able to implement the refined if sometimes delayed decisions of a tender conscience, and thus to rectify injustice or damage in a manner of which the civil law of that day, or any day, was quite incapable.

The executor's first duty was to see to the funeral and burial of the deceased and to arrange for masses and prayers for his soul.   Then he was expected to acquit the testator's debts and to assign portions to his wife and children if they survived.[243]   Here various arrangements were used.   Sometimes the obligations of the deceased were estimated and portions of the property that remained after the amount of the debt had been deducted were immediately assigned to the surviving members of the family, with the proviso that they would be expected to contribute if the testator's debts proved more than had been anticipated.   Another arrangement was to assign sufficient goods for the maintenance of the wife and children pending final arrangements for the distribution of the

---

240 "Si quid autem ex causa racionabili in testamento hoc fuerit emendandum discretioni executorum & prouisioni committit" (T. 31).   Sometimes the disposition of goods was left to the executors where the testator's intention was not clear; e.g., "Item lego omnia mobilia & immobilia indistincte legata, quod uendantur & distribuantur secundum disposicionem exsecutorum meorum" (T. 82a).

241 In 1266, the executors of John de Gray were instructed to deliver the castle of Nottingham with its armour to Reynold de Gray (*C.P.R.*, V, 570); for other examples, see *ibid.*, V, 141; VI, 509; and (Edward I), II, 424.   The executors of Reynold de Cobham and his under-sheriff rendered account at the exchequer in 1257 (*C.P.R.*, IV, 609); similarly in *C.P.R.* (Edward I), I, 317.   Executors were often instructed to deliver plea rolls, which were included among the effects of deceased justices: e.g., *C.P.R.* (Edward I), II, 84, 85, 131, 179, 220.

242 E.g., "quicquid fuerit in residuo sit in disposicione eorum ad distribuendum pro anima sua, augendo siue diminuendo prout prouiderint anime congruere" (T. 75a); other exs. T. 12, T. 47a, T. 53a, T. 71b, T. 99a, etc.   Late in the fourteenth century the residue began to be left to the executor as a legacy.   For the details of this process, see Caillemer, "The Executor in England and on the Continent," *Select Essays in Anglo-American Law*, III. 764-769.   It is not correct to say that thirteenth-century wills rarely disposed of the residue (*ibid.*, p. 764).

243 See the Exeter statutes of 1287, Wilkins, II, 156.

estate. The executor then began to collect the debts owed the testator and to deliver legacies of money and goods.[244] During the time of administration, the executor occasionally loaned the money or goods of the deceased.[245] In all of these transactions he issued and received receipts, which protected him against later claims and were presented when accounts were rendered to the ordinary.

In the delivery of tenements bequeathed in wills, or in the sale of land to raise money for bequests, the executor exercised similar powers.[246] He gave livery of seisin in some boroughs, issued charters as evidence of transactions, and made arrangements with potential claimants to ensure the success of the donation he sought to complete. Occasionally he confirmed the sale of property by the widow or heir of the testator. The executor purchased land and conveyed it to religious institutions to establish mass-endowments and chantries.[247] At the end of the period under discussion, he is to be found obtaining licence for the alienation of land in mortmain.[248] He might even establish the monastery that his testator had hoped to found.[249]

In the course of administration executors made various agreements among themselves:[250] one might be appointed to act for the group in certain matters; another might assume special responsibilities for a certain portion of the estate of the deceased; a third might agree with his associates to withdraw from further activities, but to appear with them when accounts were rendered. Executors named procurators to

---

[244] Documents touching the delivery of chattels, etc., are printed below, Appendix C, pp. 316-319.

[245] In 1232 or earlier, Robert de Aumary, executor of Sir John de St. John, borrowed twelve and a half marks from the goods of the deceased. His bond, given to the other executors, is calendared by W. H. Turner and H. O. Coxe, *Calendar of Charters and Rolls preserved in the Bodleian Library* (Oxford, 1878), p. 319, no. 291. The executors of Archbishop Boniface loaned 3000 marks to Edmund, earl of Lancaster in 1271 (*C.P.R.*, VI, 568). See Archbishop Pecham's receipt, printed below, p. 319.

[246] Typical documents touching the bequest and sale of land are printed below, Appendix C, pp. 319 ff.

[247] An early example (1218-22) is printed in *Early Charters of St. Paul's*, ed. Marion Gibbs, pp. 87-90, nos. 116, 118, 119.

[248] E.g., *C.P.R.* (Edward I), II, 392 (1290).

[249] On the Cistercian abbeys founded by the executors of Peter des Roches, see *Annales Monasterii de Waverleia*, ed. Luard in *Annales Monastici*, II, 323.

[250] In the register of Bishop Sutton of Lincoln is a letter in which William of Benneworth complained to the bishop that he and John Haket, monk of Louth Park, had been named executors, but that he had given most of the administration to John, who died before fulfilling his office: *The Rolls and Register of Bishop Oliver Sutton*, ed. Rosalind Hill, Vol. IV, 113-114; see below, Appendix C, p. 321.

act in their name, who issued and received receipts in the exercise of their office. If an executor died before his administration of a will was complete, his own executors continued to act in his place.[251]

When the executors had completed their work, they were expected to render an account of their activity to the ordinary. This obligation was mentioned in the Burton Annals as one of the items of the inquiry in 1253.[252] It also appears in the Lambeth statutes of 1261; in this case accounts were to be rendered only when demanded.[253] Later statutes presented the account as the regular final stage in the execution of wills.[254] According to the Exeter statutes of 1287, it was to be rendered within a year; otherwise the executors were considered to be negligent and were replaced.[255] But the administration of large and involved holdings can often be shown to have required longer than a year. The delay was countenanced by the ecclesiastical authority.[256] Assets that remained after the delivery of legacies and the acquittal of all the obligations of the testator were stated in the account. They were normally distributed by the executors according to the directions of the residue clause in the will or, failing that, after consultation with the bishop. In the meantime these goods remained in the custody of the executors.[257]

Once the account had been accepted, the executors were acquitted. Sometimes the ordinary commissioned an official to discharge them; on other occasions the prelate chose to do so himself.[258] The ordinary or

251 The testator of T. 78b asks his executor to complete work of administration that remained. The executor's right is transmissible to his executor at Ipswich in 1291; cf. B.C., II, 196-197 and p. 197, n. 2.

252 Annales Monastici, ed. Luard, I, 310.

253 Wilkins, I, 754.

254 Lyndwood questioned whether executors were bound to render an account if the testator had excused them from doing so; see Provinciale, p. 168, gl. ad verb. rationem, and p. 183, gl. ad verb. fideliter.

255 Wilkins, II, 156.

256 Thus in the register of Archbishop Pecham there are many examples of administrations that extended for several years after the death of the testator.

257 The executors of Ralph II, bishop of Chichester (d. 1244), considering that he had benefited from his church for twenty years, presented the residue of his estate, 140 pounds, to the fabric of the cathedral: The Chartulary of the High Church of Chichester, ed. W. D. Peckham, Sussex Rec. Soc., XLVI (1942-3), p. 9. When the accounts of the executors of Sir Thomas Hook were rendered (Nov. 1286), a residue of more than 178 marks remained. The sum was left in the hands of the executors who were to devote it to pious uses, having consulted the bishop: Register of John le Romeyn, Archbishop of York, ed. W. Brown, 2 vols., Surtees Society, CXXIII, CXXVIII (1913-7) I, 19-20, 77-78.

258 The Memoranda Rolls of Bishop Oliver Sutton contain many commissions of discharge and several letters of absolution.

his commissary issued letters of acquittal. Armed with them, the executors were ordinarily free of further claim.[259]

The executor was developed so that, within the framework of English law, a testator was free to choose a person of trust to act for him after his death. During the thirteenth century, the executor assumed remarkable power: his representation of the testator became so complete that he was able to accomplish most of the legal acts that were possible to that individual during his lifetime. Such a position of trust was necessarily open to abuse: the dishonest executor appeared almost immediately.[260] In the second half of the thirteenth century, didactic literature began to find one of its commonplaces in him. General warnings and a delightful tale of his crimes appeared in *Le Manuel des pechiez*, in the third quarter of the century.[261] These passages were translated and expanded a generation later in Robert of Brunne's *Handlyng Synne* and remained a favourite subject of the moralist during the rest of the Middle Ages.[262]

It would be a mistake to conclude from this literature that the institution was a failure. There were abuses and it was the moralist's task to condemn them, but they did not characterize the activity of the executor during the thirteenth century. Lyndwood's wise remark that the executor was a person who had been chosen and approved by the testator should not be forgotten.[263] Nevertheless, the "sticky-fingered executor" was a danger, and we find that, as his powers became explicit, a body of law to control his activity was established in diocesan synods and provincial councils.

---

[259] In *Y.B.*, 31 Edward I (ed. Horwood, pp. 238-240) executors show the bishop's letter of acquittal to prove that they have no further assets of the deceased. The letter of acquittal, printed below, Appendix C, p. 323, left the executor liable to further claim by the legatees or the creditors of the testator.

[260] In one of the earliest appearances of executors in the Plea Rolls (1219), they are found using the seal of the deceased to forge charters disposing of his estates (*C.R.R.*, VIII, 280-281).

[261] Ed. F. J. Furnivall, lines 5254-5263, 5264-5311, 1688-1834, pp. 195-203; cf. E. J. Arnould, *Le Manuel des péchés: étude de la littérature religieuse anglo-normande* (Paris, 1940), p. 122.

[262] *Handlyng Synne*, lines 6227-6515; ed. Furnival, pp. 195-203. Similar opinions are expressed in Br. Mus. MS. Royal 7.D.1, fol. 123: "tales executores, qui pocius traditores dici possunt" (dated 1270-79; cf. Arnould, *op. cit.*, p. 290, n. 4); *Les Contes moralisés de Nicole Bozon* (1320-5), ed. Lucy T. Smith and P. Meyer, Soc. des anciens texts français (Paris, 1889), pp. 103, 156, 181; *Instruction for Parish Priests* (1400-50) ed. E. Peacock, Early English Text Society, Vol. 31, p. 83 and notes. On the executor in sermons of the later middle ages, see G. R. Owst, *Preaching in Mediaeval England* (Cambridge, 1926), p. 343 and n. 2.

[263] *Provinciale*, p. 170, gl. ad verb. commissionem.

It was universally agreed that the executor was free to receive legacies from the estate of the deceased.[264] Beginning with the Worcester statutes of Walter de Cantilupe (1240), provisions were made for the executor to be indemnified from the goods of the testator for expenses incurred in performing his office. Payment was to be made under the supervision of the bishop or his commissary.[265] Fearing that executors or their friends would benefit from fraudulent purchase of the testator's goods at a low price, several statutes, including those of Worcester (1240) and Lambeth (1261), forbade any purchase from the estate by the executor, either directly or through a third party.[266] A Norwich statute of the same period ordered punishment of those involved in fraudulent purchase either as seller or purchaser.[267] But it can be shown that executors did purchase goods from the estates they administered, and a group of statutes, beginning with those of Bishop Bitton of Bath and Wells (1252-8), permitted this purchase, provided that the price was just and the transaction was performed in the presence of trustworthy witnesses.[268] The executor was expected to proceed to administration with reasonable dispatch. If he failed to do so, he was removed. According to the Exeter statutes of 1287, he was summoned, rendered an account of his administration to date, and was dismissed.[269]

Enforcement of the Will by the Courts

From the previous discussion some idea may be had of the sequence of legal acts by which a will was implemented. It is evident that, at least in the case of the wealthy testator, these proceedings could be very complicated indeed. They have been sketched in a felicitous state

---

[264] A rare example of the opposite opinion is to be found in a plea of 1210, where a defendant based his claim that he was not an executor on the fact that he had received a legacy from the testator (*C.R.R.*, VI, 79).

[265] Wilkins I, 674. This rule reappeared in the statutes derived from these of Cantilupe, namely those of Bishop Bitton of Bath and Wells (fol. 112r), Archbishop Ludham of York (fol. 251r) and Bishop Gervais of Winchester (Wilkins, II, 298). It remained the rule throughout the Middle Ages; cf. *Provinciale*, p. 178.

[266] Wilkins, I, 674, 754. This rule was imposed by borough authority at Torksey, *ca.* 1345; cf. *B.C.*, II, 197-198.

[267] Wilkins, I, 735.

[268] References to the statutes of Bath and Wells, York, and Winchester are as indicated in n. 255 above. Other examples are the statutes of Exeter (1287), John of Acton (pp. 109-110) and Lyndwood in *Provinciale* p. 178, *gl. ad verb.* tituli exemptionis. Several examples of purchase of movable property by executors are mentioned in *Select Cases in the Exchequer of Pleas*, ed. Jenkinson and Formoy, p. 12.

[269] Wilkins, II, 156.

where all those concerned with the will—executors and heir, legatees and debtors—were in agreement on what was to be done and proceeded to do it. In practice, of course, the will could be attacked at every stage of its execution. It was the duty of the courts to defend and enforce it. During the thirteenth century they developed procedures which, with varying degrees of success, were used to establish the facts in each dispute, judge where justice lay, and enforce compliance by the parties concerned.

In the first part of this chapter we saw the important developments that took place towards the end of King John's reign: an extrinsic control of the will passed to the courts of the Church. The right and duty to enforce the delivery of legacies had many ramifications; some were perhaps unforeseen in those years when ecclesiastical jurisdiction was first extended into this area. But it soon became evident that the obligation to acquit the debts owed by the testator was prior to the delivery of his legacies. Furthermore, if the testator's desires were to be fulfilled, it was necessary to recover all his movable assets, no matter where they might be. Thus a procedure was needed to prove by judicial enquiry both the debts and obligations of the deceased, and to enforce their payment.

About the middle of the thirteenth century it seemed possible that all these matters might eventually be included in that class of pleas which Bracton called *spiritualibus annexa*.[270] It is clear from Bracton's treatise and from other writings of the time that jurisdiction over some pleas, which were indirectly necessary as a prerequisite to the delivery of legacies, had passed to the courts of the Church and that this jurisdiction might be extended to others as well. It is not known whether those directing the policy of ecclesiastical courts in Bracton's time gave thought to the limits of the jurisdiction they sought. Perhaps they already saw, as did the cleric who drew up a group of petitions forty years later, that it was desirable, if only for reasons of efficiency and expense, that all pleas arising from the execution of wills be received by the court entrusted with their supervision.[271] At any rate, early in the

---

[270] *De Legibus*, fol. 407b.

[271] "Preterea cum una et indivisa esse debeat finalis expedicio testamenti per finalem compotum executorum, oportet quod omnia testamenta vel ejus finalem expedicionem tangentia sub uno judice in recognocendo tractentur, et sicut ad ecclesiasticum judicem spectat principium, videlicet recepc[i]o, probacionis testamenti et tradicio administrationis, et finis videlicet recepcio compoti et finalis de administracione liberacio, ita et medium ad eum spectare debet similiter exactio debitorum." The list of petitions is published in *Registrum Johannis de Pontissara, episcopi Wyntoniensis*, ed. C. Deedes, 2 vols., Canterbury and York Soc.,

reign of Edward I, the expansion of the testamentary jurisdiction of the Church courts was arrested and, after a period of hesitation, certain pleas were withdrawn from this jurisdiction to that of the king.

It is the purpose of this study of the will in the courts to show how the bequests of the deceased were enforced at each stage of execution. Most steps were supervised by the courts of the Church.[272] Others belonged to the civil courts. Some, for a time at least, fell under both jurisdictions. The courts' basic function was to see that the debts owed by the deceased and the legacies indicated in his will were delivered to those who had a right to them. This involved the power to coerce executors and any persons or corporations who hindered them in their administration. Episcopal statutes returned again and again to those executors, debtors, and false creditors who, by their delay and unjust claims, made the execution of wills impossible.[273] The penalty for these crimes was excommunication. Excommunicates who remained contumacious for forty days were denounced to the king. A writ *de excommunicato capiendo* was obtained and the criminal was imprisoned.[274] Civil courts enforced their decisions by the usual sanctions of fine and imprisonment.

The first duty of those charged with the enforcement of legacies was to prevent the suppression of the will by interested parties. In the fourteenth century, the apparitor summoned executors to present the will for probate.[275] It is likely that an arrangement of this sort was made soon after the non-contentious probate of wills had become general. When a will was suppressed, the legatee who knew of it could demand its production. An example of this procedure is to be seen in a suit

XIX, XXX (1915-30), II, 773, *sub anno* 1295; cf. H. G. Richardson and G. Sayles "The Clergy in the Easter Parliament of 1285," *EHR*, LII (1937), p. 228.

272 No attempt will be made here to discuss the different ecclesiastical jurisdictions involved, their procedure and the process of appeal.

273 The statutes of St. Richard de Wych, bishop of Chichester (1244-53), excommunicated those "qui rationabilia defunctorum testamenta malitiose impediant" (Wilkins, I, 693). A similar clause appeared in the *Statuta Legenda*, attributed to Stephan Langton in Wilkins I, 593; cf. Cheney, *Synodalia*, p. 53. Beginning with the statutes of Bishop Bitton of Bath and Wells (fol. 112r) and their derivatives at York (fol. 250r) and Winchester (Wilkins II, 228), this prohibition was expanded to include the negligent executor, the fictitious creditor and the debtor who refused to acquit his obligations; on these statutes see n. 8 above.

274 R. C. Fowler, "Secular Aid for Excommunicates," *Trans. Royal Historical Soc.*, 3rd Series, VIII (1914), pp. 113-117. Many examples of excommunications resulting from the execution of wills are to be found in episcopal registers.

275 *C.A.*, II, 181-182 and *The Register of Henry Chichele*, ed. E. F. Jacob, II, xxix.

before the official of the bishop of Norwich about the middle of the thirteenth century.[276] Eva Peche died and was buried at Barnwell Priory, near Cambridge, in the presence of her sons. After the funeral they left without mentioning her will. But the prior, who had been informed by others, knew that a legacy had been left his house. After two years he forced the executors to produce the will and come to an agreement about the payment of the legacy. A similar procedure existed in borough court. By the writ *ex gravi querela* legatees could demand the production and probate of a will as the first stage in the recovery of a bequest.[277]

Once the executor had received administration of an estate he proceeded to acquit the obligations of the testator and to recover his debts. Both these acts were preliminary to the delivery of legacies. Their supervision was the area of jurisdiction that was disputed between the courts of the Church and the king. In an earlier chapter dealing with the rise of the executor, it was shown that common law was very slow to admit representation of the deceased. In as much as it did so, it preferred the heir, thus creating the awkward situation in which executor and heir were dependent on each other for the completion of their administration. It was probably to remedy this situation that the ecclesiastical courts sought to extend the executor's power to represent the deceased. The courts of the king finally admitted the executor's capacity early in the reign of Edward I. Long before that, however, the Exchequer had begun to deal with the executor and, in the process, had developed procedures for dealing with certain testamentary cases that touched the king's revenue.

It was generally accepted that obligations to the king should be acquitted before all others. This principle applied to the property of the deceased: royal debts were to be paid before distribution began. If by some oversight executors had already begun to distribute property, their activity was suspended by a temporary prohibition until the claims of the king were satisfied.[278] Thus there are hundreds of letters in the rolls of the Chancery and the Exchequer instructing officials to perform one of a number of commissions that affected the administration of the property of testators. These proceedings were often long, and officials

---

[276] *Liber Memorandorum Ecclesie de Bernewelle*, ed. J. W. Clark (Cambridge, 1907), p. 176.

[277] See above, p. 205, and n. 178. For an early example see *Calendar of Early Mayor's Court Rolls*, ed. Thomas, Vol. I, 82 (1300), and *Calendar of Plea and Memoranda Rolls*, ed. Thomas, Vol. I, 157 (1343).

[278] See G. B. Flahiff, "The Writ of Prohibition to Court Christian in the Thirteenth Century," *Mediaeval Studies*, VI (1944), p. 270 and n. 45.

tended to be unnecessarily severe in their efforts to protect the interests of the king. The criticism that resulted in the fifteenth clause of the Articles of the Barons (1215) and in one of the *gravamina* of 1257 and the following years was aimed at the manner of exercise of this right.[279] But the right itself was not seriously challenged. On royal demand debts of testators were paid at the Exchequer, and when there was dispute as to the obligation, it was settled before the court that sat there.[280]

The ramifications of this jurisdiction were many. It existed to recover the king's revenue, but it could be of assistance to royal officials and favourites and, occasionally, to executors. The Exchequer was happy to collect debts owed the deceased, so that the funds realized might be used to acquit his obligations to the king. However, it is clear that all debts were sometimes collected, so that part remained at the disposition of executors for the payment of legacies or for other purposes.[281] One of the problems faced by executors was the protection of the chattels of the deceased from those who sought to carry them off. In the case of royal debtors, officials could use the machinery of local administration to recover this property. This was done not only as a preliminary to the payment of debt to the king, but, in a few cases, even after the property had been handed over to the executors. An example is provided by the Patent Roll of 1260: the king had ordered his bailiffs at Southampton to deliver the goods of Claramunda to her executors, having obtained security for royal debts. But a chest of treasure was missing, so the bailiffs were ordered to empanel a jury to discover it and to cause delivery to the executors.[282] On the other hand, royal officials were sometimes instructed to cause executors to acquit their testator's obligation to a third party so that this person, in turn, would be able to pay his debts at the Exchequer.[283] Finally, they might even enforce

---

279 Stubbs, *Select Charters*, p. 287; *gravamina* 1257, no. XXIV, Wilkins, I, 728; *gravamina* 1280, no. XIV, *Letters from Northern Registers*, ed. Raine, p. 76.

280 Many examples of pleas before the Exchequer, that arose from the collection of royal debts from executors, are printed in *Select Cases in the Exchequer of Pleas;* e.g., regarding the will of Richard de Brome (1236), nos. 1, 23, 24, 25, 36, 38, and pp. xlv-xlvi, lv-lvi.

281 E.g., in 1266 sheriffs were ordered to distrain to obtain all debts of Richard de Clare that they might be used for the soul of the deceased and for the king's needs (*C.P.R.*, 5, 660). In 1215 sheriffs were instructed to distrain all debtors of the bishop of Ely to pay his executors (*Rot. Lit. Claus.*, p. 188).

282 *C.P.R.*, 5, 92-93; similarly the bailiff of Gillingham was ordered to restore all goods which belonged to Lucas de Drumar to his executors, and, if anything had been removed, to see that it was replaced (*C.C.R.*, 4, 260). A similar case appears in the Close Roll of the following year (1242), *ibid.*, pp. 418-419.

283 An interesting example is provided by the Patent Roll of 1286: the executor of

the delivery of a bequest so that the legatee could employ it to acquit his obligation to the king.[284]

The powers of the Exchequer were extended even further, to the wills of those who had no obligations to the king. Officials, who were creditors of the deceased or his executors, could sometimes obtain royal aid to help them recover their debts or carry out administration.[285] Finally, it can be seen in the Exchequer Plea Rolls, that merchants who for one reason or another were close to the king obtained his assistance in vindicating their claims against the executors of their debtors.[286] These claims as well as those of the king were sometimes disputed. The resulting plea was held before the Exchequer court.[287]

In these ways the machinery of royal government was sometimes used to provide an efficient though special means of enforcing the execution of a will. Normally other procedures were employed, and our attention must now be turned to them. However, it is important to note the rapidity with which the Exchequer began to deal with the executor It was suggested in the previous chapter, that this recognition was one of the causes of the increased importance of the executor in the first half of the thirteenth century.[288] In the present context it seems reasonable to suggest that the Exchequer's willingness to accept him as representative of the testator, prepared the way for the courts of justice to do likewise.

A necessary preliminary to the execution of a will was the collection of the debts and the acquittal of the obligations of the deceased. At first this office pertained to the heir, but by Bracton's time passive and active representation in ecclesiastical courts was permitted the executor

Master Nicholas de Marleberg was ordered to pay 34 pounds owed by the deceased to Mabel, late wife of Emericus, to Mabel's executors, that they might be able to acquit her obligation to the king (*C.P.R.*, Edward I, II, 219).

[284] An early example from the Memoranda Roll of 28 Henry III is printed by Madox in *Formulare*, cxxiii, no. 8: the archbishop elect was ordered to cause the executors of his predecessor to appear before the barons of the Exchequer "ad respondum Regi de xx l. quos idem E[dmundus] reliquit Willelmo Tabebot in ultima voluntate sua, in parti solutionis debitorum quae idem Willelmus Regi debuit."

[285] See the discussion of this matter in the introduction to *Select Cases in the Exchequer of Pleas*, pp. xci ff.

[286] Several examples of pleas resulting from claims by merchants are printed *ibid.*, nos. 150, 157, 160. A letter of 1287 is printed in the register of Bishop Swinfield of Hereford (ed. Capes, p. 143); the bishop was instructed to distrain the executors of Roger de Clifford to appear before the Exchequer regarding Roger's debt to William Barach, royal chamberlain, and his associate, Eymer de Ponte, merchant.

[287] On the establishment, personnel, and jurisdiction of this court, see *Select Cases in the Exchequer of Pleas*, Introduction.

[288] See above, pp. 156-158.

in certain circumstances. With regard to active representation the executor could collect those debts of which judgment had been recovered during the testator's lifetime, or to which the debtor had admitted by recognizance. In these cases the debt was already regarded as part of the property of the deceased and, as such, could be considered to be a legacy.[289] But unacknowledged debts could not be bequeathed. They pertained to the inheritance and were claimed by the heir in the temporal courts. This arrangement sometimes proved quite awkward, for it meant that the executor had to act through the heir to obtain chattels or money that were necessary for the implementation of a will. The courts of the Church seem to have sought to overcome this difficulty by expanding their jurisdiction to include those pleas concerning the unacknowledged debt. This is implied by the royal answer to one of the *articuli cleri* of 1280. That year when granting a subsidy to the king, the clergy presented a series of *gravamina*. Among other things, they complained that the execution of wills was delayed by writs of prohibition preventing the recovery of debts in court Christian.[290] The royal answer showed some hesitation, but it implied that proof of debt was too easy in these courts, so that claimants had an unfair advantage. It stated that the executor's position would have been better than that of the testator, since proof of debt could be had by two witnesses even though they were of doubtful quality (*minus idoneos*). This remark seems to refer to an attempt by the Church courts to hold pleas concerning unacknowledged debts.[291] In the meantime part of the inconvenience that lay behind the complaint of the clergy was being

---

289 Bracton, *De Legibus,* fol. 407b; cf. P. and M., II, 344-348; Holdsworth, *History,* III, 573-575; Plucknett, *History,* 741-742. An example of a plea by executors in ecclesiastical court is contained in the *Liber Memorandorum Ecclesie de Bernewelle,* pp. 146-147: the executors of William de Kilkenny, bishop of Ely, sued the prior and convent of Barnwell before the commissary of the papal nuncio for 100 marks, which the defendants had owed the testator. The latter admitted the obligation in part, and claimed a legacy which was admitted by the executors.

290 "Item cum executores alicujus testamenti agant contra testamenti debitores. ut ex eorum debitis compleant voluntatem ipsius, etiam si fidei commissa respiciant vel legata, proponitur prohibitio contra eos" (no. III, *Letters from Northern Registers,* ed. Raine, p. 71). On the date of these articles see G. B. Flahiff, "The Writ of Prohibition," p. 304. n. 94. Cf. Douie, *Archbishop Pecham,* pp. 121-122 and Powicke, *The Thirteenth Century,* p. 479.

291 "Ad tertium nondum est responsum finaliter: dicebatur tamen quod non debuit esse melioris conditionis executor in præjudicium debitores quam fuit testator" (*Letters from Northern Registers,* p. 71). On the recovery of debts where the plaintiff could not rely on a sealed document or previous judgment against the defendant, see P. and M., II, 214-215. As a general rule the defendant could deny the obligation by waging his law; see *Y.B.,* 20-21 Edward I, ed. Horwood, pp. 304-306.

removed. The executor's task was simplified, for a writ became available by which he could claim all the debts of the testator. But the plea was to be held in the temporal courts.[292] When the complaint of the bishops was repeated in 1285, there was no hesitation; the royal reply stated that the plea of debt did not belong to the jurisdiction of the ecclesiastical court.[293]

The temporal courts came to the assistance of the executor in other ways as well. The Second Statute of Westminster (1285) gave him a writ by which he could demand an account of bailiffs and others who had acted for the deceased during his lifetime.[294] Much earlier in the century, the king can be seen aiding executors to obtain accounts in individual cases,[295] but the opinion seems to have been growing that the account was more properly an ecclesiastical matter. This was shown by the bishops' strenuous reaction to the article in the statute of 1285, and by the fact that a collection of writs from the early years of Edward I denied the action of account to the heir, considered the possibility that the executor should have it, and concluded that the suit was more properly an ecclesiastical matter *racione testamenti*.[296] But whatever the strength of the opinion in favour of the Church courts may have been, all hesitation ended and the matter passed to the temporal jurisdiction. Executors sometimes needed assistance when they sold some of the property of the deceased to raise money for legacies, and the buyer refused to pay. During the reign of Henry III a plaint to recover the purchase price was sometimes moved in the courts of the Church, but

[292] See P. and M., II, 346-347 and the examples cited in the Year Books, *ibid.*, p. 347, n. 2. On the important increase in the attorney's power in Second Statute of Westminster, c. 10 (1285), see Brunner, "The Early History of the Attorney in English Law," *Illinois Law Rev.*, III (1909), 274.

[293] "Quod praelati habeant cognitionem de debitis defunctorum non conceditur" (response to article IX, Wilkins, II, 115). Cf. Douie, *op. cit.*, pp. 302-309.

[294] C. 23, *Statutes of the Realm*, I, 83; P. and M. II, 347.

[295] E.g., in 1242 the custodians of the see of Canterbury were ordered to constrain the bailiffs and receivers of the late archbishop to render account to his executors (C.C.R., 4, 418-419). The future Edward I gave his executors the right to demand an account in his will (T. 72b).

[296] The negotiations before and after the publication of the statute are described by H. G. Richardson and George Sayles in "The Clergy in the Easter Parliament of 1285," EHR, LII (1937), 220-234. The bishops presented articles against certain clauses of the statute, including clause 23. The articles are missing but can be reconstructed in general from the royal replies (published *ibid.*, pp. 233-234). The reply maintained the position of the statute. The clergy then repeated their claim on this matter in the revised version of their articles against the statute (Wilkins, II, 119, no. 2). On the Register of Writs, see Holdsworth, *History*, II, 614. An early example of a plea of account is in Y.B., 20-21 Edward I, ed. Horwood, p. 181.

by the end of the century the testator is to be found proceeding against the purchaser in the courts of the king.[297]

Episcopal statutes and practices, as indicated by model *wills*, show that the executor's first obligation was to pay the debts of the deceased.[298] The development of procedure for the enforcement of this payment followed a course similar to that outlined above for the recovery of debts by the executor, although the courts of the Church were perhaps less unwilling to lose the jurisdiction that they had gained in this matter. Bracton held that obligations, admitted by the testator during his lifetime or mentioned in his will, were similar to legacies and could be recovered in ecclesiastical court.[299] Unacknowledged debts were to be sought from the heir before the temporal court. But here too the matter refused to stand; during the last quarter of the thirteenth century, writs of prohibition drew these claims out of the ecclesiastical courts, while, at the same time, the temporal courts admitted passive representation of the deceased by his executor.[300] By the end of the century, the heir was liable only for those debts to which he had been bound by his ancestor.[301]

The recovery of legacies from the testator was the testamentary plea that most properly pertained to the courts of the Church. Here their

297 The steps of a case of this sort in court Christian can be followed in a group of documents in the Public Record Office (E-135. 21/38 [1-3]): the executors of William de Treygoz sued William of Winchester, spicer of Oxford, for the purchase price of the grain of the deceased which they had sold the defendant—"quam idem testator in pios usus per ipsorum executorum manus erogari precepit." The defendant's failure to pay had impeded the execution of the will. He was summoned, admitted the obligation, and arranged for payment. Another example is in the *Cartulary of the Monastery of St. Frideswide*, ed. S. R. Wigram, Oxford Historical Society, XXVIII (1895), pp. 224-226. Here legatees had been granted a right of pre-emption at a low price, but had defaulted in payment. For an example of the plea in temporal court, see *Y.B.*, 31, Edward I, ed. Horwood, pp. 391-392.

298 See above, p. 194.

299 *De Legibus*, fol. 407b; see P. and M., II, 346, and n. 1. A plea of debt against executors in court Christian can be followed in a group of documents at the Public Record Office: Amfrey, rector of Hoathly, Sussex, claimed a debt from the executors of Sir Thomas de Gatesden, offering a writing of the deceased as proof. His claim was admitted. The suit, which was begun before the testator's death, lasted from 1256 to 126. (London, PRO, DL-25.166, 167, 169 and DL-36.1 [94-95]). For another plea of debt against executors in court Christian, see PRO, DL-25.1295, dated 1273.

300 P. and M., II, 347.

301 See the discussion of this matter, *ibid.*, and in T. F. T., Plucknett, *Legislation Edward I*, (Oxford, 1949), pp. 9-10, 75. On *Fleta*'s uncertainty, (as seen in Bk. II, chs. 5, 62 and 70), the attitude of *Britton*, and the evidence of the Year Books, see P. and M. II, 347, n. 2, and Caillemer, "The Executor in England," p. 761. On the later development of the executor as representative of the testator, see Holdsworth, *History*, III, 574-58.

jurisdiction began, and to it (as the petition of 1295 foresaw)[302] they were eventually to be limited. When this jurisdiction was admitted during the last years of King John it was intended to apply only to bequests of chattels. An attempt seems to have been made to extend it to the supervision of bequests of any kind. The numerous writs of prohibition against testamentary suits touching lay fee supply abundant evidence of this.[303] An early plea concerning a bequest of land was held before the dean of Oxford in 1231.[304] Even Bracton seems to have been of the opinion that since the burgage was bequeathed as a quasi-chattel the supervision of the bequest should pertain to the spiritual court.[305] However, this jurisdiction was not yielded to the Church, but remained to the borough courts.

As a general rule, the delivery of all other legacies was supervised by the Church. There are a few exceptions however. Manorial courts can sometimes be found enforcing the terms of a will. As was suggested above, villeins' wills, numerous though they may have been, remained matters of privilege and were made under the conditions permitted by the manorial lord. Thus it is not surprising to find in the rolls of some manorial courts that legacies were enforced there.[306] These courts also supervised the recovery of debts owed the testator and the acquittal of his obligations by the executors of his will.[307] The London borough court occasionally enforced the delivery of bequests of chattels in the fourteenth century; the practice may have had its beginnings in the earlier period which is of interest to the present investigation.[308]

[302] "Item quod corrigatur mala interpretacio que fit contra testamenta, videlicet quod nulla causa est testamentaria nisi causa legatorum in testamento..." (Registrum Pontissara, ed. Deedes, Vol. II, 773).

[303] The most interesting case, indicative of the attempt to extend ecclesiastical testamentary jurisdiction over the legacy of tenements, is included in Bracton's Note Book (no. 73): bequeathed land was assigned an estimated money value and the case was received as a plea of chattels (1219); see Maitland's note, Vol. II, 65, n. 2.

[304] Cartulary of Oseney Abbey, ed. Salter, I, 137-138.

[305] P. and M., II, 330. Bracton dealt with this matter in De Legibus, fols. 407b and 409b; the second text may be an interpolation; see the introduction to Woodbine's edition, Vol. I, 417. Jurisdiction in this matter was claimed in the articles of 1280 (no. IV, Letters from Northern Registers, pp. 71-72).

[306] There are several examples in Court Rolls of the Abbey of Ramsey and the Honor of Clare, ed. W. O. Ault, Yale Historical Publications, Manuscripts and Edited Texts IX New Haven, 1928): at Chatteris in 1270 and 1288 (pp. 260, 274) and at Weston in 1294 (p. 216).

[307] See Court Rolls of the Manor of Wakefield, ed. W. P. Baildon, et al., Yorkshire Archaeological Society, XXIX, XXXVI, LVII, LXXVIII, CIX (1900-15): claim of testators' debts by executors in 1297 and 1298 (I, 294 and II, 32), and demand that the testators' obligations be paid, moved against the executors in 1298 and 1308 (II, 42-43, 139).

[308] Calendar of Mayor's Court Rolls, ed. Thomas, I, 151: the court enforces the delivery of

When the executor had completed all the acts of administration, or when there was suspicion that he had failed in his task, he was summoned to render an account before the ordinary or his commissary. At times executors may have had good reason to seek to avoid this last act in the administration of the will, but obedience was enforced by the threat of excommunication.[309]   When the account had been rendered, letters of acquittal were issued and the execution of the will was complete.

The year 1285, when a writ of account was given the executor, has been chosen as the terminal date of this discussion.   By that time the basic legal procedures for the enforcement of the will had been established, the different pleas had been distinguished, and the courts to whose jurisdiction they pertained had been determined.   It was agreed that in most cases the production of the will, the delivery of its legacies, and the rendering of account should be supervised by the courts Christian.   There had been an area of dispute: who was to represent the deceased in pleas of debt and where were the pleas to be received?   Early in the century the temporal courts had favoured the heir.   The choice was an unfortunate one: the distribution of legacies passed to the executor, and he was necessarily concerned with the efforts to acquit the obligations of the deceased and to collect his debts. The courts of the Church sought to eliminate this awkward situation by allowing the executor to sue and be sued for unacknowledged debts. But this development was prevented by writs of prohibition.   At the same time the royal courts abandoned their preference for the heir, allowing the executor to act for the testator before them.   It would be many years before the executor's powers as personal representative of the deceased would be fully realized, but the essential steps had been taken by 1285.   Thus the executor, who was in so many ways the creature and darling of the ecclesiastical courts, was to see the final growth of his powers in the courts of the king.   Though the bishops were to complain again and again that the supervision of wills had been divided, their complaints would be in vain.   A limit to the expanding testamentary jurisdiction of the courts Christian had finally been set.

a bequest for paving Bishopsgate (1303); also *Calendar of Plea and Memoranda Rolls*, ed Thomas, I, 113 (1339).

309 There are many examples of summons to render account in *The Rolls and Register of Bishop Oliver Sutton,* ed. Rosalind Hill, Vol. III, 12-13, 145 (see p. 21), 155, 156, etc.   On page 101 is a memorandum dealing with the excommunication of Gilbert de Pinchbeck, who had refused to appear to render account.

CHAPTER VI

THE USE OF THE POWER OF DISTRIBUTION OF
PROPERTY AT DEATH DURING THE FIRST
TWO CENTURIES AFTER THE CONQUEST

I N the preceding analysis of the different legal acts used to bequeath
property at death, we have seen the theoretical distinction between
the *post obit* gift, the death-bed gift and the canonical will, and have
investigated the normal procedures of execution and enforcement. It
remains to consider these legal acts in relation to the society in which
they were used. Our interest, then, must turn to the makers and the
beneficiaries of the wills, the property of which free disposition was
allowed, the various groups and pressures, social and economic, that
sought to enlarge the personal and material freedom of testation, and
the motives that lay behind the different acts.

During the twelfth and thirteenth centuries the fundamental motive
for the distribution of property at death remained a religious one.[1]
Most men desired to devote part of their wealth for the good of their
souls. At first sight this desire to make bequests in alms seems to have
been more dominant throughout northern France and in England after
the Conquest than among the Anglo-Saxons. That impression is
probably false: information about bequests, during the period from the
arrival of the Normans to the late twelfth century, is derived almost
exclusively from the cartularies of ecclesiastical institutions, and their
compilers were usually content to mention only the gifts of which their
own church was beneficiary. For the Anglo-Saxon period the *cwide*
provides a unique source of evidence: occasionally at least it describes
many or perhaps all of the bequests made by a testator. Thus gifts to
those more distant relatives who would not benefit from a division of
property made in the customary way, bequests to friends, and rewards
for faithful service find mention there. For the Anglo-Norman world
no such information exists. But when written *wills* appear late in the
twelfth century it becomes evident that, although bequests in alms were
still the main preoccupation, considerable care was taken to provide
for friends, for servants, even for public works. Of the interval it is not

---

1 Holdsworth, *History,* III, 541 ff.

possible to speak with certainty, though it is very likely that friendship, affection, and the recognition of services found expression in many of the death-bed gifts of that period as well.   But be this as it may, it is at least certain that during these two centuries the dying usually wished to bequeath part of their property to pious causes.   Their desire was an imperious one.   It was attached to the preparation for death, a moment of supreme importance.   Nor docs it undermine the religious character of the act, to point out that it was made when the testator was capable of a disinterested view of possessions that was impossible to most men at other times.   He foresaw no further need for his property, and was all the more willing to give part of it away to provide for the one need that remained to him.   The desire to give alms could be present in every adult, no matter what his status or his wealth.   Even the monk, who had resigned the right to possess, knew that when he died alms would be given to the poor for the good of his soul.[2]

This personal motive impelling to the acquisition of a right to bequeath property was accepted and enforced by society as a whole. There is much evidence that intestacy under any circumstances was a great evil in the popular mind.   Even where more careful distinctions were made, it was understood that to die without a will, with full intention, was tantamount to rejecting the ministry of the Church; the consequences were burial in unconsecrated ground and confiscation of property by the lay authority.[3]   References to intestacy appearing in chronicles, royal letter books, reports of juries, and canon and civil law show that those free to make a will were expected to do so.   To refuse was to harm oneself or at least one's family.

Reinforced in this way, the power of bequest was of considerable importance in the social structure and the economy of the time.   The contribution of wills to the establishment and upkeep of public services was immense.   The bequest in alms was a form of voluntary taxation devoted to social needs which no government of those days desired or

[2] *The Monastic Constitutions of Lanfranc,* ed. Knowles, p. 131.   In the thirteenth century, it was customary to feed 100 poor men on the funeral day of a monk, and in many abbeys a poor man was fed and clothed for a year after the death of one of its members; see Knowles, *The Monastic Order,* p. 484.   At the Abbey of Lacock, a mite or a dry loaf was given to each of 100 poor persons on the day of burial of one of the nuns; see Eileen Power, *Medieval English Nunneries* (Cambridge, 1922), p. 121.

[3] Raymundus de Pennaforte, *Summa,* Bk. I, ch. 16, *De Sepulturis* (Rome, 1503), pp. 140-141.   On the problem of intestacy and the rather exaggerated treatment that the matter has too often received at the hands of the historians, see R. Caillemer, *Etudes sur les successions au moyen âge,* II: Confiscation et administration des successions par les pouvoirs publics au moyen âge (Lyons, 1901), pp. 43-53; also *B.C.,* II, cxli-v.

was equipped to supply. On the other hand these legacies tended to diffuse family holdings and to prevent the accumulation of capital. Last of all the desire to exercise a power of bequest extended to those who, according to custom and common law, did not and could not own property. It led to a long dispute, lasting through the thirteenth century and beyond, to determine which members of society should be allowed to make wills.

I. Personal Limitations in the Making of Wills

Thirteenth-century canonists expressed the personal extension of the power of bequest by the simple statement that all were free to make wills who were not prohibited by some rule of law.[4] This approach to the problem, one which was adopted by Lyndwood, would be adequate to provide a speculative presentation of the law on the matter from the time of Glanvill and even earlier.[5] But it would not indicate the extent to which that law was applied in practice. Nor would it give sufficient emphasis to the powerful movement to extend the right of bequest to persons who were forbidden to exercise it by custom or common law. Thus it is necessary to proceed in a somewhat laborious fashion interpreting the law in terms of the indications of practice that are available. Taken as a whole, it can be said that the centuries under consideration were characterized by two movements. The first was the successful effort to state the right of bequest and to establish safeguards to protect the wills of free men and unmarried women who owned property. The second was a steady application of pressure by the bishops and the canonists during the thirteenth century to extend the use of the will to wives and the servile classes. So far as the law was concerned, this effort failed. In practice, however, wills were often made by such persons.

The Wills of Free Men

The first unquestionable indications of a right to make a will appear in the Coronation Charter of Henry I. Some historians would find such evidence even earlier, in the reign of his father. In the London Charter's assurance that children would inherit their father's possessions,

---

[4] E.g., Durandus, *Speculum Iuris* (Venice, 1516), I, 678-680.

[5] *Provinciale*, p. 167, *gl. ad verb.* condere testamentum, and p. 173, *gl. ad verb.* propriarum. Freedom of donation in general is presented in Bracton, fols. 11b-12; *Fleta*, Bk. III, ch. 3 (ed. Selden, p. 178); *Britton*, Bk. II, ch. 3. See Holdsworth, *History*, III, 541 ff. and P. and M., II, 429-430.

they see a continuation of Cnut's defence of the family of the intestate against those who would seize his estate. This would imply that it was normal to make a will.[6] But the more obvious interpretation, that the charter ensured the child's right to inherit, seems in accord with the general tone of the document. Therefore we must turn to the statement of Henry I that vassals may make wills.[7] It implies that at least an offering in alms is expected, and provides a system to supply where the deceased has been negligent. The extent to which this freedom extended beyond the tenants-in-chief to sub-vassals and the lower free classes generally is not always clear. Glanvill presumes that all free men may make wills (VII, 5). Our knowledge of older Anglo-Saxon and Norman practice, charter evidence of gifts of land, information derived here and there from accounts of ecclesiastical income from wills and the rights of sepulchre,[8] when taken as a whole, provide a basis for the opinion that Glanvill's dictum is of general application in the interval between the Conquest and his writing. It is scarcely necessary to mention that during a period that saw so many wars and internal troubles this right was, in fact, very often defeated. Of the capacity of the free man to make a will in the century following Glanvill there is no question. This testamentary capacity extended to aliens and Jews.[9]

The Wills of Free Women and Minors

Is is generally accepted that the status of the woman in the Anglo-Norman world was considerably lower than that which her sister had enjoyed in Anglo-Saxon society. She found herself in a feudal world, a world organized for war, which tended to concentrate economic power in the hands of men. This resulted in a limitation of the woman's right to own and control property, and influenced her capacity to bequeath.[10] The married woman had no right to dispose of property

---

6 *Gesetze*, I, 486. Such was the opinion of Ballard, *British Borough Charters*, I, 74 ff.; but see *Gesetze*, III, 276, and Plucknett, *History*, p. 13, n. 5, and p. 726.

7 The text is quoted above, p. 110, n. 13.

8 The right of sepulchre and the income derived therefrom was jealously defended by the churches. Reference has been made to this problem among the Anglo-Saxons, above, p. 80. It was dealt with by Anselm's London Council of 1102 (c. 26, Wilkins, I, 383). and by councils of the following century; *Regesta*, I, no. 220 contains the account of a judgment before William the Conqueror (*ca.* 1086), between William de Briouze and the abbey of Fécamp, touching land and churches in Sussex: all income "de sepulturis de wacis, de signis sonatis," was to be surrendered to the plaintiff, and bodies were to be exhumed and transferred to the proper churchyard.

9 See P. and M., I, 459 ff. The Patent Roll of 1270 mentions that Cresseus the Jew of London made his will according to the custom of the Jewry (*C.P.R.*, VI, 463).

10 Doris M. Stenton, *The English Woman in History*, pp. 29-33; also J. Reeves, *History of*

without her husband's consent. Common law came to look upon the husband as the guardian of his wife, entitled him to the fruits of her lands, and gave him ownership of all chattels that she had or that came to her during marriage. Glanvill, Bracton and *Fleta* begin their treatment of this matter with the remark that no married woman may make a will without the consent of her husband.[11] Widows and unmarried adults were free to own property and to dispose of it by donation or sale *inter vivos,* or by will. But conditions of the time were such that women were married very young and thus passed directly from the guardianship of their fathers to that of their husbands. Nor did a wife usually enjoy her freedom very long after the death of her husband. During the twelfth century widows possessed of any degree of wealth were quickly married at the demand of the king or the lesser lord from whom they held their property. Some widows purchased the right to remain unmarried. In 1215 Magna Carta decreed that in future they would be free to live without a husband, though, if they chose to marry, they would be obliged to obtain the consent of the lord. But the responsibility of directing a great inheritance was often too much for them; in the first years after the decree of 1215 many widows preferred not to avail themselves of their new privilege.[12]

Maitland analyzed the causes and consequences of the attitude of the common law to the married woman. He showed that its final position was not as inevitable as it may seem to appear, that there were moments of hesitation when the English solution to the problem of the rights of the wife could have gone in the direction of common property, as was the case in France.[13] It is beyond doubt that, beneath the seemingly clear and consistent statement of the law, there were several currents of thought and desire that considerably modified practice in the matter. Some of these currents are reflected by Glanvill and later by Bracton. Having made the categorical statement of the wife's incapacity to make bequests without her husband's consent, they immediately add that, as a mark of respect for her (*propter honestatem*), she is sometimes allowed to make a will of that part of her husband's movable property that would be hers if she survived him.[14] Bracton went on to add that this

English Law, ed. Finlason, 5 vols. (Philadelphia, 1880), IV, 119-121; P. and M., II, 427-436; Holdsworth, *History,* III, 526-527, 544.

[11] Glanvill, Bk. VII, ch. 5; Bracton, fol. 60b; *Fleta* (which follows the text of Bracton very closely here), Bk. II, ch. 57, ed. H. G. Richardson and G. O. Sayles, Vol. II, 191.

[12] Stenton, *op. cit.,* pp. 51-52.

[13] P. and M., II, 427; cf. *B.C.,* II, xcviii.

[14] "... scilicet usque ad tertiam partem rerum suarum quam viva quidem obtinuisset si

was particularly fitting in the case of those goods that were considered to be especially her own—clothing and articles of personal adornment.[15]

That husbands frequently allowed their wives to bequeath property is evident from the remarks of Glanvill and Bracton, from references to wives' bequests in deeds and cartularies, and from their wills. The wife's share of her husband's property consisted of chattels. Since there is very little information touching the bequest of chattels throughout the twelfth century, evidence of her exercise of testamentary capacity during those years is quite limited. Information can be derived only from records of bequests of land; of these there is a not inconsiderable number.[16] As a general rule mention is made of the consent or confirmation of the husband. The attitude of the day is exemplified by a chirograph of about 1165 in which a husband states that he confirms the bequest of land made to Southwark priory by himself and his wife in his wife's will.[17] In thirteenth-century *wills* the testatrix usually states that she has her husband's permission, or she at least makes him her executor.[18]

These bequests and wills, made by dispensation as they were, preserved the theory of the law. But there was in addition a current of thought opposed to the very notion that the wife owned no chattels. It will be recalled that Glanvill and Bracton spoke of her bequests of "her husband's goods," though Bracton did suggest that she had a somewhat stronger claim to certain items of personal use. There are signs here and

maritum suum supervixisset . . ." (Glanvill); Bracton and *Fleta* are similar. For the special rules controlling the bequest of tenements in boroughs, see p. 276.

15 ". . . et maxime de rebus sibi datis et concessis ad ornatum, quæ sua propria dici poterunt sicut de robis et iocalibus" (fol. 60b). In the constitutions of Bishop Peter Quivil of Exeter (1287) those goods "quae ad usum uxoris, utputa supellectilia, vestes muliebres, monilia, annuli," were to be withdrawn from the husband's goods before the division in thirds was made (Wilkins, II, 156). On the wife's paraphernalia, see *Provinciale*, fol. 173, *gl. ad verb.* propriarum. At Bristol the wife could bequeath reasonable funeral expenses without permission (*ca.* 1240): *B.C.* II, 108-109.

16 E.g., Dugdale, *Monasticon*, III, 330, no. iii (1121-35) ; *Cart. Sancti Johannis Colechestria*, I, 159-160 (1146-61), see above, p. 115, n. 35; *Early Charters of St. Paul's*, pp. 175-176, n. 221 (1215-1219); *EYC*, VI, 117, no. 36; *Annales Monastici*, I, 113-114 (1239), etc.

17 ". . . donationem quam fecimus ego et uxor mea Goldeburga in testamento eius extremo" (*ca.* 1160-65); *Facsimiles of Royal and Other Charters in the British Museum*, ed. G. F. Warner and H. J. Ellis (London, 1903), I, no. 47.

18 The permission of the husband is mentioned in T. 23, T. 99a, etc. He is made executor in T. 23, T. 67a, T. 99a and in *Bracton's Note Book*, no. 550 (before 1231). In T. 81, which is but a fragment, there is no mention of the permission of the husband, nor is he named executor. In the distribution of the residue, however, he is to aid the executors.

there that the lawyers' view of the husband as the owner of all his wife's movable property was not entirely accepted. Remarks made more or less in passing, such as that of the Pipe Roll of John's eleventh year, which speaks of the common chattels of husband and wife, or a letter patent of 1253 informing Queen Eleanor that she might make a will not only of "her own goods," but also of the king's property to the extent of 3000 marks, are indications of another point of view.[19] Of greater interest, however, is one of the earliest wills of the thirteenth century (T. 23), made by Agnes de Condet during the lifetime of her husband, Walter Clifford. It includes a bequest of land which was part of her inheritance, legacies in money totalling about eighty pounds, and a few other gifts of jewellery. At the end of the *will* are several clauses describing the sources from which the money required for her legacies was to be drawn: the husband granted one half of the chattels of all his lands; the total income of her manor of Caenby for one year after her death was to be devoted to the completion of her will, as was the income of a wardship which she had purchased from her husband.[20] Finally those chattels which were her own (*omnium que mea sunt*)—gold and silver, vessels and clothing—were to be sold for the same purpose. The executors of the will, of whom the husband was the first named, were to devote the residue of her property to the needs of her soul. Here a distinction is quite clearly made between the wife's share of her husband's goods, and income and chattels that were her own. The husband, who appears to have been closely associated with the making of this will, can be presumed to have agreed. There are other examples later in the century: in a *will* of 1269 household linen was to be divided between husband and daughters at the discretion of the executors,[21] and in another of 1298 the wife left her spouse a golden buckle and a girdle of silk.[22] Wills of this sort show not only that the wife was allowed to dispose of her share of her husband's goods, but that some chattels were considered to be her own. Otherwise the husband is put in the unreasonable position of allowing his wife to bequeath his own property to himself.[23]

[19] "...et quod debita que pater suus R. debuit reddantur de communibus catallis que fuerunt tam patris sui quam Milicent uxoris patris sui:" Publications of the Pipe Roll Society, N.S., XXIV (1946), 50; *C.P.R.*, IV, 213 (July, 1253).

[20] The phrase reads: "et wardam de le Graye quod emi a domino meo;" in this context *domino* usually means husband.

[21] T. 67a; the husband was one of the executors.

[22] T. 99a.

[23] Maitland illustrated most of these qualities from *wills* of the fourteenth century (P. and M., II, 428-429).

Religious motives and ecclesiastical law also tended to foster the wife's right to make a will. There was first of all the fear of intestacy. Whatever the extremes and abuses to which this matter descended, it was ultimately based on the notion that a dying Christian should make some offering in alms to be devoted to social and liturgical purposes. Such a notion was not easily restricted and applied only to those with full power over property. A twelfth-century charter from Colchester prefaced the account of a bequest of land by a married woman with the remark that it is fitting that all the dying should make some offering for the soul.[24] Glanvill shows the power of that argument in his distinction between the testament and the last will, and in his insistence that even the latter is forbidden the wife without her husband's permission.[25] In the second half of the thirteenth century the effort to establish a testamentary capacity in the married woman was reinforced by canon law.[26] One of the earliest examples is found in the Lambeth statutes of Archbishop Boniface (1261). There it is stated that those who impede the "just customary and free" making of a will by a married woman, are excommunicated.[27] It is implied that there has been some loss of freedom, that an established custom is under attack. This or a similar canon appears in several of the synodal collections of the time, and was to be repeated until it found a place among the provincial statutes of Archbishop Stratford in 1342.[28] However, the synodal

24 "Sicut decet omnes morientes ut quisquis potest de suis rebus elemosinas pro se faciat:" *Cart. Sancti Johannis Colechestria*, I, 159.

25 "...nihil sine viri sui auctoritate facere potest etiam in ultima voluntate de rebus viri sui."

26 During the first half of the century, canonists developed the notion that the wife was free to choose her place of burial. Gratian had taught that she should be burica with her husband (C. 13, q. 2, c. 3), but the decretalists maintained that this was true only where she died without manifesting her intention; see X, III, 28, 7, and the *Glossa Ordinaria* thereto; also Bernard, *op. cit.*, p. 91.

27 C. 21: "Item statuimus, ne quis alicujus solutae mulieris, sive conjugatae, alienae vel propriae, impediat vel perturbet, seu impediri aut perturbari faciat, seu procuret justam et consuetam testamenti liberam factionem; quod si fecerit, sciat se excommunicationis innodatum sententia ipso facto" (Wilkins, I, 754). Cf. P. and M., II, 429.

28 A statute attributed to Giles of Bridport, bishop of Salisbury (1257-62): "Similiter de testamento mulieris desponsatae, et omnium parochianorum, tam masculorum quam foeminarum, eadem fiat executio testamenti" (Wilkins, I, 714; on this collection, see Cheney, *English Synodalia*, p. 49); a statute of John Gervais, bishop of Winchester (1262-5): "Sub poena insuper anathematis inhibemus, ne quis solutae, vel conjugatae propriae, vel alterius personae, cujuscunque conditionis extiterit, impediat, vel perturbet, contra regni consuetudinem, testamentum" (Wilkins, II, 298). A similar position was adopted in the Exeter statutes of Bishop Peter Quivil (1287), in which it is stated that anyone may make

statement of the wife's testamentary capacity—as customary (Lambeth, 1261), or as the right to bequeath her own property (Exeter, 1287)—was easily met by the common lawyers. They pointed out that the wife had no such customary right, and that she could not be expected to bequeath the property that, by her state, she was excluded from owning.[29] In spite of the threat of excommunication clearly stated in episcopal statutes, there is no sign of an effort to apply this sanction against husbands who refused to allow their wives to make wills. Nor, on the other hand, did the bishops claim that the wife had died intestate and, in virtue of their power to supervise the estates of such persons, seek to administer her property.[30]

Thus these and later efforts to establish a testamentary right in the married woman were successfully resisted by the common law. Glanvill's statement of her closely restricted capacity remains true for the centuries under consideration, so far as the law was concerned. However, given the frequent manifestations of another point of view, the mere statement of the law is somewhat misleading. Many married women considered themselves to have property that was their own. They made wills. There was a strongly held view that husbands should permit them to do so. And there was in the society an important body of opinion which maintained that the wife's capacity was not a matter of privilege, but of right.

Canonists taught that a person was free to make a will bequeathing his possessions when he attained his majority.[31] This, in accord with Roman civil law, they considered to occur at the completion of the fourteenth and twelfth years for males and females respectively. In England, according to common law and some customs, majority was attained somewhat later.[32] As presented in Glanvill and Bracton a

a will "de bonis, quae possidet tempore mortis" (Wilkins, II, 155-156), and which presume that wives do have such possessions. For the statute of Archbishop Stratford, see Wilkins, II, 705.

[29] *Y.B.*, 5 Edward II (1311), "mès femme ne peut propreté clamer, *nec per consequens testamentum facere*" (ed. G. J. Turner, *Year Books of Edward II*, vol. X, Selden Society, LXIII [1944], p. 241). Bishop Stratford's constitution occasioned a complaint in parliament two years later (*Rot. Parl.*, II, 149). On the later history of the testamentary capacity of the married woman, see *Provinciale*, p. 173; Holdsworth, *History*, III, 543; P. and M., II, 429-430.

[30] "E d'autrepart si femme devie intestat l'ordinarie s'entremettera point" (*Y.B.*, 5 Edward II, ed. Turner, p. 241); cf. P. and M., II, 430-431.

[31] E.g., Hostiensis, *Summa*, p. 162v; Durantis, *Speculum Iuris*, I, 769. In the thought of the canonists there was once more a close connection between free choice of place of burial and testamentary capacity: minors were not allowed to make such choice since they were not free to bequeath; see Bernard, *op. cit.*, p. 89.

[32] P. and M. II, 438; Holdsworth, *History*, II, 98; III, 510, 544-545; *B.C.*, II, cxxvii.

male heir to a military fief came to full age at twenty-one, a soccage
tenant at fifteen, and a burgess even earlier, when he was able to perform
certain tasks that proved his capacity.[33]   As for the heiress, Bracton
hesitates.   In a somewhat confused passage he shows that one opinion
would make the age of majority the same for both sexes, while another
favoured fifteen years even for the heiress to a military fief, since at
that age she can manage a household and marry a husband who can
acquit the obligation of the fief.   Bracton goes on to remark that if
maturity for marriage is the only consideration he can see no reason
why the age of twelve years should not be sufficient for majority.
Common law was, in fact, moving towards a general application of the
age required for the male heir of a military fief.[34]   What is not clear is
whether full legal capacity was required for the making of a will, or
whether the age of discretion or some later age was considered to be
sufficient.   When requirements for validity were established by the
ecclesiastical courts, there was at least the possibility of conflict, given
the difference that existed between the age of majority in the two
systems.   Of such a conflict there is no sign during the twelfth and
thirteenth centuries.   Borough courts, to which probate of bequests of
tenements pertained, often favoured an early age for the making of
wills.[35]   Thus at Wycombe in 1275, even land could be bequeathed by
a burgess in his thirteenth year.[36]   In this case the testator had full
legal capacity.   It is clear, however, that at Bristol an infant was allowed
to bequeath chattels even before attaining his majority.[37]   Coke, for
whom full age was twenty-one, spoke of the exercise of a testamentary
capacity at eighteen.   This point was made in a text in which he tried
to give such a meaning to a clause in Littleton.[38]   But the implication
of Littleton's text is that bequests could be made by those who were
fourteen years of age.[39]   Examples of wills made by the young in the

33 Glanvill, Bk. VII, ch. 9; Bracton, *De Legibus*, fol. 86b.

34 See P. and M., II, 438, and Holdsworth, *History*, III, 266 and 510; thus by Bracton's
time a tenant in soccage was no longer in ward after fifteen, yet he did not attain full legal
capacity until he was twenty-one (fol. 274b).

35 *B.C.*, II, cxxvii, 157-160.

36 *Ibid.*, p. 158.

37 E. W. W. Veale, *The Great Red Book of Bristol*, Vol. I, Bristol Record Soc., II (1931),
p. 73.

38 Coke, *A Commentary on Littleton*, sect. 123. Veale, *op. cit.*, p. 73, cites a note to the
nineteenth edition: "it is pointed out in a footnote that Coke gave no authority for the
proposition, and that the better opinion was that males could make a valid will at fourteen
and females at twelve."

39 "Et si tiel gardein maria lheire deins 14. ans, il accomptera al heire, ou a ses
executors de value del mariage ..."

period under consideration are rare;[40] but the over-all impression is that a rather strong current ran in favour of a testamentary capacity in those who had attained the age of majority as defined by canon law.

The Wills of Clerics and Religious

Other members of society—the clergy, and religious of different orders —were limited in their control of property by their status. The clergy were personally free but their freedom to dispose of the lands and goods they administered was subject to several restrictions.[41] Although there was a current of thought in the West that would have preferred that the cleric have no property of his own, the general teaching of the canonists held the opposite view. They made a distinction between the property that a cleric held as a private person (his patrimony) and his benefice.[42] The latter was expected to revert to the Church, passing to his successor; the former, which tended to include the increase in wealth derived from benefices,[43] could be freely bequeathed so far as the law of the Church was concerned. From the rather limited evidence of the devolution of property of ecclesiastics that exists from the last years of the Anglo-Saxon kingdom, it appears likely that this distinction was known and observed.[44]

With the Conquest of England the holding of property in a third capacity became general for the bishops. They were tenants-in-chief. In the eyes of the king, they were vassals who never had heirs in full age, so that at each vacancy the barony passed into the king's hands for a period that could be as long as the king's conscience would allow. From this point of view, the lands of the vacant see were held of the

---

[40] The will of Robert, son of John Deumars of London was challenged on the plea that the testator was not of full age and was *non compos mentis:* Sharpe, I, 103 (1291-2).

[41] See P. and M., II, 519-520; Makower, *Constitutional History,* p. 248, n. 21; Poole, *Domesday Book to Magna Carta,* pp. 182, 190-191; and especially F. Prochnow, *Das Spolienrecht und die Testierfähigkeit der Geistlichen im Abendland bis zum 13. Jahrhundert* (Berlin, 1919), where the general history of the *ius spolii* is presented and the properly English development is placed in the wider context (pp. 72-81).

[42] See the consideration of the matter above, pp. 72-73. The testaments of the clergy are treated in the *Decretum,* C. 12, q. 5, and in the *Decretals,* III, 26.

[43] Income from benefices that remained after the death of an incumbent was to be received by the churches from which it was drawn, according to III Lateran Council (1179), c. 15, which became X, III, 26, 7. Alexander III allowed some distribution of this income in alms, etc., by act *inter vivos,* but not by will. This letter (JL, 13842) became X, III, 26, 8. In another letter (JL, 14347) he accepted the custom that allowed some distribution of this wealth by testament to the poor, to churches, and to servants whether relatives or not (X, III, 26, 12); see *Provinciale,* p. 166, *gl. ad verb.* legitima testamenta.

[44] See above, p. 72.

16

king and existed to supply certain services to the king. But from another point of view, they belonged to the Church which had not died, and were intended to supply certain liturgical and social needs which were the Church's special obligation. Eventually it was decided that the episcopal barony should be used for the king's purpose during the vacancy, basic ecclesiastical needs being supplied, but the vacancy should be reasonably brief. The estates of the see were expected to pass to the new incumbent with necessary stock and equipment. Income produced by the estates during the interval belonged to the Exchequer by regalian right. Movable property accumulated by the late bishop during his tenure of office was seized by the king in virtue of the same prerogative or, tending to become included in the patrimony of the deceased, was claimed with it by the very dubious title of the *ius spolii*. However, during the twelfth century the prelate's patrimony was distinguished from that which he held in other capacities, and the right to bequeath it was established in principle. A system whereby the regular exercise of this right became a reality was worked out during the reign of King John. The process was a tortuous one and merits examination in some detail.

Of the Conqueror's reign there is very little evidence. He it was who wrought the changes in the constitution of the Church which prepared the way for later abuse, but he is known to have exercised considerable care to avoid the dilapidation of bishoprics during vacancy.[45] It is reasonable to suppose that the upper clergy made wills of some sort, in which they successfully arranged at least for the bequest of alms for their souls. During the reign of William Rufus the possibilities of abuse implicit in the arrangement were realized: the wealth of churches and the personal property of deceased bishops were usually seized by the king. To these crimes Ordericus Vitalis devotes several of his most moving passages.[46] Relief was promised by Henry I in his Coronation Charter: on the death of an archbishop, bishop, or abbot, nothing was to be removed from the domain of the church or from its tenants until a successor had taken his place.[47] Had the promise been kept, the interference of royal agents would have ceased, and the execution of bishops' wills by their successors or other clerics would have been possible. Once established on the throne, however, Henry reverted to practices much like those of his brother. Papal and episcopal

---

45 Ordericus Vitalis, *Hist. Eccl.*, Bk. IV, ch. 9 (ed. Le Prevost, II, 200).
46 *Ibid.*, Bk. VIII, ch. 8; Bk. X, chs. 2, 8 (ed. Le Prevost, III, 313; IV, 9-10, 54).
47 *Gesetze*, I, 521.

complaints, as well as the accounts of the chroniclers, provide ample evidence of his abuses.[48] When Ranulf Flambard, bishop of Durham, came to die in 1128, he was urged to make his peace with God, and sought to do so by the payment of his debts and the distribution of his wealth in alms. Ranulf had encouraged royal rapacity in the past and was not to escape himself, for royal agents collected even that portion of his wealth which had already been received by the donees.[49] The account adds, however, that some bequests to the poor and to certain churches were allowed to stand. There is some evidence from lists of benefactors of cathedrals and monasteries that, even during the reigns of William Rufus and Henry I, certain portions of the bishops' wealth —vestments or plate from the chapel of the deceased—were allowed to be given as legacies in alms.[50]

The testamentary capacity of the bishop was finally given explicit statement in the second charter of King Stephen (1136).[51] Here, in a series of concessions freeing ecclesiastical property and patronage from secular interference, it is stated that bishops, abbots, and other clerics were permitted to make a reasonable distribution of property by will.

[48] In *Hist. MSS. Comm. Report*, 5 (1876), p. 429 is a letter, allegedly of Honorius II (1124-30), complaining of royal seizure of the personal property of bishops; the Council of Reims (1131), at which Innocent II was present, reserved all the property of a deceased cleric to his church (c. 7, Mansi, XXI, 465); in the *Gesta Stephani* the bishops complain of Henry's practices in this regard (ed. Potter, p. 17); see Poole, *op. cit.*, p. 182 and nn. 4 and 5, and Prochnow, *op. cit.*, pp. 74-76.

[49] *Symeon of Durham: Historical Works*, ed. T. Arnold, 2 vols., RS, 75 (1882-5), I. 141. A similar procedure in the case of Serlo, bishop of Séez in Normandy, is described in Ordericus Vitalis, Bk. XII, ch. 35 (ed. Le Prevost, IV, 445): he had already manifested the intention of distributing his property in alms, but due to an interruption, died before he could do so (1123). The royal agents seized all his property; cf. Prochnow, p. 75. The despoiling of the treasure of Gilbert the Universal, bishop of London, is described by Henry of Huntingdon in *De Contemptu Mundi*, ed. T. Arnold in *Henrici Huntendunensis Historia Anglorum*, RS, 74 (1879), p. 308.

[50] Thus in a list of bequests to the church of Durham mention is made of gifts by every bishop from 1095 until 1257, with the exception of William of Ste. Barbe who died in 1152. This includes Ranulf Flambard and Hugh de Puiset, most of whose possessions were seized by the king; see *Wills and Inventories of the Northern Counties of England. Pt. 1*, Surtees Society, II (1835), pp. 1 ff; Dugdale, *Monasticon*, II, 219.

[51] "Si quis episcopus vel abbas vel alia ecclesiastica persona ante mortem suam rationabiliter sua distribuerit vel distribuenda statuerit, firmum manere concedo. Si vero morte praeoccupatus fuerit, pro solute animae ejus ecclesiae consilio eadem fiat distributio Dum vero sedes propriis pastoribus vacuae fuerint, ipsas et earum possessiones omnes in manu et custodia clericorum vel proborum hominum ejusdem ecclesiae committam, donec pastor canonice substituatur" (Stubbs, *Select Charters*, p. 144). See Poole, *Domesday Book to Magna Carta*, pp. 190-193.

Should they fail to do so, alms were to be given for their souls under the direction of the Church. The personal property of the cleric was carefully distinguished from the possession of the benefice, though it is not clear whether it included wealth accumulated from surplus ecclesiastical revenues or was limited to the patrimony of the deceased. Given the known practice of the lower clergy[52] and the attitude of bishops at the end of the century, it is reasonable to conclude that "personal property" was interpreted in the wider sense.

That Stephen and his successors always considered themselves bound by this charter was not to be expected. Stephen's own record, so far as it is known, is not an especially bad one. Even the seizure of the property of Roger, bishop of Salisbury, was provoked; according to one version at least, it was carried out in the spirit of the law.[53] Henry II did not repeat Stephen's promise in his Coronation Charter, but referred in general to the practices of the time of his grandfather. The will of Archbishop Theobald and the covering letter to the king show that even he, to whom the king owed so much, feared lest the execution of his will be prevented by royal interference.[54] It seems safe to conclude that during the reign of Henry and his sons, to die at enmity with the king, or to die intestate was to expose both the bishop's personal fortune and any accumulation of income from his benefice to seizure by royal agents.[55] There was a fairly widespread opinion that it was not fitting

---

[52] See below, p. 249.

[53]. There are two accounts of the events: according to William of Malmesbury, Roger's goods were pillaged by royal officials just before he died; in the Gesta Stephani, the king, just as always, distributed at least part of the bishop's great wealth in such a way that he compensated for past injuries, provided for the roofing of the church, saw to the needs of the canons, etc. Roger's intentions for the devolution of his property were not fulfilled, but if the latter version may be believed, his wealth was employed in the spirit of the charter of 1136; see Historia Novella, ed. Potter, p. 39; Gesta Stephani, ed. Potter, pp. 64-65. On the seizure of the wealth of William of Corbeil, archbishop of Canterbury (d. 1136), see ibid., p. 6.

[54] Theobald threatened interfering royal officials with excommunication, asked the king's confirmation of the will, and added a postscript of delightful realism: he had very little property anyway, so the king would scarcely suffer from its loss (Letters of John of Salisbury, ed. W. J. Millor, etc., Ep. 134, p. 246 and Ep. 135, p. 251); see above, p. 142.

[55] According to Ralph Diceto, Archbishop Roger of York, who died in 1181, had obtained a bull from Alexander III permitting him to seize the property of clerics who, though they had made a will, did not complete the actual distribution of property before death. Such was his own fate; the king promptly seized a very large fortune. See Ymagines Historiarum, ed. Stubbs, Radulphi de Diceto Opera Historica, II, 12. The Gesta Regis Henrici Secundi) ed. Stubbs, Chronicles of the Reigns of Henry II and Richard I, I, 289) says that

for a bishop to leave great wealth, that surplus income from his see should be given in alms during life rather than after death.[56] This could not always be done however, and by the end of the century it is evident that bishops were using wills to control the devolution of this property as well.

The case of St. Hugh of Lincoln is illustrative. Hugh had been a Carthusian and made it quite clear that he had little sympathy with the current though recently established practice of will-making by bishops.[57] So far as he was concerned, neither then, nor at any time, did he have property that he considered to be his own. But, since for him to die intestate meant that any wealth he had under his control went into the royal coffers, rather than to the poor and to churches for which he had intended it, he made a will and obtained King John's confirmation.

Bishop Hugh of Durham received 300 marks from Roger's estate and distributed it to the poor, to churches, and for the repair of bridges; royal officials seized his house. The basis of the king's seizure of Roger's property, according to this second version of events, was that clerics were not allowed to make division of their property during illness. The whole matter is obscure but the difficulty may stem from the failure to distinguish between the patrimony of the cleric and wealth obtained from his benefice. As was seen above, pp. 129-130, Alexander III allowed a cleric to give alms from the goods of the church if donation were accomplished before death by act *inter vivos*. Otherwise the property of the church and income which the late incumbent had possessed were to remain to his successor. The papal bull in question may well have given Roger the right to seize such goods. In some dioceses, however, members of the lower clergy were allowed to devote the income of their benefice for a year after death in alms and in payment of debt; see below, p. 249. Geoffrey Riddel, bishop of Ely, died intestate in 1189 and King Richard seized his property (Diceto, *Ymagines*, ed. Stubbs, II, 68). Hugh de Puiset, bishop of Durham, made a will, but his goods were seized by royal servants; the rigor of their examination of those in whose charge Hugh's property remained is described in William of Newburgh, *Historia Rerum Anglicarum*, ed. R. Howlett, *Chronicles of the Reign of Stephen, etc.*, II, 439-440. Some of the legacies had already been received by the beneficiaries of the will, but their value was collected and paid into the Exchequer; see *Pipe Roll of 8 Richard I*, Publications, N.S., VII (1930), 261.

56 The author of the *Gesta Stephani* sharply criticized William of Corbeil, archbishop of Canterbury, for failure to distribute his wealth during life: "quam si in elemosinarum largitione uiuens distribuisset, imitans euangelicum hominem, qui de mamona iniquitatis sibi amicos efficiens, ideo dispersit et dedit pauperibus, ut iustitia illius in æternum maneret..." (ed. Potter, p. 6). Archbishop Theobald distributed all his possessions with a few exceptions on two occasions. This way of thinking was probably involved in the difficulties of Roger of York mentioned above in note 55; both Diceto and William of Newburgh approved of the royal action. The latter criticized Roger for distributing his wealth only when he had no further use for it (*Chronicles*, ed. Howlett, I, 227).

57 "Tædet me sane hujus consuetudinis, jam passim in ecclesiam traductæ": *Magna Vita S. Hugonis*, ed. Dimock, p. 334. On the different accounts of John's confirmation, see p. lx; cf. P. and M., I, 519, n. 1.

The version of this event preserved in Hoveden and Matthew Paris mentions a royal promise to protect the wills of all prelates.[58]   At any rate John is known to have given permission for the making of wills to Hubert Walter in 1199 and to the bishops of Ely, London and Rochester in the following years.[59]   The Close Rolls of the last years of his reign show the king aiding the execution of the wills of other bishops as well.[60]   During the reign of Henry III bishops usually obtained royal permission to make wills. Of this the Charter and Patent Rolls provide ample evidence.[61]   Some of the letters of confirm-ation included a general permission to the grantee's successors [62]   In most cases mention was made of the bequest of movable and immovable property belonging to the bishop "whether by reason of his church or of his person."

On the death of a bishop his see and all his property were received by guardians appointed by the king. They were instructed, usually after a short interval,[63] to obtain security for the payment of royal debts from the executors, then to give them seisin of all movable property except the stock and equipment that were on the lands of the see when the late incumbent occupied it.[64]   When, as often happened, the king

---

[58] Chronica Magistri Rogeri de Houedene, ed. Stubbs, IV, 140-141; Matthæi Parisiensis Chronica Majora, ed. H. R. Luard, 7 vols., RS 57 (1872-84), II, 471.

[59] Rymer, Fœdera, I, 78; Rot. Lit. Cl., p. 39b (March 1204) and p. 99 (June 1213).

[60] E.g., Henry of Exeter (Jan. 1207), Simon of Wells, bishop of Chichester (Sept. 1207), Eustace of Ely (Feb. 1215): ibid., pp. 76a, 92a, 188a-b. John was not above enriching himself from such property: in the Pipe Roll of 10 John, Publications, N.S., XXIII (1945), p. 59, he demands 2000 marks and all the testator's jewels from the executors of Philip, bishop of Durham; Gervase of Canterbury describes a rather shallow trick by which the king took from the monks of Christchurch some 3000 marks bequeathed to them by the late Hubert Walter (Chronicle, ed. W. Stubbs, II, 98).

[61] Royal permissions occasionally referred to wills made either on the death-bed or before, a reflection perhaps of the earlier difficulties of Archbishop Roger of York: e.g., Ralph, bishop of Chichester (1229); Walter, bishop of Carlisle (1230); C. Ch. R., I, 96, 121.

[62] Thus in 1234, letters of permission, extended to successors, were received by the archbishop of Canterbury, and the bishops of Lincoln and Chichester: Wilkins, I, 630; C. C. R., IV, 148; The Chartulary of the High Church of Chichester, ed. Peckham, p. 231.

[63] Hugh Foliot, bishop of Hereford, died July 26, 1234; the letter assigning administration to his executors is dated Aug. 13 (C. C. R., II, 498). Richard Poore of Durham died April 15, 1237 and assignment was made April 28 (C. P. R., III, 181). The executors of Walter de Gray were given administration the day after his death, May 2, 1255 (ibid., IV, 408).

[64] Custody of the bishopric of Ely was given Thomas de Blumville who was ordered to give the executors seisin of all chattels less the stock on the property when received (1225): Rot. Lit. Cl., II, 38a-b. Similar directions regarding the manors held by Stephen Langton are in C. C. R., I, 110-111.

had need of some of the chattels of the deceased—grain, beasts or armour—the executors were paid for them.[65]   There were moments of friction, especially where the collection of royal debts was accomplished with undue harshness, or where the awarding of seisin to the executors was too long delayed,[66] but from the beginning of the reign of Henry III to the end of the century the general impression is one of excellent relations.   Bishops usually obtained royal permission to make wills. So far as is known, the permission was never refused.   They had established their right to make wills and had little to fear from royal interference.

Executors received both the patrimony of the deceased and any surplus that had accumulated from the income of benefices during his lifetime. Even the crops of the current year came into their hands.[67]   Of this, royal instructions leave no doubt.   During the last decades of the thirteenth century, bishops obtained papal permission before making their wills.   The popes were accustomed to distinguish various kinds of property, giving full freedom to dispose of patrimony, but limiting the disposal of income derived from "the altar" to bequests in alms and to the payment of church debts.[68]   The distinction is not discernible in

---

[65] E.g., C. P. R., III, 94, a bond to the executors of Bishop Hugh of Wells to pay for seed used by the custodians of the see.

[66] Writing of the death of Roger of Salisbury, bishop of Bath (d. 1247), Matthew of Paris remarks: "dominus rex secundum consuetudinem suam avidas manus bonis episcopatus injecit, ut quicquid abrodere posset festinanter asportaret" (Chronica Majora, ed. Luard, Vol. V, 3).   In C. C. R., VI, 19, the custodian of the see is ordered to give Roger's chattels to his executors, having obtained security "quod de primis bonis regi satisfacient." Interference with bishops' wills was also mentioned in the gravamina prepared by Robert Grosseteste (Annales Monastici, ed. Luard, I, 423) and in those of 1257 (Wilkins, I, 728, no. XXIII).

[67] All necessary equipment for harvesting and storage was put at their disposition: e.g., C. C. R., IV, 79 and 324.   Other income of the see (from courts, land held on lease by the see, etc.) fell to the king, not to executors; this is carefully stated in a letter of 1234, ibid., III, 518.   Wards, leases, etc., held by the bishop in a private capacity, were given to the executors.   Thus in C. C. R., I, 132 (1228), we learn that the custodian of the vacant see of London has seized lands held at farm by the late incumbent and, was ordered to surrender them to the executors: "et hoc idem mandatum est ei de wardis et perquisitis ipsius episcopi que non tenentur in capite de eodem episcopatu."

[68] Archbishop John Pecham, who was a Franciscan, received a papal letter permitting him to dispose of property, not acquired by his church, and of movables committed to him for life but not obtained from his order, in payment of debts, for funeral expenses, and in bequests to servants whether they were kinsmen or otherwise; Entries in the Papal Registers Relating to Great Britain and Ireland, ed. W. H. Bliss, etc. (London, 1894), I, 458; other examples, ibid., I, 174, 540; II, 46.   The distinction is made especially clear in a letter of Nicholas III to Robert, archdeacon of Canterbury in 1280: "de bonis suis licite acquisitis"

episcopal wills of this period.   Executors are usually instructed to sell most of the testator's goods, save some special objects bequeathed in detail, that they might pay debts and provide bequests from the proceeds.   The wills themselves are in the spirit of the papal distinction, however, for the greater portion of episcopal wealth was bequeathed to churches, to education, and to the poor.[69]

During the reign of Henry III, it becomes evident that the earlier efforts to preserve the minimum complement of animals and equipment on episcopal manors during vacancies were proving inadequate. Bishops complained that on entering their sees they found them dilapidated: manors stripped of animals and grain, cathedrals lacking even the vestments, plate and books needed for liturgical functions.[70] The matter merits further study; it is not clear whether the executors of the late incumbent had considered movables of any sort their property to be disposed of as needed, or whether the royal custodians of the see were pillaging it.   At any rate there is a series of agreements whereby bishops bequeathed equipment to their successors with the under-standing that executors would deliver the bequest only on receiving guarantees from the new incumbent that he in his turn would do the same.[71]   Thus once more the will was used by clerics to protect the endowment of their churches.

---

he is given full power of distribution by testament; "de bonis mobilibus ecclesiasticis sue dispensationi commissis et que non fuerint altaris seu altarium ecclesiarum ipsi commis-sarum ministratio, seu alicui speciali earundem ecclesiarum divino cultui vel usui deputata, necnon et quibuscunque bonis mobilibus ab ipso per ecclesiam seu ecclesiis licite acquisitis" may be used for the expenses of his funeral and for the remuneration of servants: *Les Registres de Nicolas III*, ed. Jules Gay et Suzanne Vitte, Bibliothèques des Ecoles françaises d'Athènes et de Rome (Paris, 1898-1938), p. 274, no. 617.

69 See below, p. 264.

70 See *C. Ch. R.*, II, 408-9, an inspeximus of a charter of Ralph, bishop of Carlisle. Here the prelate begins by remarking that bishops on entry are exposed to great poverty; "instructed by experience" he proceeds to arrange that his successor should have a chapel properly equipped, books of theology and canon law, equipment for kitchen, bakery and brewery, and the necessary animals and machines for his manors.   Hugh of Wells, bishop of Lincoln, bequeathed 26 ploughs with plough-teams to his successor (T. 33), but it is impossible to say whether they were intended as a special generosity or represent an attempt to assure adequate equipment for the manors of the see.   The practice in question can be especially well illustrated at Hereford: in 1237, Ralph Maidstone arranged for stock to be left on his manors for his successors (*Registrum Thome de Cantilupo*, ed. Griffiths, pp. 38-39); the Charter Roll of 1249 contains an *inspeximus* of a letter of Bishop Peter Aigueblanche, enjoining each bishop of the see to leave 30 plough-teams to his successor (*C. Ch. R.*, I, 346); see the following note.

71. The register of Thomas de Cantilupe, bishop of Hereford, contains a receipt in which

Very little evidence survives of the early exercise of testamentary capacity by the lower clergy. The general canonical distinction between patrimony and income from benefices would apply in their case as in the case of the bishops. There is every reason to suppose that especially during the first decades after the Conquest those charged with the care of many parishes were subject to the exercise of a *ius spolii* by the owner or patron of the church they served. However bishops tended to protect their wills, extending their capacity, in some cases at least, even to the revenue of their benefice. Such an arrangement is to be found almost immediately after the Conquest in the foundation charter of Salisbury Cathedral (1091), in which one third of the income from a canon's benefice, during the year following his death, was to be devoted to the poor for his soul.[72] In the twelfth century there are occasional references to the bequest of land and chattels by the lower clergy.[73] When written *wills* become more common during the reign of Henry III,

---

the bishop acknowledges the delivery of 500 marks, "pro instauro ipsius Episcopatus," by the executors of his predecessor, and promises to leave as much to his successor (October, 1277, *Registrum*, p. 139). In 1281 Bishop Peter Quivil of Exeter acknowledged the receipt of ten ploughs and 100 oxen from the executors of his predecessor, and gave bond that on his death they would pass to the dean and chapter to be delivered to his successor (Exeter, Dean and Chapter, MS. charter no. 2107; see *Hist. MSS. Comm. Report*, 55 [1901-14], Var. Coll., IV, 71). Arrangements made by William Wickwane, archbishop of York, are in *C. Ch. R.*, II, 268-269 (Oct. 1283); they incorporate a careful statement of the complement to be maintained on each manor, including carts, ploughs, harness, etc. On his death they were to pass to the use of the king during the vacancy, then to be surrendered to his successor. In the case of Bishop Ralph of Carlisle, cited in the previous note, the equipment or its value was to be delivered by his executors to the royal guardians by chirograph. The latter were to deliver it to the new bishop, who in his turn was to pass it on to his successor.

[72] The remaining two-thirds were conceded to the other canons. The text states merely that the third will be devoted "in usum pauperum," but it may be presumed that the grant is intended to be for the soul of the deceased; see *Register of St. Osmund*, ed. W. H. Rich-Jones, 2 vols., RS, 78 (1883-4), I, 78. Thurston, archbishop of York, granted that the whole income of a canonry for a year after the incumbent's death be devoted to the payment of debts and for bequests in alms. Other holders of benefices were allowed to devote two thirds of the year's income to these ends, the remaining third to go to the cathedral church (*Historians of the Church of York*, III, 64-66, and *EYC*, I, 129, no. 149 [1119-1135]). Honorius III confirmed a similar grant to the dean and chapter of Lichfield in 1221 (Bliss, *Entries in Papal Registers*, I, 80).

[73] E.g., the bequests of a priest of the diocese of Hereford who died at the abbey of Gloucester are reported by Abbot Gilbert Foliot (1139-48), in Ep. 64 (PL 190, 788-789). Philip, canon of Lincoln, bequeathed land and houses in 1186-9 (*Registrum Antiquissimum of Lincoln*, III, 322-323, no. 990). The will of Peter of Blois is mentioned in the Close Roll of 14 John (*Rot. Lit. Cl.*, I, 117b).

it is immediately evident that these clerics have the right to make wills and are exercising it.[74]

Members of religious orders had no testamentary capacity since by their state they were incapable of owning property.[75] "Civil death," to use an expression with which the canonists did not entirely agree,[76] was one of the results of religious profession. The postulant to the religious state could arrange for the distribution of his property; in England, one of the means whereby this was effected was the will, which was executed once civil death had taken place with religious profession.[77] Having taken vows the religious, in theory at least, lost all further power to own property and, therefore, to dispose of it. This very old rule appeared once more in the canons of the Oxford Council of 1222.[78] It was to meet opposition by the end of the Middle Ages, but during the age which concerns us here, any attempt by an ordinary religious to bequeath property would be considered a very serious infraction of the rule.

There are, however, a goodly number of references to wills made by the heads of religious communities during the twelfth and especially during the thirteenth and following centuries. In the earliest cases the abbots seem simply to have taken certain books, equipment, or money,

[74] For example, there are many priests' wills among those of London calendared by Sharpe.

[75] P. and M., I, 433-435. With regard to minor relaxations of the rule in this regard, see Knowles, *The Monastic Order*, p. 484, and *The Religious Orders in England*, 3 vols. (Cambridge, 1948-60), I, 288-289.

[76] On the canonists' attitude to this dictum, see G. Lepointe, "Réflexions sur des textes concernant la propriété individuelle de religieuses cisterciennes dans la région lilloise," *Revue d'histoire ecclésiastique*, XLIX (1954), p. 743, where the author cites *Recherches sur l'histoire de la théorie de la mort civile des religieux*, by Durtelle de Saint-Sauveur (Rennes, 1910). References to "civil death" are not uncommon in England: e.g., *C. P. R.*, I, 389 (1220), ". . . ita quod mortuus est quantum ad seculum;" Bracton, fol. 421b, etc.

[77] In 1281 Master Richard de Stratford, a Dominican novice, presented his own testament to the Court of Hustings and caused it to be proved. By its terms, his tenements were assigned to his executors to be sold (Sharpe, I, 52). The Close Roll of 1227 speaks of chattels which Robert de Ros "adhuc in seculari habitu . . . antequam habitum religionis suscepit per manum suam . . . dedit vel legavit" (*Rot. Lit. Cl.*, II, 166b). An heir succeeded to the estates of a land-owner after the latter took vows (Glanvill, Bk. XIII, chs. 5, 6); cf. P. and M., I, 434.

[78] C. 46, Wilkins, I, 593. There are occasional examples of donations to individual religious made in a form that would permit the future bequest of the gift. Thus in a charter published in *EYC*, I, 128, William Esveiliechen grants land to Alice, a nun: "et sciant omnes quod domina Alicia habet liberam potestatem dandi eandem elemosinam post obitum suum cuicumque voluerit." The monastic rule would not be affected by the form of the gift.

that they had accumulated for their own special needs, and ordered that they be given to their community or the poor. Such were the bequests of Abbot Faritius of Abingdon (*ca.* 1115) and of Ailred of Rievaulx (1167).[79] But there are other examples which show that abbots and priors were bequeathing property to a variety of beneficiaries, appointing executors and generally speaking making wills somewhat like those made by bishops.[80]

The development of the testamentary capacity of religious superiors seems to be connected with the process that went on during the first half of the twelfth century, whereby the holdings of many monasteries were divided between the abbot and the community. This *divisio* was necessitated by the feudalization of most of the greater religious houses after the Conquest.[81] Once an abbey became obliged to feudal services the abbot had to provide the financial basis for fulfilling his obligations to the feudal host. When he died a vacancy occurred and the abbey fell into the hands of the king. During the reigns of William Rufus and Henry I vacancies were often extremely long, and disastrous both financially and morally. Remedy was sought in the division of the property of the monastery. The community, which never died, held given estates dedicated to precise needs, and was responsible for their control and exploitation. Other manors were the property of the abbot; from their income he provided for his own needs and acquitted the monastery's obligations to the king. On his death they were held by royal servants until a successor was appointed. As the abbot withdrew more and more from the regular life of the monastery, he had

---

[79] *Abingdon Chronicon*, II, 290: in his last illness Abbot Faritius placed 30 pounds of gold [sic] on the altar for gilding the candlesticks, and left a sum of money for the poor; Ailred of Rievaulx ordered books, relics and a cross to be brought to him and said: "*Argentum et aurum non est michi*, unde non facio testamentum, quia nichil possideo proprium, vestrum est quicquid habeo et ego ipse" (*The Life of Ailred of Rievaulx by Walter Daniel*, ed. F. M. Powicke [London, 1950], p. 58).

[80] E.g., confirmation of the will of the Augustinian prior of Plympton by Archbishop Theobald (*Letters of John of Salisbury*, ed. W. J. Millor, etc., Ep. 119, p. 196). Abbot Samson of Bury made a will, as Jocelin of Brakelond tells us in the last pages of his chronicle (ed. Butler p. 136); reference to delivery by his monks—"palfridos abbatis qui obiit et jocalia ... que ipse domino rege legavit"—appears in *C. R. R.*, VI, 189 (Hilary, 1212). In a list of instruments published in the *Ramsey Cartulary* (I, 70), is a letter of Pope Gregory X (1271-6) for the execution of the will of Roger, head of the alien priory of Linton; a commission of acquittal of the executors of Alexander, Prior of Frieston in Lincolnshire, is in the register of Bishop Sutton (ed. Hill, vol. IV, p. 85).

[81] Knowles, *The Monastic Order*, pp. 404-410; for a detailed examination of the *divisio* as applied in an individual case, see Raftis, *The Estates of Ramsey Abbey*, pp. 34-38.

to establish a separate chapel and household, and provide them with equipment suitable to a person of his importance. Thus he found himself in a position very much like that of a bishop: he possessed manors which pertained to his office and from which he drew the income necessary for his needs; surplus income could be accumulated and used to purchase land, precious church ornaments, or other equipment, thus constituting a fortune which was not, strictly speaking, part of the permanent endowment of the office. A third type of property, owned by bishops, was that held in a private capacity. It is not known for certain, but it seems unlikely that abbots of this period were allowed to acquire possessions in this way, by inheritance from their families for instance, and thus establish a patrimony.[82] But even if this third form of property was denied him, the deceased abbot often left an estate that was over and above the strict endowment that came to him on entering office.

During the twelfth and much of the thirteenth centuries, this property seems often to have fallen to the king during vacancies. As late as 1255 a papal letter to the abbot of Westminster admitted that these goods "according to ancient custom, belonged to the royal treasury on the abbot's death." [83]   But the abbots like the bishops tried to maintain control of their acquisitions. As is well known, newly purchased estates were often assigned to the community or to individual obedientiaries.[84] Efforts were made to establish their control of the increment of movable property by means of the will. It will be recalled that a testamentary capacity was recognized in the abbot by Stephen's charter of 1136.[85] Examples of wills, cited above, indicate at least a partially successful exercise of this capacity. But the abbot's right was never established

---

[82] See P. and M., I, 438. The two papal privileges cited below, nn. 83 and 89, seem to refer only to the abbot's property derived from his office: in the first case, Alexander IV speaks of the goods of the monastery which pertain to the abbot; the second case is less clear—"de bonis mobilibus que penes eum tempore obitus sui fuerint," but given the sharply restricted use that was to be made of the property it very likely came from the same source; see Les Registres d'Alexandre IV, ed. Bourel de La Roncière, J. de Loye and A. Coulon, 3 vols., Bibliothèque des Ecoles françaises d'Athènes et de Rome (Paris, 1895-1953), I, 189-190, no. 630, and Les Registres d'Honorius IV, ed. M. Prou, Bibliothèque, etc. (Paris, 1888), p. 434, no. 613; also Bliss, Entries in Papal Registers, I, 320, 489.

[83] "... ad carissimum in Christo filium nostrum ... regem Anglorum illustrem, bona mobilia abbatum regi Anglie decedentium de antiqua et approbata et hactenus pacifice observata consuetudine pervenire noscantur propriis usibus applicanda": Les Registres d'Alexandre IV, I, 189-190, no. 630.

[84] See Raftis, op. cit., ch. 4.

[85] Quoted above, n. 51.

by law. Early in the fourteenth century it is stated that by common
law an abbot may not own property, nor may he make a will. The
same texts add that he may do so if he obtain papal and royal
permission.[86] Thus, during a serious illness of 1251, the abbot of
Westminster obtained permission of the king to devote money to the
payment of his debts, the rewarding of his servants, and for bequests
to relatives and friends.[87] He also obtained the pope's licence for his
action.[88] Somewhat later, a papal indult for the abbot of Bury
St. Edmunds permitted him to bequeath property for the payment of
debt, funeral expenses and the remuneration of servants.[89] It seems best
to conclude, then, that the testamentary capacity of the heads of religious
communities did not become general law, but remained a matter of
privilege.

The Wills of Villeins and Others of Restricted Right

Though a serf of thirteenth-century England would be very surprised
to learn that he had been compared to an abbot, his position with
regard to the making of wills was much the same as that of his more
lordly contemporary. In both cases the exercise of a power of bequest
was a matter of privilege. The basic principle that the unfree peasant
was without proprietary right against his lord was maintained. But in
practice he was very often treated, even by his lord, as though the
chattels he used were his own. It is not surprising, then, that the serf
often sought to control their devolution by will.[90] He was supported
in his intent by the same desires and pressures that defended the
testamentary right of the married woman. Such motives knew no
distinction of free and unfree: the desire to give alms, to acquit special
obligations, and to express affection, found place in the serf as in anyone
else. Ecclesiastical councils and synods of the second half of the
thirteenth century returned again and again to establish his right to

---

[86] *Y. B.*, 32-33 Edward I, ed. Horwood, p. 356; see P. and M., I, 438.

[87] *C. P. R.*, IV, 118, 200.

[88] References as in n. 83, above.

[89] *Les Registres d'Honorius IV*, p. 434, no. 613 (August, 1286); other examples of royal
permission for the wills of abbots: *C. P. R.* (Edward I), II, 222, 389; *C. C. R.* (Edward I),
II, 247, 282. On the attempts made by prioresses of later centuries to exercise this capacity,
see Eileen Power *Medieval English Nunneries* pp. 325 ff.

[90] Clear and brief introductions to the study of the testamentary capacity of the villein
are available in Miss Levett's *Studies in Manorial History*, pp. 208-234, and H. S. Bennett,
Life on the English Manor (Cambridge, 1937), pp. 248-251; also G. C. Homans, *English Villagers
of the Thirteenth Century*, (Cambridge, Mass., 1942), pp. 133-134; P. and M. I, 416-417;
Holdsworth, *History*, III, 541.

make a will.[91]   As in the case of a similar pressure on behalf of the
wife, this effort found final expression in the constitutions of Archbishop
Stratford in 1342 and, like it, was met by a demand in parliament
that such claims be denied.[92]   As far as the establishment of the serf's
right is concerned, the effort was a failure.   But this attempt represents
an important tendency in society and, in part, fostered it.   It is evident,
from a fairly large number of manorial extents of the first half of the
thirteenth century and later, that in many parts of England serfs were
allowed to make wills.[93]   Sometimes permission of the lord had to be
sought; sometimes his representative had to be present; in other cases
there is no sign of such limitations.   Most significant of all, the
peasant's testamentary capacity is often indicated in a quite different
way: it appears not in the form of a privilege, but in the statement of a
penalty exacted from those who fail to make a will.[94]

[91] References to the wills of married women and serfs usually occur together in the
various synodal collections. Bennett has collected most of the relevant texts, *op. cit.*,
pp. 249-250; to these, the following should be added: a statute of Bishop John Gervais of
Winchester (Wilkins, II, 298), a statute of Bishop Peter Quivil of Exeter (*ibid.*, II, 155)
and one of the *gravamina* of 1280 (see above, p. 226). In the last mentioned case the
royal reply maintained the lord's right to impede the peasant's will, but added: "Si tamen
permittat dominus servum suum condere testamentum, valeat et fiat voluntas testatoris, et
tale testamentum post mortem servi non debet aliquatenus impediri" (*Letters from Northern
Registers*, ed. Raine, p. 73).

[92] Wilkins, II, 705; *Rot. Parl.*, II, 149b; the royal answer in on p. 150a.

[93] Testamentary freedom under various conditions on the Ramsey manors of St. Ives,
Warboys, Caldicote and Hemingford, are mentioned in P. and M., I, 417, n. 1; to these
Ringstead and Barton should be added. In *Select Documents of the English Lands
of the Abbey of Bec*, ed. Marjorie Chibnall, Camden Third Series, LXXIII (1951), testamentary
freedom is indicated on more than a score of manors; this applies not only to virgaters,
but also to tenants of but a few acres or a toft (pp. 88, 106-107). These documents
represent practice of not later than 1248; some of them at least reflect custom established
considerably earlier. A composition before William of Blois, bishop of Worcester (1218-36),
presumes that testamentary gifts were made by rustics; see "Compositio inter nos et
sacristam super testamentis," *Registrum prioratus beatae Mariae Wignorniensis*, ed. W. H. Hale,
Camden Society, XCI (1865), p. 26. Other examples are mentioned by Miss Levett and by
Homans in the studies indicated above.

[94] Wills made with permission are mentioned in the *Vale Royal Ledger Book*, p. 119,
cited by Bennett, *op. cit.*, pp. 250-251; the presence of the bailiff was required on the Ramsey
manor of Barton (Ramsey Cart., I, 477). Penalties against the intestate peasant are
indicated at St. Ives (*ibid.*, I, 290-291) and in many of the Bec manors; e.g., at Wantage:
"et si intestatus decesserit omnia catalla sua in voluntate domini remanebunt" (*Select
Documents*, p. 50). It will be noted that the examples cited all occur on ecclesiastical
manors. However the villein's right to make a will on a manor owned by a lay lord is
indicated in the report of a plea before the justices at Westminster in 1287: in the case
between Alex de Skirbeck and the executors of Richard de Loveston, the jury reported that

Finally, there were certain groups in society who could own property and dispose of it by will under normal conditions, but who were partially or completely prevented from doing so because of some special circumstance, misfortune or crime. Thus those who accompanied Richard I on his crusade were allowed free disposal of personal equipment and one half of the other goods in their possession in the Holy Land. Even this disposition was limited in that the property might not be sent home.[95] The insane were not permitted to make wills during the time of their disability.[96] Some were excluded from the exercise of testamentary capacity because of crime:[97] the chattels of the condemned criminal fell to the king.[98] Others, while not condemned during life, did suffer treatment of penal character after death; their bodies were denied Christian burial and their chattels were confiscated by the public authority. To this group belonged the usurer, the suicide and the unconfessed.

The Christian who persisted in the practice of usury until the end of his life, whether he died intestate or not, forfeited his goods to the king.[99] If before death he repented and restored his ill-gotten gains, his will, dealing with remaining chattels, was allowed to stand. Inquiry as to his condition at the time of death was to be made by a jury of twelve men. Such is the law as presented by Glanvill and the *Dialogus de*

Richard, villein of Alex, made a will and appointed executors, who began to administer. They were impleaded by Alex, who asserted that Richard "fuisse villanum suum per quod intellexit quod omnia bona & catalla villani sui fuissent catalla sua propria." The executors caused Alex to be summoned before the official of the bishop of Lincoln. Alex claimed that Richard had once been the bailiff of his wife, before her marriage. He had not acquitted all his debts to her and was told not to make a will until he had done so. But the jury reported that Richard had rendered his account and was not in arrears. Furthermore, he was not forbidden to make a will; in that region it had been and still was customary for villeins to exercise a right of bequest (London, PRO, Just. It. 1/503 m.8).

95 Remaining property was to be received by a committee, headed by the archbishop of Rouen, and devoted to the crusade; *The Chronicle of the Reigns of Henry II and Richard I*, ed. Stubbs, II, 129-130; *Hoveden*, ed. Stubbs, III, 58.

96 Among the London wills calendared by Sharpe, those of Robert Deumars (1291-2) and Richard de Neuwerk (1294-5) were disputed because the testators were *non compos mentis* (I, 103-118). See P. and M., I, 481.

97 See R. Caillemer, *Etudes sur la succession au moyen âge*, II: "Confiscation et administration des successions par les pouvoirs publics au moyen âge."

98 Assize of Clarendon, c. 5 (Stubbs, *Select Charters*, p. 171); cf. P. and M., I, 476-477.

99 See T. P. McLaughlin, "The Teaching of the Canonists on Usury, IV: Punishment of Usurers," *Mediaeval Studies*, II (1940), 5-8; Caillemer, *op. cit.*, pp. 8-12; Hannan, *The Canon Law of Wills*, pp. 160-161. Christian burial is refused the impenitent usurer in II Lateran Council (1139), c. 13, and III Lateran (1179), c. 25 (Mansi, XXI, 529-530 and XXII, 231).

Scaccario.[100]   Glanvill does not mention the devolution of the goods of
the suicide, but in the Norman inquest of 1205 they are said to be
forfeited to the king.[101]   Given the ecclesiastical penalties attached to
the crime, it is likely that such was the arrangement in twelfth-century
England too.   In an exposition of the problem that is largely a paraphrase of a title of the *Digest*, Bracton presents four classes of suicides,
classes which can be reduced to those who are morally responsible for
their act and those who are not.   The chattels of the former group
were forfeited to the king.[102]   The excommunicate and the person who
refused the opportunity for confession at death suffered forfeiture and
denial of Christian burial.[103]   Rules intended to provide a basis for
judging the truly unconfessed are not found in England, but in the
Grand coutumier de Normandie, a period of nine days' illness was
considered necessary before it could be claimed that the deceased had
refused the ministrations of the church and had died *desperatus*.[104]

100 Glanvill, Bk. VII, ch. 16; *Dialogus*, Bk. II, ch. 10, ed. Hughes, *et al.*, pp. 98-99, where
it is suggested by the editors that the making of a will was considered to be evidence of
contrition.   That all goods were forfeited is made clear in the *Très ancien coutumier de
Normandie*, C. XLIX: "uxor enim et eius liberi nichil habebunt de catallis, nec presbyter
similiter" (ed. Tardif, p. 40).   In the inquiry of 1205 it was stated that if the usurer
distributed his goods with his own hand, though already in "lecto egritudinis," the
distribution was valid (Teulet, *Layettes du Trésor des chartes*, I, no. 785).   Inquiry as to
usurers is included in the articles of the eyres of 1194 and 1198 (Hoveden, *Chronica*, ed.
Stubbs, III, 264; IV, 61); cf. Bracton, fol. 117.

   101 *Layettes*, ed. Teulet, I, no. 785; see Caillemer, *op. cit.*, pp. 29-39.

   102 Bracton, fol. 150; *Digest*, 48, 21, 3.   *Fleta* omitted one of the classes mentioned by
Bracton: the person who commits suicide in spite (Bk. I, ch. 34, ed. Richardson and
Sayles, II, 89).   There are references to confiscation of chattels of suicides in the Close
Rolls: e.g., *C.C.R.*, III, 59, 149; also *Bracton's Note Book*, no. 1114.   An interesting case is
presented in the Close Roll of 1235: Adam de Eynesbury wounded himself unto death, but
before dying made a will and, presumably, confessed his fault; the will was allowed to
stand (*C.C.R.*, III, 209-210).

   103 Caillemer, *op. cit.*, pp. 51-53.   Seizure of the chattels of the deceased who had been
publicly excommunicated is mentioned in the Preston custumal (12th century): *B.C.*, II,
76.   Christian burial is denied them in the London Council of 1143 (Wilkins, I, 417-18); on
the date of this council, see H. Böhmer, *Kirche und Staat in England und in der Normandie
im XI und XII Jahrhundert*, p. 346, n. 5.   An interesting account of the funeral of an
excommunicate is described in the *Liber Memorandorum Ecclesie de Bernewell*, ed. Clark,
pp. 175-176: after a long dispute with the prior of Barnwell, Luke of Abingdon, vicar of
Guilden Morden, was excommunicated.   He appealed to the pope but died before the
case could be heard.   The canons of Barnwell claimed that he had died excommunicated
and refused to allow his body to enter the church or to have mass celebrated for his soul.
However, his executors made peace with the canons; his body was 'absolved' and was then
allowed into the church for the burial service.

   104 C. 20.1, ed. Tardif, II, 56.   The inquest of 1205 allowed a period of three or four
days' illness (*Layettes*, ed. Teulet, I, no. 785).

It was to these persons, under the circumstances just described, that testamentary capacity was extended in the twelfth and thirteenth centuries. Within the society of those years, the chief area of dispute concerned the two groups who had virtual ownership of chattels or used them as their own—the married woman and the serf. Powerful pressures sought to give them the right to make wills. The principle of the law was maintained against them; but practice, based on dispensation or custom, was often quite different. Both groups made wills and by these acts exerted a considerable influence on the devolution of wealth in the family and in the village. This exercise of a testamentary capacity played an important part in the centuries-long evolution that would increase the legal and economic rights of both the wife and the villein. For the moment, the law refused to respect their desire for these rights; but the desire itself became firmly established and was eventually to prevail.

To say that other members of society had established their testamentary right is not to imply the end of all concern lest their wills fail. As in Anglo-Saxon England, members of every class sought confirmation for their bequests. The pope's support was promised to the king and to others, clerics and laity, who had the means to obtain it.[105] The royal family, the nobility, bishops and abbots, large numbers of royal servants, sought confirmation from the king, confirmation that in many cases can be shown to have been efficacious.[106] Clergy obtained the support of their bishops;[107] were records available for the lower levels of society, the same preoccupation would almost certainly be seen there as well. Though the serf of certain manors was allowed by local custom to make a will without the permission of his lord or in the absence of the bailiff, even here one suspects that the wise testator would seek such permission, and make his will in the presence of any representative of the lord that was available. The will was well established in England of the late

---

[105] Henry III obtained papal confirmation for his will: see above, p. 144; also Richard of Cornwall (1238): Bliss, *Entries in Papal Registers*, I, 171, 185; Prince Edward sought papal support in T. 72b; other examples are cited above, nn. 68, 83, 89.

[106] Royal servants frequently sought permission to make a will, permission which included the promise that their executors would not be liable to further accounting at the Exchequer; there are scores of examples during the century: e.g., to Godfrey, sheriff of Oxfordshire (1228), to Ralph, son of Nicholas, a royal seneschal (1229), to Walter de Kirkeham, officer of the Wardrobe (1230): *C.P.R.*, II, 201, 250, 342. W. S. McKecknie concluded from these writs giving permission to make wills that subjects could not do so without royal consent; see *Magna Carta*, 2nd ed., p. 324. In this conclusion he failed to distinguish between that which was necessary and that which was merely a precaution.

[107] See above, p. 249.

thirteenth century, and there was a fairly efficient legal machinery to provide external defence of its execution; but men of that age knew that support of a privileged character was well worth having, and they sought it.

II. BENEFICIARIES OF THE WILLS

The medieval English will was an act characterized by religious solicitude. Provisions for the future of the soul, payment of debt, and rectification of the injustices of the past were usually its chief concern.[108] Those whose duty it was to pray, and persons and groups who had claims on the testator, whether in charity or justice, were among the principal beneficiaries.[109]

Usually the first clauses of a written *will* were concerned with the funeral and suffrages for the dead. The church chosen for burial was almost invariably stated. Occasionally, as in the case of Henry III, this choice revoked an earlier one.[110] More wealthy testators sometimes gave directions that their bodies be divided, so that different churches to which they or their families were especially attached might receive their remains.[111] A gift, which varied considerably in value, was almost always given with the body. Directions usually included the payment of an animal, a garment or a sum of money to the parish church as mortuary.[112]

Shortly after the middle of the thirteenth century, a growing interest in the details of the wake, funeral procession, office and burial is discernible. The *will* of Bishop Walter Suffield of Norwich provides an excellent example: one hundred pounds were provided for the

108 See the directions for making a will, printed below, Appendix B, p. 315. In the will of Richard I, as reported in Hoveden, *Chronica* (ed. Stubbs, IV, 83-84), one quarter of his treasure was to be given to servants and to the poor, but the special concern for the future of his soul is lacking.

109 Freedom to receive legacies extended to a much larger area of the population than freedom to make them. Persons or corporations not incapacitated by serious crime were free to receive legacies. In the *Statuta Legenda*, a collection of decrees intended to be read at synods, but of as yet uncertain origin, clerics are forbidden to bequeath property to their concubines (Wilkins, I, 596); on this text, see Cheney, *English Synodalia*, p. 40. The right of individual religious to receive bequests is discussed below, p. 262. For the general law of the Church, see Durantis, *Speculum Iuris*, Bk. II, pt. ii, De instrumentorum editione, 12 (Venice, 1576, p. 680b).

110 T. 53b. On opposition to the revocation of the choice of place of burial see above, pp. 141-142.

111 Richard I commanded that his entrails be buried at Charrou, his heart at Rouen and his body at Fontevraud (Hoveden, *Chronica*, ed. Stubbs, IV, 84); see T. 68, T. 96.

112 See pp. 298-300.

expenses of the funeral; as the body was brought from the place of death, wherever it might be, there was to be a distribution of money to the poor of the area through which it passed; a silver penny was to be given to each person who kept vigil.[113] The *will* includes the prudent reminder that no one should be paid twice. Other *wills* direct that food, cloth, shoes and other goods be purchased and given to the poor.[114] One gracious testator provided for the expenses of friends who came to his funeral.[115]

The choice of place of burial was usually related to the provision of suffrages for the soul. More wealthy members of society sought fraternity in some religious house that they might share in its spiritual benefits both in life and death. Occasionally they came to the community of their choice to die; at any rate they were buried there, and the community was expected to pray for their souls. Arrangements of this sort usually lie behind the *post obit* gifts of land that are found in the century after the Conquest.[116] In addition to their provision for mass and prayers on the day of the funeral, the authors of some of the written *wills* arranged for special prayers during periods of varied length, and for the commemoration of anniversaries.[117] A few established chantries for the permanent remembrance of themselves and their families.[118] Actually, the testators of the thirteenth century did not usually make detailed arrangements for suffrages. In the following century, very complex provisions of this sort would be of frequent occurrence; in the earlier period of interest here, they are to be found occasionally,[119] but the general impression is quite different. Testators seem to have considered the very generous gifts in alms to the poor and to large numbers of churches and religious houses to have been sufficient. Where provision of masses and prayers was mentioned, it was often left to the executors to make arrangements with those who were to say them.[120]

The acquittal of obligations of all kinds was quite obviously one of the chief concerns of testators. Both Glanvill and Bracton implied

---

[113] T. 56; also T. 68, T. 71a, etc.

[114] E.g., T. 59b, T. 68, T. 83, T. 98, etc.

[115] "Item ad expensas amicorum meorum ad exequias meas venientium" (T. 73).

[116] See above, pp. 111-113.

[117] E.g., T. 59b assigned 40 marks to ten chaplains for a year; T. 56 assigned 100 marks to twenty-five chaplains to offer mass for a year.

[118] A chantry of one priest was established by T. 47a, another of two priests by T. 96.

[119] E.g., T. 59b, an unusually detailed *will*, goes so far as to determine the collects to be recited by chaplains who were to pray for the deceased for one year.

[120] E.g., T. 67a.

that distribution might be made only of property free from the claims of creditors.[121]   Commands that debts be paid are often found among the first clauses of *wills*.[122]   Sometimes it is stated that debts must be met before the distribution of legacies;[123] in fact, one of the ways of emphasizing the importance of a bequest in the eyes of the testator was to ask that it be paid with the debts.[124]   Simon de Montfort instructed his executors to pay anyone able to prove his claim by document or witness, and requested that they be not too exacting in their demands of proof.[125]   Very often an attempt was made to make restitution.   The return of unjustly acquired land to its original holder was a not uncommon type of death-bed gift in the eleventh and twelfth centuries.[126]   King John made a general request that grants be made to the churches that he had harmed. William Longespee, earl of Salisbury, provided for the return of prizes unjustly taken in war,[127] and Hugh of Wells asked that part of the residue of his goods be given to tenants with whom he had dealt harshly.[128]   Occasionally an effort was made to repair the damages of a past generation by restoring property or goods seized by an ancestor.[129]   As death approached, those who had vowed to go on pilgrimage or crusade, realizing that their promise was no

---

121 Glanvill, Bk. II, ch. 5; Bracton, fol. 60b. Concern with the acquittal of the debts of the deceased appears in the *Leges Henrici Primi* (75. ii, *Gesetze*, I, 593) and, as will be recalled, it was one of the preoccupations of the canonists in their development of the canon law of the testament. This attitude is evident in the prologue to the constitution of Thurstan, archbishop of York, which allowed the income of a canon for the year following his death to be devoted to the payment of debts, etc.: "Solet plerumque contingere, quod clerici sicut et caeteri homines pro aliqua necessitate vel humana fragilitate, aliquibus debitis et delictis obligati de mundo transeant" (Wilkins, I, 412).

122 Thus T. 12 begins with the statement that debts to the king and pope are to be paid. Some *wills*, as the one just mentioned, merely indicate a general obligation to pay debts: e.g., T. 25, T. 33, T. 59a, etc.; other *wills*, especially those of less important persons, include a list of creditors and the amount owed them: e.g., T. 31.

123 Money was borrowed with the condition that, if the debtor died before repayment, the first claim met by his estate would be that of the creditor. Royal letters sometimes confirmed these arrangements: e.g., *C. P. R.*, III, 56, to the creditors of Eleanor, duchess of Pembroke (1234); cf. also *C.P.R.*, III, 279, 425, 447; IV, 181, etc.

124 Bishop Richard Wych of Chichester ended the list of bequests to his servants with the remark: "que debitis equipono et ascribo" (T. 53a).

125 T. 59a.

126 See above, p. 116.

127 T. 25. The suggestion that William Marshal return the booty of his many victories was refused.

128 T. 33; a similar sensitivity is to be seen in the *will* of Simon de Montfort (T. 59a).

129 E.g., T. 30.

longer possible of personal fulfilment, provided by their wills that another might go in their place.[130]   In these and in many other ways testators tried to pay all their debts to men and to God.   Not a few of them were quite willing to make payments and restitution which never would have been demanded of them by the common law.[131]

Cathedral and parish churches and religious houses were among the chief beneficiaries of wills. Bequests very often reflect building programs of the age.[132]   While an individual church or monastery was usually preferred before all others, it is remarkable how frequently testators chose to make many small bequests to different institutions. Legacies might be given to each church in a city or diocese.   Henry II remembered every monastery in England.[133]   In 1223 a married woman of Canterbury, in addition to a bequest of land to the Priory of the Blessed Trinity, made small donations to fourteen other churches and religious houses, and an offering of one shilling to each parish church of the city.[134]   There is no example of a massive bequest to a single monastery or church such as was occasionally found among the Anglo-Saxons.   The friars appear as legatees within a decade of their arrival in the country.   In many wills, a quite marked effort to be equally generous to Franciscans and Dominicans is discernible.[135]   Bequests to the Carmelites and the Austin Hermits appear less often and were usually somewhat smaller than those to the older communities of friars.[136]   As a general rule, bequests were made to a religious community or to its superior.   Mention of an individual male religious is rare,[137] but bequests to particular nuns are quite common.[138]   As the

---

[130] E.g., T. 30, T. 31, T. 53b.

[131] As in the *will* of Simon de Montfort (T. 59a).

[132] In his *will* of 1233, Hugh of Wells, bishop of Lincoln, left 100 marks and timber to the fabric of the cathedral.   Agnes de Condet left small sums to six churches for the same purpose (T. 23).

[133] See above, p. 143.

[134] T. 23.

[135] E.g., T. 31, T. 56, T. 91.

[136] E.g., T. 73.

[137] T. 83: bequest of half a mark is made to the Friars Minor of Lincoln, but in such a way that "it may be at the disposition of Friar Geoffrey Sampson;" in T. 82a the testatrix bequeathed 20 shillings to provide books for her son, a friar; she also left half a mark "ad pietanciam confratrum filii mei quacunque domo commoretur pro tempore mortis mee," an attempt to benefit the religious house in which her son happened to dwell at the time of her death.   With the coming of the friars and the greater mobility of religious that followed on their conception of religious life, direct bequest to a given house was not sufficient to ensure that a particular religious would benefit from the donation.

[138] E.g., T. 82a, T. 90, T. 92; in the last example cited, Philip le Tailor of London left

strict monastic view of communal property was weakened by the peculium and the giving of money pittances, bequests of this kind came into the possession of the legatee.   In the case of nuns at least, the capacity to receive bequests for the support of the individual religious was established by the second half of the thirteenth century.[139]   Many of the written *wills* include legacies to the recluse or the hermit.   Some testators knew these solitaries by name and, enumerating them one by one as they sometimes did, show that this must have been a fairly numerous group in thirteenth-century England.[140]

Bequests in alms of more directly social consequence were very numerous.   The hospital, the leper-house, and the orphanage find frequent mention in the *wills*.   Linked with them in a manner that is somewhat surprising to the modern reader are bequests for the building and repair of bridges and roads.[141]   The crusade and the needs of the Holy Land were not forgotten.[142]   Occasional bequests were left to religious foundations on the Continent.[143]

Legacies for pious purposes took many other forms as well.   A fairly common bequest, that sometimes at least was looked upon as an alms, was the donation of money to provide a dowry that young women might marry.   Henry II left five hundred marks of gold for the marriage of poor freewomen of England, Normandy and Anjou.[144]   Usually however, the bequest was specific: a father provided a dowry for his daughters, a wealthy member of a family arranged for the marriage of less fortunate nieces or cousins.[145]   The dowry for women wishing to become nuns

---

a rent of 55s. 4d. for the clothing of his three daughters, nuns at Clerkenwell. As the sisters died, the income was to pass to the survivors. If the last of the three died a religious, the rent remained with the community. Other examples in Sharpe, I, 145, 148, 324; see Eileen Power, *Medieval English Nunneries*, pp. 18, 325.

139 Knowles, *The Religious Orders*, I, 287-288; Power, *op. cit.*, pp. 316-340.

140 Five recluses are mentioned in T. 53a, six in T. 59b and nine in T. 71a; also in T. 23, T. 31.

141 E.g., T. 31, T. 53a, T. 56, etc.; see Sharpe, II, xvi-xx; on the inclusion of "public works" among the *piae causae*, see Lyndwood, p. 180, *gl. ad verb.* Pias causas.

142 E.g., T. 16, T. 68, T. 90, *Bracton's Note Book*, no. 1441 (1220). Bishop Peter of Hereford bequeathed a debt of forty marks, owed him by the archbishop-elect of Lyons, to the Pope, who was to collect the sum and devote it to the needs of the Holy Land (T. 68).

143 The *will* of Bishop Peter (mentioned in the previous note) includes several bequests to churches in the Savoie, the land of his birth. Bequests of this sort by an Englishman are found in T. 56.

144 See above, p. 143; another example: "Item tribus puellis maritandis triginta solidos" (T. 23).

145 T. 12, T. 53a, T. 59b.

was sometimes provided by will.[146]   A donation for the clothing of a monk might also find a place there.[147]   Bequests for the support of scholars frequently appear in the *wills* of the clergy.[148]   Debts, especially those of servants and the poor, were often remitted.[149]   Hugh of Wells asked that part of the residue of his goods be given in alms to converted Jews.[150]

Thus the concern for the future of the soul, so typical of the medieval will, decided the beneficiaries of many of the bequests.   Justice and charity expressed themselves in the choice of legatees of bewildering variety.   Of these, at least the more common types have been described. But there were other motives for the making of wills, and they find expression in a quite different choice of beneficiary.

There was, first of all, the desire to arrange the succession to chattels among the members of a family.   With regard to testators who made bequests to their children a distinction must be made.   As will be seen below, it was the custom throughout most of England to reserve one third of a man's chattels to his children and one third to his wife.[151] On the other hand, the widow and the married woman permitted to make a will were free to distribute all their chattels.   Thus children sometimes receive quite insignificant bequests in the wills of their fathers, since it was understood that a third of the estate was reserved to them.[152]   On the other hand, bequests made to their children by mothers, tended to be on a larger scale.[153]   In the wills of the well-to-do, children were often mentioned only as the legatees of some chattel of special value— military equipment, a jewel, a ring.[154]   Particular need or particular

---

[146] E.g., T. 69; See Power *Medieval English Nunneries*, p. 18.

[147] T. 59b: "Item Henrico dicto filio Fratris mei, si velit monachari in Ordine Cysterciensi, detur ei vestura ad valenciam xx solidorum: alioquin nichil habeat."

[148] T. 33, T. 47a, T. 56, T. 96. In a will of 1275, Walter de Merton, bishop of Rochester, left 1000 marks to purchase a perpetual endowment for his college at Oxford.   In a codicil of two years later, the residue of his estate was left to the college (Oxford, Merton College Charter 4234a).

[149] Remission of debts of servants: T. 59a; of the poor: T. 56.

[150] T. 33.

[151] See pp. 288-294.

[152] Mention of the children's portion was sometimes made in the *will* itself, e.g., T. 90. Children receive small bequests or none at all in T. 23, T. 30, etc.   On the other hand, some *wills* dealt with the testator's whole estate; thus in T. 60, there is provision of dower for daughters, bequests of tenements to the heir, etc.; also T. 71a.

[153] E.g., T. 82c, T. 83.

[154] T. 23: mother, sons and daughters of the testatrix received rings; one daughter was bequeathed 20 marks (see the following note).   In T. 30, daughters were given their father's emeralds.

affection is sometimes indicated by a gift of money to only one of many children.[155]   Since succession to at least a portion of the tenements held by a burgess was not controlled by custom, property of this sort was distributed to children in detail.[156] A special concern to provide suitable housing for unmarried daughters and widows is often discernible.   An excellent example is to be found in a London *will* of 1294 where the testator's residence was bequeathed to the widow, with reservation of a cellar and two solars to a daughter.[157]

The wife's dower and the reservation to her of a portion of her husband's chattels provided adequately for her support.   Some of the *wills* mention this fact, but there is often some special bequest to her as well.[158]   Though bastard children had no rights by custom, provision could be made for them by a parent in his will [159]

Freedom to bequeath property must have been especially appreciated by those numerous testators who wished to make a gift to relatives who would not have benefited from a customary distribution of goods.   Thus one finds many bequests to brothers and sisters and especially to nieces and nephews.[160]   It was to the latter, the younger members of their family, that the clergy often gave bequests.[161]   The wills of clerics of this period do not give the impression that family affection blinded them to the needs of others who had claims upon them; within the family itself, the poorer members were often remembered in a special way.[162]

Wills of the clergy are also remarkable for the number and value of bequests made to members of their households.   They are not alone in this, for generous bequests to servants characterize wills of many of the laity as well.

Such were the beneficiaries of these wills.   They ranged from the king to some choir boy whose name a bishop could no longer remember,

155 "Item Basile filie mee consulende viginti marcas" (T. 23).

156 E.g., T. 60.

157 T. 94; also T. 71b. Cf. H. S. Cowper, "Provision for Widows in Kentish Wills," *Archaeologia Cantiana*, XXX (1887), 127-131.

158 The wife's share is mentioned in T. 90.

159 E.g., about 1180, Amalric son of Ralph left ten marks to his illegitimate children (Br. Mus. Egerton MS. 3031, fol. 38); the will of Walter de Schenfeld (1349), calendared by Sharpe (I, 556), bequeathed chattels to an illegitimate son and his mother.

160 Several *wills* include bequests to the mother of the testator: T. 23, T. 31.

161 E.g., T. 59b.

162 The distribution to the poor of the family was often entrusted to one of its members as in T. 59b: "Item lego pauperibus parentibus meis et cognatis de Tottenes, Derthemuth, et parochia de Wreixham, viginti libras, distribuendas inter ea per manum Agathæ sororis meæ vel sui assignati;" see *Provinciale*, p. 180, *gl. ad verb.* consanguineis.

and they were very numerous. From many points of view, the most remarkable quality of these distributions of property was the large number of persons who benefited from them. The will of a Kentish woman of 1223 left about eighty pounds to be distributed among at least fifty-five persons and institutions, and there were, in addition, eleven bequests of chattels. In the mid-years of the century Master Martin of Sherbourne Hospital, who must have been a very meticulous cleric, left about 250 pounds to nearly one hundred persons and institutions, and arranged for the distribution of chattels to forty legatees as well.[163] Many other instances of this tendency could be given.[164] The fact is of interest, not only because it shows that very large numbers of persons benefited from the fully developed will, but also because it indicates a pronounced tendency to disperse capital. Many testators did not have the funds required by their bequests and ordered that stock and other chattels, land and houses be sold to obtain them.[165]

III.   PROPERTY DISTRIBUTED BY WILL

It now remains to consider the wills from the point of view of the property with which they dealt. The testator's capacity to control the future enjoyment of his estate was limited from a material point of view in several ways: certain forms of wealth were freely distributed; others were not. Investigation of this matter is simplified by a separate consideration of each of the two chief classes of property, land and movable wealth. The distinction is not a merely speculative one invented for the convenience of the student. It has been seen above that the almost complete practical separation of the two forms of wealth was accomplished by the end of the thirteenth century.[166] This division

---

[163] T. 59b.

[164] The *will* of William de Longespee, earl of Salisbury (T. 25), is a rare example of a magnate's will where bequests are made for the most part in farm stock. These animals included 2700 sheep, 106 oxen, 34 horses, 125 cows, 100 swine and 30 she-goats. They were distributed among nineteen religious houses. The bequest to the Carthusian house Locus Dei was large, including 1300 sheep and 48 oxen; but the other bequests were rather small. The same tendency to disperse a fortune, in this case a small one, is seen in T. 83. The inventory of goods is still extant: they were valued at 22 pounds, 5s. 9 d. There were at least twenty bequests of money and thirty in goods. The latter included 120 sheep distributed among at least twenty persons.

[165] See above, pp. 215-216. In 1234, the wife of Richard de Daggerwurth purchased grain and stock from her husband's executors. (*C. C. R.*, III, 12).

[166] Pp. 137, 287. See F. Joüon des Longrais, *La conception anglaise de la saisine* (Paris, 1925), pp. 155-166.

was already a very ancient one by that time: it can be found among the Anglo-Saxons, received a remarkably clear statement in the charter of Henry I, and was often exhibited in practice by the different procedures of recovery in use in England both before and after the Conquest. The distinction is borne out in the case of the will: land tended to be most resistant to alienation and distribution in this way; movable goods and rights proved to be much more amenable to the testator's control.

The Distribution of Land by Will

A balanced statement of the extent to which property owners of the twelfth and thirteenth centuries could dispose of their land by will is rendered quite difficult to the modern student by the many conflicting opinions on the matter that have been advanced by historians for a very long time. Scholars of the seventeenth and eighteenth centuries, possessed as they were of tidy and not entirely disinterested views of the state of England before the Conquest and after, usually presented a picture of considerable freedom of devise of land among the Anglo-Saxons. For them, the almost complete disappearance of this right was but one of the unhappy consequences of the Norman invasion. It was known that land held in burgage tenure was often devisable; but this practice was easily explained as an Anglo-Saxon survival.[167]

The facts of history, however, refuse to be amenable to such logical arrangement. It has become apparent that in Normandy itself the prohibition of the devise of land was not general until the end of the Middle Ages, and that during the late twelfth and thirteenth centuries the movement was rather to establish the free disposal of at least part of a testator's land.[168] Thus the hypothetical Norman custom, which according to the older theory produced such a fundamental change, would seem to have disappeared very quickly in the area from which it came. It has been shown above that on the eve of the Conquest the bequest of land was, in fact, far from being unknown in Normandy.[169] Furthermore, historians of the last sixty years have tended to restrict the importance of the bequest of land among the Anglo-Saxons. They

[167] See P. and M., I, 328 ff; "The Norman Conquest and Doctor Brady," in D. C. Douglas, *English Scholars* (London, 1943), pp. 148-174. In "Theory of Post-Mortem Disposition: Rise of the English Will," *Harvard Law Review*, XI (1897-8), 148-174, M. M. Bigelow held for general freedom of devise among the Anglo-Saxons. Other examples of this opinion are cited in J. H. Stephen, *New Commentaries on the Laws of England*, 12th ed., 4 vols. (London, 1895), I, 545 ff.

[168] Cf. R. Génestal, "L'interdiction du legs d'immeuble" (Semaine de droit normand, XIV), *Rev. hist. de droit français et étranger*, 4ᵐᵉ série, VII (1928), 683-684.

[169] Pp. 108-109.

admit that it was known; but such freedom was never a general custom. Written *wills* reveal an obvious fear lest the bequest of land be prevented, and seek the aid of the powerful to ensure its success.[170]

This more careful study of the evidence has corrected a serious historical error. It is perhaps true, however, that the denial of a general power of bequest of land among the Anglo-Saxons has tended to hide the rather large number of cases where, by one means or another, such a power was exercised. It should not be forgotten that charters, witness to sale of land or to donation completed *inter vivos*, often show the same fear lest the transaction fail to be effective, and seek the same protections that are to be found in the written *wills* of the age.[171] Furthermore, though the obtaining of assistance, royal or otherwise, was deemed advisable, it is especially important to remember that it was forthcoming, and that most land was held by the very persons able to obtain such support. The fact that a legal instrument had not reached the stage of general acceptance and required external aids to ensure its effectiveness need not mean that it was incapable of producing important economic and social results. The bequest of land was not a general custom in Anglo-Saxon England, but members of the upper classes had considerable experience in its use by the time of the Norman invasion.

The situation in England, then, was much the same as that in Normandy. It might have been expected that the evolution of the attitude to the devise of land would have been the same on both sides of the Channel. Such was not the case, for by the end of the twelfth century even the limited possibilities of devise known to the Anglo-Saxons had largely disappeared in England. The condition of the country during the first generation after the Conquest contributed in part to this change.[172] The Norman upper class, which knew the devise of land and which to a large extent replaced that part of the Anglo-Saxon population that was acquainted with its use, found that its position in the new country was most precarious. There was first of all the general uncertainty: the internal situation and external threats were such that for many years there was a strong possibility that the invasion would fail. The situation of the individual was also insecure: fiefs assigned by the Conqueror were sometimes taken back or re-

[170] P. and M., II, 320; Plucknett, *History*, 735, etc.

[171] E.g., R. VIII, XXI.

[172] D. C. Douglas, *Feudal Documents of the Abbey of Bury St. Edmunds*, British Academy, Records of Social and Economic History, VIII (London, 1932), cii-cv, and "The Norman Conquest and English Feudalism," *Economic History Review*, 2nd ser., IX (1957), 128; Plucknett, *History*, pp. 735-736.

arranged, and it was not for some years that tenure with right of inheritance was established. The provision of military strength and the establishment of the feudal structure on which it was based were the chief preoccupations of those years; in such a situation the partition of a fief by devise was not desirable. It is an error to say that the imposition of the feudal system destroyed all devise of land at a blow; in an earlier chapter it was shown that bequests of land were made and that permission of the king and other lords could be had for such action.[173] Nevertheless, feudal requirements of that first generation certainly militated against it. Thus, though the distribution of chattels by will was presented as the normal practice in the charter of Henry I, there was no mention of the bequest of land. Heirs were merely assured that they would inherit on the payment of a reasonable relief.[174] Of the devise of non-military tenements there is scarcely a word. In East Anglia and the Danelaw it is at least conceivable that attempts might occasionally have been made by non- military tenants and members of the free peasantry, but both desire and possibility of fulfilment must surely have been exceedingly rare among this part of the population.[175] The clauses of the charter of Henry I just mentioned, though not of direct application to them, can be taken as an accurate description of the extent of their testamentary capacity.

But with Henry I came peace and the stabilization of family holdings. Under these circumstances how would custom develop with regard to the bequest of land ? In the boroughs, freedom in this regard was to increase. Elsewhere, bequests by *post obit* gift and death-bed gift were far from being unknown.[176] There was a fairly widespread opinion that land of acquisition might be more freely alienated than inherited land.[177] This notion provided the first step in the developing freedom

---

173 See above, p. 113. On feudalism and the bequest of land, see P. and M., II, 326.

174 Chs. 7 and 3; *Gesetze*, I, 532-533.

175 Plucknett, *History*, p. 736. A rare example of a *post obit* gift of a non-military tenement is published by D. C. Douglas, *The Social Structure of Mediaeval East Anglia*, Oxford Studies in Social and Economic History, IX (1927), p. 244. The land had been bequeathed to the same legatee late in the Anglo-Saxon period (cf. W. XXXIII, XXXIV and *DdB*, II, 204b), but seems to have been obtained by the new donor before the will was executed.

176 See above, pp. 110 ff.

177 Two clauses of the *Leges Henrici* deal with the alienation of land. The first, c. 70.21, a combination of the laws of Alfred and notions and phrases of a much later date, forbids the alienation of inherited land and reserves the chief holding to the eldest son (cf. c. 88. 14a), but allows the alienation of acquisitions. William the Conqueror assigned England, an acquisition, to his second son. Similar arrangements were made by several of his vassals who held estates on both sides of the channel; see P. and M., II, 267. In 1177 the widow

of devise in the boroughs. Thus it is obvious that several forces were at work which might have led to a general increase of the bequest of land. Yet by the end of the twelfth century the common law had condemned it.

To understand the reasons for this condemnation, it is necessary to see it in relation to several developments touching the freedom and technique of alienation of land that occurred at this time. The first was a partial removal of restraints of alienation.[178] This change was connected with the establishment of inheritance by primogeniture in military tenures and the spread of the practice to most freeholds.[179] With it came the need to distribute property during the lifetime of a parent so that adequate provision might be made for younger children. Prior to this period, limitation of alienation had been applied on behalf of both the lord and the heir. As was seen in an earlier chapter, their permission was usually obtained before an attempt was made to bequeath land during the first century after the Conquest. The lord's power to prevent alienation seems to have been the first to weaken. There is no explicit statement of his right until the third issue of Magna Carta (1217), where it is declared that the tenant must retain enough land to be able to acquit his obligations as vassal.[180] It is difficult to speak of the previous century with certainty. Glanvill does not speak of feudal limitations to alienation. In spite of mention in charters of the lord's permission for the sale or gift of land, it seems correct to conclude, as Maitland did, that it was difficult for him to prevent reasonable alienation.[181] Charters of the twelfth century leave the impression that the restraint in favour of the heir was more effective, but that the

---

of Hugh Bigot proceeded against Hugh's heir, born of an earlier marriage, to defend the right of her son: "quod comes Hugo Bigot divisit filio suo quem de ea genuit, omnes emptiones et perquisitiones suos" (*Gesta Regis Henrici Secundi,* ed. Stubbs, I, 143). In the boroughs, land of acquisition was the first to be bequeathed. The second clause (c. 88, 15) provides for the institution of an heir where the land owner had no near relatives and wished to pass his inheritance on to someone who had assisted him; e.g., Ralph, son of Ralph de Gael, earl of Norfolk, is said to have been adopted by his uncle, William de Breteuil, who had no legitimate children; see William of Jumièges, *Gesta Normannorum Ducum,* Bk. VIII, ch. 15, ed. J. Marx, Soc. Hist. Norm. (Rouen, 1914), p. 290.

[178] On feudal limitation of alienation, see P. and M., I, 329-349, and Plucknett, *History,* pp. 539-543; on family limitation, see P. and M., II, 308-313, and Plucknett, pp. 526-530. Neither *retrait féodal* nor *retrait lignager* found a place in English common law.

[179] The gavelkind lands of Kent resisted this development; see T. Robinson, *The Common Law of Kent, or Customs of Gavelkind* (London, 1741), pp. 44 ff. On primogeniture, see P. and M., II, 262-278; Plucknett, *History,* pp. 527-529.

[180] C. 39; Stubbs, *Select Charters,* p. 343.

[181] P. and M., I, 343-344.

general tendency was to weaken it as well. By Glanvill's time a
landowner was permitted to alienate much of his inherited property by
gifts *inter vivos,* even against the wish of his heir.[182]   In the disposition
of acquired land, his freedom was still greater.   By the early years of the
thirteenth century, even the limitations in favour of the heir mentioned
by Glanvill had disappeared.[183]   Thus common law had given the
English landowner a power of alienation by act *inter vivos* more complete
than would be known in other Plantagenet territories for centuries.
Given this quite unusual degree of freedom, one looks for some
reflection of it in an increased right of bequest—whether the heir's hopes
were ruined one year before his father's death or on that very day would
seem to make very little difference.   But one looks in vain, for the time
of donation was allowed to make all the difference.

   This brings us to the second development of these same years.   It
was of fundamental importance, and was concerned not with restraints
of alienation, but with the technique whereby ownership was transferred.   During the reign of Henry II older customary procedures for
the conveyance of land were rejected, to be replaced by a drastically
simple and rigorously applied system.   The essential quality was an
actual transfer of seisin; without it, no matter what the intention of the
donor may have been, the donation could be recovered by the heir.[184]

   The reason for the condemnation of the devise of land by common
law is often presented as an effort to limit the effects of "ecclesiastical
greed and the other-worldliness of dying men," reinforced by the
procedural requirements for the transfer of property.   It is the author's
opinion that the basic though not the exclusive reason for this condemnation was the procedural one.   The emphasis on the limitation of
ecclesiastical greed is largely based on a text from Glanvill.   Discussing
family restraints on the alienation of land, Glanvill says that any
reasonable gift, made in the lifetime of the donor and completed by
transfer of seisin, is valid.   He then goes on to say that a person is not
allowed the same freedom on his death-bed, lest a too great concern for
the next world blind the dying man to the needs of those who come

182 Glanvill, Bk. VII, ch. 1.
183 On the later development of freedom of alienation, see P. and M., II, 311-313;
Plucknett, *History,* pp. 528-530.
184 Glanvill, Bk. VII, ch. 1: "Si vero donationem talem nulla fuerit saisina secuta, nihil
post mortem donatoris ex tali donatione contra voluntatem heredis efficaciter peti potest,
quia id intelligitur secundum consuetam regni interpretationem, potius esse nuda promissio
quam vera donatio" (ed. Woodbine, p. 97); cf. P. and M., II, 328-329, and F.M. Stenton,
Transcripts of Charters relating to Gilbertine Houses, pp. xvi-xvii.

after him. The general meaning of the text is obvious: the death-bed gift of land is effective only if confirmed by the heir. But the sentence in which the motive for the condemnation of the devise of land is stated is not clear. Unfortunately historians have tended to concentrate on establishing its meaning, rather than on examining it to see whether it is true or not. The sentence is as follows :

> "It is, moreover, generally lawful for a man to give during his lifetime a reasonable part of his land to whomsoever he will according to his fancy, *in extremis tamen agenti non est hoc cuiquam hactenus permissum,* for the donor might then (if such gifts were allowed) make an improvident distribution of his patrimony as a result of a sudden passion or failing reason, as frequently happens..." [185]

Much attention has been given to the meaning of the word *hactenus* in the section of the text which has been reproduced in the original Latin. Maitland, and others after him have translated the clause as follows: "but hitherto this has not been allowed to anyone who is at death's door." [186] In this translation they understand "hitherto" to mean that the doctrine described was not yet fully established, rather than the more obvious meaning that an established practice was being called into question.[187] Maitland found support for his opinion in an account of a dispute between the Abbey of Walden and Geoffrey Fitz Peter, during the reign of King Richard.[188] William de Mandeville had given an estate to the abbey shortly before his death, and Geoffrey, who was his successor eventually, opposed the donation. According to the monastic historian, the lawyers refused to allow the grant, citing some new rule against the donation of land by death-bed gift. Maitland's opinion that the prohibition was recent seems to be correct. The other translation implies an increased pressure to allow the bequest of land, a pressure that might eventually force concessions. From what we know of the growing power of alienation at that time, the implication is quite justified. Yet another meaning has been given the word *hactenus* by Professor Plucknett in his *Concise History of the Common Law.*[189] There it is understood to signify that the donor may alienate

---

[185] Bk. VII, ch. 1 (ed. Woodbine, p. 97).

[186] P. and M., II, 328, n. 2; this translation has been accepted in *Lincoln Wills,* ed. Foster, II, xix; *The Great Red Book of Bristol,* ed. Veale, I, xx.

[187] "The language suggests that the rule may possibly be altered in the near future:" E. Jenks, *A Short History of English Law,* 4th ed. (London, 1928), p. 38, n. 4.

[188] P. and M., II, 327; Dugdale, *Monasticon,* IV, 144-149. In the light of this account, the suggestion that Geoffrey Fitz Peter is the author of Glanvill takes on additional interest.

[189] P. 526; a similar understanding of the word is found in the translation by J. Beames, pp. 114-115.

land during life, but his freedom does not extend *that far* on his death-bed.   The term is understood in a moral, rather than a temporal sense. This translation is preferable.   It is grammatically correct and serves to divert attention from a question which has assumed undue important-tance, namely, whether the opposition to the death-bed gift of land, described by Glanvill, were recent or not.

The more basic problem is the reason for this opposition.   Glanvill has been understood to say that its chief purpose was the limitation of ecclesiastical cupidity.   The true location of the problem might be made clearer by posing a question.   If a dying man bequeathed land and made a complete conveyance of it, including a delivery of real seisin, would the bequest stand ?   Before answering it must be admitted that Glanvill expressed a strong dislike of donations of land made during mortal illness.   But the moment at which an illness becomes mortal is very hard to define.   When the question is related to the whole paragraph in which Glanvill deals with this matter, it seems necessary to answer it in the affirmative.   If the donor were in his right mind and succeeded in making a perfect conveyance, the act was valid. If either quality were lacking, the act was not valid.   But the same was true of any donation of land whether made on the death-bed or not.   There is ample proof that during the thirteenth century gifts of land were made during a last illness and they were upheld by the royal courts, if there were evidence that the donor was in control of his powers, and that the donee was in seisin when death occurred.[190]   These donations, though made during a mortal illness, were successful because they were acts completed *inter vivos*.   The acts condemned by Glanvill did not complete the conveyance of land.   The donor died in seisin and therefore, by the Assize of Northampton (1176), the heir inherited.[191] In the face of the new requirements for conveyance developed by the royal courts, the old death-bed gift proved wanting.   Glanvill disliked it because of the danger of abuse, but on his own principles he had to condemn it for a procedural reason.   It is not correct to say that he

[190] See Bracton, fols. 27b-28, 40, 373; in the *Note Book* donations of property during last illness were disallowed, because seisin did not follow or because the dying man was not *sui compos*, in nos. 104, 109, 144, 1221, 1818 (donation made eight days before death, but no taking of esplees), 1850.   In no. 1865 the donation is allowed to stand since the donee had seisin; similarly in an inquest reported in *C. C. R.*, III, 324 (1236) whether Peter of Meulent "legavit abbatisse de Tarrant Crawford cum corpore suo quandam terram."   Seisin before death was proved and the gift allowed.

[191] "Item si quis obierit francus-tenens, haeredes ipsius remaneant in tali saisina qualem pater suus habuit die qua fuit vivus et mortuus, de feodo suo ..." (c. 4, Stubbs, *Charters*, p. 179).

opposed the bequest of land as such.[192] To the *post obit* gift he made no
objection. As for the canonical will, he may have failed to understand
its distinction from the death-bed gift: in his general treatment of the
distribution of land at death, he was content to refer to the earlier
prohibition of the devise of inheritance.[193]

The understanding of the decision of the common law to disallow the
will of land is made easier by distinguishing the testator's purpose from
the means he chose to achieve it. He wanted to enjoy his estates until
death and then have them, or part of them, pass to someone other than
the heir. By the end of the twelfth century this purpose could be
achieved by three different legal acts: the death-bed gift, the *post obit*
gift and the canonical will. The first was rejected by Glanvill for the
reasons already mentioned. In his time or soon afterwards, common
law came to a decision about the other two. In the English form of
the *post obit* gift there was some uncertainty as to the rights of donor and
donee in the property. As the donor usually died in seisin, his heir had
the right to succeed, so the act proved ineffective because of the rules of
conveyance. But there was another form of this gift involving a double
act, enfeoffment of the donee followed by recovery with life interest by
the donor. Economically it produced the same effect. Adjusted to
the demands of common law in this way, the *post obit* gift continued to
be used well into the fourteenth century. To it there was no objection,
though it accomplished what was very much like a bequest of land.
The third form of act at the disposition of the testator was the canonical
will, and it was theoretically committed to the suspension of all effect
until the death of the donor. Thus it was essentially opposed to the
notions that governed the conveyance of land in the common law. It
was to become the favourite instrument for the distribution of movable
property at death, but in the areas of England under common law it
could not control the devolution of land and be itself.

The key to the attitude of the royal courts to the will of land is to be
found in the requirements of conveyance. There were other reasons
too: the danger of abuse in an act made at the point of death; the desire
to limit the acquisition of land in mortmain; the protection of the
rights of the heir and the lord. But in the early thirteenth century,

[192] Maitland's failure to distinguish between the *post obit* gift and the death-bed gift, in
his treatment of Glanvill, causes some confusion (P. and M., II, 327). This fact has been
noted by Plucknett in the third (1940, p. 660) and subsequent editions of his *Concise History
of the Common Law*.

[193] Bk. VII, ch. 5: "De hereditate vero nihil in ultima voluntate disponere potest, ut
praedictum est" (ed. Woodbine, p. 105).

18

these reasons had lost much of their cogency. The canonical will need have none of the dangers of the death-bed gift. It could be made, and often was made, well before death. Bequests of land to the Church were limited in the boroughs by simple rules controlling the legatee. The era between Glanvill and Bracton is characterized by a remarkable lack of interest in protecting the rights of the heir and the lord. Efforts made to bequeath land and the ingenious techniques used to effect it show that many desired to exercise this power during the thirteenth century. Thus older objections to the will of land weakened and disappeared; but the legal requirements for the transfer of owner-ship remained, and the two chief instruments for bequeathing property could not meet those demands. Although procedural rules are not ends in themselves, they sometimes tend to form law after the reason for their application has disappeared. It would not be the first time that common law had been formed in this way, if, as has been suggested here, the basic and permanent cause of the prohibition of the bequest of land is to be found in the rules of conveyance.

There was one important exception to the prevailing tendency to forbid the alienation of land by devise. Borough custom was generally inclined to avoid the restriction imposed elsewhere by common law and proceeded rather to facilitate the will of land.[194] By Littleton's time this freedom of bequest came to be seen as the proper quality of burgage tenure. Historians of borough customs have sought to locate the source of this freedom or to isolate the ideas and needs that caused its development. The problem has tended to became part of the larger question of the influence of the Continent and especially of Normandy on the development of English institutions. It has been made unnecessarily difficult by a tendency among some scholars to see the freedom of devise of land achieved much sooner than is warranted by the evidence.[195] This error can be traced to the effort to arrive at a definition of burgage tenure. Freedom of devise, which by Littleton's

---

[194] For detailed studies of the bequest of borough tenements, see *B.C.*, II, lxxxv-c, 91 ff; Ballard, *Borough Charters* I, xlix, 73-74; Ballard and Tait, *Borough Charters* II, lxxxviii-ix, 91-93; J. Tait, *The Medieval English Borough* (Manchester, 1936), pp. 103-105, 134, 204, 355, and M. de W. Hemmeon, *Burgage Tenures in Mediaeval England* (Cambridge, Mass., 1914), pp. 4-5, 130-153, 183-184. Borough custom in this regard is stated in relation to the general framework of English law in P. and M., II, 330; Holdsworth, *History*, III, 236-239. In Plucknett, *History*, p. 737, is a brief but excellent summary of the *status questionis*, several suggestions of which have been used below.

[195] E.g., C. Stephenson, *Borough and Town* (Cambridge, Mass., 1933), p. 88, where he speaks of a complete liberty of alienation as characteristic of burgage tenure in the twelfth century.

time and even in Bracton's was its most remarkable characteristic, was one of those qualities that were seized upon to provide this definition. The next step was to project this typical quality into a century during which there is very little evidence of its existence.[196] There is no mention of it in Glanvill [197] and, beyond occasional references of by no means certain import, there are few signs of it until the last decades of the twelfth century.

The development of freedom of devise proceeded at different rates in different boroughs. Hemmeon has shown, however, that there was a general pattern in the removal of restraints :[198] in a first stage, alienation by act *inter vivos* was permitted of acquired land, then of hereditary holdings. After a lapse of some years, devise was permitted, first of the former, then of the latter. A very early example is provided by the Oxfordshire borough of Burford, where between 1088 and 1107 Robert, son of Haimo, gave his burgesses freedom to bequeath property of any kind.[199] It is not possible to say in this case whether the family was able to impose restrictions or not. The right to bequeath acquired tenements is stated at Tewkesbury before 1183, possibly much earlier, and becomes explicit in several boroughs during the next decades.[200] Freedom to bequeath hereditary tenements as well is stated at Eynsham in 1215, and becomes widespread in a series of charters of the middle of the century.[201] It may have been just when Bracton was writing that

[196] So in Hemmeon, p. 5: "Burgage tenure may be defined as a form of free tenure peculiar to boroughs, where a tenement so held might be alienated by gift, sale, or devise to a degree regulated only by the custom of the borough...". Petit-Dutaillis, *Studies and Notes Supplementary to Stubbs' Constitutional History*, trans. W. E. Rhodes, 3 vols. (Manchester, 1908-29), I, 67 ff., objected to this tendency in the historians of the English boroughs.

[197] Cf. Plucknett, *History*, p. 737, n. 2: "The ambiguous passage in Pollock and Maitland, ii, 330, line 4, must not be read as meaning that Glanvill mentions the devisability of burgages (as Hemmeon, 130)."

[198] *Op. cit.*, p. 131.

[199] "Ut unusquisque domum et terram et omnem pecuniam suam possit vendere et in vadimonio ponere et de filio et filia vel uxore et de quolibet alio absque ipsius domini requisitione heredem faciat...": R. Gretton, *The Burford Records* (Oxford, 1920), pp. 10, 301; also *EHD*, II, 965, no. 286.

[200] Texts dealing with the devise of land are assembled in *B. C.*, I, 243, 245, 260, 268, 269; II, 90-102; and by Ballard and Tait in *Borough Charters*, I (1042-1216), 73-74; II (1216-1307), 85-95. A list of the boroughs in which devise was permitted is published by Hemmeon, *op. cit.*, pp. 183-184. The date of the Tewkesbury charter is based on the time of death of William, earl of Gloucester; the charter may have been given by him or by his father between 1122 and 1183. Ballard, *Borough Charters*, I, 74, dates it 1147-93, but see Stephenson, *op. cit.*, p. 124, n. 2. The same freedom appears of Cardiff before 1183 and at Dunwich in 1215.

[201] Ballard I, 74. He also includes texts from Chester (1190-1212) and Lostwithiel

the right to bequeath was extended to all tenements in London, though *Britton* still speaks of limiting the right to a control of acquired tenements.[202]   At any rate, by the middle of the century, a general or at least a partial right to devise burgage tenements was sufficiently common for Bracton to speak of it as characteristic.

Within this freedom of bequest there were several limitations which touched the legatee or the testator.   Thus prohibition of bequest of borough tenements to religious houses appeared well before the Statute of Mortmain.[203]   Jews and royal officials were declared ineligible receivers in several charters.[204]   At London, a husband was not allowed to bequeath more than a life estate to his wife.[205]   In several boroughs a wife, even though she was acting with her husband's permission, was subject to strict limitations in the bequest of land.[206]   Thus at London, her will could receive probate only if she had come into the Hustings and declared her intention to the court.[207]

(1190-1200).   No specific reference to the bequest of land is made in the Chester charter: "ejus testamentum racionabiliter factum ratum et firmum habeatur ubicunque ipse moriatur." Cf. *B. C.*, II, 95 and *Borough Charters* II, 87-88, 91-93.

202 The limitation to acquisitions is stated in Bracton, fol. 407b; the wider freedom in fol. 272; these and the *Britton* text (ed. Nichols, I, 174, note) are assembled in *B. C.*, II, 94-96.

203 E.g., at Weymouth and Scarborough in 1253; many other examples are indicated in *Borough Charters* II, 87-93 and *B. C.*, II, 201, n. 4.   This prohibition is met in deeds dealing with a single piece of property much earlier: e.g., at Bury St. Edmunds in a charter (1188-1200) of Abbot Samson, granting land to Ralph the Chaplain, "ipsi et ei quem ipse voluerit heredem constituere preter collegium" (*The Kalendar of Abbot Samson*, ed. R. H. C. Davis, Camden Third Series, LXXXIV [1954], p. 168, no. 161).   Exception was made of course; among the scores of licenses for donation in mortmain, many deal with the bequest of borough tenements: e.g., in *C. P. R.* (Edward I), II, 174, the abbot and convent of Hyde are permitted to retain a garden and houses in Winchester bequeathed to them by the will of William de Monemouth (1285); also *ibid.*, pp. 215, 449, 479.   Citizens of London were allowed devise in mortmain by royal charter of 1327 (*B. C.*, II, 201, n. 4).

204 Devise of land to Jews was forbidden in the charter of Burton on Trent (1278); see *Borough Charters*, II, 87.   Devise to royal ministers was forbidden at Altrincham (*ca.* 1290); *ibid.*, II, 88.   At Waterford devise was not permitted to persons too poor to fulfil obligations to the city (*ca.* 1300); *B.C.*, II, 95.

205 This London rule appears in *Ricart's Kalendar* in 1419 (p. 97), but was operative in the thirteenth century as the records of probate in the Hustings show: thus in 1291 Henry de Lewes left houses to his wife in fee and she had to renounce them in full court saying that she held only for life; see Sharpe, I, 102; other examples *ibid.*, pp. 102, 125. A similar limitation appears at Torksey *ca.* 1345 (*B.C.*, II, 119-120).

206 Limitation of the wife's power of devise took many different forms; cf. Hemmeon, *op. cit.*, p. 145, n. 2, and the discussion in *B. C.*, II, civ-cvi.

207 *Ibid.*, II, 109.   In 1256, William de Munchanesey sought probate of his wife's will; it was refused on the grounds that being in the power of her husband, she could not devise

It remains to investigate the origins of the custom of devise in the English borough. In the past, some historians have seen this special quality of borough tenure as an institution surviving from Anglo-Saxon times. Others have presented it as an importation from Normandy. Much remains to be investigated before it will be possible to do justice to this problem; but even now it can be said that the fully developed custom of devise is traceable to neither source. The older notion that it was general among the Anglo-Saxons has been abandoned, and with it one of the suggested origins of the custom. Normandy is an even less likely source; the devise of land was almost unknown in Norman towns and was actually slower to develop in the Anglo-Norman boroughs than in the older Anglo-Saxon ones.[208] But an explanation of this sort is probably unnecessary. Perhaps the most important contribution towards the understanding of this custom will be made by the borough historian who will establish a chronology of its development, one that, while admitting that years of use antedate the appearance of the custom in borough charters, will not presume forthwith that it was accepted very soon after the Conquest. In the present state of the evidence, it appears that freedom of devise of land became esablished to an appreciable extent only in the late twelfth century.[209] If that is so, then the Anglo-Saxon and Norman contributions to the spread of this custom can be seen in their proper light: both groups had some experience in the devise of land. They and their descendants continued to use it occasionally after the Conquest. During the twelfth century there was a general tendency to remove the restrictions on alienation by act *inter vivos;* it is very likely that, in accord with this development, the bequest of land was subject to fewer limitations. The special economic and social conditions of borough life caused this change to occur somewhat more rapidly in the towns than in the more rural parts of the country. As a general rule, the boroughs were less subject to feudal control; given the commercial character of many of them, it was especially desirable that the freedom of bequest be extended to tenements, which were looked upon as part of the capital holdings of the testator.[210] Late in the reign of Henry II the

tenements unless she came into the Hustings herself and made a *forisaffidatio;* see Sharpe, I, xlii, and the objection to the will of Cristiana, *ibid.,* p. 103.

208 Hemmeon, *op. cit.,* p. 135; Tait, *The Medieval English Borough,* pp. 111, 355.

209 See the suggestions in Plucknett, *History,* p. 737.

210 *Britton:* "...burgess merchants employ the half or more of their chattels in their housing, wherefore they may devise their purchased land" (ed. Nicholas, I, 174, note). Cf. Veale, *op. cit.,* p. 17.

common law condemned this newly developed freedom of alienation in so far as it extended to the devise of land. But the boroughs had their own customs, and were able to resist this decision so that the development continued.

Both Mary Bateson and Tait have emphasized that the freedom of devise was not so much an invention of the boroughs as the continuation of an old and rather general practice after it had been condemned by the common law. Both have tended to exaggerate the extent of the general freedom of devise in the twelfth century,[211] but with this limitation their opinion can be accepted as the most likely explanation of events. There was some devise of land throughout all of England in the early part of the twelfth century. As time passed it became more common and easier of accomplishment. At a certain point the development was stopped in the areas subject to common law; but in the boroughs, freedom of devise was allowed to continue its growth. By the end of the century, the canonical will was coming into use. It was among the advantages of this excellent instrument of bequest that it could be made at any time; thus it became possible to avoid the suspicions attached to decisions made by dying men. Canonists influenced borough custom through mercantile law, and it is very likely that the will of land, which was presumed in their system, provided much of the stimulus as well as the technique for an increased freedom of devise.[212] Borough custom required livery of seisin for conveyance by act *inter vivos,* but saw nothing inconsistent in the fact that a testator who continued in seisin until death, should be able to cause his property to pass to a legatee other than the heir.[213]

A freedom of devise analogous to that in the boroughs is to be found on royal demesne and ancient demesne. Examples of its exercise during the thirteenth century are rare, though in the Year Book of 1294, the

---

211 "...The burgess's freedom to devise land, subject to certain restrictions, must be regarded, not as a characteristic burghal reform, but as a retention of an old principle, *generally accepted* at one time, from which the common law came to deviate" (Mary Bateson in *Borough Customs,* II, xcii); "Thus that most characteristic feature of fully developed burgage tenure, freedom of bequest of land by will, was entirely due to the prohibition by the common law of what was *general custom down to the end of the twelfth century*" (Tait, *op. cit.,* p. 103). I have added italics in these quotations to illustrate their authors' views of the wide freedom of devise in the twelfth century.

212 This suggestion is made by Plucknett, *History,* p. 737.

213 Reference to the death of the testator while in seisin of borough tenements occurs frequently; it provided proof that he had not alienated the bequest before death. Alienation of a bequest by act *inter vivos* was one way of revoking a will.

practice is described as though it were general.[214]   During the reign of
Henry III, there are also occasional references to the will of land on
other manors.[215]   This may indicate that local custom was already
beginning to allow the bequest of land.   By the end of the fourteenth
century, this right was established on some manors at least.   As usual
it was to land of acquisition that freedom of devise was first extended.[216]

The successful assertion of the right to bequeath land in the boroughs
did not constitute the only attempt in this regard.   Though of perhaps
less common occurrence than in the towns, the desire to exercise a
similar control of property was found in landowners everywhere.   From
Glanvill's time to the Statute of Wills many attempts were made to
implement it.   The institution known as the *use* was employed with
considerable success in the late fourteenth and fifteenth centuries as a
means to this end, and Bracton implies that it was not unknown in his
time.[217]   In the era of special interest to this study however, the most
important development was the attempt to create a right of devise by
charter.   With the weakening of family restraints on the alienation of
land grew the practice whereby the donor imposed a certain law on
the estate in question, with the intention of controlling its future
destiny.   The practice was not new: many examples were to be found
among the Anglo-Saxons, and the royal charters constantly gave land
with a variety of limitations.   This, the *forma doni* as it is called, created
a considerable variety of limited estates.[218]   Its most common purpose
was to establish a restriction of alienation that the family itself could
not achieve.   But for almost a century there was an attempt to use it
to attain the opposite end, to make possible the devise of land.   Donation
clauses of charters making gift to a donee, his heirs, assigns and legatees,
appear occasionally in charters of the last years of the twelfth century

---

[214] *Y.B.*, 21-22 Edward I, ed. Horwood, p. 70.   Bequest of a grange and courtyard at
the Ramsey manor of King's Ripton (acquired from Henry I) occurred before 1301:
F. W. Maitland, *Select Pleas in Manorial and other Seignorial Courts*, Selden Society, II (1888),
p. 125.   In the same volume, a bequest of land and the dispute that followed are described
pp. 126-127.   Maitland suggests that the jurors opposed the devise of land.   Another
example on the same manor (1308-9) is cited by Homans, *op. cit.*, p. 431, n. 15.   Cf. Tait,
op. cit., p. 355 and n. 1.

[215] E.g., in the extent of the Ramsey manor of Brancaster (*ca.* 1239): "Persona nullam
terram habet nisi de testamento liberorum" (*Ramsey Cart.*, I, 412).

[216] See Homans, *op. cit.*, p. 132 and especially Levett, *op. cit.*, pp. 217 ff., where the
procedure used in the devise of land by villeins is described.

[217] Bracton fols. 12b, 29.

[218] On the *forma doni* in general, see P. and M. II, pp. 13 ff.   Its application to the
devise of land is discussed *ibid.*, pp. 26-27.

and become fairly common during the reign of Henry III.[219]   Bracton
reflects the development in his treatise and in the *Note Book*.   His
discussion of the matter is inconsistent: it may not have been finished,
or it may reflect the indecision of legal practice at the moment.   In any
event Bracton shows that the use of the *forma doni,* to establish the
devisability of a given property, was at least a possibility in his day.[220]
A grant in this form was made of the honour of Richmond to Peter of
Savoy in 1241, with freedom of bequest limited to brothers or cousins.
In a second charter of 1262, the freedom was extended so that anyone
might receive it as a legacy.[221]   It passed under his will to Queen Eleanor
in 1268; but after considerable discussion and negotiation she accepted
an alternative arrangement.[222]   It may well be that, as has been suggested
by Maitland, it was decided as a result of the inconvenience caused by
this transaction to forbid such procedure in the future.[223]   At any rate
the effort failed of general acceptance, and in the Year Books it is
clearly stated that a donor cannot make land devisable by charter.[224]

Thus, with the important exception of the burgage tenement, it can
be said that the attempts to establish a devise of land that was enforceable
against the claims of the heir failed in medieval England.   Among the
burgage tenements mentioned in wills, it can be shown occasionally
that the bequest was actually the confirmation of an earlier grant or

---

[219] Thus in a confirmation of a grant by the abbot of Marmoutier to Paulinus of
Liedes, king's clerk: "vel conferendum cuicumque ipse voluerit de fratribus vel nepotibus
suis post decessum suum" (1181-9); published in *EYC,* III, 158-159, no. 1463 and Delisle,
Recueil des Actes de Henry II, II, 374-375, no. DCCXLIII.   Similarly in a deed relating to
Robertsbridge Abbey: "Notum sit omnibus tam presentibus quam futuris quod ego
Aluredus de Sancto Martino dedi ... Roberto de Waliland et illi quem dictus Robertus
heredem suum facere voluerit ..." (*ca.* 1180); see *Hist. MSS. Comm. Report,* 77, Lord De
L'Isle and Dudley, Vol. I (1925), 35.   Several examples of the thirteenth century are
mentioned in P. and M., II, 27, n. 1.   The clause appears in a precedent book, assembled
after 1280, which was published by Maitland, "A Conveyancer of the Thirteenth Century,"
Collected Papers, II, 198; he suggests that by the date of composition the form was no longer
in use; see P. and M., II, 27, n. 4.

[220] In fol. 18b Bracton seems to consider the devise valid but admits that there was,
as yet, no writ enabling the devisee to recover, though it might yet be made; in fol. 49, the
devise is considered invalid; in fol. 412b, the opposite position is taken and the writ of
recovery indicated.   Cf. two references to the *forma doni* in the *Note Book* (nos. 867, 1906)
and Maitland's discussion of the various opinions adopted by Bracton, *ibid.,* I, 36-37.

[221] Rymer's *Fœdera,* I, 417, 475, 482; *C. Ch. R.,* I, 259 (1241).   He also bequeathed the
honours of Laigle and Hastings to his brothers; see *C.P.R.,* VI, 487.

[222] *C.P.R.,* VI, 310-311, 383, 433.

[223] P. and M., II, 27.

[224] *Y.B.,* 21-22 Edward I, ed. Horwood, p. 70.

sale.[225] Marriage settlements and other similar arrangements were also confirmed in wills.[226] Several documents illustrate an interesting procedure whereby provision was made for reversion of a property after the death of the first legatee. Thus at Oxford, Henry de Lincolnia bequeathed tenements to his brother with remainder to the Hospital of St. John the Baptist.[227] The ultimate beneficiary was to be put in seisin, then to convey the property to the testator's brother with a life estate. Similar arrangements were made to provide for the legatee who was to receive property after the death of a husband who held in courtesy.[228] Occasionally testators instructed their executors to sell certain properties to raise money needed for the payment of debts and the execution of legacies.[229] Bequests of non-burgage tenures were made quite often; there is adequate evidence of this in written *wills* and in other sources.[230] But these bequests were successful because of some external support; on rare occasions, those who were close to the king obtained his permission to bequeath land;[231] at other times, the heir was willing to confirm such a devise made by will or as a death-bed gift.[232] The fundamental fact remains—the common law was opposed to the bequest of land.

[225] T. 47b: William de Skelmerskerth bequeathed land to Furness Abbey, but from the previous document in the cartulary it is evident that a property with the boundaries described in the *will* had already been granted the abbey the same year. The charter of donation includes a warranty clause. Several of the bequests of land to the church of St. Frideswide, Oxford, mentioned in T. 75a, were actually donated as much as a decade before the making of the will, as the previous charter demonstrates.

[226] T. 33: Hugh, bishop of Lincoln, confirms a donation of land at Dornford, given with his niece in marriage, with reversion to the hospital at Wells if she dies without heirs of her body; also T. 30.

[227] T. 75b: "Uolo autem quod fratres dicti hospitalis ponantur primo in saisinam dictarum domum cum pertinenciis & postea recipiet dictus Willelmus frater meus ipsas domos de predictis fratribus quas sibi lego in presenti testamento, tenendas & habendas toto tempore uite sue...".

[228] T. 81.

[229] E.g., T. 82a. Sometimes this instruction might take the form of a right of pre-emption at a price somewhat lower than the market value of the land: e.g., T. 65.

[230] E.g., T. 23, bequest of a manor, part of a wife's inheritance, with the permission of her husband; T. 30, several small bequests of land, without indication of permission; a most interesting example from the Selby Coucher Book is quoted P. and M. II, 325 and n. 3; *ibid.*, p. 329; in the extent of the Ramsey manor of Brancaster (*ca.* 1239) we read: "Persona nullam terram habet nisi de testamento liberorum" (*Ramsey Cart.*, I, 412).

[231] Thus in 1232 Henry III confirmed the conveyance of Dadford Manor to Simon de Montfort by the executors of Ranulf of Chester. Joan, queen of Scotland, bequeathed land in Staunton to the abbess and convent of Tarrant, with the permission of Henry III, her brother (1238); see the confirmation in *C. Ch. R.*, II, 227.

[232] An example from the Winchcomb Landboc (I, 156-159) is quoted in P. and M., II, 329, n. 1.

The Distribution of Movable Property by Will

Lawyers of the thirteenth century found it convenient to speak of the borough tenement as a quasi-chattel.[233] In this they likened it to that part of a person's property to which testamentary capacity was limited under ordinary circumstances. Chattels remained all through the period of this study, the common matter with which wills of any sort were concerned. They probably found a place in every *post obit* division of property, and in the vast majority of cases they alone were there. Yet for that reason we are almost completely ignorant of the details of their distribution for about one hundred and fifty years after the Conquest. Except for occasional mention in narrative sources, most evidence about the bequest of chattels appears as an accidental remark in a document concerned with the bequest of land. Where information does occur, it is usually in very general terms, indicating a portion of goods bequeathed to some ecclesiastical institution.[234] Whether testators exercised considerable care in their final distribution of property; whether individual pieces of equipment, the ordinary as well as the precious, were bequeathed so as to show special affection or to ensure their possession by those best able to use them; these are questions to which no satisfactory answer can be offered. One of the more remarkable qualities of written *wills* of Anglo-Saxon times and of the thirteenth century was the very large number of legatees indicated there.[235] Testators sought to distribute chattels rather widely among family, friends, servants and churches. The extent to which this was true of the interval cannot be said with certainty. It is quite probable that the simple statement found in twelfth-century documents, that a third of the testator's goods was to be received by the church of burial, is an accurate description of the distribution of his chattels; the deceased's portion was given as a unit to the church in question. On the other hand, there are indications that some testators divided their chattels among a quite large and varied group: the priest of whom Gilbert Foliot wrote left most of his possessions to Gloucester Abbey, but one third of them was

---

233 See Bracton, fol. 407b: "cum sint quasi catalla testatoris;" *ibid.*, 409b, which is probably an interpolation (ed. Woodbine, I, 417; IV, 273). A burgage is simply called a chattel in the Eyre Roll of 1221: *Rolls of the Justices in Eyre, 1221, 1222*, ed. Doris Mary Stenton, Selden Society, LIX (1940), no. 290.

234 See above, p. 109. Manorial court rolls of the thirteenth century give a great deal of information about the movement of land after the death of tenants, but rarely indicate distribution of chattels in detail.

235 See above, pp. 74-76.

to be distributed among his servants; some of the bishops' wills of the twelfth century sought to bequeath chattels to their churches, the poor, their friends, servants and family.[236]

Even in those rare cases where there is evidence of a multiple distribution of movable property, detailed enumeration of the chattels themselves is lacking. With the thirteenth century, written *wills* appear once more; in them much is to be learned of the succession to chattels and of the testator's attitude towards them. Some testators were quite uninterested in the lot of individual chattels. Thus in the first *will* of Hugh of Wells, there are more than fifty bequests expressed in terms of money, some 5000 marks in all.[237] The only particular pieces of equipment mentioned are books and clothing, and their distribution is left to the discretion of the executors. This was a somewhat extreme case: the testator was in exile and, as his estates were in royal hands, the goods actually in his possession were probably very limited. But the second *will*, made under happier circumstances, reveals much the same point of view.[238] There are several important bequests of plate, liturgical equipment and plough-stock, but most legacies are expressed in money and his executors are instructed to raise the required sum by the sale of his goods. This will is typical of those of the well-to-do, where the only chattels mentioned specifically are those of considerable value.[239] At the other extreme are documents which read like an inventory of household effects: spoons, barrels, beds, sheets, household linen, uncut cloth, garments, vessels of every shape and size are sent off to different legatees in a bewildering line. Wills of this sort are not common and they are usually made by women.[240] The vast majority of testators were content to express most of their bequests in money or, occasionally, in animals and grain, making specific mention of furniture or equipment of unusual value.

Jewellery, plate, precious vessels of many kinds are among the most frequent specific bequests of the wills.[241] Rings, usually of gold and often decorated with precious stones, appear very often among the legacies of wealthy testators.[242] Hugh of Wells left one to each of his

---

[236] See above, pp. 242-245.

[237] T. 12.

[238] T. 33.

[239] T. 23: there are about fifty-five legacies of money, while the only bequests of particular chattels are a palfrey with harness as a mortuary and rings to the members of her family. Instructions for the sale of goods are included. Similarly, T. 30.

[240] E.g., T. 82a, T. 83, T. 99a.

[241] E.g., T. 25, T. 30, T. 53a, T. 56.

[242] E.g., T. 23, T. 33, T. 53a, T. 56, T. 59b.

confrères in the province of Canterbury, and the distribution of the rings of Richard Wych, bishop of Chichester, was sufficiently involved to require statement on a schedule attached to his *will*.[243]   References of this sort are numerous enough to show that in the thirteenth century a considerable amount of wealth was collected in this fairly mobile form. There are a few specific bequests of swords and other military equipment, but the *wills* of the thirteenth century reveal none of the special concern with arms that is so remarkable among the Anglo Saxons.[244] Vestments, liturgical vessels, and relics are bequeathed in considerable details in episcopal wills, and are also to be found in the wills of the laity.[245]   Books too are frequently mentioned.   Bishop Richard Wych distributed sixteen of them by name to as many legatees, and bequests of several others are indicated as well.[246]   For the testator of more humble means the specific bequest of more valuable garments was usually his chief concern.[247]

Legacies of farm-stock appear most frequently in *wills* of the less well-to-do.   Here a few sheep, a cow or two, an ox, are bequeathed to the place of burial, to members of the family and to friends.[248] Occasionally, the wills of the wealthy distribute stock in this way.   Thus Hugh of Wells left twenty-six team of oxen to his successor.[249]   The *will* of William Longespee, earl of Salisbury, is unique in that it includes the bequest of more than three thousand animals, mostly sheep, to nineteen ecclesiastical institutions.   Usually the wealthy were content to instruct their executors to sell their stock and devote the proceeds to the execution of their bequests.[250]   The specific bequest of a horse of special value as a mortuary or as a heriot appears in many of the *wills*.[251]

The bequest of grain and hay followed much the same pattern as that of farm-stock.   Commonly it was sold and the proceeds, often a considerable sum, were devoted to the payment of legacies.   But *wills* of less important folk sometimes mention quite small bequests of grain

---

[243] T. 33, T. 53a.

[244] Nicholas Longespee, bishop of Salisbury, bequeathed body-armour and horse-armour to his men-at-arms in T. 96.

[245] E.g., T. 25.

[246] T. 53a. Books appear in many other *wills*.

[247] E.g., T. 74.

[248] See above, p. 265, n. 164.

[249] T. 33.

[250] T. 25.

[251] See below pp. 298-302, on the mortuary and pp. 296-298, on the heriot.

—a bushel of wheat or oats.[252] The ownership of crops that had already been harvested presented no difficulty, but there was some question about the distribution of those planted by an individual who died while they were still growing in the field. A solution was quickly found for the holders of ecclesiastical benefices: if they died before Michaelmas, the income of that year was devoted to their needs.[253] By the early thirteenth century it is evident that such had become general procedure. Even a lessee could bequeath a growing crop.[254] Widows were not allowed such control over the crops of dower land until 1236, when the right was extended to them by the Statute of Merton.[255] However, during most of the thirteenth century, lessees and recipients of royal grants often saw fit to obtain the statement of this right of bequest in deeds of donation or contract. Arrangements for harvest were made by executors; equipment required for the gathering and storing of grain and hay was sometimes placed at their disposition.[256]

During the early thirteenth century, many rights came to be considered as chattels, and therefore as objects of bequest.[257] Thus in Bracton's time the term of years, the estate *pur autre vie*, and probably the mortgage, were devisable.[258] Somewhat allied to this form of bequest, and very much like it in its intention to provide income for the payments of debts and legacies, is a series of arrangements whereby testators used their wills to establish what amounted to a term of years in their executors. As the representation of the testator by the executor was asserted, the testator seems to have realized that, since his real estate was thus escaping liability for debts, all payments had to be

---

252 E.g., T. 76.

253 See above, p. 249.

254 Bracton, *Note Book*, no. 221 (1224). This right was sometimes stated in deeds: e.g., in 1286 Isabel, widow of Walter, was given a life interest in a property with the right to bequeath the fruits of the year of her death (*The Great Chartulary of Glastonbury*, ed. Watkin, II, 377-378, no. 661).

255 *Statutes of the Realm*, I, 6; see Bracton, fol. 96 and the *Note Book*, no. 1409, with the remarks of the annotator; also *C. P. R.*, III, 43, 46.

256 See above, p. 247, n. 67.

257 For a general discussion of this matter see P. and M., II, 113-117, and F. W. Maitland, "The Seisin of Chattels," *Collected Papers*, I, 353.

258 Bracton, fols. 407b, 13b, 27, 263; on the bequest of a mortgage, see Bracton, *Note Book*, no. 559 (1231). Bracton calls these rights "quasi chattels" (fol. 407b), and in *Y.B.*, 33-35 Edward I, ed. Horwood, p. 165, we find "la terme nest qe chattel;" a wardship is described in the same way in *Y.B.*, 32-33 Edward I, ed. Horwood, p. 245. Similar to a term of years in real estate was a grant of the income of the mint to Richard of Cornwall for twelve years, with the provision that it would pass to his executors, in the event of his death before the completion of the term (*C. P. R.*, III, 511).

drawn from his movable wealth. This left an insufficient amount for bequests to charity and to other legatees.[259] Those close to the king proceeded to adjust to this new situation by obtaining royal permission that, for a given length of time, the income of their estates might pass to their executors. The latter were to devote this money to the payment of debts and the execution of their wills. Thus in 1236, Simon de Montfort obtained permission to devote the issues of the honour of Leicester to that purpose for four years after his death, and in 1248 the privilege was extended to eight years.[260] Occasionally the consent of the heir was obtained as well.[261]

The rights to marriages and wardships were also distributed by will. An example of the bequest of a wardship is found during John's reign, and the Patent Roll of the early years of Henry III, in recording grants of custodies, frequently includes the statement of the right to bequeath them.[262] Royal instructions to escheators after the death of tenants-in-chief often contain the order to respect such bequests.[263] As a general rule, these rights were placed in the hands of executors who sold them or exercised them in the usual way, devoting the income to the payment of the debts and the bequests of the deceased. Their value was considerable, as is evident not only from the prices paid to acquire them but also from the very large legacies for which they were expected to supply the funds: by the will of William Longespee, earl of Salisbury, royal and other debts, the restoration of prizes unjustly taken in war, the payment of servants, and the chief legacies were all to be drawn from the income of several important wardships.[264] It was the special

259 On the charging of land with the payment of debt in the fourteenth century, see Holdsworth, *History*, III, 576.

260 *C.P.R.*, III, 155; IV, 26. There are many other examples in the Patent Rolls: in 1233 to Philip de Albiniaco for three years (III, 21); in 1238 to Joan, queen of Scots, for ten years (III, 210); in 1242 to Margaret Biset for three years (III, 286), etc. In a plea, described in the *Curia Regis Rolls* of 1210 (*C.R.R.*, VI, 79), a testator is said to have bequeathed thirty marks, "assigning some land from which the money could be received." With the permission of her husband, the testatrix of T. 23 assigned the income of a manor for one year to the payment of her legacies. Many more examples could be given.

261 E.g., *C. C. R.* (Edward I), 332 (1276): William de Warenne, son of John, earl of Surrey, confirms his father's grant of income for ten years after his death, promising to protect and warrant the executors. There is another example *ibid.*, p. 346. In the *will* of Margery de Creke (T. 82c) a manor is assigned her executors for three years. The *will* mentions that she had obtained the permission of the heir and that he confirmed it in writing.

262 *Rotuli Chartarum*, ed. T. D. Hardy, Record Commission, 25 (London, 1837), p. 108; examples for the reign of Henry III: *C.P.R.*, II, 12, 472-473; IV, 478; V, 193, etc.

263 E.g., *C.C.R.*, I, 204 (1229); III, 11 (1234).

264 T. 25.

custom of some boroughs that a burgess might choose the ward of his children, giving to them the marriages and the custody of their lands. This choice could be made by will.[265] A similar privilege was occasionally granted by the king to favoured individuals.[266]

Such were the different forms of wealth distributed by the wills of the twelfth and thirteenth centuries. From the foregoing analysis it becomes apparent that, in so far as freedom of bequest was concerned, the distinction between movable and immovable property was meaningful all through the period under consideration.

The bequest of movable property was accepted in principle by the Normans as by the Anglo-Saxons. As time went on rights of various sorts came to be considered as chattels, so that by the middle of the thirteenth century almost all private sources of income, including leased land, were reckoned among movables and distributed by will. Among the chattels and rights bequeathed at this time, there is one significant omission. It will be recalled that the slave appeared very often in the Anglo-Saxon *cwide*. There is scarcely a single reference to villeins in wills of the period under discussion; they are mentioned neither as legacies, nor as those to whom freedom was given. Whether the omission occurred because villeins were annexed to the freehold of the land, as *Britton* said,[267] or whether there was some quite different reason, cannot be discussed here. But the omission is beyond question and can be used, perhaps, to assist in understanding the position of the villein in the society of the time.

Another significant fact is the extent to which the wills of the thirteenth century reveal the workings of a money economy. A very large proportion of the legacies, even those in the wills of persons of quite modest circumstances, were gifts of money. Where bequest was made of furnishings or farm-stock, testators often assigned a cash value to each item. The liquid capital required to execute many wills was considerable. Where it was not available, it was the general practice to obtain it by the sale of chattels and land. Executors were often counselled to do so by the wills they administered.

---

[265] This right is stated at Pembroke 1173-89 (for the date see *Borough Charters* II, xlv), Dunwich 1215, London 1243; the relevant texts are printed in *B.C.*, II, 145-147 and *Borough Charters*, I, 75-79. The general European background to the English examples of this practice is discussed in *B.C.*, II, cxxviii-ix.

[266] E.g., to Peter of Savoy (1253), to Robert Aquilon "for long service" (1266) and to William of Valence (1270); *C.P.R.*, IV, 181; VI, 19, 451.

[267] Bk. I, ch. 32; a villein is bequeathed in the will of Robert, son of Alan de Fordham (*ca.* 1200): "lego ... totum servicium Eadmundi filii Alexandri stutard' cum homagio suo et tota sequela sua" (Oxford, Bodleian MS. Charters, Norfolk a. 6 [614]).

The demands made on the movable portion of a testator's estate were so great that the desire to supplement it was undoubtedly one of the forces conducing to a greater freedom of bequest of land. In the era following the Conquest, the devise of land was exceptional, and was usually made with the permission or confirmation of the lord and the heir, the two parties interested in preventing alienation. As the twelfth century drew to a close and the freedom to dispose of real estate increased, there was a strong possibility that the older limitations of bequest would weaken. In fact, this did occur in the boroughs and other communities that maintained local custom. But common law opposed the devise of realty; in spite of several attempts to circumvent it, the decision stood throughout the period of interest to the present study. Even when land was required to provide the permanent endowment of a chantry or a mass foundation, it could not be obtained from the estate of the deceased; executors were required to purchase it.

Further demands on the movable portion of the testator's property were made during the thirteenth century as the executor replaced the heir as the one responsible for the debts of the deceased. Many testators tried to oppose this development, obtaining royal permission that all the outstanding obligations at the time of their death be acquitted by the heir, so that the executors might devote that portion of the estate that came to them to the pious works and other bequests of the will. This attempt indicates a keen awareness of the fact that the movable property of the deceased was sometimes not able to support the demands that were made on it.

The thirteenth century also witnessed the beginnings of a practice that was to bring about an important increase of the funds available to the executor: permission was obtained that, for a given number of years, the income of the testator's land be devoted to the payment of his debts and legacies. Thus executors became trustees of the landed property of the deceased, administering it for the purposes which he had set out in his will. This development, partially circumventing the effects of the prohibition of the devise of land, was to increase in importance in the following century.

IV. MATERIAL LIMITATIONS IN THE WILLS OF THE TWELFTH AND THIRTEENTH CENTURIES

The discussion of the bequest of movable property may seem to have implied that, whatever the limitations of the devise of land, a testator was entirely free to distribute his chattels as he wished. Such was not the case. Many testators could bequeath only a portion of their goods, and almost all of them found that they were required to make certain payments to the Church and often to their lord. When discussing the extent of the material freedom of bequest among the Anglo-Saxons, mention was made of a customary division of movable property in thirds, whch was described by Glanvill in the twelfth century, and which, despite some indications to the contrary, was not rooted in a general Anglo-Saxon practice.[268] It now remains to see to what extent evidence of this quota system, or one like it, can be found in the first century after the Conquest, and to discover, if possible, the source from which it was derived.[269]

Documents illustrative of the practice of *post obit* distribution in the second generation after the Norman invasion speak of a portion of movable property that was especially at the disposition of the dead. It is possible that a general practice of this sort is indicated in the Coronation Charter of Henry I.[270] There the phrase *pecuniam suam* is used to describe the property which was to be distributed by will. It may refer to all the chattels of the testator, some of which were usually distributed in alms, while the rest were received by his wife and children. But it is also possible that the share of this property reserved to the wife and children by custom is presumed to have been deducted. In that case *pecuniam suam* would refer to a portion of the chattels of the deceased that was especially his own in the sense that he could alienate it at will. In the first half of the clause this meaning is far from evident. Yet even here, the alternative seems to be a freedom to dispose of all chattels, an arrangement that is not plausible. It is when the second part of the clause is read that the suggested meaning becomes more convincing: there it is said that in the case of intestacy, distribution is to be made of this same *pecuniam suam* for the good of the soul of the deceased. It is inconceivable that all the movable property of the intestate with dependents was devoted to religious purposes. The conclusion that a customary division of chattels was already established by the year 1100 would be difficult to avoid were it not for the fact that in the next clause of Henry's charter, the same phrase is used to denote movable property in general.[271] Yet when the text dealing with the distribution

---

[268] See above, pp. 76 ff.

[269] The limitation of the testator's right to dispose of movable property is discussed in the general context of family law in P. and M., II, 348-356; Holdsworth, *History*, III, 550-563; Plucknett, *History*, pp. 743-746.

[270] C. 7; quoted above, p. 110, n. 13.

[271] C. 8: "Si quis baronum ... forisfecerit, non dabit vadium in misericordia pecuniae suae, sicut faciebat tempore patris mei vel fratris mei ...".

of property at death is considered in relation to the donation clauses of
deeds of Henry's reign, the interpretation favouring a fairly general
establishment of a customary division of chattels becomes quite plausible.
Thus in 1100 when Hugh de Lacy and his wife were received into
fraternity by the monks of Gloucester Abbey, they granted their bodies
for burial "and all that part of their goods which belonged to them."[272]
In the same year or earlier, a similar arrangement was made between
Ranulf the Dapifer and his wife and Ramsey Abbey, in which donation
was made of their bodies and "the part of the property which belonged
to each of them." [273]

Other references to the bequest of chattels indicate that the share of
the individual was one third of his movable property. Perhaps the
best known example is to be found in the last decade of the eleventh
century in the "foundation charter" of St. Werburgh's Abbey, Chester:
Earl Hugh and his men arranged that on the death of barons, knights,
burgesses and other free men, the body of the deceased and one third of
his substance were to be given to the abbey.[274] The interpretation of
this charter presents many difficulties, but its testimony to a division of
property in thirds is beyond question. Other examples are to be found
in such widespread centres as Salisbury, Gloucester, Ramsey and
Rochester.[275] A letter of Osbert of Clare of about the year 1135 provides

272 *Gloucester Cart.*, I, 326: "et rerum suarum partem universam quæ eis contigeret."

273 *Ramsey Cart.*, II, 259: "et quantum possessionis ad utrumque eorum pertinebit, cum
ipsis funeribus, eidem loco attribuatur." Other examples: in a charter of Peter of Valognes
to Benham Priory: "et pars eorum totius suæ substantiæ illorum tantum maneriorum . . .
ecclesiæ sanctæ Mariæ reddi et offeri debet" (Dugdale, *Monasticon*, III, 345-346, dated 1101-7);
an agreement shortly after 1121 between Abbot Vincent of Abingdon and Simon Dispenser:
"non alias quam hic sepeliretur, cum tota mobili suæ partis pecunia. Quod si extra
Angliam [vita] fungetur, eadem tamen suæ partis hujus patriæ portio tota Abbendonensi
loco cederet" (*Abingdon Chronicon*, II, 168). An interesting development is to be seen in
the Burton Cartulary: a charter of 1094-1113 mentions all chattels—"cum autem mortuus
fuerit, deferre ad nos se faciet cum tota pecunia sua ad sepeliendum"—while two others
of 1114-1150 mention the part of the deceased—"tota pars eorum pecuniae;" see *The
Burton Chartulary*, ed. G. Wrottesley, Coll. Hist. Staffordshire, V, pt. i (1884), 30, 34, 35-36.

274 "Insuper constituerunt ut singuli barones et milites darent Deo et S. Werburgae
post obitum suum sua corpora et tertiam partem totius substantiae suae" (*Cartulary of the
Abbey of St. Werburgh,* ed. Tait, I, 17, 31-32). See above, p. 112, n. 19. The reference is
almost certainly to chattels alone; the cartulary does not indicate donations of land on the
scale that would follow if the reference were to landed property. See Bruck, *Kirchenväter*,
p. 275, n. 49. It is not clear whether the charter speaks of a permission or a command;
Pollock and Maitland favour the second interpretation (II, 324) suggesting that it is a
case of Palatine law. Bruck, *op. cit.*, p. 276 cites an order of Radulf Taisson, founder of
Fontenay Abbey, forbidding his men to give or sell to any other church (1047).

275 In Bishop Osmund's charter of Salisbury Cathedral (1091) one third of the income

much precious information.[276]   Roger of Sommery had died, and after his burial a day was set for the distribution of his chattels.   All goods, even household equipment, were placed in public view and the division was begun.   A cup that had belonged to St. Anselm was especially desired by the widow of the deceased.   It was suggested by certain monks who were present that she take it since its monetary value was slight; but, not wishing to interfere with the goods that her husband had intended to be distributed she refused.   She let it be known, however, that she would purchase the cup, if the portion of the goods in which it was included "fell to her husband."   This did not prove to be necessary, for in answer to her prayer the portion that included the cup was awarded to her.   The narrative is concerned with the woman's devotion to St. Anselm, and details of the distribution of the husband's property are included only incidentally.   It does show, however, that division was made with considerable care and formality, and implies that the reservation of a third of the movable property for the soul of the deceased was of common occurrence.   This last point, and it is of chief interest here, is especially clear in the opening words of the narrative: "dies abbati fratribusque statuitur ut tertia pars totius peculii pro defuncti remedio dividatur." [277]

These examples are sufficient to indicate a widespread practice established in England by the end of the reign of Henry I and probably somewhat earlier.   The fact of the usage seems clear enough, but its source has proved very difficult to find.   As was seen in an earlier chapter, the occasional appearance of a division in thirds among the Anglo-Saxons does not warrant the conclusion that the custom of the twelfth century was derived from them.[278]   If some remnant of Bede's

of a prebend was to be devoted to the poor for a year after the death of an incumbent (*Register of St. Osmund,* ed. Jones, I, 199-200); a charter of 1128 in the Gloucester Cartulary reads: "Et ipse Robertus dedit pro anima uxoris suæ totius substantiæ suæ tertiam partem, et ipse etiam, ubicumque sepeliatur, dabit partem substantiæ suæ quæ in Anglia fuerit" (I, 232-233); the description of the purchase of a third of the fishery of Lothewere by Abbot Reginald of Ramsey Abbey (1114-30) includes the information that the other two thirds had been given to the abbey at the death of the father and mother of the seller (*Ramsey Cart.,* I, 134); at Rochester before 1124, Wlfuuardus de Hou, receiving fraternity from the monks, gave "tertiam partem substantie sue post mortem suam" (Dugdale, *Monasticon,* I, 168, no. XXXIII).   Other examples: *Abingdon Chronicon,* II, 124 (1100-15); *Leges Henrici,* 70.22, a text based on the Lex Ribuaria in which a widow is allowed one third of jointly acquired chattels ("de omni collaboracione"), her clothes and bed (*Gesetze,* I, 590).   This may be the complement of a distribution in which one third was reserved to the husband.

276 *The Letters of Osbert of Clare,* ed. E. W. Williamson, (London, 1929), pp. 70, 201.

277 *Ibid.,* p. 70.

278 See above, pp. 76-77.   The suggestion that the reservation of a third for children

division in thirds or other similar practices survived until the Conquest, they would undoubtedly facilitate the adoption of the notion that a third of a dead man's property should be devoted to the good of his soul; but they would not explain the general adoption of the custom.

The third for the soul is not derived from Canon law. It has been shown that Gratian's limitation of the bequest in alms was rejected by the decretists. They supported the testamentary freedom of Roman law, claiming that all property might be alienated except the *pars legitima* reserved to the heir. It is significant, however, that canonists of the second half of the twelfth century indicate that the reserved portion had recently been changed from a quarter to a third of the testator's property.[279] This observation reflects the adoption of a division in thirds by the customary law of many parts of Europe, a development in which the canonists seem to have played no direct part.

As for Normandy, it is difficult to avoid the conclusion of Pollock and Maitland that there is no proof that the division in thirds ever prevailed there.[280] Yet the possibility that Normandy was the source of the custom, or at least the road by which it came to England, must not be rejected too quickly. In the case of the Anglo-Saxons, where several collections of laws and many hundreds of charters and *wills* survive yet fail to indicate a division of property in thirds, the argument from silence is a strong one. There are few documents from Normandy in the period before and immediately after the Conquest. There as elsewhere chattels were rarely mentioned until the appearance of the *will* late in the twelfth century. Hence the argument from silence is of little value; we simply do not know how the Normans dealt with the movable property of the dead. Nor is it likely that the evidence of law or charter will ever provide us with this information. However, in recent years a different approach permits some helpful suggestions. Due to several circumstances the Normans were exposed to strong influence by Christian teachers and by laws that reserved a third of a man's property for the good of his soul. This influence was brought to bear in two quite different ways. First, Professor Bruck has shown that the teaching of the Fathers on the share of the soul was spread through northern Europe by Irish missionaries.[281] Their influence and

in London is a survival from Roman times was examined and rejected by W. G. Hart in "Roman Law and the Custom of London," *Law Quarterly Review*, XLVI (1930), 49-53.

279 See above, pp. 127-128; Bruck, *op. cit.*, pp. 241-256.

280 II, 349; cf. Bruck, *op. cit.*, p. 274, n. 47.

281 *Op. cit.*, pp. 229-240 and especially 265-271; cf. Schultze, *Augustin und der Seelteil*, pp. 93-117. See above, pp. 12-16.

the penitential literature that embodied their ideas were especially prominent in the northern part of France from pre-Carolingian times to the eleventh century. As we have seen, documentation is not sufficient to show whether this influence fostered a division in thirds or not. Yet it is very likely that it had some effect. Secondly, the Normans came in contact with a legal system that embodied the teaching of the Fathers on the share of the soul. During the eleventh century, as settlers in southern Italy or on crusade they became acquainted with Byzantine law in which a third of a testator's property was reserved for bequests in alms. This provision was later included in the laws of the crusader kingdoms and the kingdom of Sicily and it is probable that it had some effect in the Norman homeland.[282] Given the strong possibility that these ideas and examples were influential in Normandy, and given the fact that most of the earliest English examples of reservation of the third for the soul involved members of the Anglo-Norman upper class,[283] it is tentatively concluded that the immediate source of the practice was Normandy and that it was introduced into England by her new aristocracy.[284]

In most of the examples cited above, the third in question was to be used exclusively for the soul and was received by a single beneficiary. This would mean that, if the testator chose to express his affection for other institutions or persons, it would be necessary for him to alienate more than a third of his chattels. It seems to have been presumed that the power of bequest was to be used exclusively for donations in alms.[285] Glanvill's account has a different tone. There it is stated that, excepting certain local usages, it was the general custom of the land that freemen with dependents, having acquitted their debts, were permitted to distribute a third of their movable property as they chose.[286] The remaining thirds, the legitim, were to be reserved for the wife and the heir. When only the latter survived, one half of the

---

[282] Schultze, op. cit., pp. 117-127; Bruck, op. cit., p. 272.

[283] But cf. H. Round, "The Burton Abbey Surveys," EHR, XX (1905), 275-289, where he concludes that the Burton examples, cited above, n. 273, involving an English house, English priors and English tenants illustrate the terms on which land was held "even before the Conquest."

[284] This was Brunner's conclusion, though he related the practice to the Germanic custom of grave endowment; see "Der Totenteil in germanischen Rechten" ZRG Germ. Abt., XIX (1898), 111 and "Beiträge zur Geschichte des germanischen Wartrechts," Abhandlungen, II, 240.

[285] Similarly the charter of liberties of Henry I presumes that the goods of the intestate are to be distributed for his soul; see above, p. 110, n. 13.

[286] Bk. VII, ch. 5.

chattels was set aside as legitim, while the remainder was at the disposition of the testator. It will be noted that the rights of wife and heir are carefully stated. The free portion of the estate is to be distributed as the testator wishes; there is no question of it being devoted exclusively to the good of the soul. The only demand of this sort was the mortuary.[287]

Bracton and *Fleta* agree with this statement of customary usage, adding that the testator without dependents might dispose of all his movable property.[288] References to the portions reserved for the soul, to the wife and to the children are to be found in several *wills* of the thirteenth century.[289] Bracton also mentions that local practices sometimes overrode the general custom. The only example cited by him was that of London, where the testator could dispose of all his chattels by will except those that were already committed to his wife in dower. Bracton and *Fleta* spoke of this arrangement, and the family discipline that it imposed, with enthusiasm. London was eventually to prove most tenacious in maintaining the reservation of legitim for wife and children, but the time and manner of its introduction are not known.[290] Bracton's statement of the custom is confirmed by a document of 1246 where a widow's claim to more than her dower was disallowed.[291] Limitation of the right of the testator is probably implied in a case of intestacy in 1419, where a division of property in thirds is indicated.[292] A London *will* of 1290 actually reads like the text of Glanvill: debts are to be paid and of the remainder, one portion is to be received by the wife, one by the children, and the third devoted to the funeral and the bequests of the deceased;[293] but whether this distribution was simply

---

[287] Bruck suggests (*op. cit.*, pp. 278-280) that Glanvill's limitation of the power of devise is part of a general reaction to excessive donation to pious causes.

[288] Fols. 60b-61; *Fleta*, Bk. II, ch. 57 (ed. Richardson and Sayles, II, 193). Glanvill actually reserves one portion to the heir: "una debetur heredi;" Bracton and *Fleta* speak of "pueri." For a discussion of the meaning of these words, see P. and M., II, 350. In a canon of the Council of Cashel (1172), which according to Giraldus Cambrensis imposed the customs of the English Church on Ireland, the term used is "liberi" (c. 6, Wilkins, I, 472-473). The courts of common law showed themselves quite unsympathetic to legitim in the fourteenth century, refusing to allow that the tripartite division was the "custom of the realm;" for a discussion of this problem see P. and M., II, 351-352, and Plucknett, *History*, pp. 744-745.

[289] E.g., T. 90.

[290] On the later history of legitim see P. and M., II, 349-356.

[291] The text from the *Liber de Antiquis Legibus*, is quoted in *B.C.*, II, 121.

[292] See *ibid.*, II, p. 136 and the discussion, pp. xcvii-xcviii.

[293] T. 90: "Item debitis prius solutis volo quod omnia bona mea diuidatur in tres partes videlicet Alicie vxori mee vnam partem Iohanni et Dyonisie pueris meis aliam

the choice of the testator or represents a recently enforced custom, it is not yet possible to decide.

Scraps of evidence here and there point to other limitations of the testator. Thus a Cambridge custom of 1299 and several *wills* mention the reservation of one half the chattels to the wife.[294] As the children's portion is not discussed in these cases, it is impossible to know whether a diminution of the testator's share resulted, though it seems most likely. Several other local variants are assembled by Miss Bateson in her study of borough customs.[295] Except for the portion reserved to the wife in dower, those borough tenements which had been declared devisable were entirely at the disposition of the testator.

The right to bequeath chattels was subject to one further limitation by local custom. It was in favour of the heir and took the form of a reservation of certain chattels to his use. These are the *principalia,* the tools of the heir, or "heirlooms." [296] Equipment needed for the household, for the tilling of the soil, and for the trade of the burgess, was reserved in this way. Very often the best example of each type of chattel was set apart as an heirloom. The devolution of arms and goods of special value was sometimes controlled in this way, but the custom was particularly concerned to prevent the alienation of those tools and utensils that were needed for the livelihood of the heir. The heirloom might be a ship, a cart, a plough, or a pot or pan needed in the kitchen, but in any case its value and economic necessity are evident. The rules governing the devolution of these chattels appear in several borough charters of the thirteenth century.[297] Heirlooms of the type that might be styled family treasure appear occasionally in the written *wills:* thus in 1259 a cleric bequeathed a drinking horn decorated in silver to his sister, with the instruction that it remain the property of their heirs forever.[298]

---

partem michi vero ad exequias meas faciendas et testamentum meum supplendum terciam partem."

[294] See *B.C.,* II, xcviii, and T. 23, T. 67c.

[295] II, xcvi-xcix.

[296] P. and M., II, 363; *B. C.,* II, xcix-c; Homans, *English Villagers of the Thirteenth Century,* pp. 133-134, where the custom of heirlooms, as it touched the succession to the goods of villeins, is discussed.

[297] *B. C.,* II, 125, 138-144. On the setting aside of the *principalia* which passed to the heir with a villein holding, see Homans, *op. cit.,* and Levett, *Studies in Manorial History,* pp. 190-1, where fourteenth-century lists are summarized.

[298] T. 59b, also in T. 94: "Item, lego Waltero, filio meo, coffrum meum et gladium; et, si infra etatem obierit, volo quod Hugo, filius meus, ea habeat."

In considering the distribution of chattels by will, a word must be said of the part of the deceased's wealth that was alienated, not by free bequest, but in the form of an exaction by the lord or the Church. These payments were the heriot and mortuary. It will be recalled that by the end of the Anglo-Saxon period it was not uncommon for wills to mention a heriot which was to be paid to the lord. During the tenth century the soul-scot or mortuary, which at first had been a free offering to the church of burial, became a regular charge enforced by the law of the land.[299] To the extent that these exactions became customary and fixed, they are not of special interest to this study. However, there was a certain degree of freedom execised in their payment and to this we must turn.

Pollock and Maitland have shown that the legal writings of the first generations after the Conquest tended to confuse the heriot of Cnut's law with the feudal relief.[300] By the time of Glanvill, the two payments were clearly distinguished. Writing of the freeman's will, he tells us that it is customary to leave the best possession to the lord. There is a hint, however, that the usage is not universal. Bracton, who actually employs the term "heriot," flatly states that the payment to the lord is by grace rather than by law, and *Britton* concedes that it is generally paid by the villein rather than by the freeman.[301]

Thus the heriot, which in the beginning was an offering of the free warrior to his lord, became by the thirteenth century an exaction especially associated with the lowest classes, where it assumed the form of a tax on a holding rather than on a person.[302] At the death of the villein householder one of his best beasts or implements, or a money payment, was received by the lord according to the usage proper to the manor. There is some possibility that, where villeins were permitted to make wills, the heriot was looked upon as a means of obtaining the lord's support for the other bequests.[303] Free peasants were also obliged to this

---

299 See above, pp. 79-81.

300 P. and M., 316-318; II, 338; cf. F. M. Stenton, *The First Age of English Feudalism* (Oxford, 1932), p. 22 and Plucknett, *History*, p. 739.

301 Glanvill, Bk. VII, ch. 5: "... dominum suum primo de meliore et principaliore re quam habet recognoscat;" Bracton, fols. 60, 86. In the second text, Bracton distinguishes the heriot from the relief and concludes: "magis fit de gratia quam de iure, et quæ heredem non contingit;" *Fleta* reproduces both texts, Bk. II, ch. 57 and Bk. III, ch. 18; *Britton*, ed. Nichols, II, 51.

302 Levett, *Studies in Manorial History*, p. 245. On the payment of a heriot by customary tenants when they sold their holding, see M. M. Postan and J. Titow, "Heriots and Prices on Winchester Manors," *Economic History Review*, 2nd Ser., XI (1958-9), 393-411.

303 Miss Levett cites a case of 1273 at Kingsbury where mention is made of the sale of

payment in many manors.[304]   It was exacted in several of the boroughs, although exemption from it was more typical of that tenure.[305]   It is very difficult to discover whether the heriot was demanded of the free-holder or whether it was received only where he chose to give it.   If the lord's right is approached from the point of view of his claims on the property of a vassal who died intestate, it is seen to be very strong. Glanvill said that he was to have all the property, and Bracton reserved the heriot to him.[306]   Yet there are very few examples of this exaction from the deceased vassal.   It had probably declined steadily during the twelfth century so that the second description of it by Bracton, as a grace rather than a right, was correct in his day.[307]

Several of the episcopal *wills* of the thirteenth century contain the bequest of a palfrey and other goods to the king.[308]   Coke and others after him concluded that this offering was required of the bishops as the price of their freedom of devise.[309]   But there is no reference to this payment in the various royal permissions to make wills.   On the other hand, it is clear that Edward I and his successors regularly received some of the more precious chattels from the estates of deceased bishops.[310] It seems best to conclude that a tax, similar to the heriot, was imposed after the death of these prelates.   Some of them chose to leave a bequest to their royal lord; some did not.   But the success of the will does not seem to have depended on the legacy to the king.   It does not follow, however, that the bishop who left a bequest to the king always did so from motives of the purest friendship.   If such a legacy obtained an

---

a cow, which ought to have been saved "pro herietto et pro testamento," and suggests that the phrase means that the heriot was given for permission to make a will (*Studies*, p. 216 and n. 6).   The analogy with Anglo-Saxon practice is evident.

[304] *Ibid.*, p. 193.   Examples of the obligation to pay the heriot by free peasants are found in many monastic cartularies: e.g., the extents of *Gloucester Cart.*, III, 133, 170, 184 *et passim*.

[305] *B. C.*, II, 80-83; *Borough Charters*, I, 75-76, 95, 192; II, 95-97, 207.

[306] Glanvill, Bk. VII, ch. 16; Bracton, fol. 60b.

[307] T. 30 included the bequest of a coat of mail and spurs; this was probably intended as a heriot.

[308] T. 33, T. 56.

[309] Coke, *The Fourth Part of the Institutes of the Laws of England*, p. 338.   The opinion is discussed by Makower, *Constitutional History*, p. 248, n. 21.

[310] See W. S. Walford "The Rights of Christ Church Canterbury, on the Death of Bishops of the Province," *The Archaeological Journal*, XI (1854), pp. 273-277.   The seal and second best ring of bishops of the province of Canterbury were received by the archbishop. From the *Liber quotidianus contrarotulatoris garderobae, 28 Edward I*, Soc. of Antiquaries (London, 1787), p. 348, it becomes evident that the king received jewels from the estates of deceased abbots as well; see above, p. 251, n. 80.

additional defender of his will, the testator had an excellent reason for making it.

The second exaction from the estate of the deceased, the mortuary, was made by the Church. Within the framework of this study it is of greater interest than the heriot, for it was demanded from a larger portion of the population and, although minimum offerings were established by custom, testators very often exercised some freedom of choice in its regard.[311] Among the Anglo-Saxons, bequests to the parish church became so general that they were eventually required by law. Though the Fathers and the canonists encouraged these donations, they were aware of the danger of abuse that was involved. Their attempt to avoid it is evident in a very long list of decrees of popes and canons of councils that prohibit the exaction of burial fees.[312] In the age that concerns us here this restriction was part of the general law of the Church. It appears in Gratian and in the canons of the second, third and fourth Councils of the Lateran. As a general rule, it was admitted that voluntary offerings might be accepted. This was explicitly stated at the fourth Council of the Lateran, with the addition that, where the offering had become customary, the bishops were free to enforce it.[313] The prohibition of the exaction of a burial fee was equally frequent in England after the Conquest; it is included among the canons of five Westminster councils of the twelfth century.[314] Yet, with some exceptions, it can be said that the burial fee was exacted throughout England. It provided one of the chief sources of parish income, so that churches sought to have cemeteries and demanded that their parishioners be buried there.[315] This defence of the right of the parish was made necessary by the increased freedom to choose a place of

---

311 P. and M., II, 338, 431; B.C., II, cxl-cxli, 78, 85, 140, 211; see J. Moorman, *Church Life in England in the Thirteenth Century* (Cambridge, 1945), p. 130, n. 2 for more recent bibliography.

312 See Bernard, *La Sépulture*, pp. 141-149.

313 *Decretum*, C. 13, q. 2, cc. 12-15; II Lateran (1139), c. 24; III Lateran (1179), c. 7; IV Lateran (1215), c. 66 (Mansi, XXI, 352; XXII, 221, 1054). Cf. Raymundus de Pennaforte, *Summa Iuris*, ed. Serra, *Opera Omnia*, I, 143.

314 The references to these councils are as follows: 1125, c. 2; 1138, c. 1; 1173, c. 9; 1175, c. 7; 1200, c. 8; Wilkins, I, 408, 415, 474, 477, 506. For later legislation, see Bernard, *op. cit.*, pp. 145-149. Bracton was aware of the general law of the Church on this matter: "Et quamvis non teneretur quis aliquid dare ecclesiæ suæ nomine sepulturæ, tamen cum consuetudo illa laudabilis existat, dominus papa non vult eam infringere" (fol. 60).

315 E.g., in Anselm's council of 1102: "Ne corpora defunctorum extra parochiam suam sepelienda portentur, ut presbyter parochiae perdat quod inde illi juste debetur" (c. XXVI, Wilkins, I, 383). On the income from sepulchre, see Bernard, *op. cit.*, p. 72.

sepulchre, already remarked in Anglo-Saxon times, but especially developed in the twelfth century.[316] Monasteries and convents were attractive places for burial, and many were of the opinion that monks took unfair advantage of the pious fears of the dying and robbed the parish priest in the process. The same charge was laid against the friars when they established themselves in England.[317] A solution was found in the reservation of an offering to the parish church, even though burial was not in its cemetery. The whole tenor of this dispute, as well as its solution, demonstrates that the avoidance of the payment of the burial fee was very difficult. It had become so much a matter of custom that it was exacted even when burial did not take place.[318]

The mortuary was originally intended as a free offering in charity. In the second half of the thirteenth century, the opinion became current that it was to serve as restitution to the parish church for any failure to pay tithes or other dues, whether by inadvertence or by intent. Thus the preoccupation with the repair of injustice, typical of the wills of the period, appears here as well. This view of the mortuary was stated in the statutes attributed to Robert of Bingham, bishop of Salisbury (1238-44).[319] It is to be found in several other collections of statutes, was mentioned in a papal letter of 1282, and duly appeared in the *wills* of the second half of the century.[320]

The persons to whom the obligation extended, as well as the amount of the offering, were established by local custom. Glanvill and Bracton mention the mortuary in their treatment of the will of freemen.[321]

---

[316] See above, pp. 141-142.

[317] The monks are satirized in the *Satira Communis* of Henry of Huntingdon, ed. T. Wright in *The Anglo-Latin Satirical Poets and Epigrammatists of the Twelfth Century, RS*, 59 (1872), II, 165. The notion stressed is that the monks were receiving bequests from those for whom they had no care during life. In his turn, Matthew of Paris criticized the friars: *Chronica Majora*, ed. Luard, IV, 280.

[318] E.g., an agreement whereby Easby Abbey allowed Torfin, son of Robert, to build a chapel in his house under various conditions, one of which was that he be buried at the Abbey or give 20s. (*EYC*, V, 61, no. 154, dated 1162-94).

[319] London, Br. Mus., Harl. MS. 52, fol. 119v; on the date and authenticity of these statutes see Cheney, *English Synodalia*, pp. 73-74.

[320] The statute was repeated at Salisbury by Giles of Bridport (1257-62); the text is available in Wilkins, I, 718. Similar canons appeared in the collection of Bishop Bitton of Bath and Wells (fol. 112r) and in its derivatives, the collections of Archbishop Ludham of York (fol. 251r) and Bishop Gervais of Winchester (Wilkins, II, 298); these collections are described above, p. 185, n. 82. The letter of Martin IV is printed in Wilkins, II, 66. Among the *wills*, see T. 78b, T. 94. Cf. P. Haensel, "Die mittelalterlichen Erbschaftssteuern in England," *Deutsche Zeitschrift für Kirchenrecht*, XX (1910), 1-50.

[321] Glanvill, Bk. VII, ch. 5; Bracton, fol. 60.

They do not exclude the possibility of its payment by the servile classes, and the customs of many manors as well as ecclesiastical law show that it was usually expected.[322] In fact, the farm-animal demanded of many peasants was a very large proportion of their wealth. Bracton held that a mortuary need be given for a wife only if her husband consented. This was admitted in the constitutions of Giles of Bridport in the middle of the thirteenth century.[323] Some local customs were stricter, however: at St. Ives, for instance, where the best plough-animal was exacted as the mortuary of the husband, the second best was demanded as an offering for his wife.[324] Is is difficult to establish the extent to which those who were not householders were obliged. Children were specifically excluded in some cases, but according to other customs an offering was expected of everyone who owned property.[325] In some parishes there was no obligation to give a mortuary. This fact was respected in the Exeter constitutions of Bishop Peter Quivil (1287), though it was strongly recommended that the payment be made freely.[326] Once the notion had been accepted that the mortuary was intended as restitution for omissions in the past, the moral obligation to pay it extended into areas where custom did not permit that it be exacted.[327] The Exeter constitutions show that those obliged to make this offering sometimes sought to avoid it by alienating all of their possessions by specific bequests, none of which was given to the parish church.

The minimum value of the mortuary was established by custom.[328]

---

322 See Bennett, *op. cit.*, p. 144 and Homans, *op. cit.*, p. 132. Record of a discussion of the obligations of villeins is found at Evesham in 1271 and at Pershore Abbey *ca.* 1284 (Dugdale, *Monasticon*, II, 31, 420).

323 Wilkins, I, 718. In the Bath and Wells statutes of Bishop Bitton, and in the collections derived therefrom, the obligation is extended to men and to widows; see above, n. 320.

324 *Ramsey Cart.*, I, 281-2 (1251); similarly at Broughton and Holywell (1252), *ibid.*, I, 294, 331-332; see P. and M., II, 431, n. 2.

325 Children were excused at Torksey in 1345 (*B. C.*, II, 211). In an Evesham register we find: "judicatum fuit in pleno capitulo ... quod quicunque fuerit et cujuscunque ætatis et habuerit bona propria ex legatione vel aliunde patris vel matris dabit heriectum sanctæ ecclesiæ in morte sua" (Dugdale, *Monasticon*, II, 32). In this context *heriectum* means a mortuary. Wives and children were freed from payment of the mortuary by the statute of 21 Henry VIII (c. 60).

326 Wilkins, II, 158, c. LII.

327 "Et quanquam ista provisio esset aliqualiter fructuosa omnibus christianis" (*ibid.*). This was the basis of Lyndwood's objection to the decision to excuse wives from the payment of the mortuary unless their husband consented (*Provinciale*, p. 21, *gl. ad verb. minime*).

328 Pleas touching the exaction of the mortuary pertained to the ecclesiastical forum

Glanvill said that it was usually the second best possession of the deceased. Bracton repeated the statement, adding that according to local usage it varied from areas where the best beast was offered to others where nothing was demanded. When freemen were not required to leave a heriot to their lord, the mortuary was often their best beast. During the thirteenth century there is some evidence of a tendency to establish a fixed minimum offering, replacing an earlier arrangement whereby the testator decided what would be given to his parish church.[329] Several episcopal statutes ruled that where less than three animals were possessed by the deceased, no mortuary other than specific legacies would be demanded.[330] An entirely different point of view is revealed in a few areas where payment was claimed of as much as a third of the movable property of the deceased.[331] This custom is an interesting example of the tendency to identify the freely distributed portion of an estate with the alms to be given at the time of burial.

The most common offering of freemen and of peasants who could afford it was a horse or an ox. These animals were placed before the body of the deceased in the funeral procession;[332] the terms *principale*

(London, PRO, KB 26/129, m. 9, Easter, 1243); but the royal courts decided whether its payment was customary or not, according to *Y. B.*, 30-31 Edward I, ed. Horwood, pp. 442-444.

[329] This change is indicated in an inquisition made at the Ramsey Abbey manor of Broughton in 1252: having stated that a husband or widow must leave the best plough-animal to the church, the text continues: "et tempore W. de Eboraco, quando fuit ejusdem ecclesiæ firmarius, inolevit ista consuetudo, quia pro voluntate antea decedentium respicie-batur ecclesia in denariis, vel blado, vel pannis, et non in averiis" (*Ramsey Cart.*, I, 330-331); an earlier attempt of 1197 and the following years is indicated in *The Chartulary of the High Church of Chichester*, ed. Peckham, p. 7.

[330] Wilkins, I, 718; II, 278, etc.

[331] In 1248, Innocent IV ordered the archdeacon of Canterbury to decide a case in the archdeaconry of Richmond which involved the claim of as much as one third of the personal property of the deceased (*Registre*, ed. Berger, II, 57, no. 4409, and Bliss, *Entries in Papal Registers*, I, 252-3). For other examples, see *B. C.*, II, cxl-cxli; *Rot. Parl.*, II, 38a (1330). For examples on the Continent, see Bernard, *op. cit.*, pp. 155-156, and especially, Bruck, *Kirchenväter*, pp. 217-240; cf. G. G. Coulton, *Ten Medieval Studies* (Cambridge, 1930): pp. 126-131. In 1271, it was decided at Evesham that, where a villein died possessing only one animal, its value was to be divided between the lord and the parish church (Dugdale, *Monasticon*, II, 31).

[332] Where the body of the deceased had to be carried a considerable distance for burial, the animals used for this purpose were given as a mortuary: e.g., in a list of offerings made by the bishops of Durham—"et equos deportantes corpus ejusdem Patris." (*Wills and Inventories*, ed. J. Raine, pp. 1 ff.), and in the *Liber ecclesie de Bernewelle*—"et duo equi qui portabant loculum," and "Duo quidem palefridi, qui corpus portauerunt, remanserunt" (pp. 176, 223). A well known example of the presence of the mortuary beast in the funeral procession is that mentioned in the account of the death of Hamo Blunt in the

and *corse-present* express both the quality of the offering and the occasion when it was made.[333]   The written *wills* of the thirteenth century reveal a considerable variety of donations to the church of burial.   The animal to go before the body of the deceased was the most common, but donations of the best garment or of money were also of frequent occurrence.   The wills of the thirteenth century leave the impression that testators usually preferred to specify the offering that was to be made rather than leave it to be determined by custom.   It is perhaps correct to discern in this the desire to maintain a certain freedom in the last grant of alms for the soul.   In so far as the mortuary was to survive until modern times, it was as a free bequest.[334]   With this donation to the Church, the English will had its beginning.

Chronicle of Jocelin of Brakelond (ed. Butler, pp. 91-92); the same notion is sometimes expressed in *wills:* e.g., T. 90, etc. Money and other offerings are mentioned as though they preceded the body of the deceased: e.g., "item, ad altare ante se dimidam marcam" (T. 60); "ante corpus meum quinque marcas" (T. 67b). In some cases at least, they were carried in the funeral procession; thus in a statement of custom at Pershore Abbey we read : "dicit quod principale legatum debet deferri ante corpus defunctorum" (Dugdale, *Monasticon,* II, 420).

[333] T. 71a: "pro suo principali meliorem pannum;" T. 91: "Item nomine sui principalis equus suus." The term *corspresent* came into use in the fourteenth century; cf. the Torksey custom of 1345, *B. C.,* II, 211. *Mortuarium* is explained by Lyndwood in a sense similar to that of corspresent: "quia cum mortuo tempore sepulturæ consuevit ad Ecclesiam deferri" (*Provinciale,* p. 21).

[334] On the later history of the mortuary, see *Lincoln Wills,* ed. Foster, II, xxiii.

CONCLUSION

THE last will of English common law provides an interesting example of a legal instrument born of the meeting of the three great cultural strains of medieval Europe. Christians of the Mediterranean basin had developed the practice of bequeathing part of their property in alms, but this practice when applied in England collided with Germanic family custom and rules regulating the ownership of property and with ancient beliefs about the after-life. However, the desire to give alms at death, supported by legal notions derived from Roman law, was strong enough to modify the Germanic customs of succession in use among the Anglo-Saxons and their Norman conquerors. These Germanic customs did not entirely disappear; they survived and, moulding the influence brought to bear on them, made their proper contribution to the English will of the thirteenth century.

The will was introduced into England as an instrument for the giving of alms. As would be expected, other advantages of a power of bequest were quickly recognized and acted upon. They assumed considerable importance and reinforced the demand to extend testamentary capacity. The somewhat detailed examination of the English will in previous chapters has perhaps tended to obscure the original and constant motive of the institution. It was intended as one of the means whereby the Christian might perform the charitable acts that were required of him. In this it was successful. The will retained a distinctly religious tone throughout the period of interest to the present study and, within it, the bequest in alms remained of prime importance. In England as elsewhere, the will supplied one of the chief supports of the vast voluntary projects of the medieval world—projects of prayer and education, of care for the weak, even of holy war.

The impact of Christian teaching on the bequest of alms had more far-reaching consequences in England and in northern Europe generally than in the Roman Empire. This teaching did not require important changes in the law of succession within the Empire; the Christian, who already possessed testamentary freedom, was urged to devote a portion of his estate to pious purposes. If he chose to do so, he simply exercised a right that he normally possessed. Bishops eventually became the special protectors of these bequests, but their support was merely subsidiary to institutions already in existence and capable of defending a valid testament. Conditions were different in England. There, the implementation of a bequest in alms involved freeing part of a believer's property from family claims so that it might be alienated. In this case, the demands of Christian teaching involved an adjustment of ancient notions of property and of the individual's control of it.

During the years when the rules governing the bequest of property were elaborated, the English clergy were able to draw on new ideas that often had an important bearing on the problem. These notions were not usually of the religious order—there was nothing specifically Christian about them—but they were part of the common property of the Church which she had acquired in her vast experience with different races, customs and systems of law. It is remarkable how frequently innovations touching the theory and practice of the will were first used by the clergy themselves in their efforts to protect their property and supervise the bequest which controlled its devolution.

In the beginning the chief contribution of the clergy was the presentation of a motive for the bequest in alms. It helped the Anglo-Saxon to realize that a distribution of property at death was a possibility and implied the assertion of a greater right of private property against the claims of the family group. But the bequests themselves were usually legal acts in accord with the Germanic conception of donation. They were contractual, irrevocable transactions, performed orally and with the observance of certain formalities. These qualities remained typical of most of the acts by which bequests were made from the first appearance of the will, immediately after the Conversion, until the second half of the twelfth century. But the influence of the clergy was to go much further. In a second step, the legal notions at their disposition were applied not only to the motive of the bequest in alms, but to the act itself. The last will of the canonists, revocable and ambulatory as was the Roman testament, but simplified in its requirements for validity, slowly replaced the older acts which had been in use for centuries. The will thus conceived became a permanent contribution of the canonists to English common law.

Early in the thirteenth century, the enforcement of bequests passed into the jurisdiction of the courts Christian. The implementation of the will was entrusted to the executor, and as the years passed his powers were increased until he became an excellent instrument for this purpose. Before the century ended, royal courts had begun to supervise certain aspects of the executor's activity. He would grow in their hands until his powers over the movable portion of an estate would bear remarkable resemblance to those of the heir in Roman law. In later centuries the clerical control of the will would be undermined by the temporal courts, but at the terminal point of the present study the testamentary jurisdiction exercised by the Church was more complete in England than in any other kingdom of Europe.

The religious motive for asserting a right of bequest was one of the causes of the dispute over the persons to whom this right should be extended. Testamentary power was first admitted in those who controlled most of the wealth of society. But if the motive for seeking this power was repentance, it could not be limited to the wealthy any more than the need of repentance could be limited to them. Furthermore the claim that every adult should make a gift for pious purposes involved the suggestion that every adult should have the right to control property that he might be free to donate it. Thus officials of the Church and those members of society who had come to see the fittingness of the bequest in alms began to apply pressure to extend the right of bequest to all adults. This demand became explicit only gradually. There was no doctrinaire attempt to deduce precise and immediately practical conclusions from the teaching that all Christians were obliged to acts of charity. But these consequences eventually became apparent; in thirteenth-century England a right of bequest was claimed for the married woman and the villein. Common law refused to allow it, but the claim was made and was to be of some importance in the future.

The distinction between movable and immovable property, already evident in Anglo-Saxon wills, became more pronounced in the period after the Conquest. The bequest of land did not become a general practice. In spite of a tendency to remove obstacles to the alienation of land during the lifetime of the owner, the development of a similar freedom of alienation by will was prevented. There were many motives for this restriction, but it seems best to conclude that its most enduring cause was a procedural one: the requirements for livery of seisin, as developed by common law, made the transfer of land by will technically impossible. In the boroughs and other areas not subject to common law a right of devise of land slowly developed so that by the middle of the thirteenth century the bequest of land was of common occurrence. Yet even here the distinction between movable and immovable property was maintained; these legacies were supervised by the temporal courts, even though the implementation of the bequests lay with the executor.

The medieval English will was primarily concerned with the distribution of movable property. In Anglo-Saxon times the testator seems to have made reasonable provision for the future needs of his wife

20

and children, but so far as can be seen the part of his chattels over which he had full power of alienation was not limited to a precise portion. An important change is discernible after the Conquest: it became a general, though not universal, custom that the testator with dependents could dispose of one third of his movable property. The remaining portions were reserved to his wife and children. Those who died without dependents were free to dispose of all their chattels except those claimed as a mortuary or as a heriot. This arrangement was probably derived from a teaching of some of the Fathers that the Christian should bequeath one third of his property in alms. When this notion appeared in England it had undergone many changes. The third was no longer the part of an estate to be bequeathed in alms, but was the total amount that could be bequeathed for any purpose. In fact this portion was sometimes exclusively devoted to charity, but if this occurred it was by the free choice of the testator. The Church in England never made a general claim to more than the mortuary, a tax that lay heavily on the poor though not on the more wealthy members of society.

When one considers the medieval English will in all its ramifications it becomes apparent that the influence of the Church on its development was very great. Christian teaching provided the original motive for donations in alms at death, and a cosmopolitan clergy eventually supplied most of the notions that lay behind the theory of the act and the manner of its implementation and control. But decisions touching the kinds and amount of property over which the power of bequest was extended were less subject to this clerical influence; they were made in terms of the military, economic and family needs of the time.

APPENDICES

APPENDIX A

A LIST OF WILLS CITED IN CHAPTERS THREE TO SIX

In the preparation of this study, texts of wills of the late twelfth and thirteenth centuries were collected. A preliminary list of 161 documents was published in the *Genealogists' Magazine*, March, 1961 (Vol. XIII, no. 9, 259-265). These texts will provide the basis of a future edition of early medieval wills. The following group was selected from them for use in the present study. Preference has been shown for texts which are already available in print.

T. 12 ...First will of Hugh of Wells, bishop of Lincoln, 1212; Wells, Library of the Dean and Chapter, Liber Albus, R. III, fol. 284v; summarized in *Hist. MSS. Comm. Report*, 28, *Calendar of the Manuscripts of the Dean and Chapter of Wells*, 2 vols. (1907-14), I, 431-432.

T. 16 ...Will of John, king of England, 1216; Rymer, *Fœdera*, Record Commission, 11, Vol. I, 144.

T. 23 ...Will of Agnes de Condet, wife of Walter Clifford, 1223 or earlier; ed. Foster, *Registrum Antiquissimum of the Cathedral Church of Lincoln*, I, 293-295.

T. 25 ...Will of William de Longespee, earl of Salisbury, 1225; *Rot. Lit. Cl.*, II, 71.

T. 26 ...Will of Philip de Sancte Marie Ecclesia, 1226; London, St. Paul's, Dean and Chapter Library, Box A 66, no. 1.

T. 28 ...Will of Richard Elmham, 1228; ed. *The Archaeological Journal*, XXIV (1867), 343-344.

T. 30 ...Will of Bartholomew de Legh, *ca.* 1230; ed. Madox, *Formulare Anglicanum*, no. DCCLXVIII, pp. 423-424.

T. 31 ...Will of John of St. John, 1231; ed. Salter, *Cartulary of Oseney Abbey*, I, 135-136.

T. 33 ...Second will of Hugh of Wells, bishop of Lincoln, 1233; ed. Foster, *Registrum Antiquissimum*, II, 70-75.

T. 37 ...Will of William, constable of Wirneris, *ca.* 1237; Oxford, Bodleian MS. Charters, Essex a. 2 (37).

T. 47a ...Fragment of will of Lawrence, archdeacon of York, *ca.* 1247, ed. Raine, *Historians of the Church of York*, III, 165-167.

T. 47b ...Fragment of will of William de Skelmerskerth, 1247; ed. J. C. Atkinson, *The Coucher Book of Furness Abbey,* Vol. I, pt. ii, Chetham Soc., N.S., XI (1887), 411.

T. 53a ...Will of St. Richard Wych, bishop of Chichester, *ca.* 1253; ed. W. H. Blaauw, *Sussex Archaeological Collections,* I (1848), 164-192.

T. 53b ...Will of Henry III, king of England, 1253; Rymer, *Fœdera,* I, 496.

T. 56 ...Will of Walter Suffield, bishop of Norwich, 1256; summarized in F. Blomefield, *Topographical History of Norfolk,* 5 vols. (Fersfield, etc., 1739-75), II, 345-346.

T. 59a ...Will of Simon de Montfort, 1259; ed. C. Bémont, *Simon de Montfort,* trans. E. F. Jacob (Oxford, 1930), pp. 276-278.

T. 59b ...Will of Martin, master of Holy Cross, 1259; ed. Raine, *Wills and Inventories,* I, 6-11.

T. 60 ...Will of Henry Perle, 1260; ed. Salter, *Cartulary of the Hospital of St. John the Baptist,* I, 466-477.

T. 65 ...Will of John Hammond, 1265; ed. Wigram, *Cartulary of the Monastery of St. Frideswide at Oxford,* II, 215-217.

T. 67a ...Will of Cecily, wife of Geoffrey Huse, 1267; London, PRO, E-210. 291.

T. 67b ...Will of Richard son of Robert, 1267; London, Br. Mus., Eger. Ch. 528.

T. 67c ...Will of John de Doulys, 1267; London, Br. Mus., Add. Ch. 27523.

T. 67d ...Will of Sir Hugh de Nevill, 1267; ed. M. S. Guiseppi, *Archaeologia,* LVI (1899), 352-354.

T. 68 ...Will of Peter of Aigueblanche, bishop of Hereford, 1268; ed. C. E. Woodruff in *The Camden Miscellany,* XIV, Camden 3rd Ser., XXXVII (1926).

T. 69 ...Will of William son of Richard, 1269; London, PRO, LR-14. 16.

T. 71a ...Will of Nicholas de Weston, 1271; ed. Salter, *Cartulary of Oseney Abbey,* II, 562-565.

T. 71b ...Will of Henry de Colebi, 1271; ed. Foster, *Lincoln Wills,* II, 215-217.

T. 72a ...Will of Adam Cornwaleys, 1272; London, St. Paul's, Dean and Chapter Library, Box A 66, no. 2.

T. 72b ...Will of Prince Edward, later King Edward I, 1272; Rymer, *Fœdera,* I, 495.

T. 73 ...Will of Thomas son of Peter de Aldeburgh, 1273; London, PRO, E-40. 11569.

T. 74 ...Will of Simon Swyn, proved 1274; Oxford, Bodleian, MS. Rolls, Norfolk 13 (b).

T. 75a ...Will of Reginald the Mason, 1270-5; ed. Wigram, *Cartulary of the Monastery of St. Frideswide*, I, 375-376.

T. 75b ...Fragment of the will of Henry de Lincolnia, 1275, ed. Salter, *Cartulary of the Hospital of St. John the Baptist*, I, 270-271.

T. 76 ...Will of Eva Poer, 1276; London, Br. Mus., Harl. Ch. 112.C.17.

T. 77 ...Will of Abel de St. Martin, proved 1277; London, St. Paul's, Dean and Chapter Library, Box A 66, no. 5.

T. 78a ...Will of Walter de Vaus, 1278; *ibid.*, Box A 66, no. 6.

T. 78b ...Will of Robert le Pere, 1278; abstract by C. E. Woodruff, *Archaeologia Cantiana*, XLVI (1903), 28-31.

T. 81 ...Will of Agnes Punchard, 1281; ed. Salter, *Cartulary of the Hospital of St. John the Baptist*, I, 320-321.

T. 82a ...Will of Juliana Wyth, 1282; ed. Salter, *Cartulary of Oseney Abbey*, I, 411-413.

T. 82b ...Will of Lawrence of St. Michael, 1282; London, PRO, E-315. 46.

T. 82c ...Will of Margery de Creke, 1282; London, Br. Mus., Camp. Ch. III, 1.

T. 83 ...Will of Christiana, relict of John de Bennington, 1283; ed. Foster, *Lincoln Wills*, I, 2-4.

T. 86 ...Will of John son of Thomas of Woodstock, 1286; Oxford, Magdalen Coll. Ch., Hosp. in Gen. 6.

T. 89a ...Will of Anian II, bishop of St. Asaph, 1289; Canterbury, Dean and Chapter Library, Sede Vacante Scrap Book, II, 187.

T. 89b ...First will of Richard de Gravesend, bishop of London, 1289; London, St. Paul's, Dean and Chapter Library, Box A 66, no. 14a.

T. 90 ...Will of Henry de Enfield, 1290; ed. Hassall, *Cartulary of St. Mary Clerkenwell*, pp. 256-257.

T. 91 ...Will of Edmund de Watford, 1891; London, PRO, E-40. 11568.

T. 92 ...Fragment of will of Philip le Tailor, 1292; ed. Hassal, *Cartulary of St. Mary Clerkenwell*, pp. 259-260.

T. 93. ...Will of Hugh de Panebrok, 1293; printed below, pp. 314-315.

T. 94 ...Will of Henry de Collecote, 1294, ed. F. C Hingeston-Randolph, *Episcopal Register of the Diocese of Exeter, Walter Bronescombe and Peter Quivil*, pp. 435-436.

T. 95 ...Will of William de Arundel, 1295; ed. Madox, *Formulare*, no. DCCLXXI, p. 425.

T. 96 ...Will of Nicholas Longespee, bishop of Salisbury, 1296; ed. A. R. Malden, *EHR*, XV (1900), 523-528.

T. 98 ...Will of Robert le Seneschal, 1298; London, St. Paul's, Dean and Chapter Library, Box A 66, no. 10.

T. 99a ...Will of Lucy Lundreys, 1299; Wells, Library of the Dean and Chapter, Liber Albus, R. I, fol. 128; summarized in *Hist. MSS. Comm. Report*, 28, Vol. I (1907), 165-166.

T. 99b ...Will of William de Wobourn, 1299; London, St. Paul's, Dean and Chapter Library, Box A 66, no. 12.

T. 99c ...Will of John Brommere, 1299; London, Br. Mus., Cott. Ch. VIII. 23.

APPENDIX B

SELECTED DOCUMENTS CONCERNING THE BEQUEST
OF PROPERTY

1 An Irrevocable Bequest

Charter of Margaret, late wife of Sir Walter Clifford, granting her heart for burial in Aconbury Priory church, and providing an irrevocable bequest of fifteen marks, and funeral expenses.   Dec. 16, 1263
(London, Br. Mus., Harl. Ch. 48. C.31).

Notum sit omnibus sancte matris ecclesie filiis, quod ego Margareta, quondam uxor domini Walteri de Clifford', in libera viduitate mea, do, lego cor meum Deo et Beate Marie et omnibus sanctis, ad sepeliendum in ecclesia priorata sanctimonialium de Acornebire prope Her[e]ford'. Et cum dicto corde meo in elemosinam, quindecim marcas sterlingorum eidem domui celerius persolvendas una cum aliis expensis, de bonis que me contingunt, honorabiliter ad exequias circa predictum cor meum sepeliendum perficiendas, secundum discretam prudenciam executorum meorum in ultima voluntate mea constituendorum. Ita quod, si forte per oblivionem vel quocumque alio casu per testamentum vel aliquam aliam ordinacionem contra presentem donacionem contravenerim, nullum obtineat robur firmitatis. In huius rei testimonium... .

2 Nuncupative Wills

(a)
Concerning the last will of Gerard de Ugina

Memorandum concerning the examination of those present when Gerard de Ugina made arrangements for the distribution of his property, during his last illness in his manor near Paris.   April 3, 1291
(Printed in *Registrum Ricardi de Swinfield*, ed. Capes, p. 251).

De ultima voluntate Girardi Defuncti,—Memorandum quod tercio die mensis Aprilis, anno Dom. MᶜCCᵒ nonagcsimo primo, Thomas Emme de Prestebury, quondam famulus Gyrardi de Ugina, personaliter constitutus coram domino in manerio suo de Colewelle, juratusque et examinatus, deposuit in virtute prestiti sacramenti quod idem Girardus, dominus suus, die Martis proxima ante festum annunciacionis dominice, anno eodem, cum in manerio suo de Cumbs villa, Parisiensis diocesis, aliquamdiu jacuisset infirmus, tradidit sibi quandam pixidem in quam posuerat quasdam litteras canonicales vel obligatorias, et injunxit eidem quod ipsam pixidem cum predictis litteris celeriter deportaret magistro Gilberto de Suynefeud, cancellario Herefordensi, tunc Parisius commoranti, et sibi diceret quod pecuniam in litteris ipsis contentam idem magister Gilbertus exigeret a debitoribus suis, et medietatem ejusdem pecunie ipse haberet de dono dicti Geraldi, et aliam medietatem solvi faceret pro salute anime sue matrici ecclesie Herefordensi. Et cum idem Thomas quod sibi injunctum fuerat complevisset, in crastino rediens invenit dominum suum predictum defunctum. Johannes de Wolvinehope, famulus ejusdem Girardi, juratus et examinatus super premissis dixit quod presens fuit quum dominus suus misit predictum Thomam Parisius, concordans cum dicto Thoma de die et loco, pro quo tamen negocio ignoravit. Requisitus de causa sciencie dixit quod fuit in camera cum eisdem, et audivit dominum suum injungere dicto Thome quod festinaret redire ad ipsum, quia antequam ipse rediret credidit moriturum. Requisiti ambo singillatim in quo statu idem Girardus fuit, cum hec injungeret et diceret, dixerunt quod fuit compos mentis, et sane et aperte loquebatur, sed de convalescencia desperabat. Obiit Girardus predictus xxij° die mensis Marcii, hoc est xj° kal. Aprilis, anno Dom. M°CC° nonagesimo finiente.

(b)
The nuncupative will of Hugh de Panebrok

Notice by Richard de Clyve, commissary of Canterbury, sede vacante, that he has examined the witnesses present when Hugh de Panebrok made a nuncupative will, and has given administration to the executors. Dec. 11, 1293
(Canterbury, Dean and Chapter Library,
Sede Vacante Scrap Book, II, 189).

In Dei nomine, Amen. Anno Domini M°CC° nonagesimo tercio, die veneris proxima ante festum sancte Lucie virginis, in Ecclesia Christi Cant' constituti, coram nobis fratre Ricardo de Clyve, commissario Cant', sede vacante, magister Thomas de Uptone, rector ecclesie de Adesham, magister Philippus de Pette, clericus, et Walterus, nepos magistri Hugonis de Panebrok', asserverunt prefatum magistrum Hugonem, rectorem ecclesie de Ivecherche, viam universe carnis esse ingressum, ipsumque testamentum condidisse nuncupativum, ipsosque dicti testamenti executores constituisse. Productis super hoc quatuor testibus omni exceptione maioribus, quibus admissis, iuratis, examinatis, et eorum dictis publicatis, invenimus quod prefatus magister Hugo, sane mentis et lingue expedite, testamentum suum condidit sub hac forma, non tamen in scriptis redactum.   Ego Hugo de Panebrok', rector ecclesie de Ivecherch[e], ordino, facio, et constituo magistrum Thomam, rectorem ecclesie de Adesham, magistrum Philippum de Pette, clericum, et Walterum, nepotem meum, executores meos de omnibus bonis meis mobilibus et immobilibus quibuscumque, et committo eadem omnia bona mea in disposicionem et ordinacionem predictorum executorum meorum; ratum et stabile habens quicquid iidem executores mei, in pios usus pro anima mea et in debitis meis solvendis ac aliis rebus necessariis faciendis, disposuerint et ordinaverint, de bonis memoratis. Unde nos frater Ricardus, commissarius supradictus, audita probacione predicta, pro dicto testamento sententialiter pronunciavimus, et prefatos magistros Thomam, rectorem ecclesie de Adesham, et Philippum de Pette ad administracionem dictorum bonorum admisimus tamquam executores, et adhuc sufficientes, prestitoque ab eisdem de fideli inventario faciendo in bonis predictis sacramento corporali.   Quo quidem facto et nobis liberato, eisdem executoribus administracionem dictorum bonorum plenam et liberam concessimus in forma iuris.

3   Directions for Making a Will

Text serving as introduction to a model will (printed in the Archaeological Journal, *XXI [1865], 58-62), in which rules are given for the testamentary distribution of property.*   ca. *1300*
(London, Br. Mus., Add. MS. 41201, fols. 3-4).

In testamenti cujuslibet exordio vel primordio duo sunt principaliter cuilibet testatori, antequam suum condat testamentum, consideranda, videlicet, debita in quibus aliis tenetur, et debita in quibus alii sibi tenentur.   Hoc facto, an habeat uxorem an non.   Si non habeat, tunc condere debet testamentum suum de omnibus bonis suis, mobilibus et immobilibus, nisi consuetudo patrie repugnet.   Si habeat uxorem et pueros, tunc resecanda est equaliter et proportionaliter tertia pars omnium bonorum suorum ad opus uxoris, omnibus suis debitis prius solutis, et alia tertia pars ad alimentum puerorum suorum.   Et ex alia tertia parte testator suum condet testamentum.   Si habeat uxorem et non pueros tunc omnia bona sua in duas partes dividantur, quarum una pars uxori sue remanebit, quam illa invita et non spontanee, nullo modo legare poterit.   Sed ex una debita portione suum condere debet testamentum, facto prius inventorio omnium bonorum suorum ex una portione debita antequam fiat testamentum; quod sic incipit... .

APPENDIX C

SELECTED DOCUMENTS CONCERNING THE EXECUTION OF WILLS

1 Grant of Administration

Letter granting administration of the estate of Walter Marshal to his executors, by Bishop Godfrey Giffard of Worcester; the executors are to render account of their administration when required. **April 24, 1286**

(Worcester, Giffard Register, fol. 251r; calendared by J. W. Willis Bund, Vol. I, 285).

G. etc., dilectis in Christo filiis Johanni le Breun, Johanni de Mechinges, et Petro Flory Glouc', executoribus Walteri Marescalli de Weston', salutem, gratiam et benedictionem. Quia dictus Walterus, condicionis humane et fragilitatis proprie reminiscens, sib providit dum viverit testamentum condendo, et de bonis suis prout salubrius credidit disponendo, secundum quod per assertiones legittimas et documenta verius nobis constat, vobis tam de bonis presentialiter sub manu sua inventis, quam in terra crescentibus, administrationem liberam concedimus per presentes. Ita quod ipsius defuncti legitime exequamini voluntatem et super vestra administratione fidele reddatis compotum, cum inde fueritis requisiti. Dat. apud Weston', viii. kal. Maii. anno xviii.

2 Acknowledgement of Payment by Executors

Selections from a file of forty-eight receipts given to the executors of Roger son of Benedict, former mayor of Lincoln, by those who had benefited from his will. **1287-8**

(Lincoln, Dean and Chapter D ij/50/2/4).

(a)

Receipt from a priest offering prayers for the soul of the deceased.

Per presens scriptum pateat universis quod ego Thomas de Welton, capellanus, recepi per manus executor' domini Rogeri filii Benedicti, civis Linc', defuncti, quinque marcas sterlingorum pro quodam annuali quod celebravi a festo sancti Michaelis anno Domini M^oCC^o lxxx^{mo} septimo pro anima eiusdem defuncti usque ad eundem festum sancti Michaelis anno Domini M^o CC^o lxxx^{mo} octavo. In cuius rei testimonium presentibus sigillum meum apposui. Dat' Linc', crastino sancti Michaelis, anno Domini supradicto.

(Sept. 30, 1288).

(b)

Receipt from a creditor of the deceased.

Omnibus Christi fidelibus ad quos presens scriptum pervenerit, Robertus, filius Goderiki de Barru(?), capellanus, salutem in domino. Noveritis me recepisse de domino Nicholao de Hybaldstowe, capellano, Thoma de Wollington, Henrico de Schadwerth executoribus testamenti Rogeri filii Benedicti de Linc' tres solidos et sex denarios pro quodam debito in quo dictus Rogerus mihi tenebatur dum vixit, et pro omnibus actionibus et demandis quas erga predictos executores habui vel habere potui seu potero. In cuius rei testimonium presentibus sigillum meum apposui. Dat' die sabbati proxima ante festum beate Katerine virginis, anno Domini M° CC° octogesimo septimo.

(Nov. 22, 1287).

(c)

Receipt from a legatee.

[Pate]at universis tenore presencium quod nos Isabella, priorissa, et conventus de Goucwell' recepimus domino Nicholao, capellano et executore testamenti domini Rogeri filii Benedicti, civis Lincoln', defuncti, cuius anime propicietur Deus, .v. solidos sterlingorum, quos dictus Rogerus nobis in testamento suo legavit. In cuius rei testimonium has literas nostras dicto domino Nicholao et coexecutoribus suis de aquietancia fecimus patentes. Dat' apud Goucwell', die sancti Barnabe apostoli, anno Domini M° CC° octogesimo septimo.

(June 11, 1287).

3   Acknowledgement of Return of Borrowed Property by Executors

The priory of Durham acknowledges the return by the executors of Robert Marsh, late dean of Lincoln, of three books borrowed from the priory by the testator. **1262**

(Printed in *Durham Annals and Documents of the Thirteenth Century*, ed. F. Barlow, Surtees Soc., CLV (1945), no. 17, p. 93)

Omnibus etc., H*ugo*, prior etc. Noueritis nos recepisse a domino W*illelmo* de Hemmingburg', canonico Linc*olniensi*, executore bone memorie magistri Roberti de Marisco, quondam decani Linc*olniensis*, tria uolumina theologie, scilicet quatuor ewangelia glossata in vno uolumne, xij prophetas, Iob, libros Salomonis et epistolas canonicas in alio, actus Apostolorum et Apocalipsim in tercio; que quidem volumina dictus magister habuit de commodato nostro. Vnde uolumus et concedimus, quod si aliqua obligacio dicti magistri de supradictis libris, sibi commodatis, penes nos uel nostros inuenta fuerit, vacua penitus remaneat et inefficax.

In cuius etc. Dat' etc.

4 Acknowledgement of Payment to Executors

The executors of Master Robert acknowledge the delivery of seven pounds, eight shillings from the estate of the deceased by his son.   *Nov. 30 1296*
(London, PRO, C-146. 6818).

Omnibus Christi fidelibus presens scriptum visuris vel audituris, Johannes de Scriis, rector ecclesie de Knapetoft, Robertus de Bymh', executores testamenti domini Roberti filii Walteri de Strell, salutem in domino   Noveritis nos recipisse de domino Roberto de Strell, filio eiusdem Roberti filii Walteri, septem libras octo solidos sterlingorum, in quibus finebatur dictis executoribus de bonis predicti Roberti patris sui, quod dicti executores solvebant; videlicet Mabilie de Blakeburne .xlii. solidos, Ade de Clocherum de Strell .xli. solidos, et pro viridi cera .lxv. solidos.   In cuius rei testimonium huic scripto sigilla nostra sunt appensa.   Dat' apud Strell, die sancti Andree apostoli, anno regni Regis Edwardi filii Regis Henrici, vicesimo quinto.

5 Loan of Testator's Property by Executors

(a)

Loan of money

The Dean and Chapter of Lincoln pay to Bishop Oliver Sutton, executor of Master William de Sherwood, ten pounds which they had borrowed from the goods of the deceased.   *Sept. 12, 1287*
(Lincoln, Dean and Chapter, D.ij/81/3/7).

Pateat universis per presentes quod cum venerabilis pater dominus O., dei gratia episcopus noster Linc', nuper coram nobis N. decano et capitulo Linc' literam nostram, per quam apparebat ipsum decem libras sterlingorum de bonis testamentariis quondam magistri Willelmi de Shyrewode, cuius executor existit, ecclesie nostre fabrice dedisse mutuo, exhiberet, et peteret sibi de eisdem satisfieri.   Dominus Ric' de Wynchecumb', concanonicus noster et custos operis antedicti, dictam pecuniam de bonis fabrice de consciencia nostra sibi statim exsolvi fecit et literam supradictam in capitulo cancellari.   Super quibus testimonium perhibemus per presentes sigillo nostro communitas.   Dat' Linc', ii. idus Septembris, anno Domini M°CC° octogesimo septimo.

(b)
Loan of goods

Acknowledgement by John Pecham, archbishop of Canterbury, that he has borrowed a glossed Bible from the estate of Nicholas of Ely, late bishop of Winchester, and that he will return it to the executors on demand.

Dec. 16, 1281 (?)

(London, Lambeth Palace, Pecham's Register, fol. 142r).

Universis etc. Noverit universitas vestra nos nomine commodati recipisse a discretis viris domino R. et magistro Hug', executoribus bone memorie domini N. Wynton' episcopi, unam bibliam glosatam in duobus voluminibus, quam promittimus bona fide per presentes eisdem nos velle restituere quandocumque a nobis eam duxerint requirendam, et eos super hoc conservare indempnes. In cuius rei t' etc. Dat' apud Ixhull, xvii. kal. Januarii.

6 Administration of Immovable Property

(a)
Sale of land by executors

Sale by the executors of the will of Baldwin de Sympling of three acres of arable in the fields of St. Edmund to the prior and brethren of the Hospital of St Peter at Bury St. Edmunds.   ca. 1250

(Oxford, Bodleian MS. Chart. Suffolk, a.l (68).

Sciant presentes et futuri quod nos Mabilia, quondam uxor Baldewyni de Sympling, Radulphus Hereward, Rogerus Sumer, et Rogerus de Lausel, executores testamenti predicti Bald[e]wyni defuncti, concessimus, vendidimus, et hac presenti carta nostra confirmavimus priori et fratribus [h]ospitalis sancti Petri in suburbio sancti Eadmundi extra portam de Risebi, et eorum successoribus pro undecim marcis argenti, quas nobis dederunt pre manibus, tres acras terre arabilis in campo sancti Eadmundi versus occidentem; jacentes inter terram que quondam fuit Symonis le Speru' et terram Matilde, relicte Johannis de Neketon. Et habuttant ad unum caput super viam que tendit de sancto Eadmundo versus Cheventon' et ad aliud caput super terram Luce filii Johannis, sive ibidem sit plus sive minus. Quam quidem terram predictus Baldewynus in ultima voluntate sua ad testamenti sui completionem per visum nostrum et dispositionem nostram venditione disposuit et legavit; habendam et tenendam predictis priori et fratribus et eorum successoribus, libere, quiete, bene, in pace, in feodo et hereditate, faciendo capitalibus dominis illius feodi servicia inde debita et consueta. In cuius... .

(b)
Executors confirm a sale of land

The executors of the will of Abel the Goldsmith give notice that with their consent and advice Dionisia, widow of the testator, sold land to Andrew Bokerell to acquit the debt of the deceased to him.   1222/3

(London, Br. Mus., Add. Ch. 7594).

Omnibus ad quos presens scriptum pervenerit, Ricardus de Greneford, canonicus de sancto Paulo, et Willelmus, capellanus hospitalis sancti Johannis de Clerkenewell, et Johannes de Woburn', et Willelmus Juvenal, executores testamenti Abel aurifabri, salutem. Noverit universitas vestra quod Dionisia, quondam uxor dicti Abel aurifabri, assensu et consilio nostro vendidit et quietam clamavit, et forisaffidavit Andree Bokerll' totam terram suam quam habuit in parochia sancti Egidii extra Creplegate, prope Everardes welle, que videlicet terra fuit dicti Abel, quondam viri sui; videlicet quicquid ibidem habuit, in terris, in lingnis et lapidibus, in gardinis et virgultis, in longitudine et latitudine et in rebus cunctis, cum omnibus pertinentiis suis, sine aliquo retinemento. Ad aquietanda debita eiusdem Abel viri sui, sicut coram nobis testatum fuit. Salvo servicio capitalium dominorum. Et ut hec venditio et quietaclamatio, et forisaffidatio, omnibus sit nota, presenti scripto sigilla nostra apposuimus. His testibus... .

(c)
Grant of land by executors for the soul of the testator

The executors of William Blund, late precentor of Lincoln, grant a toft and ten acres of land for the soul of the deceased to John de Hauuill. John shall give a candle of a pound's weight each year to burn on the vigil and feast of the Assumption for William's soul.   1245-50

(Printed in the *Registrum Antiquissimum of the Cathedral Church of Lincoln*, Vol. VII, ed. Kathleen Major, pp. 156-157).

Omnibus Christi fidelibus ad quos presens scriptum pervenerit. Willelmus Linc' ecclesie subdecanus Rogerus Blundus eiusdem ecclesie canonicus Willelmus presbiter rector ecclesie sancti Rumwaldi et Ricardus de Retford ecclesie sancte Trinitatis in Wycford Linc' executores testamenti bone memorie magistri Willelmi Blundi quondam precentoris Linc' cuius anime propiciet deus salutem in domino. Noueritis nos in capitulo Linc' et de assensu eiusdem concessisse ac dedisse pro anima eiusdem Willelmi Johanni de Hauuill' quondam familiari seruienti eius vnum toftum in villa de North Rouceby quod Adam Welle aliquando tenuit et quod idem Willelmus comparauit a Galfrido

filio Walteri de eadem villa cum decem acris terre arabilis iacentibus
in campis utriusque ville de Rouceby quas prenominatus Willelmus a
Rogero Haket de eadem villa et a predicto Galfrido comparauit.
Habend' et tenend' sibi et heredibus suis vel assignatis suis quibus vel
cui vel quando ea assignare voluerit exceptis viris religiosis et Judeis
libere quiete plenarie et integre cum omnibus pertinentiis suis et liber-
tatibus infra villam et extra sicut melius et plenius et liberius sepedictis
Willelmus ea tenuit et eciam cum omnibus aisiamentis in viis semitis
campis pasturis que ad tantam terram pertinent vel pertinere poterunt.
Reddendo inde annuatim pro omni seruicio seculari secta curie et
demanda maiori altari ecclesie Linc' pro anima sepedicti Willelmi vnam
cereum ponderis vnius libre in vigilia assumpcionis beate Marie virginis
ad ardendum in vigilia nocte et die sequenti continue in honore beate
virginis Marie In cuius rei robur et testimonium presenti scripto sigilla
nostra apposuimus.   Testibus... .

7   Relations between Executors

*Letter to the archdeacon of Leicester by which Roger de Clifford, executor
of William de Treygoz, constitutes William Cantrem, his co-executor, to be his
proctor for receiving money deposited in the Abbey of Leicester. Oct. 19, 1258*
(London, Br. Mus., Harl. Ch. 48 C 34).

Viro venerabili et discreto, archidiacono Leycestr'... Rogerus de
Clifford, miles, executor testamenti bone memorie Willelmi de Treygoz... .   In omnibus causis motis et movendis coram vobis diebus quibuscumque et locis, et precipue in causa executionis testamenti dicti
defuncti, fratrem Willelmum Cantorum de Dora, coexecutorem meum,
procuratorem meum constitui, et ad recipiendum pecuniam in Abbatia
Leycestr' per ipsum depositam... .

8   A Final Account

*The inventory of the goods of Reginald Labbe, with the executors' account
of their expenses and the list of legacies.*   *1293*
(Printed in the *Archaeological Journal*, III [1846], 65-66).

Inventarium bonorum Reginaldi Labbe defuncti anno domini M.°CC.
nonagesimo tercio die quo obiit.

Imprimis j. vacca precii v.*s.*   Item j. vitulus precii iiij.*s.*   Item ij. oves
et iij. agni precii xli.*d.* precium capitis x.*d.*   Item iij. galline precii vj.*d.*
Item, j. busellum .di. frumenti precii xv.*d.* j. summa ordei precii v.*s.*
iiij.*d.* Item, j. summa di. pabuli precii vi.*s.* Item, j. summa drag. precii
iiij.*s.* Item, j. taberd et j. tunica precii xij.*d.* Item, j. collobium precii

xij.*d.* Item, j. bolster. precii xij.*d.* Item, j. tapetum et ij. linteamina
precii x.*d.* Item, j. patella enea precii iij.*d.* j. tripod. precii. ob. Item,
sal precii ob.   Summa xxxiij.*s.* viij.*d.*

Walterus Noreys et Yda relicta dicti defuncti, executores testamenti
ejusdem defuncti cumputant in expensis . . . . . die sepulture ipsius.   In
bella pulsanda, ij.*d.* In cera, x.*d.* In j. . . . . j.*d.* ob. In sepulcro ejus
fodiendo, j.*d.* In pane, iiij.*s.* ij.*d.* In cervisia, xvj.*d.* In caseo, vj.*d.* In
testamento faciendo, vj.*d.*

                       Summa vij.*s.* viij.*d.* ob. Ecclesie
                 Est porcio dicti defuncti, xvj.*s.* x.*d.* ob. qa.
Expense ⎰ Iidem computant in expensis die mensis dicti defuncti.
[redd.] ⎱ In pane, xvj.*d.* In servisia, viij.*d.* In caseo, viij.*d.* In expensis
de probacione testamenti, cum consilo clericorum viij.*d.* In oblacion-
ibus ad vj. missas, vj.*d.*

                                          Summa iij.*s.* x.*d.*

Legata soluta] Iidem computant solutum secundum legata, videlicet
ad Summum altare Ecclesie de Newe[ton] j. ovis precii x.*d.* Item, solutum altari et fabrice Ecclesie de Eakewode j. ovem precii x.*d.* Item,
vicario de Neweton, vi. *d.* Item, clerico suo, ij.*d.* Item domino Simoni
capellano, vj.*d.* Item, solutum Yde uxori mee [sic] totam partem ipsius
unius vacce precii [v.*s.*] pro medietate. Item solutum Thome filio
Noreys quarta pars j. vituli precii . Item, solutum Yde relicte dicti
defuncti pro residuo, iij.*s.* ob. qa.
Summa vj.*s.* j.*d.*

                                          Summa, ix.*s.* ij.*d.* ob.
In stipendio clerici pro compoto isto faciendo, iij.*d.*

9   Discharge of Executors

(a)

Discharge of the executors of Master Roger

*Letter patent of Bishop Oliver Sutton of Lincoln announcing the discharge
of the executors of Master Roger of Cave. The residue from the estate is
to be kept by one of the executors until the bishop arranges for its use.*

                                          Oct. 4, 1291
               (Printed in the *Rolls and Register of Bishop Oliver
               Sutton*, ed. Rosalind Hill, III, 151-152).

Universis pateat per presentes quod nos Oliverus permissione divina
Lincoln' episcopus, audita ratione administrationis domini Willelmi
rectoris ecclesie de Wykingby, executoris testamenti quondam magistri
Rogeri de Cava canonici ecclesie Lincoln' alias in diocese nostra benefi-

ciati, germani sui, et Willelmi de Brumpton' rectoris ecclesie de Bihamel in locum quondam Roberti de Clisseby rectoris ecclesie de Carleton' coexecutoris ejusdem testamenti per nos auctoritate ordinaria subrogati, quia omnimodis receptis ac liberationibus et expensis eorundem ac aliis predictum testamentum qualitercumque contingentibus, computatis et allocatis de jure allocandis, invenimus quod penes dictum Willelmum de Wykingby VI libre XIII denarii et quadrans dumtaxat residebant de claro, de quibus juxta ordinationem nostram alias faciendam disponet ubi et quando videbitur oportunum, dicto Willelmo rectore ecclesie de Bihamel de bonis dicti defuncti nichil penes se prorsus habente, memoratos rectores de hiis que pervenerunt ad eosdem ratione dicti testamenti bene et fideliter administrasse nostro judicio reputantes, ipsos ab onere redditionis ratiocinii administrationis sue in omnibus aliis receptis per eosdem preterquam de summa pecunie pretacta duximus absolvendos. In cujus rei testimonium eisdem litteras nostras fieri fecimus patentes. Datum apud Parcum Stowe, IIII nonas Octobris anno domini M. CC. nonagesimo primo et pontificatus nostri XII.

(b)
Conditional discharge of the executor of Walter

Letter patent of Bishop Godfrey Giffard of Worcester announcing the discharge of William Frebodi, son and executor of the deceased. He shall remain liable to claims by creditors and legatees. July 16, 1285

(Worcester, Giffard Register, fol. 230r; calendared by J. W. Willis Bund, II, 262).

Universis pateat per presentis quod nos Godefridus, dei gratia ecclesie Wyg' minister, Willelmum Frebodi de Doddeleye, executorem testamenti W. patris sui, defuncti, audita ratione super administracione eiusdem in bonis dicti defuncti, per sequestratorem nostrum, ad hoc auditorem datum, eo quod in nullo inveniebatur reliquator, eundem ab onere dicti testamenti absolvimus, salva tamen, actione creditoribus et legatariis, si qui appareant in futurum. Dat' ... .

BIBLIOGRAPHY

BIBLIOGRAPHY

MANUSCRIPT SOURCES

Cambridge
    University Libr.
      Dd. 7. 6.
    Corpus Christi Coll.
      297
    Fitzwilliam Mus.
      329
    Gonville and Caius Coll.
      205

Canterbury
    Dean and Chapter Muniments
      Scrapbooks A, B, and C
      Sede Vacante Scrap Books I, II, and III
      Chartae Antiquae

Chichester
    Diocesan Record Office
      Regist. Episcop. Rede E
      Liber Y

Douai
    Bibliothèque municipale
      640

Durham
    Dean and Chapter Muniments
      Charters and deeds

Exeter
    Dean and Chapter Muniments
      Charters and deeds
    Records of the Vicars Choral
      Charters and deeds
    Public Library
      Mayor's Court Rolls

Gloucester
    Dean and Chapter Muniments
      St. Peter's Abbey, Reg. A, and Reg. B

King's Lynn
    Town Hall
      Charters and deeds

Lincoln
    Dean and Chapter Muniments
      Registrum Magnum
      Charters and deeds

London
    British Museum
      Add. 41201
      Cotton Faust. B.11
      Egerton 3031
      Harley 52, 1708, 5019
      Lansdowne 207a, 397
      Royal 9.E.vii
      Charters, deeds and rolls
    Corporation Library
      Hustings Rolls 1-29
      Bridge House Deeds
      Large Register
    Lambeth Palace
      Pecham's Register
    Public Record Office
      Exchequer Treasurer of Receipt Books, Vol. 274 (E-36.274)
      Charters, deeds and rolls
    St. Paul's, Dean and Chapter Muniments
      Charters and deeds; Boxes A 66, A 68
    Westminster Abbey, Muniments
      Charters and deeds
Norwich
    Castle Museum
      Charters and deeds of St. Giles' Hospital
Oxford
    Bodleian Libr.
      Rawlinson G. 5
      Selden Supra 87
      Charters, deeds and rolls
    Magdalen Coll.
      Charters and deeds
    Merton Coll.
      Charters and deeds
Paris
    Bibliothèque Nationale
      Lat. 3892, 3967, 5660, 15000
Rouen
    Bibliothèque municipale
      743
Salisbury
    Cathedral Libr.
      Charters and deeds
    Dean and Chapter Muniments
      Liber Evidentiarum C
      Charters and deeds, Press 4, Box W
Vatican City
    Biblioteca apostolica
      Ottobon. lat. 742

Wells
>Dean and Chapter Muniments
>>Liber Albus R I, III
>Museum
>>Charters and deeds

Worcester
>Dean and Chapter Muniments
>>Charters and deeds
>Record Office
>>Register of Bishop Giffard (MS. 713)

York
>Borthwick Institute of Historical Research
>>Registers of Archbishops Giffard, Wickwane and Romeyn
>Dean and Chapter Muniments
>>Domesday Book

PRINTED ORIGINAL SOURCES

A.   Public Records

Abbreviatio Placitorum Richard I — Edward II, ed. G. Rose and W. Illingworth, Record Commission, 5 (1811).

Calendar of Charter Rolls, Vols. I and II, PRO (1903-6).

Calendar of Close Rolls, Henry III, Vols. I-XIV; Edward I, Vols. I-IV, PRO (1900-38).

Calendar of Patent Rolls, Henry III, Vols. I-VI; Edwards I, Vols. I-III, PRO (1893-1913).

Casus Placitorum and Reports of Cases in the King's Courts, 1272-78, ed. W. R. Dunham jr., Selden Soc., LXIX (1952).

Curia Regis Rolls, Vols. I-X, PRO (1923-59).

Domesday Book seu Liber censualis Wilhelmi Primi regis Angliæ, Vols. I-II, ed. A. Farley (London, 1783); Vols. III-IV, ed. H. Ellis, Record Commission, 6-7 (1816).

Fœdera, Conventiones, Litteræ, etc.; or Rymer's Fœdera, 1066-1383, ed. A. Clarke, J. Caley *et al,* 4 vols. in 7, Record Commission, 11 (1816-69).

Inquisitio comitatus Cantabrigiensis; subjicitur Inquisitio Eliensis, ed. N. E. Hamilton (London, 1876).

Liber quotidianus contrarotulatoris garderobæ, 28 Edward I, A. D. 1299-1300, Society of Antiquaries (London, 1787).

Memoranda Roll for the Michaelmas Term of the First Year of the Reign of King John, 1190-1200, ed. H. G. Richardson, Pipe Roll Soc., N.S., XXI (1943).

Memoranda Roll for the Tenth Year of the Reign of King John, 1207-8, ed. R. A. Brown, Pipe Roll Soc., N.S., XXXI (1956).

Memoranda Roll of the King's Remembrancer for Michaelmas 1230-Trinity 1231, ed. C. Robinson, Pipe Roll Soc., N.S., XI (Princeton, 1933).

Pipe Rolls, 5 Henry II-13 John and 14 Henry III, Pipe Roll Soc. (1884-1953).

Rôles Gascons, 3 vols., ed. F. Michel and C. Bémont, Documents inédits (Paris, 1885-1906).

Rolls of the Justices in Eyre... Lincolnshire, 1218-9, and Worcestershire, 1221, ed. Doris M. Stenton, Selden Soc., LIII (1934).

Rolls of the Justices in Eyre... Yorkshire, 1218-9, ed. Doris M. Stenton, Selden Soc.,
LVI (1937).
Rotuli Chartarum in Turri Londinensi Asservati 1199-1216, ed. T. D. Hardy, Record
Commission, 25 (1837).
Rotuli Litterarum Clausarum, ed. T. D. Hardy, 2 vols., Record Commission, 15
(1833-44).
Rotuli Litterarum Patentium, ed. T. D. Hardy, Record Commission, 17 (1835).
Select Cases in the Exchequer of Pleas, ed. H. Jenkinson and Beryl Formoy, Selden
Soc., XLVIII (1932).
Select Cases of Procedure without Writ under Henry III, ed. H. G. Richardson and
G. O. Sayles, Selden Soc., LX (1941).

B.   *English Legal Materials*

Ancient Laws and Institutes of England, ed. B. Thorpe, Record Commission, 28
(1840).
Die Gesetze der Angelsachsen, ed. F. Liebermann, 3 vols. (Halle, 1903-16).
The Laws of the Earliest English Kings, ed. and trans. F. Attenborough (Cambridge,
1922).
The Laws of the Kings of England from Edmund to Henry I, ed. and trans. A. J.
Robertson (Cambridge, 1925).
Select Charters and other Illustrations of English Constitutional History, ed. W.
Stubbs, 9th ed. by H. W. C. Davis (Oxford, 1913).
Statutes of the Realm, ed. A. Luders *et al.,* 11 vols., Record Commission, 8 (1810-28).
Borough Customs, ed. Mary Bateson, 2 vols., Selden Soc., XVIII, XXI (1904-6).
Bracton Henry de, *De Legibus et Consuetudinibus Angliæ,* ed. G. E. Woodbine,
4 vols., Yale Historical Publications, MSS. and Edited Texts, III (New Haven,
1915-42).
Bracton's Note Book, ed. F. M. Maitland, 3 vols. (London, 1887).
British Borough Charters, ed. A. Ballard and J. Tait, 2 vols. (Cambridge, 1913-23).
Britton, ed. F. M. Nichols, 2 vols. (Oxford, 1865).
Calendar of Early Mayor's Court Rolls, ed. A. H. Thomas, Vol. I, 1298-1309 (Cam-
bridge, 1924).
Calendar of Plea and Memoranda Rolls of the City of London, ed. A. H. Thomas,
Vols. I-II, 1323-81 (Cambridge, 1926-9).
Court Rolls of the Abbey of Ramsey and of the Honor of Clare, ed. W. O. Ault,
Yale Historical Publications, MSS. and Edited Texts, IX (New Haven, 1928).
Court Rolls of the Manor of Wakefield, Vols. I-II, ed. W. P. Baildon; Vols. III-IV,
ed. J. Lister; Vol. V, ed. J. W. Walker, Yorkshire Arch. Soc., Rec. Ser., XXIX,
XXXVI, LVII, LXXVIII, CIX (1900-45).
De Necessariis Observantiis Scaccarii Dialogus, ed. A. Hughes, C. Crump and C.
Johnson (Oxford, 1902).
De Necessariis etc., ed. and trans. C. Johnson (London, 1950).
Fleta, ed. Selden (London, 1647).
Fleta, ed. and trans. H. G. Richardson and G. O. Sayles, Vol. II, Selden Soc. LXXII
(1955).
Glanvill, *De Legibus et Consuetudinibus Regni Angliae,* ed. G. E. Woodbine, Yale
Historical Publications, MSS. and Edited Texts, XIII (New Haven, 1932).
Glanvill, *De Legibus,* ed. Tottel (London, 1555).

Glanvill, *A Treatise on the Laws and Customs of the Kingdom of England*, trans. by J. Beames, with introd. by J. H. Beale (Washington, 1900).

The Great Red Book of Bristol, ed. E. W. Veale, 5 vols., Bristol Rec. Soc., II, IV, VIII, XVI, XVIII (1931-53).

Munimenta Gildhallæ Londoniensis, ed. H. T. Riley, 3 vols., RS, 12 (1859-62).

Placita Anglo-Normannica, ed. M. M. Bigelow (Boston, 1877).

Records of the Borough of Leicester, ed. Mary Bateson (London, 1899).

Recueil des Actes de Henri II, ed. L. Delisle and E. Berger, 4 vols. (Paris, 1909-27).

Regesta Regum Anglo-Normannorum, Vol. I, ed. H. W. C. Davis; Vol. II, ed. C. Johnson and H. A. Cronne (Oxford, 1913-56).

Royal Writs in England from the Conquest to Glanvill, ed. R. C. Van Caenegem, Selden Soc., LXXVII (1959).

Select Pleas in Manorial and other Seignorial Courts, ed. F. W. Maitland, Selden Soc., II (1889).

Some Documents of Barnoldswick Manor Court of Probate, ed. G. E. Kirk, in *Miscellanea*, Vol. VI, ed. C. E. Whiting, Yorkshire Arch. Soc., Rec. Ser., CXVIII (1953).

Traités sur les coutumes anglo-normandes, ed. D. Hoüard, 4 vols. (Paris, 1776).

Year Books, Edward I, ed. A. V. Horwood, 5 vols., RS, 31 (1866-79).

Year Books, Edward II, Vol. X, 5 Edward II, ed. G. J. Turner, Selden Soc., LXIII (1947).

C.   Canonistic Sources

1   PAPAL REGISTERS

Entries in Papal Registers relating to Great Britain and Ireland, Vol. I, 1198-1304, ed. W. H. Bliss (London, 1894).

Regesta pontificum romanorum ab condita Ecclesia ad annum post Christum natum MCXCVIII, by P. Jaffé; 2nd ed. W. Wattenbach, S. Lœwenfeld, F. Kaltenbrunner, P. Ewald, 2 vols. (Leipzig, 1855-8).

Regesta pontificum romanorum inde ab anno post Christum natum MCXCVIII ad annum MCCCIV, by A. Potthast, 2 vols. (Berlin, 1874-5).

Les Registres d'Alexandre IV, ed. Bourel de la Roncière, J. de Loye et A. Coulson, 3 vols., Bibliothèques des Ecoles françaises d'Athènes et de Rome (Paris, 1895-1953).

Les Registres d'Honorius IV, ed. M. Prou, Bibliothèques etc., (Paris, 1888).

Les Registres d'Innocent IV, ed. E. Berger, Bibliothèques etc., 4 vols. (Paris, 1884-1921).

Les Registres de Nicolas III, ed. J. Gay et Suzanne Vitte, Bibliothèques etc., (Paris, 1898-1938).

Registrum Innocentii III Papae super negotio Romani Imperii, ed. F. Kempf (Rome, 1947).

Selected Letters of Innocent III, ed. C. R. Cheney and W. H. Semple (London, 1953).

2   EPISCOPAL REGISTERS

Bath and Wells
   Registers of Walter Giffard, 1265-6, and of Henry Bowett, 1401-7, ed. T. S. Holmes, Somerset Rec. Soc., XIII (1899).

Canterbury
 Registrum epistolarum Johannis Peckham, archiepiscopi Cantuariensis, ed. C.
  T. Martin, 3 vols., RS, 77 (1882-6).
 Registrum Johannis Pecham, Canterbury and York Soc. (1908- —).
 Registrum Roberti Winchelsey, Cantuariensis archiepiscopi, A.D. 1294-1313, ed.
  Rose Graham, 2 vols., Cant. and York Soc. (1952-6).
 The Register of Henry Chichele, archbishop of Canterbury, ed. E. F. Jacob,
  4 vols., Cant. and York Soc. (1937-47).

Exeter
 *Registers of Walter Bronescombe, 1257-1280, and Peter Quivil, 1280-91, with
  some Records of the Episcopate of Bishop Thomas de Bitton, 1292-1307,* ed.
  F. C. Hingeston-Randolph (London, 1889).

Hereford
 *Registrum Thome de Cantilupo, episcopi Herefordensis, A. M. MCCLXXV-
  MCCLXXXII,* ed. R. G. Griffiths, Cant. and York Soc. (1907).
 *Registrum Ricardi de Swinfield, episcopi Herefordensis, A. D. MCCLXXXIII-
  MCCCXVII,* ed. W. W. Capes, Cant. and York Soc. (1909).

Lincoln
 Rotuli Hugonis de Welles, episcopi Lincolniensis, A. D. MCCIX-MCCXXXV,
  ed. W. P. Phillimore and F. N. Davis, 3 vols., Lincoln Rec. Soc., III, VI, IX
  (1912-4).
 Rotuli Roberti Grosseteste, episcopi Lincolniensis, A. D. MCCXXXV-MCCLIII,
  ed. F. N. Davis, Lincoln Rec. Soc., XI (1914).
 Rotuli Ricardi Gravesend, diocesis Lincolniensis, ed. F. N. Davis, C. W. Foster
  and A. H. Thompson, Lincoln Rec. Soc., XX (1925).
 The Rolls and Register of Bishop Oliver Sutton, 1280-1299 ed. Rosalind M. T.
  Hill, 4 vols. to date, Lincoln, Rec. Soc. XXXIX, XLIII, XLVIII, LII (1948-
  58).

Winchester
 *Registrum Johannis de Pontissara, episcopi Wyntoniensis, A. D. MCCLXXXII-
  MCCCIV,* ed. C. Deedes, 2 vols., Cant. and York Soc. (1915-24).

Worcester
 *Episcopal Registers, diocese of Worcester: Register of Bishop Godfrey Giffard,
  1268-1301,* ed. J. W. Willis Bund, 2 vols., Worcestershire Historical Soc.
  (Oxford, 1898-1902).

York
 The Register of Walter Giffard, lord archbishop of York, 1266-1279, ed. W.
  Brown, Surtees Soc. CIX (1904).
 The Register of William Wickwane, lord archbishop of York, 1279-1285, ed. W.
  Brown, Surtees Soc., CXIV (1907).
 The Register of John le Romeyn, lord archbishop of York, 1286-1296, ed. W.
  Brown, 2 vols. Surtees Soc., CXXIII, CXXVIII (1913-7).

3 COUNCILS

Haddan, A. W., and W. Stubbs, *Councils and Ecclesiastical Documents Relating to
 Great Britain and Ireland,* 3 vols. (Oxford, 1869-78).
Hardouin, J., *Acta Conciliorum et Epistolæ Decretales ac Constitutiones Summorum
 Pontificum,* 12 vols. (Paris, 1714-1715).

Mansi, J. D., *Sacrorum Conciliorum Nova et Amplissima Collectio,* 31 vols. (Florence and Venice, 1759-98).

Wilkins, D., *Concilia Magnae Britanniae et Hiberniae, 446-1718,* 4 vols. (London, 1737).

4 COLLECTIONS, COMMENTARIES, ETC.

Archidiaconus, *Lectura Guidonis de Baysio* (Lyons, 1516).

Bartholomew of Exeter, *Penitential;* in A. Morey, *Bartholomew of Exeter, Bishop and Canonist. A Study in the 12th Century* (Cambridge, 1937).

Bernardi Papiensis, *Summa Decretalium,* ed. E. A. Laspeyres (Graz, 1956).

Burchard of Worms, *Decretum,* PL 140.

Collectio Brugensis, ed. E. Friedberg in *Die Canonessammlungen zwischen Gratian und Bernhard von Pavia* (Leipzig, 1897).

Die Collectio Wigorniensis, ed. H. E. Lohmann, *ZRG Kan. Abt.,* XXII (193), 36-187.

Corpus Iuris Canonici, ed. E. Friedberg, 2 vols. (Leipzig, 1879-81).

Decretales Pseudoisidorianae, ed. P. Hinschius (Leipzig, 1863).

Durantis, William, *Speculum Iuris* (Venice, 1576).

Finsterwalder, P. W., *Die Canones Theodori Cantuariensis und ihre Überlieferungsformen* (Weimar, 1929).

Hostiensis, *Summa Domini Henrici Cardinalis Hostiensis* (Lyons, 1542).

Innocentius IV, *In Quinque Libros Decretalium Commentaria* (Venice, 1578).

Ivo of Chartres, *Decretum,* PL 161.

—. *Panormia,* PL 161.

John of Acton, *Constitutionis Legatinæ Othonis et Othoboni, cum Annotationibus Johannis de Athona* (Oxford, 1679).

Lanfranc, *The Monastic Constitutions of Lanfranc,* ed. D. Knowles, (London, 1951).

Lyndwood, W., *Provinciale (seu Constitutiones Angliæ)* continens *constitutiones provinciales... cum annotationibus, auctore Gul. Lyndwood* (Oxford, 1679).

MacNeill, J. T., and Helena M. Gamer, *Medieval Handbooks of Penance,* Columbia University Records of Civilization, Sources and Studies, XXIX (New York, 1928).

Ordo Iudiciarius Bambergensis, ed. J. F. v. Schulte, Sitzungsberichte der kaiserlichen Akademie der Wissenschaften in Wien (Phil.-Hist. Kl.) XXX (Vienna, 1872).

Papal Decretals relating to the Diocese of Lincoln in the Twelfth Century, ed. W. Holtzmann and E. W. Kemp, Lincoln Rec. Soc., XLVII (1954).

Papsturkunden in England, ed. W. Holtzmann, Vols. I-II (Berlin, 1931-5), Vol. III (Göttingen, 1952).

Paucapalia, Die Summa des, ed. J. F. v. Schulte (Giessen, 1890).

Peter of Blois, *Speculum Iuris Canonici,* ed. Remarius (Berlin, 1837).

Quinque Compilationes Antiquae, ed. E. Friedberg (Leipzig, 1882).

Raymundus de Pennaforte, *Summa* (Rome, 1503).

—. *Summa Iuris,* ed. J. R. Serra, *Sancti Raymundi de Penyafort Opera Omnia,* Vol. I (Barcelona, 1945).

Reginon of Prüm, *Reginonis Abbatis Prumensis Libri duo de Synodalibus Causis et Disciplinis Ecclesiasticis* ed. F. G. Wasserschleben (Leipzig, 1840).

Regularis Concordia Anglicae Nationis, ed. T. Symons (London, 1953).

Rufinus, *Die Summa Decretorum des Magister Rufinus,* ed. H. Singer (Paderborn, 1902).

Schmitz, H. J., *Die Bussbücher und die Bussdisciplin der Kirche* (Mainz, 1883).

—. *Die Bussbücher und das kanonische Bussverfahren* (Düsseldorf, 1898).

Stephan of Tournai, *Die Summa des Stephanus Tornacensis,* ed. J. F. v. Schulte (Giessen, 1891).
The Summa Parisiensis on the Decretum Gratiani, ed. T. P. McLaughlin (Toronto, 1952).
Theodore of Canterbury, *Penitential,* ed. P. W. Finsterwalder in *Die Canones Theodori Cantuariensis und ihre Überlieferungsformen* (Weimar, 1929).
Vetus Liber Archidiaconi Eliensis, ed. C. L. Feltoe and E. H. Minns, (Cambridge, 1917).
Wahrmund, L., *Quellen zur Geschichte des römisch-kanonischen Processes im Mittelalter,* 5 vols. (Innsbruck, Heidelberg, 1905-31).
Wasserschleben, F. W., *Die Bussordnungen der abendländischen Kirche* (Halle, 1851).
—. *Die irische Kanonensammlung,* 2nd ed. (Leipzig, 1885).
William of Drogheda, *Summa Aurea,* ed. L. Wahrmund, in *Quellen,* Vol. II, pt. 2.

D.   Other Legal Materials

Azo, *Summa* (Venice, 1566).
Corpus Juris Civilis, ed. stereotypa quarta decima, T. Mommsen, P. Krueger et R. Schoell, 3 vols. (Berlin, 1915-28).
Coutumiers de Normandie, ed. E. J. Tardif, 2 vols. (Paris-Rouen, 1881-96).
Fontes Iuris Romani Antejustiniani, ed. S. Riccobono, J. Baviera, G. Ferrini, J. Furlani and V. Arango-Ruiz, 3 vols. (Florence, 1940-3).
Formulae Merowingici et Karolini Aevi, ed. K. Zeumer, *MGH,* LL. Form. (1886).
Layettes du Trésor des Chartes, ed. A. Teulet et de Laborde, 3 vols. (Paris, 1863-75).
Lex Ribuaria, ed. R. Sohm, *MGH, LL, V* (1874-89).
Lex Salica, ed. J. R. Behrend, 2nd ed. (Weimar, 1897).
Vacarius, *Liber Pauperum,* ed. F. de Zulueta, Selden Soc., XLIIII (1927).

E.   Cartularies, Charters, Deeds and Wills

Anglo-Saxon Charters, ed. Agnes J. Robertson, Cambridge Studies in English Legal History (Cambridge, 1939).
Anglo-Saxon Wills, ed. Dorothy Whitelock, Cambridge Studies in English Legal History (Cambridge, 1930).
Anglo-Saxon Writs, ed. Florence E. Harmer (Manchester, 1952).
Antiquus Cartularius Ecclesiae Baiocensis (Livre noir), ed. V. Bourienne, Soc. Hist. de Normandie, 2 vols. (Rouen, 1902-3).
Burton Chartulary, An Abstract of the Contents of, by. G. Wrottesley, William Salt Archaeological Soc., V (1884).
Calendar of Charters and Rolls preserved in the Bodleian Library, ed. W. H. Turner and H. O. Coxe (Oxford, 1878).
Calendar of Wills Proved and Enrolled in the Court of Husting, London, 1258-1688, ed. R. R. Sharpe, 2 vols. (London, 1889-90).
Cartulaire de l'Abbaye de Beaulieu, ed. M. Deloche, Collection de Documents Inédits (Paris, 1859).
Cartulaire de l'Abbaye de Redon, ed. A. de Courson, Collection de Documents Inédits (Paris, 1863).
Cartulaire de l'Abbaye de Saint-Bertin, ed. M. Guérard, Collection de Documents Inédits (Paris, 1840).

Cartulaire de l'Abbaye de Saint-Georges de Rennes, ed. P. De La Bigne Villeneuve (Rennes, 1876).

Cartulaire de l'Abbaye de la Sainte-Trinité du Mont de Rouen, ed. A. Deville; appendix to *Cartulaire de l'Abbaye de Saint-Bertin,* ed. M. Guérard.

Cartularium Monasterii de Rameseia, ed. W. H. Hart and P. A. Lyons, 3 vols., RS. 79 (1884-94).

Cartularium Monasterii S. Johannis Baptiste de Colecestria, ed. S. A. Moore, 2 vols., Roxburghe Club (London, 1897).

Cartularium Saxonicum, ed. W. de G. Birch, 3 vols. (London, 1885-93).

The Cartulary of Darley Abbey, ed. R. R. Darlington, 2 vols., Derbyshire Archaeological and Natural Hist. Soc. (1945).

Cartulary of the Hospital of St. John the Baptist, ed. H. E. Salter, 3 vols., Oxford Hist. Soc., LXVI, LXVIII, LXIX (1914-6).

Cartulary of the Monastery of St. Frideswide, ed. S. R. Wigram, 2 vols., Oxford Hist. Soc., XXVIII, XXXI (1895-6).

Cartulary of Oseney Abbey, ed. H. E. Salter, 6 vols., Oxford Hist. Soc., LXXXIX-XCI, XCVII-VIII, CI (1929-36).

Cartulary of St. Mary Clerkenwell, ed. W. O. Hassal, Camden Soc., 3rd Ser., LXXI (1949).

Charters and Documents Illustrative of the History of the Cathedral City and Diocese of Salisbury, ed. W. Rich-Jones and W. D. Macray, RS, 97 (1891).

The Chartulary of the High Church of Chichester, ed. W. D. Peckham, Sussex Rec. Soc., XLVI (1946).

The Chartulary or Register of the Abbey of St. Werburgh Chester, ed. J. Tait, 2 vols., Chetham Soc., N.S., LXXIX, LXXXII (1920-3).

Codex Diplomaticus Ævi Saxonici, ed. J. M. Kemble, 6 vols., English Hist. Soc., (London, 1839-48).

A Collection of the Wills of the Kings and Queens of England from William the Conqueror to Henry VII, ed. J. Nichols (London, 1780).

The Coucher Book of Furness Abbey, Vol I, ed. J. C. Atkinson, 3 vols.; *Vol. II,* ed. J. Brownbill, 3 vols., Chetham Soc., N.S., IX, XI, XIV, LXXIV, LXXVI, LXXVIII (1886-1919).

The Coucher Book of Selby, ed. J. T. Fowler, 2 vols., Yorks. Arch. Soc., Rec. Ser., X, XIII (1891-3).

The Coucher Book of Whalley Abbey, ed. W. A. Hulton, 4 vols., Chetham Soc., X, XI, XVI, XX (1847-9).

The Crawford Collection of Early Charters and Documents, ed. A. S. Napier and W. H. Stevenson, Anecdota Oxoniensia, Med. and Mod., VII (Oxford, 1894).

Diplomatarium Anglicum Ævi Saxonici, ed. B. Thorpe (London, 1865).

Documents Illustrative of English History in the Thirteenth and Fourteenth Centuries, ed. H. Cole, Record Commission, 33 (1844).

Documents Illustrative of the Social and Economic History of the Danelaw, ed. F. M. Stenton, British Academy Records, V (London, 1920).

Dugdale, W., *Monasticon;* new ed. by J. Caley, H. Ellis and B. Bandinel, 6 vols. (London, 1846).

Early Charters of the Cathedral Church of St. Paul, London, ed. Marion Gibbs, Camden Soc., 3rd Ser., LVIII (1939).

Early Charters of Essex: the Saxon Period, ed. C. Hart, Department of English Local History, Occasional Paper, X (Leicester, 1957).

Early Yorkshire Charters, Vols. I-III, ed. W. Farrer (Edinburgh, 1914-16), Vols. IV-X, ed. C. T. Clay, Yorkshire Archaeological Society, Rec. Ser., extra Ser., II-IX (1935-55).

English Historical Documents, Vol. I, 500-1042, ed. Dorothy Whitelock; *Vol. II, 1042-1189,* ed. D. C. Douglas and G. W. Greenaway (London, 1953-5).

Eynsham Cartulary, ed. H. E. Salter, 2 vols., Oxford Hist. Soc., XLIX, LI (1906-8).

Facsimiles of Ancient Charters in the British Museum, ed. E. A. Bond, 4 vols (London, 1873-8).

Facsimiles of Anglo-Saxon Manuscripts, ed. W. B. Sanders, 3 vols. (Southampton, 1878-84).

Facsimiles of Royal and Other Charters in the British Museum, ed. G. F. Warner and H. J. Ellis, Vol. I (London, 1903).

Feudal Documents from the Abbey of Bury St. Edmunds, ed. D. C. Douglas, British Academy Records, VIII (London, 1932).

Formulare Anglicanum, ed. T. Madox (London, 1702).

The Great Chartulary of Glastonbury, ed. A. Watkin, 3 vols., Somerset Rec. Soc., LIX, LXIII, LXIV (1944-56).

Historia et Cartularium Monasterii Sancti Petri Gloucestriæ, ed. W. H. Hart, 3 vols., RS, 33 (1863-7).

The Kalendar of Abbot Samson of Bury St. Edmunds and Related Documents, ed. R. H. C. Davis, Camden Soc., 3rd Ser., LXXXIV (1954).

Liber Eliensis, Bks. I-II, ed. D. J. Stewart, Anglia Christiana Soc. (London, 1848).

Liber Memorandorum Ecclesie de Bernewelle, ed. J. W. Clarke, (Cambridge, 1907).

Lincoln Wills, Vols. I-II, ed. C. W. Foster, Lincoln Rec. Soc., V, X (1914-8).

Memorials of Beverley Minster, ed. A. F. Leach, 2 vols., Surtees Soc., XCVIII, CVIII (1898, 1903).

Pipe Roll of the Bishopric of Winchester 1208-9, ed. H. Hall, (London, 1903).

Recueil des Chartes de l'Abbaye de Saint-Germain-des-Prés, ed. R. Poupardin, 2 vols. (Paris, 1909).

Register of New Minster and Hyde Abbey, ed. W. de G. Birch, Hampshire Rec. Soc., V (1892).

The Register of St. Augustine's Abbey Canterbury, commonly called the Black Book, ed. G. J. Turner, H. E. Salter, 2 vols., British Academy Records, II (London, 1915-24).

Registrum Antiquissimum of the Cathedral Church of Lincoln, Vols. I-III, ed. C. W. Foster, Vol. IV, ed. C. W. Foster and Kathleen Major, Vols. V-VII, ed. Kathleen Major, Lincoln Rec. Soc., XXVII-IX, XXXII, XXXIV, XLI-II, XLVI (1931-53).

Registrum Roffense, ed. J. Thorpe (London, 1769).

Registrum sive Liber Irrotularius et Consuetudinarius Prioratus Beatae Mariae Wigorniensis, ed. W. H. Hale, Camden Soc., XCI (1865).

Select Documents of the English Lands of the Abbey of Bec, ed. Marjorie Chibnall, Camden Soc., 3rd Ser., LXXIII (1951).

Select English Historical Documents of the Ninth and Tenth Centuries, ed. Florence E. Harmer (Cambridge, 1914).

Testamenta Eboracensia, Pt. I, ed. J. Raine, Surtees Soc., IV (1836).

Testamenta Vetusta, ed. N. H. Nicolas, 2 vols. (London, 1826).

Textus Roffensis, ed. T. Hearne (Oxford, 1720).

Transcripts of Charters relating to Gilbertine Houses, ed. F. M. Stenton, Lincoln Rec. Soc., XVIII (1922).

Two Cartularies of the Benedictine Abbeys of Muchelney and Athelney, ed. E. H. Bates, Somerset Rec. Soc., XIV (1899).

Two Cartularies of the Priory of St. Peter at Bath, ed. W. Hunt, Somerset Rec. Soc., VII (1893).

Vetus Registrum Sarisberiense, alias dictum Registrum S. Osmundi Episcopi, ed. W. H. Rich-Jones, 2 vols., RS, 78 (1883-4).

Wills and Inventories of the Northern Counties of England, Pt. I, ed. J. Raine, Surtees Soc., II (1835).

F. *Literary Materials*

Acta Sanctorum, ed. Bollandists, 67 vols. to date (Antwerp, Brussels, 1643- —).

Ælfric, *Die Hirtenbriefe Ælfrics in altenglische und lateinische Fassung,* ed. B. Fehr, Bibliothek der angelsächsischen Prosa, IX (Hamburg, 1914).

Alcuin, *Alcvini Epistolae,* ed. Dümmler, *MGH,* Epp., IV.

—. *Expositio in Epistolam Pauli Apostoli ad Hebræos,* PL 100.

Anglo-Latin Satirical Poets of the Twelfth Century, ed. T. Wright, 2 vols., RS, 59 (1872).

The Anglo-Saxon Chronicle, ed. B. Thorpe, 2 vols., RS, 23 (1861).

Annales Monastici, ed. H. R. Luard, 5 vols., RS, 36 (1864-9).

Anselm, *Sancti Anselmi Cantuariensis Archiepiscopi Opera Omnia,* ed. F. S. Schmitt, 5 vols. (Edinburgh, 1946-51).

Arnold Fitz-Thedmar, *De Antiquis Legibus Liber: Cronica Maiorum et Vicecomitum Londoniarum,* ed. T. Stapleton, Camden Soc., XXXIV (1846).

Asser, *Life of King Alfred,* ed. W. H. Stevenson (Oxford, 1904).

Baldwin, *Liber de Sacramento Altaris,* PL 204, 642-771.

Bede, *Epistola Bede ad Ecgbertum Episcopum,* ed. C. Plummer in *Venerabilis Baedae Opera Historica,* 2 vols. (Oxford, 1896).

—. *Historia Abbatum,* ed. Plummer, *ibid.*

—. *Historia Ecclesiastica Gentis Anglorum,* ed. Plummer, *ibid.*

—. *The Old English Version of Bede's Ecclesiastical History,* ed. T. Miller, Early Eng. Text Soc., 2 pts. (1890-8).

Beowulf and the Fight at Finnsburg, ed. F. Klaeber, 3rd ed. with Supplements (New York, 1951).

The Blickling Homilies of the Tenth Century, ed. R. Morris, Early Eng. Text Soc. (1880).

Boniface, *S. Bonifatii et Lulli Epistolae,* ed. M. Tangl, *MGH,* Epp. Selectae, I (1916).

Bozon, Nicole, *Les Contes moralisés de Nicole Bozon,* ed. Lucy Smith and P. Meyer, Soc. des anciens textes français (Paris, 1889).

Caesarius of Arles, *Sancti Caesarii Episcopi Arelatensis Opera Omnia,* ed. G. Morin, 2 vols. (Maretioli, 1937-42).

The Chronicle of Battle Abbey 1066-1176, trans. M. A. Lower (London, 1851).

Chronicon Abbatiæ de Evesham, ed. W. D. Macray, RS, 29 (1863).

Chronicon Abbatiæ Rameseiensis, ed. W. D. Macray, RS, 83 (1886).

Chronicon Monasterii de Abingdon, ed. J. Stevenson, 2 vols., RS, 2 (1858).

Chronicon Monasterii de Melsa, ed. E. A. Bond, 3 vols., RS, 43 (1866-8).

Cuthbert, *Epistola Cuthberti de Obitu Bedae,* ed. E. v. K. Dobbie, *The Manuscripts of Caedmon's Hymn and Bede's Death Song,* Columbia Studies in English and Comparative Literature, 128 (New York, 1937).

Durham Annals and Documents of the Thirteenth Century, ed. F. Barlow, Surtees
     Soc., CLV (1945).
Eadmer, *Historia Novorum in Anglia et Opuscula duo De Vita Sancti Anselmi et
     Quibusdam Miraculis ejus*, ed. M. Rule, RS, 81 (1884).
—. *Vita Sancti Oswaldi*, ed. J. Raine, in *Historians of the Church of York*, Vol. II.
Eddi, *Vita Wilfridi Episcopi Eboracensis Auctore Eddio Stephano*, ed. W. Levison,
     MGH, SS, Merov., VI, pp. 163-263.
—. *The Life of Bishop Wilfrid by Eddius Stephanus*, ed. and trans. B. Colgrave
     (Cambridge, 1927).
Epistolæ Cantuariensis, ed. W. Stubbs, in *Chronicles and Memorials of Richard I*,
     Vol. II, RS, 38 (1865).
Florence of Worcester, *Chronicon ex Chronicis*, ed. B. Thorpe, English Hist. Soc.,
     2 vols. (1848-9).
Gervase of Canterbury, *The Historical Works*, ed. W. Stubbs, 2 vols., RS, 73 (1879-
     80).
Gesta Henrici Secundi Benedicti Abbatis, ed. W. Stubbs, 2 vols., RS, 49 (1867).
Gesta Stephani, ed. and trans. K. R. Potter (London, 1955).
Gilbert Foliot, *Epistolae*, PL 190.
Grosseteste, Robert, *Letters of Robert Grosseteste Illustrative of the Social Conditions
     of his Time*, ed. H. R. Luard, RS, 25 (1861).
Henry of Huntingdon, *Historia Anglorum*, ed. T. Arnold, RS, 74 (1879).
Herbert de Losinga, *The Life, Letters and Sermons of Bishop Herbert de Losinga*,
     ed. E. M. Goulburn and H. Symonds, 2 vols. (Oxford, 1878).
L'Histoire de Guillaume le Maréchal, ed. P. Meyers, 3 vols., Soc. de L'Histoire de
     France (Paris, 1891-1901).
Historians of the Church of York, ed. J. Raine, 3 vols., RS, 71 (1879-95).
Homilies of the Anglo-Saxon Church, ed. B. Thorpe, 2 vols., Ælfric Soc. (London,
     1844-6).
Hugh of Lincoln, *Magna Vita Sancti Hugonis Episcopi Lincolniensis*, ed. J. F.
     Dimock, RS, 37 (1864).
Jocelin of Brakelond, *Chronica Jocelini de Brakelonda de Rebus Gestis Samsonis
     Abbati Monasterii Sancti Edmundi*, ed. and trans. H. E. Butler (London, 1949).
John of Salisbury, *Epistolae*, PL 199.
—. *The Letters of John of Salisbury*, ed. W. J. Millor and H. E. Butler, reviewed
     by C. N. L. Brooke (London, 1955).
Lanfranc, *Epistola B. Pauli Apostoli ad Hebræos cum Interjectis B. Lanfranci Glos-
     sulis*, PL 150, 375-406.
Letters from Northern Registers, ed. J. Raine, RS, 61 (1873).
Literæ Cantuarienses, ed. J. B. Sheppard, 3 vols., RS, 85 (1887-9).
Matthew of Paris, *Chronica Majora*, ed. H. R. Luard, 7 vols., RS, 57 (1872-84).
Memorials of St. Dunstan, ed. W. Stubbs, RS, 63 (1874).
Myrc, John, *Instructions for Parish Priests*, ed. E. Peacock, Early Eng. Text Soc.
     (1868)
Ordericus Vitalis, *Historia Ecclesiastica*, ed. A. le Prevost, 5 vols. (Paris, 1838-55).
Osbert of Clare, *Letters*, ed. E. W. Williamson (London, 1929).
Petrus Comestor, *De Sacramentis*, ed. R. Martin, in H. Weisweiler, *Maître Simon et
     son groupe De Sacramentis*, Spicil. Sac. Lovaniense, Etudes et Documents, XVII
     (Louvain, 1937).
Ralph de Coggeshall, *Chronicon Anglicanum*, ed. J. Stevenson, RS, 66 (1875).

Ralph de Diceto, *Opera Historica*, ed. W. Stubbs, 2 vols., RS, 68 (1876).
Robert Mannyng of Brunne, *Handlyng Synne*, ed. F. J. Furnivall, Roxburghe Club (1862).
Roger de Hoveden, *Chronica*, ed. W. Stubbs, 4 vols., RS, 51 (1868-71).
Sedulius Scotus, *Collectanea in Epistolam ad Hebræos*, PL, 103, 251-270.
Symeon of Durham, *Opera Omnia*, ed. T. Arnold, 2 vols., RS, 75 (1882-5).
Tacitus, *Germania*, ed. and trans. H. Goelzer, Collection des Universités de France (Paris, 1922).
Walter Daniel, *The Life of Ailred of Rievaulx*, trans. F. M. Powicke (London, 1950).
William of Jumièges, *Gesta Normannorum Ducum*, ed. J. Marx, Société Hist. Norm. (Rouen, 1914).
William of Malmesbury, *De Gestis Regum*, ed. W. Stubbs, 2 vols., RS, 90 (1887-9).
—. *Historia Novella*, ed. and trans. K. R. Potter, (London, 1955).
William of Newburgh, *Historia Rerum Anglicarum*, ed. R. Howlett, in *Chronicles of the Reigns of Stephen, Henry II and Richard I*, Vols. I-II, RS, 82 (1885).
William of Wadington, *Le Manuel de Pechiez*, ed. F. J. Furnivall, Roxburghe Club (1862).
Wulfstan II, archbishop of York, *The Homilies of Wulstan*, ed. Dorothy Bethurum (Oxford, 1957).
—. *Sermo Lupi ad Anglos*, ed. Dorothy Whitelock, 2nd ed. (London, 1952).
Wyclif, John, *Select English Works of John Wyclif*, ed. T. Arnold, 3 vols. (Oxford, 1869-71).

SECONDARY WORKS

A. *Monographs*

Arnould, E. J., *Le Manuel des Péchés: étude de littérature religieuse Anglo-Normande* (Paris, 1940).
Auffroy, H., *Evolution du Testament en France des origines au XIIIᵉ siècle* (Paris, 1899).
Ballard, A., *The Domesday Boroughs* (Oxford, 1904).
—. *The English Borough in the Twelfth Century* (Cambridge, 1914).
Bémont, C., *Simon de Montfort, Earl of Leicester 1208-1265*; trans. E. F. Jacob (Oxford, 1930).
Bennett, H. S., *Life on the English Manor*, A Study of Peasant Conditions 1150-1400 (Cambridge, 1937).
Berger, A., *Encyclopedic Dictionary of Roman Law*, Transactions of the American Philosophical Soc., N.S., XLIII, pt. 2 (Philadelphia, 1953).
Bernard, A., *La Sépulture en droit canonique du décret de Gratien au Concile de Trente* (Paris, 1933).
Beseler, G., *Die Lehre von den Erbverträgen*, 3 vols. (Göttingen, 1835-40).
Blackstone, W., *Commentaries on the Laws of England*, 4th ed., 4 vols. (Dublin, 1771).
Böhmer, H., *Kirche und Staat in England und in der Normandie im XI und XII Jahrhundert* (Leipzig, 1899).
Bosworth, J., and T. N. Toller, *An Anglo-Saxon Dictionary* (Oxford, 1898); *Supplement*, by T. N. Toller (Oxford, 1921).
Bouwens, B. G., *Wills and their Whereabouts*, 2nd ed. by Helen Thacker, Society of Genealogists (London, 1951).

Bresslau, H., *Handbuch der Urkundenlehre für Deutschland und Italien*, 2 vols., 2nd ed. (Leipzig, 1912-31).

Brissaud, J., A. *History of French Private Law*, The Continental Legal History Series, III (Boston, 1912).

Brooke, Z. N., *The English Church and the Papacy* (Cambridge, 1931).

Bruck, E. F., *Kirchenväter und Soziales Erbrecht* (Berlin, 1956).

—. *Die Schenkung auf den Todesfall im griechischen und römischen Recht*, Teil I (Breslau, 1909).

—. *Totenteil und Seelgerät im griechischen Recht* (München, 1926).

Brunner, H., *Abhandlungen zur Rechtsgeschichte gesammelte aufsätze*, ed. K. Rauch, 2 vols. (Weimar, 1931).

—. *Forschungen zur Geschichte des deutschen und französischen Rechtes* (Stuttgart, 1894).

—. *Zur Rechtsgeschichte der römischen und germanischen Urkund*, Vol. I (Berlin, 1880).

Caillemer, E., *Le droit civil dans les provinces Anglo-Normandes au XIIe siècle*, in *Mémoires de l'Académie Natonale... de Caen* (Paris, 1883).

Caillemer, R., *Etudes sur les successions au moyen âge* : II, Confiscation et administration des successions par les pouvoirs publics au moyen âge (Lyon, 1901).

Cambridge Medieval History, ed. H. M. Gwatkin *et al.*, 8 vols. (New York, 1911-36).

Chadwick, H. M., *Studies in Anglo-Saxon Institutions* (Cambridge, 1905).

Cheney, C. R., *English Bishops' Chanceries 1100-1250* (Manchester, 1950).

—. *English Synodalia of the Thirteenth Century* (Oxford, 1941).

—. *From Becket to Langton*, Ford Lectures, 1955 (Manchester, 1956).

Chenon, E., and Olivier-Martin, *Histoire générale du droit français public et privé des origines à 1815*, 2 vols. (Paris, 1926-9).

Churchill, Irene, J., *Canterbury Administration*, 2 vols. (London, 1933).

Cokayne, G. E., *Complete Peerage*, 2nd ed., 12 vols. (London, 1910-40).

Coke, E., *The First Part of the Institutions of the Laws of England or a Commentary on Littleton*, 3rd ed. (London, 1633).

—. *The Institutes of the Laws of England*, 18th ed., 4 vols. (London, 1797-1823).

Collingwood, R. G., and J. N. L. Myers, *Roman Britain and the English Settlements*, Oxford History of England, I, 2nd ed. (Oxford, 1937).

Coote, H. C., *The Practice of the Ecclesiastical Courts* (London, 1847).

Coulton, G. G., *Ten Medieval Studies*, 3rd ed. (Cambridge, 1930).

Crabb, G., *A History of English Law* (London, 1829).

Deanesly, Margaret, *The Pre-Conquest Church in England*, An Ecclesiastical History of England, I (London, 1961).

Dictionnaire de droit canonique, ed. A. Villien, E. Magnin and R. Naz (Paris, 1935, in progress).

Douglas, D. C., *English Scholars* (London, 1943).

—. *The Social Structure of Mediaeval East Anglia*, Oxford Studies in Social and Economic History, IX (Oxford, 1927).

Douie, Decima L., *Archbishop Pecham* (Oxford, 1952).

Duckett, Eleanor, *Anglo-Saxon Saints and Scholars* (New York, 1947).

Dugdale, W., The *English Baronage*, 2 vols. (London, 1675-6).

Dulac, L., *Développement historique et théorie de l'exécution testamentaire* (Toulouse, 1899).

Earle, J., *A Handbook of the Land-Charters and other Saxonic Documents* (Oxford, 1888).

Edwards, E., *Ecclesiastical Jurisdiction* (London, 1853).

Edwards, Kathleen, *The English Secular Cathedrals* (Manchester, 1949).

Essays in Anglo-Saxon Law (Boston, 1905).

Falco, M., *Le Disposizioni 'pro anima', Fondamenti dottrinali e forme giuridiche* (Turin, 1911).

Finberg, H. P. R., *The Early Charters of the West Midlands,* Studies in Early English History, II (Leicester, 1961).

Flower, C. T., *Introduction to the Curia Regis Rolls,* Selden Soc., LXII (1943).

Foreville, Raymonde, *L'Eglise et la royauté en Angleterre sous Henry II Plantagenet* (Paris, 1942).

Fournier, P., *Les Officialités au moyen âge. Etude sur l'organisation, la compétence et la procédure des tribunaux ecclésiastiques ordinaires en France de 1180 à 1328* (Paris, 1880).

Fournier P., and G. Le Bras, *Histoire des collections canoniques en Occident depuis les Fausses Décrétales juqu'au Décret de Gratien* 2 vols. (Paris, 1931-2).

Gibbs, Marion, and Jane Lang, *Bishops and Reform 1215-72* (Oxford, 1934).

Gierke, O., *Schuld und Haftung in älteren deutschen Recht,* Untersuchungen zur deutschen Staats- und Rechtsgeschichte, Heft 100 (Breslau, 1910).

Glasson, E., *Etude sur les donations à cause de mort* (Paris, 1870).

—. *Histoire du droit et des institutions politiques, civiles et judiciaires de l'Angleterre,* 6 vols. (Paris, 1882-3).

Goffin, R. J., *The Testamentary Executor in England and Elsewhere* (London, 1901).

Gretton, R. H., *The Burford Records* (Oxford, 1920).

Gurdon, T., *The History of the High Court of Parliament and the History of the Court Baron and the Court Leet* (London, 1731).

Hagemann, H. R., *Die Stellung der Piae Causae nach justinianischen Rechte* (Basel, 1953).

Hanna, J. D., *The Canon Law of Wills,* Catholic University of America, Canon Law Studies, LXXXVI (Washington, 1934).

Hart, C. H., *The Early Charters of Essex, the Saxon Period,* Leicester University, Department of English Local Hist., Occasional Papers, X (Leicester, 1957).

Haskins, C. H., *Norman Institutions* (Cambridge, Mass., 1925).

Hazeltine, H. D., *Geschichte des englischen Pfandrechts,* Untersuchungen zur deutschen Staats- und Rechtsgeschichte, Heft 92 (Breslau, 1907).

Hefele, K. F. v., H. Leclercq, *et al., Histoire des conciles,* 11 vols. (Paris, 1907-52).

Hemmeon, M., *Burgage Tenure in Mediaeval England* (Cambridge, Mass., 1914).

Heusler, A., *Die Gewere* (Weimar, 1872).

—. *Institutionen des deutschen Privatrechts,* 2 vols. (Leipzig, 1885-6).

Hodgkin, R. H., *History of the Anglo-Saxons,* 2nd ed., 2 vols. (Oxford, 1939).

Holdsworth, W. S., *A History of English Law,* 12 vols. (London, 1903-38); 7th rev. ed., ed. A. L. Goodhart and H. G. Hanbury (London, 1956 ff.).

Homans, G. C., *English Villagers in the Thirteenth Century* (Cambridge, Mass. 1942).

Hone, N. J., *The Manor and Manorial Records* (London, 1906).

Huebner, R., *Die Donationes Post Obitum,* Untersuchungen zur deutschen Staats- und Rechtsgeschichte, Heft 26 (Breslau, 1888).

—. *A History of Germanic Private Law,* The Continental Legal History Series, IV (Boston, 1918).

Jenks, E., *A Short History of English Law,* 4th ed. (London, 1928).

John, E., *Land Tenure in Early England,* Studies in Early English History I (Leicester, 1960).

Jolliffe, J. E. A., *The Constitutional History of Medieval England from the English Settlement to 1485* (London, 1937).

Joüon des Longrais, F., *La Conception anglaise de la saisine du XII⁰ au XIV⁰ siècle* (Paris, 1925).

Kantorowicz, H., *Bractonian Problems* (Glasgow, 1941).

Kenny, C. S., *The History of the Law of Primogeniture* (Cambridge, 1878).

Knowles, D., *The Monastic Order in England* (Cambridge, 1940).

—. *The Religious Orders in England,* 3 vols. (Cambridge, 1948-60).

Kuttner, S., *Repertorium der Kanonistik I,* Studi e Testi, LXXI (Vatican City, 1937).

Laplanche, J. de, *La Réserve coutumière dans l'ancien droit français* (Paris, 1925).

Laurence, P. M., *The Law and Custom of Primogeniture* (Cambridge 1878).

Leeds, E. T., *Early Anglo-Saxon Art and Archaeology* (Oxford, 1936).

Lesne, E., *Histoire de la propriété ecclésiastique en France,* 6 vols. (Lille, 1910-46).

Levett, Ada Elizabeth, *Studies in Manorial History,* ed. H. M Cam, M. Coate and L. S. Sutherland (Oxford, 1938).

Levison, W., *England and the Continent in the Eighth Century,* Ford Lectures, 1943 (Oxford, 1946).

Levy, E., *West Roman Vulgar Law: The Law of Property* (Philadelphia, 1951).

Lingard, J., *The History and Antiquities of the Anglo-Saxon Church,* 2 vols. (London, 1845).

Lot, F., *Etudes critiques sur l'Abbaye de Saint-Wandrille,* Bibliothèque de l'Ecole des hautes études, Sciences historiques et philologiques, CCIV (Paris, 1913).

Madox, T., *The History and Antiquities of the Exchequer of England* (London, 1711).

Maine, H. S., *Ancient Law,* 3rd American ed. (New York, 1879).

Maitland, F. W., *Collected Papers,* ed. H. A. L. Fisher, 3 vols. (Cambridge, 1911).

—. *Domesday Book and Beyond* (Cambridge, 1897).

Makower, F., *The Constitutional History and Constitution of the Church of England* (London, 1895).

McKechnie, W. S., *Magna Charta,* 2nd ed. (Glasgow, 1914).

McLaughlin, T. P., *Le très ancien droit monastique de l'occident,* Archives de la France monastique, XXXVIII (Paris, 1935).

Miller, E., *The Abbey and Bishopric of Ely,* Cambridge Studies in Medieval Life and Thought, N. S., I (Cambridge, 1951).

Moorman, J. R. H., *Church Life in England in the Thirteenth Century* (Cambridge, 1945).

Mortimer, R. C., *The Origins of Private Penance in the Western Church* (Oxford, 1939).

Oakley, T. P., *English Penitential Discipline and Anglo-Saxon Law in their Joint Influence* (New York, 1923).

Oleson, T. J., *The Witenagemot in the Reign of Edward the Confessor* (London, 1955).

Owst, G. R., *Preaching in Mediaeval England* (Cambridge, 1926).

Palgrave, F., *The Rise and Progress of the English Commonwealth,* Anglo-Saxon Period, Pt. II, Proofs and Illustrations, in *The Collected Historical Works of Sir Francis Palgrave,* ed. R. H. I. Palgrave (Cambridge, 1921).

Palumbo, L., *Testamento Romano e Testamento Longobardo* (Lanciano, 1892).

Perraud, A., *Etude sur le testament en Bretagne* (Rennes, 1921).

Petit-Dutaillis, C. E., *Studies and Notes Supplementary to Stubbs' Constitutional History*, trans. W. E. Rhodes, 3 vols. (Manchester, 1908-29).

Phillips, G., *Englische Reichs- und Rechtsgeschichte*, 2 vols. (Berlin, 1827-8).

Plucknett, T. F. T., *A Concise History of the Common Law*, 5th ed. (London, 1956).

—. *Legislation of Edward I*, Ford Lectures, 1947 (Oxford, 1949).

Pollock, F., and F. W. Maitland, *The History of English Law*, 2nd ed., 2 vols. (Cambridge, 1911).

Poole, A. L., *From Domesday Book to Magna Carta, 1087-1216*, Oxford History of England, III (Oxford, 1951).

Poole, R. L., *The Exchequer in the Twelfth Century* (Oxford, 1912).

Potter, H., *An Historical Introduction to English Law and its Institutions*, 3rd ed. (London, 1948).

Poudret, J. F., *La Succession testamentaire dans le pays de Vaud à l'époque savoyarde* (XIIIᵉ-XVIᵉ siècle), Bibliothèque historique vaudoise (Lausanne, 1955).

Power, Eileen, *Medieval English Nunneries* (Cambridge, 1922).

Powicke, F. M., *The Thirteenth Century, 1216-1307*, Oxford History of England, IV (Oxford, 1953).

Prochnow, F., *Das Spolienrecht und die Testierfähigkeit der Geistlichen im Abendland bis zum 13 Jahrhundert* (Berlin, 1919).

Prynne, W., *An Exact Chronological Vindication of our King's Supreme Ecclesiastical Jurisdiction over all Religious Affairs*, 3 vols. (London, 1665-8).

Raftis, J. A., *The Estates of Ramsey Abbey*, The Pontifical Institute of Mediaeval Studies, Studies and Texts, III (Toronto, 1957).

Reeves, J., *A History of the English Law*, ed. W. F. Finlason, 3 vols. (London, 1869).

Robinson, J. A., *Gilbert Crispin, Abbot of Westminster*, Notes and Studies relating to Westminster Abbey, III (Cambridge, 1911).

—. *St. Oswald and the Church of Worcester*, Br. Academy, Supplemental Papers, V, (London, 1919).

—. *Somersetshire Essays* (London, 1921).

—. *The Times of St. Dunstan* (Oxford, 1923).

Robinson, T., *The Common Law of Kent, or Customs of Gavelkind and Borough English* (London, 1741).

Saltman, A., *Theobald Archbishop of Canterbury* (London, 1956).

Schröder, R., *Lehrbuch der deutschen Rechtsgeschichte*, 7th ed. (Leipzig, 1932).

Schulte, J. F. v., *Die Geschichte der Quellen und Literatur des canonischen Rechts*, 3 vols. (Stuttgart, 1875-1880).

—. *Lehrbuch der deutschen Reichs- und Rechtsgeschichte*, 5th ed. (Stuttgart, 1881).

Schultze, A., *Augustin und der Seelteil des germanischen Erbrechts: Studien zur Entstehungsgeschichte des Freiteilsrechtes* (Leipzig, 1928).

—. *Die langobardische Treuhand und ihre Umbildung zur Testaments Vollstreckung*, Untersuchungen zur deutschen Staats- und Rechtsgeschichte, Heft 49 (Breslau, 1895).

Scrutton, T. E., *Land in Fetters* (Cambridge, 1886).

Selden, J., *Of the Disposition or Administration of Intestates' Goods*, in *Works*, 3 vols. (London, 1726), III, 1664-74.

—. *The Original of the Ecclesiastical Jurisdiction of Testaments*, ibid., III, 1676-1685.

Select Essays in Anglo-American Legal History, 3 vols. (Boston, 1907-9).

Somner, W., *A Treatise on Gavelkind* (London, 1726).

Spelman, H., *Of the Original of Testaments and Wills and of their Probate*, in *The English Works of Sir Henry Spelman*, 2nd ed. (London, 1727), pp. 127-132.

Stenton, Doris M., *The English Woman in History* (London, 1957).

Stenton, F. M., *Anglo-Saxon England*, Oxford History of England, II, 2nd ed. (Oxford, 1947).

—. *The Early History of the Abbey of Abingdon* (Oxford, 1913).

—. *The First Age of English Feudalism* (Oxford, 1932).

—. *Latin Charters of the Anglo-Saxon Period* (Oxford, 1955).

—. *Types of Manorial Structure in the Northern Danelaw*, Oxford Studies in Social and Legal History, II (Oxford, 1910).

Stephen, H. J., *New Commentaries on the Laws of England*, 12th ed., 4 vols. (London, 1895).

Stephenson, C., *Borough and Town* (Cambridge, Mass., 1933).

Stickler, A. M., *Historia Iuris Canonici Latini*, Vol. I, *Historia Fontium* (Turin, 1950).

Storey, R. L., *Diocesan Administration in the Fifteenth Century*, Publication of the Borthwick Institute of Historical Research (York, 1959).

Stubbs, W., *The Constitutional History of England*, 5th ed., 3 vols. (Oxford, 1891-1903).

Studia Gratiana, ed. J. Forchielli and A. M. Stickler, 7 vols. (Bologna, 1953-9).

Swinburne, H., *On Wills, a Briefe Treatise of Testaments and Last Willes* 2nd ed. (London, 1611).

Tait, J., *The Medieval English Borough* (Manchester, 1936).

Thompson, A. H., ed. *Bede, His Life, Times, and Writings*, Essays in Commemoration of the Twelfth Centenary of his Death (Oxford, 1935).

—. *The English Clergy and Their Organization in the later Middle Ages*, Ford Lectures, 1933 (Oxford, 1947).

Thrupp, Sylvia L., *The Merchant Class of Medieval London, 1300-1500* (Chicago, 1948).

Tierney, B., *Foundation of the Conciliar Theory*, Cambridge Studies in Medieval Life and Thought, N. S., IV (Cambridge, 1955).

Van Hove, A., *Commentarium Lovaniense in Codicem Iuris Canonici*, I, i, *Prolegomena* (Rome, 1945).

Vetulani, A., *Dekret Gracjana* (Breslau, 1955).

Vinogradoff, P., *English Society in the Eleventh Century* (Oxford, 1908).

—. *The Growth of the Manor*, 2nd ed. (London, 1911).

—. *Roman Law in Medieval Europe*, 2nd ed. (Oxford, 1929).

—. *Villainage in England* (Oxford, 1892).

Vogel, C., *La Discipline pénitentielle en Gaule des origines à la fin du VIIe siècle* (Paris, 1952).

Vries, J. de, *Altgermanische Religionsgeschichte*, 2 vols. (Berlin, 1956-7).

Whitelock, Dorothy, *The Beginnings of English Society*, Pelican History of England, II (London, 1952).

Wood, Susan, *English Monasteries and their Patrons in the Thirteenth Century* (Oxford, 1955).

Woodcock, B. L., *Medieval Ecclesiastical Courts in the Diocese of Canterbury* (London, 1952).

B. *Articles*

Ballard, A., "The Laws of Breteuil," *EHR*, XXX (1915), 646-658.

Bateson, Mary, "The Laws of Breteuil," *EHR*, XV-XVI (1900-1).

Bigelow, M. M., "Theory of Post-Mortem Disposition: Rise of the English Will," *Harv. Law Rev.*, XI (1897-8), 69-80.

Böhmer, H., "Das Eigenkirchentum in England," in *Festgabe für Felix Liebermann* (Halle, 1921), pp. 301-353.

Brooke, C. W. L., "Canons of English Church Councils in the Early Decretal Collections," *Traditio*, XIII (1957), 471-479.

Bruck, E. F., "Foundations for the Deceased in Roman Law, Religion and Political Thought," in *Scritti in Onore di Contardo Ferrini* (Milan, 1942), pp. 1-42.

—. "The Growth of Foundations in Roman Law and Civilization," *Seminar* VI (1948), 1-19.

—. "Kirchliche-soziales Erbrecht in Byzanz," in *Studi in Onore di Salvatoro Riccobono* (Palermo, 1933), III, 377-423.

—. "Zur Entwicklungsgeschichte der Testamentvollstreckung in Römischen Recht," *Zeitschrift für das Privat- und offentlich Recht in Gegenwart*, XL (1914), 533-59.

Brunner, H. "The Early History of the Attorney in English Law," *Illinois Law Rev.*, III (1908), pp. 257-279.

—. "Das rechtliche Fortleben des Toten bei den Germanen," *Deutsche Monatsschrift für das gesamte Leben der Gegenwart*, XII (1907), 18-32.

—. "Der Totenteil in germanischen Rechten," *ZRG Germ. Abt.*, XIX (1898), 107-139.

Buckstaff, W., "Essay on Married Women's Property," *Annals of the American Academy of Pol. and Soc. Sciences*, IV (1893), 35-51.

Caillemer, R., "The Executor in England and on the Continent," in *Select Essays in Anglo-American Law*, III, 746-769.

Campbell, A., "A Old English Will',, *Journal of Eng. and Germ. Philology*, XXXVII (1938), 133-152.

Cheney, C. R., "Legislation of the Medieval English Church," *EHR*, L (1935), 193-224, 385-417.

—. "Norwich Cathedral Priory in the Fourteenth Century," *Bull. of the John Rylands Lib.*, XX (1936), 93-120.

Cheney, Mary, "The Compromise of Avranches of 1172 and the Spread of Canon Law in England," *EHR*, LVI (1941), 177-197.

Colgrave, B., "Bede's Miracle Stories," in *Bede, His Life, Times, and Writings*, ed. A. H. Thompson, pp. 201-229.

Coote, H. C., "On the Legal Procedure of the Anglo-Saxons," *Archaeologia*, XLI, pt. i (1867), 207-218.

Cowper, H. S., "Provision for Widows in Kentish Wills," *Archaeologia Cantiana*, XXX (1887), 127-131.

Deanesly, Margaret, "The Familia at Christchurch, Canterbury, 597-832," in *Essays in Medieval History Presented to Thomas, Frederick Tout*, ed. A. C. Little, F. M. Powicke (Manchester, 1925), pp. 1-13.

Desjardins, A., "Origine de la règle 'Donner et retenir ne vaut'," *Revue critique de législation*, XXXIII (1868), 267-293, 311-335.

Douglas, D. C., "The Norman Conquest and English Feudalism," *Ec. Hist. Rev.*, 2nd Ser., IX (1957), 232-254.

346   BIBLIOGRAPHY

Duff, P. W., "The Charitable Foundations of Byzantium," in *Cambridge Legal Essays* (Cambridge, Mass., 1926), pp. 83-99.

Flahiff, G. B., "The Writ of Prohibition to Court Christian in the Thirteenth Century," *Mediaeval Studies*, VI (1944), 261-313.

Fowler, R. C., "Secular Aid for Excommunicates," *Trans. Royal Hist. Soc.*, 3rd Ser., VIII (1914), 113-117.

Galbraith, V. H., "Monastic Foundation Charters of the Eleventh and Twelfth Centuries," *Cambridge Historical Journal*, IV (1934), 205-222, 296-298.

Genestal, R., "L'Interdiction du legs d'immeuble" (Semaine de droit normand, XIV), *Rev. hist. de droit français et étranger*, 4e série, VII (1928), 683-4.

Gross, C., "The Mediaeval Law of Intestacy," in *Select Essays in Anglo-American Legal History*, III, 723-736.

Haensel, P., "Die mittelalterlichen Erbschaftssteuern in England," *Deutsche Zeitschrift für Kirchenrecht*, XIX (1909), 171-195, 376-397; XX (1910), 1-50.

Hart, W. G., "Roman Law and the Custom of London," *Law Quarterly Rev.*, XLVI (1930), 49-53.

Holmes, O. W., "Early English Equity," *ibid.*, I (1885), 162-174.

—. "Executors in Early English Law," *Harvard Law Rev.*, IX (1895-6), 42-48.

Holtzmann W., "Über eine Ausgabe der päpstlichen Dekretalen des 12 Jahrhunderts" Nachrichten des Akademie der Wissenschaften in Göttingen, Phil.-Hist. Kl. (1945), pp. 15-36.

Jolliffe, J. E. A., "English Book Right," *EHR*, L (1935), 1-21.

Kuttner, S., "Notes on a Projected Corpus of Twelfth-Century Decretal Letters," *Traditio*, VI (1948), 345-351.

—. "Quelques observations sur l'autorité des collections canoniques dans le droit classique de l'Eglise," *Actes du Congrès de Droit canonique* (Paris, 1947), pp. 303-312.

Kuttner, S., and Eleanor Rathbone, "Anglo-Norman Canonists in the Twelfth Century," *Traditio*, VII (1949-51), 279-339.

Laird, C., "Character and Growth of the Manuel des Pechiez," *Traditio*, IV (1946), 283-306.

Laughlin, J. L., "The Anglo-Saxon Legal Procedure," in *Essays in Anglo-Saxon law*, pp. 183-305.

Le Bras, G., "Notes pour servir à l'histoire des collections canoniques: VII Les collections canoniques en Angleterre après la conquête normande," *Rev. Hist. de dr. français et étranger*, 4e série, XII (1932), 144-153.

Lepointe, G., "Réflexions sur des textes concernant la propriété individuelle de religieuses cisterciennes dans la région lilloise," *Rev. d'Hist. Eccl.*, XLIX (1954), 743-769.

Levy, J. P., "La pénétration du droit savant dans les coutumiers angevins et bretons au moyen âge" *Tijdschrift voor Rechtsgeschiedenis*, XXV (1957), 1-53.

Lodge, H. Cabot, "The Anglo-Saxon Land Law," in *Essays in Anglo-Saxon Law*, pp. 55-119.

Maitland, F. W., "A Conveyancer in the Thirteenth Century," *Law Quarterly Rev.*, VII (1891), 63-69; *Collected Papers*, II, 190-201.

—. "The History of the Register of Original Writs," *Collected Papers*, II, 110-173.

McLaughlin, T. P., "The Teaching of the Canonists on Usury," *Mediaeval Studies*, I (1939), 81-147; II (1940), 1-22.

Meyer, H., Review of *Anglo-Saxon Wills*, ed. Dorothy Whitelock, *ZRG Germ. Abt.*, LI (1931), 695-699.

Michel, J., Review of E. F. Bruck, *Kirchenväter und Soziales Erbrecht, Latomus,* XVI (1957), 529-532.

Morgan, Marjorie, "Early Canterbury Jurisdiction," *EHR,* LX (1945), 392-399.

Morris, C., "The Commissary of the Bishop in the Diocese of Lincoln," *Journal of Ecclesiastical Hist.,* X (1959), 50-65.

Myres, J. N. L., "The Present State of Knowledge: Archaeological Evidence of the Anglo-Saxon Conquest," *History,* N. S., XXI (1937), 313-330.

Plucknett, T. F. T., "Bookland and Folkland," Revisions in Economic History, III, *Ec. Hist. Rev.,* VI (1936), 64-72.

—. "The Relations between Roman Law and English Common Law down to the Sixteenth Century: a General Survey," *University of Toronto Law Journal,* III (1939-40), 24-50.

Pollock, F., "Anglo-Saxon Law," *EHR,* VIII (1893), 1-17.

—. "Notes on Maine's Ancient Law," *Law Quarterly Rev.,* XXII (1906), 73-78.

Poole, R. L., "St. Wilfrid and the See of Ripon," *EHR,* XXXIV (1919), 1-24.

Postan, M. M., and J. Titow, "Heriots, and Prices on Winchester Manors," *Ec. Hist. Rev.,* 2nd Ser., XI (1958-9), 383-411.

Quasten, J., "Vetus superstitio et nova religio: The Problem of Refrigerium in the Ancient Church of North Africa," *Harvard Theol. Rev.,* XXXII (1940), 253-266.

Raftis, J. A., "The Trend towards Serfdom in Mediaeval England," *Report of the Canadian Catholic Hist. Assoc.,* XXII (1955), 15-25.

Richardson, H. G., "The Oxford Law School under John," *Law Quarterly Rev.,* LVII (1941), 319-338.

—. "Studies in Bracton," *Traditio,* VI (1948), 61-104.

Richardson, H. G., and G. O. Sayles, "The Clergy in the Easter Parliament of 1285," *EHR,* LII (1937), 220-234.

Rietschel, S., "Der Totenteil in germanischen Rechten," *ZRG Germ. Abt.,* XXXII (1911), 297-312.

Robinson, J. A., "The Early Community at Christ Church, Canterbury," *Journal of Theological Studies,* XXVII (1926), 224-240.

Rue, Abbé de la, "Memoir on the Celebrated Tapestry of Bayeux," *Archaeologia,* XVII (1814), 85-109.

Schultze, A., "Der Einfluss der Kirche auf die Entwicklung des germanischen Erbrechts," *ZRG Germ. Abt.,* XXXV (1914), 75-110.

Senior, W., "Roman Law in England before Vacarius," *Law Quarterly Rev.,* XLVI (1930), 191-206.

Stenton, F. M., "Medeshamstede and Its Colonies," in *Historical Essays in Honour of James Tait,* ed. J. G. Edwards, V. H. Galbraith and E. F. Jacob (Manchester, 1933), pp. 313-326.

Stickler, A. M. "Ordines Judiciarii," *Dictionnaire de droit canonique,* Vol. VI (1957), 1132-1143.

Stubbs, W., "Report on Ecclesiastical Courts," in *Report of Commisioners on the Constitution and Working of the Ecclesiastical Courts; Evidence, Historical Appendices and Index,* 2 pts. (London, 1883), Pt. I, 21-51.

Stutz, U., "Das Eigenkirchwesen in England," *ZRG Kan. Abt.,* XII (1922), 409-415.

Turner, G. J., "Bookland and Folkland," in *Essays in Honour of James Tait,* pp. 357-386.

Ullmann, W., "Canonistics in England," in *Studia Gratiana,* II (1954), 519-528.

Vetulani, A., "Les manuscrits du Décret de Gratien et des œuvres des décrétistes dans les bibliothèques polonaises," *ibid.*, I (1953), 217-287.

Vinogradoff, P., "Folkland," *EHR*, VIII (1893), 1-17.

—. "Transfer of Land in Old English Law," *Harvard Law Rev.*, XX (1907), 532-548.

Walford, W. S., "The Rights of Christ Church Canterbury on the Death of Bishops of the Province," *The Archaeological Journal*, XI (1854), 273-277.

Wallach, L., "Der älteste chronikalische Beleg für Salmannus," *ZRG Germ. Abt.*, LIV (1934), 240 ff.

Wells, B. W., "Eddius, Life of Wilfrid," *EHR*, VI (1891), 535-550.

Würdinger, H., "Einwirkungen des Christentums auf das angelsächsische Recht," *ZRG Germ. Abt.*, LV (1935), 105-130.

Young, E., "The Anglo-Saxon Family-Law," in *Essays in Anglo-Saxon Law*, 121-182.

Zinkeisen, F., "The Anglo-Saxon Courts of Law," *Pol. Sc. Quarterly*, X (1895), 132-144.

INDEX

Innocent II, Pope (1130-43), 243n.
— III, Pope (1198-1216), 170, 215n.
— IV, Pope (1243-54), 134-5, 301.
Inquisitio comitatus Cantabrigiensis, 99n.
Intestacy, 68-70, 174-5, 211-2, 232-4, 238, 245n, 289, 297.
Intestatus, see Intestacy.
Inventory, 211-4, 321-2.
Irrevocability, *see* Will.
Ius ecclesiasticum, 94-5.
Ius spolii, 241n, 242, 249.
Ivo of Chartres, 131, 135n; *Collectio tripartita*, 121, 124n; *Decretum*, 121, 124n; *Panormia*, 122-4.

Jews, prohibition of bequest of land to, 276; *see* Testator.
Joan, queen of Scots, 286n.
John, K. of England, 245; *see* Testator.

King as witness and protector of wills, 43-4, 49, 257.
Kirkeham, Walter de, 257n.

Laesio fidei, 30.
Lambeth, Council at (1261), 198, 208, 212-4, 218, 220.
Land : alienation *inter vivos*, 269-70 ff., 275, 277-8; sale by executors, 319-21; *see* Bequest, *land*.
Landbook, 21, 91n.
Langton, Stephen, abp of Canterbury, 180n; *see* Testator.
Language of written *wills*, 21-3, 192-3.
Lateran, II Council (1139), 255n, 298; III Council (1179), 132, 255n, 298; IV Council (1215), 298.
Launegild, see Counter-gift.
Legatee, 74-6, 258-65, 282-3; children, 77-9, 263-4; church and monastery, 74-5, 258-62 *passim*; Crusade, 262; executor, 220; friars, 261; hospital, 262; illegitimate children, 75, 264; Jews, 263, 276; leper-house, 262; nuns, 261-3; orphanage, 262; poor, 13-5, 74-5, 258-64 *passim*; public works, 74, 262; recluse, 262; royal officials, 276; scholars, 263; servants, 215n, 264; slave, 75, 104-5; wife, 75, 77-9, 263-4.
Leges Henrici primi, 260n, 268n, 291n.
Legitim, 127-8, 216, 292-5.

Leofflæd, daughter of Brihtnoth, 56n.
— wife of Thurkil, 50.
Leofric, abbot of St. Albans, 42n.
Leofsunu, 64.
Lex ribuaria, 10, 291n.
Lex Salica, 10.
Liability of testator, 30.
Liedes, Paulinus of, 280n.
Littleton, *Tenures*, 240, 274-5.
London, bequest of land in, 276; Council of (1102), 234n; (1143), 256n; Hustings, *see* Courts; legitim in, 294.
Losinga, Herbert de, bp of Norwich, 142.
Ludham, Godfrey, abp of York, Statutes (1259?), 185n, 197, 213, 220n, 222n 299n.
Lufu, bequest (?) by, 57.
Lyndwood, William, *Provinciale*, 147n, 161, 163, 177, 180, 214n, 218-9, 220n.

Magna Carta, 154-5, 174, 196-7, 213, 215.
Mainz, Council of, 130-2 *passim*.
Majority, 72, 239-41.
Mandeville, Geoffrey de, 139n.
— William de, 271.
Le Manuel des pechiez, 219.
Marculfi formulae, 90.
Margaret, wife of Walter Clifford, irrevocable bequest by, 313.
Married woman, 235, 238n, 281, 300; *see* Husband and wife, Testator.
Marshal, William the, earl of Pembroke, 146-7, 184n, 260n; *see* Testator.
Martin IV, Pope (1281-5), 299n.
Mauclerc, Walter, bp of Carlisle, 246n.
Mepeham, Simon, abp of Canterbury, Statutes (1328), 206n.
Merton, Statute of, 285.
Mildenhall, Ogga of, 50.
Mildred, bp of Worcester, 64.
Miles, earl of Hereford, 142.
Modbert, 168.
Montfort, Henry de, 193n.
— Simon de, 184n, 286; *see* Testator.
Morning-gift, 46, 79.
Mortimer, Hugh, 160n.
Mortmain, bequest in, 217, 273, 276; Statute of, 276.
Mortuary, 194, 258, 289, 294, 296-302 *passim; see* Sawolsceatt.